DEMOGRAPHY

The Study of Human Population

Fourth Edition

Jennifer Hickes Lundquist
University of Massachusetts, Amherst

Douglas L. Anderton
University of South Carolina

David Yaukey
late of University of Massachusetts, Amherst

WAVELAND
PRESS, INC.
Long Grove, Illinois

For information about this book, contact:
Waveland Press, Inc.
4180 IL Route 83, Suite 101
Long Grove, IL 60047-9580
(847) 634-0081
info@waveland.com
www.waveland.com

Cover design: Eiko Strader

10-digit ISBN 1-4786-1306-8
13-digit ISBN 978-1-4786-1306-0

Printed in the United States of America

7   6   5   4   3   2   1

Careers in Demography

Contents

Preface

"Demography is changing" is the sentence that opened the last three editions of this book, and it remains appropriate. In just the eight intervening years since the last edition, our world has experienced a number of major demographic milestones. The global population reached and surpassed the 7 billion mark. For the first time in human history, more people began living in cities than in rural areas. Although the HIV/AIDs epidemic remains a significant mortality threat, it reached its peak and has begun to decline. A major financial crisis took place that has had demographic reverberations throughout the world. And long-term trends intensified in the two interrelated demographic processes of aging and fertility decline. For example, the world's growth rate continues to slow and very soon the elderly will outnumber young children in the world. Almost half of the global population living in every region of the world now has below-replacement fertility. Health, education, and income gains have accelerated over recent years for many developing countries. Nevertheless, global poverty and disease remain pressing issues and environmental concerns stemming from rising global consumption continue to mount. All of these trends have been incorporated into the newest edition of this text as well as a discussion of their important social policy implications.

Although demography is not an undergraduate major, we believe that it should be. As the above trends make clear, the ability to understand and shape human population processes is crucial to the future. Demographers have the tools and global perspective to improve the lives of current and future generations. Using empirical, evidence-based data, demographers shape government policy and contribute ideas to the betterment of society. At its core, demography is an interdisciplinary field drawing from a diverse array of disciplines, including the health sciences, epidemiology, economics, sociology, anthropology, history, public policy, mathematics and statistics.

In this edition we have updated and expanded our introduction to fundamental demographic issues, trends, and methods to include emerging demographic issues as above, as well as additional recent topics of interest to demographers. The chapter structure and basic design of the textbook remain as in the past edition. We have made three principal changes. First, we have added new text, examples, exercises, data, and discussion throughout the text. Clearly this effort is challenging. Textbook data will never be as current as those available online, and that is not the objective of our revision. Keeping data up to date, however, is important in making the text relevant to students and for illustrating the continued relevance of theoretical arguments and methodological tools to recent population trends. This text continues to encourage, and give direction to, the comparative inclusion of more recent online data.

Second, we have included a new feature entitled *Careers in Demography*. We conducted interviews with thirteen well-known or rising demographers so that students could learn more about some of the people behind the important research that informs this textbook. These career profiles range from demographers working in academic settings, to those working for think tanks and nonprofits, to those working for government and intergovernmental agencies. We think students will enjoy learning directly from these individuals about how they first came to the field of demography and the ways in which their work has shaped the field. We certainly enjoyed the opportunity to interact with these demographers during the creation of their profiles.

We have also created a website to accompany this textbook. All of the data tables, example exercises, figures, and an erratum file* can be accessed by students and instructors at www.demographytextbook.com. In addition, we post links there to many of the reports, articles, and publicly accessible data that we reference throughout the textbook. We hope that our new companion website will allow instructors to easily integrate our graphs and tables into their lectures and encourage students to further their interest in demography.

Since the last edition of the book, each of the authors has undergone a personal demographic change. Jennifer Lundquist reached replacement level fertility and is enjoying her aging process. Douglas Anderton experienced an internal migration, moving from Massachusetts to South Carolina where he is now Chair of the University of South Carolina Sociology Department. And lastly, we are deeply saddened to say that David Yaukey died before the writing of this Fourth Edition. At its core, this book continues to be shaped by David's original vision.

In memory of David, we would like to say a few words about his life and career. David was born in Japan, the son of China missionaries and the nephew of Pearl S. Buck. His early experiences led to a career in international demography and he lived at various periods of his life in Lebanon, China, Pakistan, Chile, and Switzerland. He was a professor of sociology at the University of Massachusetts Amherst from 1964–1991 and had various foreign assignments with the United Nations and other organizations throughout his career. His primary research accomplishment was carrying out a pioneering fertility survey in Lebanon in 1958, supported by the Population Council. The report of this survey, written at the Office of Population Research, Princeton University, was the first of his three books. David will be missed by many but his memory lives on in the foundation of this textbook.

There are many to thank (and those to whom we should apologize for imposing our schedules upon them). Foremost, we should thank the continued users of the textbook who continue to fight the good fight of population science and whose loyalty and suggestions inform the core of our textbook revision. We are particularly indebted to our brilliant graduate research assistant Eiko Strader, who helped with the revisions

---

*If readers spot errors in the data or text, we would very much appreciate notification to our publisher at info@waveland.com so that we can correct it in our online erratum.

and tracked down demographic data in order to whip it into the elegant visuals you'll find sprinkled throughout the book. There is little she cannot do and, as such, she is also to be credited for the design of the book cover. We further thank Arya Mohanka, an undergraduate student who helped out in the initial stages of the revision, and Chris Strader, who designed the textbook website.

We are grateful to the thirteen demographers who generously agreed to let us profile them in this edition. We appreciate the continuing support of Waveland Press in its efforts to keep the textbook up to date, accessible, and affordable. Doug also wants to be clear for those who appreciate this edition of the textbook that Jen bore the brunt of this revision (to say the least) and improved upon past editions significantly.

And we each have our personal thanks. Jen is grateful for the support she has received from her partner Eric, even if, in the course of this revision, he began referring to demography as "demonology." She also notes the demographic wisdom of her young children, Ursula and Elias, who pointed out that some population pyramids are really rectangles. Doug continues to draw his inspiration and support from his spouse, Terri, who offers an indefatigable model of growth and fulfillment in the face of life's challenges. And, of course, we all appreciate that demography and the study of human populations offer an important perspective to serve and sustain future generations.

Careers in Demography

Samuel H. Preston

Professor of Demography and Sociology, University of Pennsylvania
Director, UPenn Population Studies Center, 1982–1990
President, Population Association of America, 1984

How did you decide that being a demographer was the career path for you?

In 1965, when I entered graduate school in economics at Princeton, I intended to become a labor economist. In fact, demography was the only course offering I had crossed off among the courses offered. But a fellow graduate student recommended that I take a course in demography taught by Ansley Coale since the subject was somewhat related to labor economics. It was clear after two lectures that my career path had shifted: a genuine conversion experience. Births and deaths were far more appealing subjects than wages and interest rates. Careful measurement seemed more worthwhile than speculative hypothesizing. And population mathematics had at its core a beautiful construction, the stable population model.

What kind of education and training did you pursue to get to where you are in your career?

My dissertation topic, recommended by Ansley and enthusiastically adopted by me, was on the mortality effects of cigarette smoking as they were manifesting themselves in international mortality patterns. Why this topic was acceptable for a dissertation in economics is a mystery to me, but I'm grateful that it was. This research began a life-long interest in mortality analysis, which at the time was a neglected field.

I was fortunate to receive a job offer from the Department of Demography at Berkeley, the only such department in the U.S. then or now. I was one of three members of the department, with Nathan Keyfitz and Judith Blake. So by the time I was twenty-four years old, I had studied with one of the two leading technical demographers in the world and had become a colleague of the other. They set a standard of excellence in research and citizenship that provided a wonderful example for a budding demographer.

Describe your work/research as a demographer. What do you consider your most important accomplishments?

My first project was an effort to assemble, publish, and interpret all the data that had ever been collected on mortality rates by cause of death, age, and sex. This was a project that an older and wiser person would never have attempted, but it led to two useful books and provided some infrastructure for later volumes by Chris Murray and colleagues on the Global Burden of Disease.

In 1975 I published an article called "The Changing Relation between Mortality and Level of Economic Development," which is my most-cited work. It argued that technical improvements in medicine and public health had been the principal factors responsible for 20th century mortality improvements, rather than increases in income. Angus Deaton of Princeton has dubbed the graphical core of the analysis "The Preston Curve," a term that has caught on without resistance from me. I followed up this paper with more research with Michael Haines, Doug Ewbank, and Gretchen Condran. We concluded that the germ theory of disease, embodied in public health practices but also in health behaviors within the home, was the principal source of advance. This work was aided by samples that drew from U.S. censuses of 1900 and 1910, the first historical census samples to be publicly released.

In December 1980 I was on an airplane returning from a conference in Manila, musing over a mathematical equation developed by Shiro Horiuchi and Neil Bennett. I started fiddling around with it and realized in a flash that the three basic equations characterizing a stable population were a special case of an (almost) equally simple set of equations that characterize any population. This was a moment of joy and transcendence that I haven't felt before or since. I still can't shake the idea that I was being rewarded for returning to cold Philadelphia to teach my last class of the semester, while all of my demographer friends stayed in Manila to splash in the hotel pool and eat mahi-mahi. The expressions have proven useful in understanding population behavior and in estimating demographic parameters in countries with flawed data.

During the 1980s I became involved in two research projects that had public policy implications. In the first project I asserted that the well-being of American children was suffering because of family change and policy neglect, while conditions among the elderly were improving because of successful policies aimed at them. Because the lobby for older people benefitted from the perceptions of widespread elderly poverty, *Modern Maturity*, the official organ of AARP, called me in an editorial "America's leading crusader against the elderly."

The second project was a National Research Council publication entitled Population Growth and Economic Development. This was presented in a monograph written by Ron Lee, Geoff Greene, and me that seemed to many people to diminish the importance of population growth as an obstacle to economic advancement. Such a diminution was not appealing to agencies and individuals with a stake—financial or intellectual—in magnifying the threat of the "population explosion." Although I did not enjoy participating in the public fray surrounding these projects, I was pleased to be contributing to the analysis of important issues.

From 1998 to 2005, I took a seven-year sabbatical from demography when I served as Dean of Arts and Sciences at Penn. Returning from that hiatus was difficult. I told someone that it was like coming out of graduate school all over again, but without a dissertation. Whether consciously or not, I responded by returning to the subject of the dissertation, the mortality effects of cigarette smoking. Those effects had been primarily visible among men in the late 1960s, but by 2006 they were clearly visible among women as well. A National Research Council committee that I co-chaired with Eileen Crimmins attempted to account for the poor ranking of the United States in life expectancy. My work with Dana Glei and John Wilmoth estimating the impact of smoking on life expectancy played an important role in explaining the U.S. shortfall.

What do you see as the field's most important contribution as well as its greatest challenge?

I think my career illustrates that there are huge opportunities for demographers in the field of population health. This was an unknown term twenty years ago but the field has taken off. Studies of population health use quantitative measures to describe levels of health, identify their determinants, and explain how and why they vary across and within populations. There are terrifically interesting research questions in the area of population health. There are also large numbers of undergraduates who are interested in health, especially global health. There is a great opportunity for demographers to teach large-enrollment undergraduate courses in the health of populations. Reproductive health fits comfortably into such a course, and undergraduates are always interested in reproduction. Being able to teach large-enrollment undergraduate courses is an advantage for any discipline—just ask a dean. Demography lost enrollments when populations stopped exploding. Now is the hour for population health.

1

Introduction

Most of you will be reading this book as a text for a course, rather than on your own. You may already have attended one or more class sessions. If so, what were the first things you noticed about that class? Probably you looked around to see how large the class was and whether the room was crowded. Perhaps you noted what proportion of the students were men and women, or whether the other students seemed to be older or younger than yourself. You may have chatted with neighbors to find out what their intended majors were. If so, what you did was demography. You studied the size and composition of a specific population—your class.

Most of us unconsciously sketch a quick **demographic description** as a first step in approaching a new social situation. We know intuitively that the size and composition of groups with which we are dealing are important. The same logic applies on a larger scale to communities, regions, nations, even planets.

If demographic analysis is a widespread human tendency, what then is demography as a discipline?

Demography Defined

First let's start with an *informal* definition. Let us define demography in terms of the questions it tries to answer. In the vernacular, these are:

- How many people, of what kind, are where?
- How come?
- And so what?

1

More *formal* definitions of demography (e.g., MPIDR, 2013; Pressat, 1985; IUSSP, 1982) say much the same thing in a bit more precise terms. **Demography** is the science of populations that examines:

1. the *size* and *composition* of populations according to diverse criteria: age, ethnicity, sex, union (marital or cohabiting) status, educational attainment, spatial distribution, and so forth;
2. dynamic life-course processes that *change* this composition: birth, death, unions, migration, etc.; and
3. relationships between population composition and change, and the broader social and physical environment in which they exist.

Understanding these processes sheds light on important social, economic, political, and environmental issues and their impacts, such as population growth, urbanization, family change, immigration, and human health and longevity. One of the most fascinating things you will find about demography is that almost every topic is relevant to something you have experienced or will experience at some point in your life. Consider the following, somewhat nosy, questions (adapted, in part, from McFalls, 2007):

1. When and where were you born? How many others were born in your generation? What conditions will your generation face that distinguish it from other generations?
2. What is your gender and how will that identity shape the rest of your life?
3. How old were you (or will you be) when you first had sex? How often do you have sex and do you use contraception?
4. What's the likelihood you will move in with an intimate partner, ever get married, get divorced? Remarry?
5. Will you have kids? How many? Will you have grandkids? Will you be alive to see your great grandkids?
6. What kind of job will you have? How often will you change jobs? At what age will you retire?
7. How many times will you move in your lifetime? Will you ever move abroad?
8. How long will you be healthy in your life? When will you die? How will you die?

Each of these is a relevant demographic question. To paraphrase Joseph McFalls (2007), if you are not interested in demographic phenomena, then you are not interested in yourself.

Demography overlaps with many neighboring disciplines. Most demographers—at least in the United States—also identify themselves as sociologists, economists, anthropologists, geographers, historians, biologists, and so on. Demographic inquiry may be narrowly focused on demographic variables alone or broadly concerned with society, economy, and culture. The terms *pure demography* and **formal demography** are sometimes used to distinguish more narrowly focused interests in population composition and demographic dynamics, dealing entirely with **demographic variables**. An example of formal demographic analysis would be developing a theoretical model specifying the relationship between changes in fertility (treated as a cause) and changes in age composition (treated as an effect). A more extensive and less narrowly focused approach to demography is implied by the phrase **population studies**, which includes all of the above but also encompasses the study of relationships between demographic and non-demographic variables. The far-reaching implications of demographic variables in other disciplines have generated broad interest in such fields of study as social demography, economic demography, anthropological demography, biodemography, and historical demography, to name a few.

Two more preliminary remarks need to be made. Though you will undoubtedly find personal relevance to the topics throughout this textbook, one of the strengths of demography is that it allows us to see how the individual and his or her experiences fit into the larger demographic framework of the world. Demography takes these intensely personal experiences and considers them at the *aggregate* level of people, not the individual level. The very term "population" refers to the numbers of people resident in some specified geographic area, be it a classroom or a nation. Likewise, demography describes characteristics of populations, not of individual members in those populations. Thus, the cartoon shown in Figure 1-1 is something of a demographers' inside joke.

The second point is that demography is generally *quantitative* and statistical, although some demographers also use qualitative methods (see Petit and Charbit, 2013; Kertzer and Fricke, 1997; Obermeyer, 1997; Bogue et al., 1993, ch. 27). Demography deals with populations, and the features of populations are most often measured by counting the people in the total population, or in segments of it, and comparing those counts. Thus demography can easily present basic population descriptions in tables and graphs. Paging ahead through the tables and figures of this text will illustrate the quantitative nature of demographic descriptions to the reader.

Furthermore, because the subject is numerical, readers will get used to following simple demographic arithmetic during the course of reading this text. Almost all chapters end with straightforward exercises that provide guidance and practice. By doing these exercises, you will have accumulated a basic set of demographic tools by the time you reach the end of this book.

Figure 1-1

"They Tell Me You're a Demographer . . ."

"They tell me you're a demographer. Whatever happened to Fred Biddlingmeyer?"

Source: Cartoon by Peter Steiner, *Science '83.*

Current Population Size and Composition

Absolute Size, Distribution, and Density

Population size has three facets. First is *absolute size*. The absolute size of the earth's population reached 7.2 billion in 2014 and is expected to grow to close to 11 billion people by next century. The ten countries with the largest populations in the world are shown in Table 1-1, with the absolute size of their population in column 1.

Absolute size has its own consequences. To use our classroom illustration, large classes have to be taught differently than small classes, more by lecture or in an online venue than by face-to-face discussion. The immense cities of today have different problems than the villages and towns of yesterday, and they have developed different kinds of governments to handle them. Both China and India are home to well over a billion people, and in both cases very large population size has had significant effects on the politics, culture, and economic development of these nations.

A second facet of population size is *distribution*, or relative size. If we compare the populations in Table 1-1, we see that China and India together have well over a third of the world's entire population. These ten countries together have more than half (4.3 billion) of the world's population living in them. Although the United States is third largest in size, it is only a quarter the size of India's population.

Distribution, as well, has its own consequences. For instance, citizens of Western countries are sometimes alarmed that citizens of non-Western countries outnumber them now and will outnumber them by even more in the future (see chapter 3). Distribution of population within nations also is a subject of concern. For example, many less-developed countries are worried about premature and extreme urbanization (see chapter 10).

The third facet of population size is *density*. One of the main consequences of large size and uneven population distribution is that it can lead to crowded, or densely settled, populations. In our classroom illustration, if you noticed how crowded (or if it's

Table 1-1   Ten Countries with Largest Absolute Population Size, and Their Population Density, 2014

Country	Population in Millions (1)	Density per Square Mile (2)	Density per Square Kilometer (3)
China	1,364	372	143
India	1,296	1,025	394
United States	318	86	33
Indonesia	251	343	132
Brazil	203	62	24
Pakistan	194	635	244
Nigeria	177	499	192
Bangladesh	158	2,864	1,101
Russia	144	21	8
Japan	127	874	336

Source: Population Reference Bureau, 2014 (using midyear 2014 measurements).

an 8 AM class, uncrowded) the room was, you were noticing density. It refers, in its most restricted use, to the relationship between population size and the space in which the population is located. For large geographic units, one might measure density in persons per square mile or kilometer.

The largest populations of the world are not those with the highest density. In fact, some of the very smallest countries in terms of geographic area and population are the densest—for instance, Monaco and Macao have more than 50,000 people per square mile. The second and third columns of Table 1-1 show the density for the ten largest populations. Of these countries, Bangladesh is by far the most densely settled because it has an unusual combination of both a large population and a small land area.

Density, too, has its own negative and positive consequences. For people who face daily crowds, noise, and environmental pollution, the negative aspects of density are most obvious. Indeed, the concept of *overpopulation* (chapter 3) implies a concern over too dense a population in a given environment. For example, epidemic diseases can spread more easily in densely settled populations. But on the positive side, innovation, knowledge, and ideas also spread quickly and easily in densely populated areas.

Composition

The topic of composition recalls our first demographic question, with added emphasis: How many people, *of what kind*, are where? In our classroom illustration, you were observing composition when you took note of the women and men, those younger and older than yourself, and the numbers from various majors. Demographers go beyond simply counting the absolute numbers in categories to *comparing* the numbers, focusing on the *relative* size of categories. Thus, you will see frequent use of percentage distributions and various ratios in demographic descriptions of population composition.

Which traits do demographers use to classify **population composition**? The list is potentially limitless; however, some kinds of characteristics turn out to be more useful than others. For example, characteristics that either do not change easily or change in a predictable fashion tend to be useful. Therefore, sex, age, and ethnic identity are more useful than body weight, satisfaction with the president, or whether one owns a car and how many.

Demographers also focus on traits that are inherently related to altering population size and composition, such as giving birth, dying, or moving from one population to another. Variables like age and, in some cases, sex are again important in this context since these traits are related to basic biology. As the students in your class grow older they will face an increasingly higher chance of dying each year. Most college students also are approaching the ages at which they may have children. Women in the class will have different lives, in part, due to childbearing if they decide to become mothers and differing experiences related to societal gender norms. This affects the different subcultures of men and women, even for those who choose not to have children. In fact, because age and sex shape so many aspects of life, we can make reasonable guesses about some of the major characteristics of people's lives knowing only their age and sex.

Demographers also have concern for characteristics of a given composition that are used as a basis for ascribing societal roles. Because so much of behavior is related to age and sex, these characteristics are also used by people to ascribe social roles. Few of the people in your class are "children" or "elders," but most are young adults. Role ascription, to sociologists, means assigning people to roles on the basis of traits over which the individual has little control. All societies use sex and age to some degree in ascribing roles, whether we like it or not.

Although age and sex are basic dimensions of population composition, many other social and economic characteristics also are used to ascribe social roles; for example, how people categorize other people and what their social roles may be are influenced by their ethnicity, literacy and education, generational wealth, occupation, and income. This is how social inequality and stratification often starts.

Governments are concerned with the economic welfare of their populations and with their populations as workforces for their economies. So most demographic censuses collect information on the economic composition of the population. Governments also are concerned with identifying vulnerable groups that have special policy needs and the characteristics of these groups; thus, many demographic surveys are focused on such specific groups and policy-relevant population characteristics. And, finally, the public is concerned with the size and distribution of identifiable subgroups within the nation, so most national censuses deal in some way with the subject of ethnic identity, be it race, ethnicity, religious affiliation, national origin, or native language.

Age and sex are the most universally studied dimensions of population composition because they change predictably, are related to demographic behavior, and shape the social construction of societal age and gender roles. However, the study of population composition is not a closed book. The characteristics related to behavior and used to ascribe social roles can, and do, change over time and vary across cultures.

Population Change

So far, we have been dealing with population description within a given moment. Clearly, that can be only the beginning. The future population is the one we anticipate and plan for, not the present one. Indeed, describing a present population helps mainly to the degree that it tells us something about that population in the future. Thus, most demography focuses on the study of population change, including change in size.

Population Growth and Its Components

To demographers, **population growth** means change in population size. It is called growth even if it is negative growth. The amount of growth is obtained by subtracting some earlier population count (P_1) from some later count (P_2). Clearly, the difference can be either positive or negative. Most populations in developing countries are experiencing positive growth, but some of the more-developed countries are, in fact, experiencing negative growth.

What are the immediate causes of population growth? That is, what could happen to alter a population size from P_1 to P_2? Common sense furnishes the answer. If we are considering the world's population, it can change in only two ways: People are born into the world, increasing the population, and people die, decreasing the population. Any population (such as the world's) in which people cannot come or go is a *closed population* and can increase or decrease only through births or deaths. In terms of an equation:

$$P_2 - P_1 = B_{(1,2)} - D_{(1,2)}$$

which says simply that the population change in a closed population from an earlier (subscript 1) time to a later (subscript 2) time is increased by the number of births that occurred between the two times and decreased by the number of deaths between the two times. The difference between births and deaths is called the **natural increase** of the population. Thus, in a closed population, population growth is the natural increase, that is, the difference between births and deaths *(B – D)*.

Figure 1-2 dramatizes this imbalance on the world level for the year 2014. The figure shows the births (*B*), deaths (*D*), and natural increase (*B – D*) for the world's population in the year 2014, as well as for an average month, day, hour, minute, and second of that year. In the average minute, for example, there were about 273 births and 108 deaths, resulting in a natural increase, or growth, in the world's population of about 165 people per minute.

Most populations, however, are not closed. That is, people also come and go. In an *open population* there are four—and only four—ways in which a geographic area can add or subtract from its population. Again, people can be born into it or can die out of it. But in addition, people can cross a border into it or people can cross a border out of it. In this case the **growth equation** is a bit more complicated:

$$P_2 - P_1 = B_{(1,2)} - D_{(1,2)} + M_{(1,2)}$$

Figure 1-2

Growth and Natural Increase for the World per Year, Month, Day, Hour, Minute, and Second, 2014

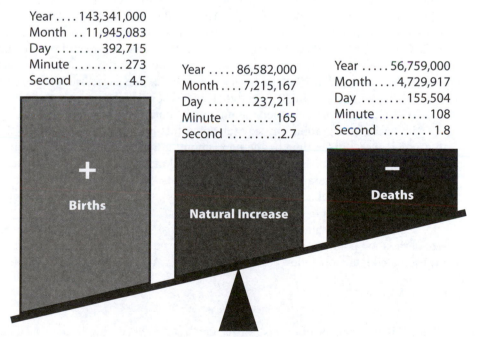

Year 143,341,000
Month . . 11,945,083
Day 392,715
Minute 273
Second 4.5

Year 86,582,000
Month 7,215,167
Day 237,211
Minute 165
Second 2.7

Year 56,759,000
Month 4,729,917
Day 155,504
Minute 108
Second 1.8

+

Births

Natural Increase

–

Deaths

Source: Data from PRB, 2014. *2014 World Population Data Sheet.*

In words, this growth equation for an open population says that the change in size of the population of a specified area during a specified time interval equals the number of births (B) over that time, minus the number of deaths (D), plus the net migration into the population (M) over the same period of time. **Net migration** is the imbalance between the movers-in and the movers-out and can, of course, be either positive or negative. Thus, even a population with a negative natural increase can grow or maintain its size with a substantial net migration of others into the population. This is, in fact, the case for countries in some of the more-developed regions of the world. An exercise at the end of this chapter offers practice in using these equations.

Growth Components as Population Processes

So far, we have been talking about the causes of population growth as events. Each birth, each death, each move across a border is a **population event**. However, demographers—and indeed the general public—are accustomed to thinking of these individual events as expressions of underlying collective processes. That is, we think of the number of births that occur in a population as an expression of the collective *fertility* of that population; the number of deaths is the manifestation of its *mortality;* and the number of moves across the border (in and out) is the process of *migration*.

The simplest measure of a population process is a *crude rate*. But before we discuss it, we should ask: Why construct rates at all? Why not simply count the number of events and let that total be the measure of the process? Perhaps the best answers to these questions may be obtained by asking you to think about the following reasoning: Suppose that exactly the same number of deaths occurred in the United States during 1900 as occurred during 2010. Can one conclude that the mortality of the United States was the same in 1900 as in 2010? Most readers will recognize that such a statement is misleading. Due to population growth, there were many more people available to die in the year 2010 than there were in 1900. If the same number of people had actually died in both years, then a much smaller percentage of the population would have died in 2010 than did in 1900. Or, as demographers would express it, the population at *risk* of dying was greater in 2010, and that should be taken into account when measuring the likelihood of a certain population event occurring.

The basic demographic strategy for doing this is to divide the number of events that occur over a given time by the population that was at risk of experiencing those events. This step produces one of the fundamental measurements demographers use—that is, *rates*. The numerator is the number of events; the denominator is the population at risk. Generally speaking, rates tell us the probability of a member of the population at risk of participating in one of the events.

A crude approximation of the population at risk for demographic processes is the size of the total population during the specified year. Dividing the number of events by the estimated total population produces **crude rates**. A general formula for crude rates is

$$\frac{E}{P_m} \times n$$

where E is the number of events (births, deaths, etc.) occurring in the specified place and year. P_m refers to the estimated total population. Since the size of the population varies throughout the year, the midyear population (indicated by the subscript m) is often used as a representative figure for the total population at risk during the year. Yearly demographic data are sometimes reported for the calendar year and sometimes reported for other annual periods, such as from July 1 of one year to July 1 of the next, and may even be reported for other periods, such as five-year intervals. It is important to remember that the midyear population refers to the population midway between the beginning and end of the period for which the data are reported.

Most crude rates are multiplied by a number or *base* of the rate, n, to express the rate as the number of events occurring for every n people. A common convention, for example, is to multiply by 1,000, which makes the rate the number of events per 1,000 population members, which is quite reasonable for births, deaths, and migration. The base can be changed to give the rate per $n = 1$ person, as a percentage of every $n = 100$ persons, or, for very rare events, per 100,000 people. The base is chosen to minimize the decimal places in crude rates or, equivalently, to adjust for the fact that some events occur to only small fractions of the population at any given time.

The adjective "crude" in these rates is not accidental. Not everybody in the total population is equally at risk of dying, or of producing a baby, or of migrating. We will introduce more refined demographic rates and measures in later chapters. Crude rates, however, provide a quick, and for many purposes adequate, measure of demographic processes. An exercise at the end of this chapter offers practice in constructing crude rates.

The growth equation, which we expressed earlier in terms of absolute numbers, can also be written in terms of crude rates. If we take each term in the growth equation and divide by the midyear population, P_m, like this

$$\frac{P_2 - P_1}{P_m} = \frac{B_{(1,2)}}{P_m} - \frac{D_{(1,2)}}{P_m} + \frac{M_{(1,2)}}{P_m}$$

each of these terms becomes a crude rate. We can, of course, also multiply each term by a base such as 1,000 to express them as rates per 1,000 population. In either case, in words this equation says:

growth rate = birth rate – death rate + rate of net migration

To illustrate this form of the growth equation, Figure 1-3 traces components in the population growth history of the United States from 1910 to 2010. Each of the components is expressed as a crude rate per 1,000 population. The top panel of the graph shows the **crude birth rate** (the highest line) and the **crude death rate** (the lowest line) over this period. The higher birth rate at the turn of the 20th century and the baby boom of the late 1940s and early 1950s can be seen in the crude birth rate. The effects of the worldwide influenza epidemic and World War I can be seen in the peak of the crude death rate just before the 1920s. The difference between these birth and death rates is the rate of natural increase in the population. Note the reduction in natural increase, for example, that occurred at the time of World War II. During this time deaths rose at the same time births declined, minimizing the imbalance. Then, in the postwar years, births rose dramatically as deaths declined slowly and steadily, resulting in a large imbalance and natural increase.

The second panel of Figure 1-3 shows the net migration rate (the lower line), which is added to the natural increase from the previous panel to give the population growth rate (the higher line). Notice that growth rates prior to the Great Depression, before the 1930s, were erratic and highly affected by changes in the year-to-year net migration rate. Twice in the 1930s–1940s net migration dropped below zero, indicating a net loss of migrants. But the fact that the net migration rate is well above zero for most of the past century indicates that the U.S. is an immigrant-receiving more than an

Figure 1-3

U.S. Birth, Death, Natural Increase, Net Migration, and Growth Rates, 1910–2010

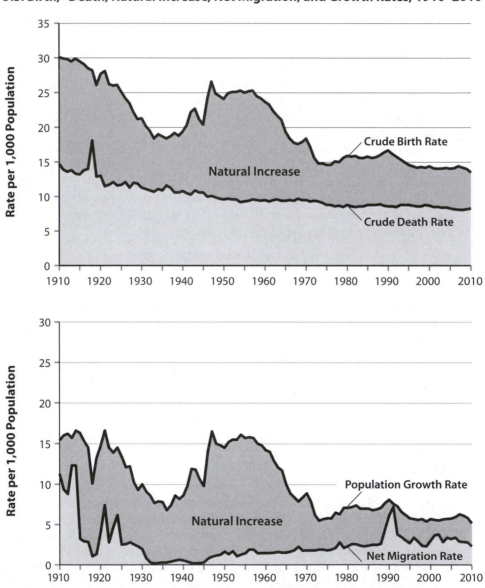

Source: Data from U.S. Census Bureau, 2011, 2012, 2013. Figures produced by Eiko Strader.

emigrant-sending society. After the early 1930s the growth rate is more heavily dependent upon the rate of natural increase, and net migration is more stable than the rate of births, except for the half-decade following the Immigration Reform and Control Act of 1986, where we see a surge in net migration. Nevertheless, net migration is responsible for a significant proportion of the United States' positive growth rates.

Population Change: Growth and Reclassification

Thus far we have been dealing only with population growth, that is, change in population size. Demographers also study change in population *composition*. What are the processes involved in a change in population composition?

All four **components of population growth** can affect the size of a population category or subpopulation, just as they do the size of a total population. For instance, the number of Catholic Americans grows (positively or negatively) in response to births and deaths among Catholic residents and the international migration patterns of Catholics into or out of the United States. However, unlike the case for total population growth, category growth can be influenced by an additional process, which we will call **reclassification**. Thus, Catholics can choose not to baptize their children as Catholic, they can change their religious affiliation, and others can become Catholics, thereby influencing the size of the Catholic population without involving mortality, fertility, or migration. Reclassification is, in a sense, a migration of meaning among subpopulations.

The process of classification is hard to simplify. For some traits, such as sex, the changes produced by reclassification are still very limited. For other traits, such as age, reclassification proceeds predictably. And for still others, such as occupation, it involves individual choices that follow no simple pattern. In fact, the study of changing subpopulation composition, and the complex forces that may affect the demography of subpopulations (such as occupational groups, income groups, educational attainment groups, etc.), is a prominent research topic throughout the social and behavioral sciences.

One reclassification process has enjoyed special attention from demographers. It is **nuptiality**, the process of changing marital status. Marriage is of special interest for several reasons. One is that marital status (as well as other unions, such as cohabiting or same-sex couples) has direct and indirect impacts on the growth processes, as it influences birth, death, and migration. Another reason is that such unions imply a jointly functioning social unit that shares resources and demographic decisions. It is also the case that couples are viewed differently by governments and that conventional demographic data systems often gather evidence about union formation and relations within households.

Population Problems

In each chapter of this book we discuss not only demographic methods, statistics, and trends, but what may be called population "problems." **Population problems** are socially defined, just as are other social problems. They may seem to be self-evident and beyond dispute at a given moment of public consensus, but the history of population problems shows that a public can be alarmed about a given population trend and then, some years later, view the same trend with indifference. Moreover, one public's problem may be another public's blessing. To understand this, let us look sociologically at the mechanics of defining population problems.

Careers in Demography

Christine Almy Bachrach

Co-Director, Robert Wood Johnson Foundation Health & Society Scholars
  Program
Research Professor, University of Maryland
Branch Chief at NIH and Acting Director of OBSSR, 1992–2010
President of the Population Association of America, 2013
Demographer/Statistician, National Center for Health Statistics, 1979–1988

How did you decide that being a demographer was the career path for you?

In part, it was the sexual revolution, which was in full swing during my years as an undergraduate at Harvard. It inspired me to volunteer at Planned Parenthood—my first foray into reproductive health issues. This could have led nowhere—but fortuitously I was becoming disenchanted with my major in psychology. I decided to finish up my requirements and spend my senior year in college getting a liberal arts education. I took a wide range of courses—Shakespeare, history, and a course in demography taught by David Heer.

After my first class I was hooked—demography provided a way to study human behavior that was straightforwardly quantitative and methodologically rigorous. What's more, it dealt with deeply important aspects of human life—birth, death, and migration. I resolved to work in the field after graduation, and set out to write to every population-related organization in Washington, DC to ask for a job.

What kind of education and training did you pursue to get to where you are in your career?

As it turns out, no one would hire a college graduate with one course in demography for a job in a population organization. I got three responses: a letter from the head of the Population Crisis Committee telling me to get a PhD, an offer of a secretarial position ("college gals make great secretaries!"), and a possible work-study arrangement at the Population Division of the U.S. Agency for International Development if I went to graduate school. I enrolled at the master's program in demography at Georgetown University, and worked two days a week at USAID. I then went to the Johns Hopkins School of Public Health for a PhD in population dynamics.

Describe your work/research as a demographer. What do you consider your most important accomplishments?

I've had a career in public service, and I've loved every minute of it. My professional life has consisted of three distinct "careers." The first was dedicated to the development and analysis of survey data on U.S. fertility with the National Survey of Family Growth in the National Center for Health Statistics. One of my first jobs was to redesign the survey, which had originally included only married women and never-married women with children, to include single women. This was in response to evidence that, by 1979, was irrefutable: single women were having sex and getting pregnant.

My second career, from 1988–2010, was at the National Institutes of Health (NIH). This job was completely different. Instead of creating science, I was now funding it. In this job, my goal was to advance demographic research. I worked first as a program official, and then as Branch Chief of the Demographic and Behavioral Sciences Branch (DBSB) at the National Institute of Child Health and Human Development (NICHD).

During my years at NICHD my branch supported large-scale data projects that provide the foundation for demographic research; expanded research on families and children, intimate relationships, and immigration; led the incorporation of social science into AIDS research; and expanded our support for demographic research on health.

Perhaps the most dramatic aspect of my tenure at NICHD was the periodic requirement to defend the research we were supporting in the face of congressional attacks. We were funding research on sexual behavior, a basic element in understanding both fertility and reproductive health. But sexual behavior studies sometimes attract the attention of members of Congress, especially around election time. They can easily be taken out of context to be made to sound prurient or unnecessary.

The most serious attack occurred in relation to a large new survey on teenagers' sexual behavior. The American Teenage Study was designed by top scientists to provide definitive answers on the causes of teen pregnancy. But, soon after I arrived, the study came to the attention of conservatives in Congress who objected to asking minors explicit questions about sex. After the Secretary of Health and Human Services was told about it on a talk show, the survey was shut down. The press erupted in outrage over political interference in science and our office was inundated by mail from conservative groups.

We provided the NIH leadership with ammunition to defend the research and worked behind the scenes with advocacy groups who rallied to our cause. After three years of effort, Congress passed a law requiring the NIH to conduct a new comprehensive study of adolescent health—described in terms that left no doubt that a study like the American Teenage Study, but with a general focus on health, would be appropriate. We received and funded a new proposal to conduct what is now the National Longitudinal Study of Adolescent Health (Add Health). When it came time to release the first results of Add Health, the findings emphasized the importance of parents for protecting adolescent health—drawing praise from the very same conservative groups who had shut down its predecessor.

In 2008, I was appointed Acting Associate Director of the NIH for Behavioral and Social Sciences and Acting Director of the NIH Office of Behavioral and Social Sciences Research (OBSSR). My main focus here was to support and leverage the work of behavioral and social scientists across the NIH; and to amplify the message that health is a function not only of molecules and cells but also of behavior, social systems, and human environments. We launched the NIH Basic Behavioral and Social Science Opportunity Network (OppNet), a five-year, trans-NIH initiative with $120 million in funding.

I retired from federal service at the age of 59, recognizing that I had an opportunity to explore other aspects of a career in demography. Since that time, I have taught a course in health disparities, done research exploring models of culture in demography, co-directed a fellowship program in population health, and served as President of the Population Association of America. It's been grand!

What do you see as the field's most important contribution as well as its greatest challenge?

Demography is interdisciplinary. It is a great place for creative people who don't want to be boxed in by any specific discipline, but are willing to take the best scientific approaches and the most useful knowledge from each. Integrating some fields (anthropology, for example) is harder because of differences in methods, but still very important because of the insights other fields bring.

Demography has a willingness to tackle new problems outside of our traditional core of fertility, mortality, and migration. We have addressed all sorts of population issues—creating productive adults, understanding the determinants of health, changes in marriage, the impact of immigration, and poverty and inequality. We've brought demography into the conversation in other fields and made tremendous contributions.

Public Definition

"Problem" is a label awarded by the public. That labeling requires two mental steps by the public: (1) accepting some belief of cause and effect, and (2) passing a negative value judgment on the alleged effect. Let us elaborate the role of the cause-effect belief, using as an illustration the aging U.S. population. As we shall see in chapter 4, the average age of the U.S. population is increasing and will increase in the future if our fertility remains low. That, in itself, is not a problem unless the U.S. public believes one or more of the various theories about how that change in age composition will influence other variables. For instance, one theory posits that the increase in the proportion of the population that is of retirement age will shrink the proportional size of the workforce and thus the collective productivity of the economy. Another theory views aging populations as costly, both in economic terms, because of increased healthcare and retirement pension costs, and in social terms because of reduced quality of life for the elderly. The point is, each of these theories or beliefs represents a statement of a relationship between some demographic variable (population aging in our example) that is seen as a cause, and some nondemographic social or economic variable that is seen as an effect.

Those things we choose to label as population problems depend on our population theories, our beliefs about cause and effect, and even the adequacy of the demographic information we have available. That has important implications. It means that the accuracy of pinpointing population problems depends on our success in what we have defined earlier as population studies, which examine the relationships between demographic and nondemographic variables. It also means our definition of population problems at a given moment may be based upon a fallacy, an erroneous belief about a cause-effect relationship, or a lack of foresight into other effects that change the equation of our anticipations. Indeed, population studies can solve population problems simply by disproving fallacious beliefs about cause and effect, and can also refocus our anticipation of problems by helping us understand the variety of influences that might alter demographic trends in the near future. On the other hand, it means that as-yet unknown consequences of population trends would be labeled "problems" if our theories were better.

Let us turn to the value judgment component of the problem-definition process. It is easy to overlook the fact that every definition of a problem involves an implicit value judgment regarding the alleged effect of the population trend. The main reason for this is that people tend to talk to other people who share their own values and consequently are unaware that somebody else might evaluate the trends quite differently. A simple illustration is the concern over the changing ethnic composition in Western Europe. In the recent past these countries welcomed ethnic immigrants as migrants, farm workers, and "guest" workers. Ethnic immigrants were perceived as filling a necessary labor need in the developed economies. However, more recently some European host countries have become alarmed that those guests have stayed, are introducing new cultural influences, and are seeking full citizenship (Ceobanu and Escandell, 2010). This is viewed as a problem to some natives. This has also been the case in the U.S. Even though the United States has a long immigration history, Americans were uneasy throughout the 19th- and early-20th-century immigration of Chinese, Mexicans, and

Southern and Eastern Europeans, reflected by periods of highly restrictive migration policy (Foner, 2005). Anti-immigrant concern continues in the U.S. today, with renewed restrictionist policies recently enacted that reduce the social benefits available to immigrants. But it is likely that immigrants do not consider themselves to be the problem as seen by some segments of the native population. Thus, those population trends one calls "problems" depends very much on where one sits. A great way to become familiar with debates around demographic issues is to check out the population-related blogs shown in Box 1-1.

Box 1-1	Blog Sites about Demography	
	Demographer.com (methods)	http://www.demographer.com
	Demography Is Destiny	http://www.mercatornet.com/demography
	Demography Matters	http://demographymatters.blogspot.com
	Demographics Revealed	http://demographicsrevealed.org
	Family Inequality	http://familyinequality.wordpress.com
	Pew Research Social & Demographic Trends	http://www.pewsocialtrends.org
	Population Reference Bureau Blog	http://prbblog.org
	United States Census Research Matters	http://researchmatters.blogs.census.gov
	Urban Demographics	http://urbandemographics.blogspot.com
	GAPMINDER for a fact-based world view	http://www.gapminder.org/
	Weeks Population	http://weekspopulation.blogspot.com

Population Problems in This Textbook

In decades past, concern over population problems was the impetus for introductory courses in demography or population studies. In our own university—and, we will wager, most others—such courses used to be titled "Population Problems," or something very similar. A focus on what was then considered the single most important demographic problem—the world population explosion alarm of the late 1960s—led to demography courses that were universally oversubscribed by socially and ecologically minded young people.

Things have changed. World population growth has slowed (but by no means stopped yet). In addition, some conditions, such as global poverty and human development, have improved despite growing populations. And a more nuanced perspective on the connection between the environment and population has evolved, acknowledging that unsustainable resource use must be considered alongside population growth. Panic over a looming population catastrophe has, as a result, become less prevalent. Today, demographic concern with population growth tends to center on insuring universal opportunities for human development and empowerment, and a more reasoned concern over the cumulative environmental effects of economic development. Demographers have come to appreciate the complexity of human demographic systems and the likelihood of an unanticipated future turn when making long-range demographic forecasts.

Similarly, most students turn to this course for more pragmatic reasons than in the past. Some are looking for demographic literacy, while others seek an understanding of demographic effects on our lives and environment or the fundamental skills that are useful in virtually any career. Accordingly, they are less likely to focus on population problems. Or, to state it more positively, they may be more inclined to recognize the subjective and relative nature of population problems and to consider a whole range of potential problems rather than follow any one current public obsession.

This book's treatment of population problems is based on this framework. The subject of population problems is reserved until the end of the chapter, after important trends have been described in detail. Then, emphasizing the subjective nature of demographic problems, we ask three questions regarding each potential problem raised for discussion: Who is alarmed by the trend? What specific effects do these people consider problematic? And, why do they judge these effects to be negative? Each chapter also contains discussion topics that focus on possible population problems. We have chosen these topics to stimulate discussion of alternative perspectives and to illustrate the fact that identifying population problems generally involves making value judgments.

SUMMARY

Demography is the study of the size and composition of populations, the processes that change this size and composition, and the relationships of population characteristics with the broader social and cultural environment. A narrow definition, formal demography, emphasizes the study of the demographic variables and their interrelationships. A broader definition, population studies, includes the study of the nondemographic determinants and consequences of the demographic variables. There are many population characteristics of demographic interest when describing population composition, but age and sex are the most fundamental.

Demography not only describes population traits at a given moment, but also analyzes the dynamic processes by which populations change in size and composition. The growth equation is a fundamental feature of demography and describes the relation between growth and births, deaths, and migratory moves. Collectively, such population events are seen as manifestations of population processes: fertility, mortality, and migration. Demographers employ rates to measure the force of these processes, the simplest examples being crude rates. Change in population composition is determined not only by fertility, mortality, and migration, but also by the complex processes of reclassification.

One source of public interest in demography is concern over population problems. Population problems are social problems and as such are defined subjectively by the public and by governments. Labeling a population trend as a problem involves believing some theory about its consequences and making a negative value judgment about those consequences. Current population problems are raised for discussion in context at the end of each chapter in this textbook. However, demographers have learned to appreciate the changeable nature of demographic behavior, and the changeability of even more transitory definitions of population problems.

EXERCISES

1. Table E1-1 gives estimated midyear demographic data for the United States and Mexico for the calendar years 2012–2013. Use these data to calculate the estimated net migration for Mexico. Use the blank cells in the table for recording your computations and use the United States column as an example. Remember, the formula needed for these calculations is the growth equation for an open population:

$$P_2 - P_1 = B_{(1,2)} - D_{(1,2)} + M_{(1,2)}$$

Table E1-1   Population Data for the United States and Mexico, July 1, 2012– July 1, 2013

	United States	Mexico
2012 Midyear Population	313,847,465	114,975,406
2013 Midyear Population	316,668,567	116,220,947
Growth between Both Years	2,821,102	
Births between Both Years	4,293,433	2,169,586
Deaths between Both Years	2,633,180	563,379
Natural Increase between Both Years	1,660,253	
Net Migration between Both Years	1,160,849	

Source: U.S. Census Bureau, 2013. "International Data Base."

2. Compute the estimated crude rates for Mexico in Table E1-2. Use the data from Table E1-1 to compute these rates, and the United States column of Table E1-2 as a model. The formula* to use for each of these is

$$\frac{E}{P_m} \times 100$$

Table E1-2   Crude Rates for the United States and Mexico, 2012

	United States	Mexico
2012 Midyear Population	313,847,465	114,975,406
Crude Birth Rate	1.40	
Crude Death Rate	0.80	
Crude Rate of Natural Increase (%)	0.53	
Crude Growth Rate	0.90	

*Normally only the crude growth rate and the rate of natural increase are percentages (per hundred), while births and deaths are expressed as crude rates per thousand. In the above case, then, the U.S. CBR normally would be expressed as 14.0 and the CDR as 8.0 per 1,000 people. But for the purposes of consistency in this exercise we calculate per 100 people.

These are only rough estimates by the Census Bureau's International Data Base; round your rates to the nearest hundredth.

Source: U.S. Census Bureau, 2013. "International Data Base."

PROPOSITIONS FOR DEBATE

1. Population "problems" should not be a matter of opinion; they only appear so in the short run because of our imperfect knowledge of the future.

2. The population problems in the headlines today will still be there in ___ years.

3. A world population-explosion catastrophe is still happening; demographers just aren't paying enough attention to it anymore.

4. The demography of the population (i.e., size and composition, processes of change, and relationships of these with the environment) will, or will not, affect personal decisions I make during college.

REFERENCES AND SUGGESTED READINGS

Bogue, Donald, Eduardo Arriaga, and Douglas L. Anderton, eds. 1993. *Readings in Population Research Methodology*. United Nations Fund for Population Activities. Chicago: Social Development Center.

Ceobanu, Alin M., and Xavier Escandell. 2010. "Comparative Analyses of Public Attitudes Toward Immigrants and Immigration Using Multinational Survey Data: A Review of Theories and Research." *Annual Review of Sociology* 36: 309–328.

Foner, Nancy. 2005. *In a New Land: A Comparative View of Immigration*. New York: New York University Press.

IUSSP (International Union for the Scientific Study of Population). 1982. *Multilingual Demographic Dictionary*. English Section. Liege, Belgium: Ordina Editions.

Kertzer, David I., and Tom Fricke, eds. 1997. *Anthropological Demography: Toward a New Synthesis*. Chicago: University of Chicago Press.

McFalls, Joseph A., Jr. 2007. "Population: A Lively Introduction, 5th Edition." *Population Bulletin* 62(1). Washington, DC: Population Reference Bureau.

MPIDR (Max Planck Institute for Demographic Research). 2013. *What is Demography?* Retrieved September 20, 2013. http://www.demogr.mpg.de/en/education_career/what_is_demography_1908/

Obermeyer, Carla Makhlouf. 1997. "Qualitative Methods: A Key to a Better Understanding of Demographic Behavior?" *Population and Development Review* 23(4).

Petit, Véronique, and Yves Charbit. 2013. "The French School of Demography: Contextualizing Demographic Analysis." *Population and Development Review* 38(1): 322–333.

PRB (Population Reference Bureau). 2014. *2014 World Population Data Sheet*. Washington, DC: Population Reference Bureau.

Pressat, Roland. 1985. *The Dictionary of Demography*. Edited by Christopher Wilson. New York: Basil Blackwell Ltd.

U.S. Census Bureau. 2011. *The 2011 Statistical Abstract: Components of Population Change*. Revised August 29, 2011. Retrieved October 22, 2013. http://www.census.gov/compendia/statab/2011/tables/11s0004.xls

———. 2012. *The 2012 Statistical Abstract: Historical Statistics*. Revised August 31, 2012. Retrieved October 22, 2013. http://www.census.gov/compendia/statab/hist_stats.html

———. 2013. "International Data Base." *International Programs*. Revised August 28, 2012. Data: 12.0625. Code:12.0321. Retrieved September 20, 2013. http://www.census.gov/population/international/data/idb/informationGateway.php

2

Demographic Data

As civilizations rise and as nations develop, governments build systems for gathering information about their people. Minimally, they wish to know how many of what kind are where. The current standard data-gathering system, evolved in the West, has as its foundation the decennial census. But a census tells only about one moment. Therefore, in this system censuses are supplemented by the registration of population events (births, deaths) and/or by sample surveys. With the advent of technological literacy in modern societies there is enormous untapped potential for measuring the digital traces left behind by Internet and cell phone users, and this will be an emerging method of data collection in the near future (Palmer et al., 2013; Watts, 2007). Such emerging data sources are popularly referred to as "big data." But even with the most sophisticated combination of these elements, gaps will still remain that must be filled by estimation. This chapter treats the currently used interrelated elements in order: censuses, registration, sample surveys, and estimation.

Population Censuses

In the 1800s, the practice of taking population censuses spread through Western countries, and later from there to the rest of the world. That is not to say that earlier civilizations had not at their peaks done something very similar. Palermo stone fragments are one of the oldest records of census that still exist to this date, and Egyptologists estimate that a large-scale census was taken around 2600 BCE (before Common Era) under the reign of Sneferu (Wilkinson, 2000). But the worldwide spread of census taking, promoted by the United Nations, is primarily a post–World War II phenomenon.

The United Nations Statistics Division (2012) estimates that about 97% of the world's countries now collect a census, enumerating nearly 99% of the world's population. Only seven countries recently did not conduct a census (United Nations Statistics Division, 2012). Such countries tend to be small (e.g., Eritrea), or are those experiencing political strife (e.g., Lebanon, Iraq, Pakistan, Somalia, Uzbekistan, Western Sahara). Despite these lapses, census data are increasingly available for the world's countries.

Basic Features

What is a census? The United Nations, where international standards evolve, says that a **census** should have four basic features. First, it should be *individual;* each person is to be recorded separately along with his or her traits. This allows for later cross-classification of individuals in the tabulation process. Second, it should be *universal;* everybody in the specified territory should be similarly counted and described. Third, it should be *simultaneous;* enumerators should specify each person's location and traits as of some particular "census moment." Fourth, censuses should be *periodic;* they should be carried out at regular intervals. Regularity makes it easier to describe trends and to check on consistency between censuses. The United Nations recommends decennial censuses and, further, has nudged countries into taking them in years ending in zero to allow international comparability (United Nations, 1998, 2008).

Consistent with these goals, modern census taking has evolved into a set of conventional steps taken by the government:

1. It specifies the geographic boundaries of the area to be covered. Further, it specifies the geographic boundaries of the subareas about which it ultimately wants separate information. Subareas should be small enough so that each can be the responsibility of an individual enumerator.

2. The government decides which traits it needs to know about for each of its people and settles upon a questionnaire.

3. Simultaneously, within all of the subareas, the government sends out the assigned enumerator to visit households and to list all of the individuals in each household. At the same time, the enumerator is to gather questionnaire information about each of the individuals. Conventionally, the enumerator visits each household, finds a qualified informant there, and gathers information about each individual residing in the household, filling it into a separate row or column on the questionnaire.

4. The government compiles the information from the subareas, tabulating numbers of people by subarea (distribution) and by category of individual trait (composition).

5. The government reports the findings to the sponsoring citizenry.

Particular governments may choose, for good reason, to deviate from this set of traditions. For instance, recent U.S. censuses have deviated in two ways from the steps just summarized: (1) they have used a mail-out/mail-back procedure instead of face-to-face interviews for most of the population, and (2) they have asked some questions of only a sample of the total population. (A later section of this chapter describes the evolution of the U.S. census.) Increasingly, as populations grow and technology evolves, the question of how much information should be collected using modern sampling methods versus complete population censuses has become a central issue in designing censuses.

Census Topics

Bases for choice.   How should a government decide what topics to cover in its census? The criteria recommended by the United Nations (1998, 2008) fall into two categories, political and technical.

On the political side, the United Nations recognizes the priority of national over international needs in determining census content. Each nation should decide its questions through its normal political processes. In a democracy, this usually involves lengthy hearings and debates dealing with demographic priorities, rights to privacy, and, inevitably, financial constraints. Being political, the decisions reflect swings in public concern. For instance, U.S. censuses from the 1920s contain more coverage of ethnicity, reflecting that era's support for legislation restricting immigration (Snipp, 2003). More recently, a great deal of discussion has revolved around ethnicity and race questions because of the rising numbers of children from parents with different ethnic backgrounds, calling for the more comprehensive multiethnic classification that first appeared in the 2000 census and was repeated in the 2010 census (U.S. Census Bureau, 2001; Edmonston and Schultze, 1995).

On the technical side, demographers need data that are complete and comparable. Nations can enhance international comparability by taking censuses in standard years (those ending in zero), by covering the same topics, and by using the same definitions. They can enhance comparability across time by covering the same topics repeatedly in their census series, allowing them to identify trends. Another consideration is one the United Nations calls "suitability": a census should not ask questions that respondents are unable to answer or find offensive, as such a procedure may jeopardize the gathering of legitimate census data.

International priorities.   Box 2-1 describes the considerable international accord reached after a series of regional conferences as to which questions should be asked on current national population censuses. Some explanation about categories of questions for population censuses may help.

Box 2-1	United Nations List of Topics for 2010 Censuses
	1. Geographical and internal migration characteristics - Place of usual residence - Place of birth - Place of previous residence - Total population - Urban and rural - Place where present at time of census - Duration of residence - Place of residence at a specified date in the past - Locality

(continued)

2. International migration characteristics
- Country of birth
- Year or period of arrival
- Citizenship

3. Household and family characteristics
- Relationship to head or other reference member of household
- Household and family composition
- Household and family status

4. Demographic and social characteristics
- Sex
- Marital status
- Language
- Indigenous identity
- Age
- Religion
- Ethnicity

5. Fertility and mortality
- Children ever born alive
- Date of birth of last child born alive
- Deaths among children born in the past 12 months
- Age of mother at birth of first child born alive
- Children living
- Births in the past 12 months
- Age, date or duration of first marriage
- Maternal or paternal orphanhood
- Household deaths in the past 12 months

6. Educational characteristics
- Literacy
- Educational attainment
- School attendance
- Field of education and educational qualifications

7. Economic characteristics
- Activity status
- Industry
- Time worked
- Institutional sector of employment
- Informal employment
- Occupation
- Status in employment
- Income
- Employment in the informal sector
- Place of work

8. Disability characteristics

9. Agriculture work

Source: United Nations, 2008. *Principles and Recommendations for Population and Housing Censuses,* pp. 112–113.

Topic 1, geographical information, concerns national origins and place of current and previous residence, and allows for counting the total population of particular areas as well as for categories of areas, such as urban versus rural. Incidentally, one issue governments have to decide is whether it serves them better to record as a person's residence where he or she was found at the "census moment" (**de facto residence**) or their usual place of residence (**de jure residence**). Most nations compromise, with the United States leaning toward the *de jure* principle. Information on duration of residence and comparison of previous with present residence provide partial information on internal migration. As international migration becomes increasingly common, censuses also have begun collecting information on migration status as seen in Topic 2.

Topic 3 focuses on households rather than individuals. Knowing the relationship of each individual to the family or household head (or other reference member) allows a description of the household and family composition. A major change in the 1980 U.S. census was the elimination of the head-of-household concept and its replacement with a reference-member approach. Other social changes are currently evolving, for example the legal recognition of same-sex marriage. When social categories are in flux or contested, it can lead to data accountability challenges. At one point in the past, the census inaccurately recoded such same-sex households reporting to be married as different sex, married households (Cohn, 2011). After the Supreme Court struck down the Defense of Marriage Act in 2013, same-sex married couples are now recognized in the census.

Topics 4, 6, 7, 8, and 9 all contain questions on population composition. As one might expect, age and sex universally are top-priority topics. Some questions on economic activities and human resources (literacy and educational attainment) also are common. Questions dealing with ethnic identity (i.e., religion; language; national, ethnic, or indigenous group) are judged useful but not necessarily of highest priority for all world regions. Questions on disability were added to the United Nations recommendations for 2000 censuses; those on indigenous peoples and informal and agricultural employment were added for the 2010 censuses. In each case these questions were added because censuses were likely to be the only reliable source of data for these topics. Preliminary discussions have begun for recommendations for the 2020 censuses. In addition to new questions to be added, it is expected that alternative approaches to census data collection will be a primary topic of focus (see Box 2-2 on the following page).

Topic 5, concerning fertility and mortality, has a special purpose. Most census questions deal with traits of persons at the moment of the census. However, demographers also want to understand the processes by which size and composition change: mortality, fertility, and migration. Civil registration and sample surveys, dealt with later in this chapter, provide direct information about the population processes. To supplement and cross-check with these two sources, demographers habitually include retrospective questions about some past vital events in censuses.

Census Errors

Errors of coverage.   No census is perfect. All suffer from two kinds of errors: coverage and content. The most obvious is coverage error, counting some people more than once or not at all. In the 2010 U.S. census, undercounts and overcounts were minimal (U.S. Census Bureau, 2012). Even when coverage error is minimal, however, par-

<table>
<tr><td>

Box 2-2

</td><td>

Internet Response Options in Censuses

</td></tr>
</table>

> **Box 2-2** · **Internet Response Options in Censuses**
>
> As the Internet has become readily available in many households across the states, more people nowadays shop, communicate, and conduct official business online, such as filing taxes and renewing licenses. Therefore, it will be no surprise if the Census Bureau were to introduce Internet response options for the 2020 Census.
>
> Actually, the United States was one of the first countries to offer an Internet response option in 2000, but the Census Bureau refrained from using the Internet for the 2010 census due to emerging data security concerns. Based on the 2003 and 2005 National Census Tests, the bureau concluded that the overall Internet response rate did not differ significantly from the traditional mail-out-only format.
>
> Countries like Australia, Canada, New Zealand, Singapore, Spain, and Switzerland have successfully introduced Internet response options in censuses without major issues. While the overall use of the Internet response option ranged from merely 1% in the 2001 Spanish census to 18.5% in the 2006 Canadian census, all of these countries plan to continually invest in the online data-collection infrastructure.
>
> The U.S. Census Bureau anticipates that increased use of Internet and wireless technologies will become necessary in order to minimize the cost of censuses. Before the 2020 census design is finalized, the bureau plans to test the effectiveness of Internet data collection via smaller-scale surveys such as the American Community Survey to gauge if it is beneficial, feasible, and cost-effective.

ticular groups of people are more likely to be overlooked: renters, the homeless, and some minorities. For example, the 2010 post-enumeration survey found that 2% of the African American population and 1.5% of the Hispanic population were not covered by the census (Mule, 2012). The major problem with such coverage errors is that they are difficult to identify without eliciting additional information beyond the initial enumeration of the population.

Errors of content. Content errors arise when respondents misreport information about the people being enumerated or when the interviewer misrecords the information given. **Misreporting** can be due to ignorance of the facts, a desire to look better in the eyes of the interviewer, or a belief that the answer is none of the government's business. Such misreporting is difficult to identify even using standard Census Bureau procedures (Iversen et al., 1999). Remember, just because a government wants to gather facts from its populace does not mean that the populace has those facts to give or cares to report them accurately. For example, although most people in the world report their biological sex accurately, it is surprising how few know (or care to report) their precise age. The tendency of people to round their reported ages to even years, the nearest five years, or even the nearest ten years results in higher percentages of people reporting these ages, a phenomenon so common that demographers have a term for it, **age heaping**. Individuals also sometimes have difficulty determining which categories of race and ethnicity apply to them or resist the categories imposed upon them by the census. To address this in the United States, census respondents are now offered the chance to check more than one racial category. It is important to recognize that racial and ethnic classification schema have changed almost every decade on the U.S. census since its inception (Snipp, 2003), reflecting the constantly changing nature of society's concept of racial and ethnic identity. Some have argued that such questions should not be included in the census and that an "origins" question would be more relevant (Hirschman et al., 2000).

Estimating errors.   An integral part of the census enterprise, according to the United Nations, should be estimating such content and coverage errors. There are several ways to validate or correct census errors: post-enumeration surveys, data validation, and comparison with secondary data sources. In the first and most reliable of these methods, census bureaus can re-enumerate with special care a sample of the census respondents and compare the results with the original enumeration. The U.S. Census Bureau conducts such post-enumeration surveys regularly to obtain complete coverage and correct information for a sample of the geographic areas covered by the census.

A second way of estimating and correcting for census errors is simply to insure that the data recorded are accurate, internally consistent, and plausible. As information is collected, errors or inconsistencies are identified for correction during the data collection itself. For instance, a woman reporting her age as twenty-five years is unlikely to have twenty living children. If this information were entered by the enumerator the computer might prompt the interviewer to repeat the question or make further inquiries to resolve the inconsistency.

Finally, in countries that have good statistical infrastructure, bureaus can compare census statistics against other statistical records. For instance, the total number of children enumerated under age ten should bear some correspondence to the total number of births and childhood deaths that have been registered over the past ten years.

Census bureaus seldom can correct erroneous individual records, but they can and do correct aggregate tabulations for sets of individuals. They also pass on warnings to consumers about the degree and direction of such errors. These corrections are often in the form of estimated underreporting of various categories of people. Such revised or corrected estimates of population characteristics that adjust for estimated errors were used for most purposes in the year 2010 U.S. census.

Evolution of the U.S. Census

The United States has the longest modern series of censuses on record. The first U.S. census was taken in 1790; the twenty-third in 2010. This primacy probably is explained by the political basis for the birth of the nation. As the first European colony to establish itself as an independent nation, the United States had a strong philosophical commitment to the idea of (limited) popular suffrage. Accordingly, its very constitution provides for a census, initially for the purpose of apportioning seats in the House of Representatives and for directing taxes among the states (U.S. Census Bureau, n.d.).

However, the first census probably bore little resemblance to the last. It was not until 1902, more than halfway through the U.S. history of census taking, that a permanent census bureau was established. Prior to that, censuses were *ad hoc* affairs handled by temporary organizations. In contrast, the present U.S. Census Bureau continuously plans future censuses, processes the most recent census data, and also administers a variety of smaller, related data-gathering efforts. The cost of the census has risen dramatically, and the 2010 census was the most expensive census in history, an eight-fold increase (even after controlling for inflation) since the 1970 census (U.S. GAO, 2011). Box 2-3 has more information about this.

Box 2-3	**U.S. Census: A Costly but Necessary Operation**
	Although the U.S. Census Bureau consumes less than 1% of the federal budget, you might be surprised to hear that the 2010 census cost roughly $117 per housing unit, or about $13 billion total. Over the years, the census operation cost has steadily increased from $3.93 per housing unit in 1900 to $70.68 in 2000 (both in 2010 constant dollars).
	Why did the census become so costly? Besides the fact that the American population has grown larger and larger every year, the first and foremost reason is the growing complexity of data-collection procedures. New housing units are sprouting up across the nation and people no longer exclusively use landline phones. In order to ensure the data accuracy, the number of enumerators has increased from 650 in 1790 to over half a million in 2010, and that does not even include all the postal workers who deliver census forms! Added costs also stem from the modernization of the geographic coding system and address-mapping software.
	However, critics who argue for a more cost-effective operation point out that the per-housing-unit cost of Canadian censuses has remained about $40 since 1996. Therefore, experts anticipate the 2020 census to undergo a drastic budgetary review.
	Source: National Research Council, 2010.

Over its two centuries, the decennial census has been transformed. It has expanded its coverage in several ways. Obviously, the territory covered has spread along with national boundaries, but in addition there has been a move to cover all parts of the nation and its affiliated territories. In parallel, there has been a tendency to include all, not part, of the population therein. Content, as well, has grown from a rudimentary noting of existence and location of individuals to a detailed description of them. Since 1940 it has been a census of both population and housing. With professionalization came a steady reduction of errors over time. As public confidence in the results has grown and as the needs of modern society for information have exploded, the ways of processing the reports have also become more sophisticated and varied. The latest census information is now regularly distributed via the Internet through downloadable reports, statistical tabulations, data visualization figures, profile maps, and raw data. As the dissemination of census data has improved, and as computing facilities have become more accessible, there has been a continual growth in the use of census data in both the public and private sectors. The following sections detail these changes.

Coverage

Not only did the geographic coverage of the U.S. census follow the frontier across the coterminous United States, it also followed the expansion of the country beyond those borders.

> Alaska was first included in 1880; the Philippine Islands, Puerto Rico, Hawaii, Guam, and American Samoa in 1900; the Canal Zone and Midway in 1910; the Virgin Islands in 1920; certain small Pacific and Caribbean Islands in 1940; and the Trust Territory of the Pacific Islands in 1950. (Shryock, 1982, p. 142)

Moreover, coverage reached even beyond the American "empire" to include some Americans living outside its borders: armed forces and federal civilian employees (and their dependents), crews of merchant vessels, and so forth.

As in ancient censuses, the earlier U.S. counts did not treat all residents equally. In the first six censuses, only the head of household was listed by name; other members were simply tallied into categories for an aggregate description. Listing all persons by name, along with their characteristics, was the great innovation of the census of 1850 (Shryock, 1982, p. 138). Moreover, categories of peoples simply ignored or only partially described in the past are included in recent censuses (the homeless, Native Americans).

Attempts to expand coverage to the homeless population have included special multiple-day outreach periods to shelters, soup kitchens, and other locations based on local knowledge of where homeless individuals might congregate. "Transitory Locations Enumerations" are also used to target RV parks, motels, circuses, and campgrounds to enumerate people who do not live in traditional housing units. With recent natural disasters and home foreclosures, nontraditional enumerations such as these are particularly important. As efforts to expand coverage continue, the census is rapidly approaching universal coverage of the population. These efforts are, of course, limited by the fact that some people in the United States, such as undocumented immigrants or those suspicious of governmental intervention, may wish to avoid enumeration. But the mission of the U.S. census is to count every American, regardless of their immigration and citizenship status, and no matter whether they live in a mansion or a cardboard box.

Census Geography

Not only has geographic coverage increased but also the geographic detail of reporting. The basic census strategy is to map small geographic units of responsibility, each to be assigned to a specific enumerator. This means small units are capable of being assembled into meaningful larger units for reporting purposes. The bureau increasingly has taken advantage of this opportunity, reporting not only by administrative units (town, county, state) but also using its data partially for defining other meaningful social units (parts of cities, standard metropolitan statistical areas, census regions, divisions of the country, and so forth).

Figure 2-1 on the following page lists some of the geographical units that the Census Bureau uses to report population data. The top panel of the figure shows the hierarchy of contiguous geographic units, from largest to smallest. After the overall *nation* level, there are four census *regions* (Northeast, Midwest, South, and West) and each region has two to three *divisions* made up of anywhere from three to nine states. Almost all census data are regionally organized. However, we are most often interested in population data for smaller areas. *States* (and *territories*) form natural divisions within the regions, as do *counties* within states.

Moving to smaller areas becomes more complicated and areas delineated are often unique to the design of the census. Counties are designed by the Census Bureau in cooperation with state and local officials. For the past couple decades, all areas of the country also are divided into small areas called *census tracts*. Only portions of the country were divided into tracts in earlier censuses. Tracts are defined by local officials working within Census Bureau guidelines and so reflect, as well as any defined area, local communities or neighborhoods. Most tracts have a population of several thousand and average around 4,000 people. Much of the research conducted using census data has been done using census tracts, and computerized census data is available for these areas. For even smaller areas of analysis the Census Bureau defines *block groups* and *blocks*. Blocks are small areas bounded on all sides by visible features such as

Figure 2-1

Standard Hierarchy of Geographic Entities for the 2010 Decennial Census

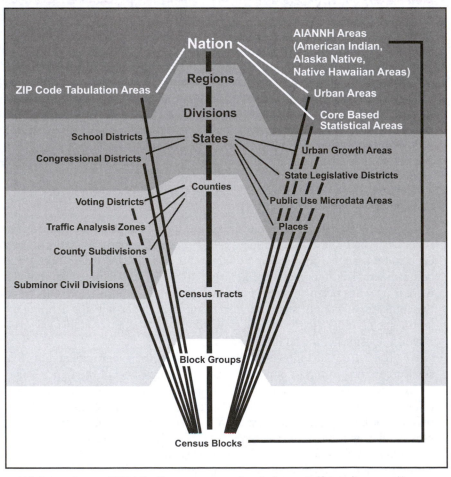

Source: U.S. Census Bureau, 2010. http://www.census.gov/geo/reference/pdfs/geodiagram.pdf

streets, roads, streams, etc., or other political property boundaries. Blocks are often used to study small areas. However, because blocks are so small, the Census Bureau regularly suppresses block-level information that might identify specific individuals.

Looking within each hierarchy level of Figure 2-1, we see that a number of other categories are used in reporting census data. Data at the national level are generally available for *core based statistical areas* consisting of a large population nucleus and adjacent communities that are socially or economically integrated with the population center. Census tabulations are frequently divided into urban and rural areas, but the Census Bureau designates *urban areas* consisting of a central place and its adjacent, densely settled, urban fringe to better capture this distinction. Less frequently used categories include *ZIP code areas, congressional districts, school districts,* and so on. As demands for data have risen, the variety of geographic areas delineated by the Census Bureau has increased, and areas identified in Figure 2-1 are just some of the more commonly used designations.

Content

Until recently, the trend has been to expand the topics covered in the census, along with the people covered. "Several of the Founding Fathers, including Thomas Jefferson and James Madison, labored mightily to persuade the Congress to add items that would provide information on manpower, industrial composition, and national origins" (Shryock, 1982, p. 138). This expansion was gradual, peaking in 1890.

But the census exists within a political context and therefore reflects the public preoccupations of the particular era in which it was developed (Snipp, 2003). For the first century, more or less, Congress was directly responsible for establishing the content. After the establishment of the Census Bureau in 1902, the director made these decisions, though undoubtedly remaining sensitive to political as well as technical considerations. Some items on the census are directly legislated by Congress. Since 1950, the process of deciding not only questionnaire content but also priorities regarding tabulations has been the work of an elaborate network of advisory committees, public hearings, and correspondence culminating in congressional approval (see U.S. Census Bureau, 1999, fig. V-1). This process now takes years before the actual census date.

As one might expect, the topics normally covered in recent U.S. censuses go beyond the priority items recommended by the United Nations in Box 2-1. Table 2-1 on the next page shows major items included in the U.S. census between 1960 and 2010. However, not all of these topics are covered for each individual in the population. From 1940 through 2000, the census questionnaires were divided into a "short form" (questions asked of everybody) and one or more "long forms" (including supplementary questions for specified samples of people). In 2010, the long form was eliminated and extensive information is now collected instead through the **American Community Survey**, which has been distributed on a rolling basis since 2005 to 250,000 households each month, rather than just once every ten years. This major innovation provides detailed information on American cities and towns annually that used to be available only on a decadal basis. With the elimination of decadal long forms, the 2010 census was heralded as the shortest census since 1790, with "10 questions in 10 minutes" (U.S. Census Bureau, 2012). Figure 2-2 on p. 31 depicts the 2010 short form version of the U.S. Census.

Table 2-1   Census Information

	1960 (1)	1970 (2)	1980 (3)	1990 (4)	2000 (5)	2010 (6)
Population Items						
Age	S	S	S	S	S	S
Sex	S	S	S	S	S	S
Race	S	S	S	S	S	S
Hispanic Origin		L	S	S	S	S
Relationship to Household Head	S	S	S	S	S	S
Age or Date of First Marriage	L	L	L			
Children Born to Mother	L	L	L	L		
School Attendance and Attainment	L	L	L	L	L	ACS
Place of Birth	L	L	L	L	L	ACS
Place of Birth Mother and Father	L	L				
Ancestry			L	L	L	ACS
Language Spoken at Home	L	L	L	L	L	ACS
Residence 5 Years Ago	L	L	L	L	L	
Work Disability		L	L	L	L	ACS
Employment Status	L	L	L	L	L	ACS
Hours Worked Last Week	L	L	L	L	L	
Year Last Worked	L	L	L	L		
Industry, Occupation, and Class	L	L	L	L	L	ACS
Means of Transportation	L	L	L	L	L	ACS
Income from Earnings	L	L	L	L	L	ACS
Farm Income, Soc. Sec., and Assistance		L	L	L	L	ACS
All Other Income	L	L	L	L	L	
Housing Items						
Owned or Rented	S	S	S	S	S	S
Number of Rooms	S	S	S	S	L	ACS
Units at Address	S	S	S	S	L	ACS
Value	S	S	S	S	L	ACS
Mortgage and Insurance			L	L	L	ACS
Detailed Utility Costs	L	L	L	L	L	ACS
Year Built	L	L	L	L	L	ACS
Number of Bedrooms	L	L	L	L	L	ACS
Source of Water	L	L	L	L		
Sewage Disposal	L	L	L	L		
Heating Fuel	L	L	L	L	L	ACS
Telephone Available	L	S	L	L	L	ACS
Automobiles	L	L	L	L	L	ACS

Note: Some items listed represent consistent blocks of multiple questions on the census. S = Short Form; L = Long Form and ACS = the American Community Survey, which replaced the long form in 2010.

Sources: Edmonston and Schultze, 1995, Appendix A, table A-2; U.S. Census Bureau, 1999, table V-1; U.S. Census Bureau, 2013.

Figure 2-2

Census 2010 Short Form

United States Census 2010

This is the official form for all the people at this address.
It is quick and easy, and your answers are protected by law.

U.S. DEPARTMENT OF COMMERCE
Economics and Statistics Administration
U.S. CENSUS BUREAU

Use a blue or black pen.

Start here

The Census must count every person living in the United States on April 1, 2010.

Before you answer Question 1, count the people living in this house, apartment, or mobile home using our guidelines.

- Count all people, including babies, who live and sleep here most of the time.

The Census Bureau also conducts counts in institutions and other places, so:

- Do not count anyone living away either at college or in the Armed Forces.
- Do not count anyone in a nursing home, jail, prison, detention facility, etc., on April 1, 2010.
- Leave these people off your form, even if they will return to live here after they leave college, the nursing home, the military, jail, etc. Otherwise, they may be counted twice.

The Census must also include people without a permanent place to stay, so:

- If someone who has no permanent place to stay is staying here on April 1, 2010, count that person. Otherwise, he or she may be missed in the census.

1. How many people were living or staying in this house, apartment, or mobile home on April 1, 2010?

Number of people = ☐☐

2. Were there any additional people staying here April 1, 2010 that you did not include in Question 1? *Mark ☒ all that apply.*

☐ Children, such as newborn babies or foster children
☐ Relatives, such as adult children, cousins, or in-laws
☐ Nonrelatives, such as roommates or live-in baby sitters
☐ People staying here temporarily
☐ No additional people

3. Is this house, apartment, or mobile home — *Mark ☒ ONE box.*

☐ Owned by you or someone in this household with a mortgage or loan? *Include home equity loans.*
☐ Owned by you or someone in this household free and clear (without a mortgage or loan)?
☐ Rented?
☐ Occupied without payment of rent?

4. What is your telephone number? *We may call if we don't understand an answer.*

Area Code + Number

☐☐☐ – ☐☐☐ – ☐☐☐☐

OMB No. 0607-0919-C: Approval Expires 12/31/2011.

Form **D-61** (1-15-2009)

5. Please provide information for each person living here. Start with a person living here who owns or rents this house, apartment, or mobile home. If the owner or renter lives somewhere else, start with any adult living here. This will be Person 1.

What is Person 1's name? *Print name below.*

Last Name

First Name MI

6. What is Person 1's sex? *Mark ☒ ONE box.*

☐ Male ☐ Female

7. What is Person 1's age and what is Person 1's date of birth?
Please report babies as age 0 when the child is less than 1 year old.
Print numbers in boxes.

Age on April 1, 2010 | Month | Day | Year of birth

→ **NOTE: Please answer BOTH Question 8 about Hispanic origin and Question 9 about race. For this census, Hispanic origins are not races.**

8. Is Person 1 of Hispanic, Latino, or Spanish origin?

☐ **No,** not of Hispanic, Latino, or Spanish origin
☐ Yes, Mexican, Mexican Am., Chicano
☐ Yes, Puerto Rican
☐ Yes, Cuban
☐ Yes, another Hispanic, Latino, or Spanish origin — *Print origin, for example, Argentinean, Colombian, Dominican, Nicaraguan, Salvadoran, Spaniard, and so on.*

9. What is Person 1's race? *Mark ☒ one or more boxes.*

☐ White
☐ Black, African Am., or Negro
☐ American Indian or Alaska Native — *Print name of enrolled or principal tribe.*

☐ Asian Indian ☐ Japanese ☐ Native Hawaiian
☐ Chinese ☐ Korean ☐ Guamanian or Chamorro
☐ Filipino ☐ Vietnamese ☐ Samoan
☐ Other Asian — *Print race, for example, Hmong, Laotian, Thai, Pakistani, Cambodian, and so on.*
☐ Other Pacific Islander — *Print race, for example, Fijian, Tongan, and so on.*

☐ Some other race — *Print race.*

10. Does Person 1 sometimes live or stay somewhere else?

☐ No ☐ Yes — *Mark ☒ all that apply.*

☐ In college housing ☐ For child custody
☐ In the military ☐ In jail or prison
☐ At a seasonal or second residence ☐ In a nursing home
☐ For another reason

→ **If more people were counted in Question 1, continue with Person 2.**

USCENSUSBUREAU

Note: Subsequent pages for each household member include a question asking what their relationship is to Person 1.

Table 2-1 shows how the content of the U.S. census has changed over time. It indicates which questions were asked of everyone on the short form and which were asked of a sample of people on one or more long forms in each U.S. decennial census from 1960 to 2000 (and for 2010 on the American Community Survey). For decennial censuses, one in six Americans received the long form, while 250,000 households receive the American Community Survey each month. Questions often get dropped when there is no legislation requiring their collection by the Census Bureau, while others are added, such as one recently mandated by Congress on caregiving by grandparents (U.S. Census Bureau, 1999). These decisions reflect both the increasing concern for the cost of conducting a census and an increasing political influence on census content. Another factor influencing census content is the usefulness of the data being collected. While the decennial census was collecting socioeconomic data once every 10 years, the American Community Survey is conducted every year. Considering the rapid pace at which the American economy changes, continual collection of income, education, and occupation-related data has been deemed more sensible than the use of decennial data, hence the discontinuation of the census long form (U.S. Census Bureau, 2010).

Data Collection

Prior to World War II, census-taking procedures in the United States were conventional; that is, they involved the gathering of full information about all individuals by means of personal interviews with household informants. Since then, a series of fundamental changes have been made.

The first innovation, started in 1940, is asking some questions about only a sample of the population and making generalizations, from the sample, about the total population. By 2000, only six items in Table 2-1 were on the census short form; the remaining long-form questions were asked of a sample containing about 17% of the nation's households (U.S. Census Bureau, 1999). The justification, obviously, is economy: by sampling, the bureau saved money that then could be spent for improving the quality of enumeration.

The second innovation is obtaining answers through the mail rather than by face-to-face interviews. Figure 2-3 shows a historical cartoon depicting the census enumerators' visits to households and the challenges they sometimes met there. Although the census has become much more accepted by the American public today, pockets of resistance and related controversies still exist, as discussed in Box 2-4.

Today, the census locates people first and foremost through their mailing addresses. The mail-out, mail-back procedure was started in 1960. In fact, 74% of the 2010 census population data was gathered in this way (U.S. Census Bureau, 2010). The remaining population was interviewed by census workers who contacted households that did not respond to the mailed census or were living in remote areas or had no fixed addresses. Obviously the mailing procedure puts a premium on the careful preparation of address lists and probably is appropriate only in a context where mail service is virtually universal.

Processing and Publication

Until 1890, U.S. census returns were tabulated by hand. This was a time-consuming and error-plagued process, and its inadequacies grew in proportion to the popula-

Figure 2-3

1880 Political Cartoon, "Wonderful effect of the appearance of the census enumerator."

"Wonderful effect of the appearance of the census enumerator."

Source: Francese, 1979, p. 34.

tion being counted. Highly motivated as it was, the Census Bureau became the source of data-processing innovations that since have spread to other organizations. Herman Hollerith developed a tabulating machine that was used from 1890 to 1910; an improved "unit counter" using punched cards was developed at the bureau and used through 1950; electronic computers were in partial use in 1950, and now virtually all census tabulations are made with them; optical scanning devices, along with pre-coded questionnaires, have been in heavy use for decades. By 1980, questions on the short form were pre-coded for optical scanning. By the 2010 census, all questions and written answers were processed first through optical scanning, with manual data entry done only to resolve difficult to process write-in items.

Box 2-4	**Census Controversies**
	Use it for GOOD, never for EVIL.
	—Official motto of IPUMS (Census Microdata for Social and Economic Research)
	As dry as a census might seem, few would expect its existence to cause so much alarm. But censuses have long been controversial because of their age-old association with war and taxes. Indeed, historical records show that the imposition of census-taking in Rome led to a number of rebellions over the centuries.
	In the crudest sense, head counts are still needed to conduct taxation and, less frequently, to raise armies. But the advent of democracy-oriented governments in recent

(continued)

centuries led to a new need for counting the population: popular representation. Censuses have become culturally accepted for this reason in many countries. As we will emphasize throughout this book, detailed population data is also crucial to ensure that government infrastructure and services are able to meet the needs of populations as they grow and change.

Resistance to census taking generally comes in two varieties. In the first instance, citizens in countries with resources often want to make sure they are counted so they can get their fair share. Local population size determines how much a particular geographical region gains in votes, subsidies, etc. Thus, it is not uncommon in the United States for political party bickering to erupt every decade or so over the census in reaction to congressional reapportioning. In Nigeria, each national census since 1960 has been challenged in part due to concerns over oil money redistribution.

The other type of resistance to census-taking relates to privacy concerns. Countries with a history of governmental corruption and population data misuse are more likely to distrust censuses. Under the Nazi regime, census data was used to track down Holocaust victims. So when the German government initiated relatively benign changes to the national census forty years later there was a nationwide boycott of the effort (Hannah, 2008). To this day, the German census bureau does not collect data on race.

The United States is not immune from such citizen privacy concerns. In fact, religious affiliation will most likely never appear on an American census due to the country's constitutional separation of church and state (its potential introduction in 1960 met with immediate popular opposition). More detailed census questions, such as those featured in the American Community Survey (ACS), are questioned by some Americans for their relevance. There has been political mobilization on the part of the Republican National Committee to make participation in the ACS voluntary rather than mandatory on the grounds that it spends "millions of tax dollars to violate the rights and invade the personal privacy of United States citizens" (Roberts, 2010). Although this level of distress might seem peculiar in an era of much more invasive information-gathering efforts, as sanctioned by the USA Patriot Act or the NSA's cell phone record surveillance, there is historical precedence for concern. For example, evidence came to light in 2007 that the U.S. Census Bureau provided data identifying the whereabouts of Japanese-Americans as part of the U.S. government's World War II internment camp policy (Minkel, 2007). Census privacy protections were restored at the end of the war.

Although filling out a census is often mandatory, with an imposed fine for noncompliance, some citizens show resistance in other ways, such as deliberately flouting census enumeration categories as a way to voice their discontent with government policy. Examples are American gay householders checking "married" even though federal law prohibited gay marriage or when 390,000 British people wrote "Jedi" in response to a 2001 census question on religious affiliation (*The Economist*, 2007). But be forewarned! In the U.S., those who "willfully give any answer that is false shall be fined not more than $500."

Despite concerns over privacy, the census has strict confidentiality policies. By law, no one is allowed to link census records back to individuals—not the IRS, not the CIA, not even the president of the United States (U.S. Census Bureau, 2013). It is generally agreed that the absence of census data would do more harm than good. Information on household income, often considered the most invasive census question, is essential to Social Security provisioning, low-income assistance program planning, and grant allocation by the Department of Education. In short, the collection of private data is incredibly important for modern societies but also requires citizens' assurance that their government can be trusted to use the information "for good and not for evil."

Modernization has also permitted a transformation in census reporting. Since 1980, when the census data were published in great detail, the Census Bureau has moved away from the production of increasingly detailed published tabulations. Instead, access to census data is now predominantly provided electronically via the Internet. An integrated system called the *American FactFinder* is used to distribute data products and tabulations from the year 2010 census and from the American Community Survey. This system provides access to census data for small geographic areas such as blocks and tracts and a sample of individual-level data with identifying information deleted (i.e., the widely used *Public Use Microdata Samples,* or *PUMS*). The interactive provision of census data has given census data users the ability to extract customized tables and to use its data visualization and **Geographical Information Systems** (GIS) tools to produce graphs and maps for standard Census Bureau geographic areas and user-defined geographic areas.

Registration and Vital Statistics

Suppose that a country does have a decennial census. A decennial census supplies information only about its population size and composition as of the "census moment." It does not tell the size and composition during the years between censuses. Nor does it tell about the events (births, deaths, migrations) that continuously are changing that population, except for the meager information from a few retrospective questions on the census.

In the Western demographic tradition, the system that has evolved to complement censuses is the **registration** of population events as they occur. The relationship between the two systems is analogous to that between stock and flow data in commerce, or to that between prevalence and incidence statistics in the study of public health (Seltzer, 1982). This registration strategy has been applied better to deaths and births than to migrations. Since these two events refer to the starting and stopping of life, counting the registered events results in **vital statistics**. Most demographers use that term more broadly to include events that change marital status, such as marriages and divorces. This inclusion is understandable since deaths, births, and marital events originally were registered as part of the same process.

Evolution of Vital Statistics Systems

For many centuries, long before Europe took censuses, Christian priests kept track of their flocks in writing. They evolved local parish registers, recording not only the existence and status of all members of the flock but also the status-changing events as they occurred. These early parish registers have provided a wealth of information for the field of historical demography. In recent years, major historical data infrastructure projects have been undertaken, which digitize and integrate massive collections of archives—including church records, genealogies, and population registers—into linked, continuous databases (European Historical Population Samples Network, 2013; Mosaic, 2013). Although most historical records are from European countries, a new historical demography database links household and individual records in China from 1750 forward (Lee and Campbell, 2012).

Careers in Demography

Victoria A. Velkoff
Chief, Social, Economic, and Housing Statistics Division, U.S. Census Bureau

How did you decide that being a demographer was the career path for you?

I knew I wanted to be a demographer when I was working on a master's in Russian and East European Studies at the University of Michigan. A demography professor, Barbara Anderson, needed a research assistant who could read Russian and she hired me to help with her research. My job was to look through Russian journals and statistical yearbooks for certain demographic topics and data. As I worked for her, Barbara began to explain the work she was doing and I found it to be extremely interesting. She encouraged me to take a few demography classes, which I did. I enjoyed the classes and I decided to pursue a PhD in demography.

What kind of education and training did you pursue to get to where you are in your career?

I have a BA in economics and an MA in Russian and East European Studies from the University of Michigan. My master's thesis examined the demographic impact of the famine in Russia and Ukraine during the 1930s. I have a PhD in sociology from Princeton University. My dissertation focused on infant mortality in the former Soviet Union. As part of my dissertation work, I spent several months in Moscow in 1989 getting data for my work. It was an interesting time to be in Moscow as there were food shortages, as well as shortages of many other products. Every time I saw a line, I would join it because sometimes it turned out that the line was for fresh fruit or some other scarcity.

When I finished my PhD, I went to work for the Census Bureau and I have worked there ever since in several positions, each with increasing responsibilities. I am now Chief of the Social, Economic, and Housing Statistics Division. As the Chief, I lead the bureau's work on income, poverty and health insurance statistics; the new measures for same-sex relationships; and the development of the new supplemental poverty measure.

Describe your work/research as a demographer. What do you consider your most important accomplishments?

My first job at the Census Bureau was in the International Programs Center (IPC), where I did research on other countries' populations. While in the IPC, my research focused broadly on the impact of aging populations worldwide; gender issues; and the collection, analysis, and dissemination of demographic data. When I first came to the Census Bureau, I analyzed demographic data and wrote reports with a special emphasis on aging and health issues in the countries of Eastern Europe and the former Soviet republics. It was a great job as I was able to focus on an area of the world in which I had an interest.

I also coordinated the gender statistics research and technical assistance program, which included developing and carrying out research projects, teaching workshops, and providing technical assistance overseas. I developed a two-week workshop on gender statistics and taught the workshop in several countries. Teaching this workshop was rewarding because not only was it about gender issues but it also taught people how to present data graphically. I served as the Chair of the UNECE's Work Sessions on Gender Statistics for several years. Working with the UNECE gave me access to people from other countries' National Statistical Offices and allowed me to see how they did their work. It also created a great network of colleagues doing work on similar topics.

One of the projects I developed while working in the IPC provided me with hands-on experience with a wide range of statistical survey methodologies. In response to a demand for data on mortality in developing countries, particularly data on AIDS mortality, I collaborated with colleagues from Measure Evaluation to design, develop, and test a sample vital registration system that uses verbal autopsies in order to obtain data on mortality by cause. This is a system designed to collect nationally representative data on mortality by broad age groups and by broad causes in developing countries.

I think that my most important demographic accomplishments are the work I led on improving the Census Bureau's annual population estimates and our work on the demographic analysis estimates used to evaluate the 2010 decennial census. The Census Bureau produces annual population estimates for the nation, states, counties, cities, and towns. These estimates are used to allocate federal funding and as statistical controls for the Census Bureau's household surveys. Every 10 years we have a census that we use to evaluate the population estimates. Over the 2000s, I led the team of people who produced the population estimates and we were continually researching ways to improve them. We focused mainly on improving the estimates of net international migration as well as the estimates of domestic migration. In 2010, the census count was 308,745,538 and the population estimate was 308,450,484. The difference between the census count and the estimate was less than 300,000 people or 0.1 percent. This was a remarkable level of agreement between a census count and a population estimate.

I also led the team that produced the demographic analysis estimates for the 2010 census. Demographic analysis estimates (DA) are developed from historical vital statistics, estimates of international migration, and other data sources that are essentially independent of the census. For 2010, we produced five series of DA estimates to show that there was some uncertainty in the estimates. We released our DA estimates prior to the release of the 2010 census and without knowledge of the 2010 census counts. As with the population estimates, the DA middle estimate was extremely close to the 2010 census counts, less than 300,000 people different or 0.08 percent.

A few things about my job have really shaped my career. First, throughout my career, I have been fortunate to work on a wide variety of topics. I also have had several wonderful mentors, each of whom provided me with valuable lessons from different perspectives. And while at the Census Bureau, I have had the opportunity to travel to many countries. Sometimes I went to teach workshops or provide technical assistance. Other times I traveled to give talks, attend professional meetings, or represent the U.S. government at meetings of international organizations. I learned a lot from these travels and I enjoyed meeting new people and learning about different countries/cultures. These elements have made for an interesting and rewarding career in demography. They also made me a better demographer because I benefited from meeting and working with demographers from around the world.

What do you see as the field's most important contribution as well as its greatest challenge?

Demography's most important contribution is providing policy relevant data and information to help decision makers make informed decisions. Doing this with increasingly limited resources is one of the biggest challenges currently facing the field. I think another challenge is maintaining the core essence of demography. However, having said that, demography is a great field to work in. As demographers our work can be critically important at several different levels. If you look in any newspaper or online news site, you can almost always find a story that uses demographic data.

Modernization secularized the Western tradition of local church registration into the modern vital statistics system. It evolved into a system of civil registration of major changes in individual status and documentation of those changes in certificates of birth, death, marriage, and divorce. The main additional step necessary for creating a *vital event registration system*, once registration is in place, is the continuous and exhaustive compilation of the local records in some central location. In the United States, birth and death certificates are collected from local registers by each state, which then transmits them to the National Center for Health Statistics, or NCHS (NCHS, 2012).

A final step in the development of vital statistics systems was to expand the information gathered about the nature of the event and the people involved; for example, the cause of death as well as its occurrence, the sex of the new child as well as its birth, and the age and marital status of the parents. It is this additional information, particularly the age and sex of those involved, that allows registration data to be combined with census data in population analysis. In the United States, NCHS provides standard forms and model procedures to the states, which administer birth and death registration. The latest revision of the standard death data collected in the United States (e.g., inclusion of a Hispanic identifier, decedents' education and socioeconomic status) occurred in 2003.

Just as with censuses, a key element in a national registration system is a system of dissemination and access to the collected data. NCHS distributes a variety of electronic reports on a regular basis from the vital registration system. NCHS also provides public-use data files from registration data for electronic download. In addition to vital statistics, NCHS oversees a number of large national surveys (e.g., some of those in Box 2-5) and, similarly, provides public-use access to these data.

Difficulties

The maintenance of an effective registration system probably is more of an administrative accomplishment than is carrying out decennial population censuses. Whereas a census can involve periodic crash efforts, civil registration requires maintaining a permanent bureaucracy in every locality in the country. Because of this, most countries have more confidence in data from their censuses than in data from their registration systems. This, combined with their costliness, has caused many countries to curtail their registration systems. As a result, in many developing countries registration is either weak or lacking. Only 25% of the world population lives in a country with high quality birth and death registry systems (WHO, 2012). A major challenge in recent years is the increasing substitution of mobile phones for landlines, making it difficult to track down households.

In the United States, the NCHS made a change of historic proportions in vital registration when it stopped collecting national marriage and divorce registration data in 1996. Marriage and divorce data had been collected by the government since 1867. NCHS discontinued this registration system "to prioritize programs in a period of tightened resource constraints" (*Federal Register*, 1995) and because of "concerns about the completeness and quality of detailed marriage and divorce data" (Broome, 1995). Changes in marital status in the United States will, as vital events in many developing countries are, have to be learned from sample surveys and limited information collected in census years.

Population Registers

While most countries with standardized reporting of vital statistics now maintain event registration systems similar to those of the United States, **population registers** provide an alternative means of monitoring vital events. Registers, much like those of early Western European parishes, are kept on a centralized, secular, national basis.

Box 2-5	Internet Access to Demographic Data Resources	
	U.S. Government Websites	
	United States Census Bureau Main	http://www.census.gov
	United States Census 2010 Gateway	http://www.census.gov/2010census
	United States Census DataFerrett	http://dataferrett.census.gov/index.html
	American FactFinder	http://factfinder2.census.gov
	Bureau of Labor Statistics	http://www.bls.gov
	Immigration and Naturalization Service	http://www.dhs.gov/immigration-statistics
	National Center for Health Statistics	http://www.cdc.gov/nchs
	U.S. Government Surveys	
	American Housing Survey	http://www.census.gov/housing/ahs
	Consumer Expenditure Survey	http://www.bls.gov/cex/home.htm
	Current Population Survey	http://www.census.gov/cps
	National Health and Nutrition Examination Survey	http://www.cdc.gov/nchs/nhanes.htm
	National Health Interview Survey	http://www.cdc.gov/nchs/nhis.htm
	National Survey of Family Growth	http://www.cdc.gov/nchs/nsfg.htm
	Survey of Income Program and Participation	http://www.census.gov/sipp
	Nongovernment U.S. Data Archives/Surveys	
	General Social Survey	http://www3.norc.org/gss+website
	Integrated Public Use Micro-Samples	https://cps.ipums.org/cps/
	Inter-university Consortium for Political and Social Research	http://www.icpsr.umich.edu
	University of North Carolina Odum Institute	http://arc.irss.unc.edu/dvn
	Selected International Data Resources	
	International Labour Organization	http://www.ilo.org
	Luxembourg Income Study	http://www.lisdatacenter.org
	Organisation for Economic Co-Operation and Development (OECD) Data Lab	http://www.oecd.org/statistics/
	United Nations (UN) Statistics Division	http://unstats.un.org
	UN Links to National Statistical Systems	http://unstats.un.org/unsd/methods/inter-natlinks/sd_natstat.asp
	UNESCO Institute for Statistics	http://stats.uis.unesco.org

They provide continuous recording of data on particular events that occur to each individual, as well as selected characteristics describing those individuals. The key difference from event registrations is that population registers organize a continuous record of events into a life history for each individual in the register. Such systems are found in some Scandinavian countries, Eastern Europe, and the Far East. Where present, they provide a data system potentially independent of that provided by the combination of the census and vital statistics.

The alert reader may notice that no mention has been made of registering the third population process: *migration*. Most nations do attempt to register crossings of their national borders, but they do this so incompletely that registration does not play a central role in measuring migration, as it does in measuring fertility and mortality. The complexities of migration estimation are treated separately in chapter 9.

Sample Surveys

Demographic sample surveys have become so globally widespread that they now are an integral part of national data systems, along with censuses and registration (United Nations, 1999). Surveys are used to improve the quality of the other data sources, even to substitute for them, and to supplement them with detail.

As we just noted, systems for registering births and deaths are especially difficult for less-developed countries to maintain. Sample surveys in these countries often substitute for registration in estimating national fertility and mortality. True, such surveys cannot provide the kind of accounting—continuous and for all localities—that a sophisticated registration system can. On the other hand, they can provide national-level data of richer detail by asking thorough retrospective questions.

Census bureaus also use such surveys as one way to form intercensal or postcensal estimates of the population (see next section). Census bureaus may have demographic questions not worth including in the census but worth answering on a periodic basis for a less expensive sample. A case in point is the U.S. Census Bureau's reliance on the rolling American Community Survey to augment its short form. It also relies on the Current Population Survey (CPS), a monthly series carried out by the Census Bureau since the 1940s, which keeps track of the labor force status of the population, among other things. The results of the CPS, published as *Current Population Reports*, have become a major bibliographic source for current descriptions of the U.S. population, supplanting for many purposes the census itself. It is likely that the same will happen with the American Community Survey.

There are a wide variety of demographic surveys that have been repeated over time and thus have come to serve as major sources of population data. While space prevents a discussion of all these resources, Box 2-5 lists Web addresses of major demographic surveys and data archives for further information and data access. Also given in Box 2-5 are the addresses for important U.S. government and international websites. Internet access to these resources is constantly evolving, and regular visits to the sites identified are one way to keep abreast of demographic developments and data in the United States. Readers will find links to these sites on the textbook website at www.demographytextbook.com.

Demographic Estimation

Why Estimates Are Needed

In many of the graphs and tables presented in the following chapters, the reader will find the word "estimated" in the title. Why can't demographers stick to hard facts rather than making guesses? There are two main reasons: (1) ten years normally elapse between most of the world's censuses, and (2) not all population data are reliable.

The ten-year gap. Because there usually is a ten-year gap between censuses, there is a need for intercensal estimates if we are interested in the past. And if we are interested in the present, there is a need for postcensal estimates. Surveys can provide current estimates, but there is another, more traditional technique. This has been labeled "direct" estimation from census and registration data. Let us assume that we are making a postcensal (vs. intercensal) estimate. The basic process is to take the latest census count as the baseline. Then we subtract people on the basis of registered deaths, add people on the basis of registered births, and subtract or add on the basis of our information about emigration and immigration. The process is very similar to that for making population projections. The difference lies in the source of input about mortality, fertility, and migration after the baseline count. In the case of projection, we employ assumptions; in the case of estimation, we optimally employ actual counts of events.

Unreliable data. The second reason for estimation is that trustworthy information may be lacking for one of the population processes, while being generally available for the others. Population size, growth, mortality, fertility, and migration form a mutually constitutive system, described in the balancing equation already discussed in chapter 1:

$$\text{crude growth rate} = \text{crude birth rate} - \text{crude death rate} + \text{crude rate of net migration}$$

In the simplest case, when one term of that equation is missing (say, net migration), it can be inferred from our knowledge of all other factors (i.e., growth, birth, and death rates). Unfortunately, data from less-developed countries often are not sufficient to allow this straightforward procedure. In many such countries, even those data that are available about population processes usually are suspect, incomplete, or in unconventional form. This situation arises, for instance, where sample surveys employing retrospective questions are used instead of registration of births. To handle this complex estimation need, formal demographers have labored to describe in more detail the interrelationships among the various demographic variables, however they are measured. With that background, they have been able to gather a growing tool kit of very indirect estimation procedures (Arriaga, 1994; Brass, 1975; Bogue et al., 1993; Hill and Zlotnik, 1982; United Nations, 1967; United Nations Population Division and the National Academy of Sciences, 1983). For an in-depth description of these various indirect estimation methods, we recommend Preston et al.'s (2001) instruction in their *Measuring and Modeling Population Processes* formal demography text.

Estimation of Historical Population Size

Chapter 3 gives an account of world population growth from around 8000 or 10,000 BCE to the present. But in the present chapter we have learned that modern population censuses, even in the more-developed countries, were a development mostly of the 1800s and that ancient censuses were taken rarely. If that is the case, how can we describe pre-modern worldwide population trends?

Part of the answer is that we cannot—not with any real confidence. Table 2-2 dramatizes the point. It shows the estimated population of the world from about 10,000 to 8000 BCE to CE 1750, giving lower and upper estimates throughout. The estimates are the extremes of what Durand calls "indifference ranges, within which there seems little basis for preference" (1977, p. 284). We have computed the percentage difference between upper and lower estimates as a rough index of the degree of indecision. It decreases from 67% for the earliest period to 9% for the 1750 estimates.

The year 1750 can be considered to be late in the era before the development of modern demographic data. How do contemporary demographers estimate the populations of the 1700s? For the Western countries, demographers have to depend on unconventional data such as partial population listings (e.g., parish christening and burial records, tax rolls, military service rolls, etc.) or listings of habitable structures. For the rest of the world, demographers combine various clues, including counts for particular cities and inference from area of cultivable land, strength of military forces, type of economy, and the nature of political organization (Durand, 1977).

Table 2-2   Range of World Population Estimates to 1750

Year	Estimate (millions)		Percentage Difference[a]
	Lower (1)	Upper (2)	(3)
10,000–8000 BCE	5	10	67
CE 0–14	270	330	20
CE 1000	275	345	22
1250	350	450	12
1500	440	540	10
1750	735	805	9

[a]Percentages computed with denominator as mean of two estimates.

Source: Durand, 1977, table 5.

The presentation of this humbling picture here has a purpose: It is to increase the reader's skepticism about sweeping descriptions of historical world population trends, including those in our next chapter. But, imprecise as they must be, those indirect historical estimates are all we have.

SUMMARY

Nations depend on regular censuses as the foundation of their demographic data-gathering systems. Ideally, censuses are taken at even intervals (usually ten years) and list each of the kinds of people residing within a defined territory as of that moment. Censuses also ask fairly standard questions about individual traits, used for description of population composition. Almost all nations of the world now take censuses, but even the best censuses have some errors both of coverage and of content. Ideally, part of the census enterprise is to estimate errors.

The United States has the longest continuous series of modern censuses, which started in 1790. Recent innovations have included the use of mail in place of most personal interviews, the use of sampling for some of the questions, the use of street surveys to enumerate transient populations, and most recently the replacement of the long form with the monthly American Community Survey. The modern Western practice has been to complement decennial censuses with registration of births and deaths. The administrative infrastructure for continuous and exhaustive registration has, however, proved difficult to maintain for less-developed countries.

Sample surveys have been used to supplement censuses or to substitute for registration. Particularly in the less-developed countries, retrospective questions about births often substitute for registration as a basis for estimating fertility. Surveys are used everywhere for evaluating censuses and providing intercensal estimates. Finally, supplementary surveys such as the U.S. Current Population Survey and the American Community Survey add regular detailed information that is too expensive or too recent to be obtained by censuses.

Although most countries now take censuses, their other data may be incomplete and questionable, especially in less-developed regions. Complex procedures have been developed for inferring missing or doubtful data from the reliable data at hand. This effort is enhanced by the close interrelationships among the various demographic variables. Where no factors are known precisely, however, such as for prehistoric times, estimation becomes very indirect indeed.

PROPOSITIONS FOR DEBATE

1. Including undocumented immigrants in the census gives some states an unfair advantage when it comes to state representation in the U.S. House of Representatives.

2. In countries that are completely mapped and where samples of subareas can be drawn, surveys can take the place of censuses.

3. Given coverage errors, U.S. courts should have the right to overturn U.S. census counts for localities, if they seem implausible.

4. The United States should maintain a national population register, as do many Scandinavian countries.

5. Little real information was lost by ending the U.S. national system of marriage and divorce registration in 1996.

6. I (name of reader) was missed in the last census of (name of country of residence).

7. The census will always undercount undocumented immigrants, the homeless, and recluses in the United States.

8. With the advent of "big data" there is no longer a need to go through the effort and cost of decadal censuses since we can collect all the information we need now from individuals' online and mobile digital traces.

REFERENCES AND SUGGESTED READINGS

Anderton, Douglas L., Richard E. Barrett, and Donald J. Bogue. 1997. *Population of the United States*. 3rd ed. New York: Free Press.

Arriaga, Eduardo E. 1994. *Population Analysis with Microcomputers*. Vol. 1 & 2. Bureau of the Census International Programs Center/USAID/UNFPA. Washington, DC: GPO.

Bogue, Donald J., Eduardo E. Arriaga, and Douglas L. Anderton, eds. 1993. *Readings in Population Research Methodology*. Vol. 1–8. Chicago: UNFPA/Social Development.

Brass, William. 1975. *Methods of Estimating Fertility and Mortality from Limited and Defective Data*. Chapel Hill, NC: Laboratories for Population Statistics.

Broome, Claire V. 1995. "FR Response, Division of Vital Statistics." FR Doc. 95-30566, filed 12/14/95.

Cohn, D'Vera. 2011. "How Accurate are Counts of Same-Sex Couples?" *Pew Research Social & Demographic Trends* (August 25). Retrieved March 15, 2013. www.pewsocialtrends.org/2011/08/25/how-accurate-are-counts-of-same-sex-couples

Durand, John D. 1977. "Historical Estimates of World Population: An Evaluation." *Population and Development Review* 3(3).

The Economist. 2007. "Counting People: Census Sensitivity." *The Economist* (December 19). Retrieved June 1, 2013. www.economist.com/node/10311346

Edmonston, Barry, and Charles Schultze, eds. 1995. *Modernizing the U.S. Census*. Panel on Census Requirements in the Year 2000 and Beyond, Committee on National Statistics, Commission on Behavioral and Social Sciences and Education, National Research Council. Washington, DC: GPO.

European Historical Population Samples Network. 2013. *Databases: Intermediate Data Structure (IDS)*. Retrieved June 1, 2013. www.ehps-net.eu/content/ids

Federal Register. 1995. "Change in Marriage and Divorce Data Available from the National Center for Health Statistics." *Federal Register* 60(241): 64437–64438.

Francese, Peter K. 1979. "The 1980 Census: The Counting of America." *Population Bulletin* 34(4). Washington, DC: Population Reference Bureau.

Hannah, Matthew. 2008. "Mapping the Underscrutinized: The West German Census Boycott Movement of 1987 and the Dangers of Information-Based Security." *Geospatial Technologies and Homeland Security* 94: 301–314.

Hill, Kenneth, and Hania Zlotnik. 1982. "Indirect Estimation of Fertility and Mortality." In John A. Ross, ed., *International Encyclopedia of Population*. Vol. 1. New York: The Free Press.

Hirschman, Charles, Richard Alba, and Reynolds Farley. 2000. "The Meaning and Measurement of Race in the U.S. Census: Glimpses into the Future." *Demography* 37(3).

Iversen, Roberta Rehner, Frank E. Furstenberg, and Alisa L. Belzer. 1999. "How Much Do We Count? Interpretation and Error-Making in the Decennial Census." *Demography* 36(1).

Lee, James Z., and Cameron D. Campbell. 2012. *China Multi-Generational Panel Dataset, Liaoning* (CMGPD-LN), 1749-1909. ICPSR27063-v7. Ann Arbor, MI: Inter-university Consortium for Political and Social Research (Distributor). doi:10.3886/ICPSR27063.v7.

Minkel, J. R. 2007. "Confirmed: The U.S. Census Bureau Gave Up Names of Japanese-Americans in WWII." *Scientific American* (March 30). Retrieved June 1, 2013. www.scientificamerican.com/article.cfm?id=confirmed-the-us-census-b

Mosaic. 2013. *Recovering Surviving Census Records to Reconstruct Population, Economic, and Cultural History*. Retrieved June 1, 2013. www.censusmosaic.org/cgi-bin/index.plx

Mule, Thomas. 2012. *Census Coverage Measurement Estimation Report: Summary of Estimates of Coverage for Persons in the United States*. DSSD 2010 Census Coverage Measurement Memorandum Series #2010-G-01.

National Research Council. 2010. *Envisioning the 2020 Census*. Washington, DC: The National Academies Press.

NCHS (National Center for Health Statistics). 2012. *Surveys and Data Collection Systems*. Retrieved June 1, 2013. www.cdc.gov/nchs/surveys.htm

Palmer, John, Thomas J. Espenshade, Frederic Bartumeus, Chang Y. Chung, Necati Ercan Ozgencil, and Kathleen Li. 2013. "New Approaches to Human Mobility: Using Mobile Phones for Demographic Research." *Demography* 50(3): 1–24.

Preston, Samuel H., Patrick Heuveline, and Michel Guillot. 2001. *Demography: Measuring and Modeling Population Processes*. Oxford: Blackwell.

Roberts, Sam. 2010. "Census Survey Asks Too Much, G.O.P. Says." *The New York Times* (August 19). Retrieved June 1, 2013. www.nytimes.com/2010/08/20/us/politics/20census.html

Seltzer, William. 1982. "Data Collection: National Systems." In John A. Ross, ed., *International Encyclopedia of Population*. Vol. 1. New York: The Free Press.

Shryock, Henry S. 1982. "Data Collection: United States Census." In John A. Ross, ed., *International Encyclopedia of Population*. Vol. 1. New York: The Free Press.

Snipp, Matthew C. 2003. "Racial Measurement in the American Census: Past Practices and Implications for the Future." *Annual Review of Sociology* 29: 563–588.

United Nations. 1967. *Manual IV: Methods of Estimating Basic Demographic Measures from Incomplete Data*. Population Studies no. 42. ST/SOA/Series A/42. New York: United Nations.

———. 1998. *Principles and Recommendations for Population and Housing Censuses*. Revision 1. ST/ESA/STAT/SER.M/Rev.1. New York: United Nations.

———. 1999. *Concise Report on World Population Monitoring, 1999: Population Growth, Structure and Distribution*. Report of the Secretary-General. E/CN.9/1999/2. New York: United Nations.

———. 2008. *Principles and Recommendations for Population and Housing Censuses, Revision 2*. Series M, No.67/Rev.2. New York: United Nations.

———. 2012. *2010 World Population and Housing Census Programme Newsletter*. Retrieved June 2013. http://unstats.un.org/unsd/demographic/sources/census/2010_PHC/newsletter/No.11.pdf

United Nations Population Division and the National Academy of Sciences. 1983. *Manual X: Indirect Techniques for Demographic Estimation*. Population Studies no. 81. New York: United Nations.

United Nations Statistics Division. 2012. *Census Round 2010: Progression of Population Censuses and the size of the enumerated population*. Retrieved June 1, 2013. http://unstats.un.org/unsd/demographic/sources/census/2010_PHC/Census_Clock/rptEnumeratedPopulationAllCountries.pdf

U.S. Census Bureau. 1999. *Census 2000 Operational Plan Using Traditional Census-Taking Methods*. Washington, DC: GPO.

———. 2001. Prepared by Elizabeth M. Grieco and Rachel C. Cassidy. *Overview of Race and Hispanic Origin 2000*. Census 2000 Brief, issued March 2001. Retrieved June 1, 2013. www.census.gov/prod/2001pubs/c2kbr01-1.pdf

———. 2010. What Is the Census? Retrieved February 10, 2013. www.census.gov/2010census/about/

———. 2012. Census Bureau Releases Estimates of Undercount and Overcount in the 2010 Census. Newsroom, May 22. Retrieved June 1, 2013. http://www.census.gov/newsroom/releases/archives/2010_census/cb12-95.html

————. 2013. American Community Survey. Feb. 10, 2013. www.census.gov/acs/www/about_the_survey/questions_and_why_we_ask/

————. n.d. *Census in the Constitution: Why Jefferson, Madison, and the Founders Enshrined the Census in Our Constitution.* Census 2010 About. Retrieved February 10, 2013. www.census.gov/2010census/about/constitutional.php

U.S. GAO (Government Accountability Office). 2011. *2010 Census: Preliminary Lessons Learned Highlight the Need for Fundamental Reforms.* Testimony before the Subcommittee on Federal Financial Management, Government Information, Federal Services, and International Security, Committee on Homeland Security and Governmental Affairs, U.S. Senate (April 6). Retrieved June 1, 2013. www.gao.gov/new.items/d11496t.pdf

Watts, Duncan J. 2007. "A Twenty-First Century Science." *Nature* 445(7127): 489.

WHO (World Health Organization). 2012. *World Health Statistics 2012.* Geneva: World Health Organization.

Wilkinson, Toby A.H. 2000. *Royal Annals of Ancient Egypt.* New York: Columbia University Press.

3

Population Growth

This chapter starts on what may be familiar ground for some readers: a description of world population growth in the past and projection into its future. With the world's population tripling from 2 billion to 6 billion over the course of the 20th century, and then reaching 7.2 billion just 14 years later, there is no more obvious demographic trend than that of population growth. The defining demographic characteristic of recent times is the modern population explosion. The world population continues to grow today, but now its growth rate is beginning to slow. As many nations come through the other side of their demographic transitions, the main demographic preoccupation of the 21st century will eventually turn to the "graying" of the population (IIASA, 2012). A few countries have already started to confront this process. The aging global population of the near future is a direct outcome of the mortality and fertility transitions that accompanied the past century's population explosion.

Our description of population growth distinguishes between the **more-developed regions** (MDRs) and the **less-developed regions** (LDRs), since the MDRs and LDRs generally have different pasts and prospects. However, we hasten to note that there is great variation within these classifications, particularly as LDRs continue to develop rapidly and at uneven paces from one another. The chapter also distinguishes countries by their stage in the nearly universal fertility decline that has taken place over the past century. The chapter closes with analyses of the issues and challenges resulting from present and future growth in countries at different stages of development, fertility decline, and "graying."

A History of Global Population Growth

Figure 3-1 on the following page is a familiar graph in demography. It charts the size of the human population of the world from our earliest guesses to the future. The dates in this version of the graph range from between 1+ million years BCE to CE 5000. The time segment at the far left, the Old Stone Age, cannot be drawn to scale, since it would extend way off the page. From 7000 BCE, a regular time scale allows us to see the pattern of increase in population size, or population growth.

It took millions of years for the global population to reach a half billion people (about 1650), but by CE 2014 world population was over *7 billion*. In just the past century 5 billion people have been added, tripling the world's population! Since the birth of a now twenty-year-old college student, the world's population has increased by nearly as many people as were alive in the world in 1900. The population is projected to continue growing into the future, albeit more slowly, leveling out at close to 10.9 billion people by the 22nd century (United Nations, 2013).

Clearly there was a dramatic change in the nature of population growth as the world reached modern times. To discuss the two very different patterns of population growth before and after about 1650, we will describe these two periods separately as the "premodern" and then the "modern" period.

Figure 3-1

World Population Growth through History

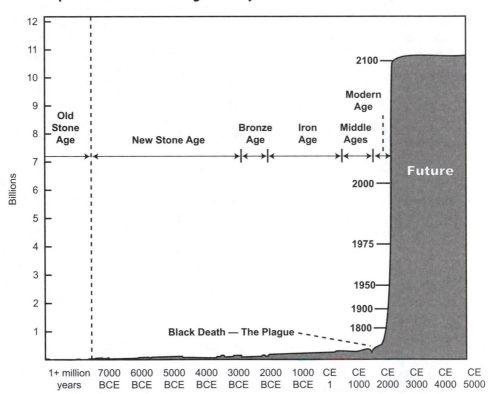

Source: Population Reference Bureau, © 2006. http://www.prb.org/presentations/gb-poptrends_all.ppt; and United Nations, *World Population Projections to 2100* (1998). Used with permission.

Premodern Growth, Before 1650

First, a warning is appropriate. To avoid distracting the reader with repeated cautions and qualifiers, we will write as though we really had a precise idea of how many people were alive in premodern times. In reality, our guesses are uncertain (see PRB, 2011 for estimates). This uncertainty is detailed in chapter 2, under "Demographic Estimation." Having said that, let us plunge boldly ahead.

In the premodern era, from about 300,000 BCE to roughly 1650, harsh living conditions resulted in extremely high mortality rates and slow growth (Collins, 1982). After thousands of years of hunting and gathering, the development of agriculture at the beginning of the New Stone Age (i.e., 8000 BCE) led to a more reliable food supply and more stable forms of social organization. Agricultural settlements in turn were followed by urban civilizations, first in Mesopotamia, then in Egypt, Crete, India, China, and Peru, wherein populations could flourish to a greater extent. With the emergence of agrarian societies, and despite continued high mortality, world population slowly increased, growing from an estimated 5 million to perhaps 200 to 300 million by CE 1.

During the early Common Era, growth was mainly held in check by infectious disease and periodic decimating epidemics that became more common as people gathered and settled in towns and cities (McKeown, 1983; McNeill, 1976). However, disease was not the only hardship of life during this slow growth period. Unfavorable climatic changes (Wrigley, 1969), periodic severe famines (Meuvret, 1965), and even lower birth rates from malnutrition (Watkins and Van de Walle, 1983) were among the myriad hardships limiting population growth. With few exceptions, this era was characterized by high birth rates and high but fluctuating death rates, resulting in slow, frequently interrupted population growth.

Modern Explosion, 1650 to the Present

Let us look more closely at the far-right segment of Figure 3-1, from 1650 to 2000. One thing to notice, of course, is the large and soaring number of people in the modern world in comparison with the premodern. The 2014 population of 7.2 billion is more than fourteen times as large as the 1650 population, the end of the premodern era. Another feature to notice, one that needs explaining, is the rapidly increasing slope of the line.

For almost all of the modern era, there are two reasons for this increasing upward slope. First is that any sustained positive *rate* of growth will result in the increasing upward slope of such a line. If people normally are behaving in such a way that they are more than replacing themselves every generation, then every generation will have more people behaving that way, producing even larger increments. By analogy, annual crude rates of population growth are like interest rates on a savings account; the rates operate not only on the original principal but also on the interest that is being reinvested continuously. The higher the growth (or interest) rate, the greater the degree of the line's concave arching that is caused by compounding alone. (Exercises 1 and 2 at the end of the chapter allow the reader to demonstrate this phenomenon.)

There is an important second reason for the upward curve of this particular line: The population **growth rate** did not simply stay stable and positive; the growth rate itself grew through almost all of this period. Table 3-1 shows that the annual rate of

Table 3-1 Annual Growth Rates of World Population and Implied Years to Double, 1650 to 2100

Period	Annual Growth Rate (percent)	Years to Double
1650–1750	0.4	175
1750–1800	0.4	175
1800–1850	0.5	140
1850–1900	0.5	140
1900–1950	0.8	88
1950–1955	1.8	39
1955–1960	1.9	37
1960–1965	2.0	35
1965–1970	1.9	37
1970–1975	1.9	37
1975–1980	1.7	41
1980–1985	1.7	41
1985–1990	1.7	41
1990–1995	1.7	41
1995–2000	1.3	53
2000–2005	1.2	58
2005–2010	1.2	60
Medium Fertility Projection		
2010–2015	1.1	61
2015–2020	1.0	67
2020–2025	0.9	75
2025–2030	0.8	84
2030–2035	0.7	94
2035–2040	0.7	105
2040–2045	0.6	118
2045–2050	0.5	135
2050–2055	0.4	156
2055–2060	0.4	179
2060–2065	0.3	205
2065–2070	0.3	235
2070–2075	0.3	272
2075–2080	0.2	315
2080–2085	0.2	359
2085–2090	0.2	408
2090–2095	0.1	485
2095–2100	0.1	630

Source: United Nations, *The Determinants and Consequences of Population Trends*, 1973, table 2-1; *World Population Prospects as Assessed in 1980*, 1981, table 1; *World Resources 1990–91*, 1990, table 16-1; *World Resources 1994–95*, 1994, table 16-1; *Revision of the World Population Estimates and Projections*, 1999; *World Urbanization Prospects*, 2004; *World Population Prospects: The 2004 Revision*, 2005; *World Population Prospects: The 2012 Revision*, 2013. Used with permission.

global population growth doubled in the three centuries between 1650 and World War II, and the postwar era witnessed an even more dramatic explosion of growth rates, peaking around 1960 to 1975.

Growth rates fell annually thereafter, and by 2005 had dropped substantially to 1.2% annually. At this writing, they are projected to continue dropping through the rest of the century and will even drop below 1650 levels by 2060. The recent drop in growth rates is due primarily to declining births in almost every country, but also, in part, to the suddenly rising number of deaths from HIV/AIDS throughout the world. The number of excess deaths due to HIV/AIDS in the forty-eight most seriously affected countries reached 9.4 million between 2005 and 2010, which is the highest recorded number of excess deaths since the discovery of the first HIV/AIDS cases in the early 1980s. Current projections show that the overall number of HIV/AIDS deaths may decline slightly in the next decade or so, but will then increase again slowly due to population growth (United Nations, 2012).

Table 3-1 also translates each of the annual growth rates into "years to double" at that rate. This is a device for dramatizing the implications of growth rates if extended over time. It is simple to make the conversion by using this formula:

$$\text{Years to double} = \frac{70}{\text{\% annual growth rate}}$$

The reason why this formula works is explained mathematically in Box 3-1 on the next page. The implication of this formula is that at the current annual growth rate (we will use the UN's estimate for 2010, 1.15%), the world's population would double in the following 61 years to just under *14 billion* by CE 2071; it would redouble to *28 billion* in the next 61 years (by CE 2132), and so on.

Such populations are unimaginable! But this exercise helps drive home an important point: As the size of the world population gets larger, the impact of *any* positive growth rate gets greater. Since the base population on which any growth rate works is now large, even a moderate rate of growth means many people are being added.

However, our example of **doubling time** assumed growth at the present rate over more than a century. Is that realistic? The consensus would seem to be "no." World mortality already is moderate or low overall, but continues to decline for most groups while rising for others (see chapter 5). World fertility is declining and will likely continue to do so even more rapidly than mortality, thus causing further erosion of the world rate of natural increase (or growth).

But a cautionary note is appropriate: Even if the world's growth rate has peaked, the world's population size certainly has not. If the world's growth rate were cut by about half—say, to 0.7% per year—the population of the globe still would double in 100 years, then redouble, then redouble. . . . To clarify, although the world growth *rate* has slowed to almost half what it was in the 1960s, it is still positive, and the *size* of the world's population has steadily increased—from 3 billion in 1960, 4 billion in 1974, 5 billion in 1987, 6 billion in 1999, and to 7.2 billion in 2014. Thus, what once took thousands and thousands of years—reaching the first billion people in the world—is now happening every twelve years or so.

Although actual population doubling and then redoubling is not necessarily inevitable, the general rapidity of population growth is why demographers are not content

Why Does the "Doubling Time" Conversion Work?

Many readers simply will be willing to take our word for the legitimacy of the conversion of annual growth rates to "doubling time." This insert is for those who want a mathematical explanation.

Here are our variables. Let

P_1 = the population at the beginning of an interval
P_2 = the population at the end of the interval
n = the number of years in the interval
r = the annual population growth rate during the interval

Now, let us take the simplest case, where the interval is one year (where $n = 1$). In that case,

$$P_2 = P_1 + rP_1$$

That is, the population at the end of the interval is equal to the population at the beginning of the interval plus the growth in between, that growth being calculated by multiplying the annual growth rate by the beginning population. This equation can also be stated as

$$P_2 = P_1(1 + r)$$

If we let n extend beyond one year, then the general formula would be

$$P_2 = P_1(1 + r)^n$$

This equation also can be stated as

$$\frac{P_2}{P_1} = (1+r)^n$$

Taking logarithms of both sides of the equation and solving for n, the equation would be as follows:

$$n = \frac{\log P_2 - \log P_1}{\log(1+r)}$$

Now let us see how many years it would take for the population to double under the conditions of an annual growth rate of 1.0%. That is, let us solve the above equation for n assuming first that the population will double, or

$$P_2 = 2P_1$$

and, second, that the annual growth rate is 1%, or

$$r = .01$$

Solving the formula with these values would produce the equation

$$n = \frac{\log 2}{\log(1+0.01)} = \frac{0.30103}{0.00432} = 69.68$$

In sum, the number of years required for a population to double at a 1% annual growth rate is precisely 69.68 years, usually rounded to 70 years.

Incidentally, if we choose to use natural logarithms rather than common logarithms, then n would equal 69.32 rather than 69.68. Some texts will treat 69.3 (rounded to 69) as the number of years required for a population to double at a 1% annual rate of growth. The difference is trivial for our purposes. We will use 70 as our "magic number."

with observing that the rate is no longer increasing; rather, they are trying to estimate when and how that rate will become *zero*, when the modern global **population explosion** will come to its end. The slowing of population growth does not mean an end to population challenges and may lead to altogether new problems, as we will discuss later in the chapter.

The term "explosion" has a hysterical ring to it that annoys some demographers (e.g., Hartmann, 1995; Simon, 1986; Lam, 2011). Moreover, it may carry a negative connotation, implying a destructive and devastating event. But in attempting to describe the dramatic population growth shown in Figure 3-1, we think the term is visually apt.

Classifying Countries

The Development Dichotomy: MDRs and LDRs

Regions of the world did not march in lockstep from the 1600s to the present through those economic and demographic changes we call "modernization" or "development." Throughout, there have been the haves and the have-nots among nations. First there were the colonial powers and the colonies they exploited. Later there were the imperial powers and their empires.

Relatedly, there were those who started early in their agricultural, industrial, and demographic revolutions and then there were those who started later. One way that distinction is captured is by the familiar dichotomy between the countries of the more-developed regions (MDRs) and the less-developed regions (LDRs). In the past, economic development and demographic development have often gone hand in hand. (*Economic* development is measured by efficiency of productive technology, while *demographic* development is measured by degree of control over death and birth.) As a result, the distinction between MDRs and LDRs has reflected many demographic, as well as economic, developmental differences between regions. The United Nations version of the classification has been widely accepted by demographers: The **MDRs** are North America, Europe, Japan, Australia, and New Zealand; the **LDRs** are Africa, Asia (less Japan), Oceania (less Australia and New Zealand), Latin America, and the Caribbean.

Recently, however, the lack of synchronization between economic development and demographic development in some countries challenges such a simple typology. And, as a larger and larger proportion of the world's countries become more developed, there are many more countries that fall in between the MDR and LDR distinction than fall within it. To illustrate this, see Hans Rosling's TED Talk: Global Population, Box by Box, on this book's website at www.demographytextbook.com under the links section of the Chapter 3 tab. Moreover, the United Nations version of the development dichotomy has classified entire world regions, rather than nations, since adjacent countries have tended to share similar economic histories. But not all regions are homogeneous: Oceania, for instance, is demographically dominated by Australia and New Zealand but also contains Micronesia and Melanesia. East Asia includes Japan, which is clearly a developed nation. Latin America, though not labeled as a mixed region, includes temperate South America (Argentina, Chile, Uruguay), which stretches the label "less-developed."

A more complex and nuanced development category that is increasingly being adopted, including by the United Nations, is the **Human Development Index** (HDI). This measure represents both social and economic development by combining a country's life expectancy, educational attainment, and national income level into a single statistic. Countries are then ranked according to whether they fall into the four following HDI tiers: very high, high, medium, and low. Generally, the continuum of the HDI falls in accordance with the LDR-MDR dichotomy, with MDRs scoring at the higher end of the scale and LDRs scoring at the lower end of the scale; however, there are a few notable exceptions. Argentina and South Korea, for example, despite being conventionally classified as LDRs, are ranked in the "very high" category of the HDI. We note this so that readers can keep in mind the generalizing nature of the classic LDR-MDR dichotomy that we rely upon for the sake of simplicity throughout this textbook.

Table 3-2 gives the current United Nations classifications for the basic LDR-MDR development dichotomy. The top rows present data for individual regions of the world. These six regions are ordered from the highest growth rate (Africa) to the lowest growth rate (Europe). In the bottom two rows of the table data is given for the more-developed and less-developed regions separately.

Table 3-2 also presents demographic rates that dramatize the contrast between classes of countries. Let us compare the MDRs and LDRs. Demographically, although there is a difference between the crude death rates (column 2), that difference is small compared with the difference between the crude birth rates (column 1). This reflects the fact that mortality has improved very quickly in LDRs while reductions in fertility are still a major transition in process. The fertility of the LDRs collectively is twice as high as that of the MDRs. The infant mortality rate (column 3), although strictly speaking a demographic measure, is often used as an index of overall well-being and of health care in nations; we see that the infant mortality rate of the LDRs is more than eight times as high as that of the MDRs. Column 4 contains the population's annual

Table 3-2   Demographic Rates for Classes of Countries, 2014

	Crude Birth Rate (1)	Crude Death Rate (2)	Infant Mortality Rate[b] (3)	Natural Increase Rate(%) (4)	Years to Double (5)
Regions[a]					
Africa	36	10	62	2.5	28
Asia (excl. China)	21	7	40	1.4	50
Latin America and Caribbean	18	6	18	1.2	58.3
Oceania	18	7	21	1.1	63.6
Northern America	12	8	5	0.4	175
Europe	11	11	6	0.0	
Less-Developed Regions	*22*	*7*	*42*	*1.4*	*50*
More-Developed Regions	*11*	*10*	*5*	*0.1*	*700*

[a]Ordered by rate of natural increase.
[b]Infant deaths per thousand births, 2013.

Source: Population Reference Bureau, 2014. *2014 World Population Data Sheet.*

growth rate and column 5 contains the years to double calculated from that growth rate. The growth rate in LDRs is 14 times greater than in MDRs. As a result, the population of the LDRs would double in only 50 years at their present rate of growth while the same doubling would require 700 years in MDRs. Not captured by these demographic statistics are the considerable differences in wealth and economic opportunity between MDRs and LDRs, nor the vulnerability of the poorest LDRs to collective and personal economic disaster, such as famine and war. Also not captured is the considerable variation among countries when considered apart from regional averages. For example, the infant mortality rate in LDRs like Cuba and Singapore is 4.6 and 2 respectively, a notably superior record to the U.S. infant mortality rate of 5.4. And there continue to be considerable differences in the health and well-being among those countries with a substantial degree of control over births and deaths. Thus, while we distinguish between LDRs and MDRs often in this textbook, the truth is that the line dividing the two typologies is often quite blurred and will only become more so in future years.

An interesting detail to note in Table 3-2 is Europe's rates. Europe is unique in that its crude death rate roughly equals its birth rate, reflecting swiftly declining fertility and an aging population structure. As a result, its population growth rate is currently zero, and if it remains at this level the European population will never double. The latest United Nations population projections indicate that Europe's future fertility rates will actually become low enough that the population will begin declining over the century (United Nations, 2013).

The regions described in Table 3-2, whether considered individually or combined into development categories, not only have different current demographic traits but also have had different demographic histories over the past two centuries. Starting in the late 1700s, one after another of the present MDRs began their **demographic transitions** from high to low death rates, and then from high to low birth rates. As regions experienced development, many countries moved gradually from *pre-transitional* to *transitional* categories. Early in this transition MDRs grew at more rapid rates than the LDRs, until about World War I. Starting with the Great Depression, and especially since World War II, the transition to lower birth rates began to slow MDR growth, while the regions with the most rapid growth since then have been the less-developed ones. The postwar rates of growth in the LDRs generally surpassed anything previously experienced by the present MDRs. This is because LDRs have benefitted from health advances far more rapidly than the pace at which health improvements occurred historically in the MDRs. The combination of rapidly increasing life expectancy, often within a single generation, and reproductive behavior that has not fully adjusted to these new conditions fueled this growth.

In the post-WWII period, most countries in the MDRs completed their fertility transitions and are now *late-transition* countries with low death, birth, and growth rates; some have even experienced negative growth rates. The MDR countries that continue to grow in population are the U.S. and Canada, and this is primarily from LDR immigration (PRB, 2008). Many countries in the LDRs have moved rapidly through similar demographic transitions, especially given where their growth rates were just a generation ago, while others are at various stages along the demographic transition. Uganda, for example, has seen a gradual decrease in its once-high mortality rate but its fertility rate still remains high. Guatemala's birth and death rates have been declining, and India's birth rate is steadily approaching the replacement rate of 2.1 (Haub and Gribble, 2011).

As a general rule, the transition from higher to lower fertility almost always happens *after* the transition from high to lower mortality. This is largely because there are many long-standing and significant societal norms that value childbearing and large families. By contrast, few individuals value poor health and short lives. Therefore, when medical technology and preventative health knowledge become available, they are generally adopted. But the existence of birth control does not necessarily mean that people will use it. Pronatalist customs that have been in place for thousands of years, in part to offset high infant and child mortality, take considerable time to reverse. Economic advancement and changing gender roles are often precursors to changes in social norms around reducing family size. The time between when MDR populations started living longer and when they stopped having as many babies sometimes lasted a century, a much longer transitional population growth period than what we are seeing in many LDRs today.

Despite many variations in timing, today there is no country left in the world that has yet to begin its demographic transition. There are a few countries at the very beginning of the transition, just starting to increase their life expectancy (Haub and Gribble, 2011), but most are well into the fertility decline phase. In fact, 48% of the world's population now lives in low-fertility countries, where women have less than 2.1 children. While most of the low-fertility population is in MDRs, nineteen Asian countries, seventeen Latin American countries, and two African countries also fit into this category (United Nations, 2013). Only 9% of the world still fits into the high fertility category, where women have five or more children.

Demographers often study countries that are now in the later stages of transition both to understand the causes of the transition and as a historical precedent for what might happen to other countries as they are becoming more economically and demographically developed. This has been the underlying rationale for the study of the historic MDR demographic transitions.

The Prototypical Historical Demographic Transition

The time and place that provides the earliest model for the demographic transition was Western Europe between 1800 and the 1930s. This was the first world region to go through the sequence (Coale and Watkins, 1986). Economically, the Western European countries already had progressed in their agricultural revolutions before the 1800s. During the demographic transition period, they were going through that complex set of changes called the industrial revolution, with accompanying social changes such as urbanization, literacy, secularization, and growing consumerism.

Description

What happened to crude death and birth rates during the European transition, along with the economic changes, is shown schematically in Figure 3-2. In pre-transition populations (left side of figure), both death rates and birth rates were high. Pestilence and famine were major causes of death. The transition generally began with a decline in epidemic mortality due to improved nutrition, sanitation, and so on. As death rates reached lower levels, remaining deaths were largely due to degenerative and human-made diseases; as death rates reached even lower levels, birth rates also fell. By the late-transition period (right side of figure), both birth and death rates were low. During the transitional phase, the model specifies that the death rate dropped before the birth rate, causing a period of very rapid natural increase—the classic population explosion. While death rates were more variable from year to year in the pre-transition phase, birth rates were more variable after the transition. The transition was not only from high to *low* rates, but also to *controlled* and more predictable mortality and fertility.

Not all Western European nations went through their demographic transitions simultaneously (Coale and Watkins, 1986). Sustained declines in death began as early as 1750 in countries as different as France and Sweden. Births generally declined much later in the transition, from 1827 (France) to 1922 (Ireland and European Russia). The gap between rapidly falling death rates and a delayed decline in birth rates led to rising population growth, with the period of greatest natural increase between 1870 and 1910 for most Western European countries.

Aside from the timing of the transition, there were many other deviations from the prototypical sequence given in Figure 3-2 within Western Europe. Pre-transition fertility was not steady, nor completely uncontrolled, as the stylized demographic transition model implies (Coale and Watkins, 1986, pp. 429–430). At times fertility fell simultaneously with mortality, or, much more rarely, even preceded it (Coale, 1975, p. 351). At

Figure 3-2

Simplified Diagram of the European Demographic Transition

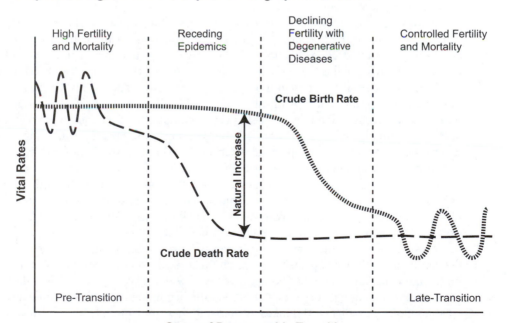

Stage of Demographic Transition

the outset of the transition, fertility was rising, compounding the impact of mortality decline (Petersen, 1975, pp. 631–637). Figure 3-2 is not a theory of how mortality and fertility declines occurred or an exact model of any one country's experience. Rather, the simplified model of Figure 3-2 is a useful device for understanding the general pattern of demographic transition and why it often resulted in explosive population growth during periods before birth rates slowed down to match lowered death rates.

Mortality and fertility declines swept across Europe steadily and by 1930 few provinces of Europe remained untouched. With few exceptions, fertility declines lagged behind mortality declines, and natural increase generated population explosions within European countries.

Demographic Transition Theories

Let us suppose that the preceding description of the European demographic transition is true, generally. What does that tell us about the future of mortality and fertility in developing countries? It tells us that many LDRs will eventually achieve low, stable mortality and low, variable fertility. But there are some important questions we must ask. *When* in the modernization and mortality-decline process will fertility decline? What *aspects* of the modernization process are crucial for triggering such a fertility decline? Is it ethnocentric to predict that LDRs will follow the same model of demographic transition as the MDRs? Given the different times and circumstances, what can we expect for transitions that are just getting underway in some LDRs?

To address such questions, we have to go beyond observing that trends coincide in time and investigate the causes of mortality and fertility declines in order to develop an analytical theory. There have been several provocative and plausible attempts to formulate such a general theory of demographic, and especially fertility, transition as well as harsh criticisms of each.

Following Mason's seminal review of demographic transition theory (1997), we can identify six major transition theories. Classical demographic transition theory emphasizes fertility decline as following mortality decline and due to changes in social life accompanying industrialization and urbanization (Thompson, 1930; Notestein, 1945). Lesthaeghe (1983) adds to modernization the importance of a shift toward self-fulfillment of parents with rising affluence. Caldwell (1982) emphasized a shift in wealth flows, brought about by such changes as compulsory education and child labor laws, which made children an economic burden, not a net benefit, to the family. The neoclassical microeconomic approach (Becker, 1981) emphasizes both the rising cost of raising children and the desire for alternative uses of family resources (e.g., rising consumerism and alternative consumption goods). Easterlin and Crimmins (1985) expand this thinking to include the psychological or social costs of limiting fertility. The ideational theory (Cleland and Wilson, 1987) attributes declining fertility to the diffusion of contraceptive information and changing childbearing norms.

Most criticisms of these general demographic transition theories arise either from the simplicity with which transitions are characterized (Mason, 1997) or from exceedingly high expectations for prediction (Feeney, 1994). As Feeney notes, even the most satisfactory transition theory may not predict the beginning of fertility decline any better than we can predict earthquakes by knowing they are caused by the shifting of tectonic plates. Although transition theories are useful to understand changes in human behavior, there is no evidence they can predict the precise timing of demographic changes in a given set of circumstances.

Mason (1997) summarizes what demographers have established about the demographic transition:

1. Mortality decline is usually a necessary, but not a sufficient, condition for fertility decline.

2. Fertility transitions occur in different circumstances when various *combinations* of conditions are sufficient to motivate or enable populations to adopt birth control.

3. A transition caused by circumstances in a given population may influence, or *diffuse* to, other regions of different circumstance.

4. Such influences may travel at different speeds depending on a variety of circumstances (e.g., state policy, information and transportation networks).

5. The number of children families can support varies across pre-transition populations.

6. If families exceed their ability to support children, parents will resort to some form of fertility control.

7. Fertility control after pregnancy or birth depends on available and acceptable forms of such control (e.g., abortion or infanticide).

8. When conditions limit such controls after pregnancy, prenatal controls such as contraception or birth spacing will be encouraged (especially if aided by state policy or programs).

This summary emphasizes the variability in circumstances of demographic transition and highlights the difficulty in identifying a single cause, or a comprehensive list of causes, for transitions. Mortality and fertility declines may have different causes in different countries or periods. Moreover, transitions are not likely to proceed in other countries exactly the same way they did in Western Europe.

There is also debate among demographers over whether a **second demographic transition** (SDT) is now emerging on the tail of the major first demographic transition just described. This is primarily characterized by a shift from traditional and universal marital households to a proliferation of different family forms and very low, unstable fertility levels (Lesthaeghe and Surkyn, 2002; Lesthaeghe and Willems, 1999; van de Kaa, 1987). In the late 20th century, new patterns of delayed marriage, nonmarital childbearing, and very low, unpredictable fertility became more common in Northern Europe, which then spread across Europe and into eastern Europe. Although it was initially argued that these patterns were idiosyncratic to Europe (Coleman, 2004), the new patterns are now proliferating in North America and appear to be under way in a number of Asian countries (Lesthaeghe, 2010).

What makes this second transition different from the first demographic transition stage? Whereas the latter transition ends with relatively stable, replacement-level fertility, the SDT describes unforeseen levels of variation in low fertility, including below-replacement fertility, which has been enabled by the revolution in modern contraceptive technology. Furthermore, the first demographic transition took place within a conservative cultural regime of traditional family and gender role norms. A defining characterization of the SDT is the new flexibility in household structures that reflects societal secularization, individualism, and increasingly egalitarian gender roles. While the first demographic transition grew out of stabilizing economic forces that met much of modern society's basic material needs, the second seems to be a function of even greater prosperity and wealth, enabling higher order needs to be met such as self-actualization and freedom of expression. It remains to be seen how distinct the SDT will be from the first demographic transition, as it is only just now beginning to manifest itself in certain regions.

Therefore, throughout this text we largely focus on the first demographic transition, which we characterize as consisting of two distinct but interrelated transitions, one in mortality and one in fertility. We will emphasize the variety of factors that have historically influenced mortality and fertility declines, rather than focus on a single example. We will revisit these in context throughout the text. In studying both mortality and fertility, later chapters of this text take European history as a point of departure. LDRs are contrasted and compared with the historical transitions in Europe and the MDRs. This is the strategy we follow in chapter 5, where we deal with the *mortality transition*, and in chapter 7, where we discuss the *fertility transition* and spread of family planning in more detail. In chapter 8 we will examine changing trends in marriage and union patterns that appear to be an initial manifestation of the second demographic transition.

Differential Growth, 1950–2100

Let us return to the description of the modern world population explosion, dramatically illustrated in Figure 3-1. But now we will distinguish between the MDRs (which have largely completed their demographic transitions) and the LDRs (which are transitioning at many different stages).

Our coverage is divided into two time periods, from 1950 to 2010 and from 2010 to 2100. The first segment brings us up to the most recent U.S. census, and for this period we can depend on actual population counts or estimates from partial information. The second segment is largely in the future, and here we must depend on projection. The source for both sets of figures is the United Nations (United Nations, 2013).

Counts and Estimates, 1950 to 2010

MDRs differ from LDRs not only in their current growth rates but also in the trends of those rates over time. The top half of Table 3-3 gives the growth rates for more-developed regions, less-developed regions, and the world as a whole up to 2010.

In the MDRs the growth rate was fairly high in the 1950s and early 1960s—by the standards of industrialized countries—but has been declining steadily since. There has been a continuous gradual decline in mortality throughout the second half of the century. The consensus is that most of the 20th century mortality decline is attributable to public health practices and medical advances even more so than rising income. Fertility, on the other hand, has had wide swings, and so has the resulting natural increase. Most MDRs had postwar baby booms (sustained, in the case of the United States) that kept natural increase higher than normal for MDRs. Fertility since the 1960s has been declining even more rapidly than mortality, shrinking the rate of natural increase.

Even at the outset of the postwar era, LDR growth rates were more than 70% higher than those for the MDRs. The gap widened for most of this period as LDR rates soared. But it is now clear that a peak rate for the LDRs was reached in the mid-1960s and has gradually retreated since then. Throughout the postwar period, overall mortality was declining substantially. True to demographic transition theory, fertility did not decline as early as mortality and generally stayed at high levels through the mid-1960s. Then it started to decline, in one country after another, eroding the overall high rate of natural increase.

There still is considerable variety among LDRs in their current growth rates. Unexpected mortality, especially from the HIV/AIDS virus, has contributed to lower growth

Table 3-3   Population Growth Rates for More-Developed and Less-Developed Regions, 1950–2100

Period	More-Developed Regions	Less-Developed Regions	World
1950–1955	1.20	2.09	1.81
1955–1960	1.17	2.14	1.85
1960–1965	1.09	2.35	1.98
1965–1970	0.83	2.51	2.04
1970–1975	0.77	2.37	1.94
1975–1980	0.66	2.09	1.73
1980–1985	0.59	2.09	1.73
1985–1990	0.60	2.05	1.72
1990–1995	0.44	1.79	1.51
1995–2000	0.33	1.59	1.34
2000–2005	0.30	1.43	1.21
2005–2010	0.24	1.34	1.14
Medium Fertility Projection			
2010–2015	0.30	1.33	1.15
2015–2020	0.24	1.21	1.04
2020–2025	0.18	1.07	0.93
2025–2030	0.12	0.96	0.83
2030–2035	0.07	0.86	0.74
2035–2040	0.04	0.77	0.66
2040–2045	0.02	0.68	0.59
2045–2050	0.01	0.60	0.51
2050–2055	−0.01	0.52	0.45
2055–2060	−0.03	0.45	0.39
2060–2065	−0.04	0.39	0.34
2065–2070	−0.04	0.34	0.30
2070–2075	−0.03	0.30	0.26
2075–2080	−0.02	0.25	0.22
2080–2085	−0.02	0.22	0.19
2085–2090	−0.02	0.20	0.17
2090–2095	−0.03	0.17	0.14
2095–2100	−0.06	0.13	0.11

Source: United Nations, 2013. *World Population Prospects: The 2012 Revision.* Used with permission.

rates than expected in some LDR countries. More important, swift mortality declines that persisted before fertility declines followed resulted in a period of much higher natural increase for some countries than in historical European transitions. The greatest influence on variability in LDR growth rates is the timing of their fertility transitions.

What do these rates mean in terms of the size and distribution of world population? A larger and larger proportion of the world's population lives in LDRs. Accordingly, what happens in the LDRs increasingly determines what happens in the world as a whole. This point is illustrated vividly in Figure 3-3, where we see that as the size of LDR populations increased from 1950 to 2005, so did the size of the world's population.

Figure 3-4 diagrams the changing distribution of population by continental areas over three centuries. By the end of this century, North America, Latin America, and Europe will have a declining proportion of the world's population. In fact, Europe is expected to shrink in total population size by -14% (United Nations, 2013). Asia, too, will become a smaller proportion of the world's population from what it was, largely driven by China's demographic trends. Africa is the region that is expected to grow most rapidly, tripling in its global population proportion by the end of the century. Growth rates are and will be highest among a subset of 49 LDR countries that continue to have very high fertility. The United Nations projects that these countries will account for most of the growth shown in Figure 3-3.

Figure 3-3

Population Growth of More-Developed and Less-Developed Regions, 1950–2100

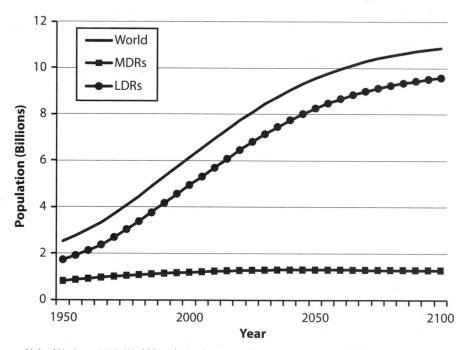

Source: United Nations, 2013. *World Population Prospects: The 2012 Revision.* Used with permission.

Figure 3-4

World Population Distribution

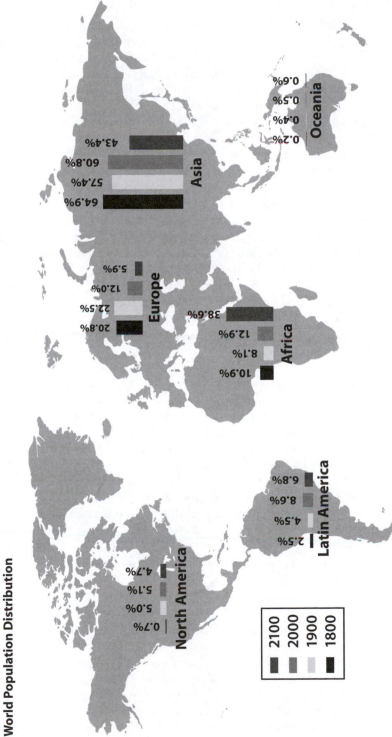

Legend:
- 2100
- 2000
- 1900
- 1800

North America
- 4.7%
- 5.1%
- 5.0%
- 0.7%

Latin America
- 6.8%
- 8.6%
- 4.5%
- 2.5%

Europe
- 5.9%
- 12.0%
- 22.5%
- 20.8%

Africa
- 38.6%
- 12.9%
- 8.1%
- 10.9%

Asia
- 43.4%
- 60.8%
- 57.4%
- 64.9%

Oceania
- 0.6%
- 0.5%
- 0.4%
- 0.2%

Source: Data from Population Reference Bureau, *Human Population* (UN Population Division Briefing Packet, 2005); United Nations, 2011. *World Population Prospects: The 2010 Revision.*

Projections, 2010 to 2100

The United Nations, by itself and occasionally in collaboration with other agencies, provides regularly updated population growth projections. Most of the projections used in this text are from its most recently revised *World Population Prospects*. Because they boldly predict into the distant future, all projections are subject to such periodic revision. The method used in making these projections is the cohort-component method, described in more detail in chapter 4. For the moment, it is enough to say that in this method, separate projections are made for the population in each age category using assumptions about its future mortality, migration, and fertility experiences.

What are the assumptions for the recent United Nations projections? Mortality is assumed to slow down as general mortality risks continue to decrease, even in the countries with high HIV/AIDS prevalence. Net migration is assumed to follow past trends and is projected to remain constant over the next decades until about 2050. Finally, fertility assumptions are more complex but are generally extrapolations of observed patterns of fertility decline within regions and countries (United Nations, 2013, 2011). In essence, these assumptions are based on the continuation of present trends.

If we accept these assumptions, what does the UN project will happen, in summary? The world's growth rate will fall to around 1% by 2015. Table 3-3 tells us that the world rate will continue to fall after 2015 and MDR growth rates will become negative by 2050. The growth rates of some high-fertility LDRs and the increase of large-population countries like the U.S. and India will boost world population to 9.6 billion by 2050, 85% of which will reside in the LDRs (United Nations, 2013). By 2100, only Africa will see its share of the world population increase dramatically, while Oceania will have a very modest increase, and other regions will have a lesser share of the world population as years go by. In terms of sheer population size, India's population is projected to surpass China's in the next few decades, while Nigeria is estimated to surpass the U.S. population by mid-century (United Nations, 2013).

But despite population *increase*, projections in Table 3-3 show that by 2070 LDR *growth rates* will be as low as MDR growth rates are today. By the end of the century global growth rates will be lower than they have ever been in recorded history. By these estimates, the global demographic transition will have just about run its full course, although population momentum growth will continue to be in swing.

Projections as Predictions

As predictions, population projections are no more accurate than the mortality, fertility, and migration assumptions they employ. How much confidence can we have that the UN's current assumptions will turn out to be true over the next century? As we have said, the projections essentially assume that present trends will continue. They also implicitly assume that mortality and fertility in the LDRs will follow some version of the sequence we call the demographic transition.

There are, however, many differences between the demographic history of MDRs from 1850 to 1900 and the experience of contemporary LDRs from 1950 to 2010, differences that affect the course of both the economic development and the demographic transitions in the LDRs. LDR rates of natural increase have surged earlier in the economic development process than they did in MDRs because their death rates dropped earlier and generally faster, due to modern medical and sanitation technologies. LDRs probably will not be able to use emigration as a transitional population "safety valve" to the same degree as did Europe. Agrarian densities at the outset are higher in many LDRs, and the prospects for industrialization are quite different, with current LDR attempts taking place in a world economy already dominated by the industrialized MDRs. Nevertheless, LDRs appear to be moving through their demographic transitions twice as fast as the MDRs did.

Finally, past projections that simply assumed the continuation of present trends have proved abysmally wrong as long-term predictions. For instance, projections made in the 1930s did not consider the postwar Western baby boom; most world projections made in the 1960s did not dare to assume the LDR fertility decline that even then must have been starting in some countries. Even recent assumptions understated the magnitude of LDR fertility declines and the dramatic rise of a worldwide HIV/AIDS epidemic. How future climate change, for example, will specifically impact population dynamics is difficult to predict; however, predictions by the Intergovernmental Panel on Climate Change (IPCC) forecast global population upheaval due to unpredictable weather patterns and their impacts (IPCC, 2007, 2012, 2013). But, at the very least, projections accurately reflect current information as a best collective guess of what will happen in the future. It is wise to view these projections not so much as scientific predictions but as statements about what would happen if current trends continue. Perhaps our greatest challenge as demographers is predicting the demographic future of countries that have begun the unprecedented transition into negative population growth.

Problems of a Changing World Distribution

In chapter 1 we took the position that analysis of any population problem involves addressing a set of three questions: *Who* is concerned about the population trend in question? *What* do these concerned observers believe to be the consequences of the trend? *Why* do they dislike those consequences? Try to keep those questions in mind as we discuss the problems associated with world population growth.

There are three interrelated aspects of world population growth trends that seem to excite concern: (1) the size and density of the world population, or of LDR national populations; (2) the rate of growth of national populations; and (3) the changing **population distribution** around the world. Let us treat problems of distribution first, since we have just described relevant trends in Table 3-3 and Figures 3-3 and 3-4. The feature of these trends that arouses the most concern is the progressive postwar tendency of LDR populations to outnumber MDR populations. This changing distribution of the world population is projected to continue indefinitely.

Who seems to be worried about the changing world population distribution? Leaders of the LDRs may be concerned about the density or growth rates of their populations (discussed later), but not about international distribution per se. There are few statements from LDR leaders decrying their increase in the proportion of the future world's population. Rather, it is the MDRs for whom the changing distribution is a problem.

What unwanted consequences do the MDR publics anticipate? Interestingly, the rationale behind the concern is seldom stated. Rather, the facts of the changing distribution simply are presented and the unhappy consequences are assumed to be self-evident. The LDR publics, naturally, have their suspicions as to underlying motives behind the MDR concerns (Hartmann, 1995). Let us consider and analyze some of these possible MDR motives.

Can it be that MDRs fear a shifting population distribution will diminish their role in the global balance of power? The recognition that population is related to power lies behind some of the earliest demographic censuses, which tallied national populations available for industry and soldiering. If we define power as being able to influence others' behavior, then (other things being equal) population probably still contributes to national power. For instance, MDR nations treat mainland China with more care than they do Singapore, even though the latter is more developed. Given this, perhaps MDR publics are concerned that the changing world population distribution also means a changing world power distribution, to their disfavor.

Can it be that MDRs are worried about becoming an even smaller minority? Are Westerners concerned about the submerging of Western culture? Or do they worry about preserving their own socioeconomic privileges in the face of shifting population distributions? One clearly stated public concern in MDRs is a fear that immigration will rise as the share of population in LDRs continues to increase, eventually making many historically majority groups a minority in their "own" country. However, MDR immigration policies do not always match public concern over immigration since labor migration generally proves so economically useful for MDRs. We will treat this in detail in chapter 9.

It may also be that MDRs are concerned about being globally overwhelmed by the poverty or economic development of some LDRs. Do they see the rich countries as a shrinking, embattled enclave in a poorer world? Do they fear that their higher standard of living and past economic dominance will no longer be tolerated under the new population circumstances? Such concerns appear reasonable given the resource consumption and waste production in MDRs. Although MDRs comprise just a small percentage of the global population, their resource consumption and pollution generation are disproportionately large (Ewing et al., 2010). Per capita water consumption by MDR residents is thirty to fifty times that by LDR residents, while per capita carbon dioxide emissions are triple that of LDRs (The Royal Society, 2012; UNESCO, 2003). If LDRs tried to strictly emulate MDRs, at the very least resource constraints would require MDRs to reduce their privileged, and wasteful, use of world resources. This speculation about the basis of MDR concern over world *distribution* is not very flattering.

Speculations about the basis for MDR concern regarding LDR population *size* and *growth rates* are not so unflattering. They could range from simple humanitarian desire to improve lives in LDRs, to a desire to cut down on the costs of international foreign aid, to a desire to reduce LDR-to-MDR migration pressures.

Whatever the basis for the concern, the reasoning behind defining overpopulation and rapid growth as LDR problems is not as simple as it may seem. In an attempt to inject order into this discussion, let us separate our treatment of population size problems from that of population growth problems.

Problems of Population Size

Carrying Capacity, Population Density, and the Ecological Footprint

The popular notion of overpopulation is vague. It suggests that the population of an area is too large. The closest demographic specification of that fear is population density, or the size of a population within a given area. Indeed, one notion of overpopulation is the idea that a population is too densely settled.

Chapter 1 defines density as the relationship between a population's size and the space it inhabits. Thus defined, density can be measured by this ratio:

$$\frac{\text{population size}}{\text{space (e.g., land area)}}$$

This is sometimes called the population per area.

But a concept that better captures the impact of population on its resources is known as the **carrying capacity**. For our purposes it is sufficient to define carrying capacity as the maximum population size within a given area that can sustain itself indefinitely without damaging its existing resources, given its technology and consumption patterns. Since at least 1679, there have been many estimates of the earth's carrying capacity for human populations, ranging in size from below to well above the current world population (Cohen, 1995). One recent calculation estimates that the global carrying capacity has already been overshot by 30% (Rees, 2010). We can crudely generalize the ratio as follows:

$$\frac{\text{population size}}{\text{resources}}$$

The resources depend on both technology and consumption behavior. In the case of an agricultural economy, it may be primarily land, but the concept is meant to include all natural resources considered essential for human well-being and production (e.g., water, fresh air, a nonpolluted environment, and energy sources). It also includes the other nonlabor determinants of productive capacity (e.g., investment capital, education, and health services). The total area of land needed to sustain many populations often reaches far beyond its immediate geographic borders to include other lands and resources. This is particularly true for the MDRs. Thus, a closely related concept to carrying capacity is the **ecological footprint**, which specifies how environmentally sustainable a given population is (Rees and Wackernagel, 1992). Originally called the "appropriated carrying capacity," but renamed to the more policy-friendly "ecological footprint" (EF), the EF calculates the per-capita amount of consumption relative to the environment's ability to regenerate needed resources. Specifically, it is a natural resource accounting tool that measures how quickly resources are being regenerated and waste is being absorbed in a given time period. These are generally divided into types of renewable resource usage, including cropland, grazing land, timber, fishing, and land development. The EF also includes a measure for carbon, the by-product of burning fossil fuels, which is defined as the amount of forest land required to absorb the amount of carbon emissions (for more details see Ewing et al., 2010).

As a general rule, higher income countries consume many more resources than lower income countries when measured on a per-person basis. For example, lower income countries like Bolivia have 16.3 hectares of excess biocapacity, whereas high-income countries like Qatar record 8 hectares of ecological deficit due to extensive use of renewable resources. A significant portion of the ecological footprint can be attributed to carbon emissions, especially for high-income countries. Not all high-income countries produce the same carbon footprint. To list a few, the United Arab Emirates produced 8.1 hectares and the United States produced 5.5 hectares per capita worth of carbon emissions in the early 21st century, whereas Norway only produced 1.4 hectares (Ewing et al., 2010).

The relationship between population and its consumption impact on world resources has been recognized by the United Nations. Among its current Millennium Development Goals is ensuring environmental sustainability and reducing biodiversity loss at the same time that it advocates for ameliorating global poverty. Thus, economic development should be directly linked to the environment, ensuring that current development needs do not compromise the potential for future generations to meet their needs as well.

From Malthus to Marx to the Neo-Malthusians

Historically, the judgment of overpopulation necessarily focused on scarcity: too large a numerator (population) and too small a denominator (resources). Overpopulation can be eased either by decreasing the numerator or by increasing the denominator. Labeling a high ratio as overpopulation amounts to blaming the large numerator rather than the small denominator. Such a judgment often is made not only where the density is high but also where the denominator is difficult to expand given current technology and consumption behavior. The classic instance is an agricultural economy with no unused arable land to plow and not enough to go around among the potential farmers. In England at the end of the 18th century, for example, changes in agricultural technology came slowly, requiring the importation of grain for sustenance (and exportation of emigrants). The tendency to blame the population size for shortages in the means for subsistence owes much to the theories of Thomas Malthus, which were formulated at just this time in English history.

Thomas Malthus's first and second essays on the principles of population (published in 1798 and 1803) were landmarks in the development of population theory. He was not the first to include demographic variables in economic and social analysis; in fact, his essays were partially in refutation of competitive theories by Godwin, Condorcet, and others. But the role of population size and growth was so prominent in Malthus's theory, and he spent so many years and later editions of his essays (seven in all) trying to test, polish, and defend his theory, that it could not be ignored.

Box 3-2 provides a summary of Malthus's central thoughts on the subject of overpopulation. Malthus's theory, as summarized, was simplistic and demonstrably wrong in many ways. Population does not increase geometrically. Nor does subsistence on resources increase arithmetically. These erroneous simplifications by Malthus do not, however, alter the force of his central argument that, without checks, a population will tend to outgrow its available resources (i.e., the numerator will increase more rapidly than the denominator).

Two important critics of Malthus, Karl Marx and Friedrich Engels, were both teenagers in Germany when Malthus died in England in 1834. Malthusian theory was

Box 3-2

Thomas Malthus's Principle of Population

According to Malthus, populations tend to grow more rapidly than do the means for their subsistence; that is, unless checked in some way, populations tend to grow in a geometric progression (1, 2, 4, 8, etc.). On the other hand, there is no such tendency for the means of subsistence to expand by geometric progression; rather, they expand by arithmetic progression (1, 2, 3, 4, etc.). Moreover, where resources are finite and limited, such as arable land in an already densely populated country, then a principle of diminishing returns will apply: The best land will be plowed first and each successive acre plowed will be of poorer land. By "means for subsistence," Malthus meant—ultimately—food supply, so this agricultural example is apt.

Population is kept within the limits of the means for subsistence mainly by **positive checks**, those operating through the death rates. When the means for subsistence are not adequate to take care of a population at a given size, the death rate will go up until the population has shrunk to a supportable level.

By the same token, whenever a surplus might appear in the means for subsistence, this will tend temporarily to lower the death rate (and raise the rate of natural increase) until the population has grown to the limits of the new means for subsistence. This is the "Malthusian dilemma."

Hypothetically, the way out of the dilemma is through the application of "preventive checks" on population growth, operating through the birth rate. These fall into two categories: "moral restraint" and "vice." They are quite distinct in terms of how they correspond to the improvement of humanity (says the Reverend Malthus). Humanity differs from animals, at least potentially, in terms of its ability to foresee the consequences of its actions and to guide its current behavior accordingly.

"Moral restraint," as advocated by Malthus, consists of not marrying until one can support the resulting children and of remaining sexually chaste outside of such marriage. Clearly this appeals to the best in human nature, as Malthus saw it. Moreover, if marriage and sexual companionship must be earned, then people will work harder to win this prize, thereby increasing aggregate means of subsistence.

"Vice," according to Malthus, includes promiscuity, homosexuality, adultery, and birth control (including abortion). Undoubtedly Malthus did not foresee the degree to which the technology of contraception would develop over the next century and a half, nor the growing social acceptability of his other forms of "vice." His stated objection was on moral grounds. Engaging in any of these vices represented an indulgence in sexual appetites without an acceptance of the responsibility for the consequences of such indulgence. It was a rejection of individual responsibility, and Malthus saw acceptance of such responsibility as—in the long run—humanity's only hope for emerging from the dilemma. This pessimism seemed to soften over his seven consecutive editions of the essays.

Such a brief summary is clearly only a simplification of Malthus's life's work. What you have here is undiluted Malthusian thought, as it is preserved in demographic theoretical tradition.

Sources: William Petersen's summary (1975); his volume titled, simply, *Malthus* (1979; see reviews by Dupâquier, 1980, and Keyfitz, 1980); and a volume of essays, *Malthus Past and Present,* edited by Dupâquier (1983).

dominant both in their native country and in England, to which they each moved. What little Marx and Engels said about demography was in rejection of Malthus (Meek, 1954). Within the socialist theory that Marx and Engels were developing, the effect of population size on subsistence and wealth depended on the kind of social organization a society had. What were considered population problems by Malthus were actually results of an unwise and unjust social organization of production and distribution. Humanity is not universally trapped in the Malthusian dilemma. Marx and Engels believed we can escape the supposed negative consequences of population density by reordering society, specifically by socialist control over the means of production and distribution. Some classical Marxist scholars might go further and point out that the labor theory of value leads to the conclusion that "people are wealth," generally, and that population growth is never a root source of poverty. Some conservative "capitalist" economists have reached the same basic conclusion (e.g., Simon, 1986). The contributions of Malthus's critics, including Marx and Engels, were to remind us that population size is only half of the density, or carrying capacity, equation.

The tension between fears of overpopulation and the alternative of blaming current social organization of production and distribution has been echoed in all subsequent discussions of population growth and development. In recent decades a *neo-Malthusian* perspective has used part of Malthus's theory as a justification for worldwide family-planning programs. *Neo-Marxian* perspectives, and economic development theory, have meanwhile promoted development policies such as improved agricultural technology, opportunities and access to credit for marginalized social groups, and efficient social distribution systems within LDRs. Not surprisingly, these two perspectives are complementary, reflecting the numerator (i.e., population size) and the denominator (i.e., means of subsistence) in our general formula for population density. Both clearly have a role in concerns over population growth. Malthus's contribution was to bring attention to the importance of population growth in this equation.

We can assume that Malthus would applaud the recognition that many countries have given to the importance of population growth. China, for example, came to recognize its huge population and rapid growth as a cause of continued underdevelopment and took measures in the form of fertility regulation to counteract it (however, evidence shows that fertility decline began in China prior to regulation). Though few countries have taken an approach as extreme and controversial as China's, officials in many countries have respect for the possible negative consequences of entirely unchecked population growth.

Malthus would not, however, applaud the family-planning policies that countries have implemented to address concerns with population growth. These policies are examples of neo-Malthusianism, which openly advocates the use of **preventive checks** to escape the Malthusian dilemma. That includes, prominently, birth control, which Malthus called "vice." A product of the Victorian era, Malthus instead advocated "moral restraint" through abstinence and delayed marriage. In spite of this difference, neo-Malthusians and the modern family-planning movement are directly descended from Malthus and rely on a general notion of his "principle of population" as pointing to the need for family-planning programs.

Global Overpopulation and the Environment

In the mid-20th century, those alarmed over rapid population growth were writing books and founding population study centers. There was much discussion of how the 20th-century population explosion would inevitably lead to food shortages, depleted resources, and growing poverty. But despite the doubling of the global population in a very short period, global food production during that time outpaced population growth, resources became cheaper, not more expensive, and global poverty actually decreased (Lam, 2011). This is not to suggest that the overpopulation voices of the period were off base, as their warnings are arguably what led to agricultural innovations and proactive attempts to prevent growing poverty. And there is little question that the environmental repercussions of rapid population growth and the consumption patterns of wealthier countries are harsh and potentially catastrophic. However, in terms of food production and economic growth, it is an important lesson in how prediction-making is highly dependent on an unchanging context.

When talking about long time spans and speaking on a global level, it is easy to envision finite limits of arable land, water, clean air, any given natural resource, and ultimately living space itself. Thus, those most sensitive to the problem of potential overpopulation are those most conscious of such limits, such as environmentalists, human ecologists, and international development organizations (Catafaro and Crist, 2012; Ehrlich and Ehrlich, 2012; Robertson, 2012; United Nations Secretary-General's High-level Panel on Global Sustainability, 2012). Rather than focusing on overpopulation in terms of too many people in one place, measures such as the ecological footprint make clear that overconsumption and lack of sustainability among even a small population can have devastating effects on the global environment.

There are a variety of views about how global population size might respond to the earth's carrying capacity. Four such models of population limits are graphically depicted in Figure 3-5 on the following page.

The two models at the top of this figure are stable, or *adaptive equilibrium*, models. In these models population growth responds to environmental conditions and grows up to, but not beyond, the carrying capacity. The models differ in whether carrying capacity increases as technology and culture develop (upper left) so that population can also continue to grow, or whether the carrying capacity is really an overall fixed limit that population size will approach as it grows (upper right). The central feature of both models is that population growth responds to limited carrying capacity before reaching limits to growth.

The two basic models at the bottom of this figure are unstable, or *overshoot*, models. In both of these cases population growth is not aware of, or at least not responsive to, limits to growth until it has exceeded the carrying capacity. Based on current population and consumption trends, some estimate that the earth's sustainable carrying capacity has already been overshot, but that the population has not yet been affected because it has not yet depleted its remaining stores of nonrenewable energy sources (Ewing et al., 2010).

These two models differ in how population growth responds once the carrying capacity of the population is exceeded. The first possibility (lower left) is that population drops off (i.e., negative growth) once it exceeds carrying capacity, perhaps with

Figure 3-5

Global Population Size and Carrying Capacity: Four Models

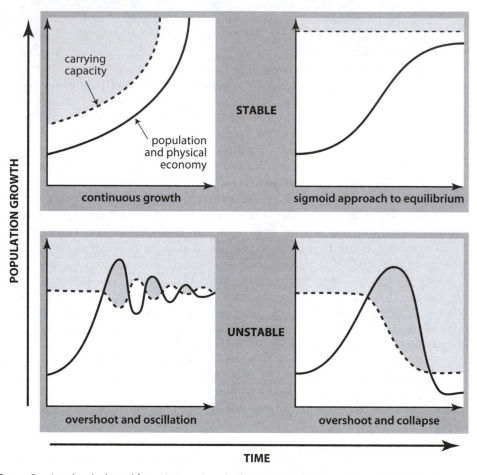

Source: Reprinted and adapted from *Limits to Growth: The 30-Year Update,* copyright © 2004 by Meadows, Meadows, and Randers. With permission from Chelsea Green Publishing Co.

some damage to the environment, and oscillates above or below carrying capacity until, perhaps, an eventual equilibrium is reached. This model is often characterized as a population learning its carrying capacity by trial and error. It is also the model that is closest to what Malthus might have envisioned.

The second possibility (lower right) is the bleakest of all. In this model, once the population exceeds its carrying capacity there is catastrophic damage to the environment. Once this happens, both the carrying capacity and the population collapse in ruin or extinction. It is not farfetched to imagine increasing world conflict over limited natural resources prior to a collapse. This model is, of course, only the most pessimistic possibility. In a bit more optimistic view, those who believe that there are fixed limits to growth often point out that, with exceptions, humanity would not likely reach limits simultaneously all over the world. Depending on both population and technology, some regions would encounter limits earlier than others. Already, some countries are facing severe water shortages (World Water Assessment Programme, 2012). If other regions with excess resources were willing to share them unselfishly, limits to growth, or possible overshoot, might be postponed and eventually avoided altogether. Can we have faith in such interregional altruism, and on the massive scale required as additional "overpopulated" regions are added, including ever larger proportions of the world's population? Even if it were only a problem of redistribution of resources, it is a massive and difficult one to resolve.

Other demographic-environmental concerns have more immediate global implications. Carbon emissions and resulting climate change is a major example. While population growth and energy consumption have by now been well documented as causes of climate change (IPCC 2007, 2013; Pachauri and Jiang, 2008; National Research Council, 2008), research is needed on the extent to which demographic characteristics of populations—such as age structure, household size, and urbanization—may predict differing energy consumption patterns (Jiang and Hardee, 2011). The "feedback" effects of future climate change are even more difficult to predict. The United Nations' Intergovernmental Panel on Climate Change (IPCC) estimates that immediate effects will be felt differentially across the globe (IPCC, 2007, 2012, 2013). Regions located near the equator are likely to experience worsening conditions, whereas regions in higher latitudes may experience some short-term agricultural benefits. Unfortunately, those countries who will bear the immediate brunt of global warming are LDRs, which not only produce the lowest amounts of greenhouse gases in the first place, but also have fewer resources to protect themselves from related agricultural and economic instability. Longer term, however, the accelerating impacts of climate change will likely be felt globally. The IPCC predicts increasing frequency of extreme weather events, unpredictable weather patterns, rising sea levels, and water shortages. Potential consequences, such as impaired agricultural productivity and food shortages, altered infectious disease prevalence, and environment-related mass migrations would impact global sociopolitical stability, and we could certainly expect them to also influence classic demographic trends, such as migration, mortality, and perhaps even fertility.

One of the greatest challenges to resolving population-related environmental degradation is the phenomenon known as the **tragedy of the commons**, which describes how individual interests are often at odds with the collective best interest. A classic example is fisheries. Fish are a global resource and, in the absence of international regulation, each nation will seek to expand its yield, because if it does not, another nation will. However, the end result will be overfishing and fishery depletion, which is ultimately in no nation's interest. The same is true of climate change, where each nation has an economic stake in energy consumption and little short-term disincentive to check their global greenhouse gas emissions.

Recent international cooperation on other environmental matters provides reason for optimism, however. The Montreal Protocol globally banned the production of ozone-depleting CFC aerosols, remedying what was thought to be a potentially intractable environmental disaster (Sarma and Andersen, 2011). Although the causes of climate change are more complex and the political and economic stakes of reducing reliance on nonrenewable fuels are much higher, there are nascent signs of emerging international cooperation. The Kyoto Protocol is the first international attempt to limit global carbon emissions through a system of reduction goals, caps, and emissions trading. Because the United Nations is unable to enforce participation, however, some of the most significant carbon-emitting countries, like the United States, have opted out. As climate change becomes a more visible risk, the hope is that all nations can be persuaded to participate before the repercussions of climate change are too severe. Evolving technologies, such as the development of renewable energy sources, including wind, solar, bioenergy, hydropower, biothermal, and ocean energy, also have the potential to reduce global reliance on fossil fuels (IPCC, 2011).

National Overpopulation

Countries vary greatly in their population densities, as Figure 3-6 dramatizes. The bars in the graph measure the population-per-area ratios of twenty countries, from MDRs and LDRs, which were selected for their widely varying densities. Australia, Canada, Brazil, and the United States, **frontier regions/nations**, appear at the sparsely populated extreme. Singapore and Hong Kong are at the other extreme, far outstripping even the Netherlands and Japan.

Figure 3-6

Population Density in Twenty Selected Countries, 2014

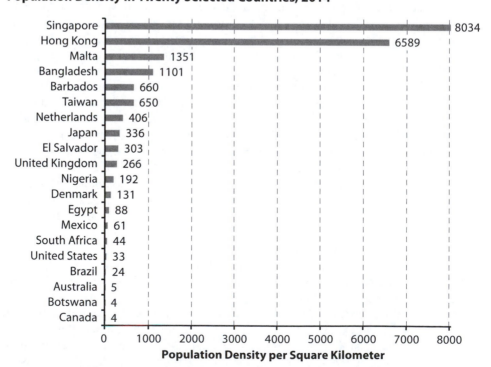

Source: Data from Population Reference Bureau, 2014. *2014 World Population Data Sheet.*

Are the more densely settled of these countries "overpopulated"? The debate over this issue is often in terms of economics and health. For example, if country X had fewer people and a lower density, would that increase the wealth of the country and living standards of its citizens? Would lower density improve the available housing for the population? Would lower density improve health or lower death rates? Any number of such questions may be raised.

A large, densely settled population is deemed to both help and hurt the pursuit of national and personal wealth. On the benefit side, a large population, settled together in space, increases the possibility for division of labor and specialization of producing units; it also makes possible large enterprises that produce economies of scale. On the cost side, a large, densely settled population may limit the productivity per worker by limiting the resources per worker. The balance between these pros and cons depends on the basis of the economy. In countries based on industry, the problem of undersupplying workers with the means for production may be less pressing because those means (capital, equipment, skills, and energy) are expanded and relocated more flexibly. In countries with extractive economies, on the other hand, the resources that make workers productive are less expandable and more easily outstripped in a given location. The classic example of a nonexpandable resource is agricultural land, but one also could include mineral wealth, forests, and fossil fuels.

Aside from its effect on economic productivity, population density has complex effects on living standards and health. Local densities, such as those associated with urbanization, have their advantages as well as their disadvantages, as we will explore in chapter 10. And density has been historically related to mortality and health (chapters 5 and 6).

With all of these dimensions of overpopulation, the problem on a national level is either confined to, or more acute in, the densely settled LDRs. In some of these countries, the benefits of size and density can be outweighed by the detriments. Bangladesh is still commonly cited as the classic case of an overpopulated country, a country in the Malthusian dilemma. It is a small country with a proportionally large population size and, until recently, its economy was almost entirely agricultural. Living standards were marginal, public services were underdeveloped, and it has experienced a number of cyclones, military conflicts, and famines that have aggravated public health concerns. But in recent decades it has made extraordinary development gains that contradict its reputation as a country overburdened by population problems. Thanks largely to the government's investment in women's education and public health, fertility has fallen to almost replacement levels and life expectancy has increased dramatically (*The Economist*, 2012).

The Netherlands and Japan, on the other hand, although fairly heavily settled, have seldom ever been referred to as "overpopulated" because their economies are not basically extractive. Even more dramatic cases of heavily populated but not "overpopulated" countries would be Singapore and Hong Kong, because of their commercial-industrial economies. Again, there are some negative costs of density in these countries, but they are limited compared to those in many LDR urban centers where infrastructure has not always been able to keep up with growth. There also are some LDRs that, though they have extractive economies, are not yet so densely populated that they would be considered as having an "overpopulation" problem; Bolivia is one such example.

Careers in Demography

Wendy Baldwin
President, Population Reference Bureau
Program Director, Population Council, 2006–2012
Executive Vice President for Research, University of Kentucky, 2003–2006
Deputy Director, NIH and NICHD, 1994–2002

How did you decide that being a demographer was the career path for you?

In my sophomore year in college I took a course on population and knew immediately that it combined my interest in social issues with quantitative methods. I was hooked!

What kind of education and training did you pursue to get to where you are in your career?

As part of my BA program I was able to do a five-week self-directed activity. I chose to do all the research I could on how family planning became an issue in the U.S., how it evolved, what the challenges were, and so forth. I augmented that with visiting and talking with the local family-planning program.

I felt strongly that if women could not control that fundamental aspect of their lives, they would be unable to control others, such as investing in education and professional lives. That said, I worked for a year and then went to graduate school to build more skills. My experiences while doing dissertation research in Bogotá, Colombia, reinforced my view of the key importance of understanding how women and couples made decisions about family and how they were able to implement them.

After graduate school I went to the NIH on a two-year appointment—and stayed for 30 years. I was able to develop a research program on adolescent sexual and fertility behavior, advance our understanding of AIDS risk behaviors, and much more. It was a great experience. Now, I have been able to extend those interests in my work at the Population Council and most recently at the Population Reference Bureau.

Describe your work/research as a demographer. What do you consider your most important accomplishments?

My work has been largely in research administration—which sounds dull, but is anything but! It has placed me at the interface of academic research advances and the process of getting those advances known and understood by policy makers. There is a great need for demographic information in many sectors and there is a need for those who can help translate information for those audiences.

As president of the Population Reference Bureau (PRB) in Washington, DC, we get data to decision makers to inform, empower, and advance population issues in the United States and around the world—actions that are critical to the support of strong, effective policies and programs to advance reproductive health and the well-being of populations.

In my past work at NIH, I helped to craft the policies on sharing data and on the inclusion of women and minorities in research, both key issues for how research is done to the benefit of all. At the Population Council, I worked toward helping adolescents make the transition to healthy, productive adulthood.

The kinds of problems we deal with take a long time to address but we have seen success. There may be long-standing traditions of child marriage, for example, but families and communities can learn ways to redefine those traditions that also protect young girls from marriage. The younger the girl, the greater the age gap between her and her spouse, the less voice she is likely to have in the decision to marry, the end of schooling, and the beginning of very early childbearing. So, when we see communities that begin to value their daughters more, provide alternatives for them, support their schooling, and open up new opportunities for them . . . well, that looks like success to me!

I believe that whether or not girls are valued is an issue that everyone can relate to. Too often problems in developing countries seem so far away and it isn't clear what can be done to make the lives of girls better. I have seen programs that have a transformative effect on girls; I've talked with fathers who were so appreciative of the help in finding a better life for their daughters. There is a fundamental satisfaction that comes from such work and this is an important way to spread a vision of the compassion of people for others.

What do you see as the field's most important contribution as well as its greatest challenge?

The field of demography faces several challenges. While there are massive amounts of data available, they are not necessarily easily available. We should always be looking for ways to ensure that data are truly available and accessible to "end users," not just demographers! Also, demography deals with fundamentally personal topics—sex, fertility, marriage, and death. We must forge strong alliances with many disciplines so that we can obtain the most valid information in a way that protects the sensibilities and rights of respondents.

It is again important to remember that there are many costs and benefits of density. To have a particular problem that is aggravated by population density does not necessarily make a clear case for overpopulation. If that were so, then only the areas inhabited by hermits would not be overpopulated. As a result, demographers have gotten out of the habit of thinking in simple terms of overpopulation and underpopulation. This is more a layman's definition of the problem. It is difficult to arrive at a defensible all-purpose "optimum" population figure for any given area. Instead, most demographers focus on the specific effects of population growth rates.

An alternative definition of overpopulation is the ecological footprint measure. That is, how environmentally sustainable is a population, regardless of its density? Does the population consume more resources than it renews? By this measurement, then, Figure 3-6 would look quite different, with countries like the United Arab Emirates and Belgium topping the most "overpopulated" countries in the world (Ewing et al., 2010).

Problems of Growth Rates

Too-Rapid Growth

Who defines rapid growth as a problem for the less-developed countries? Such a belief is widespread in the Western press, which is given to statements like this: "And to cap off the economic problems of impoverished (insert name of LDR country), it is burdened with a population growth rate of more than 2% per year. Thus, every advance in its economy is gobbled up by its burgeoning masses." Many demographers, developmental economists, and population policy planners share the belief that rapid population growth may limit or constrain economic development. Poverty in LDRs may be both worsened and made more difficult to redress by rapid population growth.

An alternative, optimistic point of view, championed by Julian Simon (2006, 1986, 1981, 1977; see also Lal, 2006), argues that evidence shows that human ingenuity is "the ultimate resource"; the more people we have thinking about how to solve problems of production, the greater will be the improvement of technology and economic development. This view is not always met with much sympathy among the demographic establishment (see reviews by Anderton, 1988; Cutright, 1982; Timmer et al., 1982; Coleman and Rowthorn, 2011). A similar sentiment has also been associated with conservative think tanks that seek to deny the seriousness of related environmental concerns (Jacques et al., 2008).

But, despite a recent history of debate over the effects of population growth on economic development, many scholars now agree that rapid population growth is not the *primary* obstacle to economic development. Other factors, such as institutional contexts, labor markets, and social policies are as important as the effects of population growth on economic development (Coleman and Rowthorn, 2011; Das Gupta et al., 2011; Kelley and Schmidt, 2005; Weil and Wilde, 2009; National Research Council, 1986). For example, while rapid postwar economic growth in East Asia was accompanied by drastic decline in population size, shifting from an average of six or more children per woman to two or less in a couple of decades, scholars believe that fertility decline was not the only condition for this economic growth (Mason, 2003). Economists and demographers also pay attention to other facets of economic development, such as resource dilution and diversion, social expenditure, welfare state policies, and so forth, and they differentiate between short- and long-term effects of population growth on economic development (Headey and Hodge, 2009).

Many LDR governments—presumably advised by their own economists (and often under pressure from the West)—have come to view rapid population growth as one of many potential obstacles to economic development. The number of LDR governments concerned that their growth rates were too high increased significantly throughout the latter half of the 20th century. During this time, LDR growth rates decreased significantly, on average from 2.4% in 1971–1975 to 1.4% in 2005–2010 (United Nations, 2010). Today about half the governments of developing nations think that their population growth rate is too high and believe that managing population growth must be a part of LDR strategies for economic development (United Nations, 2010).

Given the relationship between population growth and development, it is reasonable to ask how, theoretically, rapid population growth rates might result in slower economic development in the LDRs. Traditional arguments fall into two categories, one dealing with youth dependency and the other with the productivity of the workforce (Birdsall, 1977; Boserup, 1981; Coale and Hoover, 1958; Crenshaw et al., 1997; Lee, 1983, 1986; McNicoll, 1998).

Strictly speaking, the **youth dependency** problem results from high fertility rather than high growth rates. Rapid growth rates in the modern world are caused by high birth rates coupled with much lower death rates, as shown in the demographic transition in Figure 3-2. The number of new babies added to the population every year is progressively larger. It is true, as Marx pointed out, that each of these babies comes equipped with only one mouth but two hands. But, mouths become operative immediately (ask any parent) while the hands become productive only after a long immaturity.

Society has to treat these babies as consumers immediately and as producers only later in their lives. First, society has to bear the costs of their mothers' pre- and postnatal care, the babies' own infant care, and so on through their years of education and job training. It is only much later that children start to pay back the societal investment. In short, high-fertility populations tend to have large proportions of people at young, dependent ages (see chapter 4 on age and sex structure).

Importantly, if fertility decreases, LDR economies may profit from a temporary economic boost as these young dependents become adults, enter the productive labor force, and are replaced by smaller numbers of dependents in coming generations (Gribble and Bremner, 2012; Crenshaw et al., 1997). This has been referred to as the **demographic dividend**. Theoretically, curtailing rapid population growth, then, may both reduce the immediate burdens of youth dependency and also provide a transition generation with unusually low burdens of youth dependency. Both outcomes would, hypothetically, increase the capital and labor resources available for investment in economic development.

The second explanation of how rapid growth rates inhibit development focuses on the capacity of the economy to improve worker productivity. Theoretically, productivity per worker is related to how many workers share the means for production, the capital. This can be expressed as a version of the general density ratio encountered earlier:

$$\frac{\text{workforce}}{\text{capital}}$$

(Economists sometimes use the inverse of this ratio, capital available per worker, or the *capital–labor* ratio.) Economic development results from expanding capital by providing better tools, better training, improving the transportation infrastructure, and so forth. But some argue that the more rapidly the population—and thus the workforce (in the numerator)—grows, the more rapidly the capital (in the denominator) has to grow in order to decrease the ratio between the two. This is less of a problem where capital is easily expandable, but the economic consensus seems to be that, by their very nature, technologically underdeveloped economies do not expand their capital flexibly; they are more extractive economies, relying on agriculture, mining, forestry, and fishing. Indeed, most LDRs already suffer from high rates of unemployment and underemployment, unable to keep their existing workforces supplied with the capital for production (United Nations, 2009). Controlling rapid population growth theoretically gives LDRs a greater amount of capital per worker, or *capital intensification*, which should allow for greater economic development.

In simple form, the arguments of youth dependency and worker productivity seem convincing. Unfortunately, reality is much more complex and hard evidence supporting these theories is lacking (McNicoll, 1998; Crenshaw et al., 1997). Indeed, some demographers have argued that the realities of population growth and various aspects of economic development are so complex as to defy any formal analysis (e.g., Rodgers, 1989). Even ardent supporters of these theories acknowledge that there is, as yet, little quantitative cross-national evidence for them. Yet, the lack of evidence is also, in large part, due to a lack of detailed longitudinal data and the result of seeking a single model that would apply across all LDR countries. Careful historical observation of individual countries does lend some support for these theories (McNicoll, 1998). Demographers have shown an increasing appreciation for how complex these relationships can be, even if "complexity does not imply inconsequence" (McNicoll, 1998, p. 4).

Beyond these reactions, some scholars are skeptical about Western economic development theory generally as it applies to contemporary modernizing LDRs. Those theories were formulated domestically in countries whose economic development occurred in quite a different era, one ripe for industrialization and imperial exploits. In contrast, contemporary LDRs are trying to scratch out a foothold in a world whose economic institutions are already shaped by the West. In particular, capital-intensive industrial production is dominated (and outsourced) by the MDRs. Therefore, world economic development in the future could take quite a different form than what occurred during Western modernization. It might involve an unprecedented pattern of economic development for the LDRs, one with more emphasis on labor-intensive production and the development of human capital (Sadik, 1991). Policies promoting women's economic development and providing agricultural education are examples of such human capital investments (Kristof and WuDunn, 2010; World Bank, 2006).

Too-Slow Growth

As Table 3-3 shows, the population growth rates of MDRs are low relative to the LDRs, and getting lower. Between 2005 and 2010, the rates were 0.86% for North America and 0.11% for Europe as a whole (United Nations, 2011). Eastern Europe even had a negative growth rate (-.17%), making a platform of population growth stimulus a major factor in Russia's 2011 presidential election (Parfitt, 2011). As one might expect, the current definition of population growth problems is quite different in the MDRs than in the LDRs. The problem, where one is acknowledged, is "stagnation." In 2009, 47% of governments believed their population growth rates were too low (United Nations, 2010). Thus, compared with LDRs, the MDRs have the opposite concern about population growth.

As Espenshade (1978, p. 645) points out, the MDRs have not always been very calm about slow population growth:

> When the Great Depression had plunged the Western world into a protracted period of sluggish economic growth and high unemployment, it was fashionable among academic economists in the United States and Western Europe to attribute these conditions partly if not wholly to the unprecedented low rates of population growth. This view, popularly known as the "stagnation thesis," held that population growth stimulated business investment in factories and machines; and by contributing to business optimism, in which investment misallocations were likely to be regarded less seriously than if population were to slow to nil.

The reaction to the current slow growth is calmer, informed by the Depression experience. The MDRs lived through the period of slow population growth in the 1930s without apparent damage. And, although critics of the prevailing views on population growth might take heart in such an explanation for the Great Depression, hindsight blames many other factors in addition to slow population growth. Economic growth of MDRs has not appeared to suffer inordinately from slowing population growth (Coleman and Rowthorn, 2011), particularly as long as the influx of immigrants from LDRs is able to fill MDR labor force gaps.

To the degree that slow growth is seen as a source of social and economic problems, the short-term path of its negative effect is largely through the transitioning age composition of the population. Contemporary slow growth is achieved by low birth rates, which generate a population whose average age is older. There is some evidence that recent financial crises in Japan, the Asian Tigers,[1] and the United States stem from the transition from a large young adult population (ages fifteen to twenty-four) to a smaller one (Macunovich 2012, 2007). This age group tends to consume significant amounts in terms of new households formed and educational investments. Failure to forecast the contraction of this young adult population may lead to unexpected inventory build-up and production cutbacks. Furthermore, an aging population can create its own problems through the disproportionate dependence of the elderly on the working-age population. This can undermine the stability of various country-level policies, such as social security and healthcare systems, among others, which we revisit at the end of chapter 4.

In the long term, however, if population growth rates continue to slow and eventually become negative, as they are projected to do in some countries, a more grave concern is population decline. Just as the doubling-time equation demonstrates how quickly a growing population can expand, populations with negative growth can halve and then halve again just as suddenly. For example, if current fertility rates in Europe were to continue, the European population is just past its peak and will have 199 million *fewer* people by the year 2100 (United Nations, 2013).

Historic concern with **underpopulation** has often been fueled by an "us versus them" mentality, where MDRs feared being eclipsed culturally and politically by quickly growing LDR populations (Teitelbaum and Winter, 1985). But it has become clear in recent years that population decline no longer falls only in the domain of MDR concerns. Underpopulation has the potential to become a global issue, albeit occurring much sooner for some countries than others. Most of the world's population resides in countries that have undergone or are undergoing fertility transition, and evidence from MDR fertility transitions suggests that very low fertility levels are an inevitable outcome. A world with high fertility may eventually become a historical footnote (Morgan, 2003; Bongaarts and Bulatao, 2000; United Nations, 2003).

Just as the dialogue on overpopulation has sometimes been accused of having a sensationalist overtone, the same is true of the dialogue on underpopulation. Titles of popular books like *What to Expect When No One's Expecting*, *How Civilizations Die*, and *Shock of Gray* are in direct contrast to classic overpopulation standards of earlier decades, such as the well-known *The Population Bomb*. Hyperbole often factors prominently in such missives, with the word "plummeting" taking the place of the word "explosion." While *The Population Bomb* compared growth rates to a "cancer" with the potential to expand at the "speed of light" (Ehrlich, 1968, p. 152), underpopulation characterizations are equally bleak. For example, in *What to Expect When No One's Expecting: America's Coming Demographic Disaster*, the author writes, "Throughout recorded human history, declining populations have *always* followed or been followed by Very Bad Things. Disease. War. Economic stagnation or collapse" (Last, 2013, p. 7). These issues, as it turns out, also make great fodder for fiction novels with grim demographic themes (see Box 3-3).

---

[1] Named *Asian Tigers* for their rapid economic transition during the 1960s–1990s, these include Singapore, Taiwan, South Korea, and Hong Kong.

Box
3-3

Demography in Fiction

> Because beneath the field's dry statistical surface, there teems an irresistible Pandora's Box of paranoia, nationalism, rivalrous ambition, misanthropy, and apocalyptic dread, demography is sure to tempt fiction-writing dabblers to prize open the lid.
>
> —Lionel Shriver, award-winning novelist and journalist

Once loosely associated with eugenics in the early 20th century, the field of demography began self-consciously differentiating itself from the movement by the 1930s. Nonetheless, demographers are still sometimes nefariously associated with eugenicists of the past who promoted the reproduction of some groups and discouraged the reproduction of others. Thus, in the popular imagination, novels with demographic themes tend to gravitate toward the post-apocalyptic and the dystopian. The following works of fiction are just a sampling of many that explore basic demographic questions of humanity and morality.

Reproductive Genetic Engineering Themes

Brave New World (1931). A classic by British author Aldous Huxley, this book was among the first to imagine a future of state-regulated fertility using reproductive technology. In the year 2540, natural reproduction no longer exists. Instead, children are genetically engineered to fit a particular social caste, "decanted," and then raised in "conditioning centres."

The First Century after Beatrice (1994). Novelist Amin Maalouf picks up on the theme of sex selection and carries it out to its disturbing conclusion. A medicine is developed that results only in boy births. Industrialized countries deliberately market the pill to less developed countries in the hopes of drastically cutting their fertility rates, which ultimately leads to a doomed all-male world.

Never Let Me Go (2005). Kazuo Ishiguro writes an emotionally devastating book exploring the use of cloned humans as organ donors. Life expectancy for "originals" is extended well beyond the age of 100 by harvesting organs from one's clone, who is fated to die by early adulthood.

Overpopulation Themes

Make Room! Make Room! (1966). Harry Harrison's novel takes place in 1999 in the midst of environmental catastrophe and dwindling resources due to global overpopulation (the population had reached 7 billion people, slightly less than today's population size!). The better known movie version, *Soylent Green* (1973), introduces the sinister twist of secretly terminating the elderly and making them into a food source for the starving population.

Game Control (1994). Lionel Shriver features a whole cast of real-life demographers. The main protagonist is a villain who advocates for ignoring high infant mortality in the developing world in order to avoid overpopulation. He develops a virus designed to kill 2 billion humans in the name of sustainability.

Inferno (2013). Dan Brown's latest novel is about an overpopulation "cure," a purposefully-released virus that induces sterilization in a third of the global population. One of the characters is the head of the World Health Organization (WHO), who becomes infected with the virus. The larger premise is that this virus is the only way to prevent an overpopulation crash and allow the human race to evolve into the next stage of "transhumanism."

Underpopulation Themes

Earth Abides (1949). In George R. Stewart's novel a plague causes the collapse of North American society, and with too small of a population, society cannot sustain itself. This book allegedly inspired Stephen King's 1978 post-plague apocalypse *The Stand*.

The Children of Men (1992). Also made into a 2006 film, P. D. James paints a world where mass infertility has beset the population, giving a heartbreaking description of the final generations of people facing their extinction. "Omegas" are the last generation of humans to be born and are treated by the rest of society as celebrities, while pets are coddled and treated like infants.

Aging Themes

Diary of the War of the Pig (1969). In this harrowing depiction of the future, Adolfo Bioy Casares describes a rapidly aging population where the elderly are scorned and persecuted. Society, governed by youth, has decided that the elderly do not contribute to society and should be systematically exterminated.

Death with Interruptions (2005). Immortality is finally achieved in José Saramago's disturbing novel. The development is only fleetingly celebrated because it becomes clear that the environment cannot sustain an undying population. Furthermore, the healthcare system cannot provide for the terminally frail elderly population that is permanently suspended in the act of dying.

Sources: Brown, Dan. 2013. *Inferno.* Bantam Books; Domingo, A. 2008. "Demodystopias: Prospects of Demographic Hell." *Population and Development Review* 34: 725–745; Kuijsten, Anton C. 1999. "Demografiction." In Anton Kuijsten, Hans de Gans, and Henk de Feijter (eds.), *The Joy of Demography . . . and Other Disciplines: Essays in Honour of Dirk van de Kaa.* Amsterdam: Thela Thesis, pp. 83–102; Shriver, Lionel. 2003. "Population in Literature." *Population and Development Review* 29(2): 153–162; Ramsden, Edmund. 2009. "Confronting the Stigma of Eugenics: Genetics, Demography and the Problems of Population." *Social Studies of Science* 39: 853–884.

But sometimes a tendency toward hyperbole provides a needed catalyst in bringing about social change. The overpopulation movement of the 1960s and 1970s inspired a vast body of writings and research in the Malthusian tradition, which quickly gained widespread currency among the mainstream public. This, in turn, has inspired governments and nonprofit organizations around the world to make family planning a top funding priority, arguably paving the way for the newest concern over falling fertility rates.

What is a measured response to these population debates? Although the transition to population decline is a potential future problem, the immediate ramifications of rapid population growth is a pressing issue that many countries must face in the present. Of the two extremes, a future of global population decline is arguably more desirable than one of unchecked population growth like that experienced over the past fifty years. In his address to the Population Association of America, Philip Morgan summed it up this way:

> In my view, low fertility is not a twenty-first-century crisis—not yet, anyway. It is a genuine problem, but the kind of problem we want to have. That is, it is the result of solving a bigger, more threatening social problem: the crisis of continued population growth. Low fertility is also a problem that can be addressed through public policy and institutional adjustments. Finally, low fertility is a problem that befalls developed countries that, by and large, have the resources to respond. (2003, p. 600)

SUMMARY

After millennia of slow growth, the world's population took off at an unprecedented rate starting in the 1600s and peaking in the late 1960s. Population consumption patterns—more so than population growth—may challenge the carrying capacity of the planet, even though fertility has begun to decline worldwide. Concerns about population overconsumption patterns include carbon emissions leading to climate change, the exhaustion of fisheries and freshwater resources, and so forth. The modern population explosion has not been equally intense worldwide. It started in what are now the more-developed countries. They have experienced, with their modernization, a sequence of declines in death and birth rates described as the demographic transition. A few of these countries even now have below-replacement fertility. Many MDRs today are experiencing significant changes in union and householding patterns, what has been called the "second demographic transition."

After World War II the less-developed countries replaced the more-developed as those with quickly growing populations. Although most LDR countries have now begun to move into the demographic transition, the ramifications of rapid population growth will continue through the 21st century and growth will decline only slowly.

The recent explosive growth of many LDRs has theoretical consequences that are sometimes defined as potential problems. The fact that much of this growth is concentrated in LDRs means that the distribution of world population is changing. MDRs are becoming an ever smaller minority of the world's peoples, a fact that may strain the past privileged position and political dominance of MDRs. Some MDRs and LDRs are densely settled, and are increasingly so. Population density may place strains on resources, living standards, and a population's health, especially in less-developed countries. The rapid natural increase (with accompanying high birth rates) in many LDRs means that economically dependent segments of the population are large relative to the economically mature, or productive, segments. In addition, rapid population growth makes it difficult for governments to supply growing workforces with capital, or the means for production. These economic concerns are largely based on the historical experience of Western economies.

There is still much debate as to the causes of and solutions for these problems and even as to whether they really are "problems" for contemporary LDRs and MDRs. There is an acknowledged relationship between rapid population growth and challenges to economic development; however, it is increasingly recognized that population growth rates are not the primary barriers to economic development in LDRs. The relationships between population growth and development are complex, depending on other characteristics of the specific population involved and requiring demographic policies suited to the unique challenges and resources of contemporary LDRs. Among MDRs and a few LDRs, challenges related to rapidly aging populations are a final legacy as the demographic transition plays itself out.

Among some demographers, there is growing concern about eventual population decline once fertility transitions have run their course around the world. This possibility is far enough in the future, however, that it is difficult to give it too much credence yet, especially when so many countries are just now dealing with the repercussions of rapid population growth. In any case, the causes and consequences of underpopulation are generally preferable to those of overpopulation.

EXERCISES

1. Table E3-1 shows what would happen to the total population of Japan if it started at 127,587,800 at the midyear of 2012 and decreased by –0.2% (i.e., 2 per thousand or .002) every year until midyear through 2017. Copy the same procedure and apply it to Bangladesh, filling in the blanks in the table. Assume an annual growth rate for Bangladesh of 1.6% (i.e., 16 per thousand). Figures are provided for the year 2012 to get you started. Round off the increment figure to the nearest thousand before adding it to the population as of the beginning of the succeeding year.

Table E3-1   Projected Population at Constant Growth Rates

	Japan		Bangladesh	
Midyear	Midyear Population	Increment During Year	Midyear Population	Increment During Year
2012	127,587,800	–255,175.6	152,875	2,446
2013	127,333	–255		
2014	127,078	–254		
2015	126,824	–254		
2016	126,570	–253		
2017	126,317	–253		

Note: After Japan 2012, all figures in thousands.

2. Plot the projected population of Bangladesh for every year from 2012 to 2017 in Figure E3-1 on the following page. Connect the dots with a freehand line.

3. The implications of a constant growth rate can be expressed dramatically in terms of the years to double at that rate. The formula is:

$$\text{years to double} = \frac{70}{\%\ \text{annual growth rate}}$$

Suppose that the annual growth rates for the United States and Mexico in 2012 were 0.9% and 1.1%, respectively. How many years would it take for the populations to double? Round to one decimal place.

U.S. doubling time _____ (years)

Mexico doubling time _____ (years)

4. Go to the textbook website at www.demographytextbook.com to the exercises section under the Chapter 3 tab to view Exercise 4, which shows carbon emissions over time. On the right hand select tool, select China, United States, United Kingdom, Brazil, and Botswana. Click play to see the cumulative CO_2 emissions from 1800–2011. Describe the trends you see.

Now change the Y-axis measurement on the left hand side from cumulative emissions to emissions per person by changing the Y-axis to "CO_2 emissions (tonnes per person)." Click play. Describe the trends you see compared to the previous example.

Figure E3-1

Graph of Projected Population of Bangladesh, 2012–2017

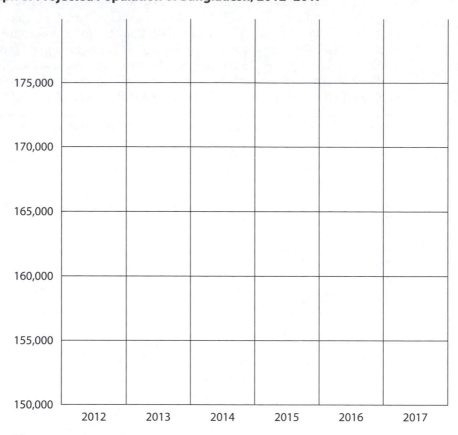

Note: All figures are in thousands.

PROPOSITIONS FOR DEBATE

1. Thomas Malthus's principle of population is wrong.
2. World population is more likely to overshoot carrying capacity than stabilize below it, but it will not be too late to avoid a population collapse.
3. Those who view overpopulation and rapid population growth as problems lack sufficient faith in human ingenuity and technological development.
4. The motivation of MDR leaders in viewing LDR rapid growth as a source of problems is basically selfish, concerned only with the privileges and power of the MDRs.
5. It is not rapid population growth in the LDRs that is slowing development; rather, it is domination of the world economy by the MDRs.
6. Explore your ecological footprint here:
   http://www.footprintnetwork.org/en/index.php/GFN/page/calculators/

REFERENCES AND SUGGESTED READINGS

Anderton, Douglas L. 1988. "Review of 'Theory of Population and Economic Growth,' by Julian L. Simon." *Contemporary Sociology* 17(4).

Becker, Gary S. 1981. *A Treatise of the Family*. Cambridge, MA: Harvard University Press.

Birdsall, Nancy. 1977. "Analytical Approaches to the Relationship of Population Growth and Development." *Population and Development Review* 3(1–2).

Bongaarts, J., and R. A. Bulatao, eds. 2000. *Beyond Six Billion: Forecasting the World's Population*. Washington, DC: National Academy Press.

Boserup, Ester. 1981. *Population and Technological Change: A Study of Long-term Trends*. Chicago: University of Chicago Press; and Oxford, England: Basil Blackwell.

Caldwell, John C. 1982. *Theory of Fertility Decline*. London: Academic Press.

Catafaro, Philip, and Eileen Crist. 2012. *Life on the Brink: Environmentalists Confront Overpopulation*. Athens: University of Georgia Press.

Cleland, J., and C. Wilson. 1987. "Demand Theories of the Fertility Transition: An Iconoclastic View." *Population Studies* 41(1).

Coale, Ansley J. 1975. "The Demographic Transition." In *United Nations: The Population Debate*, Vol. 1, pp. 347–355. Population Studies, No. 57. New York: United Nations.

Coale, Ansley J., and Edgar M. Hoover. 1958. *Population Growth and Economic Development in Low-income Countries*. Princeton: Princeton University Press.

Coale, Ansley J., and Susan Cotts Watkins, eds. 1986. *The Decline of Fertility in Europe*. Princeton: Princeton University Press.

Cohen, Joel E. 1995. *How Many People Can the Earth Support?* New York: W. W. Norton.

Coleman, David. 2004. "Why We Don't Have to Believe without Doubting in the 'Second Demographic Transition'—Some Agnostic Comments." *Vienna Yearbook of Population Research*, Vol. 2, pp. 11–24.

Coleman, David, and Robert Rowthorn. 2011. "Who's Afraid of Population Decline? A Critical Examination of Its Consequences." *Population and Development Review* 37: 217–248.

Collins, Lynn. 1982. "World Population." In John A. Ross, ed., *International Encyclopedia of Population*. New York: The Free Press.

Crenshaw, Edward M., Ansari Z. Ameen, and Matthew Christenson. 1997. "Population Dynamics and Economic Development: Age-Specific Population Growth Rates and Economic Growth in Developing Countries, 1965 to 1990." *American Sociological Review* 62(6).

Cutright, Phillips. 1982. "The Best of All Possible Worlds." A Review of "The Ultimate Resource" by Julian L. Simon. *Contemporary Sociology* 11(6).

Das Gupta, Monica, John Bongaarts, and John Cleland. 2011. *Population, Poverty, and Sustainable Development: A Review of the Evidence*. Policy Research Working Paper 5719. Washington, DC: The World Bank.

Dupâquier, Jacques. 1980. "Malthus Reconsidered." A Review of "Malthus" by William Petersen. *Contemporary Sociology* 9(4).

Dupâquier, Jacques, ed. 1983. *Malthus Past and Present*. New York: Academic Press.

Easterlin, Richard A., and Eileen M. Crimmins. 1985. *The Fertility Revolution: A Supply-Demand Analysis*. Chicago: University of Chicago Press.

The Economist. 2012. *The Path Through the Fields* (November 3).

Ehrlich, Paul. 1968. *The Population Bomb*. New York: Ballantine.

Ehrlich, Paul, and Anne H. Ehrlich. 2012. "Solving the Human Predicament." *International Journal of Environmental Studies* 69(4): 557–565.

Espenshade, Thomas J. 1978. "Zero Population Growth and the Economics of Developed Nations." *Population and Development Review* 4(4).

Ewing, Brad, David Moore, Steven Goldfinger, Anna Oursler, Anders Reed, and Mathis Wackernagel. 2010. *The Ecological Footprint Atlas 2010*. Oakland, CA: Global Footprint Network.

Feeney, Griffith M. 1994. "Fertility Decline in East Asia." *Science* 226(2).

Gribble, James N., and Jason Bremner. 2012. "Achieving a Demographic Dividend." *Population Bulletin* 67(2).

Hartmann, Betsy. 1995. *Reproductive Rights and Wrongs: The Global Politics of Population Control*. Boston: South End Press.

Haub, Carl, and James Gribble. 2011. "World at 7 Billion." *Population Bulletin* 66(2). Washington, DC: Population Reference Bureau.

Headey, Derek D., and Andrew Hodge. 2009. "The Effect of Population Growth on Economic Growth: A Meta-Regression Analysis of the Macroeconomic Literature." *Population Development Review* 35(2): 221–248.

IIASA (International Institute for Applied Systems Analysis). 2012. *Population Forecasting and Aging* (November 5). Retrieved February 19, 2013. http://www.iiasa.ac.at/web/home/research/researchPrograms/WorldPopulation/Research/Population-Forecasting-and-Aging.en.html

IPCC (Intergovernmental Panel on Climate Change). 2007. *Climate Change 2007: Impacts, Adaptation, and Vulnerability*. Cambridge, UK: Cambridge University Press.

———. 2011. *Mitigation, Climate Change: IPCC Special Report on Renewable Energy Sources and Climate Change Mitigation*. Cambridge, UK: Cambridge University Press.

———. 2012. *Managing the Risks of Extreme Events and Disasters to Advance Climate Change Adaptation*. Special Report of the Intergovernmental Panel on Climate Change, edited by Christopher B. Field, Vincente Barros, Thomas F. Stocker, Qin Dahe, David Jon Dokken, Kristie L. Ebi, Michael D. Mastrandrea, Katharine J. Mach, Gian-Kasper Plattner, Simon K. Allen, Melinda Tignor, and Pauline M. Midgley. Cambridge: Cambridge University Press.

———. 2013. *Climate Change 2013: The Physical Science Basis*. IPCC Working Group I Contribution to Fifth Assessment Report, edited by Thomas F. Stocker, Qin Dahe, Gian-Kasper Plattner, Melinda Tignor, Simon K. Allen, J. Boschung et al. Switzerland: IPCC.

Jacques, Peter J., Riley E. Dunlap, and Mark Freeman. 2008. "The Organisation of Denial: Conservative Think Tanks and Environmental Scepticism." *Environmental Politics* 17(3): 349–385.

Jiang, Leiwen, and Karen Hardee. 2011. "How Do Recent Population Trends Matter to Climate Change?" *Population Research and Policy Review* 30(2): 287–312.

Kelley, Allen C., and Robert M. Schmidt. 2005. "Evolution of Recent Economic-Demographic Modeling: A Synthesis." *Population Economics* 18: 275–300.

Keyfitz, Nathan. 1980. "Petersen on Malthus." A Review of "Malthus" by William Petersen. *Contemporary Sociology* 9(4).

Kristof, Nicholas D., and Sheryl WuDunn. 2010. *Half the Sky: Turning Oppression into Opportunity for Women Worldwide*. New York: Vintage Books.

Lal, Deepak. 2006. "India: Population Change and Its Consequences." *Population and Development Review* 32(1): 145–182.

Lam, David. 2011. "How the World Survived the Population Bomb: Lessons From 50 Years of Extraordinary Demographic History." *Demography* 48(4): 1231–1261.

Last, Jonathan V. 2013. *What to Expect When No One's Expecting: America's Coming Demographic Disaster*. New York: Encounter Books.

Lee, Ronald. 1983. "Economic Consequences of Population Size, Structure, and Growth." *Newsletter of the International Union for the Scientific Study of Population* 17.

———. 1986. "Malthus and Boserup: A Dynamic Synthesis." In David Coleman and Roger Schoefield, eds., *The State of Population Theory: Forward From Malthus*. Oxford: Basil Blackwell.

Lesthaeghe, R. 1983. "A Century of Demographic and Cultural Change in Western Europe: An Exploration of Underlying Dimensions." *Population and Development Review* 6(4).

———. 2010. "The Unfolding Story of the Second Demographic Transition." *Population and Development Review* 36(2): 211–251.

Lesthaeghe, R., and J. R. Surkyn. 2002. "New Forms of Household Formation in Central and Eastern Europe: Are They Related to Newly Emerging Value Orientations?" *UNECE Economic Survey of Europe*, Chapter 6, pp. 197–216. Geneva: United Nations Commission for Europe.

Lesthaeghe, R., and P. Willems. 1999. "Is Low Fertility a Temporary Phenomenon in the European Union?" *Population and Development Review* 25(2): 211–228.

Macunovich, Diane J. 2007. "Effects of Changing Age Structure and Intergenerational Transfers on Patterns of Consumption and Saving." In Anne Hélène Gauthier, C. Y. Cyrus Chu, and Shripad Tuljapurkar, eds., *Allocating Public and Private Resources Across Generations*. Dordrecht, The Netherlands: Springer.

———. 2012. "The Role of Demographics in Precipitating Economic Downturns." *Journal of Population Economics* 25(3): 783–807.

Mason, Andrew. 2003. "Population Change and Economic Development: What Have We Learned from the East Asia Experience?" *Applied Population and Policy* 1(1): 3–14.

Mason, Karen Oppenheim. 1997. "Explaining Fertility Transitions." Presidential Address to the Population Association of America, *Demography* 34(4).

McKeown, Thomas. 1983. "Food, Infection and Population." In Robert I. Roberg and Theodore K. Rabb, eds., *Hunger and History: The Impact of Changing Food Production and Consumption Patterns on Society*. Cambridge: Cambridge University Press.

McNeill, William H. 1976. *Plagues and Peoples*. Oxford: Blackwell.

McNicoll, Geoffrey. 1998. "Population and Poverty: The Poverty Issues, Parts I & II." Presented at the Workshop on Population, Poverty and Environment held at FAO, Rome, October.

Meek, Ronald L., ed. 1954. *Marx and Engels on Malthus: Selections from the Writings of Marx and Engels Dealing with the Theories of Thomas Robert Malthus*. New York: International Publishers.

Meuvret, Jean. 1965. "Demographic Crisis in France from the Sixteenth to the Eighteenth Century." In David V. Glass and David E. C. Eversley, eds., *Population in History*. London: Arnold.

Morgan, S. Philip. 2003. "Is Low Fertility a 21st-Century Demographic Crisis?" *Demography* 40(4).

National Research Council, Working Group on Population Growth and Economic Development, Committee on Population. 1986. *Population Growth and Economic Development: Policy Questions*. Washington, DC: National Academy Press.

National Research Council, Board on Atmospheric Sciences and Climate. 2008. *Understanding and Responding to Climate Change: Highlights of National Academies Reports*. Washington, DC: National Academy Press.

Notestein, Frank W. 1945. "Population—The Long View." In Theodore W. Schultz, ed., *Food for the World*. Chicago: University of Chicago Press.

Pachauri, Shonali, and Leiwen Jiang. 2008. "The Household Energy Transition in India and China." *Energy Policy* 36(11): 4022–4035.

Parfitt, Tom. 2011. "Vladimir Putin Pledges to Spend £32bn on Increasing Russian Life Expectancy." *The Guardian* (April 21). Retrieved March 7, 2013. http://www.guardian.co.uk/world/2011/apr/21/vladimir-putin-increasing-russian-life-expectancy?INTCMP=SRCH

Petersen, William. 1975. *Population*. 3rd ed. New York: Macmillan.

———. 1979. *Malthus*. Cambridge, MA: Harvard University Press.

———. 1980. "Further Comments on Malthus and 'Malthus.'" *Contemporary Sociology* 9(4).

PRB (Population Reference Bureau). 2008. *World Population Highlights: Key Findings from PRB's 2008 World Population Data Sheet*. Retrieved February 19, 2013. http://www.prb.org/Publications/PopulationBulletins/2008/worldpopulationhighlights2008.aspx

———. 2011. *How Many People Have Ever Lived on Earth?* Retrieved June 6, 2013. http://www.prb.org/Articles/2002/HowManyPeopleHaveEverLivedonEarth.aspx

———. 2014. *2014 World Population Data Sheet*. Retrieved September 2014. http://www.prb.org/pdf14/2014-world-population-data-sheet_eng.pdf

Rees, William. 2010. "The Human Nature of Unsustainability." In Richard Heinberg and Daniel Leich, eds., *The Post Carbon Reader: Managing the 21st Century Sustainability Crisis.* Healdsburg, CA: Watershed Media.

Rees, W. E., and M. Wackernagel. 1992. *Ecological Footprints and Appropriated Carrying Capacity: Measuring the Natural Capital Requirements of the Human Economy.* University of British Columbia, School of Community and Regional Planning.

Robertson, Thomas. 2012. *The Malthusian Moment: Global Population Growth and the Birth of American Environmentalism.* New Brunswick, NJ: Rutgers University Press.

Rodgers, Gerry, ed. 1989. *Population Growth and Poverty in Rural South Asia.* New Delhi: Sage.

The Royal Society. 2012. *People and the Planet: The Royal Society Science Policy Centre Report 01/12.* London: The Royal Society, Science Policy.

Sadik, Nafis, ed. 1991. *Population Policies and Programmes: Lessons Learned from Two Decades of Experience.* United Nations Population Fund. New York: New York University Press.

Sarma, K. Madhava, and Stephen O. Andersen. 2011. "Science and Diplomacy: Montreal Protocol on Substances that Deplete the Ozone Layer." In Paul Arthur Berkman, Michael A. Lang, David W. H. Walton, and Oran R. Young, eds., *Science Diplomacy: Antarctica, Science, and the Governance of International Spaces,* pp. 123–132. Washington, DC: Smithsonian Institution Scholarly Press.

Simon, Julian L. 1977. *The Economics of Population.* Princeton: Princeton University Press.

———. 1981. *The Ultimate Resource.* Princeton: Princeton University Press.

———. 1986. Theory of Population and Economic Growth. Oxford: Basil Blackwell.

———. 2006. *Hoodwinking the Nation.* Piscataway, NJ: Transaction Publishers.

Teitelbaum, M. S., and J. M. Winter. 1985. *The Fear of Population Decline.* Orlando: Academic Press.

Thompson, W. S. 1930. *Population Problems.* New York: McGraw-Hill.

Timmer, C. Peter, Ismael Sirageldin, John F. Kantner, and Samuel H. Preston. 1982. "Review Symposium of Julian L. Simon, 'The Ultimate Resource.'" *Population and Development Review* 8(1).

UNESCO. 2003. "Political Inertia Exacerbates Water Crisis, Says World Water Development Report: First UN System-Wide Evaluation of Global Water Resources." Press Release, March 5. Paris: United Nations Educational, Scientific and Cultural Organization.

United Nations. 1973. *The Determinants and Consequences of Population Trends.* Vol. 1. ST/SOA/SER.A/50. New York: United Nations.

———. 1981. *World Population Prospects as Assessed in 1980.* Population Studies Series, no. 78: ST/ESA/SER.A/78. New York: United Nations.

———. 1990. *World Resources 1990–91.* A Report by the World Resources Institute. Oxford: Oxford University Press.

———. 1994. *World Resources 1994–95.* A Report by the World Resources Institute. Oxford: Oxford University Press.

———. 1999. *Revision of the World Population Estimates and Projections,* 1998 briefing packet. New York: United Nations.

———. 2003. *World Population Prospects: The 2002 Revision.* Department of Economic and Social Affairs, Population Division. New York: United Nations.

———. 2004. *World Urbanization Prospects: The 2003 Revision.* Department of Economic and Social Affairs, Population Division. New York: United Nations.

———. 2005. *World Population Prospects: The 2004 Revision.* Department of Economic and Social Affairs, Population Division. New York: United Nations.

———. 2009. *Rethinking Poverty: Report on the World Social Situation 2010.* ST/ESA/324. Department of Economic and Social Affairs. New York: United Nations.

———. 2010. *World Population Policies 2009.* ST/ESA/SER.A/293. Department of Economic and Social Affairs, Population Division. New York: United Nations.

———. 2011. *Assumptions Underlying the 2010 Revision*. Retrieved February 27, 2013. http://esa.un.org/wpp/Documentation/pdf/WPP2010_ASSUMPTIONS_AND_VARIANTS.pdf.

———. 2012. *World Mortality Report 2011*. ST/ESA/SER.A/324. Department of Economic and Social Affairs, Population Division. New York: United Nations.

———. 2013. *World Population Prospects, The 2012 Revision*. Department of Economic and Social Affairs, Population Division. New York: United Nations.

United Nations Secretary-General's High-level Panel on Global Sustainability. 2012. *Resilient People, Resilient Planet: A Future Worth Choosing*. New York: United Nations.

Van De Kaa, D. J. 1987. "Europe's Second Demographic Transition." *Population Bulletin* 42(1): 1–59.

Watkins, Susan Cotts, and Etienne Van de Walle. 1983. "Nutrition, Mortality, and Population Size: Malthus's Court of Last Resort." In Robert I. Roberg and Theodore K. Rabb, eds., *Hunger and History: The Impact of Changing Food Production and Consumption Patterns on Society*. Cambridge: Cambridge University Press.

Weil, David N., and Joshua Wilde. 2009. "How Relevant Is Malthus for Economic Development Today?" *American Economic Review* 99(2): 255–260.

World Bank. 2006. Gender Equality as Smart Economics: A World Bank Group Gender Action Plan, Fiscal Years 2007–10. Washington, DC: World Bank.

World Water Assessment Programme. 2012. The United Nations World Water Development Report 4: *Managing Water under Uncertainty and Risk*. Paris: UNESCO.

Wrigley, E. A. 1969. *Population and History*. New York: McGraw-Hill.

4

Age and Sex Structure

Demography deals not only with population size and growth but also with population composition. The most important dimensions of composition, indisputably, are age and sex. Age, in particular, is undergoing great flux, as the world's populations grow older. Population aging will be the major demographic focus of the 21st century. By 2050, for the first time in human history, there will be more elderly people than children in the world. This is due primarily to fertility reductions but it also reflects the fact that life expectancy has increased. Living longer lives is perhaps the greatest success story of modern history, thanks to innovations in public health, medicine, and economic development. At the same time, aging populations can introduce serious challenges for society. Old-age dependency may lead to lowered economic productivity and overtaxed healthcare and pension systems. But if these challenges are anticipated they can be offset with social and economic policies. There is also an argument to be made that the early aging transition from a youth-dependent to working-age population comes with great opportunity, a phenomenon known as the "demographic dividend," a concept we will explore later in the chapter.

Societies construct roles and assign status on the basis of age and sex more than on any other characteristics. Consequently, nations uniformly include questions on age and sex in their census questionnaires. So important is age-sex composition, many demographers give it a special label: **population structure**. We will use that term throughout this chapter.

The chapter proceeds from method to substance. We start with a review of census data on age and sex, noting some errors to be found there. Next we cover some of the simpler methods for describing population structure, ending with the familiar population (or age-sex) pyramid. We use these measures to describe the important contrasts between the structures of less-developed and more-developed countries, since, just as their structures differ, so do their resulting population problems. We close the chapter with an introduction to some of these challenges.

Describing Age-Sex Structure

Quality of Census Data

How, one might ask, could censuses make errors in recording something as simple as age and sex? Two kinds of errors can occur, which Shryock and Siegel call underenumeration and misreporting (1976, p. 115). **Underenumeration** of an age or sex class means failing to count somebody who would have fallen into that class. The errors arising from underenumeration are also called *coverage errors* or *undercounts*. **Misreporting** means counting somebody but misallocating him or her among the age-sex categories.

Demographers define sex as someone's biological and physiological characteristics, as opposed to gender, which refers to socially constructed roles assigned by society to women and men. As one might expect, with respect to sex, underenumeration is more of a problem than is misreporting. There is usually not much ambiguity as to a person's sex. But it is possible for someone's sex to influence whether his or her very existence will be reported. For instance, in a society with a military draft the existence of young men in the household might go unmentioned on purpose, or baby girls might be forgotten in household enumerations in societies where women are considered to have lower status. Underenumeration of women was common, for example, in U.S. censuses of the southern states prior to the Civil War.

Less frequently, coverage errors occur when the census attempts to correct what appears to be misreporting. In 1990 the census recategorized same-sex householders into opposite-sex householders for any same-sex household that reported a marital status of legally married, since same-sex marriage was still federally prohibited in the United States at the time. This resulted in sex enumeration errors as well as a 30% undercount of reported same-sex partnered households (Smith and Gates, 2001).

But generally the problems with sex data in contemporary censuses are trivial compared with those for age data. Let us look at how age is determined by enumerators. The standard census definition is clear: "Age is the interval of time between the date of birth and the date of the census, expressed in complete solar years" (United Nations, 2008 p. 135). A census enumerator can find a respondent's age by either (1) asking the age directly, or (2) asking the date of birth and letting the census office measure the difference. The United Nations recommends asking date of birth wherever circumstances permit, since it usually results in more precise reporting. Many censuses ask both to check the reliability of each.

How could there be a problem in recording responses to these questions? It is not so simple. Not everybody calibrates the calendar in exactly the same way. Nor does everybody count age the same way, according to the Western system of describing people in terms of last anniversary of birth, the last completed year of age. Not every society shares the West's fixation for precise distinctions in age and time; many might settle for those distinctions that have meaning with respect to ascribed roles in their particular cultures, such as infant/pre-adolescent, youth/post-adolescent and unmarried, youth/married young adult, and so on.

Lacking unambiguous evidence of precise age, it is tempting for respondents to bend the truth. They might intentionally report a youth of military age to be slightly too young or too old, report a middle-aged woman to be not quite middle-aged, report a sixty-four-year-old to be of retirement age (where that is sixty-five), or report a ninety-eight-year-old to be a centenarian.

Or they might unintentionally round off reports, resulting in what demographers call **age heaping**. There is an almost universal tendency to report age, or date of birth, as years ending in zero or five, or in even numbers, sometimes avoiding other numbers that are culturally tabooed (Myers, 1940; Shryock and Siegel, 1976; Ewbank, 1981).

Although misreporting and underenumeration in age and sex data cannot be eliminated totally, they have the advantage of being detectable. One way to estimate census errors is through *intercensal reconciliation*. This springs from the fact that people change their physical sex only with great difficulty and change their age only according to a fixed and knowable schedule. This allows us to trace age-sex classes of people from one census to the next, thereby detecting implausibilities (Robinson et al., 1993; Shryock and Siegel, 1976). For instance, women aged fifteen to nineteen in the 2010 U.S. census should bear some correspondence to women aged twenty-five to twenty-nine in the 2020 U.S. census, taking into account the effects of intervening mortality and migration. We also can estimate census errors using supplemental *post-enumeration samples* of the population. Intensive efforts are made to collect highly accurate data for a small statistical sample of the population. These data are then compared to the census to estimate coverage and reporting errors for various groups (Hogan, 1993; Hill, 1987; Wolter, 1986). Using both of these methods, estimates of coverage errors for the 2010 census are available by age and sex as well as for special groups such as urban minorities and the homeless (U.S. Census Bureau, 2008). Largely due to the seriousness of coverage errors in the 1990 census, post-enumeration samples have been made an integral part of all subsequent U.S. censuses (U.S. Census Bureau, 2004a; Edmonston and Shultze, 1995).

Describing Age Structure

Some of the techniques that demographers use for describing age and sex structure may be familiar. Frequency distributions, percentage distributions, ratios, and bar graphs are standard descriptive statistics. Seeing their application here will be a simple review for some readers.

The first step in constructing a **frequency distribution** is categorization or grouping of cases. Conventionally, census tabulations dealing with age alone, or with age and sex together, use year intervals or age groups, as illustrated in Table 4-1. At the youngest end, the under-five category is sometimes divided into under-one and one-through-four years of age because of the importance of separate figures on the first year of life, infancy. At the oldest end, because there are so few survivors in the very old categories, demographers conventionally use an open-ended category, such as 80+ or 85+. As a reflection of worldwide expanding life expectancies, many sources of population data are in the process of extending the open-ended age category to 100+.

The first three columns of Table 4-1 present the projected frequency distributions by age class, according to the U.S. Census Bureau, first for both sexes together and then separately for men and for women as of 2020. We can look down one of those columns, note the relative size of the figures, and get some notion of the shape of the age distribution. However, if we wanted to compare the same age class in two columns, for instance, males versus females aged five to nine, we would have to correct for differences in the total size of the population being distributed. That is the purpose of **percentage distributions**, shown in columns 4 and 5.

To compute the percentages, we multiply the entry in each age-sex category by one hundred, then divide every such product by the total of the population in that same sex category. The formula would be

$$\frac{(\text{population in age and sex class}) \times 100}{\text{population in all age classes of same sex}}$$

Columns 4 and 5 of Table 4-1 are percentage distributions of males and females. It is legitimate to compare male and female percentages for any given age class in those columns. We see, for instance, that in the contemporary United States, relatively larger percentages of men are in the younger categories and larger percentages of women are in the older categories.

There are twenty-one categories, however, in each of the distributions of Table 4-1. For many purposes, that is so much detail that it leads to confusion. Demographers often combine age categories to make certain comparisons more salient, using certain cutoff points in the age continuum that are more important than others. For example, age fifteen has become an arbitrary cutoff point for eligibility for adult economic roles. In many countries age sixty-five means eligibility for retirement, although retirement still tends to occur at earlier ages in many LDRs and is increasingly occurring beyond age sixty-five in MDRs. So a conventional way to describe what proportion of the total population is "young" is the percentage aged fifteen or less; this is 19% in Table 4-1. At the other extreme, the proportion that is "old" is measured by the percentage who will be aged sixty-five and over; this is about 17% in the table.

Such percentages in broad categories, however, do not give an overall picture of the age distribution; for that we need some summary measures. It is conventional to use the median to summarize age distributions. Although the computation of the median is too complex to show here, the meaning of the measure is straightforward: The median is the age above which and below which precisely half of the population falls. (The average, or arithmetic mean, would be misleading in this context because of the generally skewed shape of age distributions.) Table 4-1 shows that the projected 2020 U.S. male median age (37.0 years) will be less than the female median (39.6 years). This confirms our impression from scanning the percentage distributions.

A convenient way to compare the relative size of any two numbers is by constructing a **ratio**, dividing one number by the other. When applied to age distributions, the most frequently used is the **age-dependency ratio**. In the numerator are dependents, defined as those considered too young and too old to be fully economically productive. In the denominator is the rest of the population of working ages, i.e., those aged fifteen through sixty-four. The formula is

$$\frac{P_{0-14} + P_{65+}}{P_{15-64}} \times 100$$

where

P_{0-14} = population aged under fifteen years
P_{65+} = population aged sixty-five or more years
P_{15-64} = population aged fifteen through sixty-four

The age-dependency ratio in Table 4-1 shows that there are 55.88 dependents for every 100 persons of working age. The concept of dependency is, of course, culturally specific and may change over time. For example, in many societies children begin working for wages younger than age fifteen, while other countries may have labor protection laws prohibiting child employment. In many such countries, young adults do not begin to earn incomes until their mid-twenties. Similarly, many adults continue working well into their seventies and would take offense at being considered a dependent. As the

Table 4-1   Projected Age-Sex Distribution of U.S. Population, 2020

	In thousands			Percentages		
	(1)	**(2)**	**(3)**	**(4)**	**(5)**	**(6)**
Age[a]	**Both Sexes**	**Male**	**Female**	**Male**	**Female**	**Sex Ratio**
All Ages	333,896	164,812	169,084	100%	100%	97.47
0–4	21,808	11,150	10,658	6.77%	6.30%	104.62
5–9	21,307	10,896	10,411	6.61%	6.16%	104.66
10–14	20,616	10,538	10,078	6.39%	5.96%	104.56
15–19	20,806	10,640	10,166	6.46%	6.01%	104.66
20–24	21,651	11,109	10,541	6.74%	6.23%	105.39
25–29	23,366	11,994	11,372	7.28%	6.73%	105.47
30–34	22,906	11,653	11,253	7.07%	6.66%	103.55
35–39	21,869	10,991	10,877	6.67%	6.43%	101.05
40–44	20,361	10,158	10,203	6.16%	6.03%	99.56
45–49	20,008	9,907	10,101	6.01%	5.97%	98.08
50–54	20,467	10,103	10,363	6.13%	6.13%	97.49
55–59	21,747	10,599	11,148	6.43%	6.59%	95.08
60–64	21,017	10,103	10,914	6.13%	6.45%	92.57
65–69	18,052	8,515	9,538	5.17%	5.64%	89.27
70–74	14,744	6,839	7,905	4.15%	4.68%	86.51
75–79	10,010	4,487	5,523	2.72%	3.27%	81.24
80–84	6,470	2,748	3,722	1.67%	2.20%	73.83
85–89	3,934	1,520	2,414	0.92%	1.43%	62.97
90–94	2,008	667	1,340	0.40%	0.79%	49.78
95–99	645	173	472	0.10%	0.28%	36.65
100+	106	22	85	0.01%	0.05%	25.88

Under 15	63,731 (19.09%)	
15 – 64	214,198 (64.15%)	Age-dependency ratio = $\dfrac{63,731+55,969}{214,198} \times 100 = 55.88$
65 and over	55,969 (16.76%)	

Median Ages	38.3	37.0	39.6

[a]Since entries for particular age categories are rounded to thousands, they may not add up precisely to the subtotals and totals presented.

Source: U.S. Census Bureau, 2012c. *Projections of the Population by Age and Sex for the United States: 2015 to 2060.*

human life course continues to expand, the age brackets for the age-dependency ratio will be reconfigured in turn.

Describing Sex Structure

Demographers often describe the sex composition of populations by comparing the number of persons of each sex with a ratio. The **sex ratio** is the number of men divided by the number of women multiplied by a constant of 100:

$$\frac{\text{Men}}{\text{Women}} \times 100$$

In column 6 of Table 4-1, we see that the sex ratio for the total U.S. population in 2020 is projected to be 97.47, meaning that there will be about 97 men for every 100 women in the population.

Sex ratios can be computed not only for total populations but also for classes within those populations. Demographers frequently find it helpful to pay attention to sex composition at different age levels. Column 6 of Table 4-1 dramatizes how the sex ratio will vary by age class in the United States in 2020. This decreasing sex ratio with aging is a reflection of the slightly younger overall age of the U.S. male population in contrast with the female. (The relative youth of the male population is explained primarily by differential mortality risks, described in chapter 5.)

Population Pyramids

By far the most familiar way of depicting age and sex structure together is with **population pyramids**, which are composed of bar graphs. Bar graphs make it possible for one to compare visually the sizes of a series of classes. They can be used to compare the classes in any frequency distribution or percentage distribution.

A population pyramid consists of a bar graph showing the age distribution of both men and women, presented together in a particular way. The age categories proceed from the bottom to the top. The male bars proceed from a vertical center line leftward; the female bars proceed from a vertical center line rightward. Pyramids can be constructed from either frequency distributions or from percentage distributions. One could, for instance, construct a population pyramid directly from columns 2 and 3 of Table 4-1. The length of each bar would be proportional to the number of thousands in each age-sex class. Such absolute-number pyramids are particularly useful for registering changes in the sizes of age-sex classes over time.

More frequently, however, we see population pyramids representing percentage distributions. Note, however, that the percentages are not of age distributions for men separately and for women separately; they represent age-sex percentage distributions for the population of both sexes together. For instance, it would be incorrect for us to construct a percentage population pyramid from Table 4-1 by juxtaposing a bar graph for column 4 with a bar graph for column 5. Rather, we would have to construct a new percentage distribution by dividing each figure in columns 2 and 3 by the total population (333,896) and multiplying it by one hundred. Then the length of any bar would be proportional to this percentage.

Percentage pyramids have the advantage of not being influenced by the total size of the population. The area of all percentage pyramids is the same if they are all drawn on the same scale. The feature to notice is the *shape* of the pyramid, which registers only the relative sizes of the age-sex classes in that pyramid. Percentage pyramids are particularly useful in comparing populations of considerably different size. The population pyramids shown in Figure 4-1 on the following page are good examples. The leftmost and middle pyramids are based on actual populations in 1950 and 2000. The rightmost pyramids are projected for the year 2050 (we will explain more about projections later). As you might notice, by 2050 a more apt description of population pyramids might be "population rectangles," but alas, the term lacks the same appealing alliteration. "Pyramid," as you have probably guessed, comes from the fact that in times past under conditions of population growth and higher mortality there were more young people than old people in most populations, and thus the younger (lower) bars were longer than the older (upper) ones. Thus, the classic shape of population age structures before moving through their demographic transitions is pyramidal, rising regularly from a broad base to a sharp peak. The figure shows that at the turn of the century, current LDR populations still had a pyramidal shape to them, but by 2050 they will become much more rectangular, indicating fewer children being born and more people living into older ages.

Similarly, the MDRs in 1950 were pyramidal, indicating population growth. In many MDR countries the baby boom was just underway in 1950 and you can see how this baby boom "bulge" moves up through the population figures over time. At the turn of the century, the largest proportion of the MDR population was in their late thirties and early forties, with a smaller proportion of younger generations being born afterward. Another characteristic of future population pyramids is the "roof" at the top. This indicates the ever-increasing maximum life span, with more people surviving into older years of life. If the top age brackets were broken into separate intervals running through age 100, rather than combined into an eighty and over age category, the figures would retain a pyramidal shape at the very top.

The best way to make sure that you understand these measures is to compute examples. Exercises at the end of the chapter offer practice in all of the measures in this section, including population pyramids.

Contrasts Between More-Developed and Less-Developed Countries

Age Structure

Table 4-2 on p. 101 presents dramatic evidence of world contrasts in **age structure**. Each column gives one measure of age structure introduced in the preceding section. The table presents projected age measurement for world regions in 2020, including the two categories of world regions, less-developed (LDRs) and more-developed (MDRs). We have ordered them from youngest populations to oldest populations.

Let's compare the two extremes, Africa at the younger end, and Europe at the older end. Africa has more than twice Europe's zero to fourteen proportion, while Europe has almost five times Africa's proportion of people age sixty five and older. In regions such as Latin America and the Caribbean, Asia, Oceania, and Northern Amer-

Figure 4-1

Population Age-Sex Structure in Less-Developed and More-Developed Countries, 1950, 2000, and 2050

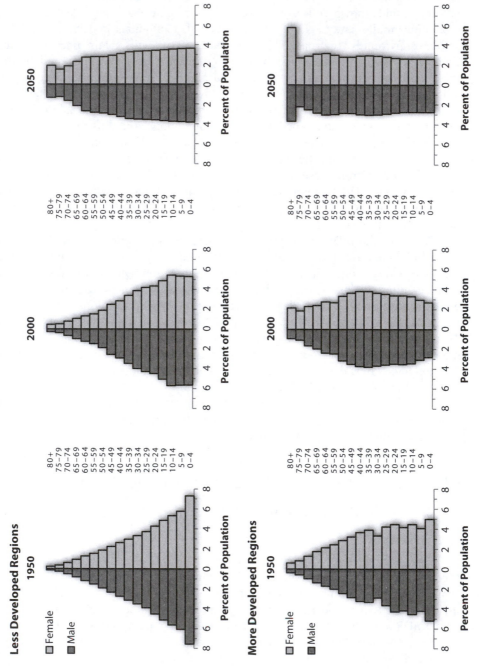

Note: UN projection with medium fertility rate was used for 2050 figures.

Source: Data from United Nations, 2013. *World Population Prospects: The 2012 Revision, Detailed Indicators.* Graphs created by Eiko Strader.

Table 4-2   Summary Measures of Age Structure, World Regions, 2020

Regions[a]	0–14 (1)	15–64 (2)	65+ (3)	Age-Dependency Ratio (4)
Africa	38.87%	57.38%	3.75%	74.29
Latin America and Caribbean	23.63%	67.49%	8.88%	48.16
Asia	22.92%	67.93%	9.15%	47.20
Oceania	21.41%	64.87%	13.72%	54.16
Northern America	19.41%	64.00%	16.59%	56.24
Europe	15.60%	65.36%	19.04%	52.99
Less Developed Countries	26.44%	65.93%	7.63%	51.67
More Developed Countries	16.46%	64.27%	19.27%	55.60

[a]Ordered by percentage less than fifteen years old.

Source: Data from U.S. Census Bureau, 2013a. *International Programs: International Database.*

ica, the percentage under age fifteen falls in a closer range from higher to lower (at 24%, 23%, 21%, and 19%, respectively). With respect to older ages, Europe is the only country with a greater proportion in the older ages than in younger ages, although Northern America will soon follow. While still a small proportion of the population in Table 4-2, the elderly in Asia and Latin America are growing quickly due mostly to falling birth rates. China in particular has transitioned into an aging population more quickly than has any other country as a consequence of its shift to one-child households (Yi and George, 1999; PRB, 2010).

Generally, the less-developed regions have a higher proportion of their population under fifteen years of age. In contrast, the more-developed regions generally have higher proportions aged sixty-five and over. Column four shows that Africa has by far the highest age-dependency ratio at 74.29, and this is almost entirely due to youth dependency. Northern America has the second highest ratio, at 56.24, and this is due to both large proportions of youth and elderly. By 2020, Latin America and Asia will benefit from the lowest age-dependency ratios, which means that they will have the largest proportion of working-age people among all the regions.

Despite differences across MDRs and LDRs, one trend that will become clear to you by the time you finish reading this textbook is that there is tremendous variation within any one given region and even within a single country. Often this variation has to do with social and economic disparities. For example, as can be seen from Figure 4-2 on the following page, even though Malawi has a very young age structure, if you divide the population pyramid into one for the wealthiest (left) and one for the poorest (right), it becomes clear that wealthy Malawians have substantially fewer percentages of young-age dependents than poor Malawians. This is because wealthier families in Malawi are going through the demographic transition earlier, reducing their fertility at faster rates and living longer than those who have fewer resources. Often, the overall demographic differences we see between MDRs and LDRs are echoed on a smaller scale within individual countries due to social class and urban-rural status differences.

Figure 4-2

Malawi Age Structure by Wealth, 2010

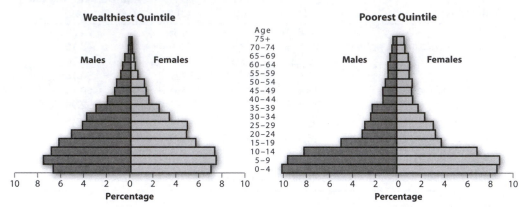

Source: Population Reference Bureau, 2012. *2012 World Population Data Sheet,* prepared by Carl Haub and Toshiko Kaneda. Used with permission.

Sex Structure

The population pyramids in Figure 4-1 also allow us to see the nature of **sex-structure** contrasts between the less-developed and more-developed regions. For the less-developed regions, the pyramid is almost symmetrical, with little change between 1950 and 2000. In contrast, by 2000 the pyramid for the more-developed regions has a marked rightward, or female, lean as it rises to the older age categories. In both regions, men are slightly more predominant in the earliest ages. In the higher ages, women tend to outnumber the men more and more. But the degree to which this is true varies greatly with the level of development of the region. Female predominance in the older age categories is a feature of more-developed countries where aging of the population emphasizes the greater longevity of women. This feature was also demonstrated for the United States in Table 4-1, showing sex ratios by age.

Projected Changes to 2050

Modern methods of population projection specify not only future population sizes but future population structures. The most widely accepted method for making projections, the **cohort-component method**, is explained in Box 4-1 and illustrated in Table 4.3 on p. 105. Any projection, of course, depends upon the fertility, mortality, and migration assumptions employed. The 2050 projection shown in Figure 4-1 is based on the assumptions that the United Nations considers most likely at the current time, which is a general continued slow decline in worldwide mortality and in the fertility of less-developed regions.

As one can see, the pyramids for the less-developed and more-developed regions are projected to change in the same direction (see Figure 4-1), but at each date they are caught at different points in that change. To simplify, the more-developed regions will evolve from a tall bell shape to a slightly inverted shape that is becoming more top-

Box 4-1

Projecting Age-Sex Structure

The most generally accepted modern method for projecting national populations is the *cohort-component method*. It has the advantage of providing figures not only on total size but also on age-sex structure.

A **cohort** is a set of people identified on the basis of having experienced a specified demographic event in the same short interval of time. Thus, a **birth cohort** is a set of people born in the same short interval and, of course, having similar present ages. We also could identify marriage cohorts, immigration cohorts, and so on. But when demographers use the word "cohort" unmodified, they mean birth cohort.

Each cohort is projected forward separately. Specific assumptions about future mortality, fertility, and migration are applied to each cohort, and these determine its projected size at points in the future. That is, separate assumptions are made about the *components of growth* (or population processes) for each cohort.

Although the actual production of a projection can be technically complex, the underlying strategy is simple. It can be summarized in a series of five steps. An actual projection of the population of Mexican women from 2010 to 2035, shown in Table 4-3, serves as a concrete example.

1. *Make a baseline estimate of the population and its age-sex distribution.* Estimate the number of people in each age-sex class for the most recent date possible. If your baseline date happens to be the date of a census count, then no further estimation is required; you use the count. But if you want to start with some postcensal date, then you have to estimate by taking into account information about deaths, births, and migrations since the census. In our illustrative table, the baseline figures are derived from the 2010 Mexican census adjusted for under-enumeration.

2. *For each existing birth cohort, add and subtract members according to migration and mortality assumptions.* Let us illustrate with the youngest existing birth cohort in the baseline year, 2010, that aged zero through four years (<5). *Fertility* can no longer influence this cohort (or any older one) since its members are born already. *Mortality* is usually the major factor influencing the future size of existing national cohorts. On the basis of assumed sequences of *age-sex-specific death rates* (see Box 4-2 for details), demographers estimate how many of the children aged zero through four in 2010 would survive to be five through nine in 2015, ten through fourteen in 2020, and so on. However, regarding *migration,* some of those surviving to older ages will emigrate out of the region's population while others will immigrate into the region's population. The difference between those moving in and out of the population as the cohort is projected forward is the *net migration*. Migration data are often difficult to obtain and projections make simplified assumptions about *age-sex-specific net migration rates*. Applying these rates to the cohort gives an estimate of the number of net migrants that will be added or subtracted from the surviving population while moving that cohort through the time intervals. You can follow the combined influence of mortality and migration on this (initially <5) cohort just below the stepped line in Table 4-3. Each existing birth cohort is followed forward through the series of five-year steps in the same manner.

3. *For cohorts yet unborn in the baseline year, project births by sex of child.* The cohorts yet unborn in 2010 are those above the stepped line in Table 4-3. The future fertility assumptions are stated in terms of the *age-specific fertility (birth) rates* (see Box 4-2 for details) for each five-year age interval of women from fif-

(continued)

teen to forty-five years of age. The assumed specific birth rates are multiplied by the number of women projected to be in each of the age categories (i.e., for ages at which women are assumed fecund), after which the number of births to all women are totaled. How many of these projected total births will be boys and how many girls is estimated by applying an assumed sex ratio at birth, normally something like 105 men per 100 women.

4. *Add and subtract members from the new cohorts on the basis of migration and mortality assumptions.* Not all of the birth cohorts projected in step three will survive to be counted at the end of the projection interval into which they are born. Each birth cohort will be depleted by mortality during its first interval of life, just as in all the later ones. Thus, we subtract members of these new cohorts on the basis of assumptions about infant mortality (death before age one) and early childhood mortality (death at ages one through four). Children and infants also migrate, as do all age groups, and the numbers carried forward to the next interval of life are thus also modified by net migration rates in these early years of life.

5. *Carry out step two for each of the new cohorts.* For example, those 5,638 (thousand) members of the 2010–2014 birth cohort surviving to 2015 are projected forward to 2035. Their path is seen just above the stepped line in Table 4-3. The cohort survivors are depleted according to assumed age-sex-specific death rates and either depleted or increased by assumed age-sex-specific migration rates.

For further details, see Bogue et al., 1993, chapter 17; or Shryock and Siegel, 1976, chapter 23.

heavy as the average age of the population gets older. The growing percentage of the population over eighty years of age is evident in the apparent "T" shape of future population pyramids in the developed regions. This is also accompanied by substantially more women than men surviving into the eighty-and-over age range. The less-developed regions will move from their triangular or pyramidal shape to one that is very similar to the 2000 pyramid of the developed regions. This emerging long-term trend toward global aging is unparalleled in human history. The global elderly population tripled over the past half century and is projected to triple again by 2050.

Evolution of the U.S. Structure

Figure 4-3 on p. 106 presents six successive percentage pyramids for the United States, from 1900 to 2050. Together this sequence shows the structural changes already experienced in one Western country as it developed economically and demographically, along with future expectations.

Each of the bars in a given pyramid refers to a **birth cohort**, a set of people born about the same time. In later pyramids, the same birth cohort climbs up the pyramid because it has moved into older age brackets. Figure 4-3 illustrates this by identifying the cohort of 1955 to 1959 (shown in black bars) as it climbs the last four pyramids. The number of survivors of the birth cohort who will remain to be included in a pyramid depends on how many it had at birth (fertility), how many died off since birth (mortality), and how many moved in or out of the country since birth (net migration).

Table 4-3   Illustrative Cohort-Component Projection, Mexican Women, 2010–2035

Age	2010	2015	2020	2025	2030	2035
Total	60,845	64,531	67,898	70,999	73,694	75,910
0–4	5,638	5,421	5,245	5,071	4,873	4,646
5–9	5,799	5,610	5,395	5,223	5,051	4,854
10–14	5,846	5,762	5,573	5,365	5,194	5,022
15–19	5,668	5,789	5,706	5,526	5,319	5,148
20–24	5,308	5,578	5,700	5,631	5,453	5,246
25–29	4,870	5,167	5,438	5,583	5,515	5,338
30–34	4,660	4,723	5,021	5,315	5,460	5,393
35–39	4,823	4,593	4,658	4,964	5,258	5,405
40–44	4,109	4,778	4,551	4,621	4,927	5,222
45–49	3,360	4,064	4,730	4,509	4,581	4,888
50–54	2,739	3,308	4,007	4,669	4,455	4,530
55–59	2,392	2,677	3,238	3,929	4,585	4,381
60–64	1,671	2,306	2,589	3,141	3,820	4,468
65–69	1,388	1,578	2,190	2,468	3,007	3,670
70–74	948	1,270	1,455	2,032	2,304	2,821
75–79	737	826	1,119	1,293	1,822	2,083
80–84	496	577	659	907	1,064	1,519
85–89	271	323	387	453	638	764
90–94	86	139	172	213	256	371
95–99	30	33	55	70	90	112
100+	6	9	10	16	22	29

Note: Since entries for particular age categories are rounded to thousands, they may not add up to precisely the subtotals and totals presented.

Source: United Nations, 2013. *World Population Prospects: The 2012 Revision.* Used with permission.

The shape of the pyramid in any given year is determined by the relative sizes of all sur-viving cohorts.

What happened in the United States during the past century? The U.S. population pyramid of 1900 is shaped more like the 2000 LDR pyramid shown in Figure 4-1 than the contemporary MDR one. Fertility was still relatively high, considerably higher than mortality. Net immigration was heavy in the U.S. at this time and favored young peo-ple. The first major departure from that pyramidal shape came during the Great Depression. Both fertility and migration declined drastically. The cohorts of 1930 through 1939, aged zero through nine in 1940, are markedly slimmer than the preced-ing ones. These Depression cohorts were aged thirty to thirty-nine in the 1970 pyramid. In spite of the small proportion of the population at reproductive ages, as these cohorts moved through childbearing they managed to create a baby boom (Bouvier, 1980). Childbearing that had been delayed during World War II by these Depression cohorts, combined with early marriage and prolific fertility of younger cohorts entering repro-ductive ages in the prosperous postwar decades, contributed to the baby boom seen in

Figure 4-3

Population Pyramids for the United States, 1900 to 2050

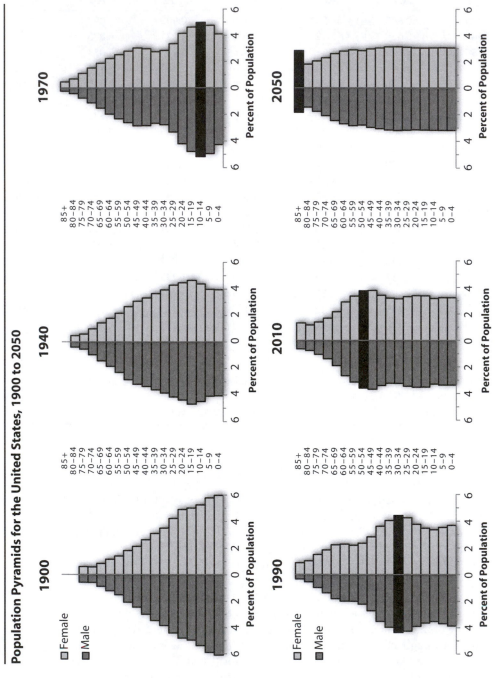

Source: Data from U.S. Census Bureau, 2004b. "National Estimates by Age, Sex, Race: 1900–1979", 2001, "Resident Population Estimates of the US by Age and Sex: April 1, 1990 to July 1"; 2009, "National Population Projections July 1, 2000 to July 1, 2050: Constant Net International Migration Series," Table 2. Graphs created by Eiko Strader.

the large cohort of infants and children in the 1970 pyramid. By 1990, both the slim Depression cohorts and the fat baby-boom cohorts marched up the pyramid but had less pronounced effects on the composition of the entire population. Recent cohorts in the youngest ages of the 1990 pyramid reflect both the baby bust of the late 1960s and 1970s (i.e., those aged ten to twenty-four) and the slight baby-boom echo of the 1980s (i.e., those born to baby boomers and aged zero to nine).

By 2010 and projected to 2050, the main new feature in these pyramids is the change from a youthful one to an aged one. The broad base of the 1900 pyramid has shrunk to a narrow band. The pyramidal shape of 1900 has changed to an increasingly more rectangular one, and the population at older ages has increased. In 2010, the first of the baby-boom population reached retirement age.

Americans are now staying in the workforce longer, a reversal of a trend toward an early retirement "golden age" over the past forty years. This is due to a combination of factors. Increasing life expectancies and better health enable more people to continue working who wish to do so; at the same time, many others have little choice due to the erosion of the American pension system and the fact that the U.S. health insurance system has long been tied to employment (DiCecio et al., 2008; Jacobsen et al., 2011; Johnson et al., 2008). Children were clearly the majority of dependents in 1900, while the elderly will be a growing proportion of dependents in the future. Once the baby boomers have exited the workforce, their added weight to the age-dependency ratio will be felt intensely by programs that provide for the elderly (e.g., pension funds, Medicare, Social Security).

By 2050 the surviving cohort of 1955–59 will have reached the oldest-old category. Compared to all earlier pyramids, 2050 will have the highest proportions of elderly. The 2050 projection assumes a constant set of age-specific fertility rates, just high enough for replacement, resulting in about 2.1 children born per woman in her lifetime. Mortality is assumed to decline slightly with the typical age of death (i.e., life expectancy) rising from about seventy-six to just under eighty-three years old. Documented immigration is presumed to stay near its recent level of 974,885 immigrants per year.

In this descriptive account of the changing structure of the U.S. population, we have made passing reference to the proximate causes of the changes—swings in U.S. migration, fertility, and mortality rates. These three population processes are the only forces that can change population structure. Now is the time for a more theoretical treatment of their impact.

How Structure Affects the Population Processes

The likelihood of dying, giving birth, or migrating varies with age and sex. Thus, all of the crude rates are affected by the age-sex structure of the population. Structure is not the only determinant of mortality, fertility, and migration, but it is an important one.

Figure 4-4 on the following page graphs the Japanese age pattern of mortality, by sex, and of fertility using the 2010 population census data. Each line connects **age-sex-specific rates** for one of the sexes. (This important kind of rate is explained in Box 4-2 on p. 109.) These rates register the probability of dying and of giving birth at each of the ages specified on the x-axis of the graph.

Figure 4-4

Age-Sex-Specific Death Rates and Age-Specific Birth (Fertility) Rates for Japan, 2010

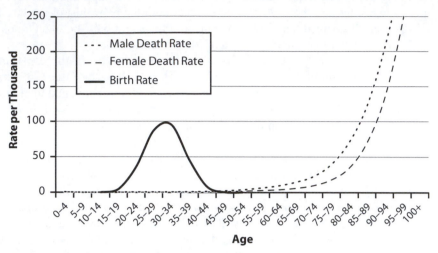

Source: Data from Statistics Japan, 2012. Graph created by Eiko Strader.

Mortality

In Figure 4-4, the very small mortality rate during infancy declines to almost no mortality during youth, climbs gradually through the middle years, and then rises more rapidly thereafter. Though the shape of that curve is similar for both sexes, mortality for men is higher than for women. The general "J" shape of these age distributions of mortality is almost universal, though the lean of the "J" may vary. Everywhere, sex influences mortality, although not always in precisely the pattern shown in Figure 4-4. (More about this in chapter 5.)

Fertility

Only women give birth, and generally only over about a thirty-year span. Moreover, the tendency to give birth, even within that span, varies considerably with women's age. We can see in Figure 4-4 that fertility rises rapidly in the late teens to a peak in the late twenties to early thirties, then declines to negligible levels in the mid-forties. The general shape of this curve, as well, is universal; but again there are variations in overall fertility level and the number of women having births at later ages. The advancement of fertility medical technology and its increasing use in some countries may eventually play a bigger role in driving later ages at childbearing. (More about this and other variations in chapter 7.)

Migration

Although the ways that age and sex influence mortality and fertility are fundamentally biological, it may come as a surprise that age also strongly affects migration. Universally, contemporary mobility is at its peak between the late teens and the mid-thirties. This corresponds to the life-cycle phases in which men and women are taking on adult roles, finding their places in the workforce, and forming new households. Mobility also differs by sex, but here the nature of the difference varies by cultural variations in women's and men's social roles. (More about this in chapter 9.)

Box 4-2

Age-Sex-Specific Rates

Age-sex-specific rates are used for two main purposes. One is to describe the impact of age and sex upon the population process in question. The second purpose is to discount, or "control" for, the influence of age-sex structure while measuring some other population process.

Demographers use rates in general to discount the influence of specified factors on measures of the population process (Preston et al., 2001; Ross, 1982). In the case of *crude* rates, treated in chapter 1, the factor being discounted was the size of the total population. When we compare two crude rates, we know that whatever may be causing them to differ, it cannot be the sizes of the total populations producing the events in question. In the case of *age-sex-specific* rates, the factor being discounted is the structure of the population. When we compare two specific rates for the same age-sex category, we know that whatever may be causing them to differ, it cannot be the proportion of the total population that falls into the age-sex category.

For either of these purposes, specific, separate rates are computed for each pertinent age class in the population; that is, for each bar of the population pyramid. Rates normally are constructed for one sex at a time. For each age category, the general formula is

$$_nr_x = \frac{_nE_x}{_nP_x} \times 1{,}000$$

where x is the initial age, n is the number of years in the age category, E is the number of events (e.g., births or deaths) occurring to persons in the age category, and P is the number of persons in the age category (Shryock and Siegel, 1976). For example, the age-specific birth rate for women aged 20–24 in the United States in 2015 would be obtained by solving the following formula:

$$_5r_{20} = \frac{_5B_{20}}{_5P_{20}} \times 1{,}000$$

where B is the number of children born in 2015 to women aged 20–24 and P is the number of women aged 20–24 in the 2015 population. Exercises at the end of the chapter illustrate these computations with real data and provide the reader a chance to construct some rates.

Figure 4-4 is a graph of age-sex-specific rates. Death rates are computed for each sex and age interval. In the case of births, however, rates do not have to be constructed for all age-sex classes. Although it certainly can be argued that both sexes participate in the production of children, the number of women available is the more limiting factor (so far). Moreover, female fertility is so low as to be negligible before age fifteen and after age forty-five (so far). Therefore, conventionally, age-specific birth rates are computed only for women, one each for the six five-year age intervals between ages fifteen and forty-five. Conventionally such rates are called fertility rates.

How the Population Processes Determine Structure

It requires imagination to assess the hypothetical impacts of mortality, fertility, and migration changes on **age-sex structure**. One takes a given population pyramid and imagines what it would look like at some specific future date if certain events were assumed to happen to its population processes during the interval (Bogue, 1993; Coale, 1972; Stolnitz, 1956). The projection can be done either precisely, with numbers, or approximately, in the head, as we ask you to do here.

What kind of assumptions should we make? Remember that only the three components of growth (mortality, fertility, and migration) can influence the size of either the total population or any age cohort within it; therefore, if you are trying to imagine the separate influence of any one component on the future age structure, the simplest strategy is to assume that the other two components will not change, or at least not change in such a way as to alter the shape of the projected pyramid. Then you specify an assumed change in the one remaining population process and imagine the results of that assumed change.

The following examples start by assuming changes that generally occur normally in the demographic transition that accompany economic development: mortality decline and fertility decline. So what you are getting here is also a formal demographic explanation of the main changes in population pyramids as they go through their transitions, the kind of change presented in Figure 4-3 for the United States. It is also an explanation of the current difference between MDR and LDR pyramids, summarized in Figure 4-1.

Mortality Decline

Effect on age.   Suppose that we have an absolute-number population pyramid for an imaginary country in 2015. The length of each of the bars in the pyramid represents the number of people in a five-year age category as of 2015.

Now, let us make some simplifying assumptions about migration and fertility. Let us assume that there is no net migration for any of the cohorts during the five-year span from 2015 to 2020. Fertility changes between 2015 and 2020 could affect the size of only the youngest age category in 2020, that is, those aged zero to five in 2020. Therefore, the length of the bar for each of the 2015 already-born cohorts (or age categories over five years old) as of 2020 will be determined solely by the death toll during the five-year time span.

Now let us try to imagine what that pyramid would look like in 2020 if overall mortality were to decline between 2015 and 2020, rather than stay at prior levels. The impact of the decline would depend upon the relative shrinkage of the specific death rates for the various ages.

Let us first suppose that mortality declined so as to improve life chances equally, across the board. For instance, try to imagine what would happen if age-specific death rates declined in such a way that survivorship between 2015 and 2020 doubled for every cohort. Each cohort would be larger in 2020 than it would have been under stable mortality conditions, larger in proportion to its original size. The size of the absolute-number pyramid would be larger, but that pyramid would have grown proportionally in each cohort or age group. The shape of the 2020 population pyramid would be the same under both stable-mortality and equally-declining-mortality assumptions; the percentage population pyramids would be identical. In other words, an equal increase in survivorship rates for all age categories would have no impact on the relative age composition of the population. Incidentally, an equal decrease in survivorship for all age categories also would have no impact.

But what if survivorship does not change equally at all age levels, as is more often the case? Then, indeed, mortality change can have an impact on age structure. In fact, during demographic transitions to lower mortality, survivorship generally improves more at the youngest ages. What would be the impact of such a disproportionate improvement of infant and early childhood survivorship? It would mean that younger birth cohorts would swell by a greater percentage than would the older cohorts during a specified interval; thus the shape of the pyramid would be made broader at the bottom after the mortality decline.

Historically, the declines in mortality that have accompanied demographic transitions have had a greater impact on infant and child mortality than on adult mortality. As a result, mortality declines have *not* been the major cause of the aging of MDR populations. Indeed, if transitional mortality declines have had any impact on percentage pyramids, it probably has been to make them slightly *younger* than they would have been.

These are not trivial facts, nor are they widely understood by nondemographers. The popular wisdom still is that the historical aging of the U.S. population, for instance, has been due to mortality decline. Not so, but it is easy to understand how that misconception arose. Mortality decline obviously does improve the life expectancy of *individuals*, but it does not necessarily affect the age structure of *collectives*. Population aging is not the same as individual aging.

Recently, however, things have changed in late-transitional MDR populations: there has been a disproportionate decline in mortality among the elderly. As can be seen from Figure 4-4, in a fully-transitioned MDR country like Japan, the mortality rate of women ages eighty-five to eighty-nine is only 69 per 1,000. When youthful and middle-age death rates are already low, there is less room for improvement at those ages and mortality decreases tend to concentrate at older-age rates. Thus, survivorship disproportionately begins to occur at the top of the population pyramid (Friedlander and Malul, 1983; Stolnitz, 1982; Treas and Torrecilha, 1995).

In sum, then, we can say that during the main demographic transition, mortality changes theoretically made little contribution to the aging of populations. However, in late-transitional countries, recent disproportionate mortality declines have indeed contributed to population aging and will do so in the future (see chapter 5).

Effect on sex.   Table 4-4 on the next page dramatizes the gradual shift from a male to female majority throughout the life span. In column 1, for the whole world projected to 2020, we see that a sex ratio of 106 in the zero-to-four age category gradually declines to a sex ratio of only 60 by age eighty-five and to 28 by age one hundred. Worldwide, there are roughly three women for every one man by the older ages.

What could be the explanation of this depletion of the world's men relative to women with age? We can proceed by process of elimination. Fertility is not a factor, since men universally outnumber women at birth. International migration is not an explanation since we are considering global sex ratios and, so far, extraterrestrial migration is not a reality. In any case, women and men are now equally likely to

Table 4-4   Sex Ratios by Age Category, Worldwide and in Regions, 2020

	World (1)	More-Developed Regions (2)	Less-Developed Regions (3)
Total, all ages	**102**	**95**	**103**
0–4	106	105	106
5–9	107	105	107
10–14	107	105	107
15–19	107	105	107
20–24	107	106	107
25–29	106	105	106
30–34	105	104	105
35–39	103	103	103
40–44	102	101	103
45–49	101	100	102
50–54	100	98	101
55–59	98	94	98
60–64	95	90	97
65–69	91	85	94
70–74	85	81	87
75–79	79	74	81
80–84	69	63	73
85–89	60	54	65
90–94	47	42	57
95–99	35	29	49
100+	28	21	47

Source: United Nations, 2013. *World Population Prospects: The 2012 Revision.* Used with permission.

migrate globally, although gender patterns of migration do vary considerably by country or origin (United Nations, 2013). That leaves higher male mortality as an explanation for the greater depletion of men at higher ages. For the world as a whole, women tend to survive longer than men.

The degree to which this is true varies internationally. The same general pattern of declining sex ratios at higher ages characterizes more- and less-developed regions (columns 2 and 3). And Table 4-4 shows that the sex ratio for the MDRs and LDRs is about the same in age groups from zero to forty-nine. However, sex ratios in these regions differ dramatically past age sixty, with ratios of only 63 by age eighty in MDRs compared to 73 in LDRs. With a faster depletion of men in late adulthood, women become a majority by age fifty in the MDRs and by age fifty-five in the LDRs.

How can we explain this difference between more- and less-developed regions? Higher fertility in LDRs could possibly increase maternal mortality, lowering the number of surviving women nearer to that of surviving men and thus keeping sex ratios more equitable into older ages. That would be consistent with higher sex ratios in LDRs. Yet, as we'll show in chapter 7, countries with the highest levels of fertility have lower, rather than higher, sex ratios from infancy through adult reproductive years.

Differences in mortality are, again, the primary explanation. Mortality in MDRs is clearly more sex-selective, being higher for men at older ages. This is especially true at the oldest ages in the MDRs, where there are twice as many women as men still living. We will leave the aspects of development in MDRs that are responsible for the lower female and higher male mortality at older ages for chapter 5.

One pattern that does not show up in Table 4-4's aggregate data is the skewed sex ratio in some countries as a result of sex-selective abortion technology. Sex ratios at birth are naturally weighted toward boys, at around 105 or 106. Ratios much above that are generally attributed to sex-selective abortion. Although this practice is associated with countries like China and India, it is also occurring in other parts of Asia, as well as in the Caucuses. For example, while China's sex ratio at birth is 118.1, it is 115.8 in Armenia and 117.6 in Azerbaijan (Guilmoto, 2012). These ratios first emerged in the 1980s when prenatal sex-identification technologies became widely available. The practice occurs most often among poorer families in societies where male children have more economic and social value than female children. In such a cultural context, the transition to smaller families can lead parents to choose boys over girls. Female fetuses are most likely to be aborted when the first child born was a girl (Gilles and Feldman-Jacobs, 2012). The World Bank estimates that 1.5 million girls are missing each year as the result of this.

Fertility Decline

Figure 4-5 shows schematically how fertility affects an absolute-number population pyramid. In it, a broad arrow arises from that segment of the pyramid representing the women of reproductive age and extends around to the base of the pyramid, where it splits into boys and girls before entering the base of the pyramid. This is meant to symbolize that final delivery of babies is confined to women (almost entirely to those aged fifteen to forty-five), that they produce babies of both sexes in almost equal numbers, and that all babies enter the pyramid at the bottom, at age zero.

The figure also dramatizes that two factors determine the number of babies that will be produced. The first is the number of women

Figure 4-5

How Fertility Influences the Age Structure

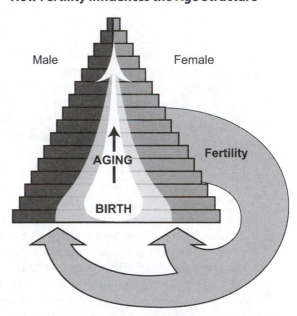

Source: Bos et al., 1994. *World Population Projections 1994–95 Edition.*

in the childbearing ages, fifteen through forty-five. The other is the level of the age-specific birth (fertility) rates being experienced by those women—the higher the rates, the more births.

Effect on age.   Just as we did in the case of mortality, let us try to imagine the changes in age composition that would result from a decline in age-specific fertility rates. Unlike the case of mortality, there is both a short-term and a long-term effect of any such change in rates. So let us proceed one stage at a time.

For the first fifteen years, a decline in age-specific fertility rates would lead to a proportional decline in the number of births entering the bottom of the population pyramid. Since the younger cohorts would be small relative to the previously born cohorts, the pyramid would become slimmer at its base than it would have if the older (higher) fertility rates had continued to prevail. That is, the percentage pyramid would look something like that for the United States in 1940, seen in Figure 4-3. That figure shows the impact of the fertility declines that reached their nadir during the 1930s (exaggerated in this particular case by the decline in immigration as well).

Remember, however, that the number of births produced is a factor not only of age-specific rates but also of the number of women in the childbearing ages. It is this second factor that leads to the delayed "echo" effect of a decline in rates. This begins some fifteen years after the initial decline in rates. At this point, daughters born over the initial fifteen years are beginning to enter their childbearing years. There are fewer of them, however, so their reduced numbers combine with the already reduced rates to produce even smaller birth cohorts.

The same kind of complementary short-term and long-term effects could occur if there were a sustained increase of age-specific birth rates. First there would be an increase in the base of the pyramid with the entry of the first, larger birth cohorts. Then, some fifteen years later, there would begin to be a compounding of this swelling at the base as the baby-boom cohorts reached their reproductive ages. Together, there would be more women of reproductive age and higher fertility rates, resulting in a squatter-shaped population pyramid.

However, the two factors also can work to oppose rather than complement each other. Generally speaking, this is the recent experience of the United States. The baby boom in the United States resulted in the population bulge at ages five to nineteen in the population pyramid for 1970, shown in Figure 4-3. That is, the baby boom began roughly twenty years earlier as the depleted birth cohorts of the Depression years were entering their childbearing ages during the 1950s. How can this be? The age-specific birth rates were raised enough during the 1950s to overwhelm the impact of there being relatively few women to experience those high rates. The baby bust of the 1970s illustrates a converse situation. The population pyramid for 1970 shows large numbers of women from the baby boom entering peak childbearing years in their late teens and early twenties. But the baby bust is already evident in the small number of infants under five years of age. This baby bust is a case of lower age-specific fertility rates offsetting an increase in the number of potential mothers. The U.S. crude birth rate would have been even lower in the recent years were it not for the **population momentum** created by the girl babies of the postwar boom just now beginning to exit the childbearing ages (see chapter 7).

Migration

Migration can affect both age and sex. Migration streams are generally comprised of young adults, and depending on whether the migration is labor related, it can sometimes be skewed toward one sex or another. The potential impact of migration on age-sex structure varies with the size of the geographic area being considered. That is because the relative size of the migrant population in comparison with the resident population tends to vary with the size of the area. The closer together the borders of an area are, the greater will be the proportion of residential movements by people who will cross these borders and thus constitute migrations.

A college town exemplifies how migration can create bizarre population pyramids for small geographic units. The age structure of such a town is often transformed every fall as the student body arrives and settles in. Although there has been a rise in older, nontraditional student enrollment, most college populations are still dominated by young adults. For the academic year, then, youth dominates the scene. Then, toward the end of the spring, the student body scatters to its summer life, leaving the relatively middle-aged or old, permanent resident population to catch its breath. Many readers of this text are familiar with the cycle from personal experience.

Figure 4-6 illustrates what may be an extreme case by using the population pyramid of Amherst, Massachusetts, according to the 2010 census. Amherst is at the center of the "Five Colleges" area. Most students of Amherst College, Hampshire College, and the University of Massachusetts, Amherst, as well as a few from Mount Holyoke and Smith Colleges, were included in this population.

Whatever impact migration has on population structure operates both directly and indirectly. It has a *direct impact* on age-sex structure only to the degree that *net* migration is *selective* with respect to sex and age. Remember that, potentially, both immigration and emigration may go on during any specified period. It is imbalance between the two processes that might affect structure. The simplest case of no age-sex selectivity in net migration is that in which each immigrant is matched by one emigrant of the same sex and age: since there is no net migration, then there can be no selective net migration. A more complicated case might occur where there was positive net migration—having more immigrants than emigrants—but where the net migration population gained through the interchange had precisely the same pro-

Figure 4-6

Percentage Population Pyramid of a College Town: Amherst, MA, 2010

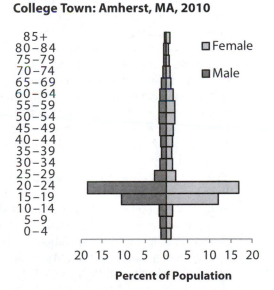

Source: U.S. Census Bureau, *American FactFinder 2010.* Graph created by Eiko Strader.

portionate age-sex structure as did the resident population. In this case, the age-sex classes in the resident population would be enlarged in equal proportions. The same non-effect would result in a negative net migration if it were proportional across age-sex classes.

The age structure of a net migrant population, however, seldom matches the age structure of a resident population. Figure 4-6 is a special case of this. Migration by students to a small college town will be composed primarily of young people in their late teens and early twenties, which creates a disproportionate bulge at the young adult ages. It is generally true that more traditional labor-related migration tends to be dominated by the young, historically by young working-age men. Thus the broad-based population pyramid for the United States in 1900, shown in Figure 4-3, is a result not only of high fertility but also of selective immigration of young adults and their children. The narrowing of the base in 1940 is a result not only of declines in fertility but also of the decline in immigration after World War I.

Indirect effects occur when selective net migration has a direct impact on population composition which, in turn, influences fertility, which then has its own effect on the age-sex structure. Suppose that migration is age and sex selective in such a way that it increases the proportion of the total female population in childbearing years. If there is no compensating decline in the age-specific fertility rates, the result will be an increase in the crude birth rate. This in turn will create larger birth cohorts.

Thus, if a country experiences heavy net immigration of young couples, that will create a bulge on the pyramid in the young adult ages (direct effect) and, in subsequent years, will produce larger birth cohorts at the base of the pyramid (indirect effect). This is precisely what happened in the United States during its peak years of immigration in the early 20th century. In contrast, the European countries of origin of these emigrants often had their young-adult categories depleted by the direct effect of emigration and their birth cohorts depleted as an indirect effect. Aging of some European countries' populations was then amplified by both direct and indirect effects of substantial emigration.

Migration effects continue to be substantial for some countries. International migration is at an all-time high, with 3.1% of the world's population living outside their country of birth or citizenship as of 2010 (United Nations, 2009). Net international migration accounted for 306% of Germany's population growth in 2011. That is, all of Germany's demographic growth, including compensation for natural decrease (the reason more than 100% of growth is accounted for) was due to migration. Similarly, Italy would have experienced negative population growth in 2011 if international migration were not taken into account. In many of the EU countries, such as Austria, Belgium, Denmark, Finland, Luxembourg, and Sweden, the majority of growth over the same period was due to net international migration (European Commission, 2013). With new population growth stemming almost exclusively from immigration, it is clear that age-sex selectivity of migration will impact population structure in such countries. But in order to counter population declines in the future, the number of immigrants to the European Union would have to drastically increase from current levels (Lesthaeghe, 2010; Martin and Widgren, 2002).

Problems of Young Populations

The definition of a population pattern as being a social problem requires two mental steps: (1) believing some theory of cause and effect, and (2) passing a negative value judgment on the supposed effect. Therefore, to understand public definitions of problems blamed on age and sex structure, we should ask questions such as these: What aspects of present and future population structures are seen as sources of social problems? What consequences are believed to flow from these structural characteristics? Why are these supposed consequences judged to be bad? Who defines the problems thus?

We have seen that more-developed countries have populations that are old and getting older, while less-developed countries have populations that are still young. As one might expect, the perceived problems for the two categories of countries are almost opposite. For LDRs, youth dependency is the overwhelming concern, although the gender imbalance due to sex-selective technologies is a severe problem for a specific group of LDRs (and some MDRs) as well.

Table 4-2 tells us that 26.4% of LDR populations in 2020 will be less than fifteen years old. Figure 4-1 shows that such a situation is projected to change only well into the present century, and only on the assumption that LDR fertility continues to decline. This implies that more than one out of every four people in LDRs is and will be a "youth dependent" through the first half of the 21st century.

Development Concerns

Youth dependency is by itself simply a structural population characteristic; but it is also seen as a source of social problems. Youth dependency can be a drain on per-capita wealth in LDRs. The larger the cohorts that are too young to work in comparison with the cohorts that are of working age, the greater the number of consumers relative to producers. But is it realistic to assume that being less than fifteen years old means being economically unproductive everywhere? While that may be true in industrialized economies, in some LDRs and especially in rural regions children begin making an economic contribution to the family much earlier and are sometimes kept out of school to do so (e.g., Visaria and Visaria, 1995). Economic development in most MDRs has meant taking the children out of the fields and factories, and putting them into schools. Thus, in these regions youth is commonly defined as an age of dependence.

There is nothing new about LDR populations being youthful; what is relatively new is the definition of youthfulness as a problem. As we saw in the previous section, the dominant cause of a young population structure is high fertility. LDRs generally have had higher fertility and it is only recently that many countries in the LDRs are experiencing fertility transitions. During the latter half of the 20th century a new kind of social and economic change was proposed for, and often imposed upon, these countries—capital-intensive modernization after the Western model. Defining a youthful population as a social problem has been, in large part, due to the implicit problems dependency presents for prevailing models of industrial development.

Social and Health Concerns

A younger population generally has a high percentage of persons in young, initially sexually active ages. A young, high-fertility population creates a number of social and health concerns (United Nations, 2011; World Health Organization, 2010; Noble et al., 1996). One in seven girls across LDRs marries before the age of fifteen, and childbearing is expected soon thereafter. The number one cause of death for girls between the ages of fifteen and nineteen in these countries is birth-related. The risk of low birth weight, infant mortality, and childhood death are all greater for the offspring of such young women. With a large reproductive-age population in a context where child marriage is accepted, these concerns comprise a greater share of health problems in LDRs and the need to address such reproductive health concerns is more pronounced.

Sexually transmitted diseases also are more frequent in a young population, with the highest infection rates among twenty- to twenty-four-year-olds followed by those fifteen to nineteen (Dehne and Riedner, 2005). HIV has spread rapidly among young women of these ages in some countries. Young adults under age twenty-five account for up to 60% of all new HIV infections, many of whom were infected in their teens.

Other problems (in both MDRs and LDRs) may be more frequent in younger populations. In many countries, for example, crime rates are highest among the young. Crime rates in the United States increased when the baby boomers were young and have declined as they have aged. These and other social problems associated with youth generate additional social and health concerns that are especially relevant for LDRs at their current stage in the demographic transition.

The Demographic Dividend as Antidote

While many LDR countries are still quite young, they are undergoing fertility transitions that pave the way for what some demographers call a demographic dividend, or demographic bonus (Gribble and Bremner, 2012; United Nations, 2011; Bloom et al., 2003). This is the window of time following rapid fertility decline in which the dependency ratio is at its lowest, with large majorities of the population at working ages. This early phase of transition from a young to an older population can result in a prolonged period of productivity and an opportunity for greater investment in children, leading to enhanced economic and social well-being. Some Asian LDRs, most notably China and South Korea, have been able to seize on this window of opportunity quite successfully (Khan, 2004, 1997). African LDRs are demographically poised to take advantage of this transition process next, with large proportions of youth entering adult working ages by 2020–2030. To make the most of this age transition period, countries must be in a position to implement social policies to support the transition to adulthood. Important infrastructure must be anticipated and put into place for youth, such as comprehensive child health programs, job-skills training, and educational policies (Agbor et al., 2012). Evidence over the decades has shown that investing in gender equality in such infrastructure build-up is a significant catalyst of investment in families, decreased fertility, improved child health and, ultimately, economic growth (Kristof and WuDunn, 2010; World Bank, 2006).

Problems of Old Populations

The problems resulting from age structure in the MDRs are the reverse of those in the LDRs. As seen in Figure 4-1, MDR population pyramids are almost columnar in shape and are projected to be even more so in the future. This means that increasingly larger proportions of their populations are growing old—however that may be defined. Many MDRs benefited from the dividends of a small dependency ratio throughout the late 20th century, but that bonus period is coming to an end for most.

This overall aging of MDR populations itself seems to raise vague alarms from Western commentators. When we look for explanations, two distinct aspects of the over-all aging process are singled out for attention. First is the changing age structure of the workforce, and second is the increasing size and visibility of the "elderly" population.

Let us discuss the two aspects separately, but first, a reminder: There is a differ-ence between the aging of individuals and the aging of populations. It is true that, in the MDRs, individuals on the average live longer and presumably will live even longer in the future; however, individual longevity is not what we are talking about in this sec-tion. Instead, we are talking about the changing age structure of the population: the increasing proportion of the population that is—at a given moment—in the older ages and the decreasing proportion that is in the younger ages. You may remember from our previous discussion that these two distinct phenomena have different causes: Increas-ing individual longevity is caused by declines in death rates, but increasing age of pop-ulations has historically been more influenced by declines in birth rates.

Productivity of the Workforce

One trend considered problematic by many is the increasing average age of those who are within the workforce ages, fifteen to sixty-five. Let us divide these fifty years into three segments: fifteen to twenty-nine, thirty to forty-four, and forty-five to sixty-four. In MDRs, the proportion of the population in each working-age group is nearly identical (i.e., just over a fifth of the population). In LDRs, the proportion of the popu-lation in the youngest working ages is disproportionately large (United Nations, 2013). But from Figure 4-1 we can see that by 2050, LDRs are projected to have a labor force structure similar to the MDRs.

If we can assume that changes in the age composition of the *total population* will result in changes in the age composition of the *workforce* (defined as people having jobs or looking for them) between the ages of fifteen and sixty-five, the MDR workforce is aging. That is, we are assuming for the moment that changes in workforce participa-tion rates through the lifecourse will not counteract the impact of aging within the con-ventionally defined labor force population aged fifteen to sixty-five.

Who is concerned about the consequences of an aging workforce? Those who pub-lish theoretical statements on the subject are predominantly Western economists. One can guess, however, that an equally—though perhaps less publicly—interested set of people are employers, eager to get maximum productivity from their workers.

What negative consequences do they see? One concern is old-age bias by employ-ers (Roscigno, 2010; Neumark, 2009; Bouvier and De Vita, 1991; AARP, 1989). Employers may believe that older workers will be less productive because they lack the technological and innovative edge of younger workers, who have more recently com-pleted their formal education. However, in a workforce where experience and seniority are highly valued, this fear is unlikely to be realized in most fields. Policy inputs that increase opportunities for training and educational advancement for older workers are one way to address this concern in fields where it might be a problem.

Careers in Demography

Tukufu Zuberi
Lasry Family Professor of Race Relations, Africana Studies and Sociology,
  University of Pennsylvania
Research Associate, Penn Population Center
Documentary film writer and producer
PBS series *History Detectives* host

How did you decide that being a demographer was the career path for you?

By my second year at the University of Chicago, I knew that demographic methods would allow me to profoundly confront my sociological interests. For me it was important that this is the only social science in the world defined by a balancing equation. The only problem we have is having data of a quality sufficient to estimate the different parameters of this equation.

We know what goes into making population numbers what they are. The distinction of this disciplinary uniqueness was attractive to my sociological imagination. I was convinced as a young man that if I were to make a contribution to understanding and society, I would need to ground my understanding of society in facts. And the basic facts of society are grounded in the human population.

What kind of education and training did you pursue to get to where you are in your career?

I entered San Jose State University in 1977 as a member of the track team. After a year of running track and actively participating on the team, I decided my future lie elsewhere. I informed the coach that I needed to spend more time with my studies, and left the team. This was the beginning of my pursuit of knowledge and understanding.

My undergraduate degree is in sociology with minors in economics and Afro-American studies. After receiving a wonderful education at San Jose State, I spent one year studying law at Martin Luther King Junior Hall at the University of California at Davis. It was during this year that my great love for sociology was confirmed. After passing my first year exams in law, I transferred to Sacramento State University where I received an MA in sociology. I next entered the University of Chicago. After four years of the most rigorous sociology training that could be offered, I left the University of Chicago for my first job as Assistant Professor of Sociology at the University of Pennsylvania.

While I attended the University of Chicago, Evelyn Kitagawa, a professor of sociology who did path-breaking work on the study of mortality, inspired me to think about demography as an essential tool in my research. It was in her methods classes that I was able to really come to appreciate the potential of the science of demography in helping us understand society. Other professors, like Dennis Hogan and Douglas Anderton, while a different generation of scholars, confirmed for me that demography was an essential method to be employed in my sociological practice.

Describe your work/research as a demographer. What do you consider your most important accomplishments?

I have thought of my contributions primarily in terms of projects. These projects always have the objective of providing education, which might help make the world a better place. My research interests have focused on racial stratification and African and African Diaspora populations.

My first major project was collaboration with Phil Morgan and Sam Preston to study racial differences in family structure using historical U.S. census data. Following the successful publication of a number of articles, this collaboration led to my next project, which examined mortality in historical Liberia. This project, in which I collaborated with Sam Preston and several graduate students, produced a number of important articles and resulted in the publication of my first book, *Swing Low, Sweet Chariot: The Mortality Cost of Colonizing Liberia in the Nineteenth Century.*

This project was followed by the study of the methods used to understand racial differences, entitled "Thicker Than Blood: How Racial Statistics Lie." This ongoing project attempts to broaden the scope of demography by suggesting a more scientific understanding of human difference. The past and current fascinations with the biological basis of human difference are misguided and reflect political and ideological orientations more than science.

To complement these efforts I have organized a number of programs to recruit more African American and Latino scholars to demography. The successes of these efforts are the significant number of students that have benefited from these programs. Some of these students and others that have been influenced by our work were part of a recent edited volume on the same topic, *White Logic, White Methods: Racism and Methodology.* This volume extended the collaboration around removing the racial logic that has distorted the science of demography.

My third major project is the African Census Analysis Project, which I founded in the 1990s. This project became an international collaboration between myself and a number of African scholars, universities, and governments. At its height, the project served as a rallying point for enhancing our understanding of African census data. In fact, the project can be credited for establishing the credibility of African census data in the understanding of African demography. The project has become dormant due to funding cuts, but I still very much believe in its aims and objectives and hope to someday reinvigorate the project.

The project helped to educate hundreds of students and provided a significant number of post-docs and visiting assistantships for African scholars at the University of Pennsylvania. The significant amount of published articles and number of students trained in the project are an apt testament for engaging in such analytical collaborations. This project also resulted in the publication of *The Demography of South Africa*, Volume 1 of the *General Demography of Africa* series, which I co-edited with Amson Sibanda and Eric Udjo.

In addition to being a professor at the University of Pennsylvania, I have been a visiting professor at Makerere University, Kampala, Uganda, The University of Dar-Es-Salaam in Tanzania, and the Universidade Federal de Minas Gerais in Brazil. My current interests and projects are concerned with population and human difference.

What do you see as the field's most important contribution as well as its greatest challenge?

The study of demography offers scientific answers to basic social questions. The actual study of demography has gone up and down in the field of demography. Much of what we consider demographic research today does not employ demographic methods. In fact, much of what is considered the most important work done in the field of demography today is done with statistical methods. The future of demographic research will rest on our ability to reintroduce demographic methods and to maintain the scientific basis of the discipline.

Employers may also have reduced incentive to retain older workers if they view them as expensive compared to a new hire who will demand lesser pay and benefits. Reflecting this age discrimination bias, it is still common in many MDR firms to engage in mandatory retirement practices, where employees are forced to retire upon turning sixty or sixty-five (Seike, 2010). In times of economic recession, is such bias against older workers magnified? In the recent Great Recession of 2007–2009, there was mixed evidence for this. Older people in the labor market were actually less likely than other groups to lose their jobs (young adults fared the worst in this respect), but those who did become unemployed were less likely than other age groups to get re-employed (Bell and Blanchflower, 2011; Van Horn et al., 2011).

A related concern, however, is individual mobility within organizations. The type and number of occupations within the organization tend to fall into a pyramid, with fewer managers over many workers. It is theorized that if changes in the age structure of the workforce as a whole are mirrored *within* organizations, then older people will hang on to their higher-status jobs while younger workers may have to wait longer to become managers (Easterlin, 1980). This effect has so far been negligible in aging societies, because large proportions of the over-sixty-five population still retire from the labor force, even despite the recent recession (Gustman et al., 2011).

Now let us relax our assumption that change in the age structure within the working ages will be faithfully reflected by a change in the age structure of the workforce. Is there evidence that there may be changes in workforce participation patterns that will blunt this effect?

In the United States, workforce participation rates have been changing in such a way as to offset partially the changing age structure of the working-age population. Although there was a decline in the retirement age up until the 1990s, labor force participation for older workers has since begun to increase. There has been an especially marked increase in workforce participation among women, almost entirely in the adult and older age categories. Between 1960 and 2010, male labor market participation declined from 83.3% to 71.2%; during the same time, women's labor market participation increased from 37.7% to 58.6% (U.S. Bureau of Labor Statistics, 2013). Age-specific participation rates, especially for young men, have dropped significantly since 2000, reflecting their weak labor market attachment in economic downturns and increasing financial returns to higher education.

For better and for worse, all of these changes in labor force participation rates currently combine to counteract the aging of the workforce in many MDRs. Aging of the population and aging of the workforce are only tenuously linked and depend heavily on prevailing labor force participation patterns. It is hoped that as the critical mass of baby-boom generations move into older ages they will challenge and reform many of the MDR old-age stereotypes and related work policies.

Increasing Size and Visibility of the Elderly Population

Let us start with some statistical elaboration about the proportionate size of the elderly population. Then we will discuss other trends that have increased the visibility of the elderly over the past half-century and specific concerns that have been voiced about the aging of the U.S. population.

Table 4-2 tells us that the proportion of the population aged sixty-five and over in 2020 will be magnified in the MDRs compared to the LDRs, particularly in Europe and

Northern America. Figure 4-7 deals with the United States in particular. The increasing proportion of elderly through the last century registered the effects of declining fertility. While the proportion aged sixty-five and over more than tripled over the century, the proportion aged eighty-five and over increased ninefold so that the population achieving extremely old ages, or **grandevity**, is increasing (U.S. Department of Health and Human Services [DHHS], 2013).

The right side of Figure 4-7 gives projections into mid-century using Census Bureau cohort-component projections. The proportion aged sixty-five and over is projected to peak in 2030, while the percentage aged eighty-five and over will continue to grow from 5.75 million in 2010 to 19 million by 2050, and is expected to increase until slightly past mid-century (U.S. DHHS, 2013).

Several other factors contribute to the visibility of the elderly population in the United States. One is that they are heavily concentrated in selected geographic regions of the country (U.S. DHHS, 2013). A useful assessment of elderly concentration is the *proportion* and the *median age* of elderly in a particular population. Florida and West Virginia are the two U.S. states with the highest proportion of elderly (at 17% and 16%, respectively), while Maine and Vermont are the two states with the oldest median ages (at forty-three and forty-two, respectively) (U.S. Census Bureau, 2011a). Regions of the country with older populations are most often those areas left by younger people, what we call negative net migration, such as in the Northeast and Midwest, rather than

Figure 4-7

Percent of the Total U.S. Population in the Older Ages, 1900–2050

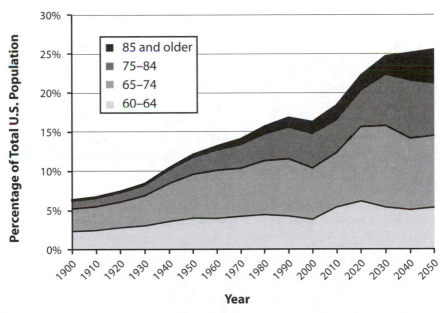

Source: Data from U.S. DHHS, 2013. *Aging Statistics: Projected Future Growth of Older Population.* Graph created by Eiko Strader.

those sought out by retirees. Generally, this out-migration represents young people in search of better jobs.

Another reason for the increased visibility of the elderly is that retirees, often equated with the elderly in popular culture, increased in number over the past forty years. Until the recession-related reversal of this trend, the average age of retirement had fallen from sixty-seven to sixty-two over the past forty years (PRB, 2011). The well-publicized "golden age" of the recent generations of retirees who have had greater disposable incomes and are in better health than past generations of retirees has made the "elderly" more visible as a segment of society.

As the full cohort of baby boomers moves into retirement age, they no doubt will shape societal norms. A larger proportion of the population than other age groups, they have influenced American culture in a variety of ways at each life stage and will likely revolutionize the way in which aging is currently conceptualized (Cohn and Taylor, 2010; Gendell, 2008; Freedman, 1999). Thus, the cultural visibility of the elderly population is likely to be even greater than their already substantial demographic increase.

Another significant change has been the increasing feminization of the elderly population. Especially in MDRs, women tend to outnumber men; the older the age category, the more the female dominance. Figure 4-8 graphs this trend and projects its continuation into the future. In 2000, in every older-age category shown, there is a higher percentage of women than men. This is most extreme at the oldest ages, with

Figure 4-8

Projected Percent Female at Older Ages, United States, 2000–2050

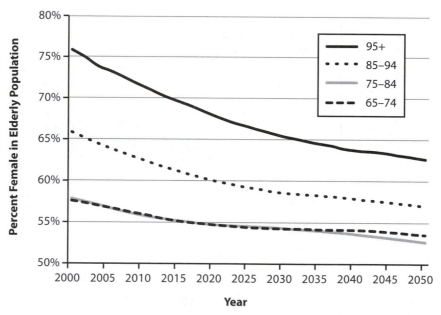

Source: U.S. Census Bureau, 2009. *National Population Projections Supplemental Files: Zero Net International Migration Series*, Table 1. Graph created by Eiko Strader.

three women for every one man at age ninety-five and older. But what we see looking into the future, is that women's edge over men in longevity will decrease. By 2050, women and men at ages sixty-five to eighty-four will be closer to parity in their population sizes, and the sex gap at ages eighty-five and over will be significantly narrower. This is part of an interesting historical pattern, where gender differences in life expectancy were close to zero historically, but widened considerably throughout the demographic transition. In recent years, continued gains against mortality have been greater for men than women and have begun to reverse this 20th century trend in the U.S. (U.S. Census Bureau, 2011a). These male gains are projected to level off toward mid-century, leaving women with a smaller but still significant longevity advantage. In the meantime, elderly women are especially prominent among those achieving grandevity.

So what is *wrong* with these trends of increasing size and visibility of the elderly population? Who is worried about them? What negative consequences are anticipated? A number of policy-related issues have dominated discussions about the elderly. Visiting a selected few of these important issues will convey the variety and range of concerns expressed about the aging of the U.S. population.

Old-Age Dependency

MDRs vary in the severity of their old-age dependency problems. Baby booms and busts have not exactly coincided internationally, so the pattern of imbalances between succeeding generations is not entirely uniform. Moreover, countries differ in their systems for providing economically for their elderly. North America has a smaller proportion of people aged sixty-five and over than Europe (see Table 4-2). In part this reflects a longer duration baby boom in the United States, which has not yet aged to the same extent as in Europe.

We should remind ourselves, however, that old age is not the only source of age dependency. There is youth dependency as well, and in many countries youth dependency is a more intensive short-term economic challenge than old-age dependency. Societies invest in youth via universal schooling and other supports with the understanding that children will grow up to become productive future citizens. Thus, few children under the age of sixteen are employed in most MDRs. By contrast, large minorities of sixty-five and over adults are still in the labor force and making immediate contributions to society.

It is time to introduce some modifications of the measure we have called the age-dependency ratio. You will remember that the numerator of that ratio combined the youth-dependent and the old-age-dependent populations; the denominator was the population in the normal working ages, conventionally fifteen through sixty-four. When analyzing the composition of age dependency, it is important to distinguish between different classifications of demographic dependency. Thus, commonly used modifications are the **young-age-dependency ratio** and the **old-age-dependency ratio**. Conventionally, the numerator consists of the population fifteen and younger or the population sixty-five and older; the denominator consists of the population aged eighteen through sixty-four. Some common variations on these themes include defining the youth dependent population as eighteen and under instead of fifteen, or the *oldest-old dependency ratio* that defines the numerator as eighty and over instead of sixty-five and over. Recognizing that there is great variability in how dependent the older population actually is, a newer innovation in the old-age-dependency ratio is the *prospective old-age depen-*

dency ratio (Sanderson and Scherbov, 2008). Instead of arbitrarily assigning all people age sixty-five and over to the numerator, this measurement instead takes into account how expanding life expectancies change across generations. Dependency is defined as all people whose additional years of life expectancy are less than fifteen years, rather than employing a fixed age cut-off in the numerator.

The Case of Japan and the United States

The Japanese old-age-dependency ratio in 1920 was only 9 per 100 persons aged fifteen to sixty-four and it took seventy-one years to double to 18 per 100 persons. But the rate of old-age dependency increased tremendously around the turn of the century and by 2010 it had quadrupled to 36 per 100 (Statistics Japan, 2012). As of now, Japan has the highest share of the sixty-five and older population across the globe. Due to decreasing fertility along with lengthening life expectancy, old-age dependency in Japan is projected to increase rapidly as baby boomers retire, to nearly 54 per 100 in 2030 and to 78 per 100 by 2060 based on 2010 estimates (Government of Japan, 2012).

Some have optimistically pointed to steady immigration streams as an effective offset to rising old-age dependency, such as in the United States. But what makes the Japanese case different from many other aging societies is its lack of immigration incorporation. Immigrants make up only about 1% of the total workforce in Japan, in large part because anti-immigration sentiment is still quite strong there. Experts therefore forecast a bleak future of high old-age dependency (Keidanren, 2008).

Although projections are not as grim in the United States, those who are alarmed about prospective old-age dependency point to the period when all the baby-boom cohorts reach elderly ages. These elderly cohorts will be supported by the small, low-fertility cohorts that followed them. However, an important implicit assumption lurks behind the idea of old-age dependency, which is that in any given year, those who have completed their working lives are to be supported by those who have not yet done so. The belief is that supporting the elderly has to be done by an intergenerational transfer of wealth, but there are alternatives to this sort of system (more on this in the next section).

There are a few reasons why growth of the elderly population may not reflect the economic dependency implicit in dependency ratios. First, elderly poverty has been dramatically reduced as Social Security has proven to be an effective social program of collective support. Second, at present there are considerable resources devoted to preparing for the coming retirement of the baby boomers. Third, labor force participation rates are flexible and adaptive in the early elderly ages. For example, 36% of men and 26% of women ages sixty-five to sixty-nine were in the labor force in 2009 (Jacobsen et al., 2011). With effective social programs in place, the resources and foresight to prepare in advance, and their individual resources of wealth and marketable skills, elderly dependents differ markedly from young dependents.

The Future of Social Security in the United States

The predominant concern over aging in the United States has been the fear that the Social Security system will be bankrupted by the burden of payments to retiring baby boomers. Payments currently being made by workers and their employers are used to support the retirement of those who already have aged out of the workforce. And, glancing forward, the implications of continuing such a system show that it is not sustainable. Figure 4-9 combines historical and projected data on Social Security and Medicare costs against Old-Age, Survivors and Disability Insurance (the trust fund for worker/employer Social Security contributions). Smaller cohorts will be strained to provide for bulging ones entering retirement if no alternative is adopted. As of 2010, more was being paid out to Social Security recipients than was being paid in by workers. The Social Security and Medicare Boards of Trustees estimates that, under current conditions, Social Security benefits will be paid in full until 2049 (U.S. Social Security Administration, 2012; Congressional Budget Office, 2011).

However, other support strategies are possible and the system will continue to be tinkered with over the coming decades. Raising the retirement age to keep up with increases in life expectancy is one possible modification. Many MDR countries have begun to modify their retirement programs, pushing back the age at which full retirement benefits can be received. Another is increasing payroll taxes. Alternatively, each cohort could be made responsible, and helped to be responsible, for saving for its retirement. This principle would eliminate the problem of irregularities in relative cohort sizes. To implement such a system would likely require a gradual transition. It would leave a generation stranded between the current pay-as-you-go system and those beginning a genuine retirement savings program. Suggested cohort savings programs are often privatized, relying on personal investment accounts, which are vulnerable to market forces. As we saw with the Great Recession, there is no guarantee that such savings will provide for retirement into the future. The most likely course of action is a more gradual move in the direction of federally backed cohort investment and savings. In the short run there will almost certainly be a continued reliance on current contributions and a guarantee through the full credit of the government.

Figure 4-9

Social Security and Medicare Costs as a Percentage of GDP

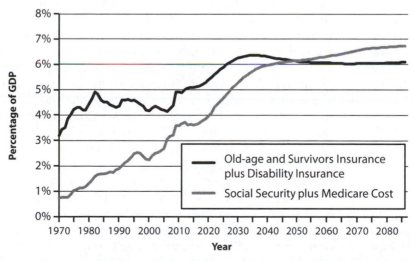

Source: U.S. Social Security Administration, 2012. *A Summary of the 2012 Annual Reports.* Graph created by Eiko Strader.

Whatever changes are made to U.S. Social Security, it is clear that the current retirement of the baby-boom cohort and the increase in life expectancy will require some revision to retirement systems. An increase in health, life span, personal wealth, education, and other personal assets means the elderly are in a position to, and now do, contribute to their own retirement support. It is likely that modifications to Social Security might eventually include adjustments for personal wealth and alternative income sources, as well as other changes reflecting the evolving meaning of "old" in the United States. In recent congressional testimony, economist Alice Rivlin noted that the Great Recession has made Social Security reform more possible politically than ever before:

> The crisis may have . . . provided an opportunity to put the system on a sound fiscal basis for the foreseeable future. Fixing Social Security is a relatively easy technical problem. It will take some combination of several much-discussed marginal changes: raising the retirement age gradually in the future (and then indexing it to longevity), raising the cap on the payroll tax, fixing the COLA, and modifying the indexing of initial benefits so they grow more slowly for more affluent people. In view of the collapse of market values, no one is likely to argue seriously for diverting existing revenues to private accounts, so the opportunity to craft a compromise is much greater than it was a few years ago. (Rivlin, 2009)

Health and Capacity in the United States

Another prominent concern with rising old-age-dependency ratios is the unique health concerns and healthcare needs in a growing elderly population. According to the Federal Interagency Forum on Aging-Related Statistics (2012), about 45% of male and 56% of female elderly suffer from arthritis in the United States. Over half of the elderly suffer from hypertension, about a third suffer from heart disease and hearing loss, and more than half of the elderly report at least one long-lasting condition or disability (Federal Interagency Forum, 2012). In short, older people require more health services because they are more likely to suffer from health problems. As a result, healthcare burdens upon the elderly and society have reached record levels as the number and proportion of elderly have increased. Just as Social Security has demanded adjustment, Medicare—the U.S. health insurance for the elderly—and the healthcare system in general are struggling to adapt to changes in population composition. In 2010 the most significant healthcare reform in the past half-century was passed, the Patient Protection and Affordable Care Act (PPACA). This new policy is intended to extend healthcare coverage to all Americans while stemming rising medical costs, including that of Medicare. Reassessment of healthcare services and delivery will be a continual process as the population ages.

Functional impairments also increase dramatically with aging. The percentage of Medicare enrollees who are unable to perform a basic physical function, such as kneeling, grasping small objects, or reaching over the head, almost double among those aged sixty-five to seventy-four and then almost double again for those over seventy-five (Federal Interagency Forum, 2012). Beyond age eighty-five, nearly 40% of men and over 50% of women have such a disability and require living assistance. These disabilities can be expected to increase as grandevity increases. Most elderly caregiving is not within institutions but is provided through informal assistance or family members, and these caregiving demands will continue to increase in the coming years. The percentage of elderly living in institutions or assisted-living centers can also be anticipated to increase after remaining relatively steady in recent years. These changes will be among many that are a part of the adapting social milieu that is arising from the aging of America. While it is easy to emphasize the potential needs of the elderly, it should be remembered that the elderly increasingly report themselves to be in better health over time (Sanderson and Scherbov, 2008). Once again, the elderly are not simply dependent on younger generations. And unlike youth dependents, the elderly vote. They will, in large part, determine the nature of changes in their own individual lifestyles and politically shape the way in which society adapts to their healthcare needs.

The Intergenerational Distribution of Wealth

A very different concern over the rising elderly population is that of an intergenerational shift in personal wealth. The issue here is not with increasing dependence of the elderly but with the increasing share of wealth held by the elderly. This viewpoint largely takes a zero-sum view of social resources—that is, those held by one generation are not available to another.

Illustrating the source of these concerns is the fact that the wealth gap between the old and the young is wider than it has ever been before. The 2010 median net worth of householders aged sixty-five and over was $170,128 while that of householders under age thirty-five was just over $5,000 (U.S. Census Bureau, 2013b). Of course, people gain assets and pay off debt as they age, so a difference is expected; however, the wealth gap between old and young has increased drastically over time. While in 1984 the elderly were ten times more wealthy than the young, today that figure has increased to *thirty-four* times more wealthy (U.S. Census Bureau, 2013b; Fry et al., 2011). This wasn't always the case. As Figure 4-10 on the following page shows, the elderly experienced the highest rates of poverty of all age groups until the 1970s. Since then, the elderly poverty level has fallen steadily while the poverty rate among children has correspondingly increased. In 1973, there was a crossover, marking the point at which child poverty rates became the highest of all groups. Figure 4-10 also indicates that the decline in old-age poverty has surpassed even that of working-age Americans (the people on whom the elderly are supposed to be dependent!), whose poverty rates began to rise in 2000 while the elderly continued their downward trend.

These trends exemplify how social policies and the redistribution of resources to reduce poverty have successfully reversed trends among one age group. It also reflects a demographic story. Larger proportions of today's U.S. elderly are living longer, healthier, and more independent lives, allowing many to accumulate and hold their wealth for longer periods of time. Lesser wealth is held by younger generations and specifically by those who are most truly societal dependents, children. It is this group that has the greatest need for similar poverty-reduction policies today. Unfortunately, U.S. assistance programs addressing young women and children in poverty have been dramatically reduced during the same time that an increasing share of social wealth is being held by older generations. The declining share of youth dependency in the U.S. aging population might, in contrast, signal a unique opportunity to address the needs of the young dependent population just as it decreases in relative size and will be more

Figure 4-10

Percent Living in Poverty by Age Group, U.S., 1966–2011

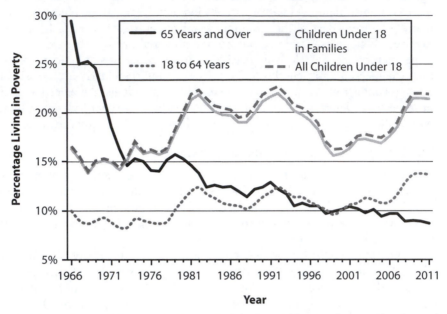

Source: U.S. Census Bureau, 2012a. *Historical Poverty Tables–People*, Table 3. Graph created by Eiko Strader.

affordable to do. Unlike the growing elderly population, there is relatively little children can do to contribute to their own support. Let us hope that concerns over the aging baby-boom cohort and their disproportionate political and cultural influence do not overwhelm commitments to address the severe needs of dependent children and young parents in poverty.

Intergenerational Perceptions and Structural Relations

An implicit conflict about the distribution of resources among generations can be seen in each of the concerns just discussed. The conflict in intergenerational distribution of resources, whether real or a zero-sum fiction, can also be seen in real cultural expressions at both ends of the age distribution. Consider property tax initiatives to support education, for example. The elderly face a conflict between their fixed incomes and rising property taxes. If they vote to stabilize property taxes they risk being viewed as miserly toward society's youth. But old age also means confronting a limited resource horizon and great financial, as well as physical, uncertainties. Being conservative with finances appears a reasonable and prudent course of action. Meanwhile, young post–baby boomers fear they will bear the burdens of caring for the elderly and be overshadowed by, or confined to, a baby-boomer-dominated culture. More importantly, they are one of the first American generations to anticipate a lower lifestyle standard than that of their parents. Many believe they are saddled with social and environmental problems created by an earlier generation that has reaped many benefits and left behind the burdens.

From a sociological standpoint these sentiments may have more to do with increasing social distance between the young and elderly than with any real inherent conflicts over social resources. What can we learn by comparing the population pyramid of 1900 in Figure 4-3 with that of 2050? At the beginning of the 20th century the vast majority of the adult population was still of working age and from a relatively narrow range of birth cohorts. That is, the members of the adult population were relatively similar to one another in age and cohort experiences with only a scattering of older generations. However, by 2050 adults will be relatively evenly distributed from ages twenty through seventy-five and there will be a substantial group of the "old-old" beyond age eighty-five. Over the past century the population, with minor fluctuations, has increasingly become one in which individuals are less similar to each other in terms of age and cohort experiences. Or, as sociologists might say, society has become more differentiated with respect to age.

Other historical changes may amplify the increasing social distance between cohorts. Rapid development and dissemination of technology, for example, has meant that the experiences and skills of one cohort are rapidly replaced by those of the next (Zickuhr, 2011). Mid-career retraining for employment is a notion that would have seemed foreign in times past. Yet, without retraining, a demographer trained in 1970 with a "slide rule" would have been left behind by those using personal computers just a decade later. The faster pace of social, technological, and historical change in recent generations has potentially amplified the structural effects of increasing social distances between cohorts. While some events and experiences may unify generations, these are less easily identified and more likely are exceptions to the rule.

Other potentially distancing generational differences pertain to political affiliation and the changing ethnic composition of the U.S. population. Generally, it is an age-old truism that the old tend to be more conservative than the young. In the 2008 U.S. presidential elections, 66% of adults under thirty voted for the Democratic Party (Obama) compared to 45% of adults sixty-five and older (Parker, 2012). In addition, because the U.S. population has become a much more ethnically diverse population over the last fifty years, there will emerge large compositional differences in ethnic makeup between the oldest and the youngest generations. As a case in point, in 2012 non-Hispanic white infants comprised a minority (albeit slight, at 49.6%) for the first time in U.S. history (U.S. Census Bureau, 2012b). This is in stark contrast with the age sixty-five and over population, who are still comprised of a large majority (80%) of non-Hispanic whites (U.S. Census Bureau, 2011b). As long as racial and ethnic identity continues to be correlated with inequality in U.S. society, it is likely that these generational differences will exacerbate social distance between population cohorts.

Problems of Fluctuations in Cohort Size in the MDRs

MDRs may experience significant fluctuations in cohort size. As we saw in chapter 1, having completed the "demographic transition" means that a country will have brought its fertility under individual voluntary control. Individually controlled fertility, however, is collectively quite variable, swinging upward and downward on the basis of whatever it is that makes couples decide to have many or few children early or late in their own lives. Because birth rates are the major determinant of the size of birth cohorts, swings in the rates are reflected as bulges and bottlenecks in the population pyramid.

That this not only *can* happen but *does* happen is well illustrated by the example of the United States in Figure 4-3, where the population pyramid for 1990 clearly identifies the baby-boom generation that peaked with the 1955–1959 birth cohort and the baby-boom echo of the 1980s. Identifiable in the pyramid as bottlenecks are two other extreme generations. Those aged fifty-five through fifty-nine in 1990 were the birth cohorts of 1930 through 1934, the Depression generation. Those aged ten through nineteen in the 1990 pyramid, born between 1970 and 1980, are the baby bust or self-labeled "generation X," allegedly reflecting anonymity in the wake of the baby boom. The lowermost rows in the pyramid represent most of "generation Y" (born starting in the 1980s), also known as the "millennium generation" or the "echo boomers." As indicated by the latter label, this generation is slightly larger than the generation X that preceded it. The 2010 pyramid shows these cohorts twenty years later. The Depression generation (now age seventy-five to seventy-nine) is no longer distinguishable as smaller than those born before it because much of the previous generation has died off. The baby boom generation is still the largest bulge in the pyramid, but they have lost some members due to mid-life mortality. The X and Millennial generations, by 2010 having reached their twenties and thirties, are now joined by the newest generation. This generation is smaller than the Millennials but not as small as the Xers. It is America's current youth-dependent age group and has yet to receive a nickname, although emerging candidates seem to be "generation Z" and "the Homeland generation."

Institutional Problems

Those who are in charge of planning for the future and preparing institutions to provide for society are repeatedly undone by having either too many or too few facilities. This is particularly true when the facilities involved are inflexible. The U.S. baby boom provides a familiar example. Educational institutions, for example, strained to meet the load of the baby boom, expanding physical facilities and welcoming new teachers into the fold. As the baby bust moved through the school years there was pressure to curtail educational expenditures. Yet, right after the bust bottomed out in elementary schools, secondary schools, and colleges, these same institutions that had cut back now faced increasing numbers of baby-boom echo students. The same experience is likely to be faced by healthcare institutions as these cohorts reach older ages and, eventually, the end of their lives.

There are other examples of wrenching adjustments in the economy. Both the size and age composition of the workforce can take wild swings. As large and small cohorts enter and leave the workforce, periods of job opportunity can alternate with periods of stagnation. Housing prices inflated wildly as the baby-boom generation bought housing only to stagnate and lose value as Generation X arrived at the usual home-buying ages of twenty to thirty. Prices will likely be affected as the Millennial generation enters the housing market and as baby boomers relocate to retirement housing. There is some indication that baby boomers prefer to retire in small, more rural towns where the cost of living is lower (PRB, 2011). If so, their outsized demand for transportation, housing, and health services has the potential both to strain small-town resources as well as to revitalize these areas. Finally, we already have discussed the potential problems of providing Social Security to the retiring baby-boom generation on the basis of the payments made by smaller subsequent generations.

Cohort Problems

So far we have discussed the problems of varying cohort size as defined by the society at large and its institutions. Do these variations also cause special problems for the members within each cohort? Richard Easterlin (1980) and others (see Macunovich 2000, 2012), stressed that the relative size of a cohort has a lot to do with the fate of its members.

Again, the most dramatic and familiar illustration in recent U.S. history is the baby-boom cohort. It was big, much bigger than the especially small Depression cohort that preceded it. It was the cohort that personally experienced, and still is experiencing, many of the institutional problems we have just described. First, it had to cope with overcrowded classrooms and teacher shortages. Yet, as a large and young generation it felt uniquely empowered to end the Vietnam War and engage in the civil rights movement. When it entered the workforce in search of first employment, labor was in oversupply. Baby boomers faced housing shortages as they entered the housing market. And, as they matured in working ages, some boomers fell victim to corporate pressures to "downsize" them from higher-paying jobs and replace them with younger, and cheaper, workers. Baby boomers will now be retiring under circumstances where cohort-related imbalances in the Social Security system are likely to lead to resentment from younger generations.

The Millennial and X generations are each living through unique demographically-influenced cohort experiences. Generation X is in an already crowded labor force and housing market. The Millennials are being educated in overcrowded colleges and universities, as was the baby boom. Despite being a larger cohort, the Millennials face less immediate competition for jobs and housing than Generation Xers, who are still in more direct competition with the immediately preceding baby boomers. On the other hand, Millennials, as the age group most vulnerable to unemployment, are entering a labor market that has just undergone a major recession. It is, as of yet, uncertain whether this generation will experience more adverse long-term economic effects than other age groups as a result.

Each of these younger cohorts has come of age in the shadow of the baby boom. As the discussion above suggests, the sheer size of the baby boom has structurally impacted both groups. In addition, the baby boom has exerted a disproportionate influence on the culture in which younger cohorts have lived. As the largest pool of consumers, the baby boom dominates commercial culture and the marketing of products.

Another potentially problematic aspect of fluctuations in cohort size comes from the sense of identity a cohort can form. A shared unique history tends to create in any cohort a sense of identity and perhaps a shared definition of the cause of its problems. Differing cohort identities can amplify the sense of conflicts between generations over resources, ideology, identity, and so forth. Just as rapid technological change may amplify the increasing social distance between cohorts as MDR populations age, fluctuations in cohort size may further emphasize unique cohort identities and further strain intergenerational relations. Baby boomers proudly identified with their uniqueness and proclaimed a "generation gap." Generational or cohort identities are clearly associated with the baby-boom, X, and Millennial cohorts. Each group has a sense of cohort identity that is frequently defined in relation, or opposition, to the others. It remains to be seen how the newest U.S. generation will be defined. But it is likely that they will in some way identify as coming of age in a post-September 11 society.

SUMMARY

One of the most important demographic trends of the 21st century will be the aging of the population. The transition to older age populations is a reflection of the combined trends of fertility reductions and increased life expectancies. The age-sex composition of a population is so important that many demographers simply refer to it as a population's "structure." In describing age or sex structure separately, demographers use familiar statistical techniques such as frequency distributions, percentages, and ratios. A particular kind of bar graph that handles age and sex simultaneously is the population pyramid.

Age and sex strongly influence the demographic processes. Demographers use age-sex-specific rates to describe age and sex differences in mortality, fertility, and migration. They also use specific rates to control the influence of age and sex while comparing the fertility or mortality of populations with different structures.

Countries of less-developed and more-developed regions generally have differing structures. Because of their higher fertility, LDRs continue to have younger populations and broader-based population pyramids. Fertility declines in the MDRs, and to a lesser degree declining elderly mortality, have aged their populations significantly and resulted in more rectangular population pyramids. Large variations in MDR population composition are usually due to intergenerational swings in fertility that show up as bulges or troughs working their way through population pyramids. Until very recently, mortality improvements for women were more extreme than those for men and have resulted in an increased feminizing of sex ratios throughout the life span, especially for MDRs.

Just as MDRs and LDRs differ with respect to their population structures, so do they differ in their resulting problems. For LDRs the overriding problem has been that of youth dependency; however, some have begun to take advantage of the demographic dividend that comes with fertility decline and the movement of the youth bulge into working ages. In a few high-population LDRs, sex-selection practices have led to gender-imbalanced populations.

The problems faced by MDRs are the converse. They are concerned about a workforce whose average age will increase along with that of the rest of the population. They also worry about the problem of old-age dependency and issues arising from the allocation of societal resources across an increasing variety of generations and cohort needs. Finally, because of fertility booms and busts, some MDRs also worry about providing for successive cohorts that vary greatly in size. Social resources like schools and healthcare facilities face the strains of adapting to changing cohort sizes.

On the individual level, members of a boom or bust cohort may face unique opportunities or shortages. The growing age diversity of MDRs and cohort identities formed from unique cohort experiences have simultaneously reinforced the cultural meaning and impact of age structures.

EXERCISES

1. Table E4-1 presents age frequency distributions for the projected 2020 population of India for men, women, and for both sexes together. Using these data, complete exercises a, b, and c by filling in the cells in the "India" column of Table E4-2 on the next page. Use the "Japan" column of that table as a model.

Table E4-1   Estimated Age-Sex Distribution of India Population, 2020

| | In Thousands | | |
| | Men | Women | Total |
Ages	(1)	(2)	(3)
All Ages[a]	698,768	654,536	1,353,306
0–4	63,084	56,925	120,009
5–9	63,664	57,257	120,921
10–14	62,673	56,331	119,004
Subtotal, 0–14	189,421	170,513	359,934
15–19	63,704	57,370	121,075
20–24	61,891	55,905	117,796
25–29	59,837	54,441	114,277
30–34	56,699	52,611	109,311
35–39	51,682	48,375	100,057
40–44	46,219	43,745	89,964
45–49	40,160	38,327	78,487
50–54	35,431	34,208	69,638
55–59	29,859	29,292	59,151
60–64	24,159	24,242	48,402
Subtotal, 15–64	469,641	438,516	908,158
65–69	17,945	18,685	36,629
70–74	10,346	11,946	22,292
75–79	6,185	7,689	13,875
80–84	3,242	4,408	7,650
85–89	1,373	1,937	3,310
90–94	469	649	1,118
95–99	120	161	282
100+	26	32	58
Subtotal, 65+	39,706	45,507	85,214

[a]Since entries for particular age categories are rounded to thousands, they may not add up precisely to the subtotals and totals presented.

Source: Data from United Nations, 2013. *World Population Prospects: The 2012 Revision, Detailed Indicators.*

a. Compute the percentages of both sexes combined under fifteen years of age, fifteen through sixty-four, and sixty-five years and over. Round the percentages to two decimal places and enter these percentages in the spaces provided in Table E4-2 on the next page.

Table E4-2   Estimated Age-Sex Structure of Japan and India, 2020

Measure	Japan	India
Percent of Total Population		
Under 15	12.63	
15–64	58.76	
65 and over	28.61	
Age Dependency Ratio	70.19	
Sex Ratio at Ages		
Under 15	105.45	
15–64	102.02	
65 and over	75.99	

Source: Data from United Nations, 2013. *World Population Prospects: The 2012 Revision, Detailed Indicators.*

b. Compute the sex ratios for each of the three age categories, round to two decimal places, and enter in the spaces provided in Table E4-2. The formula for the sex ratio is

$$\frac{\text{Men}}{\text{Women}} \times 100$$

c. Compute the age-dependency ratio for both sexes together, round to one decimal place, and enter in the space provided in Table E4-2. The formula for the age-dependency ratio is

$$\frac{P_{0-14} + P_{65+}}{P_{15-64}} \times 100$$

2. Table E4-3 classifies the projected population of India for 2050 by age and sex. Construct a population pyramid from these data, taking the following steps:

a. In the columns provided, enter the missing percentages. Remember that these percentages have as their denominators the total population of *both sexes*.

b. On the graph provided (Figure E4-1 on p. 138), draw a population pyramid, using the percentages in columns 3 and 4. Shade the area within the pyramid. Alternatively, you can construct the pyramid in Excel by following instructions here:

http://prb.org/Publications/Lesson-Plans/PopulationPyramidsExcelPPT.aspx

3. How would the Indian population pyramid for 2050 have differed from the one above if the assumptions employed had differed in the following ways?

a. If fertility had remained higher from 2020 to 2050, the average age of the population would have been

_____ younger

_____ older

_____ the same

Table E4-3   Estimated Age-Sex Distribution of India Population, 2050

| Ages | In Thousands | | Percentages | |
	Men (1)	Women (2)	Men (3)	Women (4)
All Ages	827,446	792,606	51.08	48.92
0–4	53,495	49,482	3.30	3.05
5–9	54,775	50,638	3.38	3.13
10–14	56,327	51,858	3.48	
15–19	57,852	52,971	3.57	
20–24	59,260	53,976	3.66	
25–29	60,315	54,767	3.72	
30–34	60,617	55,001	3.74	3.40
35–39	60,842	55,372	3.76	3.42
40–44	59,122	54,162	3.65	3.34
45–49	58,907	54,647	3.64	3.37
50–54	55,519	52,513		3.24
55–59	51,195	49,880		3.08
60–64	44,849	45,958	2.77	2.84
65–69	35,902	38,795	2.22	
70–74	26,189	30,241	1.62	
75–79	16,697	20,755	1.03	1.28
80–84	9,355	12,598		0.78
85–89	4,227	6,060		0.37
90–94	1,515	2,241	0.09	0.14
95–99	407	583	0.03	0.04
100+	79	108		0.01

Source: Data from United Nations, 2013. *World Population Prospects: The 2012 Revision, Detailed Indicators.*

   b. If mortality had declined to even lower levels and in equal proportion at all ages, the average age of the population would have been

      _____ younger

      _____ older

      _____ the same

4. Practice constructing age-sex-specific rates for death. Table E4-4 on p. 139 presents the necessary data for U.S. women in 2011. For each age category, column 1 tells how many women of that age died in 2011, column 2 tells the estimated number of women of that age there were to die in 2011, and column 3 tells the age-sex-specific death rate (per thousand women). Thus, to get the rate for the 5–14 row, the 2,214 deaths were divided by the 2,012,727 existing women and then multiplied by 1,000, producing a death rate of 0.11 per thousand women. Compute rates for the three rows where rates have been omitted. (Refer to Box 4-2 for an explanation of age-sex-specific rates.)

Figure E4-1

Graph for Exercise 2(b)

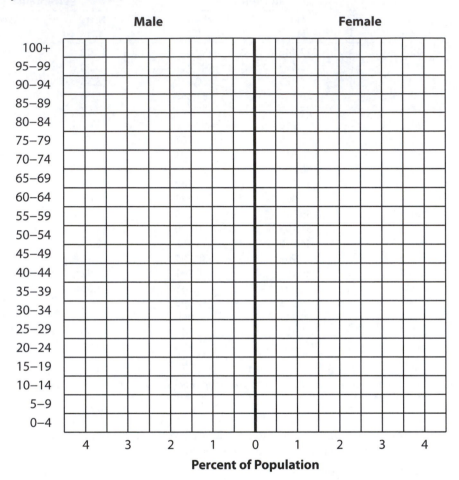

5. Calculate the implications of age-sex-specific death rates found in Table E4-4. Where the number of deaths has been omitted from column 1, multiply the death rate by the population and divide by 1000 to estimate the number of deaths which would have produced the given death rate.

Table E4-4   Computing Age-Sex Specific Death Rates for U.S. Women, 2011

Ages	Deaths (1)	Population (2)	Rate per Thousand (3)
Under 1	10,651	195,288	5.45
1–4	1,843	790,987	
5–14	2,214	2,012,727	0.11
15–24		2,135,359	0.36
25–34		2,074,277	0.66
35–44	26,594	2,040,982	1.30
45–54	71,442	2,270,162	
55–64	126,591	1,970,288	6.42
65–74	180,690	1,200,518	15.05
75–84	313,317	760,220	
85+	504,720	384,314	131.33

Source: Hoyert and Xu, 2012. "Deaths: Preliminary Data for 2011." *National Vital Statistics Reports.*

PROPOSITIONS FOR DEBATE

1. The "problem" of youth dependency in the LDRs is an illusion, based on an ethnocentric Western view of the proper roles for children.

2. The main reason for the aging of the U.S. population since 1900 has been the overall decline in mortality.

3. Given a choice, it would be nicer to belong to a small cohort than to a large cohort.

4. The U.S. view of "the elderly" as a marginalized minority will change as the baby-boom generation experiences retirement age.

5. If one is concerned about youth dependency in the LDRs and old-age dependency in the MDRs, a rational policy would be to encourage more international migration from the former to the latter.

6. If one recent cause of aging in the U.S. population has been reduction of death rates at the older ages, then a rational solution would be to stop spending scarce medical resources on old-age diseases.

7. The gender birth ratio imbalance in some countries due to sex-selection technologies will correct itself because the future dearth of women will naturally make girls and women more valued.

REFERENCES AND SUGGESTED READINGS

AARP. 1989. "Business and Older Workers: Current Perceptions and New Directions for the 1990s." Report issued by the American Association of Retired Persons, Washington, DC.

Agbor, Julius, Olumide Taiwo, and Jessica Smith. 2012. "Sub-Saharan Africa's Youth Bulge: A Demographic Dividend or Disaster?" *Africa Growth Initiative.* Washington, DC: The Brookings Institution.

Bell, D. N., and D. G. Blanchflower. 2011. "Young People and the Great Recession." *Oxford Review of Economic Policy* 27(2): 241–267.

Bloom, David E., David Canning, and Jaypee Sevilla. 2003. *The Demographic Dividend: A New Perspective on the Economic Consequences of Population Change*. Santa Monica, CA: RAND.

Bogue, Donald. 1993. "The Components Method of Forecasting: Rationale." In Bogue, Arriaga, and Anderton, eds., *Readings in Population Research Methodology*. United Nations Fund for Population Activities. Chicago: Social Development Center.

Bogue, Donald, Eduardo Arriaga, and Douglas L. Anderton, eds. 1993. *Readings in Population Research Methodology*. United Nations Fund for Population Activities. Chicago: Social Development Center.

Bouvier, Leon F. 1980. "America's Baby Boom Generation: The Fateful Bulge." *Population Bulletin* 35(1). Washington, DC: Population Reference Bureau.

Bouvier, Leon F., and Carol J. De Vita. 1991. "The Baby Boom—Entering Midlife." *Population Bulletin* 46(3). Washington, DC: Population Reference Bureau.

Coale, Ansley J. 1972. *The Growth of Human Populations: A Mathematical Investigation*. Princeton, NJ: Princeton University Press.

Cohn, D'Vera, and Paul Taylor. 2010. "Baby Boomers Approach 65 – Glumly: Survey Findings about America's Largest Generation." Retrieved June 2013. http://www.pewsocialtrends.org/files/2010/12/Boomer-Summary-Report-FINAL.pdf

Congressional Budget Office (CBO). 2011. *CBO's 2011 Long-Term Budget Outlook*. Retrieved July 17, 2013. http://www.cbo.gov/sites/default/files/cbofiles/attachments/06-21-Long-Term_Budget_Outlook.pdf

Dehne, Karl, and Gabriele Riedner. 2005. "Sexually Transmitted Infections among Adolescents: The Need for Adequate Health Services." Geneva, Switzerland: World Health Organization. http://www.who.int/maternal_child_adolescent/documents/9241562889/en/

DiCecio, Riccardo, Kristie M. Engemann, Michael T. Owyang, and Christopher H. Wheeler. 2008. "Changing Trends in the Labor Force: A Survey." *Federal Reserve Bank of St. Louis Review* 90(1): 47-62.

Easterlin, Richard. 1980. *Birth and Fortune: The Impact of Numbers on Personal Welfare*. New York: Basic Books.

Edmonston, Barry, and Charles Schultze, eds. 1995. *Modernizing the U.S. Census*. Washington, DC: National Academy Press.

European Commission. 2013. *EU Employment and Social Situation, Quarterly Review. Special Supplement on Demographic Trends*. Retrieved July 2013. http://ec.europa.eu/social/BlobServlet?docId=9934&langId=en

Ewbank, Douglas C. 1981. "Typical Patterns of Distortion in Reported Age Distributions." In *Age Misreporting and Age Selective Under-Enumeration: Sources, Patterns and Consequences for Demographic Analysis*. Washington, DC: National Academy Press.

Federal Interagency Forum on Aging-Related Statistics. 2012. *Older Americans 2012: Key Indicators of Well-Being*. Washington, DC: U.S. GPO.

Freedman, Marc. 1999. *Prime Time: How Baby Boomers Will Revolutionize Retirement and Transform America*. New York: PublicAffairs.

Friedlander, Dov, and Ruth Klinov Malul. 1983. "The Aging Society and Economic Burden." *Intercom* 11(1–2).

Fry, Richard, D'Vera Cohn, Gretchen Livingston, and Paul Taylor. 2011. "The Rising Age Gap in Economic Well-Being: The Old Prosper Relative to the Young." *Pew Research Social & Demographic Trends*. Retrieved June 21, 2013. http://www.pewsocialtrends.org/2011/11/07/the-rising-age-gap-in-economic-well-being/#overview

Gendell, Murray. 2008. "Older Workers: Increasing Their Labor Force Participation and Hours of Work." *Monthly Labor Review* (January): 41–54.

Gilles, Kate, and Charlotte Feldman-Jacobs. 2012. "When Technology and Tradition Collide: From Gender Bias to Sex Selection." Population Reference Bureau, Policy Brief. http://www.prb.org/pdf12/gender-bias-sex-selection.pdf

Government of Japan. 2012. *Kourei Shakai Hakusho (White Paper on the Aging Society)*. Office for Policies on Cohesive Society, Cabinet Office. Tokyo: Government of Japan. http://www8.cao.go.jp/kourei/whitepaper/w-2012/zenbun/index.html

Gribble, James N., and Jason Bremner. 2012. "Achieving a Demographic Dividend." *Population Bulletin* 67(2).

Guilmoto, Christophe. 2012. *Sex Imbalances at Birth: Trends, Consequences, and Policy Implications*. Bangkok, Thailand: UNFPA Asia and the Pacific Regional Office.

Gustman, A. L., T. L. Steinmeier, and N. Tabatabai. 2011. *How Did the Recession of 2007–2009 Affect the Wealth and Retirement of the Near-Retirement-Age Population in the Health and Retirement Study?* (No. w17547). National Bureau of Economic Research.

Hill, Kenneth H. 1987. "Estimating Census and Death Registration Completeness." *Asian and Pacific Population Forum* 1(3).

Hogan, Howard. 1993. "The 1990 Post-Enumeration Survey: Operations and Results." *Journal of the American Statistical Association* 88(423).

Hoyert, Donna L., and Jiaquan Xu. 2012. "Deaths: Preliminary Data for 2011." *National Vital Statistics Reports* 61(6). Hyattsville, MD: National Center for Health Statistics.

International Union for the Scientific Study of Population (IUSSP). 1982. *Multilingual Demographic Dictionary*. Liege, Belgium: Ordina Editions.

Jacobsen, Linda A., Mary Kent, Marlene Lee, and Mark Mather. 2011. "America's Aging Population." *Population Bulletin* 66(1). Washington, DC: Population Reference Bureau.

Johnson, Richard W., Mauricio Soto, and Sheila R. Zedlewski. 2008. "How Is the Economic Turmoil Affecting Older Americans?" *Urban Institute Fact Sheet on Retirement Policy*. Washington DC: Urban Institute.

Keidanren. 2008. "Jinkou Genshou ni Taioushita Keizai Shakai no Arikata (Economic System That Corresponds to the Population Decline)." *Chousa Houkoku (Survey Reports)*. Tokyo: Keidanren. http://www.keidanren.or.jp/japanese/policy/2008/073.pdf

Khan, Haider A. 1997. *Technology, Energy and Development: The South Korean Transition*. Cheltenham, UK: Edward Elgar.

———. 2004. *Interpreting East Asian Growth and Innovation: The Future of Miracles*. New York: Palgrave Macmillan.

Kristof, Nicholas D., and Sheryl WuDunn. 2010. *Half the Sky: Turning Oppression into Opportunity for Women Worldwide*. New York: Vintage Books.

Lesthaeghe, R. 2010. "The Unfolding Story of the Second Demographic Transition." *Population and Development Review* 36(2): 211–251.

Macunovich, D. J. 2000. "Relative Cohort Size: Source of a Unifying Theory of Global Fertility Transition?" *Population and Development Review* 26(2): 235–261.

———. 2012. "Relative Cohort Size, Relative Income, and Married Women's Labor Force Participation: United States, 1968–2010." *Population and Development Review* 38(4), 631–648.

Martin, Philip, and Jonas Widgren. 2002. "International Migration: Facing the Challenge." *Population Bulletin* 57(1). Washington, DC: Population Reference Bureau.

Myers, Robert J. 1940. "Errors and Bias in the Reporting of Ages in Census Data." *Transactions of the Actuarial Society of America* 41(2): 104.

Neumark, David. 2009. "The Age Discrimination in Employment Act and the Challenge of Population Aging." *Research on Aging* 31: 41-68.

Noble, Jeanne, Jane Cover, and Machiko Yanagishita. 1996. "The World's Youth 1996." Washington, DC: Population Reference Bureau.

Parker, Kim. 2012. "The Big Generation Gap at the Polls Is Echoed in Attitudes on Budget Trad-eoffs: But Public Sees Only Modest Conflict between Young and Old." *Pew Research Social & Demographic Trends*. Retrieved June 21, 2013. http://www.pewsocialtrends.org/2012/12/20/the-big-generation-gap-at-the-polls-is-echoed-in-attitudes-on-budget-tradeoffs/

PRB (Population Reference Bureau). 2010. "China's Rapidly Aging Population." *Today's Research on Aging* 20. http://www.prb.org/pdf10/TodaysResearchAging20.pdf

———. 2011. "America's Aging Population." *Population Bulletin* 66(10). Washington, DC: Population Reference Bureau. http://www.prb.org/pdf11/aging-in-america.pdf

———. 2012. *2012 World Population Data Sheet*. Washington, DC: Population Reference Bureau.

Preston, Samuel H., Patrick Heuveline, and Michel Guillot. 2001. *Demography: Measuring and Modeling Population Processes*. Oxford: Blackwell.

Rivlin, Alice M. 2009. "Budget Policy Challenges." *Testimony*. January 27, 2009. Retrieved June 21, 2013. http://www.brookings.edu/research/testimony/2009/01/27-budget-rivlin.

Robinson, J. G., P. D. Gupta, and R. A. Woodrow. 1993. "Estimation of Population Coverage in the 1990 United States Census Based on Demographic Analysis." *Journal of the American Statistical Association* 88(423).

Roscigno, Vincent, J. 2010. "Ageism in the American Workplace." *Contexts* 9:16-21.

Ross, John A. 1982. "Rates and Ratios." In John A. Ross, ed., *International Encyclopedia of Population*. New York: Free Press.

Sanderson, Warren, and Sergei Scherbov. 2008. "Rethinking Age and Aging." *Population Bulletin* 63(4). Washington, DC: Population Reference Bureau.

Seike, Atsushi. 2010. "An Economic Analysis of Age Discrimination: The Impact of Mandatory Retirement and Age Limitations in Hiring on the Utilization of Human Resources in an Ageing Society." In S. Tuljapurkar, N. Ogawa, and A. H. Gauthier, eds., *Ageing in Advanced Industrial States: International Studies in Population*, Vol. 8: 311-324. New York: Springer.

Shryock, Henry S., Jacob S. Siegel, and Associates. 1976. *The Methods and Materials of Demography*. Condensed edition by Edward Stockwell. New York: Academic Press.

Smith, David M., and Gary J. Gates. 2001 (August). "Gay and Lesbian Families in the United States: Same-Sex Unmarried Partner Households." Washington, DC: Human Rights Campaign.

Statistics Japan. 2012. "Nihon no Chouki Toukei Keiretsu (Historical Statistics of Japan)." *Sougou Toukeisho (Summary of Survey Results)*. Retrieved April 25, 2013. http://www.stat.go.jp/data/sougou/index.htm

Stolnitz, George J. 1956. "Mortality Declines and Age Distribution." *Milbank Memorial Fund Quarterly* 34(2).

———. 1982. "Mortality: Post–World War II Trends." In John A. Ross, ed., *International Encyclopedia of Population*. New York: The Free Press.

Treas, Judith, and Ramon Torrecilha. 1995. "The Older Population." In Reynolds Farley, ed., *State of the Union: America in the 1990s*. Vol. II. New York: Russell Sage Foundation.

United Nations. 2008. *Principles and Recommendations for Population and Housing Censuses, Revision 2*. Series M, No. 7/Rev.2. New York: United Nations.

———. 2009. *Trends in International Migrant Stock: The 2008 Revision*. Population Division, POP/DB/MIG/Stock/Rev.2008. New York: United Nations.

———. 2011. *Population Dynamics in the Least Developed Countries: Challenges and Opportunities for Development and Poverty Reduction*. Technical Division. New York: United Nations.

———. 2012. *2011 Demographic Yearbook*. ST/ESA/STAT/SER.R/41

———. 2013. *World Population Prospects: The 2012 Revision, Detailed Indicators*. Retrieved June 21, 2013. http://esa.un.org/wpp/unpp/panel_indicators.htm

U.S. Bureau of Labor Statistics. 2013. *Databases, Tables & Calculators by Subject*. Retrieved April 22, 2013. http://www.bls.gov/data/

U.S. Census Bureau. 2001. *Resident Population Estimates of the U.S. by Age and Sex: April 1, 1990 to July 1, 1999.* http://www.census.gov/popest/data/national/totals/1990s/tables/nat-agesex.txt

———. 2004a. *Coverage Measurement from the Perspective of March 2001 Accuracy and Coverage Evaluation.* Census 2000 Topic Report no. 4, Census 2000 Testing, Experimentation, and Evaluation Program, T4-4. Washington, DC: GPO.

———. 2004b. *National Estimates by Age, Sex, Race: 1900-1979.* http://www.census.gov/popest/data/national/asrh/pre-1980/PE-11.html

———. 2008. *2010 Census Coverage Measurement Estimation Methodology.* DSSD 2010 Census Coverage Measurement Memorandum Series #2010-E-18. Washington, DC: Decennial Statistical Studies Division.

———. 2009. *National Population Projections July 1, 2000 to July 1, 2050: Zero Net International Migration Series.* http://www.census.gov/population/projections/data/

———. 2011a. *Age and Sex Composition: 2010.* http://www.census.gov/prod/cen2010/briefs/c2010br-03.pdf

———. 2011b. *Statistical Abstract of the United States, 2012.* Washington, DC: GPO.

———. 2012a. *Historical Poverty Tables – People: Table 3: Poverty Status, by Age, Race and Hispanic Origin.* http://www.census.gov/hhes/www/poverty/data/historical/people.html

———. 2012b. "Most Children Younger Than Age 1 are Minorities, Census Bureau Reports." *Newsroom Releases.* Retrieved June 21, 2013. http://www.census.gov/newsroom/releases/archives/population/cb12-90.html

———. 2012c. *Projections of the Population by Age and Sex for the United States: 2015 to 2060.* http://www.census.gov/population/projections/data/national/2012/summarytables.html

———. 2013a. *International Programs: International Data Base.* Retrieved April 26, 2013. http://www.census.gov/population/international/data/idb/informationGateway.php

———. 2013b. *Net Worth and Asset Ownership of Households: 2010.* http://www.census.gov/people/wealth/files/Wealth_Tables_2010.xls

U.S. Department of Health and Human Services (DHHS). 2013. *Aging Statistics: Projected Future Growth of Older Population.* Retrieved April 22, 2013. http://aoa.gov/AoARoot/Aging_Statistics/future_growth/future_growth.aspx

U.S. Social Security Administration. 2012. *A Summary of the 2012 Annual Reports.* Social Security and Medicare Boards of Trustees. http://www.ssa.gov/oact/trsum/

Van Horn, Carl E., Nicole Corre, and Maria Heidkamp. 2011. "Older Workers, the Great Recession, and the Impact of Long-Term Unemployment." *John J. Heldrich Center for Workforce Development, Research Brief.* Retrieved July 17, 2013. http://www.heldrich.rutgers.edu/sites/default/files/content/Heldrich_Center_Older_Workers_Brief.pdf

Visaria, Leela, and Pravin Visaria. 1995. "India's Population in Transition." *Population Bulletin* 50(3). Washington, DC: Population Reference Bureau.

WHO (World Health Organization). 2010. *Trends in Maternal Mortality: 1990 to 2008.* Geneva: World Health Organization.

Wolter, Kirk M. 1986. "Some Coverage Error Models for Census Data." *Journal of the American Statistical Association* 81(394).

World Bank. 2006. *Gender Equality as Smart Economics: A World Bank Group Gender Action Plan, Fiscal Years 2007-10.* Washington, DC: World Bank.

Yi, Zeng, and Linda George. 1999. "Extremely Rapid Ageing and the Living Arrangements of Older Persons: The Case of China." Population Division, UN/POP/AGE/2000/8.

Zickuhr, Kathryn. 2011. "Generations and Their Gadgets." *Pew Internet & American Life Project* 20.

5

Mortality

In chapter 3 (on population growth), we were introduced to the "demographic transition" that has swept through the more-developed countries and is sweeping through the less-developed countries. According to that model, demographic transitions are heralded by gradual, then rapid, declines in mortality, followed by declines in fertility. Thus it is the drop in national mortality, not a rise in fertility, that has led to the rapid population growth that characterizes recent human history. This chapter focuses on describing and analyzing such mortality transitions.

First we will take some time to acquaint the reader with two measures of mortality: average life expectancy and infant mortality rates. These are the ones used most in international comparisons. Any mortality measure—these included—requires a count of deaths.

Measuring Mortality via Life Expectancy

Mortality, as we have said before, is one of the three processes that determine the pace of population growth, the others being fertility and migration. Demographers collectively call them the components of population growth. The pace of each of these processes is determined by the frequency of its relevant event. The event determining fertility is birth; for migration it is change of residence; for mortality it is death (not including fetal death). **Mortality**, then, refers to the frequency with which deaths occur.

Counting Deaths

In Western countries, civil registration has been the dominant system for counting deaths (see chapter 2). Ideally, each event is recorded as it occurs, along with certain characteristics of the deceased (e.g., age, sex) and of the death itself (e.g., cause). This information is funneled to statistical centers for tallying. As a result, there are often delays in obtaining mortality data. And even in more-developed countries, civil registration of vital events has been less complete than counting people in censuses; therefore, MDR demographers normally use census data to estimate the degree of underenumeration of deaths. LDR civil registration is even less complete (United Nations, 2013a; Siegel and Swanson, 2004; Bogue et al., 1993, vol. 2; Shryock and Siegel, 1976).

What kinds of errors occur? One kind is not counting a death at all. Infant deaths are most likely to go unrecorded. If the infant lives a very short time, there is a strong tendency to register neither the birth nor the death, perhaps to forget the whole tragic affair.

Even if all deaths do get registered, they can be misallocated in place and time. In urbanized countries especially, there is a tendency to register a death at the location of the hospital where it took place rather than the residence of the victim, or to register sudden deaths that occurred away from home at the place of occurrence rather than the place of residence. Where administrative systems are not well developed and the death is not registered until after some delay, there may be a temptation to record the time of the death as the time of registration rather than the time of occurrence.

Because of the extreme difficulty of running a civil death registration system well, many LDR countries rely on other data services. One involves registration but confines it to a sample of areas in the nation. Another source is sample surveys, usually asking retrospectively about all deaths that occurred within a specified, short time interval. A third method is a combination of a sample registration system and sample surveys such that we can estimate the degree of undercounting and reporting errors resulting from either source alone (Phuong Hoa et al., 2012; Vallin and Meslé, 1990, part I; Krotki, 1978).

Computing and Interpreting Life Expectancy

Let us be optimistic and suppose, for the moment, that we have ideal death data for a country; that is, let us suppose that we not only have a complete count of deaths by year, but also that we know the age and sex of each person at death. Let us also assume that we have a good estimate of the total population by year as well as the age-sex breakdown of that total. If we had all this, then we would be in a position to compute not only the crude death rates (see chapter 1) but also the age-sex-specific death rates (see chapter 4).

Both of these rates have their uses; both have their limitations. Although a crude death rate summarizes the mortality of an entire population in a single figure, it is influenced by the age-sex structure of the population. The strengths and weaknesses of age-sex-specific death rates are just the opposite: they are not influenced by the structure of the population, but it takes many of them to describe the population's mortality.

Wouldn't it be convenient if we had a measure of a population's mortality that avoided both of these limitations, and that presented a single figure not influenced by the age-sex structure of the population? **Life expectancy at birth** is such a measure.

To comprehend it, however, we need to consider not only the concept of mortality but also two related concepts: survival and longevity. A death rate measures mortality, or the risk of dying in a given year. The opposite of death is **survival.** Demographers sometimes construct survival rates, assigning the probability of avoiding death through a given year. Closely related to the idea of survival is the idea of **longevity**, the age at which one dies. Individually, one's longevity is determined by how many years one escapes (survives) death. Collectively, the average age at which a cohort of people dies is determined by its rate of death (or survival of death from age to age through its collective lifetime).

Most of us intuitively grasp this connection between a sequence of annual risks of death and average longevity. Therefore, we are prepared to use longevity itself as a way of summarizing complex information about age-specific mortality. This is what we do when we combine information contained in age-specific death rates into a measure of average life expectancy.

Life expectancy is a hypothetical figure. The mental game involved in computing it is as follows: Start with a given set of age-specific death rates for one of the sexes (life expectancy figures normally are computed separately for the two sexes due to differing mortality rates). Then conjure up an imaginary set of people and put them through a lifetime of mortality risks and resulting attrition as described by that series (or "schedule") of age-specific death rates. That is, construct a **hypothetical** or **synthetic cohort** and trace how it would shrink if it had the mortality history described in some particular schedule of age-specific death rates. Finally, note the average age at which cohort members are likely to die. This is their (average) life expectancy at birth.

Demographers use **life tables** for tracing such imaginary mortality histories. Table 5-1 on the following page gives an illustration. The life expectancy figures are those found in column 7, and the life expectancy at birth (i.e., at age zero) is the topmost figure in that column, 79.05 years. This means that, if a cohort of women actually experienced the sequence of age-specific (female) mortality rates listed in column 2, the mean age at which they would have died would be 79.05 years.

There are some important features of life tables and the life expectancy figures that result from them. First, everything in the table is generated from the schedule of age-specific death rates. Column 2 expresses these rates in terms of risks of dying (by age); all subsequent columns are derived solely from column 2. No additional information is used to arrive at column 7 (life expectancy by age), meaning nothing else has influenced the figures in column 7. That is why we can say that life expectancy figures are not influenced by age structures of populations. That is also why we say that life tables assume no net migration; migration (normally) is not allowed to add or subtract from age categories as the synthetic cohort passes through.

Second, the mortality assumptions employed in constructing any given life table are hypothetical—and probably unrealistic. There probably never will be a birth cohort that experiences precisely the schedule of age-specific death rates employed in the table. The purpose is to describe the implications of mortality during a given year, not to describe a real cohort's life experiences.

Third, life expectancy statements can be made for any age. Expectancy at birth, or at age zero (e_0), is influenced by the entire series of age-specific death rates following birth and therefore is the most frequently used. On the other hand, sometimes one needs to focus on mortality at later stages in life. It may be of interest to a life insurance company, for instance, that according to the Argentinian female life table (Table 5-1), women aged sixty-five still have 19.18 more years of life expectancy, on the average. (Incidentally, it was from life insurance actuaries that demographers borrowed the life table model and the resulting measure of life expectancy by age.) And, as we discussed in chapter 4, calculating life expectancy at older ages is likely to become a more accurate way to gauge a population's old-age dependency level than going by the proportion of people sixty-five and older.

Becoming comfortable with the use of life tables depends on understanding how they are built. That, in turn, is best learned by building them. For that reason, we have included an exercise at the end of this chapter (and on www.demographytextbook.com) that first describes the steps in constructing a life table and then gives the reader practice in filling in blank spaces in such a table. You can use the exercise to understand the details of how the life table in Table 5-1 was constructed. Resist the temptation to skip over this exercise; you will find us referring back to it.

Table 5-1   Female Life Table, Argentina, 2011

Age Interval[a] x to $x+n$ (1)	Proportion Dying[b] $_nq_x$ (2)	Number Living at Beginning of Age Interval (of 100,000 born alive) l_x (3)	Number Dying During Age Interval (of 100,000 born alive) $_nd_x$ (4)	Person-Years Lived In the Age Interval $_nL_x$ (5)	Person-Years Lived in This and All Subsequent Age Intervals T_x (6)	Average Remaining Lifetime[c] e_x (7)
<1	0.01133	100,000.00	1,132.71	98,980.56	7,905,209.00	79.05
1–4	0.00136	98,867.29	134.84	395,145.50	7,806,228.00	78.96
5–9	0.00094	98,732.45	92.85	493,430.10	7,411,083.00	75.06
10–14	0.00126	98,639.59	124.42	492,886.90	6,917,653.00	70.13
15–19	0.00219	98,515.18	215.30	492,037.70	6,424,766.00	65.22
20–24	0.00253	98,299.88	248.54	490,878.00	5,932,728.00	60.35
25–29	0.00284	98,051.34	278.39	489,560.70	5,441,850.00	55.50
30–34	0.00390	97,772.94	381.60	487,910.70	4,952,290.00	50.65
35–39	0.00553	97,391.34	538.99	485,609.20	4,464,379.00	45.84
40–44	0.00825	96,852.34	798.80	482,264.70	3,978,770.00	41.08
45–49	0.01309	96,053.54	1,256.89	477,125.50	3,496,505.00	36.40
50–54	0.01950	94,796.65	1,848.89	469,361.00	3,019,380.00	31.85
55–59	0.02982	92,947.76	2,771.32	457,810.50	2,550,019.00	27.43
60–64	0.04519	90,176.44	4,075.02	440,694.70	2,092,208.00	23.20
65–69	0.06609	86,101.42	5,690.24	416,281.50	1,651,514.00	19.18
70–74	0.10172	80,411.18	8,179.05	381,608.30	1,235,232.00	15.36
75–79	0.16232	72,232.13	11,724.76	331,848.80	853,623.70	11.82
80–84	0.28687	60,507.38	17,357.67	259,142.70	521,774.90	8.62
85–89	0.46130	43,149.70	19,905.13	165,985.70	262,632.20	6.09
90–94	0.63037	23,244.58	14,652.66	72,264.90	96,646.52	4.16
95–99	0.75889	8,591.91	6,520.28	20,138.60	24,381.62	2.84
100+	1.00000	2,071.64	2,071.64	4,243.02	4,243.02	2.05

[a] Period of life between two exact ages, stated in years.
[b] Proportion of persons alive at beginning of age interval who die during interval.
[c] Average number of years of life remaining at beginning of age interval.

Source: WHO Global Health Observatory (GHO), 2013a. Permission granted by World Health Organization, Geneva, Switzerland.

One drawback of life expectancy as a mortality measure is that it requires ideal data; that is, it requires full reporting of deaths by age and sex of the person dying. Few LDR countries have such data. This means that demographers have to develop sophisticated estimation procedures to fill the gap. Some of these procedures are described in Box 5-1.

Box 5-1

Estimating Life Expectancy

Most MDR countries gather the data necessary for constructing life tables and estimating life expectancy. But many LDRs are still less likely to have any comprehensive death registration system, much less one that records age or cause of death precisely. But they may have one or more censuses and even a sample survey, perhaps including a marital and family-building history (Silva, 2012; Vallin et al., 1990, part I; Shryock and Siegel, 1976). How can such limited data be used to estimate the age-sex-specific mortality information needed for a life table? Formal demography has developed techniques to do just this (Arriaga, 1994; Ewbank, 1990; Hill and Zlotnik, 1982). It would be confusing for us to attempt a detailed summary of these techniques here, but a few examples might illustrate the basic strategies involved.

The simplest situation arises when a country has a sequence of decennial censuses, each classifying the population by age and sex. In this circumstance, one can follow a birth cohort from the earlier census to the later one and measure its shrinkage. That shrinkage could only have been caused by age-sex-specific migration or mortality. If one knows enough about the migration pattern during the intercensal interval, one can infer what the age-sex-specific mortality must have been. We call this *direct* estimation.

A more complex situation arises when one has a single census or sample survey with incomplete information. In these data-deficient cases, one has to rely on *indirect* estimates of population characteristics. If some information about the population is available, and if we assume basic relationships among demographic measures are similar to some other populations around the world that we have observed, it may be possible to make very good guesses about other unobserved population characteristics.

An illustration is a technique developed by Brass (1975) and since modified by several others (see Arriaga, 1994; Silva, 2012). Suppose, as is frequently the case in censuses and/or surveys, women are asked (a) their own age, (b) how many children they have ever borne, and (c) how many of those children are still living. There is a logical relationship between these three factors and rates of infant and early childhood mortality. Obviously, a young woman who has borne many children but has few surviving has experienced high infant and childhood mortality among her offspring. The detailed pattern of these relationships already has been studied for countries where all factors are known; therefore, we can infer infant and child mortality rates from a few known factors.

Similar methods can use survey data about orphanhood and widowhood to estimate adult mortality (see Arriaga, 1994; Luy, 2012) and about sisterhood to estimate maternal mortality (see Simons et al., 1996) and adult mortality (Obermeyer et al., 2010). Still, any one of these indirect techniques is likely to provide death rates for only a few of the age categories. How do demographers fill in the figures for other categories?

(continued)

Empirical life tables have been accumulated for many countries over the years. These life tables demonstrate that age-specific mortality is highly predictable if we know the overall level of mortality in a population. These observed patterns have been generalized to serve as *model life tables* likely to be found at various levels of overall mortality (Coale and Demeny, 1966). We can use what is known about the mortality of a country—perhaps infant mortality or crude death rate—to determine which model table to use, then use other estimates from that table. We have made this sound much simpler than it is in practice, but the strategy is straightforward and model life tables are available in statistical data programming software (for example, see Stata Press, 2011).

Historical Mortality Transitions

Increases in Life Expectancy

In the more-developed regions.   Chapter 3 described, in broad strokes, the demographic transition that accompanied the modernization of the countries we now call "more-developed." Let us call the changes in MDR mortality and life expectancy during that era the **mortality transition** (sometimes called *the epidemiological transition*). We can divide it into three segments: a pretransitional segment of high mortality (before 1850), a transitional segment characterized by a decline in epidemic and infectious diseases (from 1850 to 1950), and a late-transition segment characterized by degenerative and human-made diseases (from 1950 to the present).

Demographic transition theory says that pretransitional mortality was high and variable from year to year. How high? In nomadic hunting and gathering societies, life expectancies were very low, with most mortality from accidents and tribal warfare (Horiuchi, 1999, although see Gurven and Kaplan, 2007). The transition to a more sedentary, agrarian lifestyle reduced injury-related mortality but brought about greater risk of infectious disease arising from increased human population density. Fragmentary data imply that, from the 13th to 17th centuries, life expectancy among Europeans ranged from twenty to forty years. In Western Europe, there seems to have been a gradual improvement in the mid-1700s, with increases in life expectancies to thirty-five to forty years (Coale, 1986, figure 1.2), and over the next century a further increase of about ten years, to between forty and forty-five years in the mid-1800s (Anderson, 1996, p. 272). Thus, overall mortality had been edging gradually downward for a century or more, even before the rapid transition started in the later 1800s.

Now let us look at the second, transitional segment. Once mortality started to fall in a given country, it fell at an increasing pace for several decades, and life expectancy soared accordingly. Figure 5-1 shows the increasing improvements in life expectancy from 1840 to 2010 for six European countries on which we have reliable data: Belgium, Denmark, France, Netherlands, Norway, and Sweden. One can see that the improvement increased decade by decade in these countries, with the fastest rate of increase between 1940–1950.

Not all more-developed regions entered their mortality transitions at the same moment. Generally speaking, Northern and Western Europe, along with what might be

Figure 5-1

Life Expectancy in Six European Countries, 1840–2010

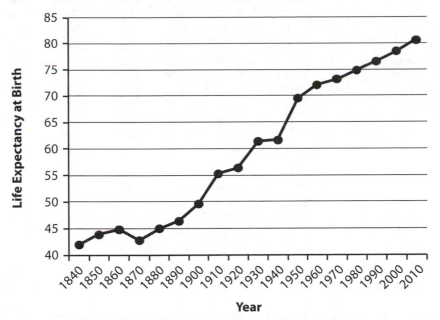

Source: Data from The Gapminder Foundation, 2013. Graph created by Eiko Strader.

called the "frontier areas" of North America, and Oceania seemed to have started earli-est. Western European mortality experienced a sustained decline in the late 18th cen-tury (Anderson, 1996); in the United States, this mortality decline began in the 1870s (Preston and Haines, 1991). Eastern and Southern Europe lagged behind (Schofield et al., 1991; United Nations, 1973). As a result of this staggered start, life expectancy ranged from forty to sixty years of age across Europe in the early 20th century (Vallin, 1991, table 3.1).

By 1950 life expectancy in all of Europe had increased to more than sixty-five years of age (see Table 5-2). During the late-transition (third) segment, improvement in life expectancy among the leading countries continued, but at a slower pace. Since 1950 there has been an improvement of about nine years in life expectancy in both Europe and North America. Although the timing of MDR mortality declines varied, there has been considerable convergence among MDRs in the last few decades. As seen in Table 5-2 on the following page, the range in differences across life expectancies between North America, Europe, and Oceania for the period 2010–2020 is only about three years (less than half what it was in 1950). Of course, such national averages mask continuing socioeconomic and racial/ethnic differentials within countries.

The main point is that during the rapid MDR mortality transition—taking little more than a century—life expectancy at birth grew by more than 50%. Such a demo-graphic event was unprecedented in world history.

Table 5-2   Life Expectancy by World Region, 1950–2020

Region[a]	1950–1960 (1)	1960–1970 (2)	1970–1980 (3)	1980–1990 (4)	1990–2000 (5)	2000–2010 (6)	2010–2020[b] (7)
World	48.16	53.79	59.76	63.20	65.19	67.91	70.51
More Developed Regions	66.18	69.88	71.52	73.37	74.42	76.23	78.15
Less Developed Regions	42.88	49.41	56.88	60.83	63.21	66.15	68.84
North America	69.14	70.31	72.33	74.74	76.22	77.87	79.48
Oceania	61.45	64.46	67.28	70.54	73.12	76.06	77.98
Europe	65.32	69.60	70.82	72.23	72.82	74.52	76.51
Latin America & Caribbean	52.86	57.92	62.13	66.18	69.80	72.80	75.28
Asia	43.44	50.37	58.88	63.07	66.03	69.53	71.92
Africa	38.63	43.31	47.55	51.18	51.94	54.24	59.07

[a]Regions listed in order of decreasing 2010–2020 life expectancy.
[b]2010–2020 estimates are based on medium fertility variant.

Source: United Nations, 2013b. *World Population Prospects: The 2012 Revision, Mortality Tables.* Used with permission.

In the less-developed regions.   The LDRs also have begun such a mortality transition. Looking at Table 5-2 we see that over the past sixty years LDRs have lengthened life expectancy by twenty-six years, to levels approaching those of the MDRs in the 1960s. The LDRs, with much later mortality transitions, have gained some ground in catching up with the MDRs. The difference between MDRs and LDRs is still about nine years of life expectancy; but back in 1950 this difference was even greater—over twenty-three years of life.

The LDRs are even more different from one another than were the MDRs during their epidemiological transitions. Today, public health and modern medicine are known technologies that can be used when resources are available. Thus, LDR mortality declines are more likely to vary directly with the level of economic development across, and within, countries. As a result, most measures of regional mortality now distinguish between high mortality LDRs, such as sub-Saharan Africa, and low mortality LDRs, such as East Asia. To illustrate, life expectancy at birth for a Costa Rican woman is eighty-two years while a woman born in Botswana can expect to live an average of only forty-seven years (PRB, 2014).

Theoretically, mortality in the LDRs should achieve life expectancies similar to those of the MDRs (some Asian and Latin American countries already have). But unfortunately, new mortality threats such as HIV/AIDS will mean significant delay in some LDR mortality declines. And although it is difficult to predict the specific and multifaceted mortality impacts of future climate change, we know that it will affect LDR countries more intensely than MDRs (UNFPA, 2011). Despite these new mortality threats, the epidemiological transition is currently in progress worldwide.

The future of life expectancy.   The last century has seen incredible increases in life expectancy to average ages that no one would have dreamed possible throughout most of human history. The question is, have we finally reached our limit? There are two competing theories among demographers and biologists. The predominating demographic, medical, and biological theory is that reaching an average life expectancy past age eighty-five (currently, Japanese women have the longest average life expectancy at eighty-five) or so is beyond the limits of our biological capacity (Olshansky, 2011; Olshansky et al., 1990, 2001). Although there are rare examples of supercentenarians who go on to live ten years or more beyond age 100, these individuals are exceptions to the norm.

Others have speculated that there is no finite limit to human longevity. Arguments have been made that diet and caloric restriction can effectively slow the process of aging, resulting in life expectancies closer to around 150 years (Walford et al., 1999; Walford, 2000), and recent experiments on mice and rhesus monkeys seem to support this hypothesis (Anderson et al., 2009). It has been claimed by some that death itself is not biologically inevitable. Mortality has been selected for because it was evolutionarily advantageous; however, what is evolutionarily advantageous for humans is likely to change over time (Klarsfeld and Revah, 2003). Perhaps most important to consider is that even if life expectancy is extended, how will longer life spans affect the demography of the population and, furthermore, how will extended life spans affect quality of life for the elderly? Although there are some debates as to whether current life expectancies into the seventies and eighties have simply prolonged frailty and disability (e.g., morbidity, see chapter 6), recent studies show that people are aging in better health and will live even longer healthier lives (Vaupel, 2010).

Proximate Causes of Death

One can think of the causes of death as falling into two categories, based on how immediate their contribution to the death was. Thus, the most immediate—or **proximate**—causes of death are the ones that finally brought about the event: cancer, heart disease, murder, or whatever. Less immediate (*nonproximate*) causes are a whole host of factors that contributed to the death only in the sense that they increased the likelihood of experiencing one of the proximate causes. For instance, chemical pollution might increase the risk of cancer, smoking might increase the risk of heart disease, or living in a rough part of town might increase the risk of being murdered. When responsible authorities register the **cause of death** for medical and legal purposes, they are recording the proximate cause of death. Some readers may prefer to think of these categories as the biological (proximate) versus the cultural (nonproximate) causes of death.

Our strategy in this section is to deal first with the proximate and then the nonproximate causes; that is, we first describe the changes in the proximate causes of death that accompanied the mortality transitions, noting which proximate causes have been brought under control in the MDRs and those LDRs that are in an advanced stage of mortality decline. Then we address the question of what cultural (including medical) changes allowed these reduced proximate causes to be brought under control.

Ideally, civil registration of deaths includes registering the proximate causes of deaths; that is, whoever registers the death (such as a coroner) not only records the event of the death and the sex and age of the deceased, but also what that person died of. In reality, historical records of causes of death are extremely hard to come by. Usually we are limited, even in the MDRs, to a few local long-time series (such as the state of Massachusetts or the city of New York in the United States). Even then we are plagued by shifts in diagnostic terminology over time that threaten to invalidate many historical comparisons (Kunitz, 1991) or require reclassifying causes of death to a consistent standard (Vallin and Meslé, 1990). In addition, social biases complicate historical mortality analysis and cause-of-death classification (Anderton and Leonard, 2004).

Omran (1982) studied the incomplete evidence to find the general pattern of change in the causes-of-death profiles that have accompanied mortality transitions throughout the world. He identified three models of change: the *Western*, the *accelerated*, and the *delayed*. Most MDRs would be described by his Western model, in which mortality started to decline early and gradually. The accelerated model describes many countries in which rapid mortality declines began later, such as the remaining MDRs (e.g., Japan or Eastern Europe), and now those LDR countries already advanced in their mortality decline (e.g., Argentina, Brazil, Costa Rica, Cuba, Cyprus, Mauritius, Thailand, or Uruguay). The delayed model refers to most LDRs that are still at the early stages of mortality decline (e.g., much of Africa and some parts of Asia and Latin America). The Western and accelerated models differ primarily in the speed with which they occurred and only secondarily in terms of the shifts in the causes of deaths.

Omran says that the "epidemiologic transition" for the Western-model countries consisted of three stages. His labels for those stages summarize the dominant causes of death in each (Omran, 1977, p. 9):

1. The age of *pestilence* and *famine*. This precedes the mortality transition. Annual life expectancy at birth vacillates between twenty and forty years.

2. The age of *receding pandemics*. A **pandemic** is an outbreak of disease that involves large proportions of the population, devastating it briefly. The resulting peaks in the mortality curve become less lofty and less frequent as pandemics recede. Life expectancy increases steadily from about thirty to about fifty years and varies less from year to year.

3. The age of *degenerative* or *human-made diseases*. Life expectancy approaches stability at more than seventy years.

Figure 5-2 illustrates a particular example that follows the Western model: New York City from about the early 1800s to 1970. Through the mid-1800s, the crude death rate line is exceedingly jagged and each peak seems clearly identifiable with a specific outbreak of yellow fever, smallpox, or cholera. Through the later 1800s and the 1900s, the line both declines and becomes less jagged. People are being spared from these proximate causes of death, these infectious diseases, to succumb later to other less sporadic killers. During the early part of the period depicted, New York City probably had higher death rates than did much of the rest of the country, especially the rural areas. Cities were not the best places to survive disease outbreaks early in the demographic transition (see chapter 10).

Caselli (1991) estimated the gains in life expectancy won from the decline of infectious diseases during the MDR mortality transition. Table 5-3 shows the estimated years added to life expectancy of men and women due to declines in several specific causes of death during the mortality transitions of England and Wales, and of Italy. The last row of the table gives the total increase in life expectancy from changes in all causes of death. Column 1, for example, shows that male life expectancy in England and Wales increased by over 26 years between 1871 and 1951. The first row of the table

Figure 5-2

Epidemiological Transition in New York City, 1800–1970

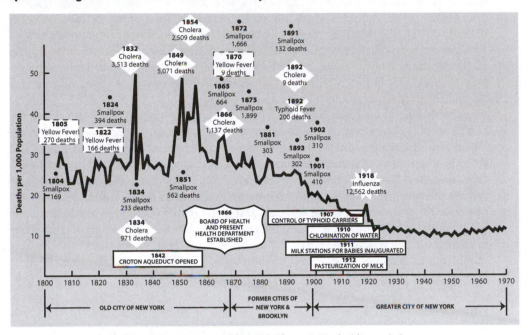

Source: Omran, 1977. "Epidemiological Transition in the U.S.," figure 3. Used with permission.

Table 5-3   Increased Years of Life Expectancy Due to Declines in Selected Causes of Death, England and Wales (1871–1951) and Italy (1881–1951)

Cause of Death	England and Wales		Italy	
	Males (1)	Females (2)	Males (3)	Females (4)
Infectious diseases	11.51	12.13	12.08	13.29
Bronchitis, pneumonia and influenza	3.47	3.78	4.74	4.64
Diarrhea and enteritis	2.01	2.01	3.13	3.72
Diseases of infancy and early childhood	1.82	1.77	2.47	2.16
Diseases of the circulatory system	0.36	0.86	0.52	1.07
Accidents	1.08	0.31	0.58	0.39
Neoplasms (incl. cancers)	−1.06	−0.46	−0.17	−0.21
Other causes	7.43	8.07	6.97	8.08
Total from all causes	**26.62**	**28.47**	**30.32**	**33.14**

Source: Caselli, 1991. "Health Transition and Cause-Specific Mortality," table 4.4.

shows the increase in life expectancy from declines in infectious disease. Looking again at the first column we can see that nearly half of the increase in male life expectancy in England and Wales, or 11.51 years, was due to declining infectious diseases. The decline of tuberculosis alone accounts for nearly four years of this added life (Caselli, 1991). The first four rows of the table are for epidemic or infectious diseases, which show a significant decline over the mortality transition. By the end of World War II, the mortality transition had created a new pattern of noninfectious degenerative or human-made diseases in MDRs that has remained relatively unchanged despite continuing increases in life expectancy (Caselli, 1991).

The decline of epidemic and infectious diseases over the mortality transition also can be seen by comparing causes-of-death profiles across world regions defined by the World Health Organization (WHO) in Figure 5-3. In Africa, the highest-mortality LDR, the percentage of deaths due to infectious diseases almost equals that of noncommunicable diseases. The most common infectious causes of death are HIV/AIDs, diarrheal-related diseases, tuberculosis, and malaria, as well as perinatal and maternal deaths associated with less adequate health care and high fertility (Lozano et al., 2012). Other LDR countries in Southeast Asia and the eastern Mediterranean that are further along in their mortality transitions have now begun to experience majorities of deaths from noninfectious diseases. By contrast, the lion's share of mortality in the primarily more

Figure 5-3

Comparable Percentage Causes-of-Death by WHO World Region, 2008

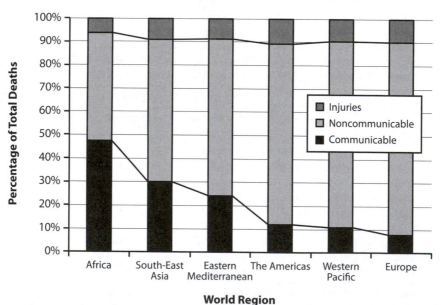

Note: Communicable diseases include maternal causes, conditions arising during the perinatal period, and nutritional deficiencies.

Source: World Health Organization, 2013b. World Health Statistics 2013.

developed regions of the Americas, the western Pacific, and Europe is caused by nonin-fectious, degenerative diseases. This includes diseases of the circulatory system, diabetes, cancers, and respiratory diseases. Four preventable behaviors are the primary causes of MDR diseases: smoking, overeating, over-consumption of alcohol, and physical inactivity (United Nations, 2012b).

Some demographers speculate that the more-developed regions are entering a new stage of mortality transition, where both new and antiquated infectious diseases will emerge (Bryant and Peck, 2009, p. 13; Olshansky et al., 1997, p. 11) and increasing obesity and physical inactivity will result in deteriorating health, and possibly lowered life expectancy (Gaziano, 2010). The past is more certain. The infectious and parasitic diseases that dominated the world before the mortality transition have been largely replaced by degenerative diseases in MDRs and increasingly also in the LDRs.

How Certain Proximate Causes of Death Were Avoided

Bringing infectious, parasitic, and respiratory diseases under control in the MDRs required profound social, economic, and medical changes. What follows is a generalized description of those changes as they occurred in the countries of Northern and Western Europe and in frontier countries such as the United States (see, for example, Corsini and Viazzo, 1997; McKeown, 1976; Preston, 1976; and Schofield et al., 1991). We treat these changes in the order in which they began to impact mortality.

Economic development and rising income levels.   Remember that Western mortality was declining gradually for a century or more prior to the more rapid decline we call the mortality transition. This early decline in mortality resulted mainly from reduction in the frequency and extent of periodic crises, such as famines and epidemics. Such escapes from mortal catastrophes were largely due to improvements in general living conditions.

For one thing, the food supply and people's diets gradually improved. The agricultural revolution brought the possibility of surpluses and thus the avoidance of periodic famines. Methods of storing food were improved. Centralization of authority on a wider, national level made it likely that food surpluses could and would be moved from localities of current surplus to localities of current shortage. The reduction in outright starvation due to famines probably was secondary in importance to the reduction of malnutrition and lowered resistance to other killers.

For another thing, people could afford better personal hygiene as their living standards rose. While the use of soap, the wearing of undergarments, and the shift from wool to cotton clothing may have been motivated on aesthetic grounds, they also discouraged lice, the carriers of typhus, and relapsing fever.

People also were able to afford better housing. Brick housing helped to thwart disease-carrying rats. Good ventilation, access to sunshine, and the reduction of crowding all probably raised general resistance to disease.

Institutionalized sanitary reforms and public health measures.   Increasingly after the 1850s, the state intervened on behalf of the public's health. We are not talking about the medical advances that followed the establishment of the germ (or microbial) theory of disease causation. Rather, we are talking about government-sponsored changes in environmental conditions based on a yet-incomplete understanding of the causes of disease. This included the removal of garbage, the building of covered sewers, and the purification of drinking water that limited cholera and waterborne diseases. Prior to these reforms, cities were stinking, filthy places in which to live.

Social reforms.   This category refers to those changes—sometimes instituted by governments—that were not directly aimed at improving longevity but did so as a by-product. The workplace was improved by reducing child labor, shortening the length of the working day, and improving workplace conditions. Housing legislation set minimum standards. Social Security schemes started providing such benefits as old-age pensions, health insurance, medical care, unemployment insurance, and payments to the indigent.

Advances in medicine.   The impact of medical advances came later than the other three categories, probably mostly in the early 1900s. Immunization against disease was, of course, a major factor. Smallpox vaccination spread before the turn of the century, and other immunizations came into use after that. Antiseptic surgery became more common. Later, in the 1930s, there were great strides in the use of drugs to cure or halt the progress of an infectious disease. There were further improvements in the use of antibiotics and "wonder drugs" during and immediately after World War II. Finally, the development of effective insecticides greatly reduced insect-borne diseases such as typhus and malaria.

In conclusion, the popular belief that improvements in medical science played a heroic role in European and American mortality transitions is generally incorrect. In fact, the contribution of medicine came relatively late in the mortality transition. Before that, there had been important social and economic changes that already had set mortality plummeting.

Mortality Declines in the Less-Developed Regions

Increases in Life Expectancy

We have seen, in Table 5-2, that the LDRs have also experienced significant mortality decline over the past six decades as they have begun mortality transitions. How does declining LDR mortality compare to the historical mortality transitions in the MDRs?

LDRs include a wide variety of countries, cultures, and environments. Despite these differences, in the past LDR countries had in common the high and fluctuating epidemic mortality that characterized most populations before mortality transition. LDR mortality did not experience any sustained decline until the 20th century. Indeed, life expectancy in 1935–1939 in the LDRs as a class was still estimated at thirty years, which is not very different from what it had been in the MDRs in the early 1800s.

But in the 1950s, after World War II, life expectancy started to soar, reflecting a mortality transition that extends to the present. Dramatic life expectancy gains of twenty to thirty years took place rapidly in such countries as Trinidad, Sri Lanka, and Taiwan (Heer and Grigsby, 1992). Since 1950, life expectancy has risen by more than twenty-five years for LDRs as a class (see Table 5-2). About half of this increase occurred in just two decades between 1950 and 1970. Stolnitz contrasts this with the prior European mortality transition:

Within a decade in numerous instances and no more than two decades in most, many of the world's low-income nations have passed through successions of longevity stages that today's highest-income nations required generations or even half-centuries to reach and leave behind. It is safe to say that nothing in world history would have prepared a pre–World War II or even a 1950 observer for the mortality trends that soon emerged. (1982, p. 465)

Because of this steep mortality drop in the LDRs, there has been a gradual and partial convergence between LDR and MDR longevity. For an excellent demonstration of the drastic improvements in life expectancy in just two hundred years across the globe by demographer Hans Rosling, go to this book's website at www.demographytextbook.com to the links section under the Chapter 5 tab. In this video on life expectancy Rosling shows the relationship between income and life expectancy, and demonstrates that, whereas two centuries ago there was no country with a life expectancy over age forty, today there is not a single country with a life expectancy *under* forty.

LDRs still vary much more with respect to mortality than do MDRs. On average African countries have the shortest life expectancy. As an example of extremes, a person from sub-Saharan Africa can expect to live an average of seventeen fewer years than a person from Central America. That said, within the African continent itself there is also extreme variation. For example, the average life expectancy in Sierra Leone is forty-five years old while in Tunisia it is seventy-five (PRB, 2014).

Some countries with the highest mortality rates are not catching up with the others, and still find themselves with brutally short life expectancies for their people, virtually the same as what present MDRs experienced a century ago. On an even grimmer note, there is evidence of a recent setback of improvement in survivorship in a few LDRs. Some countries in Africa, for example, have experienced the brunt of world mortality from recently emergent diseases, such as HIV and Ebola.

Decreases in Infant Mortality

Why infant mortality is considered so important.   In the study of mortality transitions, deaths during the first year—**infant mortality**—tend to be of greater interest than mortality at any other age. There are several reasons for this.

One is that such a large proportion of all deaths in high-mortality countries involve infants. Age-specific mortality rates are generally highest at the very youngest and oldest ages in a population. If infant mortality is lowered, children surviving the early years will likely survive until much older ages, thereby contributing substantial years to life expectancy in the population. Interventions that lower infant mortality are especially effective in extending longevity.

A common but erroneous assumption about life expectancy is that if a population's average life expectancy is say, sixty years, then most of the population will die by age sixty. In fact, the life expectancy age is weighted downward due to the number of deaths occurring at young ages. So in the previous population example, many people who survive infanthood and childhood will live substantially longer than age sixty. Figure 5-4 on the next page dramatizes this relationship.

In this figure, world regions are ordered from lowest to highest infant mortality as one reads from left to right across the page. As a general pattern, life expectancy decreases significantly as infant mortality increases. Just as Africa was the only region

Figure 5-4

Infant Mortality and Life Expectancy in World Regions, 2015–2020

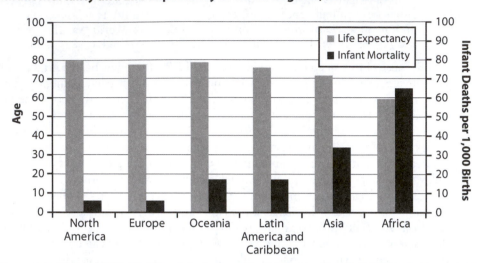

Source: United Nations, 2013b. *World Population Prospects: The 2012 Revision, Mortality Tables.* Used with permission.

where the number of deaths due to infectious causes is still very high (Figure 5-3), here we see that it is also the only region where high infant mortality rates have driven down life expectancies below age sixty.

Another reason we focus on infant mortality is its sensitivity. For instance, deaths in the first year are particularly responsive to intervention through medicine. Indeed, infant mortality often is used as an index of the general medical and public health conditions in a country. It even is used as a general indicator of socioeconomic well-being and development.

A final reason for special interest in infant mortality is the plausible relationship (or relationships) between infant death and fertility. In one direction, the chances of a couple's offspring surviving infancy have been hypothesized to influence their likelihood of choosing to have more children (e.g., Preston, 1978). We will review the evidence for this in chapter 7. In the opposite direction, closely spaced births do increase infant mortality (Wendt et al., 2012; Palloni, 1989). Family-planning programs thus provide another possible intervention to reduce infant mortality.

Measuring infant mortality.   One measure of infant mortality can be found in the first row of a life table. For instance, in Table 5-1 the first entry in column 2 tells us that, per hundred women starting their lives, 1.1 Argentinean women would die as infants, according to current Argentinean mortality risks. But, as we have stressed, such life tables require death reporting by age for all ages, a set of complex data infrequently available in LDRs and usually underestimated. An independent measure, based partially on other more reliable data, has become the standard: the **infant mortality rate**. It is simply the total deaths of infants in a given year divided by the total births in that same year, multiplied by 1,000. Box 5-2 describes the computation of and rationale behind the infant mortality rate.

**Box
5-2**

Infant Mortality Rates

The formula for the infant mortality rate (IMR) is as follows:

$$IMR = \frac{D_0}{B} \times 1{,}000$$

where

D_0 = deaths to infants (children under one year of age) in a given year
B = births in the given year

Let us take the example of the United States in 2010. There were 24,586 deaths to persons less than one year of age in 2010. In that same year, there were 3,999,386 births (NCHS, 2013). Thus:

$$IMR = \frac{24{,}586}{3{,}999{,}386} \times 1{,}000 = (.00614744) \times 1{,}000 = 6.15$$

There is an interesting difference between the logic of an IMR and the logic of an age-sex-specific death rate (or mortality rate from column two of a life table). Death rates (and mortality rates) use the population exposed to the risk of dying (i.e., the number of people in that age-sex category during the period of the deaths) as a denominator. The infant mortality rate, in contrast, *estimates* the "at-risk" denominator by the number of births during the same period.

Let us distinguish infant mortality from other early mortality. *Fetal mortality* is not included in infant mortality, nor in the demographic definition of mortality generally; it occurs before a live birth. *Neonatal mortality* refers to death between birth and the end of the first twenty-eight days of life. *Post-neonatal mortality* is that which occurs during the rest of the first year. The separation between neonatal and post-neonatal mortality has been made because the causes of death soon after birth differ from those later in infancy.

Where registration is reliable, both death and birth data for infants can come from the civil registration system. In the LDRs they more frequently come from sample surveys or censuses. Sometimes surveys involve direct questions about births and infant deaths during the preceding year. Many surveys ask the number of children ever born, the survivors by age, and the age of the mother. From these, one can estimate infant mortality rates indirectly (e.g., Box 5-1).

Regional differences in infant mortality. Figure 5-5 presents estimated infant mortality rates for world regions for the periods 1950–1955 and 2015–2020. (It also presents projections for the distant future; more on that later.) The regions are ordered from highest to lowest by infant mortality rate as of 2015–2020.

The results can be interpreted in more than one way. It is true that in all regions shown there has been a marked decrease in infant mortality rates over the period represented; the black bars are much longer than the light gray bars. But it is also the case that the percentage decline in the rate is not generally most precipitous where the rate had been highest. In other words, infant mortality may be declining across the board, but gaps in LDR infant mortality are not necessarily closing. Mortality in Africa is about 30% of what it was in the 1950s whereas it is only 7% of what it once was in Europe. But even in MDRs there have been some periods of stalling or even reversal since the 1950s. For instance, U.S. infant mortality rates increased for the first time in forty years in 2001, and there remain large disparities by race (MacDorman and Mathews, 2011; MacDorman et al., 2005).

For each region represented in Figure 5-5, the top bar is a projection into the middle of the 21st century. Remember that such predictions are speculative, and the future of mortality trends (including infant mortality trends) remains uncertain. To make intelligent guesses, it helps to study the changing profile of the proximate causes of death that has accompanied the "mortality transition" thus far.

Figure 5-5

Estimated and Projected Infant Mortality Rates for 1950, 2015, and 2050

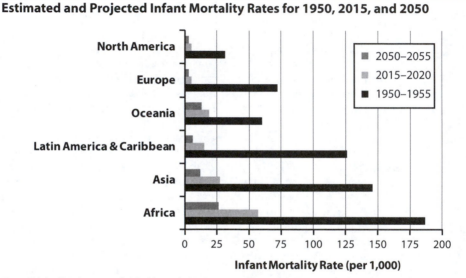

Source: United Nations, 2013b. *World Population Prospects: The 2012 Revision, Mortality Tables.* Used with permission.

Proximate Causes of Death and Their Control

What former immediate causes of death were brought under control in order to reduce mortality so drastically? Superficially, the postwar cause-of-death transition for LDRs was similar to the one experienced earlier by the MDRs. Communicable diseases—in particular, respiratory tuberculosis, bronchitis, and pneumonia—have been dramatically reduced (Frenk et al., 1996; Preston and Nelson, 1974).

However, there also seem to be some interesting differences from the MDR transitions. LDR mortality declines have owed more to programs targeted at particular killers, such as smallpox, yaws, plague, relapsing fever, polio, malaria, measles, and trachoma (WHO, 1998) and less to eradication of diarrhetic diseases than was the case in previous MDR declines (Olshansky et al., 1997). In addition, the transition has been less uniformly widespread than in the MDR declines, with greater variation from one disease to another. Some infectious diseases remain persistent or even have increased recently in LDRs. Chronic and noncommunicable diseases have also appeared early in the LDR transition, leading to a "double burden" of both infectious and noninfectious diseases (WHO, 2002, 2004, 2009; Lopez, 1993). In short, although LDR mortality decline has happened in a much shorter period, so far they are not experiencing the steady and broadly uniform epidemiological transition that characterized the MDRs.

An underlying contrast between the MDR and LDR transitions has been the role of medicine. During the slow and fitful mortality declines of the early 1900s, survival increases probably were won by gradual improvements in living conditions. Soon after World War II, however, there was a massive infusion of medical and public health technology for controlling infectious disease. Not only was the knowledge of disease control in place (unlike at the beginning of the MDR mortality transition), but also there was a foreign aid commitment by MDRs that motivated them to put their theory into practice. Thus, a striking contrast between the LDR and MDR mortality transitions has been the point at which medical and public health technology made important contributions (Olshansky et al., 1997). It was very early in the LDR transition and relatively late in the MDRs.

Rapid LDR mortality declines, and resulting population growth, have outpaced economic development in many countries. Without improvements in living standards and basic sanitation, in addition to controlling the HIV/AIDS epidemic, lowering LDR mortality further may be difficult (Mathers et al., 2009). Diarrheal diseases, largely caused by a lack of safe drinking water and poor sanitation, have been particularly resistant to control in LDRs. About 1.5 million people, mostly infants and children, die from diarrhea every year (PRB, 2010). Although there has been significant improvement in sanitation for the world population as part of the United Nation's 2015 Millennium Development Goals, almost 40% of the globe still lacks improved sanitation facilities (PRB, 2010). On the positive side, close to 90% of the world's inhabitants now have access to clean drinking water, which was a UN Development Goal that was met earlier than expected (WHO, 2013b).

Sex Differences in Mortality in the More-Developed Regions

As modernization has reduced MDR mortality, it has not been evenhanded in its distribution of additional survivorship. Female survivorship has improved more, and the improvements in age-specific rates have been greater for those under fifty than for those over fifty. Older men have benefited least from increases in survivorship. Let us start by documenting the current sex differentials in the MDRs contrasted with the LDRs. Then we will analyze how MDR patterns arose and how persistent they might be.

Current Contrasts between More-Developed and Less-Developed Regions

Table 5-4 on the next page presents estimated sex differences in life expectancy by world region. Columns 1 and 2 show estimates for men and for women; column 3 shows the difference, or the years by which life expectancy of women exceeds that of men. Females universally outlive men. But the *degree* to which that is true varies by the

Table 5-4   Sex Differences in Estimated Life Expectancy at Birth for World Regions, 2015–2020

Region[a]	Male (1)	Female (2)	Female minus Male (3)
World	68.8	73.3	4.5
More-Developed Regions	75.2	81.9	6.7
Less-Developed Regions	67.5	71.3	3.8
North America	77.6	82.1	4.5
Oceania	76.1	80.6	4.6
Europe	73.1	80.7	7.6
Latin America & Caribbean	72.8	79.0	6.2
Asia	70.5	74.5	3.9
Africa	58.5	61.3	2.8

[a]Regions listed in order of male life expectancy.

Note: 2015–2020 estimates based on medium fertility variant.

Source: United Nations, 2013b. *World Population Prospects: The 2012 Revision, Mortality Tables.* Used with permission.

development level of the region. In the LDRs as a class, women out-survive men by only 3.8 years; in the MDRs that difference is 6.7 years. Europe is the extreme example of this MDR disparity: Women outlive men by 7.6 years.

Female greater life expectancy has a cumulative impact on the sex composition in older ages. The global female sex ratio (women per 100 men) is exactly even at ages fifty to fifty-four, but rises to 150 at ages eighty to eighty-five, and to 330 among centenarians in 2010 (United Nations, 2013b).

Life expectancy figures, however, are averages, representing the whole life cycle. Let us take a longitudinal view of that cycle. The literature tells us that in the MDRs female survivorship is superior at all ages. In the LDRs the picture is not so simple. Female survivorship through the first year of life (infancy) is superior to male. During the early childhood years (ages one through four) the gap not only closes but in some countries male survivorship surpasses female's. This implies inferior allocation of scarce survival resources to female children. Later, during the reproductive ages, the female survivorship superiority again narrows and even reverses in some LDR countries due to maternal mortality and discriminatory treatment of women (Clark and Peck, 2012). **Maternal mortality** is women's deaths associated with pregnancy, labor, and the *puerperium*, the period immediately following childbirth. Thus, in the LDRs there remain life periods during which women are in greater jeopardy than they would be in the MDRs. Excess under-sixty female mortality in LDRs is estimated at 3.9 million missing women worldwide, 85% of whom are in China, India, and sub-Saharan Africa (World Bank, 2011).

Some of the missing women were never even born. Sex-selective practices at birth have led to a gender imbalance in some countries, and this practice is not limited to just LDR countries. Table 5-5 shows those countries with higher than average male to female sex ratios at birth where sex-selective practices are more common (Gilles and

Feldman-Jacobs, 2012). There is naturally a slightly higher sex ratio at birth, between 1.04–1.07, but ratios above that are usually considered to be altered by technology due to gender preferences for male children (see chapter 4 and Box 5-3).

Table 5-5   Countries with Most Skewed Sex Ratios at Birth

Azerbaijan	1.13	Vietnam	1.12	Georgia	1.10
China (Mainland)	1.12	Albania	1.11	Macedonia	1.08
India	1.12	Armenia	1.11	Kosovo	1.08

Source: CIA, 2013. *World Factbook.*

Box 5-3	**Sex-Selection Technology and Gender Preference**

Sex ratios of 1.07 and above of boy to girl births are largely attributable to the practice of sex-selective abortion. The technology to determine fetal sex, together with strong cultural preferences for sons over daughters, accounts for the high shares of baby boys in the countries shown in Table 5-5. Although most popular attention focuses on skewed sex ratios at birth (SRB) in China and India, it is clearly a problem in other countries. Of particular note are emerging SRB imbalances in the Caucasus. Some countries, such as South Korea, have successfully reversed the trend by imposing harsh penalties for the use of sex-selective technologies and because of societal attitude change that has begun to value more equal gender roles (Chung and Das Gupta, 2007).

Americans often think of child gender preference as a thing of the past, or a problem in developing countries. After all, the U.S. sex ratio at birth falls in the normal range, at 1.05. This is in spite of the curious American cottage industry in fetal sex-identification home-use kits, such as the *Intelligender,* the *GenderMaker,* and the *Gender Mentor.* In surveys, American parents report an ideal of two children and equal preference for boys and girls. However, American gender preferences manifest themselves in more sneaky ways. A recent survey showed that, if couples were only able to have *one child,* the most common preference was for a boy (Newport, 2011). These results are little changed from the same Gallup question asked of Americans in 1941.

Explaining Superior Female Longevity in the More-Developed Regions

Not only is life expectancy universally higher for women than for men in the MDRs, but that gender gap had been growing until the very recent past. The difference in MDR male and female life expectancies in 1950 was 5.1 years; by 2005–2010 it was 7.04 years (United Nations, 2013b). What are the causes of the current female survivorship superiority in more-developed regions and has it always been this way? The answer to that calls for a historical review of changes in mortality by sex in the MDRs.

Before the mortality transition, the situation in the MDRs was quite different from the present, with generally higher mortality for women. At least two changes lowered female mortality relative to male mortality during the course of the epidemiological transition. First, in the younger ages, improvements were made in economic, social, and health conditions, which had been responsible for higher female mortality among children and adolescents. The home, where girls spent more time than did boys, became more habitable and less overcrowded. At the same time, with urbanization, the external environment became more and more hazardous for the boys, who spent relatively more time outside the home (Pinnelli and Mancini, 1997). In early adulthood, the most important trend for improving female survivorship has been the decline in maternal mortality. It is usually measured by the **maternal mortality rate**, the number of maternal deaths per 100,000 live births in a specified year.

Figure 5-6 shows the dramatic drop in U.S. maternal mortality rates during the period following the end of World War I. The immediate reasons for this impressive decline are several: Expectant mothers had better nutrition because of an improved standard of living; they received better medical care before and after childbirth; and the great majority of diseases responsible for maternal mortality happened to be preventable and controllable with proper medical care. The reason for the spike in mortality was the 1918 influenza epidemic, which disproportionately killed women of childbearing ages.

In addition, maternal mortality was significantly cut by reduced childbearing. Generally speaking, the fewer children a mother has, the larger the proportion of her children born at low parities (e.g., first or second children) and born at prime maternal ages (e.g., in the mother's twenties versus her teens or late thirties). High parities and

Figure 5-6

U.S. Maternal Mortality Rates, 1915–1965

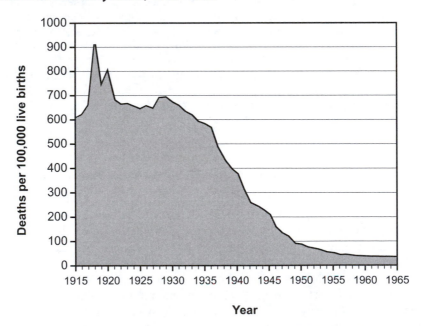

Source: Anderton et al., 1997. *The Population of the United States,* table 4-15; U.S. Census Bureau. 1960. *Historical Statistics of the United States,* Series B 101–112.

very early or late maternal age influence the risk of labor complications. Moreover, the fewer times that women subject themselves to the risk of childbearing at all—the fewer children they have—the fewer the number of women who will die of childbearing.

Beyond maternal mortality, there has been a change in the dominant immediate causes of death in the MDRs, and that has affected the sexes differently. Figure 5-3 shows that noninfectious diseases, which consist primarily of cancers and diseases of the circulatory system, have become more dominant in the MDRs; these causes have not only increased in importance, but they also seem to have turned first upon men. Before the mortality transition, infectious and parasitic diseases had a higher impact on women, so their decline especially benefited women (see Table 5-3). Overall, the shift in causes of death over the transition has benefited survivorship of women in the MDRs. There is also some speculation that women may have a biological advantage over men in the absence of high infectious disease prevalence. The source of this advantage is not yet well understood, but it may be linked to various genetic and physiological factors such as skewing of X chromosome inactivation, telomere attrition, mitochondrial inheritance, hormonal and cellular reactions to stress, etc. (see Seifarth et al., 2012).

Behaviors that vary by societal norms of masculinity and femininity also increase mortality for men relative to women. Men have higher suicide, homicide, and accident rates, as well as increased exposure to occupational hazards and lower use of healthcare services than do women. In addition, men more often engage in unhealthy lifestyle behaviors, such as drinking, smoking, and maintaining poor diets (Clark and Peck, 2012). The dramatic widening of the MDR gender gap in female survivorship has shown signs of narrowing in recent years, much of which appears to be linked to behavioral and lifestyle changes on the part of women (PRB, 2011; Trovato and Lalu, 1996, 1998). Increasing gender equity in the MDRs may have the unfortunate side effect of subjecting women to the same higher risks of mortality as men. Females have entered the labor force and participate in traditionally male occupations and behaviors. This is especially the case with tobacco usage. Female smoking rates in MDRs are now almost equal to men's and appear to be largely responsible for most of the slowdown in rising women's longevity relative to men's (PRB, 2011; Pampel, 2002; Lopez et al., 1995). In addition, many of the new major health threats cut across gender groups equally or are even more likely to impact women, like HIV/AIDS contagion.

Problems of Mortality

Defining Mortality Problems

How can the worldwide plunge in mortality cause any problems? As we have seen (chapter 3), the mortality decline contributed to rapid population growth in the LDRs, which presents a variety of challenges for their economic development and the provision of social services. We also have seen that the mortality decline has contributed, although clearly less than declining fertility, to the growing percentage of the "oldest old" in the MDRs (chapter 4), which may strain their ability to provide adequate social services (see chapter 6). All of these potential problems are *indirect* effects of mortality decline. They also are discussed in other places throughout this text. So, let us confine our attention here to the more direct, and dramatic, mortality problems worldwide.

Careers in Demography

Robert A. Hummer

Howard W. Odum Professor of Sociology and Faculty Fellow, Carolina Population Center, University of North Carolina at Chapel Hill (2015–)

Past Professor of Sociology and Faculty Research Associate, Population Research Center, University of Texas at Austin (1996–2015)

How did you decide that being a demographer was the career path for you?

I entered graduate school with the intention of becoming a sociology professor at a small liberal arts college. I had only a very vague notion of what demography was. But shortly after starting my first semester in graduate school, Professor Ike Eberstein asked if I was interested in working on a project with him and his colleague Charles Nam on patterns of infant mortality in Florida. They needed a research assistant who was not afraid to work with quantitative data. A requirement of working on that project was that I also enroll in a graduate-level course on demographic methods. Between the infant mortality project and that initial demographic methods course, I realized that demography offers a fantastic set of theories, concepts, data, and methods to understand social trends and inequalities in a concrete, quantifiable manner. Thus, by the end of that first semester, I knew that my academic future was in demography.

What kind of education and training did you pursue to get to where you are in your career?

I received a PhD in sociology, with an emphasis on demography, from Florida State University. Professors Eberstein and Nam were incredible mentors; they not only taught me all they could about demography, but they demonstrated to me on a day-to-day basis that hard work, honesty, concern for students, and humility were characteristics that helped make them both great demographers and professors. Throughout my career, I've tried to emulate their passion for research, teaching, and mentoring in the context of tremendous professional and personal integrity.

After earning my PhD, I served short stints at East Carolina University and Louisiana State University prior to spending 19 years at the University of Texas at Austin (UT). There, the Population Research Center (PRC) was a wonderful academic home. Most recently I accepted a position in the Department of Sociology and Carolina Population Center (CPC) at the University of North Carolina at Chapel Hill. In particular, the CPC is an academic context that fosters the highest level of demographic research and student training in the country and perhaps the world, and I'm looking forward to being a part of that exciting and rich research and training environment.

Describe your work/research as a demographer. What do you consider your most important accomplishments?

Since graduate school, I've worked on projects that aim to better document and understand population-based health and mortality disparities in the United States. This research area continues to capture my attention for two reasons: (1) the United States performs very poorly relative to other high-income countries in terms of our overall levels of health and life expectancy; and (2) our country is characterized by very wide disparities in health and mortality across groups.

Over the past 10 years, I've focused a great deal of attention on educational disparities in U.S. health and mortality. On the bright side, patterns of health and longevity look quite good among the highly educated in U.S. society. In this age of information, people who are fortunate enough to attend college, graduate from college, and earn advanced degrees obtain all kinds of advantages across the life course that result in better health and longer lives. On the down side, however, patterns of health and longevity look very poor for U.S. adults with low levels of education; for example, people without a high school degree live on average 12–15 fewer years than people with advanced degrees in our society. And, unfortunately, about 11% of U.S. young adults do not graduate from high school and another 28% or so graduate from high school but never go to college.

In my view, these are unacceptable figures in such a wealthy society—and we need to collectively do a much better job in making sure that all of our nation's children, adolescents, and young adults have the opportunity to obtain a quality education that helps insure their future health and long life. And for those who do not obtain high school or college degrees, we need to do a much better job of making sure that our society has policies in place so that low education is not a ticket to poor lifelong health and a short life. Together with my co-author Elaine Hernandez, I summarized research on educational attainment and U.S. adult mortality and made policy recommendations in a *Population Bulletin* (2013) published by the Population Reference Bureau.

Research-wise, I think my most important contribution to demography is the consistent message throughout my work that a highly inequitable distribution of societal resources—whether by race and ethnicity, educational level, gender, or immigrant status—results in highly inequitable levels of health and longevity across social groups. In a highly unequal society like the United States, these are troubling patterns that, in my view, require serious policy attention from federal, state, and local governments. My research attempts to place health and mortality inequalities on the public radar screen and to prevent our society from being complacent with this state of affairs.

What do you see as the field's most important contribution as well as its greatest challenge?

I think demography's most important contribution is that we have the utmost concern for getting the facts right. Demographers try very hard to collect and/or use high-quality data, to apply careful methods in our work, and to interpret our findings with substantial caution. Demographers make very useful contributions to science, policy, and humankind because we are believable. Moreover, we work on topics that are important to societies throughout the world—morbidity and mortality, reproductive health and fertility, migration, family structure, age structure, and more. In other words, we do relevant stuff!

That said, I think we face a number of challenges as a field, just two of which I'll mention here. First, federal government investments in basic science, including demographic research, have stagnated in recent years, making it increasingly difficult for researchers to obtain funding to do good science and effectively train the next generation. Forward-thinking societies need to invest substantial money in science so that we better understand ourselves and create programs and policies to insure our health and well-being into the future. Second, I think demography, as a field, needs to better serve undergraduate students in American universities. Why don't we offer students an opportunity to major in demography? Some may argue that there is not enough student demand. However, demography is a highly relevant and interesting field with well developed theories, concepts, data, and methods. Pitched this way, there is bound to be substantial interest.

There are two categories of concern with respect to mortality declines that we address in this section. First, mortality decline is not as certain to continue as one might think. Mortality improvements since the 1950s already are facing major setbacks in some MDRs and LDRs from newly emergent diseases, as well as from tobacco-related and obesity-related mortality. Second, across world regions and within countries, not all groups have benefited equally from mortality decline. Persistent, yet preventable, mortality differentials among groups remain, even in the MDRs.

Let us again go through the mental exercise of asking how these phenomena get defined as "problems." Who is concerned? What consequences are believed to follow? Why are those consequences perceived to be bad?

These questions seem almost silly when they refer to concerns about slowing or reversing declines in mortality. Nearly all of us wish for long lives, not only for ourselves but also for humanity. Most of us subscribe to the belief that the consequences of long life are happier than those of short life, at least so far. Therefore, we almost automatically define any interruption of the mortality transition as a problem.

How do our questions apply to the problem of differentials in mortality? Let us assume, from the preceding paragraph, that long life is favored over short life. Who is concerned about vast differences among nations, among classes, among gender or age or ethnic categories in life expectancy? What consequences are supposed to flow from persistence of these inequalities? These questions are seldom asked, yet they are thought-provoking. (See "Propositions for Debate" at the end of the chapter.)

Problems of Stalled Mortality Transitions

However likely, the continuing decline of mortality is not a certainty. In fact, it has been theorized that reverse epidemiological transitions may be an inevitable component of the evolution of human mortality. In Horiuchi's five-stage epidemiological model (1999), he notes that mortality reversals are not unknown historically. Increased levels of human mortality during the initial stages of the industrial revolution are but one example. He speculates that future populations may confront additional reverse transitions due to the re-emergence of infectious diseases, environmental pollution, and rising rates of homicide due to modern social alienation (Horiuchi, 1999). In fact, a recent study in Thailand suggests that the HIV epidemic has reversed the epidemiological transition for men and has slowed it for women tremendously (Hill et al., 2007).

Demographers often have failed to anticipate changes in population trends by assuming that things will continue more or less as they have in the past. But how safe are such assumptions? We focus here on two reasons for skepticism: the slowing and even reversal of European mortality declines, and the emergence of new pandemics, especially HIV/AIDS, as well as tobacco-related and diet-related illnesses. (A third reason for skepticism, the apparent intractability of higher mortality in socially underprivileged classes, is treated in the following section.)

Recent reversals in Europe.   At the turn of the 21st century, the World Health Organization reported that mortality crises in the newly independent states of central and Eastern Europe, and continuing premature death in the disadvantaged social classes of almost every European country, actually led to a decline in European life expectancy for the first time since World War II (WHO Europe, 1998). After the collapse of the Soviet Union, male life expectancy declined by six years between 1990 and 1994, and only in 2008 did Russia's life expectancy recover to the level it was in the 1970s. A number of studies have sought to uncover these recent East-West differences in mortality, and have theorized hazardous alcohol and tobacco consumption, subpar health care and treatment, as well as lower levels of education and living standards to be the possible explanations for higher mortality in former communist countries. However, more studies are needed to fully understand the variability among the European nations and the recent reversal in life expectancy (Leon, 2011).

In Europe as a whole, infectious diseases unknown for decades, such as new strains of influenza, sexually transmitted diseases, and drug-resistant strains of tuberculosis, pneumonia, and malaria, re-emerged to play a part in shifting mortality trends (European Commission, 2008). Lifestyle-related mortality also is cited as a cause of decreasing life expectancy, with high mortality from cardiovascular, obesity-related diseases, and tobacco-related deaths. The setback in European life expectancy may have been a temporary result of dramatic economic and social restructuring in Europe. But new infectious diseases such as HIV/AIDS, antibiotic-resistant disease strains, and tobacco-related deaths are neither unique to Europe nor most severe in the MDRs. Trends in Europe and elsewhere may suggest more than temporary mortality problems.

HIV/AIDS and Other Emergent Diseases

Perhaps the most obvious, and universally recognized, mortality problem is the worldwide HIV/AIDS pandemic, which has become the leading cause of death for young adults in some countries. Thirty-four million people are currently living with HIV/AIDs today (WHO, 2013b). Figure 5-7 on the following page demonstrates how quickly HIV/AIDS evolved into a global endemic. In 1981 the first few cases of HIV/AIDS came to light in the United States; just twenty years later the number of people infected by the disease worldwide had reached 40 million, with more than 20 million deaths occurring during that period (WHO, 2004). No vaccine yet exists to cure people infected with HIV/AIDS; however, antiretroviral drug therapy (ART) developed in the 1990s has proven effective in substantially slowing the progress of the disease and unprecedented gains have been made in the fight against HIV/AIDS in the last decades. Annual deaths from HIV/AIDs have decreased by 24% since 2005, the year of the disease's peak with 2.3 million deaths, according to the Joint United Nations Programme on HIV/AIDS (UNAIDS, 2012). The incidence rate of new infections has also begun to decline.

Unfortunately, the countries most in need of ART still suffer from unequal access. Only 30% of eligible pregnant women and 54% of the infected population in less-developed countries are currently being treated with ART compared to almost universal coverage for those in the MDRs (UNAIDS, 2012). Efforts to increase access are underway and the UN has made it a goal to double ART access by 2015 (UNAIDS, 2012). Treating HIV/AIDS with ART is a success story, allowing millions of people to live high-quality lives who otherwise would have died from the virus. However, antiretroviral drugs are not a cure and it is important that HIV/AIDS intervention efforts continue to emphasize prevention.

Figure 5-7

HIV/AIDS: The Evolution of an Epidemic

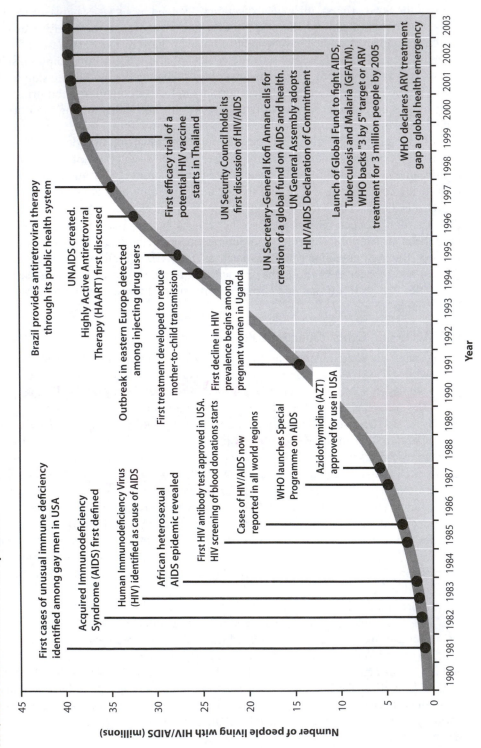

Source: World Health Organization, 2003. *The World Health Report 2003: Shaping the Future.* Permission granted by World Health Organization, Geneva, Switzerland.

In the 1980s, years of life lost to HIV/AIDS in MDRs increased rapidly in urban centers like New York City (Obiri et al., 1998). But contraction rates of HIV/AIDS plateaued with the advent of public health campaigns and availability of ART in most MDRs. (The leveling-out effect has not occurred evenly across all ethnic groups in MDRs, however, an exception to which we return in chapter 11.) It is the populations in many LDRs, especially in sub-Saharan Africa, that have been most heavily impacted by this disease. The majority of people living with HIV/AIDs are in Africa (69%), where one in twenty adults is infected (UNAIDS, 2012). The same poor economic conditions that lead to high HIV/AIDS prevalence also lead to high rates of other infectious diseases, such as malaria, bacterial diseases, and tuberculosis. Most HIV/AIDS mortality in Africa stems from the interaction of these infections with the immune system of individuals already weakened by the HIV/AIDS virus.

Figure 5-8 shows HIV/AIDS and non-HIV/AIDS mortality among African countries that have been hardest hit by the pandemic. In particular this figure illustrates the differing impact on age structure of HIV/AIDS. Whereas the other causes of death affect primarily children and elderly, HIV/AIDs hits hardest among the adult working-age population: 86% of all HIV/AIDS deaths occur between the ages of fifteen and fifty-nine. To illustrate this point, Figure 5-9 on the next page demonstrates how HIV/AIDS is expected to impact Botswana's age structure by 2020. Rather than the typical pyramid shape characteristic of most LDRs (see chapter 4), Botswana's population structure will become concave throughout the adult ages, with particularly heavy losses among young adult women, who are hit hardest by HIV/AIDS. The disease is thus even more devastating to the extent that it leaves so many dependents without support.

Figure 5-8

Percentage Distribution of AIDS Versus Non-AIDS Deaths by Broad Age Group, 48 AIDS-Affected Countries, 2010–2015

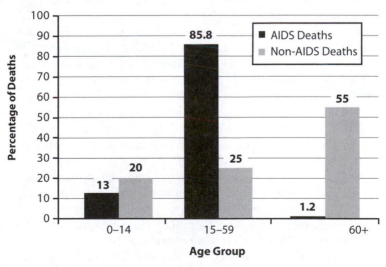

Source: United Nations, 2012b. *World Mortality Report 2011.* Used with permission.

Figure 5-9

Projected Population Structure of Botswana in 2020, with and without AIDS

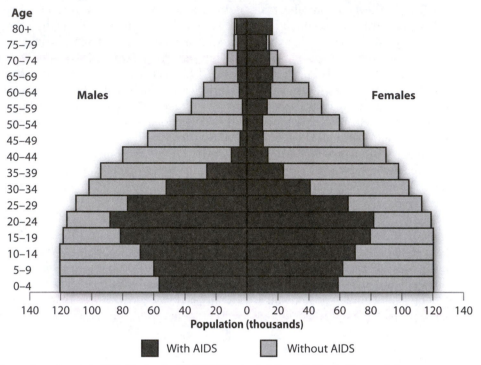

Source: Lamptey et al., 2002, "Facing the HIV/AIDS Pandemic," Figure 7. Used with permission.

Between 1990 and 2010, life expectancy in southern Africa fell from 61 to 51 due to HIV/AIDS (United Nations, 2011b). The contrast between longevity with and without HIV/AIDS is even more extreme when we consider those individual countries in Africa hardest hit by the endemic. Botswana's 2010-2015 life expectancy at birth is fifty-two years old; in the absence of HIV/AIDS it would have been sixty-nine (United Nations, 2012b). While many African populations will most likely continue to increase due to high fertility, their natural increase will be affected by the disease. Southern Africa's population, for example, is projected to be significantly smaller than it would have been without HIV/AIDS by 2050 (Lamptey et al., 2002; United Nations, 2011b). Although 69% of the world's HIV/AIDS cases are located in Africa, contraction rates have also grown in other parts of the world, predominantly central Asia and Eastern Europe.

Although HIV/AIDS has had the largest impact, the importance of other diseases should not be discounted. Around 500 million of the world's population is, for example, infected with the hepatitis B or C viruses, while tuberculosis is the world's largest infectious cause of death, killing 1.4 million people a year. Malaria kills a child every minute on average (WHO, 2012c; United Nations, 2012a).

As Europe's experience suggests, HIV/AIDS is not the only emergent or newly identified disease. In the last few decades, nearly forty new diseases have emerged.

Some of these may be familiar to the reader, such as variant Creutzfeld-Jacobs disease (the human version of "mad cow" disease), hepatitis C, avian flu, West Nile, SARS, and others (European Commission, 2008). The Ebola virus, the world's most virulent new disease, had its deadliest outbreak to date across West Africa in 2014 (WHO, 2014). The disease was continuing to spread as this textbook went to press.

Vaccination programs have made a dramatic difference in lowering the incidence of many infectious diseases. However, in part due to population growth and globalization, infectious diseases are being provided more opportunities to mutate new strains and disperse through human hosts. Over the past two decades, new diseases have begun to emerge at unprecedented rates (European Commission, 2008). Older diseases also have experienced some resurgence. For example, Africa has seen a resurgence of yellow fever and meningitis and the centuries-old human plague has reappeared in sporadic outbreaks in locations such as Madagascar and the Democratic Republic of the Congo (WHO, 2013b). Another concern is the reemergence of known infectious diseases in new drug-resistant forms due to widespread overuse of antibiotics (CDC, 2013b).

Whether human populations can continue to provide successful public health and medical measures as rapidly as diseases can adapt or reassert themselves is an open question. The 20th century, which began with an influenza pandemic and ended with the HIV/AIDS pandemic, is a sobering reminder that Malthus's positive checks on population growth (see Box 3-2) are not necessarily a thing of the past.

Tobacco-related mortality.   A second, perhaps less obvious, pandemic that nonetheless kills more than HIV/AIDS, tuberculosis, and malaria combined is the dramatically rising mortality attributed to tobacco use. Smoking is the single largest preventable cause of mortality worldwide. Killing approximately six million people a year currently and another 600,000 from second-hand smoke, the mortality impact of tobacco use is expected to double by 2020 (United Nations, 2012b; WHO, 2012b).

Tobacco-related mortality is a relatively recent problem. In the 1930s lung cancer was a rare disease in the United States and Europe. Yet over the next few decades it became one of the leading causes of death in developed countries, and is the single largest cause of premature death (Fenelon and Preston, 2012). One of every five deaths, or more than 400,000 deaths, in the United States each year is smoking related (CDC, 2013a). Europe has the highest such death rate in the world, with one of every three deaths among Europeans aged forty-five to fifty-nine due to smoking-related causes. Africans have the lowest smoking prevalence in the world. Although smoking is still a highly gendered behavior, with five male deaths for every one female death, it is becoming an equal opportunity killer as more women adopt the practice (WHO, 2011; 2012b).

In the MDRs, smoking began first with men and then, some thirty years later, became popular with women. In some countries, such as Sweden, women are now smoking more than men (WHO, 2011). In the 21st century, many MDRs have committed themselves to massive public health campaigns against the tobacco industry. As a result, smoking has declined in the United States, the United Kingdom, Australia, and Canada. Smoking currently kills the most people in the Americas and in Europe, since these are the regions where the practice has been around the longest. In the LDRs, the percentage of deaths caused by tobacco is rising quickly as other causes are brought under control, as survivorship into older ages increases, and as tobacco consumption continues to increase (WHO, 2012e). Rapid population growth and the uneven presence of anti-tobacco litigation have made LDRs an increasingly attractive market for expansion by the tobacco industry (WHO, 2012e). As a result, more men now smoke in LDRs than MDRs, although LDR women still have lower rates than MDR women (Mackay and Eriksen, 2002; WHO 2011, 2013b). If current trends continue, eight out of every ten tobacco-related deaths will take place among those living in LDRs (WHO, 2012e). By 2030 tobacco is expected to kill more people than any single disease and this trend is likely to continue to increase through at least the next quarter century.

Tobacco-related mortality tells a sobering story. It seems astounding that a clearly self-made threat to human life could loom even larger than the past century's greatest pandemic. Faced with a clearly preventable cause of death, countries have failed to stop their tobacco epidemics. In large part this is because controlling a tobacco epidemic requires either modification of individual addiction or substance-abuse regulations in economies dominated by powerful tobacco lobbies. Widespread obesity and sedentary lifestyles, unhealthy diets, alcohol and substance abuse, and so forth all suggest that longevity is not always an overriding priority at the individual level.

Obesity-related mortality.   Both LDRs and MDRs also suffer from unhealthy diets. Poor diets in LDRs primarily have manifested themselves in the form of undernourishment, whereas the opposite problem, obesity, is the biggest dietary issue in the developed world. In the poorest LDRs, childhood underweight is still the number one risk factor leading to mortality. By contrast, obesity is the third largest mortality risk factor in higher income MDRs, after tobacco use and high blood pressure (WHO, 2009). More than 35% of U.S. adults are obese (NCHS, 2012). However, the obesity epidemic is also spreading to the less developed regions of the world. Already, conditions brought on by obesity and overweight kill more people globally than do conditions brought on by underweight (WHO, 2009) and obesity has been rising in almost all low- and middle-income countries (Popkin et al., 2012).

Obesity, stemming from sedentary lifestyles and diets high in salts, fats, and sugars, leads to heart disease, stroke, diabetes, and various types of cancer, many of which are already leading causes of death in more-developed countries. The rise in obesity-related deaths has been drastic enough for demographers to begin revising life expectancy projections in some MDRs. In the United States it is now estimated that obesity will cut the life expectancy at birth by as much as ten years (Peto et al., 2010). Accordingly, the American Medical Association officially declared obesity a disease in 2013 (Pollack, 2013). The last time the United States experienced this sort of reversal in life expectancy was during the Great Depression.

Inequality of Persistent High Mortality

Another major group of mortality problems concerns classes of people whose mortality has not declined as much as others' have. Social class differences are found for most causes of death (Birchenall, 2007) and high mortality persists in many disadvantaged nations.

International inequality.   Let us review some disturbing aspects of present LDR mortality shown in Table 5-2. While the gap in life expectancy between MDRs and

LDRs has narrowed, MDR populations overall still expect to live ten years longer. Moreover, the large gap among the LDRs seems to be persisting. Africa, in particular, is falling even further behind the other LDRs, largely due to reversals in gains due to HIV/AIDS. Within all of these less-developed regions, the mortality improvements have been least for the poorest of the countries and the poorest subgroups within those countries.

The narrowing gap in life expectancy between less- and more-developed countries, and between the rich and the poor within LDR countries, largely has been due to declines in infant mortality among poor people and poor nations (Guzman, 1989). However, when inequality in life expectancy is examined for those aged ten and above, the global life expectancy gap between LDRs and MDRs looks less sanguine. While it seems to be the case that within-country inequality has narrowed over time, between-country inequality appears to have increased (Edwards, 2011).

Mortality transitions have, themselves, led to some reasons for persistent and increasing international inequalities. In many less-developed countries the increasing population resulting from the decline of communicable diseases has not met with increased economic opportunities. Instead, population increases have fueled a rapidly growing lower class with persistently higher mortality than the middle and upper classes (Taucher et al., 1996). A study shows that in many of the low- and middle-income countries, the under-five mortality rate is almost always higher for the poorest quintile than for the richest quintile of the population. This is likely due to the fact that lower socioeconomic groups often suffer from malnutrition, higher exposure to infections, and lower quality of health care (Houweling and Kunst, 2010). LDR countries thus face a dual burden of mortality, with rising health-care needs among the wealthy contesting for resources needed to combat persistent communicable diseases among the poor.

Socioeconomic class inequality.   In the MDRs as well, social class differences in mortality persist in all countries. The magnitude of difference varies widely depending on country-level policies (such as the availability of universal healthcare), and they also vary according to the specific cause considered (Elo, 2010; Marmot, 1995). Some MDR countries, such as the United States, are the wealthiest in the world and yet their high levels of inequality cause them to be ranked surprisingly low on mortality indicators relative to other less wealthy MDRs. In the United States, substantial differences in infant and maternal mortality persist by class and by ethnic group, and overall life expectancy increases have been more rapid in recent decades for wealthier than poor Americans (Singh and Siahpush, 2006; NCHS, 2011).

MDRs confront rising health costs that present difficult choices. The aging of MDR populations, in particular, strains resources. The MDR population over age seventy-five consumes many times more medical and social services than those under seventy-five. As populations continue to age, MDR countries will sometimes face difficult choices between (1) allocating resources to help socially disadvantaged groups who lag behind in life expectancy, and (2) providing for the rising chronic conditions and health-care demands of an aging population.

Vulnerable groups.   Across national and regional boundaries, and across socio-economic classes, certain segments of the population suffer disproportionately from mortality that is premature and largely preventable. The United Nations has placed particular emphasis on identifying and protecting the basic health of such vulnerable groups. Not surprisingly, these vulnerable groups also are economically disadvantaged ones with higher unemployment, lack of housing, poverty, and poor health (United Nations, 2012a).

In both the more-developed and the less-developed regions, *infants and children* suffer disproportionately from poverty and preventable mortality. Almost seven million children under the age of five died last year, the majority from preventable, infectious diseases (UNICEF, 2012). Of the world's child mortality, 99% is concentrated in less-developed countries (UNICEF, 2012). About 12% of sub-Saharan African children will die before their fifth birthday, compared to less than 1% in developed regions (United Nations, 2012a). In the LDRs, poverty-related causes of death such as diarrheal and communicable diseases, pneumonia, malaria, and HIV/AIDS are major causes of child death (United Nations, 2012a). Child and adolescent deaths occurring in the MDRs are largely from unintentional accidents. In the United States, for example, the majority of deaths to children and teens are due to motor vehicle crashes (NCHS, 2013). Reducing these largely preventable deaths at young ages would contribute substantially to increased life expectancy. Nonetheless, significant progress has been made in reducing child mortality, and that trend is projected to continue or even accelerate. Since 1990, there has been a global decrease of 41% in child deaths (UNICEF, 2012).

Concern has grown over the mortality and health of LDR *women* in the past few decades. Differential gender treatment and unequal access to resources can lead to greater female mortality (United Nations, 2010, 2011a). In some regions, such as China and India, there is a higher risk that girls, as compared to boys, will die before age five despite their natural biological mortality advantages. Reproductive biology can also burden women. Over half a million women die each year during childbirth, and these risks are highest where fertility rates are high, when mothers are under age fifteen, and where health care is lacking. Pregnancy and childbirth are the top causes of death and disability among women of reproductive ages in LDRs, and over 99% of world maternal mortality takes place in these countries (WHO, 2012a; 2012d). Fortunately, as with infant and child mortality, maternal mortality has also declined considerably (by about 50%) since the UN's 2002 Millennium Development Goals were put in place, but there is still considerable progress to be made.

In past decades, programs addressing women's health have focused on reproductive health. More recent initiatives also have focused on development initiatives, recognizing that women's educational attainment, employment, social roles, and access to resources all have considerable impact on their health and mortality, as well as on their children's (Kristof and WuDunn, 2009; United Nations, 2011a, 2012a).

Women and children, however, are not the only groups vulnerable to premature and preventable mortality. There are other clearly vulnerable groups whose health needs have been neglected or are largely unknown. One such group is *indigenous peoples*, comprising 5% of the world's population, for whom demographic data are lacking. Due to histories of colonization, dispossession of ancestral lands, and continued discrimination, many indigenous peoples are disproportionately in poverty and in poor health (United Nations, 2009).

SUMMARY

In today's more-developed countries, the "mortality transition" resulted in a near-doubling of life expectancy at birth in a little over a century. Such a sustained improvement in survivorship was unprecedented in human history and attributable to the control of infectious diseases largely through improved living standards, sanitary reforms, and public health measures. Advances in medicine, such as mass immunization against disease, made their contribution relatively late in the MDR mortality transition.

In today's less-developed countries, in contrast, innovations in medical technology made an early and significant contribution to mortality transitions. Although there had been a gradual, fitful decline in LDR mortality in the early 1900s, medicinal advances following World War II were largely responsible for the universal and rapid decline in LDR mortality during the following decades.

There continues to be considerable variety among LDR countries regarding mortality. The poorest still have life expectancies that are distressingly short by modern standards. Continuing substantial improvements in LDR mortality cannot likely be achieved by waving the medical wand; improvement in living standards is a prerequisite. The LDRs and some MDRs also have suffered some setbacks in their mortality transitions. Foremost among these have been the HIV/AIDS pandemic and resurgences of other infectious diseases. The consequences have been dramatic, as gains in life expectancy in some African countries reversed due to these diseases. Preventable mortality stemming from the tobacco and obesity epidemics is prevalent in the MDRs and spreading to LDRs.

Even within nations, vast differentials (related to socioeconomic status, age, and sex, among other social distinctions) in preventable mortality persist. Most infant and child mortality and many persistent causes of mortality among women are preventable. Regarding sex, female survivorship has improved more with development than has male, largely due to declines in maternal mortality. But this pattern of longer lives for women has not been as prevalent in LDRs as in the MDRs, because women there continue to face a number of gender status-related mortality disadvantages and significant maternal mortality.

The mortality transition has been a revolutionary worldwide historical event that continues to unfold. Epidemic mortality will not necessarily disappear as this transition continues. The threats of Malthus's positive checks on population remain with us in the 21st century. Continuing mortality disparities between rich and poor nations, and rich and poor people within those nations, are prevalent within LDRs and MDRs. Speculating from recent history, it is most likely that the mortality transition will continue to progress throughout the world. Yet, new threats to mortality will almost certainly be encountered, and societies may have to shift their allocations of scarce health resources. The course of future mortality decline remains far from certain.

EXERCISES

1. Table E5-1 on p. 181 is a male life table for Sweden according to the age-sex-specific death rates of 2011. Some blanks intentionally have been left in columns 3, 4, 6, and 7 of the table. Your task is to fill in those blanks, copying the computations used for

determining the other entries for the same columns. What follows is an explanation of each of the columns, from left to right:

- Column 1 simply lists the age intervals. With two exceptions, we have used five-year intervals rather than single-year ones; thus, this is an "abridged" life table. The exceptions are at either end of the age range. Infant mortality (age zero to one) is separated from early childhood mortality (age one to four). The terminal category (100 and over in this table) is open-ended.

- Column 2 ($_nq_x$) presents the assumed risk of dying over the n years beginning at age x for each of the age intervals. Each such "mortality rate" is based on an age-sex-specific death rate. The entire rest of the table is generated from column 2.

- Column 3 (l_x) and column 4 ($_nd_x$) are best explained together. We start at the top of column 3 with an arbitrary, large, hypothetical cohort (or "radix"); this table follows the convention of using 100,000. Then we trace what the fate of this hypothetical cohort would be if it experienced the probabilities of death listed in column 2. For instance, the 100,000 men born experienced a probability of death of 0.00235 until their first birthday. This would result in 235.21 deaths by the first birthday. This is the entry for column 4 for the first age interval. How many men would start their second year of life? We subtract the deaths (235.21) from those who started the first interval (100,000) and get 99,764.79, the next entry in column 3. Multiplying these 99,764.79 survivors by the probability of dying between the ages of one and four, or 0.00064, we find that 64.15 of them will die, the next entry in column 4, and so on, back and forth between columns 3 and 4. Algebraically stated,

$$_nd_x = (_nq_x)(l_x)$$

and

$$l_x + n = l_x - _nd_x$$

where
x = exact age at the beginning of the age interval
n = number of years in the age interval

- Column 5 ($_nL_x$) is the number of person-years lived in the age interval by the survivors of the hypothetical cohort. In the first row, if there were 100,000 babies born and 99,788 survived the whole first year, how many person-years did they collectively live during that one-year age interval? It depends on when during the year death occurred. Because of the unusual pattern of death during infancy, demographers use a complex procedure to arrive at an estimate for the top entry in column 5. For subsequent age intervals, however, deaths are more evenly spread throughout the interval. Thus, for most of the age intervals beyond infancy, the entry will be very close to the average of (1) the number of people alive at the beginning of the interval and (2) the number alive at the end of the interval. You are not required to make such a complex interpolation here.

- Column 6 (T_x) is derived entirely from column 5 ($_nL_x$). It tells how many *person-years* will be lived by the survivors of the hypothetical cohort from any specified age until all are dead. Thus, the entry 7,978,689 at the top of column 6 indicates this hypothetical cohort collectively will have that many years of life among them before the last one dies. Arithmetically, the column is constructed by summing the number of years lived in each interval from the bottom row upward to the top in column 5. Stated algebraically,

$$T_x = \sum_{x=100+}^{0} {}_nL_x$$

- Column 7 (e_x) tells the life expectancy remaining after each specified birthday. Take the top entry as an illustration, the life expectancy at birth (e_0). If there were 7,978,689 person-years of life to be shared among the 100,000 males who were born

Table E5-1   Male Life Table, Sweden, 2011

Age Interval[a] x to x + n (1)	Proportion Dying[b] $_nq_x$ (2)	Number Living at Beginning of Age Interval (of 100,000 Born Alive) l_x (3)	Number Dying during Age Interval (of 100,000 Born Alive) $_nd_x$ (4)	Person Years Lived in the Age Interval $_nL_x$ (5)	Person-Years Lived in This and All Subsequent Age Intervals T_x (6)	Average Remaining Lifetime[c] e_x (7)
<1	0.00235	100,000.00	235.21	99,788.31	7,978,689.00	79.79
1–4	0.00064	99,764.79	64.15	398,905.20		78.97
5–9	0.00022	99,700.63	22.41	498,447.20	7,479,996.00	
10–14	0.00046		45.52	498,277.30	6,981,549.00	70.04
15–19	0.00160	99,632.71	159.12	497,765.80	6,483,271.00	65.07
20–24	0.00314	99,473.59	312.63	496,586.40	5,985,505.00	60.17
25–29	0.00350	99,160.96		494,937.10	5,488,919.00	55.35
30–34	0.00329	98,813.88	325.13	493,256.50	4,993,982.00	50.54
35–39	0.00347	98,488.74	341.62	491,589.70	4,500,725.00	45.70
40–44	0.00568	98,147.13	557.21	489,342.60	4,009,135.00	40.85
45–49	0.00962	97,589.91	938.45	485,603.40		36.07
50–54	0.01636	96,651.46	1,581.62	479,303.30	3,034,189.00	31.39
55–59	0.02660	95,069.84	2,529.28	469,026.00	2,554,886.00	
60–64	0.04425		4,095.26	452,464.70	2,085,860.00	22.54
65–69	0.06832	88,445.30	6,042.83	427,119.50	1,633,395.00	18.47
70–74	0.11183	82,402.48	9,215.26	388,974.20	1,206,276.00	14.64
75–79	0.19166	73,187.21		330,868.30	817,301.50	11.17
80–84	0.31949	59,160.13	18,900.81	248,548.60	486,433.20	8.22
85–89	0.48416	40,259.31	19,491.82	152,567.00	237,884.60	5.91
90–94	0.63729	20,767.49	13,234.85	64,132.92	85,317.54	4.11
95–99	0.76100	7,532.64	5,732.32	17,600.11	21,184.62	2.81
100+	1.00000	1,800.33	1,800.33	3,584.51	3,584.51	1.99

[a] Period of life between two exact ages, stated in years.
[b] Proportion of persons alive at beginning of age interval who die during interval.
[c] Average number of years of life remaining at beginning of age interval.

Source: WHO Global Health Observatory (GHO), 2013a. World Health Organization, Geneva, Switzerland.

into the hypothetical cohort (see column 3), then there were about 79.8 years per man. Algebraically stated,

$$e_x = \frac{T_x}{l_x}$$

- It can be thought of as the average number of years men in the hypothetical cohort would live, according to the death rates assumed in column 2. Life expectancies can be computed for later ages as well, and they frequently are. The exercise requests that you do so for ages five and fifty-five.

2. Consult Table E5-1 to arrive at the following figures:

   a. From the $_nq_x$ column, find the percentage of the cohort reaching their sixty-fifth birthday that would survive to their seventieth birthday: _____

   b. From the l_x column, find the percentage of the cohort who would reach their sixty-fifth birthday: _____

   c. What number of cohort members die between their sixty-fifth and seventieth birthdays: _____

   d. What is the number of person-years lived by the cohort between ages sixty-five and seventy: _____

   e. What is the average remaining years of life at age sixty-five and what is the total life expectancy a sixty-five-year-old can expect: _____ and _____

3. Go the textbook website at www.demographytextbook.com to the exercises section of the Chapter 5 tab. Go to exercise 3, Gapminder's global child mortality rates, which are interactively graphed against total fertility rates. We are focusing on four countries: Bangladesh, China, Niger, and United Kingdom from 1840 through 2012. Hit play at the bottom left. After the interactive chart plays itself out answer the following questions:

   a. Write down the year and associated fertility rate and child mortality rate for each country at the beginning of the period and at the end of the period shown on the chart. What is their relationship with each other?

   b. Why do you think the time periods all have different starting points?

   c. What is the relationship between fertility and child mortality rates?

   d. Which of the countries experienced the largest total decline in child mortality from beginning until end of the periods graphed?

   e. Now click on the y-axis and change the measure from fertility to income per person. Click play. How do the trend lines change when using income instead of fertility? Why?

PROPOSITIONS FOR DEBATE

1. In a life table, the life expectancy at age one (e_1) logically can never exceed the life expectancy at age zero (e_0).

2. LDR life expectancy will continue to increase rapidly until it is about the same as MDR life expectancy.

3. Medical science is eliminating communicable diseases worldwide as major proximate causes of death and they will never again be as important on the national level.

4. Glaring international and socioeconomic differentials in mortality both could be eliminated by redistributing resources from the rich to the poor.

5. Less attention should be paid in the MDRs to reducing women's mortality since they are now living longer than men anyway.

6. As U.S. life expectancy increases and its population ages (see chapter 4), efforts to decrease mortality rates in the senior years will diminish.

7. The competition for national health resources will decline, both within MDR and LDR countries.

8. The average human life expectancy has the potential to extend well beyond 100 years and should be prioritized.

REFERENCES AND SUGGESTED READINGS

Anderson, Michael. 1996. *British Population History from the Black Death to the Present Day.* Cambridge: Cambridge University Press.

Anderson, Rozalyn, Dhanansayan Shanmuganayagam, and Richard Weindruch. 2009. "Caloric Restriction and Aging: Studies in Mice and Monkeys." *Toxicologic Pathology* 37(1): 47–51.

Anderton, Douglas L., and Susan Hautaniemi Leonard. 2004. "Grammars of Death: An Analysis of Nineteenth-Century Literal Causes of Death from the Age of Miasmas to Germ Theory." *Social Science History* 28(1): 111–143.

Anderton, Douglas L., Richard E. Barrett, and Donald J. Bogue. 1997. *The Population of the United States.* 3rd ed. New York: Free Press.

Arriaga, Eduardo E. 1994. *Population Analysis with Microcomputers.* Vol. I. Washington, DC: International Programs Center, Population Division, Bureau of the Census.

Birchenall, Javier A. 2007. "Economic Development and the Escape from High Mortality." *World Development* 35(4): 543–568.

Bogue, Donald J., Eduardo E. Arriaga, and Douglas L. Anderton, eds. 1993. *Readings in Population Research Methodology.* Vol. 1–8. Chicago: UNFPA/Social Development Center.

Brass, William. 1975. *Methods of Estimating Fertility and Mortality from Limited and Defective Data.* Chapel Hill, NC: Laboratories for Population Statistics.

Bryant, Clifton D., and Dennis L. Peck, eds. 2009. *Encyclopedia of Death and the Human Experience.* Thousand Oaks, CA: SAGE Publications.

Caselli, Graziella. 1991. "Health Transition and Cause-Specific Mortality." In Roger Schofield, David Reher, and Alain Bideau, eds., *The Decline of Mortality in Europe.* Oxford: Clarendon Press.

CDC (Centers for Disease Control). 2013a. "Adult Cigarette Smoking in the United States: Current Estimate, Adult Data Fact Sheets." *Smoking & Tobacco Use.* Retrieved June 1, 2013. http://www.cdc.gov/tobacco/data_statistics/fact_sheets/adult_data/cig_smoking/

———. 2013b. "Antibiotic Resistance Threats in the United States, 2013." Retrieved September 25, 2013. http://www.cdc.gov/drugresistance/threat-report-2013/pdf/ar-threats-2013-508.pdf

Chung, W., and M. D. Das Gupta. 2007. "The Decline of Son Preference in South Korea: The Roles of Development and Public Policy." *Population and Development Review* 33(4): 757–783.

CIA (Central Intelligence Agency). 2013. *CIA Factbook.* Retrieved April 2014. https://www.cia.gov/library/publications/download/download-2013/index.html

Clark, Rob, and B. Mitchell Peck. 2012. "Examining the Gender Gap in Life Expectancy: A Cross-National Analysis, 1980–2005." *Social Science Quarterly* 93(3): 820–837.

Coale, Ansley J. 1986. "The Decline of Fertility in Europe since the Eighteenth Century as a Chapter in Human Demographic History." In Ansley J. Coale and Susan Cotts Watkins, eds., *The Decline of Fertility in Europe*. Princeton, NJ: Princeton University Press.

Coale, Ansley J., and Paul Demeny. 1966. *Regional Model Life Tables and Stable Populations*. Princeton, NJ: Princeton University Press.

Corsini, Carlo A., and Pier Paolo Viazzo, eds. 1997. *The Decline of Infant and Child Mortality—The European Experience: 1750–1990*. Dordrecht, The Netherlands: Martinus Nijhoff.

Edwards, Ryan D. 2011. "Changes in World Inequality in Length of Life: 1970–2000." *Population Development Review* 37(3): 499–528.

Elo, Irma T. 2009. "Social Class Differentials in Health and Mortality: Patterns and Explanations in Comparative Perspective." *Annual Review of Sociology* 35: 553–572.

European Commission. 2008. *Emerging Epidemics Research: EU-Funded Projects 2002–2008*. Luxembourg: Office for Official Publications of the European Communities.

Ewbank, Douglas C. 1990. "Evaluation of Model Life Tables for East Africa." In Jacques Vallin, Stan D'Souza, and Alberto Palloni, eds., *Measurement and Analysis of Mortality: New Approaches*. Oxford: Clarendon Press.

Fenelon, Andrew, and Samuel H. Preston. 2012. "Estimating Smoking-Attributable Mortality in the United States." *Demography* 49(3): 797–818.

Frenk, Julio, José Luis Bobadilla, and Rafael Loranzo. 1996. "The Epidemiological Transition in Latin America." In Ian M. Timæs, Juan Chackiel, and Lado Ruzicka, eds., *Adult Mortality in Latin America*. Oxford: Clarendon Press.

Gaziano, Michael, J. 2010. "Fifth Phase of the Epidemiologic Transition: The Age of Obesity and Inactivity." *The Journal of the American Medical Association* 303(3): 275–276.

Gilles, Kate, and Charlotte Feldman-Jacobs. 2012. "When Technology and Tradition Collide: From Gender Bias to Sex Selection." Population Reference Bureau, Policy Brief. http://www.prb.org/pdf12/gender-bias-sex-selection.pdf

Gurven, Michael, and Hillard Kaplan. 2007. "Longevity among Hunter-Gatherers: A Cross-Cultural Examination." *Population and Development Review* 33(2): 321–365.

Guzman, José Miguel. 1989. "Trends in Socio-economic Differentials in Infant Mortality in Selected Latin American Countries." In Lado Ruzicka, Guillame Wusch, and Penny Kane, eds., *Differential Mortality: Methodological Issues and Biosocial Factors*. Oxford: Clarendon Press.

Heer, David M., and Jill S. Grigsby. 1992. *Society and Population*. 3rd ed. Englewood Cliffs, NJ: Prentice-Hall.

Hill, Kenneth, and Hania Zlotnik. 1982. "Indirect Estimation of Fertility and Mortality." In John A. Ross, ed., *International Encyclopedia of Population*. Vol. 1. New York: The Free Press.

Hill, Kenneth, Patama Vapattanawong, Pramote Prasartkul, Yawarat Porapakkham, Stephen S. Lim, and Alan D. Lopez. 2007. "Epidemiologic Transition Interrupted: A Reassessment of Mortality Trends in Thailand, 1980–2000." *International Journal of Epidemiology* 36(2): 374–384.

Horiuchi, Shiro. 1999. "Epidemiological Transitions in Developed Countries: Past, Present and Future." In *United Nations Health and Mortality Issues of Global Concern*. New York: UN.

Houweling, Tanja A., and Anton E. Kunst. 2010. "Socio-Economic Inequalities in Childhood Mortality in Low- and Middle-Income Countries: A Review of the International Evidence." *British Medical Bulletin* 93(1): 7–26.

Klarsfeld, André, and Frédéric Revah. 2003. *The Biology of Death: Origins of Mortality*. Ithaca, NY: Cornell University Press.

Kristof, Nicholas D., and Sheryl WuDunn. 2009. *Half the Sky: Turning Oppression into Opportunity for Women Worldwide*. New York: Vintage Books.

Krotki, Karol J., ed. 1978. *Developments in Dual System Estimation of Population Size and Growth*. Edmonton, Alberta: University of Alberta Press.

Kunitz, Stephen J. 1991. "The Personal Physician and the Decline of Mortality." In Roger Scho-field, David Reher, and Alain Bideau, eds., *The Decline of Mortality in Europe*. Oxford: Clarendon Press.

Lamptey, Peter, Merywen Wigley, Dara Carr, and Yvette Collymore. 2002. "Facing the HIV/AIDS Pandemic." *Population Bulletin* 57(3). Washington, DC: Population Reference Bureau.

Leon, David A. 2011. "Trends in European Life Expectancy: A Salutary View." *International Journal of Epidemiology* 40: 271–277.

Lopez, Alan D. 1993. "Causes of Death in Industrial and Developing Countries: Estimates for 1985–1990." In Dean T. Jamison et al., eds., *Disease Control Priorities in Developing Countries*. Oxford: Oxford University Press.

Lopez, Alan D., Graziella Caselli, and Tapani Valkonen, eds. 1995. *Adult Mortality in Developed Countries: From Description to Explanation*. Oxford: Clarendon Press.

Lozano, Rafael, Mohsen Naghavi, Kyle Foreman, Stephen Lim, Kenji Shibuya, Victor Aboyans, and Jerry Abraham, et al. 2012. "Global and Regional Mortality from 235 Causes of Death for 20 Age Groups in 1990 and 2010: A Systematic Analysis for the Global Burden of Disease Study 2010." *The Lancet* 380(9859): 2095–2128.

Luy, Marc. 2012. "Estimating Mortality Differences in Developed Countries from Survey Information on Maternal and Paternal Orphanhood." *Demography* 49(2): 607–627.

MacDorman, Marian F., Joyce A. Martin, T. J. Mathews, Donna L. Hoyert, and Stephanie J. Ventura. 2005. "Explaining the 2001–02 Infant Mortality Increase: Data from the Linked Birth/Infant Death Data Set." *National Vital Statistics Reports* 53(12). Hyattsville, MD: Centers for Disease Control and Prevention.

MacDorman, Marian F., and T. J. Mathews. 2011. "Understanding Racial and Ethnic Disparities in U.S. Infant Mortality Rates." *NCHS Data Brief* 74. Hyattsville, MD: Centers for Disease Control and Prevention.

Mackay, Judith, and Michael Eriksen. 2002. *The Tobacco Atlas*. Geneva: World Health Organization.

Marmot, Michael. 1995. "Social Differentials in Mortality: The Whitehall Studies." In Alan D. Lopez et al., eds., *Adult Mortality in Developed Countries: From Description to Explanation*. Oxford: Clarendon Press.

Mathers, Colin D., Ties Boerma, and Doris Ma Fat. 2009. "Global and Regional Causes of Death." *British Medical Bulletin* 92: 7–32.

McKeown, Thomas. 1976. *The Modern Rise in Population*. New York: The Academic Press.

NCHS (National Center for Health Statistics). 2011. *Health, United States, 2010: With Special Feature on Death and Dying*. Hyattsville, MD: Centers for Disease Control and Prevention.

———. 2012. "Prevalence of Obesity in the United States, 2009–2010." *NCHS Data Brief* 82. Hyattsville, MD: Centers for Disease Control and Prevention.

———. 2013. "Deaths: Final Data for 2010." *National Vital Statistics Reports* 61(4). Hyattsville, MD: Centers for Disease Control and Prevention.

Newport, Frank. 2011. "Americans Prefer Boys to Girls, Just as They Did in 1941." Gallup. Retrieved October 3, 2013. http://www.gallup.com/poll/148187/americans-prefer-boys-girls-1941.aspx

Obermeyer, Ziad, Julie Knoll Rajaratnam, Chang H. Park, Emmanuela Gakidou, Margaret C. Hogan, Alan D. Lopez, and Christopher J. L. Murray. 2010. "Measuring Adult Mortality Using Sibling Survival: A New Analytical Method and New Results for 44 Countries, 1974–2006." *PLOS Medicine* 7(4).

Obiri, G. U., E. J. Fordyce, T. P. Singh, and S. Forlenza. 1998. "Effect of HIV/AIDS Versus other Causes of Death on Premature Mortality in New York City, 1983–1994." *American Journal of Epidemiology* 147(9).

Olshansky, S. J., 2011. Aging, Health, and Longevity in the 21st Century. *Public Policy & Aging Report* 20(4): 3–13.

Olshansky, S. J., B. A. Carnes, and C. Casse. 1990. "In Search of Methuselah: Estimating the Upper Limits to Human Longevity." *Science* 250(4981).

Olshansky, S. J., B. A. Carnes, and A. Désesquelles. 2001. "Prospects for Human Longevity." *Science* 291(5508).

Olshansky, S. Jay, Bruce Carnes, Richard G. Rodgers, and Len Smith. 1997. "Infectious Diseases—New and Ancient Threats to World Health." *Population Bulletin* 52(2). Washington, DC: Population Reference Bureau.

Omran, Abdel R. 1977. "Epidemiological Transition in the U.S." *Population Bulletin* 32(2). Washington, DC: Population Reference Bureau.

———. 1982. "Epidemiological Transition." In John A. Ross, ed., *International Encyclopedia of Population.* New York: The Free Press.

Palloni, Alberto. 1989. "Effects of Inter-birth Intervals on Infant and Early Childhood Mortality." In Lado Ruzicka, Guillame Wusch, and Penny Kane, eds., *Differential Mortality: Methodological Issues and Biosocial Factors.* Oxford: Clarendon Press.

Pampel, Fred C. 2002. "Cigarette Use and the Narrowing Sex Differential in Mortality." *Population and Development Review* 28(1).

Peto, Richard, Gary Whitlock, and Prabhat Jha. 2010. "Effects of Obesity and Smoking on U.S. Life Expectancy." *New England Journal of Medicine* 362(9): 854–856.

Phuong Hoa, Nguyen, Chalapati Rao, Damian G. Hoy, Nguyen Duc Hinh, Nguyen Thi Kim Chuc, and Duc Anh Ngo. 2012. "Mortality Measures from Sample-Based Surveillance: Evidence of the Epidemiological Transition in Viet Nam." *Bulletin of the World Health Organization* 90: 764–772.

Pinnelli, Antonella, and Paola Mancini. 1997. "Gender Mortality Differences from Birth to Puberty." In Carlo A. Corsini and Pier Paolo Viazzo, eds., *The Decline of Infant and Child Mortality—The European Experience: 1750–1990.* Dordrecht, The Netherlands: Martinus Nijhoff.

Pollack, Andrew. 2013. "A.M.A. Recognizes Obesity as a Disease." *The New York Times* (June 18).

Popkin, Barry M., Linda S. Adair, and Shu Wen Ng. 2012. "Global Nutrition Transition and the Pandemic of Obesity in Developing Countries." *Nutrition Reviews* 70(1): 3–21.

PRB (Population Reference Bureau). 2010. "World Population Highlights: Key Findings from PRB's 2010 World Population Data Sheet." *Population Bulletin* 65(2).

———. 2011. *Population Bulletin: America's Aging Population* 66 (10). http://www.prb.org/pdf11/aging-in-america.pdf

———. 2014. *2014 World Population Data Sheet.* Washington, DC: Population Reference Bureau.

Preston, Samuel H. 1976. *Mortality Patterns in National Populations, with Special Reference to Causes of Death.* New York: Academic Press.

———, ed. 1978. *The Effects of Infant and Childhood Mortality on Fertility.* New York: Academic Press.

Preston, Samuel H., and Michael R. Haines. 1991. *Fatal Years: Child Mortality in Late Nineteenth-Century America.* Princeton, NJ: Princeton University Press.

Preston, Samuel H., and Verne E. Nelson. 1974. "Structure and Change in Causes of Death: An International Summary." *Population Studies* 28(1).

Ruzicka, Lado, Guillame Wusch, and Penny Kane, eds. 1989. *Differential Mortality: Methodological Issues and Biosocial Factors.* Oxford: Clarendon Press.

Schofield, Roger, David Reher, and Alan Bideau. 1991. *The Decline of Mortality in Europe.* Oxford: Clarendon Press.

Seifarth, Joshua E., Cheri L. McGowan, and Kevin J. Milne. 2012. "Sex and Life Expectancy." *Gender Medicine* 9(6): 390–401.

Siegel, Jacob S., and David A. Swanson, eds. 2004. *The Methods and Materials of Demography.* 2nd ed. New York: Academic Press.

Silva, Romesh. 2012. "Child Mortality Estimation: Consistency of Under-Five Mortality Rate Estimates Using Full Birth Histories and Summary Birth Histories." *PLOS Medicine* 9(8): e1001296.

Simons, Harmen, Laura Wong, Wendy Graham, and Susan Schkolnik. 1996. "Experience with the Sisterhood Method for Estimating Maternal Mortality." In Ian M. Timæs, Juan Chackiel, and Lado Ruzicka, eds., *Adult Mortality in Latin America*. Oxford: Clarendon Press.

Singh, Gopal K., and Mohammad Siahpush. 2006. "Widening Socioeconomic Inequalities in US Life Expectancy, 1980–2000." *International Journal of Epidemiology* 35(4): 969–979.

Stata Press. 2011. *Survival Analysis and Epidemiological Tables Reference Manual, Release 12*. College Station, TX: Stata Press.

Stolnitz, George J. 1982. "Mortality: Post–World War II Trends." In John A. Ross, ed., *International Encyclopedia of Population*. New York: The Free Press.

Taucher, Erica, Cecilia Albala, and Gloria Icaza. 1996. "Adult Mortality from Chronic Diseases in Chile, 1968–90." In Ian M. Timæs, Juan Chackiel, and Lado Ruzicka, eds., *Adult Mortality in Latin America*. Oxford: Clarendon Press.

The Gapminder Foundation. 2013. *Life Expectancy at Birth in Gapminder World, Version 6*. Data released on July 23, 2013. http://www.gapminder.org/data/documentation/gd004/

Trovato, F., and N. M. Lalu. 1996. "Narrowing Sex Differentials in Life Expectancy in the Industrialized World: Early 1970s to early 1990s." *Social Biology* 43.

———. 1998. "Contributions of Cause-Specific Mortality to Changing Sex Differences in Life Expectancy: Seven Nations Case Study." *Social Biology* 45.

UNAIDS (Joint United Nations Programme on HIV/AIDS). 2012. *Global Report: UNAIDS Report on the Global AIDS Epidemic, 2012*. Geneva, Switzerland: UNAIDS.

UNFPA (United Nations Population Fund). 2011. *Population Dynamics in the Least Developed Countries: Challenges and Opportunities for Development and Poverty Reduction*. Technical Division, Population and Development Branch. http://unfpa.org/public/home/publications/pid/7599

UNICEF. 2012. *Levels & Trends in Child Mortality, Report 2012: Estimates Developed by the UN Inter-Agency Group for Child Mortality Estimation*. New York: United Nations Children's Fund.

United Nations. 1973. *The Determinants and Consequences of Population Trends: New Summary of Findings on Interaction of Demographic, Economic and Social Factors*. Vol. 1. Population Studies series, no. 50. ST/SOA/SER.A/50. New York: United Nations.

———. 2009. *State of the World's Indigenous Peoples*. ST/ESA/328. New York: United Nations, Department of Economic and Social Affairs, Division for Social Policy and Development.

———. 2010. *The World's Women 2010*. ST/ESA/STAT/SER.K/19. New York: United Nations.

———. 2011a. *Sex Differentials in Childhood Mortality*. ST/ESA/SER.A/314. New York: United Nations, Department of Economic and Social Affairs, Population Division.

———. 2011b. *World Population Prospects: The 2010 Revision*. Population Division of the Department of Economic and Social Affairs. http://esa.un.org/wpp/.

———. 2012a. *The Millennium Development Goals Report 2012*. New York: United Nations.

———. 2012b. *World Mortality Report 2011*. ST/ESA/SER.A/324. New York: United Nations.

———. 2013a. *Principles and Recommendations for a Vital Statistics System, Revision 3 (Final Draft)*. United Nations, Department of Economic and Social Affairs. http://unstats.un.org/unsd/demographic/standmeth/principles/unedited_M19Rev3en.pdf

———. 2013b. *World Population Prospects: The 2012 Revision, Mortality Tables in EXCEL-Format*. Retrieved June 23, 2013. http://esa.un.org/wpp/Excel-Data/mortality.htm

Vallin, Jacques. 1991. "Mortality in Europe from 1720 to 1914: Long Term Trends and Changes in Patterns by Age and Sex." In Roger Schofield, David Reher, and Alain Bideau, eds., *The Decline of Mortality in Europe*. Oxford: Clarendon Press.

Vallin, Jacques, Stan D'Souza, and Alberto Palloni, eds. 1990. *Measurement and Analysis of Mortality: New Approaches*. Oxford: Clarendon Press.

Vallin, Jacques, and France Meslé. 1990. "The Causes of Death in France, 1925–1978: Reclassification According to the Eighth Revision of the International Classification of Diseases." In Jacques Vallin, Stan D'Souza, and Alberto Palloni, eds., *Measurement and Analysis of Mortality: New Approaches*. Oxford: Clarendon Press.

Vaupel, J. 2010. "Biodemography of Human Ageing." *Nature* 464: 536–542.

Walford, R. L. 2000. *Beyond the 120-Year Diet*. New York: Four Walls Eight Windows.

Walford, Roy, D. Mock, T. Maccallum, and J. Laseter. 1999. "Physiologic Changes in Humans Subjected to Severe, Selective Calorie Restriction for Two Years in Biosphere 2: Health, Aging and Toxicologic Perspectives." *Toxicological Sciences* 52(2).

Wendt, Amanda, et al. 2012. "Impact of Increasing Inter-pregnancy Interval on Maternal and Infant Health." *Pediatric and Perinatal Epidemiology* 26: 239–258.

WHO (World Health Organization). 1998. *World Health Report 1998: Executive Summary*. Geneva: World Health Organization.

——. 2002. *World Health Report 2002: Reducing Risks, Promoting Healthy Life*. Geneva: World Health Organization.

——. 2004. *World Health Report 2004: Changing History*. Geneva: World Health Organization.

——. 2009. *Global Health Risks: Mortality and Burden of Disease Attributable to Selected Major Risks*. Geneva: World Health Organization.

——. 2011. *WHO Report on the Global Tobacco Epidemic, 2011: Warning About the Dangers of Tobacco*. Geneva: World Health Organization.

——. 2012a. *Maternal Mortality, Fact Sheet No 348*. Media Centre. Retrieved June 1, 2013. http://www.who.int/mediacentre/factsheets/fs348/en/

——. 2012b. *Mortality Attributable to Tobacco*. Geneva: World Health Organization.

——. 2012c. *Prevention & Control of Viral Hepatitis Infection: Framework for Global Action*. WHO/HSE/PED/HIP/GHP 2012.1. Geneva: World Health Organization.

——. 2012d. *Trends in Maternal Mortality: 1990 to 2010*. Geneva: World Health Organization.

——. 2012e. *Confronting the Tobacco Epidemic in a New Era of Trade and Investment Liberalization*. Geneva: World Health Organization.

——. 2013a. Global Health Observatory (GHO) Data Repository. Retrieved June 17. http://apps.who.int/gho/data/node.main

——. 2013b. *World Health Statistics 2013*. Geneva: World Health Organization.

——. 2014. *Ebola Virus Disease, West Africa—Update*. Global Alert Response Report. http://www.who.int/csr/don/2014_07_08_ebola/en/

WHO Europe. 1998. *Health in Europe 1997: Report on the Third Evaluation of Progress Towards Health for all in the European Region of WHO (1996–1997)*. Copenhagen: World Health Organization.

World Bank. 2011. *World Development Report 2012: Gender Equality and Development*. Washington, DC: World Bank.

6

Morbidity and Health

"Morbidity" probably is not so familiar a term to most readers as is "fertility" or "mortality." Therefore, let us start with a tentative definition: **morbidity** refers to the prevailing condition of disease in a population. In this context, *disease* is defined broadly, to include *disability* and *illness*. More specifically, morbidity refers to the *frequency* of disease, both its *incidence* (how diseases spread through a population over time) and its *prevalence* (how much disease is encountered in a population at a given moment). One can think of morbidity as the opposite of *health* in a living population.

Morbidity is closely related to mortality, but it is not the same. Disease and disability often do hasten death, but not always. Death often follows disease and disability, but sometimes occurs without them.

Why Demographers Study Morbidity

Let us recall the guiding questions for demography, introduced in chapter 1: How many people, of *what kind*, are where . . . ? That is, demography is charged with studying not only population size, but also population composition. We already have treated two dimensions of composition in chapter 4: age and sex. These take priority in our text because they have such immediate impact on the population growth processes we are explaining. But what about morbidity; why does it get its own chapter?

We begin with the most obvious reason: disease is universally abhorred. Any incidence or prevalence of disease in a society is a "problem," almost by definition. The societal stake in knowing the incidence and prevalence of disease conditions is self-evident. In fact, the fields of demography and public health developed largely in tandem during modernization, motivated by a common purpose of improving the human condition.

189

A second reason is the relation between morbidity and the population processes. The close relation between morbidity and mortality (and thus population growth) is only the most obvious. Disease and disability also affect the likelihood of successful childbearing, as well as cohabitation, marriage, divorce and widowhood, migration, and indeed most of the processes treated in this text.

Morbidity and Mortality in the Epidemiological Transition

Let us adopt, somewhat arbitrarily, the following terminology. **Epidemiology** is a branch of medical science that deals with the incidence, distribution, and control of disease in a population. The **epidemiological transition**, as that term is used by demographers, consists of both the familiar Western *mortality transition* described in chapter 5 and the parallel *morbidity transition* described here.

Sources of Data

Where do we get data on the morbidity transition? Since mortality data are more commonly available for historical populations than are data on health and morbidity, much of what we know about disease in past times comes from mortality trends and causes of death. Yet, as we have cautioned, it is a mistake to equate rates of mortality and morbidity. Mortality measures often understate the health impact of disease. Morbidity was as high as 55% during the 1720–1722 plague in France, while mortality was as low as 8% (Benedictow, 1987). Morbidity and mortality trends also can follow different paths: Alter and Riley (1988) found that morbidity in England increased during the period from 1840 to 1890 as mortality rates were falling. When 19th-century urban conditions in the United States improved, mortality declined but morbidity from infectious diseases, such as tuberculosis, continued long after (Preston and Haines, 1991).

Fortunately, mortality data are not our only sources to study historical health. Human populations leave behind many pieces of evidence regarding historical morbidity, including skeletal remains, institutional health records, diaries and personal accounts, records of physicians and clinics, newspapers and public health records, and so on (Barbiera and Dalla-Zuanna, 2009; Signoli et al., 2002; Armelagos, 1990; Vargas, 1990; Fogel and Costa, 1997; Porter, 1993; Morel, 1977; Alter and Riley, 1988; Rosenberg, 1987). From such sources we can derive measures of health (e.g., physical stature, frequency of epidemics, etc.) and often find accounts of morbidity and its causes (e.g., health behaviors, public works initiatives, diagnoses and treatments, etc.).

Historical evidence also reveals popular misconceptions and limitations in medical knowledge. Figure 6-1, for example, highlights the medical advice distributed in all New York City newspapers during the cholera epidemic of 1832. This advice reflects prevailing morality and mythology, but little real knowledge of the underlying causes of cholera. When reading historical accounts or using historical data, one should bear in mind the limitations of knowledge and cultural biases of the time.

Figure 6-1

Cholera Advice of the New York City Medical Council, 1832

> ❖ *Notice* ❖
>
> *Be temperate* in eating and drinking,
>
> avoid crude *vegetables and fruits;*
>
> abstain from *cold water,* when heated;
>
> and above all from *ardent spirits* and
>
> if habit have rendered it indispensable,
>
> take much less than usual.
>
> *Sleep and clothe warm.*
>
> Avoid labor in the heat of day.
>
> Do not sleep or sit in a draught of air when heated.
>
> *Avoid getting wet.*
>
> Take no medicines without advice.

Source: New York Medical Counsel, 1849. *Preventives of Cholera!*

Two Underlying Causes

From these scattered pieces of evidence it often is possible to gain a broad picture of historical health and morbidity. Two important historical morbidity issues played a major role in the mortality decline and are of special interest to contemporary demographers: (1) malnutrition and (2) environmental hazards, especially contagion.

Malnutrition posed a major threat to the health of pretransition and transitional populations (Fogel, 2004). Even where famine mortality was not apparent, health and behavior were affected in the years after food shortages (Ó Gráda, 2009; Outhwaite, 1991; Wrigley and Schofield, 1981). By some estimates, beggars constituted nearly a fifth of the population in premodern times (e.g., Spielvogel, 2008; Cipolla, 1980; Laslett, 1983). More than a quarter of the English population of 1900 suffered the effects of poverty and hunger (Bowley and Burnett-Hurst, 1915). Physiological measurements, such as the height of military recruits, suggest that European populations at the beginning of the 19th century were chronically malnourished, and that risk of chronic disease may have been related to malnutrition among U.S. Civil War recruits half a century later (see Fogel and Costa, 1997; Fogel 2004). Nutritional deficiencies also reduced resistance to infection and contributed to the frailty and poor health of historical populations (Scott and Duncan, 2002; Swedlund and Armelagos, 1990; Rotberg and Rabb, 1985).

Contagion played a dominant role in urbanizing societies. Infectious diseases had a greater chance of passing from one individual to the next in densely settled urban areas (Preston and Haines, 1991). Tuberculosis, for example, is spread by respiratory contact (e.g. sneezing, coughing) and was one of the top two urban causes of death in the 19th century (Olshansky et al., 1997). Dense urban areas with inadequate sanitation and clean water also generated breeding grounds for waterborne diseases such as cholera, typhoid, or diphtheria.

Cholera, virtually nonexistent in rural areas, was a major disease in 19th-century urban centers (Olshansky et al., 1997; Rosenberg, 1987). In a pioneering urban health study of 1855, John Snow (reprinted 1965) mapped cases of a cholera epidemic in London only to discover a single contaminated well was responsible for nearly 500 deaths (see Figure 6-2). Removing the pump handle ended the epidemic and proved a turning point in understanding urban infectious disease.

Figure 6-2

Cholera Fatalities and Water Sources in London, 1854

Note: The pump causing the epidemic is marked with an *X* within the gray circle.

Source: Snow, 1855 (1965 reprint). *Snow on Cholera.*

Contagion was not the only environmental threat to health in crowded and rapidly growing urban areas. By the middle of the 19th century, demographers were studying the connections between poverty, urban life, and health (Cassedy, 1986). Despite the growing awareness of urban health issues, conditions in emerging cities and towns often did not improve until population growth and rapid development slowed, allowing public health services to keep pace with urban growth (Hautaniemi et al., 1999; Szreter, 1997).

Infant and Child Health

Just as demographers have a particular interest in infant mortality (see chapter 5), so they do in infant and child morbidity. Again, we find that the earliest years of life are particularly vulnerable, not only to death but also to disease. By the same token, morbidity in these years is most susceptible to transitional change with modernization.

The causes of improved infant and child health from the late 18th to the early 20th century are still hotly contested. Nutrition likely played a major role and has been argued to be the major influence on improving health (McKeown, 1976; Fogel, 2004). Other studies, however, have suggested that improved nutrition and access to other material resources were not major influences, or that they improved health only where conditions had been very unhealthy (Preston and Haines, 1991; Reid, 1997). Cities were harsh environments during the 18th and 19th centuries, with elevated levels of respiratory and summer diarrheal diseases among children (Schofield et al., 1991; Preston and Haines, 1991; Woods, 1993).

Preston and Haines (1991), among others (e.g., Corsini and Viazzo, 1997; Schofield et al., 1991), argue that health knowledge and practices played a major role in improved urban infant and child health. Specific practices reduced specific diseases. Hygiene in the home, such as breast-feeding infants or heating often-contaminated milk before bottle feeding, eventually reduced summer diarrheal diseases. New medical developments such as diphtheria antitoxin limited other diseases.

Historical health studies from the now more-developed countries have greatly influenced contemporary policies in less-developed countries (Corsini and Viazzo, 1997). As we shall learn, less-developed countries face many of the same health problems pre-transition MDRs did, even as they confront ominous new health threats.

Modern Morbidity Data

Even in the more-developed regions, morbidity data-gathering is difficult to standardize. This springs partially from the difficulty in defining morbid conditions. Whereas the major demographic processes are defined by specific events—births, deaths, moves across borders—such clarity does not attend the onset and departure of disease. Moreover, the very identification of a health condition (e.g., arthritis) as a "disease" is often ambiguous; it can even change over time in the same country. As we saw in the last chapter, for example, obesity was redefined as a disease in the United States in 2013. In addition, the extreme variety in the time sequence followed by the various diseases makes it difficult to settle on a single disease monitoring system.

Nevertheless, the public concern over health that has accompanied economic development is generating a growing body of morbidity data. These data, however, are varied in source and difficult to interpret, relative to other demographic data. Three categories of sources are described in the following sections: (1) surveillance systems and registries, (2) health surveys, and (3) cause-of-death reports.

Surveillance Systems and Registries

When a particular disease becomes widespread or otherwise alarming to the medical community, it can be defined as a *reportable disease* and trigger a surveillance effort. **Surveillance systems** are established to estimate the size of a health problem, detect epidemic outbreaks, characterize disease trends, and determine the necessary public health measures to form a response. Local authorities are typically charged with collecting data on new cases of disease and reporting them to a central, or national, organization that monitors, reports, and reacts to epidemic outbreaks or health threats.

The World Health Organization maintains several disease surveillance systems for reporting countries. These systems include the 150 WHO country offices, more than 110 national influenza centers forming FLUNET, a network of national rabies reference centers forming RABNET, and more than 60 HIV sentinel surveillance sites, among others. WHO chronicles weekly outbreaks and reported cases of specific diseases in the *Weekly Epidemiological Record*.

In the United States, most surveillance systems are overseen by the Centers for Disease Control (CDC). The CDC maintains surveillance systems for such conditions as birth defects, HIV/AIDS, sexually transmitted diseases, tuberculosis, and water- and food-borne disease outbreaks. The CDC reports weekly outbreaks and the occurrence of reportable diseases in the *Morbidity and Mortality Weekly Report* (MMWR).

Some health conditions are chronic or terminal, lasting either for long periods or until death. In such cases, disease registries may be set up to monitor the progress of known cases, demographic and diagnostic details, treatments, and so forth. Registries often are maintained at a local or state level with support from central governments. Since registries are expensive and difficult to maintain, they usually are established only for diseases of great medical research concern.

In the United States, the best example of a disease registry program is that for cancer, maintained by state and territorial health departments. The National Cancer Institute's Surveillance, Epidemiology and End Results (SEER) program maintains registers of cancer occurrence, treatment, and survival in selected states and metropolitan areas of the United States. The CDC provides support and standards for registries in the states and territories not covered by the SEER program. Together, these registries provide morbidity data on all cases undergoing treatment.

Health Surveys

Surveillance systems and registries, however, track only diseases prominent enough to be defined as "reportable." A far more inclusive source of morbidity data is a health survey. Since 1984, the U.S. Agency for International Development has funded a series of *Demographic and Health Surveys* (DHS) for samples of residents in over 100 countries throughout the world. These surveys collect information on family planning, maternal and child health, AIDS/STDs, and the like. Additional surveys are often circulated by national and local governments. In the United States, the National Health Interview Survey and the National Survey of Family Growth are just a few of the many quality surveys that provide detailed demographic and health information (see chapter 2, Box 2-4). Repetitive health surveys have the potential for generating surveillance systems; such systems, of course, can monitor a broad array of health conditions, not just a few prominent reportable diseases.

Cause-of-Death Reports

As we said in chapter 5, vital statistics systems normally report not only the fact of death and facts about the victim, but also the cause of death. The value of cause-of-death reports for the study of morbidity was enhanced greatly by enriching the reporting of *multiple* causes of death. In 1949 the sixth revision of the *International Statistical Classification of Diseases, Injuries and Causes of Death* was modified to recommend recording the immediate cause of death, intervening or intermediate causes, the underlying cause of death, and a list of other unrelated but contributing causes. Tabulations by underlying causes of death were adopted the same year internationally and in the United States. Underlying causes reveal the initial health problem that started the chain of events eventually leading to death, rather than the "final straw" or immediate cause. Analyses of the multiple causes recorded in death certificates can provide a fairly detailed picture of the morbidity events leading up to mortality. Methods for analyzing such complex data are, however, in need of further development and the quality of this detailed data varies widely (Nam, 1990; Redelings et al., 2006).

Morbidity data have improved dramatically. However, the quality of data still varies greatly between more-developed and less-developed countries, and by the severity of the specific medical conditions involved. In all countries, many individuals suffer from an illness or poor health that goes unreported or unrecorded; many suffer from health impairments such as arthritis or malnourishment but regard these as normal conditions of life rather than ill health. Because of the uneven development of national health-monitoring systems, much of the data reported in this chapter for less-developed countries are only estimates from surveys or sample reporting areas.

Measuring Morbidity

With adequate data from surveillance systems, there are a variety of measures that can be used to assess morbidity, which is defined as the frequency of disease. In earlier chapters we've discussed crude rates and age-sex-specific birth and death rates. Such rates measure the frequency of *events* in an **at-risk population**. Disease, however, is not simply an event nor as clearly defined as birth and death. A person can become ill suddenly or gradually. The illness may be reported or may never be reported. One disease may kill suddenly while another may last over a considerable period of time without mortality.

Morbidity Rates

First, let us consider how to compute simple rates for the occurrence or incidence of morbidity. Since the onset of morbidity is not always observed, the best we can do is to consider a *reported diagnosis*, which may occur well after the onset of the event we wish to measure. With this provision, a similar approach to birth and death rates can be used in measuring the levels of morbidity in a population; we can compute a rate at which people are diagnosed with the illness. The numerator of this rate would be the number of *newly reported cases* of the condition in a given period (usually a year). The denominator would be the population at risk of getting the illness during the same time period. This measure is called the **incidence rate**, that is:

$$\text{Incidence Rate} = \frac{\text{Number of New Cases}}{\text{Population at Risk}}$$

Once people are diagnosed with a condition they are no longer at risk of being *newly* diagnosed cases (until they have a full recovery and re-enter the population at risk), but they may live for any number of years afterward with the condition. Thus in the incidence rate, the population at risk of new incidence is not simply the population remaining alive, but those who have not been previously diagnosed with the condition. That is, the incidence rate measures the new incidence of a condition among the population not previously diagnosed with the condition. As such, they are especially useful in detecting epidemic outbreaks and changes over time in the occurrence of morbidity. Incidence rates allow us to make predictions about the risk of contracting a disease at a specific point in time. However, they do not tell us how prevalent the morbidity condition is at any given time.

To measure prevalence, we use a more familiar sort of rate, the **prevalence rate**, which is simply the number of people with a morbidity condition divided by the total population.

$$\text{Prevalence Rate} = \frac{\text{Number of All Cases}}{\text{Total Population}}$$

Both incidence and prevalence rates may be computed for age-sex-specific groups to reveal the age and sex patterns of morbidity. Both rates are often multiplied by 1,000 to express the rate per 1,000 people (at risk or total), but the denomination chosen can vary with the size of the numerator. Prevalence rates give us a sense for how widespread a particular disease is at a specific point in time.

Because we have two common measures of morbidity frequency, it is important to remember that they measure two very different things. Since the incidence rate measures *new* cases, instead of all cases, it will usually understate the prevalence or level of morbidity in a population. Conversely, a prevalence rate will generally overstate the incidence in the population because it includes all cases rather than only new cases. There are exceptions to these expectations. If diseases have a short duration and commonly occur, such as diarrheal diseases, they will not remain prevalent in a population but might have a very high incidence. Incidence and prevalence rates provide different information, and it is important not to confuse them.

Leading Mortality Causes

Deaths and death rates for the leading worldwide causes of mortality in 2010 are presented in Table 6-1. Mortality estimates are based on vital registration, verbal autopsy, mortality surveillance, censuses, surveys, hospital, police records, and mortuary records collected from 187 countries between 1980 to 2010 (Lozano et al., 2012). Because of the difficulty in measuring morbidity rates across all countries, global incidence and prevalence rates are shown only for some diseases in the table.

Aside from the substantive mortality information it provides, Table 6-1 allows us to contrast some incidence and prevalence rates. For instance, diarrhea is one of the leading causes of global morbidity, yet since this disease can be very short-lived, individuals could have had more than one episode during the year. The incidence does not imply that 1.7 billion different people had a single episode. The global prevalence rate for diarrhea is unknown because diarrheal diseases are of such short duration that their incidence rates will almost always be higher than prevalence rates. By contrast, for diseases of much longer duration, such as HIV-AIDS, which has no known cure, prevalence rates are much higher than incidence rates. Moreover, given the tremendous incidence of diarrheal diseases, the death rate is relatively low, showing that diarrhea, although a major cause of morbidity, is not as lethal per episode as are many other leading causes of morbidity. Cancer, for instance, has a much lower incidence, but the death rate from cancer is nearly six times as high as that for diarrhea.

Other morbidity causes may last a very long time yet not directly cause death, resulting in high rates of prevalence but low rates of death, and thus they are not listed

Table 6-1   Incidence, Prevalence, Deaths, and Age-Standardized Death Rates from Leading Mortality Causes, World, 2010

	Incidence (1,000s)	Prevalence (1,000s)	All Ages Deaths (1,000s)	Death Rates (per 100,000)
All Causes			52,769.7	784.5
Communicable Diseases				
Lower Respiratory Infections			2,814.4	41.0
HIV/AIDS	2,500	34,000	1,465.4	21.4
Diarrheal Diseases	1,700,000		1,445.8	20.9
Tuberculosis	8,800	12,000	1,196.0	18.0
Malaria	219,000		1,169.5	16.7
Hepatitis		500,000	307.7	4.6
Noncommunicable Diseases				
Cardiovascular & Circulatory Diseases			15,616.1	234.8
Neoplasms (Cancer)	12,662	28,803	7,977.9	121.4
Chronic Respiratory Diseases			3,776.3	57.0
Diabetes, Urogenital, Blood & Endocrine Diseases			2,726.2	41.0
Neurological Disorders			1,273.8	18.8
Digestive Diseases (Except Cirrhosis)			1,111.7	16.7
Cirrhosis of the Liver			1,030.8	15.6
Mental & Behavioral Disorders			231.9	3.5
Musculoskeletal Disorders			153.5	2.3

Note: Death rates are age-standardized. HIV/AIDS incidence and prevalence estimates are for 2011. Annual diarrheal disease incidence estimate is for around 2013. Malaria incidence estimate has an uncertainty range of 154 to 289 million. Chronic hepatitis B and C prevalence estimates for around 2010. Cancer incidence estimate is for 2008 and excludes non-melanoma skin cancer and prevalence estimate is for 5-years.

Source: Lozano et al., 2012; CDC, 2013; Ferlay et al., 2010; WHO, 2011, 2013a, 2013e, 2013g.

Careers in Demography

Monica Das Gupta
Research Professor, University of Maryland, 2012–present
Visiting Fellow, Population Reference Bureau, 2012–2013
World Bank Senior Demographer, 1998–2012

How did you decide that being a demographer was the career path for you?

I always wanted to work on development issues. Having studied social anthropology, demography seemed a good complement in quantitative methods to work on development issues.

What kind of education and training did you pursue to get to where you are in your career?

I received a bachelor's degree in social anthropology and a master's degree in demography from the London School of Economics, and then a doctorate in social anthropology and demography from the University of Sussex in the United Kingdom. Doing two years of intensive fieldwork in a North Indian village for my PhD dissertation was a huge educational experience for me, and one from which I have derived a lot of the ideas I subsequently worked on through my career. The only way I could repay the people in that village for their incredible generosity and patience with my endless questions was through my grammatical mistakes. The local language is a dialect of Punjabi and Hindi, and like French and German, has genders for most things like tables and chairs—this was something I never mastered, and it made them cry laughing.

The next crossroads moment was while working at the National Council for Applied Economic Research in New Delhi, where I was able to do a large-scale longitudinal survey to test some of the hypotheses I developed during my intensive fieldwork. It was an extraordinary privilege to be able to do both of these types of complementary research, with the in-depth qualitative research informing the quantitative data collection and analysis.

Working at the World Bank was a tremendous opportunity for me to immerse myself in development issues. There is such a wide range of areas being addressed there and so much collective expertise. I found that colleagues were enthusiastic about sharing their expertise, not worried about having their ideas "stolen." In my fourteen years there with the Development Research Group I focused on development in India, China, South Korea, Sri Lanka, Bangladesh, Pakistan, Vietnam, and Nigeria. Working there enabled me to work on many research areas in different geographical settings. This was paradise, especially the prospect of your work actually having some impact on people's thinking and policy making.

Describe your work/research as a demographer. What do you consider your most important accomplishments?

I have worked on various aspects of population, poverty, and development. I began with extensive village-level research on how communities respond to population pressure, and on community-level factors that encourage circular migration. I then did survey-based research on child health, including an apparent tendency for child deaths to cluster in a few households; and the tendency for gender bias against girls to increase with birth order.

Building on my field experience, I studied how family systems shape the life chances of different categories of household members—including gender differentials in health in Asia, as well as the household regulation of marriage and childbearing. More recently, I have also worked on public goods in health, focusing on public health systems to reduce a population's exposure to disease. This has included studying the institutional design of successful models of low-cost preventive public health systems in South Asia and other developing countries. Other recent work has been on state policies to reduce sex-selection; and a review of the interrelationships between population, poverty, and climate change.

My most useful contributions are perhaps in the fields of child health, family systems, public health systems, and the links between population, poverty, and climate change.

What do you see as the field's most important contribution as well as its greatest challenge?

The field of demography's most important contribution has been to the study of mortality. Its greatest challenge today for students is the limited number of jobs available, so the "sales pitch" to prospective demography students would be to bear in mind that the field offers infinite opportunity for multidisciplinary work in a very wide range of subject areas, and they need to be creative to benefit from this.

among the leading mortality causes shown in Table 6-1. Depression and behavioral disorders, for example, usually are neither readily cured nor lethal. As a result, the number of reported cases for mental disorders is much higher than the number of reported deaths. For example, in 2010 there were over 298 million reported cases of major depressive disorder and almost 273 million reported cases of anxiety disorders worldwide, compared to 0.2 million deaths due to mental and behavioral disorders (Lozano et al., 2012; Vos et al., 2012).

Let us turn briefly from incidence and prevalence rates to the substantive implications of the table. An obvious conclusion is the increased importance of noncommunicable diseases on a worldwide level. The three leading causes of global morbidity, ranked by age-standardized death rates, all are noncommunicable diseases: cardiovascular and circulatory diseases, cancer, and chronic respiratory diseases. Together, these three causes alone kill over 50% of people globally. The remaining top ten contributors to global mortality are infectious diseases of the respiratory system, HIV/AIDS, diarrheal diseases, tuberculosis, malaria, neurological disorders, digestive diseases, and diabetes.

Age and Sex Patterns of Morbidity

In the least-developed countries, infectious diseases dominate as the ultimate cause of death, while in high-income countries nine out of the top ten causes of death are noninfectious (WHO, 2008). Because children are particularly vulnerable to communicable diseases, children become sick and die more often than any other age group in the poorest countries (WHO, 2008). The more-developed regions, where degenerative diseases predominate, generally have the opposite age pattern.

The vast majority of people who develop serious health complications do so after age sixty. Ischemic heart disease, one of the leading causes of worldwide mortality, has an incidence rate over age sixty that is more than six times higher than in any younger age group (Murray and Lopez, 1996b; WHO, 2009). The general shift in age morbidity patterns over the course of the epidemiological transition does not, however, automatically mean that older people spend more time being ill than younger people. A lower respiratory infection in a child may lead to a lifetime of illness while an older person with ischemic heart disease could have a very short period of morbidity before death.

And what about sex patterns in morbidity? We know that women have a global advantage in overall life expectancy than men, and thus we might also expect that their (age-specific) morbidity rates would be generally lower. However, this is not always the case. In Africa, even though women have lower mortality rates than men, their higher HIV/AIDS infection rates and maternal conditions contribute to a high women's burden of disease there (WHO, 2009). Generally, women also report higher levels of depression and anxiety disorders than men (WHO, 2008). An ongoing demographic puzzle is the "gender paradox," which is based on multiple studies showing that women live longer than men yet report worse health at every age (Case and Paxson, 2005; Macintyre et al., 1999; Verbrugge, 1989). Although the so-called gender paradox is highly variable depending on what health outcome one examines (Macintyre et al., 1996), the debate centers on whether sex morbidity differences are based in biology, gendered subjectivities in well-being, or differing healthcare usage.

Morbidity Problems: Costs of Lost Life and Health

Our self-imposed exercise when defining population "problems" is to ask: Who is alarmed? What effects do these people see springing from the problematic trend or condition? What do they judge to be wrong with those effects? When dealing with morbidity problems, however, such questions are superfluous. The negative evaluation of disease and disability seems universal, not requiring rational elaboration or justification. So demographers quickly turn to the problem of measuring the *degree* of the negative impact. Many of these costs, such as anguish, lost opportunities, or suffering, are difficult or impossible to measure. Demographers can, however, provide some answers to more limited questions concerning the personal and social costs of ill health.

Years of Life Lost (YLL)

Using a life table we can estimate how many more years people might have lived if they had not died from a particular illness or cause (see chapter 5). When a person dies at age x, he or she fails to live out the average remaining lifetime, e_x, for other persons of that same age. If we sum all these years of life lost to those who died from a specific cause we would have the *total cause-specific* **years of life lost**, or YLL, to deaths from that cause:

$$\text{YLL} = \text{Sum of } e_x \text{ for all Deaths from a Cause}$$

The total YLL gives us a picture of the cost to society in lost years-lived from deaths due to a given cause. If we divide this total by the number of people dying from the cause, we would get the *average cause-specific years of life lost* to deaths from that cause. The average YLL tells us the average personal cost in lost years-lived for those who die from the cause.

Variations on the strategy are possible. Where data are limited, we might simplify the calculation of YLL by assuming all individuals are expected to live an average life expectancy at birth, e_0. In populations where life expectancies tend to be high, a single high life expectancy standard is often used. In such countries it is common to use a life expectancy of seventy-five years, referred to as **years of potential life lost** (YPLL), to gauge premature mortality occurring before age seventy-five. Or sometimes to emphasize *productive* years of life lost we might count only years of life lost up to an expected retirement age, for example, sixty-five years old.

Reliable data to compute YLL are difficult to obtain in many parts of the world. As part of a path-breaking and ambitious effort to study the burdens of disease, the World Health Organization and the World Bank used statistical models to estimate years of life lost to specific causes throughout the world. Figure 6-3 gives these estimates for the percentage of years of life lost due to ten leading causes of death in the world. The causes are listed by increasing order of the percentage of deaths for which they are responsible.

Comparing deaths to years of life lost from these leading causes shows a basic fact of morbidity. Infectious diseases and conditions that occur early in life account for a greater percentage of YLL than of deaths. Conversely, those conditions that cause high mortality concentrated in the older population—for example, heart, cerebrovascular, and chronic obstructive pulmonary diseases—account for a far greater percentage of deaths than years of life lost. In developing countries, a young population structure (see chapter 4) with a high prevalence of infectious disease deaths (see chapter 5) results in a very high number of life-years lost.

Figure 6-3

Deaths and Years of Life Lost to 10 Leading Causes, World, 2010

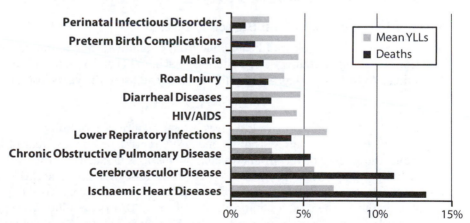

Source: Data taken from IHME, 2012b. *Global Burden of Disease Study 2010.* Percentage figures and graph produced by Eiko Strader.

Years of Health Lost

Years of life lost tell us how much life is lost due to premature death. But, strictly speaking, that is a measure of the cost of mortality, not morbidity. Where detailed survey data are available, we can ask how long a person has suffered from ill health due to a particular cause, what medical resources he or she required, how disabled he or she was during the illness, and so on. The National Health Interview Survey collects this sort of data for the population of the United States. But in areas without detailed surveys, as in many developing countries, we have to estimate morbidity impacts indirectly. Some of these complex estimation procedures are described below.

Episodes of ill health differ in their *duration* and also in their degree of *disability*, i.e., the severity of limits they place on a person's normal life activities. Missing a day of school due to a nasty cold, something we've probably all experienced, is an example of short duration with minimal disability. In other cases, which we hope not to experience, morbidity is long-term, very disabling, and life-threatening.

Let us deal with duration first. Suppose, for example, that we have medical data telling us the average incident of tuberculosis lasts for 2.1 years. If we multiply the reported occurrences of tuberculosis by this average duration, we get a crude estimate of how many years will be spent with this disability.

But to what extent were those people disabled during this time? If we knew a particular disease let a person do only half of his or her normal activities, we might estimate that for each year that person had the disease, half of a healthy year was lost to ill health. A person who was completely disabled would have lost the entire year to ill health. The *Global Burden of Disease* project estimates years of life lived with, and lost to, health disabilities of known severity and duration. This measure is called the **years lived with disability**, or YLD. Stated as a general formula,

$$YLD = occurrences \times duration \times disability$$

where disability is a percentage for degree of severity.

Years of Life and Health Lost: Burden of Disease

To measure the total loss of healthy life from disability during morbidity episodes and from resulting mortality, we can add together the YLD and YLL for a given cause. Summing all years lost to morbidity is the **disability adjusted life-years lost**, or DALY:

$$DALY = YLD + YLL$$

Disability adjusted life-years lost gives a total picture of morbidity and mortality impacts due to specific causes. That is, one DALY represents one lost year of healthy living and allows us to distinguish between those diseases that cause early death but little disability, as opposed to those that do not kill but cause disability. The DALY gives us a sense for the total burden of disease, showing how poor health impacts the quality of life of individuals. The diseases that contribute most to DALYs are different depending on the level of a country's development. Table 6-2 shows that developed countries suffered the greatest loss of healthy life due to noncommunicable diseases. Note that in this chapter our regional categories are expanded, reflecting the categorization method used by the *Global Burden of Disease Study 2010* (see the Appendix at the end of this chapter for country composition).

Over half of DALYs are due to mental and behavioral disorders, cardiovascular disease, cancer, diabetes, and musculoskeletal disorders in more-developed countries. In contrast, communicable diseases and conditions related to children or to childbearing (i.e., maternal, perinatal, and nutritional conditions) cause the greatest loss of healthy life in the less-developed regions (column 3). The biggest differences between the regions in terms of loss of healthy life are explained by the major shift from infectious diseases to degenerative diseases over the epidemiological transition. One interesting anomaly can be seen in the Caribbean region, reporting slightly over half of DALYs due to injuries (column 4). This is largely due to the fact that more than a quarter of the Caribbean population resides in Haiti, which experienced a devastating earthquake in 2010 (Murray et al., 2012).

Table 6-2   Percentage of Disability Adjusted Life-Years Lost Due to Specific Morbidity Causes by World Region, 2010

Regions (1)	Non-Communicable Diseases (2)	Communicable, Maternal, Neonatal, and Nutritional Disorders (3)	Injuries (4)	All Causes
High-income Asia Pacific	83.4%	6.4%	10.2%	100.0%
Western Europe	86.9%	4.2%	8.9%	100.0%
Australasia	85.6%	4.6%	9.8%	100.0%
High-income North America	85.3%	5.2%	9.5%	100.0%
Central Europe	84.6%	5.2%	10.2%	100.0%
Southern Latin America	77.0%	11.6%	11.4%	100.0%
Eastern Europe	76.9%	9.0%	14.1%	100.0%
East Asia	76.8%	10.3%	12.9%	100.0%
Tropical Latin America	68.8%	16.7%	14.5%	100.0%
Central Latin America	64.8%	19.5%	15.7%	100.0%
Southeast Asia	59.5%	29.9%	10.6%	100.0%
Central Asia	64.8%	23.3%	11.9%	100.0%
Andean Latin America	58.7%	29.5%	11.8%	100.0%
North Africa and Middle East	67.9%	22.3%	9.8%	100.0%
Caribbean	33.4%	16.4%	50.2%	100.0%
South Asia	45.5%	42.9%	11.6%	100.0%
Oceania	47.7%	42.0%	10.3%	100.0%
Southern sub-Saharan Africa	29.4%	61.4%	9.2%	100.0%
Eastern sub-Saharan Africa	25.2%	67.0%	7.8%	100.0%
Central sub-Saharan Africa	22.8%	68.9%	8.3%	100.0%
Western sub-Saharan Africa	21.3%	71.3%	7.4%	100.0%
World	54.0%	34.9%	11.2%	100.0%

Note: Aggregated percentages from the original 21 morbidity cause categories calculated by Eiko Strader.

Source: IHME, 2012b. *Global Burden of Disease Study 2010.*

Health-Adjusted Life Expectancy

Health-adjusted life expectancy (HALE) is a measure of life expectancy at birth minus the number of years of life spent in poor health or injured. HALE is a helpful summary measure of population health because it indicates the number of years that an individual can expect to live before the onset of morbidity. In 2010, the average health-adjusted life expectancy for the world was estimated to be fifty-eight years for men and sixty-two years for women (Salomon et al., 2012). Not surprisingly, HALE measures are greater for the more-developed regions compared to the less-developed regions of the world. While we learned in chapter 5 that overall life expectancies in MDRs are significantly greater than those in LDRs (Table 5-2), Figure 6-4 illustrates that the longer lives lived by MDR populations are also significantly healthier.

As can be seen from Figure 6-4, even among the MDRs, HALE varies greatly. For example, there is a seven-year HALE gap between Eastern and Western Europe. And Asian HALEs vary greatly by region, with East Asia (primarily China) ranked above some MDRs, while Central and South Asia are ranked closer to the bottom. Unfortunately, while we like to think that progress in reducing morbidity throughout the world has been a continuously forward process, substantial declines in HALE took place at the end of the 20th century. The ensuing social and economic instability upon the disintegration of Communism had repercussions on population health, with a decline of four years in health-adjusted life expectancy in Eastern Europe and the former Soviet Union between 1990 and 2000 (WHO, 2003a). The same regression took place in sub-Saharan Africa, where health-adjusted life expectancy in southern sub-Saharan Africa

Figure 6-4

Health-Adjusted Life Expectancy (HALE) by Regions, 2010

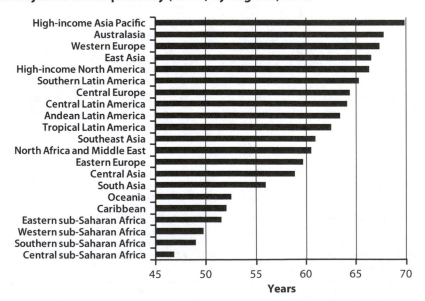

Source: Data from IHME, 2012a. *Global Burden of Disease Study 2010.* Graph created by Eiko Strader.

declined by five years between 1990 and 2010 from HIV/AIDS related morbidity (Salomon et al., 2012).

Morbidity Problems: Risk Factors

It is our habit in this text to define "problems" as unwanted consequences of demographic facts. In this chapter, we wish to broaden the discussion to include the immediate underlying *causes* of those facts—that is, morbidity *risk factors*. Partially this is because morbidity conditions are themselves so universally devalued that we can assume a universal desire to minimize them. Partially it is because such risk factors are so closely associated with unwanted morbidity conditions that the factors themselves share the negative social evaluation; malnutrition, for instance, is considered bad, irrespective of its morbidity consequences.

Relative Importance

To compare the worldwide importance of major categories of risk factors, let us employ some of the measures introduced in the previous section: percent of deaths, years of life lost, and disability adjusted life-years lost to the factor. These measures are presented for the twelve major categories of risk factors in Table 6-3, ranked in the order of deaths caused (in millions).

The leading risk factors causing death in the world are sedentary lifestyles and poor diets, which result in high blood pressure, diabetes, and high cholesterol levels, as well as high body-mass index (BMI). While childhood underweight causes a signif-

Table 6-3   Global Morbidity and Mortality Attributable to 10 Major Risk Factors and Clusters, 2010

Risk Factor	Deaths Caused (in Millions) (1)	Years of Life Lost (YLLs, in Millions) (2)	Disability Adjusted Life-Years Lost (DALYs, in Millions) (3)
Dietary Risks	10.4	210.0	229.7
High Blood Pressure	9.4	161.9	173.6
Smoking	6.3	137.8	156.8
Household Air Pollution	3.5	100.2	107.1
High Body-Mass Index	3.4	66.1	82.7
Diabetes (High Plasma Glucose)	3.4	65.8	89.0
Ambient Particulate Matter Pollution	3.2	72.4	76.2
Physical Inactivity	3.2	59.0	69.3
Alcohol Use	2.7	77.7	98.3
High Total Cholesterol	2.0	37.7	40.9
Childhood Underweight	0.86	73.0	77.3
Occupational Risks	0.85	32.3	62.5

Note: Dietary risks, smoking, and occupational risks are risk clusters.

Source: Data taken from IHME, 2012c.

icantly lower number of deaths than other risk factors, it contributes to relatively high YLLs and DALYs. This is because most of those suffering from low caloric intake and vitamin deficiencies are infants and children who go on to suffer from these child-hood conditions later in life, whereas those suffering from high BMI and cholesterol tend to be middle-aged or elderly. WHO estimates that 17%, or 99 million, of the world's children under five in developing countries were underweight in 2011, which also makes them more immediately susceptible to infectious and parasitic diseases (WHO, 2013b).

Of the remaining risk factors in Table 6-3, many reflect unhealthy behaviors, such as tobacco and alcohol consumption. These risks weigh heavily on adults and young adults in more-developed countries, but some also are major threats in less-developed countries. LDRs in particular are exposed to health threats stemming from poor infrastructure and environmental pollution, such as unclean water and compromised air quality.

Because many morbidity causes and health risks are shared by MDRs and LDRs, we will not, as in most other chapters, sharply divide our discussion of health problems by the development dichotomy. Instead, we will discuss health problems in a sort of general progression, from those that are most concentrated and severe in the least developed countries, to those that are shared health concerns, ending with those that are most concentrated in MDRs. This progression also roughly parallels the historical evolution of morbidity problems over the epidemiological transition experienced by MDRs.

Malnutrition

As part of the United Nations' Millennium Development Goals, child malnutrition has come to be recognized as a foremost indicator of a nation's overall public health well-being (United Nations, 2005; WHO, 2012). Nutritional morbidity is best identified by its universal consequence: physical growth deficiencies in children (de Onis et al., 1999; de Onis and Blössner, 2003). Figure 6-5 shows the prevalence of children in less-developed regions who suffer from malnutrition, as evidenced by moderate to severe underweight or stunting. **Stunting** is an indicator of chronic malnutrition and measures a child's shortness for age. As the figure shows, progress has been quite variable by region. Malnutrition is most prevalent in Africa, where nearly two of every ten children are underweight and more than a third of all children are stunted. Stunting prevalence is higher than underweight prevalence since it is a long term, cumulative indicator of past episodes of underweight and malnutrition.

Infant and Child Morbidity

Malnutrition and unhealthy environments are especially burdensome to the health of infants and children in the LDRs. However, since 1990 there have been considerable improvements thanks to two public health campaigns that have played major roles in reducing morbidity among children: First, immunization against major diseases (measles, tuberculosis, diphtheria, whooping cough, tetanus, and polio) increased from 20% of the world's children in 1981 to 83% in 2011 (Gelbard et al., 1999; WHO, 2004, 2013f). Second, treatment for diarrheal disease—oral rehydration therapy—has prevented millions of diarrheal deaths to young children, although the therapy still lacks widespread use where it is needed most (Forsberg et al., 2007; Gelbard et al., 1999).

Figure 6-5

Estimated Prevalence of Children Under Five Years Affected by Moderate to Severe Stunting and Underweight, Less-Developed Regions, 2011

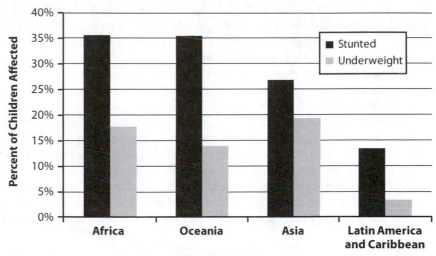

Note: Asia excludes Japan, and Oceania excludes Australia and New Zealand.

Source: United Nations Children's Fund, World Health Organization, The World Bank, 2012. *Levels and Trends in Child Malnutrition*.

Environmental Health

Table 6-3 tells us that indoor and outdoor smoke pollution are major morbidity risk factors. Population density historically has contributed to these environmental deficits and, through them, to more immediate causes of death. Infectious diseases continue to plague densely settled areas with inadequate public health services. Cholera, for example, continues to be a threat in some countries, especially in times of crisis or natural disaster, where sanitation and fresh water supplies are inadequate.

Environmental health concerns associated with density are again, generally, worst in rapidly growing urban centers of the LDRs (see chapter 10). Over half of the urban population in less-developed countries lives in extreme poverty, with billions of people lacking access to adequate sanitation and safe water supplies (WHO and UNICEF, 2006; WHO, 1997). High levels of outdoor air pollution emissions are a growing and serious problem in urban centers (WHO, 2002; World Nuclear Association, 2011). In addition, indoor air pollution from burning solid fuels for cooking and heating with inadequate ventilation is also a severe problem (WHO, 2002). Air contamination, particularly that occurring indoors where people spend most of their time, leads to respiratory infections, cancers, and pulmonary disease.

Unhealthy Lifestyles

The major sources of morbidity in more-developed countries are degenerative diseases and other health risks that are artifacts of human activity; less-developed countries also have seen a premature increase in these health threats as they have begun their mortality declines. Specifically, the HIV/AIDS and tobacco pandemics clearly are related to lifestyle behaviors—unsafe sex or illicit drug use (the major, but not the only, sources of HIV infection) and smoking. Both epidemics cause not only death but significant morbidity. Thirty-four million people currently live with HIV/AIDs, mostly in LDRs, and tobacco-related morbidity is projected to increase into the foreseeable future, causing more disability adjusted life-years lost than almost any other single disease in the MDRs (CDC, 2013; WHO, 2009).

Obesity is another example of lifestyle-related health risks in MDRs, as well as in some less-developed countries with aging populations. It is becoming a major source of disability adjusted life-years lost in MDRs and a primary risk factor globally (WHO, 2009). One of every three people in the world age twenty and older is overweight (i.e., body mass index greater than 24) and one of every ten are obese (BMI greater than 29) (WHO, 2013h). Obesity is a direct cause of disability and, more importantly, is a major contributing factor for heart disease and other degenerative diseases. In the United States, where childhood and adolescent obesity is high, new forecasting estimates suggest that future morbidity in the form of early-onset diabetes and cardiovascular disease is likely to occur earlier in the life cycle than previously (Reither et al., 2011).

Injuries

Injuries result from human activities such as automobile accidents, drowning and accidental poisonings, self-harm, and interpersonal violence. Currently, injuries account for 9.6% of total mortality, 13.5% of YLLs, 6.1% of YLDs, and 11.2% of DALYs worldwide (IHME, 2012a, 2012b, 2012c; WHO, 2013d). The majority of the world's injury-related mortality rates stem from road-traffic injuries, followed by interpersonal and personal (suicide) violence (IHME, 2012b; WHO, 2003b, 2013c). Resulting morbidity from injuries is considered a major health problem for two reasons. First, many of these risks are clearly preventable; second, younger people are particularly at risk, so the years of life lost are magnified.

The significance of injuries is apparent in Figure 6-6, which shows the years of life lost (YLL) per 100,000 population under age sixty due to injury, compared with cancer and cardiovascular and circulatory diseases, in several more-developed regions. In the United States and Canada, injuries are responsible for more YLLs than either cancer or cardiovascular and circulatory diseases, even though the mortality rate from injuries is only one-fifth that of cardiovascular and circulatory diseases and one-fourth that of cancer. Eliminating only injury mortality in North America, where men's death rates from injury are almost twice that of women's, would add more than two years to male life expectancy at birth (Rockett, 1998; WHO, 2003b). Injuries result in morbidity losses similar to those for the leading causes of death in all the more-developed countries listed in Figure 6-6.

Frail Old Age

We have seen (in chapter 4) that populations age as fertility and old-age mortality decline. As we suggested in the last chapter, it is difficult to call increasing life expectancy a "problem." However, the growing percentage of the world's population that is very old (sometimes called "grandevity") does raise morbidity concerns. According to

Figure 6-6

Years of Life Lost (before Age 60) Due to Injuries, Cancer, and Cardiovascular and Circulatory Diseases in Four More-Developed Regions, 2010

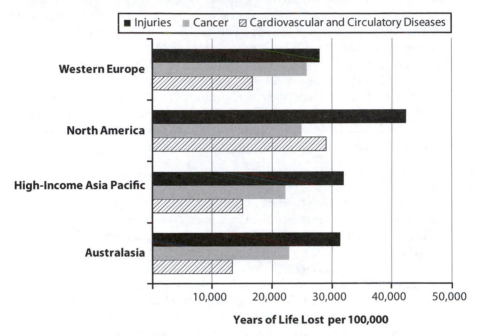

Note: High-income Asia Pacific countries include Brunei, Japan, South Korea, and Singapore.

Source: Data taken from IHME, 2012c. Graph created by Eiko Strader.

the United Nations, there were roughly 108 million people aged eighty years and older in 2010 worldwide. This number is projected to increase more than seven-fold by 2100, to 830 million, when the medium fertility projection variant is used. The number of nonagenarians (ninety to ninety-nine years of age) is projected to increase by fifteen-fold, and that of centenarians (100-plus years old) by *fifty-seven-fold* (United Nations, 2013).

Demographers debate the meaning of living longer lives in relation to morbidity. Initially, it was argued that longer life expectancies will simply force people to suffer through expanded periods of morbidity in the final segment of their lives (Gruenberg, 1977; Olshansky et al., 1991; Rothenberg et al., 1991). Others argued for a compression in morbidity—that is, that old-age disability and frailty would be compressed into a shorter period before death (Fries, 1980) or that the relationship between mortality and morbidity are proportionally linked to one another, so that as one decreases the other decreases in similar measure (Manton and Land, 2000). The good news is that most studies now show support for lessened morbidity with increases in life expectancy (Freedman et al., 2002; Freedman et al., 2007; Vaupel, 2010). Evidence shows that functional disabilities, such as decreased mobility, blindness, and deafness, have been on a constant decline for Americans at the same time that life expectancies have become elongated (Costa, 2002; CDC and the Merck Company Foundation, 2007). This is attributable to the overall reduction of some debilitative diseases that traditionally accompanied old age, as well as advances in medical technology that ameliorate the effects of old-age diseases. Even so, a quarter of the U.S. population over age sixty-five, for example, reports that they are not in good health, and more than a fifth of those over age eighty-five are confined to skilled nursing facilities (Federal Interagency Forum on Aging-Related Statistics, 2012). Grandevity also often means that an individual is more likely to require medical services. For example, in the United States almost 50% of residents over sixty-five years of age report some sort of disability (Brault, 2012).

The morbidity and attendant healthcare needs that come with very old age are largely responsible for the much higher cost of social services for those over age sixty-five in the MDRs (chapter 5). Morbidity among those who achieve grandevity will force, and has already forced, difficult policy decisions.

SUMMARY

Almost everyone has experienced, and will experience, the personal costs of ill health and morbidity during his or her life. Every population bears significant social costs from morbidity, and ill health can affect virtually all other demographic behaviors. Not surprisingly, then, morbidity historically has been of considerable interest to demographers.

Key aspects of morbidity include the *severity* of disabilities caused by the condition, the *duration* of the condition, the age of morbidity incidence, and the chances the condition will result in death. These dimensions of ill health suggest several different ways to measure morbidity, each of which captures different aspects of morbidity. *Incidence rates* tell us how frequently new cases are reported among those at risk of developing or contracting the condition in a given period of time. *Prevalence rates* measure what proportion of a population currently has the morbid condition.

Other measures estimate the costs of morbidity. *Years of life lost* (YLL) reflects the effects of a condition on life expectancy, the number of years we might have expected people to live if they had not experienced the condition. *Years lived with disability* (YLD) is a measurement that combines the effects of severity, duration, and incidence to measure the loss of healthy life to morbidity during a person's lifetime. The sum of life-years lost to mortality and years lived with disability is called the *disability adjusted life-years lost* (DALY). *Health-adjusted life expectancy* (HALE) is a measure of life expectancy at birth minus the number of years of life spent in poor health or with injuries.

The morbidities that cause the highest mortality in the world today are noncommunicable diseases instead of communicable (infectious) diseases. The three leading causes are cardiovascular and circulatory diseases, cancer, and chronic respiratory diseases. Infectious disease, accidents, and other conditions that occur early in life are responsible for a far greater percentage of years of life lost to morbidity than for deaths. Noncommunicable diseases that are concentrated in the older population, on the other hand, account for a far greater percentage of deaths than of years of life lost.

The major causes of morbidity in more-developed and in less-developed countries reflect the extent of their epidemiological transition and the decline of infectious diseases. Communicable diseases and conditions related to infancy or childbearing are responsible for the greatest loss of healthy life, or DALYs, in less-developed countries.

Noncommunicable and degenerative diseases cause the greatest loss of healthy life in more-developed countries and are rapidly increasing in many less-developed countries. Over the course of the epidemiological transition, as infectious diseases declined and degenerative ones rose, the age incidence of morbidity also changed, with morbidity among children generally falling. Prior to the epidemiological transition, the greatest *underlying* influences on levels of MDR morbidity were undernutrition and hazardous urban environments. These two factors are still significant underlying causes of world-wide morbidity and ill health. Today, widespread vaccination programs, modern knowledge of health and hygienic practices, and specific medical training programs have given LDRs advantages that MDRs did not have. The HIV/AIDS, tobacco, and obesity pandemics are, however, significant challenges to all countries today.

Sedentary lifestyles and unhealthy diets are now major contenders in underlying causes of morbidity. Injuries arising from human activities also are major underlying causes of morbidity. Most of the morbidity from lifestyle and injury is preventable. In contrast, much of the morbidity among those who achieve extreme old age is difficult to prevent and is increasing in MDRs. The healthcare needs of aging MDR populations will require difficult choices to be made in the allocation of scarce social resources.

As premature mortality has declined throughout much of the world, concerns over morbidity have risen. Ill health has both personal and social costs that often can exceed even those of mortality. And morbidity can affect every other aspect of life, including all demographic behaviors. Although the past few decades have seen dramatic successes in combating morbidity, e.g., vaccination programs and oral rehydration therapy, the rise of degenerative diseases and new emerging infectious diseases may challenge this progress in the future. If recent advances against infectious diseases and in public health continue, the aging of the world's population and lifestyle choices will likely continue to shape morbidity trends into the foreseeable future.

EXERCISES

1. Table E6-1 on the following page shows the reported prevalence and incidence of HIV/AIDS in the United States during 2009. Dividing the prevalence of AIDS in row 2 by the population (in 100,000s) of row 1 gives us the prevalence rate per 100,000 population shown in row 3 of the table. Looking at column 1, for example, 109.38 of every 100,000 adults and adolescents lived with AIDS in 2009.

   Dividing the number of people with HIV in row 4 by the population in row 1 gives the prevalence of HIV (without AIDS) in row 5.

   Finally, row 6 estimates the population at risk of contracting a new HIV infection (again in 100,000s) during the year and row 7 reports the new HIV cases reported during 2009. Dividing these new cases by the population at risk gives the incidence rates reported in row 8 of the table.

   Your exercise is to fill in the three blank cells of this table.

2. On May 4 the *Morbidity and Mortality Weekly Report* carried this story:

   Human Rabies—New York
   A 29-year-old male U.S. Army soldier with progressive right arm and shoulder pain, nausea, vomiting, ataxia, anxiety, and dysphagia was admitted to an emergency

Table E6-1   HIV/AIDS Incidence and Prevalence Estimates, United States, 2009

Population and Rate Estimates	Adults and Adolescents (1)	Children Under 13 (2)	Total (3)
1. July 1, 2009 Population (in 100,000s)	4477.38	577.87	5055.25
2. Living with AIDS at the End of 2009	489,729.00	546.00	490,275.00
3. AIDS Prevalence Rate	109.38	0.94	
4. Living with HIV at the End of 2009	805,161.00	2929.00	808,090.00
5. HIV Prevalence Rate		5.07	159.9
6. Estimated Population at Risk (in 100,000s)	4469.33	577.84	5047.17
7. HIV Cases Reported in 2009	42,440.00	185.00	42,625.00
8. HIV Incidence Rate		0.32	8.4

Note: Estimates are for 46 states and 5 U.S. dependent areas with confidential name-based HIV infection reporting.

Source: Centers for Disease Control, 2010. *HIV/AIDS Surveillance Report*, tables 1b, 17b, and 18b; U.S. Census Bureau, 2009. *Annual Estimates of the Population by Selected Age Groups and Sex for the U.S.*

department (ED) in New York for suspected rabies. An Afghanistan canine rabies virus variant was identified. The patient underwent an experimental treatment protocol but died on August 31.

From the most recent life table (use Table E5-1 of the previous chapter), how many years of life were lost due to this single death?

YLL = ⎯⎯⎯⎯⎯

3. On April 30 the *Morbidity and Mortality Weekly Report* carried this story:

Outbreak of Poliomyelitis—Angola
On March 23 the Pediatric Hospital in Luanda, Angola, reported 21 cases (three deaths) of acute flaccid paralysis (AFP). . . . By April 25, 635 AFP cases (39 deaths) were reported.

Further investigation determined that these cases occurred primarily among children under age five not fully vaccinated for polio.

a. For the cases that did not result in death, the estimated duration of poliomyelitis would be up to 58.9 years (Murray and Lopez, 1996a). (Let's assume survivors lived this long.) Using a severity, or disability, of 0.24 (24% disabled), compute how many years lived with disability could have been caused by this outbreak.

YLD = ⎯⎯⎯⎯⎯

b. If the 39 cases resulting in death had an average remaining life expectancy of 58.9 years, how many years of life were lost due to their deaths?

YLL = ⎯⎯⎯⎯⎯

c. How many total disability adjusted life-years lost (DALY) were caused by this outbreak?

DALY = YLL + YLD = ⎯⎯⎯⎯⎯

PROPOSITIONS FOR DEBATE

1. As the incidence of a lifelong disease declines, the prevalence also will decline.

2. The *best* measure of morbidity is the prevalence rate.

3. Saving individuals from death from one cause leaves them at risk of death from other causes, rather than insuring that they will live through the average remaining life expectancy. Therefore, computing years of life lost (YLL) always overstates the consequences of an illness.

4. It would be better for less-developed countries to ignore recently rising morbidity from degenerative diseases and concentrate on lowering morbidity from infectious diseases, because morbidity among the young will always cause more disability adjusted life-years lost (DALY).

5. Morbidity is under individual control in the MDRs to a greater extent than in the LDRs.

6. The likelihood of morbidity increases with extreme old age; therefore old age itself should be considered a disease.

REFERENCES AND SUGGESTED READINGS

Alter, George, and James C. Riley. 1988. "Frailty, Sickness, and Death: Models of Morbidity and Mortality in Historical Populations." *Population Association of America Meetings*, New Orleans, LA.

Armelagos, George J. 1990. "Health and Disease in Prehistoric Populations in Transition." In Alan C. Swedlund and George J. Armelagos, eds., *Disease in Populations in Transition*. New York: Bergin and Garvey.

Barbiera, Irene, and Gianpiero Dalla-Zuanna. 2009. "Population Dynamics in Italy in the Middle Ages: New Insights from Archaeological Findings." *Population and Development Review* 35(2): 367–389.

Benedictow, O. J. 1987. "Morbidity in Historical Plague Epidemics." *Population Studies* 41(3).

Bowley, A. L., and A. R. Burnett-Hurst. 1915. *Livelihood and Poverty*. London: Ratan Tata Foundation (cf. Fogel and Costa, 1997).

Brault, Matthew W. 2012. *Americans with Disabilities: 2010*. U.S. Department of Commerce, Economics and Statistics Administration, U.S. Census Bureau. Retrieved November 1, 2013 http://www.census.gov/prod/2012pubs/p70-131.pdf

Case, Anna, and Christina H. Paxson. 2005. "Sex Differences in Morbidity and Mortality." *Demography* 42(2): 189–214.

Cassedy, James H. 1986. *Medicine and American Growth, 1800–1860*. Madison: University of Wisconsin Press.

CDC (Centers for Disease Control). 2010. *HIV Surveillance Report: Diagnosis of HIV Infection and AIDS in the United States and Dependent Areas, 2010.*

———. 2013. *Global HIV/AIDS at CDC—Our Story: CDC Plays a Unique Role in the Fight Against Global HIV/AIDS*. Retrieved July 1, 2013. http://www.cdc.gov/globalaids/Global-HIV-AIDS-at-CDC/default.html

CDC (Centers for Disease Control) and the Merck Company Foundation. 2007. *The State of Aging and Health in America 2007*. Whitehouse Station, NJ: The Merck Company Foundation.

Cipolla, C. M. 1980. *Before the Industrial Revolution: European Society and Economy, 1000–1700*. 2nd ed. New York: Norton.

Corsini, Carlo A., and Pier Paolo Viazzo, eds. 1997. *The Decline of Infant and Child Mortality*. Dordrecht, The Netherlands: Martinas Nijhoff Publishers.

Costa, Dora L. 2002. "Changing Chronic Disease Rates and Long-Term Declines in Functional Limitation among Older Men." *Demography* 39(1).

de Onis, Mercedes, and Monika Blössner. 2003. "The World Health Organization Global Database on Child Growth and Malnutrition: Methodology and Applications." *International Journal of Epidemiology* 32(4): 518–526.

de Onis, Mercedes, Monika Blössner, Elaine Borghi, Richard Morris, and Edward A. Frongillo. 2004. "Methodology for Estimating Regional and Global Trends of Child Malnutrition." *International Journal of Epidemiology* 33(6).

de Onis, Mercedes, C. Monteiro, J. Akré, and G. Clugston. 1999. "The Worldwide Magnitude of Protein-Energy Malnutrition: An Overview from the WHO Global Database on Child Growth." *WHOSIS Electronic Bulletin.*

Federal Interagency Forum on Aging-Related Statistics. 2012. *Older Americans 2012: Key Indicators of Well-Being.* Washington, DC: U.S. GPO.

Ferlay Jacques, Hai-Rim Shin, Freddie Bray, David Forman, Colin Mathers, and Donald Maxwell Parkin. 2010. *GLOBOCAN 2008 v2.0, Cancer Incidence and Mortality Worldwide: IARC CancerBase No. 10.* Lyon, France: International Agency for Research on Cancer. Retrieved July 11, 2013. http://globocan.iarc.fr

Fogel, Robert W. 2004. *The Escape from Hunger and Premature Death, 1700-2100: Europe, America and the Third World.* New York: Cambridge University Press.

Fogel, Robert W., and Dora L. Costa. 1997. "A Theory of Technophysio Evolution, with Some Implications for Forecasting Population, Health Care Costs, and Pension Costs." *Demography* 34(1).

Forsberg, Birger Carl, Max G. Petzold, Göran Tomson, and Peter Allebeck. 2007. "Diarrhoea Case Management in Low- and Middle-Income Countries—An Unfinished Agenda." *Bulletin of the World Health Organization* 85(1): 42–48.

Freedman, Vicki A., Linda G. Martin, and Robert F. Schoeni. 2002. "Recent Trends in Disability and Functioning Among Older Adults in the United States: A Systematic Review." *Journal of American Medical Association* 288(24): 3137–3146.

Freedman, Vicki A., Robert F. Schoeni, Linda G. Martin, and Jennifer C. Cornman. 2007. "Chronic Conditions and the Decline in Late-Life Disability." *Demography* 44(3): 459–477.

Fries, James F. 1980. "Aging, Natural Death and the Compression of Morbidity." *New England Journal of Medicine* 303(3): 130–135.

Gelbard, Alene, Carl Haub, and Mary M. Kent. 1999. "World Population beyond Six Billion." *Population Bulletin* 54(1).

Gruenberg, Ernest M. 1977. "The Failures of Success." Milbank Memorial Fund Quarterly. *Health and Society* 55(1): 3–24.

Hautaniemi, Susan I., Alan Swedlund, and Douglas L. Anderton. 1999. "Mill Town Mortality: Consequences of Industrial Growth in Two 19th Century New England Towns." *Social History* 23(1): 1–39.

IHME (Institute for Health Metrics and Evaluation). 2012a. *Global Burden of Disease Study 2010 (GBD 2010): Healthy Life Expectancy 1990–2010.*

———. 2012b. *Global Burden of Disease Study 2010 (GBD 2010): Results by Cause 1990–2010.*

———. 2012c. *Global Burden of Disease Study 2010 (GBD 2010): Results by Risk Factor 1990–2010.*

Laslett, Peter. 1983. *The World We Have Lost: England Before the Industrial Age.* 3rd ed. New York: Scribner.

Lozano, Rafael, Mohsen Naghavi, Kyle Foreman, Stephen Lim, Kenji Shibuya, Victor Aboyans, and Jerry Abraham, et al. 2012. "Global and Regional Mortality from 235 Causes of Death for 20 Age Groups in 1990 and 2010: A Systematic Analysis for the Global Burden of Disease Study 2010." *The Lancet* 380(9859): 2095–2128.

Macintyre, Sally, Graeme Ford, and Kate Hunt. 1999. "Do Women 'Over-Report' Morbidity? Men's and Women's Responses to Structured Prompting on a Standard Question on Long Standing Illness." *Social Science and Medicine* 48(1): 89–98.

Macintyre, Sally, Kate Hunt, and Helen Sweeting. 1996. "Gender Differences in Health: Are Things Really as Simple as They Seem?" *Social Science and Medicine* 42(4): 617–624.

Manton, Kenneth G., and Kenneth C. Land. 2000. "Active Life Expectancy Estimates for the U.S. Elderly Population: A Multidimensional Continuous-Mixture Model of Functional Change Applied to Completed Cohorts, 1982-1996." *Demography* 37(3): 253–265.

McKeown, T. H. 1976. *The Modern Rise of Population.* New York: Academic Press.

Morel, Marie-France. 1977. "City and Country in Eighteenth-Century Medical Discussions about Early Childhood." *Annales E. S. C.* 32.

Murray, Christopher J. L., and Alan D. Lopez, eds. 1996a. *The Global Burden of Disease: A Comprehensive Assessment of Mortality and Disability from Diseases, Injuries and Risk Factors in 1990 and Projected to 2020* (with executive summary). Published by Harvard School of Public Health on behalf of the World Health Organization and World Bank. Cambridge, MA: Harvard University Press.

———. 1996b. *Global Health Statistics.* Published by Harvard School of Public Health on behalf of the World Health Organization and World Bank. Cambridge, MA: Harvard University Press.

Murray, Christopher J. L., et al. 2012. "Disability-Adjusted Life Years (DALYs) for 291 Diseases and Injuries in 21 Regions, 1990–2010: A Systematic Analysis for the Global Burden of Disease Study 2010." *The Lancet* 380(9859): 2197–2223.

Nam, Charles B. 1990. "Mortality Differentials from a Multiple-Cause-of-Death Perspective." In Jacques Vallin, Stan D'Souza, and Alberto Palloni, eds., *Measurement and Analysis of Mortality: New Approaches.* Oxford: Clarendon Press.

Ó Gráda, Cormac. 2009. *Famine: A Short History.* Princeton, NJ: Princeton University Press.

Olshansky, S. Jay, Bruce Carnes, Richard G. Rodgers, and Len Smith. 1997. "Infectious Diseases—New and Ancient Threats to World Health." *Population Bulletin* 52(2).

Olshansky, S. Jay, Mark A. Rudberg, Bruce A. Carnes, Christine K. Cassel, and Jacob A. Brady. 1991. "Trading Off Longer Life for Worsening Health: The Expansion of Morbidity Hypothesis." *Journal of Aging and Health* 3(2): 194–216.

Outhwaite, R. B. 1991. *Death, Public Policy and Social Disturbance in England, 1550–1800.* Cambridge: Cambridge University Press.

Porter, Roy. 1993. *Disease, Medicine and Society in England, 1550–1860.* 2nd ed. Cambridge: Cambridge University Press.

Preston, Samuel H., and Michael R. Haines. 1991. *Fatal Years: Child Mortality in Late Nineteenth-Century America.* Princeton, NJ: Princeton University Press.

Redelings, Matthew D., Frank Sorvillo, and Paul Simon. 2006. "A Comparison of Underlying Cause and Multiple Causes of Death: U.S. Vital Statistics, 2000-2001." *Epidemiology* 17(1): 100–103.

Reid, Alice. 1997. "Locality or Class? Spatial and Social Differentials in Infant and Child Mortality in England and Wales, 1895–1911." In C. A. Corsini and P. P. Viazzo, eds., *The Decline of Infant and Child Mortality: The European Experience, 1750–1990.* New York: UNICEF.

Reither, Eric N., S. Jay Olshansky, and Yang Yang. 2011. "New Forecasting Methodology Indicates More Disease and Earlier Mortality Ahead for Today's Younger Americans." *Health Affairs* 30(8): 1562–1568.

Rockett, Ian R. H. 1998. "Injury and Violence: A Public Health Perspective." *Population Bulletin* 53(4).

Rosenberg, Charles E. 1987. *The Cholera Years: The United States in 1832, 1849, and 1866.* Chicago: University of Chicago Press.

Rotberg, Robert I., and T. K. Rabb, eds. 1985. *Hunger and History.* Cambridge: Cambridge University Press.

Rothenberg, Richard, Harold R. Lentzner, and Robert A. Parker. 1991. "Population Aging Patterns: The Expansion of Mortality." *Journal of Gerontology: Social Sciences* 46(2): 66–70.

Salomon, Joshua A., Haidong Wang, Michael K. Freeman, Theo Vos, Abraham D. Flaxman, Alan D. Lopez, and Christopher J. L. Murray. 2012. "Healthy Life Expectancy for 187 Countries, 1990–2010: A Systematic Analysis for the Global Burden Disease Study 2010." *The Lancet* 380(9859): 2144–2162.

Schofield, Roger, D. Reher, and A. Bideau, eds. 1991. *The Decline of Mortality in Europe.* Oxford: Clarendon Press.

Scott, Susan, and Christopher J. Duncan. 2002. *Demography and Nutrition: Evidence from Historical and Contemporary Populations.* Oxford, UK: Blackwell Science Ltd.

Signoli, Michel, Isabelle Séguy, Jean-Noël Biraben, Olivier Dutour, and Paul Belle. 2002. "Paleodemography and Historical Demography in the Context of an Epidemic: Plague in Provence in the Eighteenth Century." *Population* 57(6): 829–854.

Snow, John. 1855 (reprint 1965). *Snow on Cholera.* New York: Hafner.

Spielvogel, Jackson J. 2008. *Western Civilization Since 1500.* 7th ed. Boston: Cengage Learning.

Swedlund, Alan C., and George J. Armelagos, eds. 1990. *Disease in Populations in Transition.* New York: Bergin and Garvey.

Szreter, S. 1997. "Economic Growth, Disruption, Deprivation, Diseases and Death: On the Importance of the Politics of Public Health for Development." *Population and Development Review* 23(4).

United Nations. 2005. *Millennium Project.* http://www.unmillenniumproject.org/goals/index.htm.

———. 2013. *World Population Prospects: The 2012 Revision.* Retrieved August 5, 2013. http://esa.un.org/wpp/index.htm

United Nations Children's Fund, World Health Organization, The World Bank. 2012. *Levels and Trends in Child Malnutrition: UNICEF-WHO-World Bank Joint Child Malnutrition Estimates.* Washington, DC: UNICEF; New York: WHO; Geneva: The World Bank.

U.S. Census Bureau. 2009. *Annual Estimates of the Population by Selected Age Groups and Sex for the United States: April 1, 2000 to July 1, 2009.* NC-EST2009-02.

Vargas, Luis A. 1990. "Old and New Transitions and Nutrition in Mexico." In Alan C. Swedlund and George J. Armelagos, eds., *Disease in Populations in Transition.* New York: Bergin and Garvey.

Vaupel, James W. 2010. "Biodemography of Human Ageing." *Nature* 464: 536–542.

Verbrugge, Lois M. 1989. "The Twain Meet: Empirical Explanations of Sex Differences in Health and Mortality. *Journal of Health and Social Behavior* 30(3): 282–304.

Vos, Theo, et al. 2012. "Years Lived with Disability (YLDs) for 1160 Sequelae of 289 Diseases and Injuries 1990–2010: A Systematic Analysis for the Global Burden of Disease Study 2010." *The Lancet* 380(9859): 2163–2196.

WHO (World Health Organization). 1997. "Health and Environment in Sustainable Development." *World Health Organization Information Fact Sheet no. 170.*

———. 2002. *World Health Report 2002.* http://www.who.int/whr/2002/annex/en/index.html. Data from Annexes 11, 12, and 13.

———. 2003a. *Healthy Life Expectancy: Measuring Average Levels of Population Health in WHO Member States.* http://www.who.int/entity/mip/2003/other_documents/en/hale.pdf

———. 2003b. *The Injury Chartbook: A Graphical Overview of the Global Burden of Injuries.* http://www.who.int/violence_injury_prevention/publications/other_injury/chartb/en

———. 2004. *Global Immunization Data.* http://www.who.int/immunization_

———. 2008. *The Global Burden of Disease: 2004 Update.* Geneva: World Health Organization.

———. 2009. *Global Health Risks: Mortality and Burden of Disease Attributable to Selected Major Risks.* Geneva: World Health Organization.

———. 2011. *Global Tuberculosis Control, 2011.* Geneva: World Health Organization.

———. 2012. *Media Centre: Millennium Development Goals (MDGs). Fact Sheet No. 290.* Retrieved July 2013. http://www.who.int/mediacentre/factsheets/fs290/en/

———. 2013a. *Global Alert and Response (GAR). Hepatitis.* Retrieved July 11, 2013. http://www.who.int/csr/disease/hepatitis/en/index.html

————. 2013b. *Global Health Observatory: Underweight in Children.* Retrieved July 3, 2013. http://www.who.int/gho/mdg/poverty_hunger/underweight_text/en/index.html

————. 2013c. *Global Status Report on Road Safety 2013: Supporting A Decade of Action.* Geneva: World Health Organization.

————. 2013d. *Health Topics: Injuries.* Retrieved July 1, 2013. http://www.who.int/topics/injuries/en/

————. 2013e. *Media Centre: Diarrhoeal Disease. Fact Sheet. No. 330.* Retrieved July 11, 2013. http://www.who.int/mediacentre/factsheets/fs330/en/

————. 2013f. *Media Centre: Immunization Coverage. Fact Sheet. No. 378.* Retrieved July 1, 2013. http://www.who.int/mediacentre/factsheets/fs378/en/index.html

————. 2013g. *Media Centre: Malaria. Fact Sheet. No. 94.* Retrieved July 1, 2013. http://www.who.int/mediacentre/factsheets/fs094/en/

————. 2013h. *Media Centre: Obesity and Overweight. Fact Sheet. No. 311.* Retrieved July 1, 2013. http://www.who.int/mediacentre/factsheets/fs311/en/index.html

WHO (World Health Organization) and UNICEF. 2006. *Meeting the MDG Drinking Water and Sanitation Target: The Urban and Rural Challenge of the Decade.* Geneva: World Health Organization.

Woods, Robert. 1993. "On the Historical Relationship between Infant and Adult Mortality." *Population Studies* 47: 195–219.

World Nuclear Association. 2011. "WHO Warns on Urban Air Pollution." *World Nuclear News* (September 28). Retrieved July 1, 2013. http://www.world-nuclear-news.org/ee-who_warns_on_urban_air_pollution-2809116.html

Wrigley, E. A., and Roger Schofield. 1981. *The Population History of England, 1541–1871.* London: Edward Arnold.

APPENDIX

Global Burden of Disease Study, 2010
Countries by Regions, Institute for Health Metrics and Evaluation (IHME).

Andean Latin America:

Bolivia   Ecuador   Peru

Australasia:

Australia   New Zealand

Caribbean:

Antigua and Barbuda   Bahamas   Barbados   Belize   Cuba   Dominica   Dominican Republic   Grenada   Guyana   Haiti   Jamaica   Saint Lucia   Saint Vincent and the Grenadines   Suriname   Trinidad and Tobago

Central Asia:

Armenia   Azerbaijan   Georgia   Kazakhstan   Kyrgyzstan   Mongolia   Tajikistan   Turkmenistan   Uzbekistan

Central Europe:

Albania   Bosnia and Herzegovina   Bulgaria   Croatia   Czech Republic   Hungary   Macedonia   Montenegro   Poland   Romania   Serbia   Slovakia   Slovenia

Central Latin America

Colombia   Costa Rica   El Salvador   Guatemala   Honduras   Mexico   Nicaragua   Panama   Venezuela

(continued)

Central sub-Saharan Africa

Angola   Central African Republic   Congo   Democratic Republic of the Congo   Equatorial Guinea
Gabon

East Asia:

China   North Korea   Taiwan

Eastern Europe:

Belarus   Estonia   Latvia   Lithuania   Moldova   Russia   Ukraine

Eastern sub-Saharan Africa:

Burundi   Comoros   Djibouti   Eritrea   Ethiopia   Kenya   Madagascar   Malawi   Mauritius
Mozambique   Rwanda   Seychelles   Somalia   Sudan   Tanzania   Uganda   Zambia

High-income Asia Pacific:

Brunei   Japan   South Korea   Singapore

High-income North America:

Canada   United States

North Africa and Middle East:

Algeria   Bahrain   Egypt   Iran   Iraq   Jordan   Kuwait   Lebanon   Libya   Morocco   Oman
Palestine   Qatar   Saudi Arabia   Syria   Tunisia   Turkey   United Arab Emirates   Yemen

Oceania:

Fiji   Kiribati   Marshall Islands   Micronesia   Papua New Guinea   Samoa   Solomon Islands
Tonga   Vanuatu

South Asia:

Afghanistan   Bangladesh   Bhutan   India   Nepal   Pakistan

Southeast Asia:

Cambodia   Indonesia   Laos   Malaysia   Maldives   Myanmar   Philippines   Sri Lanka   Thailand
Timor-Leste   Vietnam

Southern Latin America:

Argentina   Chile   Uruguay

Southern sub-Saharan Africa:

Botswana   Lesotho   Namibia   South Africa   Swaziland   Zimbabwe

Tropical Latin America:

Brazil   Paraguay

Western Europe:

Andorra   Austria   Belgium   Cyprus   Denmark   Finland   France   Germany   Greece   Iceland
Ireland   Israel   Italy   Luxembourg   Malta   Netherlands   Norway   Portugal   Spain   Sweden
Switzerland   United Kingdom

Western sub-Saharan Africa:

Benin   Burkina Faso   Cameroon   Cape Verde   Chad   Cote d'Ivoire   Gambia   Ghana   Guinea
Guinea-Bissau   Liberia   Mali   Mauritania   Niger   Nigeria   Sao Tome and Principe   Senegal
Sierra Leone   Togo

7

Fertility

Childbearing, or **fertility**, of populations has received more attention from demographers than any other topic. There are several reasons for this. First, as we discussed in chapter 4, fertility largely determines a population's age structure: high fertility is responsible for youth dependency in some regions; declining fertility is responsible for aging of populations in other regions. Variable fertility has also created major fluctuations in cohort size, such as the baby-booms, in many countries. A second reason for interest in fertility is its contribution to population growth: continuing high fertility, after mortality began to decline, has produced the most explosive population growth episodes of modern times. A final reason is that the biological potential for childbearing, or **fecundity**, has increasingly come under voluntary control over the past century. As a result, people can plan their childbearing and policy makers can reasonably attempt to influence these choices.

While fertility remains the driving force of world population growth, world fertility probably never has been as low as it is today and it is unlikely to increase much in the near future (Kinsella and He, 2009). More than a third of all nations, and practically all of the more-developed countries, have fertility levels below those which would replace their existing populations. Moreover, fertility decline has spread to many less-developed countries (United Nations, 2013b). The causes, consequences, and likely future course of this worldwide fertility transition are among the most compelling demographic questions of our time period.

In this chapter, we look first at the earliest fertility transitions of the now more-developed countries and then at fertility transitions underway in most of the rest of the world. We then introduce methods to measure fertility, and discuss how both biology and culture impact fertility. As in previous chapters, we then discuss perceived problems associated with trends in this demographic process. Finally, we describe family-planning programs and the debate surrounding them.

219

European Fertility Transitions

The European demographic transition had both mortality and fertility components. We covered the drop in mortality in chapter 5. In this section we treat the downward transition in fertility.

With few exceptions, the really steep drop in fertility in European countries started in the four decades bracketing 1900, but the beginning of this steep drop often was foreshadowed many decades earlier by more gradual declines. Conventional European demographic data do not go back far enough to cover the whole sweep of the fertility transition in some countries. By "conventional data" we mean regular censuses and continuous civil registration of vital events (see chapter 2). Both of these practices spread through Europe mostly during the 1800s (van de Walle and Knodel, 1980). In many localities, fertility started to edge downward well before that.

Historical Demography

Recently, demographers have developed methods to infer demographic behavior and population structure of earlier times from other historical data. These data and methods have come to be known as **historical demography**. One major data source for Europe is parish registers of baptisms, weddings, and burials by Catholic and Protestant clergymen. These registers record not only the event and its date, but also the crucial information of the participants' names.

Figure 7-1 gives a (typically, barely legible) example. This 1803 register was made in a parish northeast of Manchester, England. The column headings indicate, from left to right, infant's name and birth order; father's name, abode, and profession; mother's name and descent; dates of birth and baptism. In the first line, for example, Jonathan was born on the 5th of October 1803 as the third son of Thomas Finch of Wallgate, a warehouseman, and Alice his wife, who was the daughter of Thomas and Alice Barrow. Note that births without a record of the father's identity were designated as "Base" in the infant's name column, indicating "base born" at a time where births outside of marriage were considered to be illegitimate. John, the sixth listed infant, was the "illegitimate" great-great-grandfather of one of the text's authors.

One fruitful method for analyzing such parish registers is **family reconstitution**. By linking dates of births, marriages, and deaths within families, vital events can be chronicled to create many important demographic variables. These include birth intervals, family size, people's age at marriage, age of mother at each birth, infant mortality, and marital fertility (van de Walle and Knodel, 1980). The construction of individual life histories from such old records, somewhat incomplete and always difficult to read, is a tedious and time-consuming undertaking. Fortunately, digital technologies are transforming such resources into comprehensive and linked databases, leading to innovative uses of previously unexplored historical household data (Ruggles, 2012).

Historical demography also applies a variety of other methods to various data sources such as wills, genealogies, hearth and household enumerations, and organizational records, all of which contain valuable demographic data on populations in the past (Gutmann et al., 2011; Reher and Schofield, 1993; Willigan and Lynch, 1982). And, in good historical tradition, demographers also rely on observations written by persons living in the period being described. They find them in such diverse sources as letters, diaries, and

Figure 7-1

Baptismal Register, Wigan Parish, England, 1803

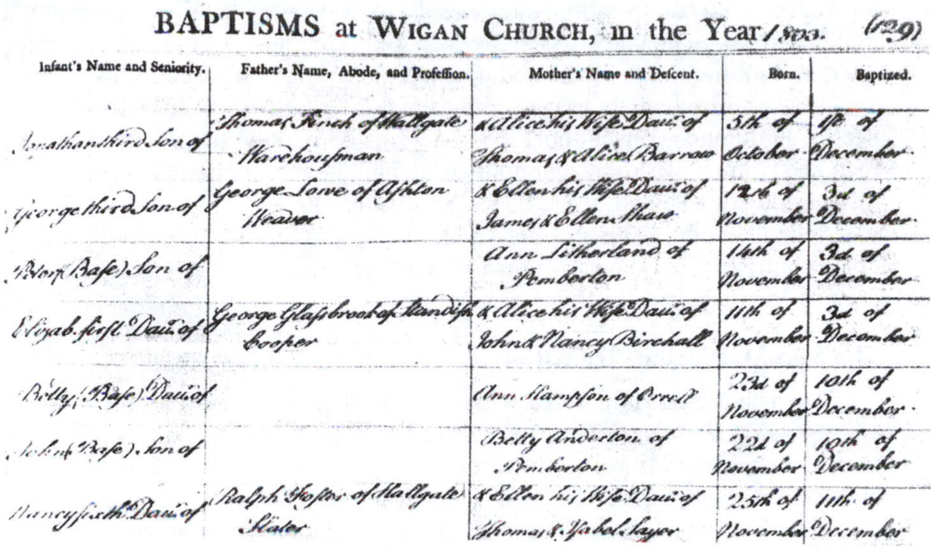

BAPTISMS at WIGAN CHURCH, in the Year 1803. (129)

Infant's Name and Seniority.	Father's Name, Abode, and Profession.	Mother's Name and Descent.	Born.	Baptized.
Nathan third Son of	Thomas Finch of Wallgate Warehousman	& Alice his Wife Dau. of Thomas & Alice Barrow	5th of October	9th of December
George third Son of	George Lowe of Ashton Weaver	& Ellen his Wife Dau. of James & Ellen Shaw	12th of November	3d. of December
Peter (Base) Son of		Ann Litherland of Pemberton	14th of November	3d. of December
Elizab. first Dau. of	George Glassbrook of Standish Cooper	& Alice his Wife Dau. of John & Nancy Birchall	11th of November	3d. of December
Betty (Base) Dau. of		Ann Hampson of Orrell	23d of November	10th of December
John (Base) Son of		Betty Anderton of Pemberton	22d of November	10th of December
Nancy sixth Dau. of	Ralph Foster of Wallgate Slater	& Ellen his Wife Dau. of Thomas & Isabel Layer	25th of November	11th of December

novels of the time and reports by trained contemporary observers (such as statisticians evaluating their own data in introductions to their reports) and by doctors reporting on their patients and on general health conditions (van de Walle and Knodel, 1980).

Much of what we know about the role of marriage and fertility limitation within marriage during the early European fertility decline comes from these historical demographic studies. The most notable collection, although far from the only study, is that of the Princeton Fertility Project.

When fertility declined in Europe, there were two components of the decline. One was delay and/or curtailment of marriage. Coale (1973) labeled this the **Malthusian transition**, after Thomas Malthus. (You will remember that Malthus hoped that delayed marriage would act as a preventive check on population growth.) The other component was the declining childbearing of married couples. Coale labeled this the **neo-Malthusian transition**. We describe each in the following sections.

The Malthusian Transition

The Malthusian transition in Europe spread what Hajnal (1965) has called the **European marriage pattern**. That pattern combines late age at first marriage (say, until the middle or late twenties) with many women never marrying (approximately 10% or more). The pattern from which the affected European provinces moved probably was similar to what we now observe in least-developed countries, early and universal marriage of women.

When did this unique European marriage pattern begin? From available data, about all we can say for sure is that the changeover in marriage patterns started after the Middle Ages and had swept through Western Europe before industrialization (Coale and Treadway, 1986). The timing was later for Eastern Europe, but the East-West gap in European marriage behavior narrowed after the 1930s as Western Europe experienced somewhat of a resurgence in early and universal marriage while Eastern Europe (most notably Russia) experienced a Malthusian decline in marriage. Despite continuing regional variations, all of the more-developed countries now have completed the Malthusian component of the fertility transition. Couples in these regions tend to marry later, and substantial numbers end up never marrying (more about this in chapter 8).

As the European marriage pattern of later marriage spread, overall fertility declined. Although conventional gender norms limited the sexual contact of unmarried men and women, we know that nonmarital childbearing nonetheless took place during this period (van Poppel et al., 2013; Shorter et al., 1971). The resurgence of earlier marriage after the 1930s did not substantially increase fertility. By that time, efficacious contraception allowed control of fertility within marriage to limit childbearing even as marriage became more common.

The Neo-Malthusian Transition

The neo-Malthusian transition was a decline in *marital* fertility—childbearing among married women. This transition represented mainly a transition from *natural fertility* behavior. Natural fertility results when couples do not attempt to terminate childbearing before the end of their biological reproductive span.

This does not mean that natural-fertility populations have as many children as possible. Most populations produce far fewer births than they could if everyone was operating at biological capacity (Henry, 1961). The Hutterites, a religious sect living in the Dakotas, Montana, and Canada in the 1950s, were considered to have the maximum fertility known for a large group—an average family size of 10.9 children—and even that was considered a couple of children below capacity (Eaton and Mayer, 1954). The Hutterites are considered a natural experiment in how fertility would look under the most optimal conditions and with strict religious norms prohibiting contraceptive use. Natural fertility, in most cases, however, simply means that couples do not try to stop having children after a given number of births or completed family size.

Parity-specific fertility limitation, in contrast, means stopping childbearing after enough children have been had. (**Parity** is simply the number of children already born.) Demographers distinguish attempts to stop at a specific number of children born from behavior that may space births but does not intentionally stop childbearing. Either stopping or spacing births can reduce the overall fertility in a population and it can be difficult to distinguish these behaviors in the early stages of fertility decline (Tsuya et al., 2010; Guinnane et al., 1994; Anderton and Bean, 1985). Some long intervals between births, for example, may reflect failed attempts to stop childbearing, and long birth intervals at older ages can mistakenly appear to be stopping behavior (Anderton, 1989; van Bavel, 2004). Once fertility transitions were underway, however, there is little doubt that efforts to stop childbearing at smaller family sizes were responsible for the dramatic fertility declines in Europe (Coale and Treadway, 1986; van de Walle and Knodel, 1980).

The timing of the Malthusian and neo-Malthusian components of fertility transition relative to each other varied among European countries, notably between Western and Eastern Europe. In Eastern Europe, the two generally overlapped, tending simultaneously to push total fertility down rapidly during the early 1900s. In Western Europe, in contrast, the Malthusian transition had an early start and tended to antedate the neo-Malthusian transition. Let us focus here on the decline in marital fertility in Western European countries.

Western European marital fertility before the neo-Malthusian transition had two important features: (1) It was high by modern standards, and (2) it varied considerably around that high average, both among nations and among localities within nations.

Figure 7-2 illustrates the differences among European nations from the mid-1800s up to 1980. The "index of marital fertility" used in the graph is too complex to explain in detail in an introductory textbook; however, it is sufficient to know that it compares

Figure 7-2

Levels and Changes in Marital Fertility, Selected European Countries, 1860–1980

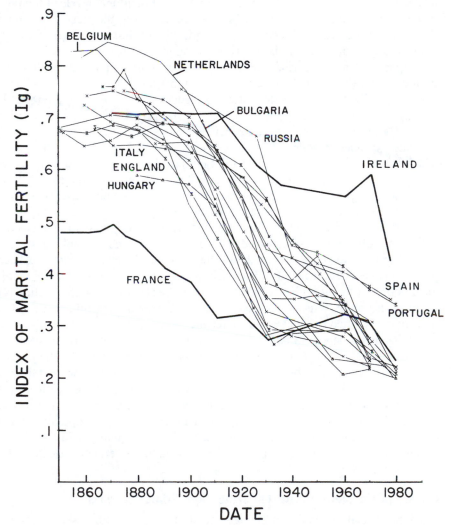

Source: Coale and Watkins, eds., 1986. *The Decline of Fertility in Europe,* fig. 2.3. Used with permission.

the total marital fertility of the countries described with that of the most fertile population on which we have complete records, the Hutterites (Shorter et al., 1971). If a European country had age-specific marital fertility on a par with the Hutterites, its index of marital fertility would be 1.0. We can see that, by 1860, France had an index of about 0.5, while the Netherlands and Belgium were above 0.8. Moreover, the Princeton University team that provided these figures also carefully studied data from localities within these countries and found considerable variation among them (Coale and Treadway, 1986).

How did these early fertility differences come about in the absence of modern birth control? Most local differences were due to variations in the "frequency and duration of breast-feeding, periods of separation due to seasonal migration of one of the spouses, variation in frequency of intercourse, customs prohibiting resumption of intercourse for some period following a birth, and nutritional levels of the population" (van de Walle and Knodel, 1980, p. 12). For our purposes, the most important observation is that these early 19th-century differentials in marital fertility were caused only to a minor degree by voluntary family size limitation.

Figure 7-2 also describes the national transitions in marital fertility during the period from 1860 to 1980. For any given country, fertility first edges gradually downward, typically drops into a steep dive, and ends at levels of marital fertility less than half what it was at the beginning of this transition (with the notable exception of Ireland). There was national variation, with France and Ireland representing the early and late extremes. Among the rest, there was a tendency for Western European countries to decline earlier and Eastern and Southern European countries to decline later. For most of the Western European nations, fertility lines converge as they reach modern times. Regardless of prior national variations, a similar change swept rapidly through the entire region in the late 1800s and early 1900s.

With the exceptions of France and Ireland, the steep national declines all started within less than a forty-year period. This point is made more graphically clear in Figure 7-3 on the next page, which shows the timing of the fertility drops for local European *provinces* within nations. The early peak in this figure is entirely composed of local populations within France. For the rest of Western Europe the decline is concentrated in a narrow time period. Nearly 60% of provinces within these nations have their first sustained decline in marital fertility between 1890 and 1920.

Not all the people in each of these localities responded with equal promptness. During the transition, fertility differentials increased temporarily. The already lower urban fertility dropped before the rural, widening that gap. The middle and upper classes restricted their fertility before the lower class did. Those involved in the new economic order—the educated and those in nonagricultural occupations—lowered their fertility first. Ethnic, religious, and racial groups in the population participated differentially in modernization and also in family size limitation. Just as the transition initially widened these differentials, its end has led to convergence (Coale and Watkins, 1986; Ryder, 1959).

Causes of the Neo-Malthusian Transition: Some Theories

What social and cultural changes made these populations start to employ birth control so suddenly? Despite the fact that the debate originated some seventy-five years

Figure 7-3

Starting Dates of Fertility Transitions in Selected European Provinces, 1780–1960

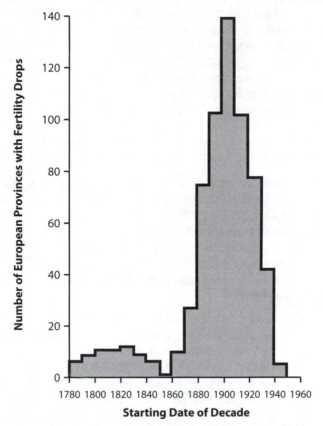

Source: Coale and Watkins, eds., 1986. *The Decline of Fertility in Europe,* fig. 2.2. Used with permission.

ago, demographers still disagree over which causes deserve the most emphasis, mainly because so many important changes happened about the same time. There was a change from rural to urban living, from agricultural to industrial occupations and economies. There was modernization of social institutions, and there evolved broader acceptance of the Western conjugal family model. There was a mortality decline, which largely preceded fertility declines (at least at the national level). Which of these changes caused individuals to limit their family size?

Mason (1997) provides a seminal review of the six leading theories of fertility decline, in Europe and subsequently elsewhere. We will rely here on a summary of her review but extend her critical comments in some cases. The reader is forewarned that the presentation that follows may seem abstract, sophisticated, and intimidating to beginning students. The summaries are presented to demonstrate the earnest attempts by demographers to explain the facets of fertility decline rather than to finally answer the question.

Classic demographic transition theory.   This theory attributes fertility decline to changes in social life associated with industrialization and urbanization (Thompson, 1930; Notestein, 1953). These changes first increased the survival rate of children, theoretically reducing the need for parents to want large numbers of children as "insurance" against child death (see discussion of the fertility-mortality link in Cleland, 2001). At the same time, these changes created a modern lifestyle in which large families became increasingly expensive. Although the classic demographic transition theory is heavily used by demographers as a general framework, it has critical flaws as a specific theory. First, the theory is so general that it does not provide sufficient detail to constitute a testable hypothesis in any one specific instance of fertility decline. Second, the classic theory is left unsupported by the relatively weak correlations between fertility and urbanization or industrialization, either in historical MDR transitions (Coale and Watkins, 1986) or in LDR transitions (Bongaarts and Watkins, 1996).

Modernization and secularization theory.   This line of thinking extends the classic theory by emphasizing the rising values of individualism and self-fulfillment that are associated with increasing affluence and secularization (Lesthaeghe, 1983, 1995). This modification of classic theory provides insight into the historical Europe fertility transitions where such factors as declining religious authority and alternative life-course possibilities were associated with fertility decline. It does not, however, fare as well in LDR countries where fertility declines have occurred with less evidence of erosion in traditional values.

Wealth flow theory.   This view argues that a key turning point in modernization occurs when changes in child labor, compulsory education, extended family structures, old-age security, and other factors shift the economic benefits of family life from the parents to the offspring (Caldwell, 1982). As children become more of an economic burden than economic benefit to parents, people choose to limit their fertility. Again, this theory works well in some countries but less well in others where fertility has declined with little change in extended family structures or in European settings where extended families were not significant even before fertility declines (Thornton and Fricke, 1987).

Neoclassical microeconomic theory.   This approach emphasizes a rational-choice model where decisions to limit fertility are contingent on fertility desires, childbearing and rearing costs, budget or income constraints, and the substitutability of children for other available goods (Becker, 1960). As with most highly generalized microeconomic approaches, one flaw of the theory is its failure to explain the historical changes in these decision-making conditions that led to fertility transitions in specific cases. The ahistorical nature of the model tends to make its application tautological and uninformative (Robinson, 1997).

Regulatory microeconomic theory.   This theory extends the neoclassical model by emphasizing more sociological interpretations of the supply, demand, and costs of children (Easterlin and Crimmins, 1985). In Easterlin's theory, the supply of children is a theoretical one, or natural fertility in the absence of deliberate decisions to limit childbearing. Demand for children is a desired surviving family size and only one proximate determinant of fertility. The costs of fertility regulation are extended to include psychic and social, as well as monetary, costs. The theory has encouraged innovative thinking about fertility decisions and provides a better explanation of fertility fluctuations than other transition theories (Abernethy, 1995). But the theory still suffers from a similar ahistoricism as neoclassical microeconomic theory.

Ideational theory. This perspective attributes fertility declines to the diffusion of innovations in birth control technologies and social norms, perhaps after mortality declines have created an excess supply of children (Cleland and Wilson, 1987). Diffusion of such information is clearly important to many fertility transitions, especially those reliant on modern technological innovations (Bongaarts and Watkins, 1996). The diffusion of norms and technologies may affect attempts to stop fertility at a desired number of children, or to space children even where desired levels have not yet been reached (Caldwell et al., 1992). Like other theories reviewed, however, the ideational theory is incomplete and doesn't identify when diffused innovations will be adopted or elaborate the institutional factors underlying the origin of such ideational changes.

It is not surprising for academics to have different theories for such complex and widespread events as fertility transitions—and the controversy among learned demographic scholars undoubtedly will continue. It may be of some relief to recognize that we do not have to choose. Some of the theories above emphasize a single underlying social change which may be very important in one historical or regional setting and less so in another. Some of these theories provide insight into one aspect of fertility decisions but are incomplete, neglecting social changes that may drive these fertility decisions. Being realistic, all of the relationships put forward by these transition theories may have been important to a different degree in different fertility transitions. This perspective does not contradict the idea that worldwide fertility transitions have been part of a common historical experience, which follow mortality transitions and are broadly similar. It does, however, suggest we should not expect any one narrow model to provide great insight into fertility declines that have taken place across vastly different times and cultures.

Measuring Period Fertility

When we turn to contemporary times we have much more, and more reliable, data available to study fertility transitions. And, as with mortality and morbidity, there are a number of different measures that can illuminate different aspects of fertility.

Do not be confused by use of the word "period" here to modify fertility. **Period rates**, such as those in earlier chapters of this book (e.g., crude birth and death rates and age-sex-specific death rates), all refer to events (such as births or deaths) that occur within a specified short period, usually a single year.

However, in studying fertility, we will also use measures that view fertility longitudinally, as childbearing accumulates in the history of an age group. For instance, we might want to measure fertility by the average number of children that women of a given cohort, such as baby boomers, bear in their lifetimes. This measure is not for a specific period but rather measures cohort fertility. We will pursue cohort fertility later in this chapter. For the moment we are simply introducing the phrase "period fertility" to be clear which type of measure we are referring to.

Getting Information about Births

The vital event defining fertility is *live birth* (not conception), and to measure fertility one first needs to record births. In the Western tradition, records of live births come mostly from the civil registration system, just as do the records of deaths (see chapter 2). Designated people likely to witness the birth are held responsible for recording its occurrence, time, and location. They normally also are responsible for recording some information about the mother, such as her age and marital status, how many children she already has (that is, the parity of this child), and even her education and/or ethnic identity.

However, as chapter 2 details, civil registration of births is incomplete, at least in the less-developed regions. The task is so difficult that many LDRs do not seriously attempt nationwide birth registration. A more manageable procedure is to select a representative sample of geographic areas within the nation for more intensive registration efforts.

Demographers also use censuses; either to check on the completeness of birth registration or to supply independent estimates of births by date (see chapter 2 and Box 5-1). The children found at the various ages below ten in a given decennial census must have been born during the preceding ten years; more precisely, they are the survivors of those born. If one has enough information about infant and childhood mortality in the population, as well as migration, one can estimate how many births must have occurred in order to leave the number of survivors found in the census.

The major technical trend in counting births in the LDRs, however, has been the introduction of retrospective sample surveys. Aside from counting births in lieu of effective civil registration systems, these surveys have been charged with gathering information on the potential determinants of fertility. Thus, survey responses conventionally provide not only a complete history of conceptions and births, but also a marital history, a contraceptive and abortion history, and information on relevant parental characteristics (such as education, ethnic status, and rural or urban residence).

The most well-known and widely administered sets of surveys with detailed fertility information are the Demographic and Health Surveys (DHS+) and, from 1972–1983, the World Fertility Surveys. Both surveys have data for a large number of developing countries with sufficient numbers of respondents for detailed fertility analyses. The basic strategy for maintaining international comparability of results has been to standardize survey questionnaires to the extent possible. While optional survey items vary across countries, a common core of information generally includes the respondent's and spouse's background, maternal and child health, contraceptive knowledge and practices, relationship history, family-planning regulation, HIV, work history, and possible determinants of fertility including socioeconomic factors and more immediate influences. One important caution regarding such surveys is that much of the fertility data collected are retrospective; that is, respondents are asked to recollect their family and fertility events and (sometimes remote) dates.

Fertility Rates

Given records of live births, how does one measure the fertility of a population in a given year? The simplest approach is to divide the number of births by the total population. The result is the crude birth rate, still one of the most useful annual measures of fertility; but people in the population contribute unequally in the production of births.

In an ultimate sense, giving birth is limited to women, though men obviously made contributions earlier in the process. Moreover, it is limited to women of reproductive age, normally considered to be ages fifteen through forty-nine (and sometimes even into the fifties in countries where assisted reproductive technology is becoming more common). Even within those childbearing years, a woman's fecundity characteristically peaks in her twenties and declines starting in her thirties. Therefore, the age-sex structure of a population partially determines how many births it will produce.

Demographers conventionally call rates applying to the total population *birth rates*. But the rate of births to just women of childbearing age is called the **fertility rate**. As we have seen, one way of discounting the influence of age-sex structure on fertility is to deal in *age-sex-specific fertility rates* (see Box 4-2). One can, for instance, classify the female reproductive cycle into seven five-year age categories and compute a separate age-sex-specific rate for each population category. This is illustrated in Table 7-1. The population counts in column 1 are estimated from censuses. Column 2 records births by age of mother, information ideally obtained from the civil registration system but often necessarily estimated from other data. Column 3 records the annual specific fertility rates, that is, the number of births per thousand women in the age category.

Table 7-1 Illustrative Computation of Total Fertility Rate, United States, 2011

Age	Female Population (as of July 1) (1)	Births (2)	Births per 1,000 Women per Year (col. 2/col. 1) (3)	Projected Resulting Births during Age Interval (col. 3 × 5) (4)
15–19	10,530,679	329,772	31.32	156.58
20–24	10,847,227	925,200	85.29	426.47
25–29	10,527,669	1,127,583	107.11	535.53
30–34	10,232,783	986,682	96.42	482.12
35–39	9,835,794	463,849	47.16	235.80
40–44	10,575,276	108,920	10.30	51.50
45–49	11,210,067	7,025	0.63	3.13
50–54	11,497,858	585	0.05	0.25
Total	**85,257,353**	**3,949,616**	**378.28**	**1891.38**

Source: National Center for Health Statistics, 2013. "Births: Final Data for 2011."

Age-specific fertility rates are not affected by population structure. One can compare the rate for U.S. women aged fifteen to nineteen with that for women of the same ages in Mexico, for instance. Any resulting difference would be due to something other than the differences in their population structures.

Total Fertility Rates

In order to compare the *overall* fertility of different populations with age-sex-specific rates, one would have to make seven comparisons, one for each of the age classes of women. A more convenient approach would be to combine these age-sex-specific rates into a single summary measure that was not influenced by population structure. The total fertility rate (TFR) is such a measure. It is the most important indicator of fertility used by demographers.

The reasoning behind the TFR is very similar to the reasoning behind life expectancy measures (see chapter 5). It involves establishing a hypothetical cohort and then following it through a specific schedule of hypothetical events to see what the end result would be. In this case, the hypothetical cohort starts out as 1,000 women, all of whom reach age fifteen simultaneously. We can trace their experience in Table 7-1 as an illustration. As they progress through the ages fifteen through nineteen, they experience *each year* the specified age-specific fertility rate (31.32 per 1,000, shown in column 3), and thereby, during the five-year age interval, produce 156 births. Similarly, for each successive age category, one computes the number of births that would result during five years to this hypothetical cohort by multiplying the age-specific rate by five. When one has carried the cohort through the end of its fecund years (age fifty-four), one can total column 4 to obtain the number of births they collectively would have produced (in this case, 1,891 babies to the 1,000 women or 1.89 births per woman).

Formally defined, the period **total fertility rate** (TFR) "measures the average number of children that would be born to a hypothetical cohort of women who survive to the end of their reproductive period and who bear children at each age at the rate observed during a particular period" (Preston et al. 2001, p. 95). A computational shortcut for determining the TFR is first to total the age-specific fertility rates and then multiply the total by five (if using five-year age groups). In our Table 7-1 illustration, that would mean totaling column 3 and then multiplying that total (378.28) by five, giving us the same 1,891 babies, and the same TFR of 1.89.

Demographers have studied enough cases to know fairly precisely the relationships among (1) the total number of births in a population, (2) the number of women in each of the age categories of the childbearing years, and (3) the total fertility rate. Therefore, if they are supplied the first two facts, they can estimate the third.

A very similar fertility measure is the **gross reproduction rate** (GRR). The GRR is identical to the TFR except that it counts only female babies. That makes the GRR a measure of the average number of daughters a woman would bear; that is, a measure of women's reproduction of themselves across generations. It is constructed by multiplying the TFR by the proportion of all births that are daughters, usually about 48%. Therefore, the GRR is about half the TFR for the same population and year.

But what if we do not have all the precise data necessary for the computation of age-specific fertility rates and, thus, total fertility rates? What if we do not have for each birth a record of the age of the mother?

It is quite normal in the less-developed regions to be missing this detail and yet to have some other useful information, such as (1) the age-sex structure of the population (obtained from censuses), and (2) the *total* number of births, irrespective of age of mother. Censuses are better developed in most LDRs than are civil registration systems. Registration systems are more likely to contain complete records of the number of births alone than information about the age of the mothers. Even failing that, total births by calendar year of occurrence can be inferred after the fact, from subsequent censuses.

Given those data, there are two options: either *estimate* indirectly what the TFR might have been (as described above) or compute a **general fertility rate** (GFR, sometimes called simply the "fertility rate"). The formula for the GFR is

$$GFR = \frac{B}{P_{15-54}} \times 1,000$$

where B is the total births for the year and P_{15-54} is the women aged fifteen through fifty-four in the year. We can illustrate its computation from data contained in Table 7-1:

$$GFR = \frac{3,949,616}{85,257,353} \times 1,000 = 46.32$$

The GFR *partially* controls for the influence of age-sex structure on fertility; that is, it accounts for differences in the proportion of the total population that consists of women in the childbearing years. But it does not control for variations from one population to another in terms of the age distribution of women between the ages of fifteen and fifty-four.

Recent Fertility Declines

In the past century, fertility decline has become a nearly universal trend. The majority of the world today experiences low to intermediate levels of fertility. Less than 20% of the world's people could be classified as "high fertility"; that is, having more than a GRR of 1.5 daughters per woman (United Nations, 2013b).

By Region

Fertility has reached dramatically lower levels than ever thought possible in many countries. A number of European countries as well as some Asian countries have TFRs of 1.3 children per woman or below (PRB, 2014). This much of a fall in fertility rates in some countries has created a new term among demographers: "lowest-low fertility" (Kohler et al., 2002).

Although childlessness is a factor, the very low fertility rates in many countries stem mostly from reductions to just one or two children per family. Small families like these reflect changing lifestyles and adjusted preferences in ideal family size that often accompany economic development. It is common for demographers to interview individuals about their desired number of children to get an idea for how it matches their actual number of children. Surveys show that the preferred family size for most people in MDRs has stabilized to an ideal of about two children (Hagewen and Morgan, 2005; Dey and Wasoff, 2010). But it appears that the ideal family size is becoming even smaller in parts of Europe, leading demographers to speculate that as fertility declines, a culture of low-fertility preference norms is adopted (Coleman, 2007; Lutz et al., 2006; Goldstein et al., 2003).

Individuals' preference in family size in these countries is often larger than their actual completed family sizes. This is quite the opposite of high-fertility countries, where family size tends to exceed the desired family size (Hagewen and Morgan, 2005; Bongaarts, 2001). We can conclude then that the very low TFRs emerging in many societies are not always deliberate. At one extreme, for example, the Chinese government imposed a one-child limit in 1979 to reduce overpopulation (although there is some evidence to suggest that fertility norms had already shifted prior to the policy, see Feng et al., 2013). But in many other countries, delayed ages at marriage and childbearing leave a much smaller window of time in which couples can achieve their family size goals. Competing demands of schooling and work during that time, as well as unanticipated obstacles like union disruption or age-related infertility, often cause people to fall short of their childbearing preferences.

Many individuals overstate their intended number of children and fail to achieve their childbearing goals. For example, only 38% of American women had met their intended family size stated at age twenty-two by age forty (Quesnel-Vallée and Morgan, 2003). While some people simply change their minds over time, some put off childbearing to ages when it becomes more difficult to conceive. Delay to older ages is estimated to account for about 15% of fertility decline in Italy and about 8% of the decline in the United States (Morgan, 2003). Although this trend has been accompanied by a rise in assisted reproductive technologies, such methods have yet to counterbalance decreases in fertility.

Fertility has also declined steadily in most of Asia, Latin America, and North Africa during the last fifty or so years. In China, with a TFR of 1.6, fertility has now fallen below that of the United States (which has a TFR of 1.9). In other developing countries, fertility has fallen by more than half since the 1950s.

Despite the spread of fertility decline, there remains a contrast between the more-developed regions as a general category and the less-developed regions. In Table 7-2, TFRs are shown for regions of the world in 1955 and 2010 with a mid-level projection to 2025. In the 1950s, MDR countries had an average of about three children per woman while LDR countries had an average of over six children per women. Today, that difference has narrowed considerably, with LDR countries averaging only about one child more per woman than MDR countries. Projected into the next decade, fertility in less-developed countries will continue to decline slightly while fertility in more-developed countries is projected to increase slightly.

Table 7-2   Estimated and Projected Total Fertility Rates for World Regions, 1955, 2010, and 2025

Region[a]	1950–1955	2005–2010	2020–2025
World	4.97	2.53	2.41
More-Developed Regions	2.83	1.66	1.74
Less-Developed Regions	6.08	2.69	2.50
Europe	2.67	1.54	1.66
Northern America	3.35	2.02	1.96
Asia	5.83	2.25	2.07
Latin America	5.86	2.30	2.00
Oceania	3.84	2.47	2.31
Africa	6.60	4.88	4.13

[a] Regions listed in order of increasing 2010 TFR.

Source: United Nations, 2013b. *World Population Prospects: The 2012 Revision.* Used with permission.

There is more variation among the less-developed regions than among the more-developed ones. In particular, despite fertility declines in the northern parts of the continent, fertility in sub-Saharan Africa remains high. For Africa as a whole the TFR is three times that of Europe.

Replacement-Level Fertility

In trying to assess whether fertility is high or low, people usually are not satisfied with simply comparing populations, as we have just done. Instead they seek some more absolute benchmark against which to compare current fertility, one that shows the implications of that fertility level for the welfare of the populace. The benchmark in current use is **replacement-level fertility**, which is the level at which women, on the average, have enough daughters to "replace" themselves in the population (U.S. Census Bureau, 2009).

Suppose we took a hypothetical cohort of women through the age-sex-specific death rates that prevailed in the United States in 2010 and recorded how many women still survived at each age, up through the end of childbearing, say age forty-nine. Given that schedule of survivorship, and given a normal sex ratio at birth (slightly fewer daughters than sons), there is some schedule of age-specific fertility rates that would result in that particular cohort of mothers collectively producing exactly one daughter per mother.

In order to be at replacement-level, total fertility rates must be above 2.0, since at least one son is born for every daughter, and some potential mothers die before they have had their children, even in the healthiest hypothetical cohort. As a general estimate, replacement TFR is taken to be 2.1 in MDRs and 2.3 in LDRs, where mortality rates are higher. Countries with TFRs below these levels are said to have below-replacement fertility. According to Table 7-2, Europe and Northern America are currently below replacement-level fertility.

Nations that find themselves with fertility *below* replacement level tend to be concerned with the problems of slow population growth and population decline (see chapter 3). There are currently eleven countries or territories that have begun to experience unprecedented lowest-low fertility levels, falling at or below 1.3 children per woman. However, fertility is only one source of change in a country's population growth. It would be a mistake to assume that below-replacement fertility always will result in declining population size. Among the seventy-five countries that now have below-replacement fertility (48% of the world's population), many will continue to experience population growth due both to immigration and to younger age structures, with large cohorts entering reproductive ages (United Nations, 2013b).

As the foregoing table showed, it is not just the more-developed regions that have low fertility. Fully one-third of less-developed countries in the world now have below-replacement fertility levels (United Nations, 2011b). These include some of the most populated developing countries, such as China, Brazil, Iran, Thailand, Vietnam, and South Korea (United Nations, 2013b).

Figure 7-4 shows a global map shaded into below replacement, replacement, medium, and high fertility countries. Higher fertility primarily characterizes African countries and a few Latin American and Asian countries. However, there has also been notable fertility decline in Africa, with many African countries now in the medium fer-

Figure 7-4

Total Fertility Estimate, 2005–2010

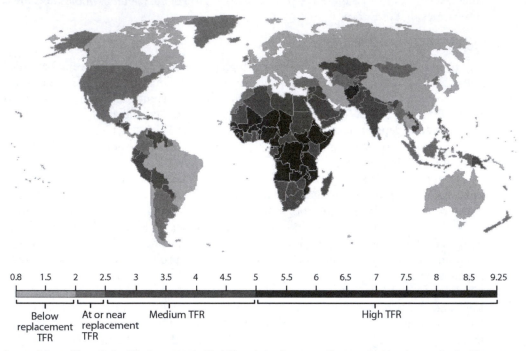

Source: Adapted from United Nations, 2013b. *World Population Prospects: The 2012 Revision*, interactive fertility maps.

tility category. And, as we have pointed out in previous chapters, region and country-level averages have a tendency to mask internal diversity. For example, Guatemala, the country in Latin America with the highest growth rate, has a TFR of 5.8 among the poorest 20% of the population and a TFR of only 1.7 among the wealthiest 20% of the population (Haub and Gribble, 2011).

Malthusian and Neo-Malthusian Components

How much of these declines in fertility are caused by delay and avoidance of marriage and how much by curtailing of fertility after marriage? The Malthusian and neo-Malthusian components of the fertility transition have overlapped far more in today's less-developed regions than they did historically in Europe. The average age at marriage for women in developed countries today is around thirty whereas in the least developed countries it is a full decade younger (United Nations, 2011d). But a large number of developing countries that have experienced rapid economic development and cultural change are seeing a rise in age at marriage that looks similar to that of developed countries. Increasing marriage age and an increase in the proportion of women remaining single accounted for much of the fertility decline in many Middle Eastern countries in recent decades (DeJong and El-Khoury, 2006; Rashad et al., 2005; Gelbard et al., 1999).

Although changing marital patterns have played an important role, it is the neo-Malthusian fertility decline that has been the more important factor in current LDR transitions. How is it being brought about? Some of it is attributable to the diffusion of family-planning programs, which are now facilitating contraception, sterilization, and abortion for people with unmet family-planning needs. There have been widespread cultural changes in the number of children desired, which then motivates the use of birth control devices. Family-planning use rose from less than 10% of married women of childbearing age in the 1960s to 63% in 2009 (United Nations, 2011b; Gelbard et al., 1999).

Projections

Demographers are mainly informed by two sets of worldwide fertility projections. The United Nations estimates population size, population growth, and population projections for all countries of the world every two years; the U.S. Census Bureau provides its own similar projections of world population trends. Both projections provide, along with population size, such indicators as population growth rate, crude birth rate, crude death rate, total fertility rate, life expectancy at birth, and age-sex distribution.

Because fertility is the major determinant of world population growth, several projections are made, each assuming different fertility trends (e.g., constant, low, medium, and high). In the recent past, medium fertility estimates have tended to provide projections slightly higher than what later occurred. However, it is not possible to be certain those trends will continue, and the medium projections are usually a "best guess" of future trends.

Column 3 of Table 7-2 predicts total fertility rates to the year 2025. Whatever their accuracy, demographic projections have become lower every decade since the 1960s. By 2025 only Africa is projected to have fertility levels significantly higher than replacement level. Asia and Latin America in 2025 would be at or below replacement fertility, more similar to levels in current-day North America.

When the worldwide total fertility rate reaches replacement levels, does that mean the world population explosion will be over? Not quite. *Crude* birth rates and *crude* growth rates could remain transitionally high for decades because of a young age structure, the heritage of previously high TFRs (see chapter 4). This point foreshadows our explanation of *population momentum* in the following section.

Explaining Period Fertility Changes: The U.S. Case

In the more-developed countries, crude birth rates dropped as part of their demographic transitions and most less-developed countries have now entered their fertility transitions as well. What are the immediate causes of these trends? How do changes in the age structure of the populations, in the number of children that couples have, and in the age when they have them, taken together, influence the crude birth rates? The interrelationships are complex.

Let us use the example of the United States to demonstrate how demographers explain fertility changes. It has already undergone its demographic transition and it has well-documented fertility data. To set the stage, what follows is a thumbnail history of the U.S. crude birth rate.

History of the U.S. Crude Birth Rate

Since the birth of the nation, the U.S. population has experienced a two-century decline in crude birth rates, interrupted in the mid-20th century by cyclical variations around that long-term trend. Although the data are incomplete, our best estimate is that the crude birth rate in 1800 was around fifty per 1,000 total population (Klein, 2012), which approximates current Niger. That probably was higher than for any Western European country at that time. But by the late 1800s, the U.S. crude birth rate was below forty, like that of Western Europe (Moore and O'Connell, 1978).

Since the establishment of vital registration in the United States in the early 1900s, we have better estimates of fertility. Figure 7-5 graphs in detail the path of the crude birth rate of the United States from then until 2011. The long-term decline continued, bottoming out early in the 1930s during the Depression. This was followed by the baby boom of the 1950s and 1960s, and that was followed by the baby bust that bottomed out in the mid-1970s. The baby-boom echo caused by childbearing of women born during the baby boom then appears to have peaked in 1990. Since 1990, fertility has declined gradually, and the 2011 estimate of 12.7 is the lowest level seen in U.S. his-

Figure 7-5

U.S. Crude Birth Rates, 1910–2011

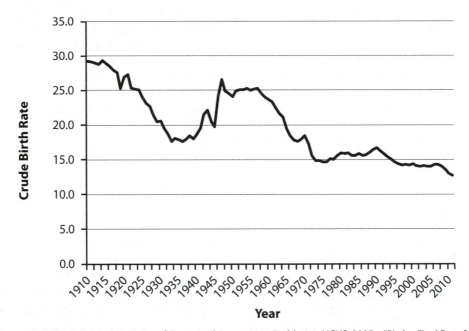

Sources: NCHS, 2002. "Vital Statistics of the United States, 2000," table 1-1; NCHS, 2005a. "Births: Final Data for 2003"; NCHS, 2005b. "Preliminary Births for 2004"; NCHS, 2013. "Births: Final Data for 2011." Graph created by Eiko Strader.

tory. There has also been a shift to older ages at childbearing during this period. Birth-rates among those in their late teens and early twenties are at historic lows, while women in their early forties recorded the highest level of childbearing in four decades (NCHS, 2013).

Fertility decline continues in the United States at this writing and has been particularly affected, as in other countries, by the Great Recession starting in 2007 (Livingston, 2011; Lanzieri, 2013). Over almost a two-century span, the United States saw its fertility drop to less than 30% of its original high level but it ended up with unstable fertility, subject to up-and-down cycles around the new low level. The worst of the "bulge" effects from the U.S. fertility transition are likely in the past now (see chapter 4) and projections into the distant future predict there will be a continual gradual decline through the 21st century (United Nations, 2013b).

The Influence of Age Structure on Period Fertility

One factor that influences a crude birth rate is the proportion of the total population consisting of women in their childbearing years. The greater that proportion, the higher the crude birth rate, all else being equal. That proportion, in turn, can be influenced by migration and by fertility itself.

First, let us take migration. Through most of its history, the United States has had heavy positive net migration—more people moving in than out. Moreover, immigration has been dominated by young people willing and able to start lives in a new world. Thus, the net effect of migration has been to add to that part of the population pyramid "at risk" of childbearing. This, in turn, tended to peg the U.S. crude birth rate at a higher level than it would have been without age-selective net immigration.

On the other hand, throughout U.S. history the *proportion* of the population who were new immigrants has decreased. That meant the upward pressure of new immigration on fertility became less and less. Thus the decline in the U.S. net migration rate contributed to the decline in the U.S. crude birth rate.

Second, fertility change can create its own momentum via the age structure. A reduced crude birth rate produces a birth cohort at the bottom of the population pyramid that is smaller than it would have been with a higher birth rate. This shrunken cohort ages upward through the population pyramid until it reaches its childbearing ages. Then, because it is smaller in number than it would have been at old fertility levels, it produces fewer children, who in turn form an even smaller birth cohort at the bottom of the pyramid, and the cycle is repeated.

This mechanism has given momentum to all long-term fertility transitions. It did so in Europe and in the United States until their crude birth rates temporarily bottomed out in the 1930s. This momentum effect means that fertility trends take some time to have significant impact.

Aside from such long-term trends, more-developed countries seem subject to short cycles in crude birth rates. Such cycles, by creating peaks and valleys in the population pyramid, can create **echo effects** in the crude birth rate a generation later. The United States is a good example, since its recent fertility cycles have been extreme.

Table 7-3 on the following page allows us to specify the timing of the positive and negative effects of past fertility cycles on crude birth rates via the age structure. Whereas age structure does influence the crude birth rate, it does not influence the total fertility rate. Thus, if we construct a ratio in which the crude birth rate is the numerator and the total fertility rate is the denominator, the size of the ratio is an index of the degree to which the age structure was enhancing the crude birth rate. We have done this in column 3 of Table 7-3.

In that column, we see that the ratio stayed stable until the late 1940s. Then it started a decline that was not to hit bottom until the early 1960s. Subtracting between twenty-five and thirty years as an average time between childbearing generations, we can figure that this decline was an echo of the smaller generations born during the declining fertility of the 1930s. The ratio then rose into the mid-1980s. Again, this is clearly an echo effect as larger numbers of women born during the baby boom were in childbearing ages. Finally, the more recent decline in the ratio has begun to reflect another echo of earlier fertility, this time of declining fertility during the baby bust in the late 1970s.

Although there clearly are direct echo effects of past fertility cycles, fertility behavior may also respond to these cycles in such a way as to dampen, or enhance, the full

Table 7-3   Comparison of U.S. Crude Birth Rates with Total Fertility Rates, 1920–2024

Years[a]	Crude Birth Rate (CBR) (1)	Total Fertility Rate (TFR) (2)	Ratio of CBR/TFR (3)
1920–24	26.8	3.248	8.25
1925–29	23.2	2.840	8.17
1930–34	19.7	2.376	8.29
1935–39	18.8	2.235	8.41
1940–44	21.2	2.523	8.40
1945–49	24.1	2.985	8.07
1950–54	24.9	3.337	7.46
1955–59	24.9	3.690	6.75
1960–64	22.4	3.459	6.48
1965–69	18.2	2.636	6.90
1970–74	16.2	2.016	8.04
1975–79	15.0	1.774	8.46
1980–84	15.9	1.817	8.75
1985–89	15.9	1.900	8.37
1990–95	16.1	2.060	7.82
1995–99	14.1	1.950	7.23
2000–04	14.2	2.040	6.96
2005–09	14.0	2.060	6.80
2010–14	13.2	1.970	6.70
2015–19	13.1	1.980	6.62
2020–24	13.0	1.980	6.57

[a]Five-year averages.

Sources: Moore and O'Connell, 1978. *Perspectives on American Fertility,* table 1-2; NCHS, 1998. "Report of Final Natality Statistics," tables 1 and 4; United Nations, 2013b. *World Population Prospects: The 2012 Revision.*

effects of such cycles indirectly. In the United States, they seem more often to dampen the effects of past fertility and population structure. The 1970s baby bust, for instance, occurred when the baby-boom cohorts were in their early childbearing years. In the 1980s there was some rise due to delayed childbearing among the baby boomers. Baby boomers limited and delayed their fertility, reducing the full impact their rising numbers might have had on crude birth rates. Indeed, there is some theoretical basis for saying that couples adjust how many children they have, and when they have them, on the basis of the relative size of their birth cohort in comparison with their parents' cohort (Easterlin, 1968, 1978; Ryder, 1979). That is, there may be an automatic tendency for past fertility cycles to suppress rather than reinforce future fertility cycles.

The *degree* of impact of age structure on crude birth rates, however, is generally minor compared with the impact of cohort fertility patterns. That is, how many children couples have in their lifetimes, and when they have them, remain the major causes of trends and cycles in period fertility. For the rest of this section, let us measure fertility with total fertility rates (TFRs) rather than crude birth rates. The TFR is not affected by the age structure of the population. By using it, therefore, we are able to explore what, *beyond age structure*, can have an immediate impact on fertility trends.

The Influence of Cohort-Completed Fertility

Another fertility measure that would not be affected by age structure of the population would be the eventual number of children ever born to a generation, or *birth cohort*, of women who had completed childbearing. This measure would not be affected by age because women belonging to the birth cohort are all nearly the same age, and because women of the birth cohort have already passed through all ages of childbearing. When we follow a cohort of women through their lives and observe, on average, how many children they have had when they are at the end of childbearing ages, we have a measure of their **cohort-completed fertility rate** (Shryock and Siegel, 1976). Currently, the end of childbearing years is generally assumed to be around age fifty.

This rate is similar to the total fertility rate in many ways. As you may recall, the shortcut we used to compute the TFR was to add age-specific fertility rates across all ages (and then to multiply by the number of years in each age category). That is, we added up the fertility a woman would eventually have if she went through life and experienced the current age-specific fertility rates for each year of her life as she grew older.

To compute the cohort-completed fertility rate (CCFR), we actually follow women through their lives and add up the effects of their own age-specific fertility rates across time as the cohort ages. If we take, for instance, the cohort of women born between 1950 and 1954, they would begin significant childbearing at ages fifteen to nineteen during the years 1965–1969; ages twenty to twenty-four during 1970–1974; ages twenty-five to twenty-nine during 1975–1979, and so on, until they reached the final years of childbearing. To compute their completed fertility we would add the 1965–1969 age-specific rate for women aged fifteen to nineteen to the 1970–1974 rate for women aged twenty to twenty-four, and so on, then multiply by five (the number of years in the birth cohort and each age group).

In sum, the computation is the same as that for the TFR; what is different is the age-specific rates we are cumulating. In the case of the cohort-completed fertility rate, we are adding up the rates experienced by an actual cohort of women during their lives.

One frustrating limitation of cohort-completed fertility rates is that they cannot measure completed fertility until the cohort has passed through childbearing ages. This problem can be dealt with in two ways.

The first way is component projection. We can assume, on whatever basis, a schedule of age-specific fertility rates that a currently childbearing cohort will experience for the remainder of its childbearing ages, add those to the rates recorded for ages already passed, and obtain a partially projected cohort-completed fertility rate. Recent methodological estimation innovation allows researchers to project cohort fertility for women who have not yet passed through their reproductive years (Max Planck Institute for Demographic Research, 2013).

The second way is deceptively simple. It consists of asking (in survey interviews) not only how many children women have had, but also how many children the women expect to have before they complete their childbearing. Obviously, women in their forties will be better able to make such a determination than women just starting their fecund years, and obviously younger women will have more time to change their minds or fail to fulfill their expectations. But this is a straightforward way of using subjective plans for prediction in societies where families are largely preplanned.

To what degree are the ups and downs in 20th-century U.S. total fertility rates explained by ups and downs in cohort-completed fertility? Figure 7-6 presents total fertility rates for 1925 through 1999 and cohort fertility rates for women who recently completed their childbearing and are now in their sixties.

Some technical comments are necessary to understand this figure. In comparing period and cohort trends, we are faced with a technical difficulty: What *date* do we assign to a cohort rate? Women who were born between 1945 and 1949, for example, were of childbearing ages all the way from the early 1960s to the mid-1990s. A fairly arbitrary answer is to assign cohort fertility rates to the date of the cohort's approximate median female age of childbearing; thirty has been chosen as that age in Figure 7-6. This is why the dates in the two time scales of Figure 7-6 differ consistently by thirty years.

This also explains why the CCFR graph ends in the late 1970s. The birth cohort of 1945–1949 only completed childbearing in the 1990s, but the TFR when these women were about age thirty would be that from 1975–1979. This illustrates the frustrating limitation of cohort rates, mentioned above, that they measure events which could be long past.

We can see that U.S. cohort-completed fertility made significant swings, but within the limited range of about 3.2 live births to 2.2 live births per woman. The timing of the upward and downward swings certainly was such that the changing tendencies of American women to have large, then small, then large, then small families helped explain the changes in total fertility rate. Finally, if the graph included a longer historical span, it would reveal a long-term secular decline in the average cohort-completed fertility, probably extending from the birth of the nation.

A disclaimer may be appropriate. Our task has been to see whether the relation between these two trends was such that changes in CCFR could have caused observed changes in TFR, and that has been demonstrated to some extent. However, it is equally logical—given no further data—to say that changes in period total fertility rates eventually caused the swings in cohort-completed fertility.

Figure 7-6

Total Fertility Rate, 1925–1999, and Cohort-Completed Fertility Rates, 1895–1949

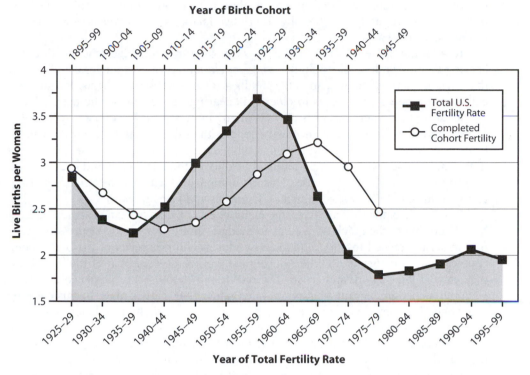

Source: Adapted from Anderton et al., 1997. *The Population of the United States,* tables 6-2 and 6-13.

The Influence of Timing

The other aspect of cohort childbearing that can influence the total fertility rate is the timing of childbearing. It makes a difference whether women bear their children early or late in their fecund ages. First, we will describe how this works in the abstract; then we will describe how it has influenced U.S. total fertility rates in the past few decades.

Everything else being equal, a population where older women bear the children will have lower period fertility than will a population where younger women bear the children. There are two factors causing this.

Call the first the "prematernal-death" factor. Death erodes any cohort of women through its collective lifetime. That means that at every successive age between, say, fifteen and forty-nine there will be fewer women surviving. If that cohort bears its children at older ages, fewer of them will be alive to participate in the childbearing and they collectively will produce fewer children. (This will not be reflected in a lower cohort-completed fertility rate, since that describes the fertility only of the women who survived.)

Call the second the "baby-spread" factor. If women bear their children at older ages and so do their daughters, and then so do their daughters, the result will be that those children will be spread over a larger number of calendar years. That means that the total fertility rate for any given year involved will be lower than it would have been under a regime of early childbearing. These two factors are *permanent* as long as the timing does not change.

In addition, there is a *transitory* effect of moving from one age schedule of childbearing to another. If an older childbearing population moves to younger childbearing, there will be more of an overlap in the childbearing of successive cohorts. If a younger childbearing population moves to older childbearing—for example, the deferment of childbearing until later ages as is now occurring in most countries—there will be less overlap in the childbearing of successive cohorts than there would have been with no transition. Short-term period fertility measures during changing age schedules of fertility would underestimate actual levels of fertility in the latter case and overestimate fertility levels in the former case. This estimation problem can be remedied using tempo-adjusted fertility measurements (Bongaarts and Feeney, 1998).

In the case of the United States, the major effects of changes in age at childbearing have been due to the quick transitions in modern times. During the Depression, couples generally tended to delay childbearing; during the prosperity of the baby boom, couples started earlier and earlier; during the worldwide recession of the baby bust, they started later again, and so on. The recent baby-boom echo happened at a time when women were bearing children at later rather than earlier ages. In this case the older baby boomers finally entered into these ages and had children before they considered it too late to do so. Most of these transitory effects have acted to *enhance* the effect of changes in U.S. cohort-completed fertility. This is true even in cases such as the baby-boom echo where they may have dampened changes in period fertility.

Figure 7-6 graphs this. In this figure, the degree to which the total-fertility-rate line veers above or below the cohort-completed-fertility-rate line is an index of the influence of changes in the timing of cohort fertility. Thus, the TFR dipping below the CCFR line during the Depression would result from delays in childbearing. The soaring of the TFR above the CCFR during the baby boom would be due to the late appearance of children delayed from their normal expectation during the Depression, plus the early appearance of baby-boom childbearing. The downward plunge of the TFR since 1965, even below the CCFR, registers the gap left by early-appearing baby-boom babies, plus the progressive delay of childbearing during the baby bust. The effects of the baby-boom echo on completed fertility will not be seen until those women complete their childbearing. These echo effects can be estimated using the methods discussed above and show a continuing cyclical pattern. However, just as recent swings in TFR have been less extreme, so will be the anticipated echo effects.

Nevertheless, the potential impact of changes in timing is particularly strong in a society such as the United States. Only a portion of American women's fecund years normally are taken up with childbearing. In a few less-developed countries, in contrast, almost all of women's fecund years are taken up with childbearing. When women are reproducing at all ages in the reproductive lifestage, there is very little room to shift the timing of their childbearing. In the United States, women have greater latitude about when to have their comparatively fewer children, and their decisions can have real impact on period fertility.

The Influence of Age Structure on Cohort Fertility

Here is another example of how the various immediate determinants of the crude birth rate may be subtly interrelated with each other: The relative size of birth cohorts may influence both the completed fertility of cohorts and the timing of their childbearing. How this might happen has been outlined by Richard Easterlin (1978).

Start with the observation that job opportunities for cohorts maturing into the workforce depend, everything else being equal, on the size of the cohort. Under the same business conditions, a large cohort will have to share available jobs among more people; members of a small cohort will have more choice of jobs.

Members of a cohort will see their economic situation as hopeful or hopeless, not only on the basis of their actual opportunities but also by comparing those prospects with some other standard. That standard, says Easterlin, is their family of orientation, their parents. If they see their prospects as better than those of their parents, they tend to be optimistic about improving their economic status; if they see no such chance, they respond with pessimism. Thus, the relative economic opportunity of successive generations, partially determined by the relative sizes of those cohorts, influences economic optimism and pessimism.

Members express their optimism or pessimism reproductively. If they are pessimistic, they will tend to feel they can afford fewer children, voluntarily decreasing the cohort-completed fertility rate for their generation. More immediately, they will tend to put off the start of childbearing until they feel more economically secure (Ryder, 1979). Both responses, of course, will reduce period fertility.

The theory is basically cyclical. Pessimistic generations (such as those becoming adults during the Depression) will produce small birth cohorts; those children, one generation hence, will see themselves as having better opportunities than their parents. They optimistically will marry earlier and have more children, creating a larger birth cohort whose members, one generation hence, will see themselves as having poorer opportunities than their parents. They pessimistically will delay marriage and have fewer children (such as in the recent baby bust), thus creating a small birth cohort, and so on. Easterlin's theory is generally supported by the demographic evidence (Jeon and Shields, 2005; Slack and Jensen, 2008).

One interesting, highly hypothetical implication is that this "Easterlin effect" might serve to explain the dampening of the "echo effect" of peaks and valleys in the population pyramid. Everything else being equal, a relatively small birth cohort maturing into the childbearing ages is likely to produce fewer children. But here we see that a small cohort of potential parents also is likely to be economically optimistic, starting childbearing earlier, and having more children. Of course, many other things besides cohort size can influence economic optimism, and many influences other than optimism can affect childbearing decisions, particularly as women become increasingly important economic earners for their families.

Figure 7-7 on the next page shows the percentages of women at age forty to forty-four by child parity. The major demographic story of the U.S. modern day is the dominance of the two-child norm. In the past, when fertility was higher, there was greater diversity in parity, with four-child families being most common, but also with a high prevalence of two-child and three-child families. Today, having four children or more is

Figure 7-7

Percent of Women Ages 40 to 44 by Number of Children Ever Born, by Birth Cohort

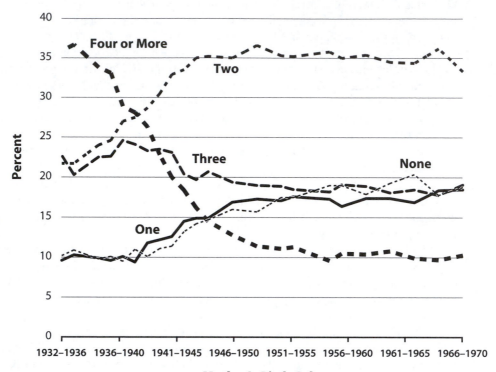

Mother's Birth Cohort

Source: Jacobsen et al., 2012. "Household Changes in the United States." *Population Bulletin* 67(1). Used with permission of Population Reference Bureau.

even less common than having no children. The percentages of women with no children or one child have doubled over the past century, but two-child families have become the most common form of households with families. American norms around what is "too few" and "too many" children have also changed accordingly during this period.

Explaining Cohort Fertility

As we trace back through the causal chain that determines period fertility, what are the next links to study? We have established that differences in total fertility rates are caused by differences in two aspects of cohort fertility: the number of children born and the timing of the childbearing. What, then, causes these to vary?

Explanation by Background

Merely to describe fertility differences is to "explain" them in a primitive sense. Take, for instance, general fertility differences between the LDRs and the MDRs.

Knowing the characteristics of people who tend to have higher fertility, for example, we might say that LDRs have higher fertility because people there are likely to be poorer, less access to resources, more likely of pronatalist religion, more likely to live in an agricultural economy, and so on. We can call this "explanation by background." It is a first step.

The limitations of that kind of explanation become clear as soon as we undertake to *influence* fertility levels, to design fertility policies. Suppose, for instance, a country decides it wants to reduce its fertility levels. The only guidance provided by the preceding kind of explanation in designing a policy is to suggest they change a maximum number of people from high-fertility categories to low-fertility categories. That is, make people richer, provide them with different sorts of jobs, and so on.

Policies that attempt to change people's fertility by changing their characteristics are indirect and gradual. When focused on particular aspects of social change, such policies can be popular among policy makers and supportive of other programs. An example is LDR policies for improving women's educational levels. But note that choosing a focus implies accepting some theory of how that background factor influences human behavior and thus fertility.

"Explanation by background" is simply not sufficient if we want to understand how group differences come about, or if we seek more effective ways to help people have the number of children they desire (Bulatao, 1984; Bongaarts and Potter, 1983; Burch, 1975; Casterline and Sinding, 2000). How many children a woman bears, and when, is the result of complicated patterns of actions. She has sex or she doesn't, uses contraception or doesn't, induces an abortion or doesn't, to mention just a few of the determining acts. Those kinds of actions that have direct impact on the reproductive process we can call the *proximate determinants* of fertility levels. A more satisfactory explanation of fertility differences involves not only stating what characteristics are associated with higher or lower fertility (describing background differentials) but also specifying how they do it (specifying differentials in the proximate determinants).

The Proximate Determinants of Fertility

Kingsley Davis and Judith Blake (1956) outlined which categories of behavior should be taken into account in seeking to understand fertility. They saw the proximate determinants of fertility levels as *finite* and *limited*; there are only so many things that individuals can do to influence how many children they have and when. They listed these proximate determinants of fertility in order of the time sequence involved in producing babies through three stages: (1) intercourse, (2) conception, and (3) gestation and parturition. Their original list is presented in Box 7-1 on the next page. In the years since these proximate determinants were first introduced, it has generally been determined that five of these factors explain the vast majority of variation in fertility across groups: proportion in unions (items 1 & 2); contraceptive usage (item 8); postpartum infecundability (item 7); and abortion (item 11) (Bongaarts, 1982).

Davis and Blake called these proximate determinants "intermediate variables." This is because the explanation of fertility up until the introduction of their list had been largely explanation by background. They stressed that the *only* way that a background difference (e.g., in wealth, religion, etc.) could produce a fertility difference was by causing variation in one or more of the proximate determinants on their list.

Box
7-1

The "Intermediate Fertility Variables" of Davis and Blake

I. Factors affecting exposure to intercourse ("Intercourse Variables")

   A. Those governing the formation and dissolution of unions in the reproductive period

      1. Age of entry into sexual unions

      2. Permanent celibacy: proportion of women never entering sexual unions

      3. Amount of reproductive period spent after or between unions

         a. When unions are broken by divorce, separation, or desertion

         b. When unions are broken by death of husband

   B. Those governing the exposure to intercourse within unions

      4. Voluntary abstinence

      5. Involuntary abstinence (from impotence, illness, or temporary separations)

      6. Coital frequency (excluding periods of abstinence)

II. Factors affecting exposure to conception ("Conception Variables")

      7. Fecundity or infecundity, as affected by involuntary causes

      8. Use or non-use of contraception

      9. Fecundity or infecundity, as affected by voluntary causes (sterilization, subincision, medical treatment, etc.)

III. Factors affecting gestation and successful parturition ("Gestation Variables")

      10. Fetal mortality from involuntary causes

      11. Fetal mortality from voluntary causes

Source: Davis and Blake, "Social Structure and Fertility: An Analytic Framework," 1956, p. 212.

If we specify the proximate determinants of too-high or too-low cohort fertility for a group of people, we are in a better position for targeting a policy for influencing that fertility. If poor people have more children because they have less access to modern contraceptives, we can more easily provide such contraceptives than we can improve the standard of living, although the latter is certainly a worthy goal in its own right. Indeed, most modern fertility reduction policies in the LDRs have been family-planning programs based on this causal explanation.

Voluntary versus Involuntary Factors

Davis and Blake (1956) consistently attempted to distinguish between *voluntary* and *involuntary* intercourse variables, conception variables, and gestation variables. Let us take "voluntary" in this context to mean that the couple was adjusting its behavior with the intent of influencing how many children it would ultimately have and/or when those children would arrive. Induced abortion would be a clear case of a voluntary factor; impotence due to illness would be an extreme case of an involuntary factor.

What difference does the voluntariness of factors make? It makes a lot, not only in how you explain intercultural fertility differentials but also in what policies you might employ to influence fertility levels. For instance, if you believe that the circumstances keeping fertility high are mostly voluntary (people want to have large families early), then your strategy for lowering fertility would require inciting cultural change in fertility desires—not an easy task. If, on the other hand, you think the high fertility is involuntary and couples would like to have fewer children, then you undertake policies to change each one of these factors in a fertility-lowering direction. For instance, you might make contraceptives more easily available or make induced abortion easier to obtain.

The motive for a couple to voluntarily alter its fertility isn't necessarily to reduce completed family size. Couples may delay the next child to give the mother more time to recover her health, to improve the next child's chances for survival, or to afford themselves temporary flexibility in responding to occupational or educational opportunities. None of these motives necessarily involves a desire to end up with a smaller family.

Let us now employ the Davis-Blake taxonomy and consider, in order, the impacts of intercourse variables, conception variables, and gestation variables on cohort fertility.

Intercourse Variables

The pattern of intercourse that would maximize a population's fertility is well known. It is one in which all the women in a population are sexually active throughout their fecund years and in which intercourse is optimally frequent throughout all those years. Technically, there are about six days during a woman's menstrual cycle when she can conceive (Wilcox et al., 1995). For most couples who are not keeping track of ovulation cycles, however, a sexual frequency of two to three times per week is considered optimal for reproduction (Trussell and Westoff, 1980).

Some deviations from patterns of intercourse that would maximize fertility have more impact on fertility than do others. Interruptions of sexual activity during ages of greatest fecundity, that is, among women in their twenties and early thirties, would have the most severe impact. Interruptions among women who are physiologically unlikely to conceive after birth (during postpartum amenorrhea and depending on the specifics of breast-feeding; see Zohoori and Popkin, 1996), suffering from secondary sterility, or at less fecund ages would have less impact. What follow are some of the major types of deviation from an optimal intercourse pattern that have impacted fertility in some cultures.

Being in Sexual Unions

Late entry into stable sexual unions.   The term "sexual union" here refers to a heterosexual relationship in which the partners are committed to having access to each other sexually, among other things. The most common kind of sexual union leading to fertility is marriage, although sizable groups participate in nonmarital sexual unions of varying stability in many countries (and as you will see in chapter 8, nonmarital childbearing is more common than marital childbearing in a few European countries).

The age at which women first enter such stable sexual unions influences period fertility rates in two ways. First, it influences completed fertility of cohorts. If a cohort of women would have borne children throughout its fecund years, getting a late start would tend to reduce their completed family size. In addition, that late start will tend to increase the average age of mothers at childbearing and, as we have seen, late child-bearing has its own direct impact on period fertility above or beyond its impact on completed family size.

Delayed entry into unions has less impact on fertility in societies where contraceptives are widely used and couples normally have small families. Nevertheless, differences in age at first marriage are partially responsible for some of the major world fertility differentials. The low modern fertility of Western countries is attributed partially to the "European marriage pattern," that is, late women's age at marriage and relatively larger proportions of women never marrying.

Interruption of stable sexual unions.   Sexual unions can be broken, either by the death of the partner (widowhood) or by union dissolution. Whatever the precipitating event, how long such people stay single obviously depends on how rapidly and completely a new union takes place (see chapter 8). Widowhood during childbearing ages is declining on a worldwide level as mortality declines. Moreover, the negative impact of widowhood on fertility always has been limited by the fact that women are widowed mostly after their most fecund years.

The fertility impact of worldwide trends in divorce, remarriage, and cohabitation defies easy generalization. Some LDR countries (such as those with Muslim cultures) have very low levels of divorce while others have a high incidence. MDRs generally have a much higher prevalence of divorce as well as cohabitation in their countries.

Sexual union variables as cultural, not "intermediate."   Strictly speaking, those "intercourse variables" on the Davis-Blake list in Box 7-1 ("Those governing the formation and dissolution of unions . . .") do not logically belong on the list of "intermediate variables" but rather among the cultural factors that must operate through the intermediate variables. Every other variable on the Davis-Blake list has the potential for direct impact on fertility. The variables in category I.A., in contrast, can influence fertility only by influencing one of the remaining variables on the list.

Exposure within Unions

Postpartum abstinence.   Sexual abstinence for one, two, or even three years after giving birth is normal in many societies due to norms and taboos against postpartum sexual activity (Heer and Grigsby, 1992). Such customs are most common in sub-Saharan Africa, but also have been found in other LDRs (Jolly and Gribble, 1993; Cleland et al., 1999; Dada et al., 2002). Such abstinence delays subsequent childbearing by increasing birth intervals in between children, which also improves infant survival. How much of an impact it has on completed family size depends on how long abstinence goes on after the mother stops breast-feeding.

Periodic abstinence.   In Davis and Blake's list, periodic abstinence does not refer to either short-term interruptions of intercourse directed at contraception nor long-term interruptions that are effectively disruptions of sexual unions. We are referring here to seasonal abstinence in such countries as Mozambique (Agadjanian et al., 2011) and Mexico (White and Potter, 2013; Lindstrom and Saucedo, 2007), where men commonly seasonally migrate in search of employment, leaving their partners behind. With rising demand for female labor migration as well, especially from countries with established domestic-worker traditions as in Indonesia, the Philippines, and Bangladesh, the fertility-reducing effect may become even stronger (Azarnert, 2012).

Infrequent intercourse. It can be difficult to get reliable representative data on the frequency of sexual intercourse. One consistent finding, however, is that sexual frequency varies by age and by whether one is in a stable sexual union. Those in sexual unions generally have more intercourse (although those outside unions may have more sexual partners), and intercourse is less frequent at older ages. Some variation in the frequency of intercourse seems to exist cross-nationally, and studies suggest cultural contexts may matter. The Global Study of Sexual Attitudes and Behaviors (GSSAB), an international survey taken from twenty-nine countries among adults aged forty to eighty, finds that East Asians report lesser frequency of intercourse on average than Europeans, non-European Westerners, Central/South Americans, Middle Easterns, and Southeast Asians (Nicolosi et al., 2004). Similarly, studies in the United States find that Asian Americans tend to have more conservative sexual behaviors and fewer lifetime partners than Euro-Americans or Hispanics (Meston and Ahrold, 2010). However, whenever sensitive matters are explored in studies, we need to be wary of potential bias in the data collected due to cultural norms in social desirability. For example, men and women from more gender-conservative cultures may respectively overreport and underreport their frequency of intercourse and number of partners.

There are also gender differences in reported sexual behaviors. Data from the National Survey of Family Growth in the United States shows increased frequency of intercourse after marriage for women, whereas men's reported coital frequency is not influenced by marriage. Among men ages twenty-five and forty-five, increased height, less than high school education, and younger age are all associated with greater reported sexual frequency, while these factors do not significantly predict frequency of intercourse for women (Eisenberg et al., 2010).

Intercourse frequency may clearly affect a woman's fertility. However, to significantly delay the average time to conceive among any large social group, coital frequency would have to be extremely low—lower than has been found on the average in any societal segment.

Conception Variables

Under a given pattern of sexual intercourse, individuals and populations differ in the rate at which conception occurs. The factors that determine the differences in these conception rates are what Davis and Blake mean by "conception variables." These causes can be involuntary (such as sickness or malnutrition) or voluntary (such as contraception). Or, as in the case of breast-feeding, they can be a combination of the two. We will start with the clearly involuntary factors influencing conception.

Involuntary Factors

A woman is said to be fecund if she is able to conceive. The range of biological factors that could influence fecundity is wide. We will focus on disease and malnutrition, both of which more often threaten fertility among the underprivileged.

As a starter, it helps to imagine a population with maximum fecundity. In this hypothetical population, women have early **menarche** (the onset of menstruation) and thus start their conception period young. Moreover, they have late **menopause** (cessation of menstruation), allowing them to bear children late in their lives. In between these events, they have a high probability of conceiving every time they have intercourse. As part of this, they recover their capacity to conceive rapidly after each of their childbirths, having a very short period of **postpartum amenorrhea** (delay of the re-onset of menstruation) and very few anovulatory cycles (menstrual cycles in which ovulation and thus conception do not occur). In this hypothetical population, male partners produce sperm adequate to their coital frequency and also of high motility. Now let us describe deviations from this maximum-fecundity population.

Length of the fecund period.   The average age of menopause is generally around age 50, although there is some variation depending on an individual's smoking and childbearing history (National Institute on Aging, 2013; Sievert, 2006). Humans are the only species where menopause occurs well before the end of life. Evolutionary hypotheses attribute this to the "grandmother effect," where it is more advantageous to put resources into ensuring the survival of grandchildren than to continue producing more offspring (Hawkes, 2003; Hill and Hurtado, 1991).

Fecundity peaks in a woman's twenties and declines after the age of thirty (Leridon, 2004; Menken et al., 1986). The rise of fertility medications and **assisted reproductive technologies**, such as *in vitro fertilization*, has thus far had only a minor impact on fertility. In their current state, these inputs are unable to fully compensate for age-related declines in fertility (Leridon, 2004). Nevertheless, in countries where women delay fertility for educational and career reasons, such technologies are estimated to account for about 7% of births and are likely to play an increasing role in future fertility trends (Sobotka et al., 2008).

Fertility demographers have a tendency to focus exclusively on women; however, recent findings indicate that fertility impairments may be just as prevalent among men and that their fecundity also declines with age (Macaluso et al., 2010; Maheshwari et al., 2008). Although there is no absolute cut-off for men as there is for women, men's fecundity starts declining around age thirty-five (Matorras et al., 2011; Balasch, 2010), with sperm quality playing a major role in infertility cases (Nallella et al., 2006).

Age of menarche, unlike age at menopause, varies both internationally and historically. Teenage females universally become fecund over a progression of years during which they experience decreasing adolescent sterility. Age of menarche is linked to nutrition and thus generally decreases with modernization (Heer and Grigsby, 1992; Nag, 1980). The onset of menarche decreased two to three months per decade in Europe and the United States in the 20th century (Parent et al., 2003). Poland, for example, saw steady decline from 13.1 years in 1983 to 12.7 years in 2010 (Kowal et al., 2013).

Evidence indicates that these changes are, in part, due to the obesity epidemic, with BMI (body mass index) associated with early onset of puberty (Currie et al., 2012). Some developing countries are also witnessing steady declines. The average onset of menarche in Bangladesh decreased from 15.8 years in 1976 to 12.8 years in 2005, as a case in point (Rah et al., 2009). How much of an impact age at menarche has on fertility depends, of course, on how much intercourse, contraception, and abortion also take place in the teen years.

Subfecundity due to morbidity.   Disease and malnutrition can reduce fecundity. Infectious diseases have greater impact during reproductive ages than do degenerative diseases. Both smallpox and tuberculosis, for example, produced subfecundity well into the 20th century. Any infection accompanied by high fever can threaten spermatogenesis. Malaria is a good and pertinent illustration. In addition, some diseases can interfere with the transport of sperm or ova by inflaming or scarring the epididymis or the Fallopian tubes. Probably the most important attackers of transport are STDs (sexually transmitted diseases). HIV/AIDS and many other diseases also can lower fecundity through both wasting and secondary infections (Mascarenhas et al., 2012; Magadi and Agwanda, 2010).

How much impact do infectious diseases actually have? Without the influence of these diseases, LDR fertility would tend to be higher, especially in parts of central Africa. A study showed that over 85% of infertility among women in Africa was due to infectious diseases (Ombelet et al., 2008). Disease, with its threat to conception, also undoubtedly helps to explain conception differentials between social classes within societies, including the MDRs.

Very severe stoppages of nutritional intake, such as occur in famine, may cause cessation of ovulation, as well as loss of libido and reduced sperm production (Menken et al., 1981). The effect of malnutrition is more speculative and more updated research is needed. Frisch (1975) suggests that women need to maintain a certain critical body weight in order to have the fat reserves necessary for regular ovulation. Coale (1974) notes that there is a tendency for malnourished women to have longer periods of post-partum amenorrhea. But all investigators seem to agree that the major cause of long periods of postpartum amenorrhea is not caused by poor nutrition so much as breast-feeding (Menken et al., 1981).

Breast-Feeding

Generally, menstruation begins again about six weeks after birth (Jackson and Glasier, 2011). But if a woman nurses a child after giving birth, her hormonal reaction to lactation delays considerably the return of her menstrual cycles and thus her ovulation and fecundity. This tendency varies considerably among individuals and breast-feeding methods. It does not normally work indefinitely, but on the average it can have considerable impact on birth intervals, and can lower fertility proportionately more than other noncontraceptive family-planning methods (Sipsma et al., 2013; Dewey et al., 2001; Cooney, 1992). Bongaarts and Potter (1983) estimate that, with no use of contraceptives, uninterrupted breast-feeding could add eighteen months or more to average birth intervals.

Traditionally, women in less-developed countries have breast-fed in larger proportions and for longer durations than women in more-developed countries; however, there is considerable variation, even among LDRs (Arabi et al., 2012; Sharma et al., 1991; London et al., 1985; Bongaarts and Potter, 1983). The availability of manufactured baby food, and the strong marketing presence of infant formula companies in many countries, led to a large-scale decline in breast-feeding practices (Dobbing, 1988). Another factor that affects the length of breast-feeding and the timing at which breast-milk substitute is introduced is women's labor force participation. Studies have shown that the sooner women go back to work, the sooner and more likely breast-milk substitutes are introduced (Arabi et al., 2012). Lactation is a labor intensive process, requiring feedings that last from 20 to 45 minutes each and that occur at an average of eight times a day (and often in the middle of the night!). It is no surprise then that women's entrance into the industrialized labor market, where paid parental leave policies are rare outside of the European context, has severely curtailed breast-feeding practices.

Although some researchers predicted a continuing decline in breast-feeding for these reasons, acknowledgement that breast-feeding is a key contributor to infant and maternal health has led to concerted efforts by the World Health Organization, the United Nations, and many governments to increase breast-feeding rates around the globe (United Nations, 2011a; WHO, 2007; Lewis, 2003). The U.S. Department of Health and Human Services (2013) has set very specific breast-feeding goals for American mothers by 2020, aiming for an 82% initiation rate with 62% continuing to breast-feed at six months and 34% for a year. American breast-feeding practices are beginning to increase as a result of this public health campaign, although they are still below the set goals. For babies born in 2010, 76.5% of Americans breast-fed, 49% continued to breast-feed at six months, and 27% breast-fed through the first year (CDC, 2013a).

Interestingly, immigrants to the United States tend to have among the highest breast-feeding rates, but those rates decrease with each generation (Sussner et al., 2008). Part of this may relate to cultural stigmas against public breast-feeding that continue to operate in the United States. Only 43% of Americans believe that women have the right to breast-feed in public and women often report embarrassment and fear of stigma as their reason for discontinuing (Office of the Surgeon General, 2011). Paid maternity leave offered by some private companies and the advent of the electric breast pump, which enables mothers to produce milk while at work (Rasmussen and Geraghty, 2011), help some U.S. women to continue breast-feeding. Unfortunately, most women lack private offices or spaces for breast pumping in their workplace and paid leave is available only for some professionals.

Many developing countries have adopted the use of breast-feeding, or the Lactational Amenorrhea Method (LAM), as a heavily promoted family-planning method because it is not only inexpensive but is also believed to be 98% effective when used correctly (Fabic and Choi, 2013; Shane, 1997). In a high-fertility country like Niger where LAM is widely promoted, about half of women self-reported its practice (Sipsma et al., 2013). Among the LDRs, breast-feeding is most prevalent in Asian and Latin American countries and least prevalent in Africa. Among the MDRs, countries with longer periods of maternity and parental leaves, such as Norway, Denmark, and Sweden tend to have higher proportions of children who are breast-fed. Initiation rates ranged from nearly 100% in Norway to slightly above 40% in Ireland (OECD, 2012).

Historically, in both LDRs and MDRs, urban and more educated women were less likely to nurse and/or likely to nurse for shorter periods (Hirschman and Butler, 1981; Jain and Bongaarts, 1980; Knodel and Debavalya, 1981). These educational differences, however, have reversed along with findings on the medical benefits of breast-feeding over formula feeding. According to the latest National Immunization Survey, 85% of college-educated women in the United States initiated breast-feeding compared to 66.2% of women with less than a high school diploma (CDC, 2010).

Contraception

The geographical pattern of contraceptive use among the nations of the world probably corresponds very closely to the pattern of low fertility. Effective use of contraception is the main reason for low fertility in the nations where it is found. Box 7-2 presents a list of the prevalent contraceptive methods, ordered on the basis of when in the reproductive process they work.

Box 7-2	**Prevalent Contraceptive Methods and How They Work**

Prevention of Ovulation, Spermatogenesis, or Transport

Oral Hormonal Contraceptives. The "pill" is a compound of synthetic hormones that suppress ovulation by keeping the estrogen level high. Although contraception is achieved primarily by suppressing ovulation, the pill also operates by keeping the cervical mucus in a state the sperm cannot penetrate and by making the lining of the uterus unsuitable for implantation. Actually, there are many different types of pills, using various combinations and doses of estrogen, progestin, and other agents.
Perfect use efficacy rate: 99%

Other Hormonal Contraceptives. These are similar in composition and action to oral contraceptives and are primarily distinctive in their long-term action, which does not require daily dosages. Some are wearable, such as the "patch" (Ortho Evra) or the "ring" (NuvaRing); some are implantable (Implanon or Nexplanon); while others are injectable (Depo-Provera).
Perfect use efficacy rate: 99%

Surgical Sterilization. In women, sterilization consists of cutting, tying, and removing a portion of the oviduct. In men, sterilization (called "vasectomy") consists of cutting, tying, and removing a portion of the spermatic duct, or vas deferens. Male sterilization is a much simpler (and thus safer) surgery than female sterilization, but many women opt for sterilization as part of the procedure when they have their last birth. In either case, transport to the potential place of union, and thus conception, is blocked.
Efficacy rate: 100%

Breast-feeding. Sometimes called the Lactational Amenorrhea Method (LAM), this is a natural way to prevent ovulation post-birth. Breast-feeding must be continuous to be effective and is best not relied on after six months postpartum.
Perfect use efficacy rate within first 6 months: 99%

Prevention of Contact between Sperm and Ova

Fertility Awareness Methods. Also known as *natural family planning* or *periodic abstinence,* this method capitalizes on the long-known fact that ova are available for fertilization during only a few days of the menstrual cycle. The strategy is to avoid intercourse during those few days, and the trick is to find the exact interval in which to avoid intercourse. This is attempted through estimating time of ovulation from records of past menstrual cycles, noting minor changes in the woman's temperature that signal hormonal changes following ovulation, and noting mucosal changes in the vagina throughout the entire cycle.
Efficacy rate with error: 76% (perfect use is, in theory, 100%)

Withdrawal. Known more demurely as *coitus interruptus,* the method consists simply of removing the penis from the vagina before ejaculation.
Perfect use efficacy rate: 96%

(continued)

Vaginal Contraceptives. Spermicides that are placed in the vagina, creating a barrier to sperm and killing or immobilizing them. The chemicals are contained in suppositories, gels, and creams.

Perfect use efficacy rate: 85%

The Diaphragm, Cervical Cap and Sponge. These operate by covering the cervix tightly, preventing the sperm from entering the uterus. The diaphragm is a shallow silicone cup with a spring reinforcing the rim. The cervical cap (FemCap) is a small, thimble-shaped cup made of silicone that blocks the cervix. The Sponge (Today Sponge) is a sponge made of plastic foam that blocks the cervix. All of these barrier methods are used with spermicide.

Perfect use efficacy rate: 91–96%

Condoms. The male condom is a latex barrier that fits snugly over the penis and prevents the ejaculated sperm from entering the vagina. Such condoms made from the intestines of sheep and other animals first appeared in the 18th century, but it was not until the vulcanization of rubber in the 19th century that use of condoms on a large scale became possible. Hence the popular name, the "rubber." There is also a female condom. It is a pouch that is inserted into the vagina prior to intercourse.

Perfect use efficacy rate: 95–98%

Prevention of Implantation of the Ovum in the Uterus

Intrauterine Devices (IUDs). The idea of placing objects in the uterus to avoid pregnancy is fairly old. IUDs are T-shaped devices (Paragard and Mirena) that must be inserted by a medical professional. They interfere with sperm mobility, making them unable to reach the egg.

Efficacy rate: 99%

Morning-after Pill. This pill, made of synthetic estrogen, can be taken up to five days after coitus. Properly administered doses of oral contraceptives can provide a similar effect to morning-after pills. These medications to avert implantation (Plan B and Next Choice) are distinguished from Mifepristone (formerly RU-486), which aborts an already implanted fetus.

Efficacy rate: 86%

How widespread is contraception? A majority of couples use it: at 72% in MDRs and 61% in LDRs, a dramatic increase in LDR usage over just the last few decades (United Nations, 2011b). The most commonly used forms of contraception used worldwide are (1) sterilization, (2) intrauterine devices (IUDs), (3) oral contraceptives, and (4) male condoms (United Nations, 2011b). These trends are shown in Figure 7-8.

As this figure shows, there is considerable variation in the practice of modern forms of contraception despite the spread of such methods to less-developed countries. Figure 7-8 shows levels of contraception divided into modern forms and traditional forms, the most common of the latter being withdrawal and fertility awareness methods. While modern contraceptive usage is a little bit higher for MDRs than LDRs, it may be surprising that traditional methods are also quite high for some European MDRs. This may be a legacy of Catholicism and Communism. In Southern Europe, the role of the Catholic Church is more prominent than in the rest of Europe. And under Communist rule, Eastern European countries had little contraceptive access (Alan Guttmacher

Figure 7-8

Percentage of Married Women Aged 15 to 49 Currently Using Contraception, 2012

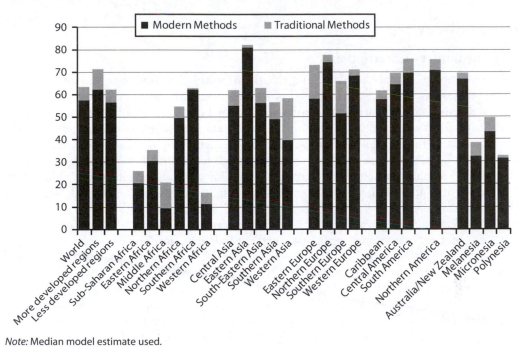

Note: Median model estimate used.

Source: Data from United Nations, 2012. *World Contraceptive Use 2012.* Graph created by Eiko Strader.

Institute, 1999). Albania and Bosnia Herzegovina, for example, have considerably lower modern contraceptive usage than the rest of the more-developed regions.

Difference in modern contraceptive usage among LDRs is extreme. The percentages of married, reproductive-age women using contraception in some regions of Africa as well as Oceania remain the lowest in the world. Yet eastern Asia, which is dominated by China, has the highest modern contraception usage rates in the world. This is in part due to the one-child population control policy begun by the Chinese government in 1979.

Variation in modern contraceptive use among individual countries within the same region is even more dramatic. The prevalence of modern methods in Iran, for example, is three times higher than in neighboring Afghanistan (United Nations, 2011b). Relatedly, Afghanistan has a total fertility rate of 5.1 children per woman compared to Iran's underreplacement rate of 1.8 (PRB, 2014). According to the most recent fertility surveys, only a small percentage of women use any contraceptive methods at all in the world's most populous countries, such as Pakistan (25% modern and 10% traditional) and Nigeria (9% modern and 6% traditional).

Contraception will continue to be one of the most important proximate determinants of fertility throughout the 21st century. In determining future fertility trends, the efficacy with which families can achieve lower desired family sizes is second only to having those desires in the first place. We will discuss unmet contraceptive needs and family-planning programs as a fertility "problem" later in this chapter.

Gestation Variables

Involuntary Interruption

Demographers have come to divide the nine-month gestation period into two segments, drawing the line at the end of the twenty-eighth week. Pregnancy loss before that time is called **early fetal death** and corresponds to the popular notion of miscarriage. Loss after the twenty-eighth week of gestation, called **late fetal death**, corresponds to the popular notion of stillbirth. The demographic reason for dividing the gestation period for separate study of subperiods is that the dominant causes of death shift. The causes of late fetal death are so similar to those for a newborn child's first week that late fetal mortality and neonatal mortality are sometimes studied together as *perinatal mortality.*

Fetal mortality is a potent force in limiting fertility. As much as 40% of conceptions may not survive through birth, even without induced abortion. Yet, since fetal deaths are relatively evenhanded across countries and are resistant to external interference, they are not a major explanation of differences in national fertility levels.

A variety of factors influence fetal mortality. One clearly is the age of the mother (Tafari and Zerihun, 1993); the risk curve is generally J-shaped. In the case of the United States, fetal mortality rate for mothers under fifteen is twice the rate of those aged twenty-five to twenty-nine (5.47 per 1,000). After that, the rate continues to rise and reaches about 15.5 per 1,000 live births for mothers aged forty-five and over (Mac-Dorman and Kirmeyer, 2009). A recent study finds that while fetal mortality increases as the maternal age increases, the rate greatly varies cross-nationally. Experts suggest that societal level demographic composition, such as the prevalence of conception at old ages in a given society, also influences fetal mortality rates at older maternal ages (Anthony et al., 2009).

Another fetal mortality factor is gender; male fetuses seem to be more vulnerable than female fetuses. Women carrying male fetuses face higher probabilities of gestational diabetes, fetal macrosomia, cord prolapse, and so on (Di Renzo et al., 2007). Mental and emotional stress can have physiological consequences that affect fetal health. A variety of stressful life circumstances are more prevalent in developing countries and increase fetal mortality there, including infectious diseases, wars, short birth intervals, malnutrition, and limited access to health care (Schwartz, 2013; Tafari and Zerihun, 1993).

In all regions, smoking increases fetal mortality (Hoyert, 1996). A recent study from the United States estimates that cigarette smoking may increase the incidence of low birth weight by up to 25% due to fetal growth restriction and preterm birth, increasing infant mortality rates (Brown and Graves, 2013).

Voluntary Interruption

Definitions are important here. As used by the medical profession, the term **abortion** denotes the termination of a pregnancy after the implantation of the blastocyst (fertilized egg) in the endometrium (uterine wall) but before the fetus has gained viability. This definition distinguishes abortion from the last category of contraception described in Box 7-2: those methods that operate by preventing implantation of the ovum in the uterus, such as the IUD or the morning-after pill. Traditionally, a fetus has been considered "viable" (able to survive outside the mother) after twenty-eight weeks, although intensive care technology has moved the viability period increasingly earlier (Vavasseur et al., 2007). An abortion is either induced or spontaneous (as in a miscarriage), depending on whether anything was done with the *intention* of ending the pregnancy. When proper medical facilities are used or an abortion pill (Mifepristone) is consumed for earlier gestation pregnancies, intention is unambiguous. On the other hand, there is a category of things that women can do that might result in abortions and where their intentions are not self-evident.

Induced abortions can be either legal or illegal. Most countries—97%—allow for abortion in cases where the mother's life is endangered. However, only 30% allow abortion on request (United Nations, 2013a). The grounds on which abortion is permitted vary widely from country to country. Less-developed countries generally have more restrictive policies than do more-developed countries. Over 70% of MDR countries, for example, permit abortion for any reason while only 16% of those in LDRs permit abortion under similar circumstances (United Nations, 2013a). The incidence of abortion has been decreasing globally primarily due to simultaneous increase in contraception (Sedgh et al., 2012).

The incidence of abortion can be measured by **abortion rates** very similar to those we use for fertility. That is, we can construct crude abortion rates, general abortion rates, age-specific abortion rates, and even total abortion rates. The United States had an abortion rate of 19.6 abortions per 1,000 women of reproductive age in 2000 (Sedgh et al., 2012).

Abortion rates vary widely. European abortion rates range from a low of 1.4 in Austria to a high of 37.4 in Russia. Most high-fertility countries have low reported abortion rates. For example, India has an abortion rate of only 2.2. Abortion is legal in many Asian countries but illegal in most Latin American and African countries. Accordingly, the prevalence of unsafe, high-risk abortions is highest there. Each year 47,000 women die from unsafe abortion, almost all in Latin America and Africa (United Nations, 2013a).

Reported abortion data, however, should be interpreted cautiously. It is estimated that between 40% and 50% of abortions performed worldwide are illegal, indicating that the prevalence of abortion is much higher than reported in countries with restrictive abortion policies (Sedgh et al., 2012). And because abortion is stigmatized, the completeness of reporting even legal abortions is also questionable. Therefore, in countries where abortion is legal it is likely that most abortion statistics are underreported and almost certain in countries where abortion is illegal (Sedgh et al., 2012).

Abortion data for the MDRs are more reliable than those for most developing countries. Although American and European teens have similar ages at sexual initiation, American teens are less likely to use contraception and have almost twice the abortion prevalence (Sedgh et al., 2012). Even so, most abortions take place among adult women, not among adolescents.

The majority (92%) of abortions in the United States take place in the first trimester, most (64%) within the first eight weeks of gestation (CDC, 2012a). Looking at trends over time, the abortion rate in the United States went from about 13 in 1972 up to 25 in 1980 and has since declined slowly to just under 20 abortions per 1,000 women at the time of this publication. There is great regional variation in U.S. reported abortion rates. The declining availability of abortion services along with restrictive policies appears to be a major influence on the variability of abortion rates from one area of the country to the next (Alan Guttmacher Institute, 2009; Wetstein, 1996).

Another way of measuring abortion prevalence is by means of the **abortion ratio**. The numerator of the ratio is the number of abortions. The denominator is the number of births and abortions, rather than reproductive-aged women. Thus, abortion ratios refer to the relative probability that any given pregnancy will end in an induced abortion. Since we might expect abortion to vary in response to the rate of pregnancies, the abortion ratio is often preferred to the abortion rate. The abortion ratio in the United States was around 180 abortions per 1,000 live births in 1972, rose to 359 in 1984, then fell slowly to 227 by 2009 (CDC, 1998, 2002, 2013b).

Even with adequate data, is difficult to know the exact effects of abortion on overall fertility in the United States. First, efficacious contraceptive options are widely available. Second, not all abortions are of viable fetuses; 17% of abortions are for medical reasons (CDC, 2013b).

Finally, the dividing line between abortion and contraception is becoming increasingly blurred by a range of orally administered contraceptives and abortifacients. For example, Mifepristone (formerly known as RU-486) is an abortion pill that can be used outside of medical facilities to terminate pregnancies early in their gestation period. Despite the emotion and political rancor surrounding induced abortion, it is only one of a range of fertility options exercised by women in the United States and certainly not the most important determinant of fertility.

Fertility "Problems"

Fertility, Age Structure, and Population Growth: A Review

As we discussed in chapters 3 and 4, youth dependency is caused by sustained high birth rates in many less-developed countries. In the more-developed countries, the problems of an aging population are due primarily to decreases in birth rates. The imbalance between the sizes of succeeding cohorts in MDR countries is due to modern short-term cycles in fertility.

It is common to point a finger at fertility for problems of population growth, discussed in chapter 3, but with only partial justification. Modern population explosions have been caused by changes in mortality, not in fertility, yet we tend to blame sustained high fertility for the problem. Of course, it is more palatable to advocate a solution that decreases childbearing rather than one that shortens human lives.

Population growth and population structure are the major purely demographic impacts of fertility trends, but there are other outcomes of a more personal nature.

Maternal and Child Mortality and Morbidity

Sustained, rapid childbearing can threaten the health of mothers and babies alike. The chances of the mother and the infant surviving improve significantly if the woman does not marry as a teenager and is not giving birth continuously throughout her life into older ages. Longer intervals between births (at least two years) improve mothers' and babies' chances of surviving as does being in good maternal health.

Access to contraceptives can prevent more than a fourth of all maternal deaths by allowing women to space children, to avoid unwanted pregnancies and unsafe abortions, to protect themselves from sexually transmitted diseases and HIV/AIDS, and to stop childbearing once a desired family size has been reached (UNFPA, 2012; Shane 1997). Ensuring universal access to family-planning resources in LDRs would save an estimated $11.3 billion annually in maternal and newborn healthcare (UNFPA, 2012). Moreover, family planning is linked to basic women's rights and their access to education and employment. In countries where teen marriage is common and fertility rates are well above replacement, women tend to have lower social status, poorer health, and worse socioeconomic status (United Nations, 2010).

This is a case where humanitarian concern for human rights and health runs parallel with collective concern over population growth and youth dependency. If women married later and had fewer children, they would not only be reducing overall fertility rates, but also protecting mother and infant health and well-being. Policy makers, thus, frequently use health and human rights considerations as a politically acceptable justification for fertility reduction aims in the less-developed countries (Kristof and WuDunn, 2010; Sadik, 1991). For example, the USAID website, the American government's foreign aid office, mentions population growth last (and only then obliquely) in its family planning aid goals. Highlighted first are: (1) protecting the health of women by reducing high-risk pregnancies; (2) protecting the health of children by allowing sufficient time between pregnancies; (3) fighting HIV/AIDS through providing information, counseling, and access to male and female condoms; (4) reducing abortion; (5) supporting women's rights and opportunities for education, employment, and full participation in society; and lastly, (6) mitigating the impact of population dynamics on economic growth, natural resources, and state stability (USAID, 2013).

Unmet Contraceptive Needs and Unwanted Pregnancies

If women continue to have children after they have achieved their desired family size, it can place a strain on both the parents and offspring. It is this discrepancy between wish and reality that formed the ideology of the Planned Parenthood movement. At least originally, the movement goals were not necessarily to decrease aggregate fertility levels, but rather to minimize discrepancies between desired and actual family sizes and timings of births. That is why the movement was careful to include among its goals helping women who had *fewer* children than they wanted as well as those who were at risk of having *more* than they wanted.

Again, those in favor of fertility-reduction programs for the LDRs have been able to appeal to this concern about couples' unmet contraceptive needs and unwanted pregnancies as a justification for reducing aggregate fertility. It is a lot easier to argue for helping couples implement their own family-size goals than it is to argue for imposing a collective low-fertility goal on them.

A woman is considered to have unmet contraceptive needs if she is fecund and sexually active but would prefer to control fertility, either by spacing or limiting births, and is not currently using contraception (United Nations, 2011c). Unwanted pregnancies may occur to a woman with unmet contraceptive needs or through contraceptive failure. Although surveys can obtain information on unmet contraceptive needs, it is difficult to measure the extent of unwanted pregnancies. Not all pregnancies to women with unmet contraceptive needs are unwanted. And, many women may change their preferences depending on when they are asked. A previously unwanted pregnancy often becomes a wanted one once it has occurred.

Nevertheless, the estimated unmet contraceptive needs of women in less-developed regions are shown in Figure 7-9. The bars show the proportion of sexually active women aged fifteen to forty-nine who report that they do not currently desire a pregnancy but who are not using any form of contraception. The percentage of women whose contraceptive needs are presently unmet range from 4.3% in East Asia to 41.5% in Polynesia. Given high failure rates associated with traditional forms of contraception, it is arguable that women using these methods seeking to avoid pregnancy should also be included in estimates of unmet need (United Nations, 2011b; Singh et al., 2003). If that were the case, unmet needs for African women (in middle Africa especially) and Middle Eastern women would be much higher.

Figure 7-9

Unmet Need: Percent of Women Aged 15 to 49 at Risk of Unintended Pregnancy Using No Contraceptive Methods, 2012

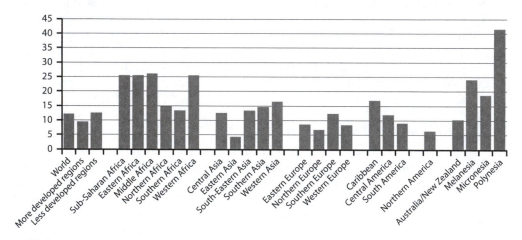

Note: Median model estimate used.

Source: Data from United Nations, 2012. *World Contraceptive Use 2012.* Graph created by Eiko Strader.

Adolescent Fertility

The extent to which adolescent fertility is considered to be a problem varies from country to country. In some countries early marriage and early childbearing are culturally desirable. Early marriage norms are the greatest cultural cause of adolescent fertility. Yet, regardless of cultural support for early marriage and adolescent fertility, there are significant health threats associated with these births, which are high-risk for both mother and child.

In the United States, which has always had the highest adolescent pregnancy and STD rates in the developed world, teen births have recently reached historic lows (CDC, 2012b; PRB, 2012; NCHS, 2003). Most adolescent childbearing occurs in the developing countries of South Asia, sub-Saharan Africa, and Latin America although this, too, is beginning to decline (Haub, 2013). The adolescent fertility decline in less-developed regions has been even more rapid than declines there in the fertility of older women.

Despite these recent declines, some groups of young women continue to experience higher fertility rates, unwanted pregnancies, and resulting health problems. Prominent among these are women in the highest fertility countries and in rural areas of developing countries. With less access to family planning, these women typically have higher adolescent fertility rates. Young women who give birth before their twenties are at twice the risk of maternal mortality (Haub, 2013). Becoming a parent as a teen also greatly reduces the likelihood that she will complete her education (UNFPA, 2012). Because of the negative consequences for the health and well-being of mothers and children, and the especially heavy burden of adolescent fertility on disadvantaged social groups, it remains a major concern.

In sum, when we go beyond blaming sustained high fertility for its contribution to age structure and population growth problems, we tend to focus on its negative consequences for women and maternal and child health. It is not surprising that the constituencies most concerned with this category of problems would be the health and medical professions and women's rights advocates. Indeed, within the history of the postwar family-planning movement we see a shift in emphasis from population explosion concerns to what we might call "the health and reproductive rights agenda." This shift is traced in the following section.

Family-Planning Programs in the Less-Developed Regions

Historically, nations have tried to raise as well as lower their fertility. During the 1930s, for instance, European policies were likely to be pronatalist, however ineffective. National policies in the post–World War II decades, however, have been largely confined to the less-developed regions, and they universally have aimed at enhancing women's reproductive control for the purposes of limiting fertility and improving maternal and child health and well-being (Haub and Gribble, 2011).

Such family-planning programs have proven very successful over the past several decades. In retrospect, seldom has a social invention swept through so much of the world in such a short period with such a significant impact as has family planning. For a time, it had a high degree of political acceptability, congruence with widespread social values, and technical appeal. Still, family planning has had its critics, and the politics of family planning have changed significantly over recent years.

Careers in Demography

Mohammad Jalal Abbasi-Shavazi

Professor of Demography, University of Tehran, Iran
Director, National Institute of Population Research
Founder and Past President of the Asian Population Association
Laureate of the United Nations Population Award

How did you decide that being a demographer was the career path for you?

"Introduction to Demography" was one of the first courses I took as an undergraduate at the University of Isfahan. My interest was further fueled by the debate on the population explosion going on at that time in post-revolutionary Iran. I then entered the demography program at the University of Tehran (UT), becoming the program's first MA student in demography where I defended my thesis under the supervision of Mohammad Mirzaie, who was a graduate of the University of Pennsylvania. That was the beginning of my career in demography.

What kind of education and training did you pursue to get to where you are in your career?

I have had a long journey to get to where I am now! In 1970, I started my primary education in Shavaz, a small village with around 150 households but with more than 1,000 years of history. There was no secondary or high-school there, and after finishing primary school I moved to Yazd city as an 11-year-old student to continue my education. I had to work and manage my own life during my secondary and high school education. After completing my undergraduate study, I got a job as a high school teacher in the Hormozgan province. When I was admitted to my demography MA program, I continued to teach high school two days a week and traveled 800 miles by bus to Tehran to take my classes (the equivalent of travelling between Rochester, New York, and Iowa City, Iowa!).

In 1994 I received a scholarship to the demography PhD program of the Australian National University. I was fortunate to meet Peter McDonald, the past President of the IUSSP, who advised me to study the fertility patterns of Australian immigrant groups for my dissertation thesis. This marked a milestone in my academic life as I continued working with Peter in a very productive and fruitful collaboration for the next two decades.

Describe your work/research as a demographer. What do you consider your most important accomplishments?

My early research on immigrant fertility in Australia showed that second-generation Lebanese and Turkish women adopted Australian patterns of lower childbearing. This work is often cited as an example of demographic adaptation even in societies where multiculturalism is the official policy, as in Australia.

During my studies, I noticed the dearth of knowledge on the demography of the Middle East, and of Iran in particular. As a result, my colleagues and I were among the first scholars to examine available demographic evidence in-depth, revealing that Iran's fertility had dropped by 70% between 1980 and 2000, the fastest fertility decline ever recorded in the Muslim world. With Djavad Salehi-Isfahani and Meimanat Hosseini, I found that Iran's proactive strategy of seeking out women in rural areas to provide them with maternal and child health care reduced mortality and supported the expansion of family planning.

Aware of the importance of considering cultural aspects in developing effective programs, we documented how a pragmatic religious approach to population policy was compatible and supported the expansion of family planning in Iran. Our decade-long research resulted in the 2009 book, *The Fertility Transition in Iran: Revolution and Reproduction*, among the few case studies of contemporary fertility decline outside the West.

My ongoing collaborative research on Muslim demography has shown that the social, economic, and cultural differences among Middle Eastern countries are more important than religion as determinants of differences in population dynamics. My research in this area has demonstrated the fallacy of assuming that Islamic teaching is incompatible with low fertility and also pointed out that higher educational attainment for women in Iran is associated with democratization.

I am a member of the Developmental Idealism Study Group based at the University of Michigan led by Arland Thornton, which explores the ideas of social and economic development held by people in everyday life. I have been involved in the design and implementation of this data collection in Iran. We are investigating how developmental values influence marriage, childbearing, divorce, health behaviors, and health outcomes.

I have become increasingly concerned with increasing refugee and forced migration movements. With a team of demographers, sociologists, and anthropologists, I conducted four major surveys on the 2.5 million Afghan refugees living in Iran since 2004. Our published research has become the primary reference point on the status of Afghan refugees in Iran. I am chairing an IUSSP Scientific Panel on Demography of Refugees, and with Graeme Hugo, I am editing a volume on the *Demography of Refugee and Forced Migration*.

I believe that research should result in policy. This can be done through advocacy, resource mobilization, and institution building. Despite the importance of Asia in global population issues and policy, there was no regional population association to mobilize demographers in the region. I played a major role in the establishment of the Asian Population Association. I also have been involved in population policy design and advocacy in Iran, and have collaborated with national and international organizations toward this end. I was honored to recently receive the United Nations Population Award in recognition of my contribution to Iranian and Asian demography.

What do you see as the field's most important contribution as well as its greatest challenge?

Demographers can greatly influence the development of societies and improve the lives of current and future generations. Their research can lead to better policies and are able to evaluate the success and failures of development plans. As countries enter new eras of social change, expanded theories explaining demographic behaviors are needed. For example, currently some Asian and Muslim countries are experiencing low or ultra-low fertility, the level that demographers could not anticipate four decades ago. The fall of fertility in these settings cannot be fully explained by the conventional demographic transition theory, and thus, it is a theoretical challenge for the discipline.

Also, my research shows that refugee and involuntary migrations have increased substantially in scale, complexity, and diversity in recent years. While other disciplines have made major contributions to refugee and forced migration studies, a demographic approach is sorely missing. Demographers are needed to develop innovative methods of data collection and data analysis during war, conflict, and disasters. Understanding how such refugees adapt to new societies is another unresolved matter that should be the focus of demographers and policy makers.

The Goals of Family Planning

The rationale for the existence of family planning has gone through several distinctive stages. In the 1960s through the mid-1970s these policies were dominated by concern over the need to limit population growth in developing countries.

The **family-planning** agenda rested on an elegantly simple rationale: The desired number of children per couple is generally less than the actual number of children per couple. Thus, implementing individuals' and couples' wishes should simultaneously eliminate couples' future unwanted pregnancies and also reduce high growth burdens in developing countries.

Emphasizing knowledge and practices of contraception, family-planning programs were "designed to provide the information, supplies, and services of (modern) means of fertility control to those interested" (Watson, 1982, p. 205). A key feature was voluntariness, relying on the individual's (or couple's) motivation for limiting fertility. This could be aided by non-coercive persuasion; programs included varying degrees of propaganda for small families, but they ideally only educated individuals to their own self-interest. Another feature was the advent of modern contraceptive methods as a means of achieving the desired family size. A key aspect of these programs was government sponsorship, either directly or in combination with voluntary agencies.

Critics and Compromises

Even as family-planning programs were spreading through the LDRs, demographic critics were questioning their adequacy. One attack was directed at the underlying assumption that the collective demographic good would be served by simply implementing existing individual desires (e.g., Blake, 1969; Davis, 1967; Demerath, 1976; Hauser, 1967). Critics argued that the cultures of LDRs had evolved in the context of high mortality and high fertility norms; without higher fertility, the societies would not have survived. There is, therefore, no escape from the necessity for basic cultural change as a prerequisite for durable and substantial fertility reduction. To these critics, the supply of contraception was not the issue. Instead, what was important was to change the social conditions generating high fertility demand (Simmons, 1986). Critics were not even necessarily convinced by the decline of fertility in many LDR countries that did have family-planning programs; they suspected that much of this decline would have occurred without the programs, due to other more fundamental cultural changes.

Another source of suspicion involved doubts about the motives of program advocates. Let us call this the "genocide threat" (Darity et al., 1971; Hartmann, 1995). To understand this perspective, it helps to recall the intellectual history of American demography during the first half of the 20th century. Much of what were seen as population "problems" in the MDRs late in their demographic transitions were based on the belief that the "higher quality" people were having fewer children than the "lower quality" people, a *eugenics* concern. Now the critics once again saw demographers advocating smaller families—but for whom? For the citizens of the less-developed countries, who also happened to be predominantly nonwhite. Moreover, within any country, the programs were aimed mainly at those below the local (Westernized) middle class. It did not help, of course, that the programs were being advocated by former colonial or imperialist powers.

The Health and Reproductive Rights Agenda

Partly in response to criticisms, but also due to rising knowledge of the negative health impacts of high fertility for women, in the mid-1970s attention shifted to the maternal and child health aspects of family planning (Sadik, 1991; Shane, 1997). Since the mid-1980s, a series of international population and development conferences has moved the family-planning agenda to a focus on human rights, predominantly centering on women's reproductive rights, autonomy, status, education, and reproductive health (Center for Reproductive Rights, 2012; Murthy and Smith, 2010; Harcourt, 1999; Hardee et al., 1999). This culminated in 1994 when 179 governments adopted the Program of Action, which officially endorsed the new rights-based orientation of family planning. The United Nation Population Fund's most recent *State of the World Population* publication, for example, is subtitled *By Choice, Not By Chance: Family Planning, Human Rights and Development* and describes the connection between women's reproductive rights and other women's rights:

> When a woman is able to exercise her reproductive rights, she is more able to benefit from her other rights, such as the right to education. The results are higher incomes, better health for her and her children and greater decision-making power for her, both in the household and the community. When women and men together plan their childbearing, children benefit immediately and in their long-term prospect. (UNFPA, 2012)

Despite this dramatic change in emphasis, echoes of the earlier family-planning criticisms remain. Some critics maintain that current programs still have the goal of imposing Western perspectives of human rights and reproduction on other cultures. Others argue that our primary concern in less-developed countries should be with developmental, rather than reproductive health and contraceptive, agendas.

Although the newer emphasis on human rights and reproductive health is laudable in its own right, it is not without controversy among the advocates of family-planning programs and more traditional agendas. Caldwell (1997), for example, warns that these goals may be obstacles to the completion of the demographic transition and that developed country governments may "never again emphasize the need for family-planning programs in developing countries."

The rhetoric of these debates has often been heated. Those advocating an emphasis on women's rights and autonomy sometimes decry the provision of contraception as an attempted cultural intrusion or genocide, while those advocating family planning often argue that the new agenda is an attempt to hijack successful programs and their support by those with a different political agenda.

This controversy, however, may be overstated in the long run. Efforts to improve reproductive health, reproductive rights, and the overall status of women will most likely find few programs as helpful as family-planning programs in achieving those objectives. And, as we have seen (see Figure 7-9), there is already considerable demand for family planning in most regions of the world. Based on past history, this demand and the diffusion of contraceptive technology are likely to increase rather than retreat over the 21st century.

Support for Family-Planning Programs

A key element of family-planning programs is government sponsorship. In Table 7-4 government perspectives on current birth rates (column 3) and support for family planning (column 5) are given for regions of the world alongside indicators of fertility, contraception, and maternal mortality.

The less-developed regions, primarily African countries, have the highest fertility and highest maternal mortality. Correspondingly, they are those with the highest proportion of governments that consider the birth rate to be high and that support family planning programs.

Though the relationship between high fertility and governmental family planning policies may seem logical, this was not always the case. Until the 1960s, Latin American governments were generally unsupportive of contraception. Many African countries until very recently considered their fertility to be low and a number had laws prohibiting contraceptive usage. Even the few LDR governments that classified fertility levels as too high often lacked sufficient resources and commitment to family-planning programs. Historically, support for family planning was greater in Asia than in other LDRs.

Today, most LDR countries have come to see contraception and family planning as an important policy input for economic development and sustainable population growth. And indeed, Table 7-4 shows that modern contraceptive use has bypassed that of Europe in Asia and Latin America. Africa still has the lowest modern contraceptive use among all the regions, despite having the highest levels of governmental acknowledgement of and second highest support for family planning. While this might indicate that high birth rates in Africa remain a strong cultural norm and are thus unresponsive to government attempts at fertility reduction, measurements of unmet needs show that many women in Africa simply still do not have access to modern forms of contracep-

Table 7-4   Government Support for Family Planning, and Related Demographic Measures, by World Region

Region	Total Fertility Rate (1)	Maternal Deaths per 100,000 Live Births (2)	Percent of Governments that Consider Birth Rate High (3)	Percent of Married Women Using Modern Methods of Contraception (4)	Percent of Governments that Directly Support Family Planning (5)
Africa	4.88	460	75.5	26.8	88.7
Asia	2.25	150	31.9	61.4	83.0
Europe	1.54	15	0.0	60.6	38.6
Latin America	2.30	80	30.3	67.1	90.9
North America	2.02	20	0.0	70.8	50.0
Oceania	2.47	93	50.0	55.1	75.0
Data Years	**2005–10**	**2010**	**2009**	**2012**	**2009**

Sources: United Nations, 2011c. *World Fertility Policies 2011*; 2012, *World Contraceptive Use 2012*; 2013b, *World Population Prospects: The 2012 Revision*; WHO, 2012. *Trends in Maternal Mortality.*

tion. Recall from Figure 7-9 that unmet needs are most pervasive in Africa. It is estimated that 222 million women worldwide lack access to modern methods of contraception (Singh and Darroch, 2012). Clearly, even when governments commit themselves to family-planning policies, the efficacy of such commitments varies by country and requires substantial time to come to fruition.

Family planning has been one of the most successful social inventions of the past century. Although the self-defined unmet needs in the LDRs remain evident, U.S. international support for family-planning programs remains a politicized issue. Under the 1984 "Mexico City Policy," the United States retracted all funding for international family-planning programs that offered abortions or provided related counseling or referrals, even if this was done with non-U.S. funds (USAID, 2009). This global gag rule policy has waxed and waned along with domestic politics, rescinded in 1993, reinstated in 2001, and rescinded again in 2009.

Turning to the more-developed world, Table 7-4 shows that in contrast to LDRs, MDR governments do not consider fertility levels to be high. (In fact, most European governments consider their national birth rates to be too low.) As a result, Europe has the least direct governmental support for family-planning policies. While in some cases this might reflect pronatalist policies of reduced government funding for contraception, it largely indicates that private providers of family-planning services have arisen to meet the demand.

SUMMARY

Part of the demographic transitions that accompany modernization are fertility transitions from high to low levels. These transitions theoretically start with gradual declines, followed by steeper drops, then level off around replacement levels. For European nations, initiation of the steep fertility declines bracketed the turn of the 20th century. The transitions involved a Malthusian component, which started operating centuries ago, caused by a shift to the "European marriage pattern" of late average age at marriage and widespread nonmarriage. European fertility transitions also involved a neo-Malthusian component, the largely voluntary curtailing of marital childbearing through birth control. The social and cultural changes theorized to support the shift to family limitation are complex, including improved infant survivorship, decreasing economic valuation of children, increasing nonmaternal role options for women, the spread of contraceptive technology, and so forth.

The first step in explaining differences in period fertility is to specify the demographic causes. In explaining crude birth rates, one such demographic factor is the proportion of the total population consisting of women in the childbearing ages. The other demographic factors are two distinct aspects of cohort fertility performance: the average number of children born to women in the birth cohort and the timing of their childbearing.

The next step in explaining these differences lies in cohort fertility patterns. A satisfactory explanation means specifying the actions that result in different cohort fertility. The proximate determinants of cohort fertility can be classified, following Davis and Blake, into intercourse variables, conception variables, and gestation variables. In each category, some are voluntary and some involuntary from the perspective of the couple. The importance of the fertility variables varies widely across different settings and historical periods. Some such variables, but not all of them, are changing in such a way as to continue the worldwide fertility transition and reduce birth rates in less-developed countries.

In many less-developed countries fertility declines are well underway. An increasing number of these countries have reached replacement fertility levels and some have even fallen below replacement levels. Family-planning programs have been a major part of demographic policies during this fertility decline in less-developed countries. They have spread quickly and now involve much of the LDR population. Exactly how much of the current LDR fertility transition can be credited directly to family planning is debatable, but family planning appears to have been an effective component of the current worldwide fertility decline.

Fertility transitions underway in less-developed countries have benefited from the availability of modern, more effective contraceptive methods. Much of this demand is for the spacing or timing of births, which can also lower overall fertility and improve maternal and child health. Increasingly, fertility reduction policies are advocated not only on the basis of too-rapid growth rates and youth dependency but also on the basis of concerns for maternal and child health, avoidance of unwanted pregnancies, and the promotion of women's reproductive and human rights. There remains considerable need for family-planning assistance in countries with limited resources and competing demographic priorities.

EXERCISES

1. Table E7-1 presents all of the information necessary for computing a general fertility rate (GFR) and a total fertility rate (TFR) for Brazil for 2015. (The table is similar in structure to Table 7-1.)

   a. There are two missing entries each in columns 3 and 4. Fill them in, following the directions at the head of each column.

   b. Compute the *general fertility rate* (GFR) by using the formula

   $$\text{GFR} = \frac{B}{P_{15-49}} \times 1,000$$

   where B is the total births in the year and P_{15-49} is the total number of women aged fifteen through forty-nine in the year. Be sure to use the total of column 2 for the annual births and round to one decimal place.

   GFR = _____

   c. Compute the *total fertility rate* (TFR) by totaling column 4 and dividing by 1,000. Or you can add column 3, then multiply the total by 5 and divide by 1,000. Round to one decimal place.

   TFR = _____

   d. Compute the *gross reproduction rate* (GRR) by assuming that the proportion of total births that are female is .48. That is, multiply the (unrounded) TFR by that proportion. Round to two decimal places.

   GRR = _____

Table E7-1   Age-Specific Fertility Rates, Brazil, 2015

Age	Midyear Female Population (1)	Births (2)	Births per 1,000 Women (col. 2 ÷ col. 1 × 1000) (3)	Projected Resulting Births during Age Interval (5 × col. 3) (4)
15–19	8,479,000	562,800	66.4	331.9
20–24	8,084,000	844,800	104.5	522.5
25–29	8,441,000	727,200		
30–34	8,741,000	462,400	52.9	264.5
35–39	8,034,000	232,200		
40–44	7,138,000	69,600	9.8	48.8
45–49	6,629,000	12,000	1.8	9.1
Total	55,546,000	2,911,000		

Source: United Nations, 2013b. *World Population Prospects: The 2012 Revision.*

2. Table E7-2 presents the data necessary for computing legal abortion rates and ratios for 2009. Compute the missing rates and ratios for the "Non-Hispanic Black," "Non-Hispanic Other," and "Hispanic" categories. Follow the computations provided for whites. Enter your answers in the blank spaces in the table.

Table E7-2   Estimated Abortion Rates and Ratios by Ethnic Category, U.S. 2009

Race/Ethnic Category	Number of Abortions (in 1,000s) (1)	Women Aged 15–44 (in 1,000s) (2)	Rate (per 1,000) (3)	Live Births (in 1,000s) (4)	Ratio (per 1,000 Live Births) (5)
Non-Hispanic White	164	19,291	9	1,171	140
Non-Hispanic Black	154	4,747		323	
Non-Hispanic Other	27	1,548		113	
Hispanic	90	4,655		461	

Note: California, Connecticut, Delaware, Florida, Hawaii, Illinois, Iowa, Louisiana, Maryland, Massachusetts, Michigan, Nebraska, Nevada, New Hampshire, New Mexico, North Carolina, Oklahoma, Pennsylvania, Rhode Island, Vermont, Washington, Wisconsin, and Wyoming were not included in this CDC data due to some data quality issues, thus the figures are based on 27 reporting states. For each state, abortions for women of unknown race/ethnicity were distributed according to the distribution of abortions among women of known race/ethnicity for that state.

Source: Centers for Disease Control, 2012a. "Abortion Surveillance–United States, 2009."

PROPOSITIONS FOR DEBATE

1. With modernization, most of the changes in the involuntary proximate determinants of fertility are in the direction of increasing rather than decreasing fertility.

2. Malthusian transitions do not necessarily have to decrease fertility levels.

3. The more liberated women are, the fewer children couples will have.

4. LDR fertility cannot approach MDR fertility unless and until LDR societies modernize.

5. Family-planning programs are a vestige of racism and privilege on the part of the former powers of imperialism.

6. LDR fertility control policies should aim to help couples to have their desired number of offspring, not convince them to have fewer.

7. The abortion rate is a superior measure to the abortion ratio.

REFERENCES AND SUGGESTED READINGS

Abernethy, Virginia. 1995. "The Demographic Transition Model: A Ghost Story." *Population and Environment* 17(1).

Agadjanian, Victor, Scott T. Yabiku, and Boaventura Cau. 2011. "Men's Migration and Women's Fertility in Rural Mozambique." *Demography* 48(3): 1029–1048.

Alan Guttmacher Institute. 1999. *Sharing Responsibility: Women, Society and Abortion Worldwide.* http://www.guttmacher.org/pubs/sharing.pdf

———. 2009. *Abortion Worldwide: A Decade of Uneven Progress.* New York: Guttmacher Institute.

Anderton, Douglas L. 1989. "Starting, Stopping and Spacing: A Commentary." *Demography* 26(3): 467–470.

Anderton, Douglas L., Richard E. Barrett, and Donald J. Bogue. 1997. *The Population of the United States.* 3rd ed. New York: Free Press.

Anderton, Douglas L., and Lee L. Bean. 1985. "Birth Spacing and Fertility Limitation: A Behavioral Analysis of a Nineteenth Century Frontier Population." *Demography* 22(2).

Anthony, Sabine, Gert W. Jacobusse, Karin M. van der Pal-de Bruin, Simone Buitendijk, and Jennifer Zeitlin. 2009. "Do Differences in Maternal Age, Parity and Multiple Births Explain Variations in Fetal and Neonatal Mortality Rates in Europe?—Results from the EURO-PERISTAT Project." *Paediatric & Perinatal Epidemiology* 23(4): 292–300.

Arabi, Mandana, Edward A. Frongillo, Rasmi Avula, and Nune Mangasaryan. 2012. "Infant and Young Child Feeding in Developing Countries." *Child Development* 83(1): 32–45.

Azarnert, Leonid V. 2012. "Male versus Female Guest-Worker Migration: Does It Matter for Fertility in the Source Country?" *Research in Economics* 66(1): 1–6.

Balasch, Juan. 2010. "Ageing and Infertility: An Overview." *Gynecological Endocrinology* 26(12): 855–860.

Becker, Gary S. 1960. "An Economic Analysis of Fertility." In *Demographic and Economic Change in Developed Countries.* Princeton, NJ: Princeton University Press.

Blake, Judith. 1969. "Population Policy for Americans: Is the Government Being Misled?" *Science* 164(19).

Bongaarts, John. 1982. "The Fertility-Inhibiting Effects of the Intermediate Fertility Variables." *Studies in Family Planning* 13(6/7): 179–189.

———. 2001. "Fertility and Reproductive Preferences in Post-Transitional Societies." *Population and Development Review* 27 (suppl.).

Bongaarts, John, and Griffith Feeney. 1998. "On the Quantum and Tempo of Fertility." *Population and Development Review* 24(2).

Bongaarts, John, and Robert G. Potter. 1983. *Fertility, Biology, and Behavior: An Analysis of the Proximate Determinants of Fertility*. New York: Academic Press.

Bongaarts, John, and Susan Cotts Watkins. 1996. "Social Interactions and Contemporary Fertility Transitions." *Population and Development Review* 22(4).

Brown, Haywood L., and Cornelia R. Graves. 2013. "Smoking and Marijuana Use in Pregnancy." *Clinical Obstetrics and Gynecology* 56(1): 107–113.

Bulatao, Rodolfo A. 1984. "Reducing Fertility in Developing Countries: A Review of Determinants and Policy Levers." *World Bank Staff Working Papers no. 680, Population and Development Series no. 5*. Washington, DC: World Bank.

Burch, Thomas. 1975. "Theories of Fertility as Guides to Population Policy." *Social Forces* 54(1).

Caldwell, John C. 1982. *Theory of Fertility*. London: Academic Press.

———. 1997. "Reaching a Stationary Global Population: What We Have Learnt, and What We Must Do." *Health Transition Review* 7: Suppl. 4.

Caldwell, John C., I. O. Orubuloye, and Pat Caldwell. 1992. "Fertility Decline in Africa: A New Type of Transition?" *Population and Development Review* 18(2).

Casterline, John B., and Steven W. Sinding. 2000. "Unmet Need for Family Planning in Developing Countries and Implications for Population Policy." *Population and Development Review* 26(4): 691–723.

CDC (Centers for Disease Control). 1998. "Abortion Surveillance: Preliminary Analysis—United States, 1996." *Morbidity and Mortality Weekly Report* 47 (December 4).

———. 2002. "Abortion Surveillance—United States, 1999." *Morbidity and Mortality Weekly Report* 51 (November 29).

———. 2010. "Racial and Ethnic Differences in Breastfeeding Initiation and Duration, by State – National Immunization Survey, United States, 2004–2008." *Morbidity and Mortality Weekly Report* 59 (March 26).

———. 2012a. "Abortion Surveillance—United States, 2009." *Morbidity and Mortality Weekly Report* 61 (November 23).

———. 2012b. *Teen Pregnancy: About Teen Pregnancy*. Last Updated November 21, 2012. Retrieved August 12, 2013. http://www.cdc.gov/TeenPregnancy/AboutTeenPreg.htm

———. 2013a. *Breastfeeding Report Card 2013*. Retrieved August 22, 2013. http://www.cdc.gov/breastfeeding/pdf/2013BreastfeedingReportCard.pdf

———. 2013b. *Reproductive Health: Data and Statistics*. Last Updated April 11, 2013. Retrieved August 12, 2013. http://www.cdc.gov/reproductivehealth/Data_Stats/#Abortion

Center for Reproductive Rights. 2012. *Global Advocates: Family Planning Summit Must Put Women's Human Rights First*. (Press Release). Retrieved August 12, 2013. http://reproductiverights.org/en/press-room/global-advocates-family-planning-summit-must-put-womens-human-rights-first

Cleland, John. 2001. "The Effects of Improved Survival on Fertility: A Reassessment." *Population and Development Review* 27 (Supplement: Global Fertility Transition): 60–92.

Cleland, John, Mohamed M. Ali, and Virgile Capo-Chichi. 1999. "Post-Partum Sexual Abstinence in West Africa: Implications for AIDS-Control and Family Planning Programmes." *AIDS* 13(1): 125–131.

Cleland, John, and Chris Wilson. 1987. "Demand Theories of the Fertility Transition: An Iconoclastic View." *Population Studies* 41(1).

Coale, Ansley. 1973. "The Demographic Transition." *Proceedings of the International Population Conference, Liege*. Vol. 1. Liege: IUSSP.

———. 1974. "The History of Human Population." In *The Human Population: A Scientific American Book*. San Francisco: W. H. Freeman.

Coale, Ansley J., and Roy Treadway. 1986. "A Summary of the Changing Distribution of Overall Fertility, Marital Fertility and the Proportion Married in the Provinces of Europe." In A.

Coale and S. Watkins, eds., *The Decline of Fertility in Europe*. Princeton, NJ: Princeton University Press.

Coale, Ansley J., and Susan Cotts Watkins, eds. 1986. *The Decline of Fertility in Europe*. Princeton, NJ: Princeton University Press.

Coleman, David. 2007. "The Road to Low Fertility." *Ageing Horizons* 7: 7–15.

Cooney, K. A. 1992. "The Contribution of Breastfeeding and Lactational Amenorrhea Method to the Reduction of Fertility Worldwide." *Institute for Reproductive Health Occasional Paper no. 3*. Washington, DC: Institute for Reproductive Health.

Currie, Candace, Naman Ahluwalia, Emmanuelle Godeau, Saoirse Nic Gabhainn, Pernille Due, and Dorothy B. Currie. 2012. "Is Obesity at Individual and National Level Associated with Lower Age at Menarche? Evidence from 34 Countries in the Health Behaviour in School-Aged Children Study." *Journal of Adolescent Health* 50(6): 621–626.

Dada, O. A., F. A. Akesode, D. M. Olanrewaju, O. A. Olowu, O. Sule-Odu, T. A. Fakoya, F. A. Oluwole, B. V. Odunlami, and WHO Task Force on Methods for the Natural Regulation of Fertility. 2002. "Infant Feeding and Lactational Amenorrhea in Sagamu, Nigeria." *African Journal of Reproductive Health* 6(2): 39–50.

Darity, William, C. Turner, and H. Thiebaux. 1971. *Race Consciousness and Fears of Black Genocide as Barriers to Family Planning*. Population Reference Bureau Selection no. 37. Washington, DC: Population Reference Bureau.

Davis, Kingsley. 1967. "Population Policy: Will Current Programs Succeed?" *Science* 158.

Davis, Kingsley, and Judith Blake. 1956. "Social Structure and Fertility: An Analytic Framework." *Economic Development and Cultural Change* 4(4).

DeJong, Jocelyn, and Golda El-Khoury. 2006. "Reproductive Health of Arab Young People." *British Medical Journal* 333(7573): 849–851.

Demerath, Nicholas J. 1976. *Birth Control and Foreign Policy: The Alternatives to Family Planning*. New York: Harper and Row.

Dewey, Kathryn G., Roberta J. Cohen, Kenneth H. Brown, and Leonardo Landa Rivera. 2001. "Effects of Exclusive Breastfeeding for Four versus Six Months on Maternal Nutritional Status and Infant Motor Development: Results of Two Randomized Trials in Honduras." *Journal of Nutrition* 131(2): 262–267.

Dey, Ian, and Fran Wasoff. 2010. "Another Child? Fertility Ideals, Resources and Opportunities." *Population Research and Policy Review* 29(6): 921–940.

Di Renzo, Gian Carlo, Alessia Rosati, Roberta Donati Sarti, Laura Cruciani, and Antonio Massimo Cutuli. 2007. "Does Fetal Sex Affect Pregnancy Outcome?" *Gender Medicine* 4(1): 19–30.

Dobbing, John, ed. 1988. *Infant Feeding: Anatomy of a Controversy, 1973–1984*. New York: Springer-Verlag.

Easterlin, Richard A. 1968. *Population, Labor Force, and Long Swings in Economic Growth*. New York: Columbia University Press.

———. 1978. "What Will 1984 Be Like? Socioeconomic Implications of Recent Twists in Age Structure." *Demography* 15(4).

Easterlin, Richard A., and Eileen M. Crimmins. 1985. *The Fertility Revolution*. Chicago: University of Chicago Press.

Eaton, Joseph, and Albert Mayer. 1954. *Man's Capacity to Reproduce*. Glencoe, IL: The Free Press.

Eisenberg, Michael L., Alan W. Shindel, James F. Smith, Benjamin N. Breyer, and Larry I. Lipshultz. 2010. "Socioeconomic, Anthropomorphic, and Demographic Predictors of Adult Sexual Activity in the United States: Data from the National Survey of Family Growth." *Journal of Sexual Medicine* 7(1): 50–58.

Fabic, Madeleine Short, and Yoonjoung Choi. 2013. "Assessing the Quality of Data Regarding Use of the Lactational Amenorrhea Method." *Studies in Family Planning* 44(2): 205–221.

Feng, Wang, Yong Cai, and Baochang Gu. 2013. "Population, Policy, and Politics: How Will History Judge China's One-Child Policy?" *Population and Development Review* 38: 115–129.

Frisch, Rose E. 1975. "Demographic Implications of the Biological Determinants of Female Fecundity." *Social Biology* 22(1).

Gelbard, Alene, Carl Haub, and Mary M. Kent. 1999. "World Population Beyond Six Billion." *Population Bulletin* 54(1). Washington, DC: Population Reference Bureau.

Goldstein, Joshua, Lutz Wolfgang, and Maria Rita Testa. 2003. "The Emergence of Sub-Replacement Family Size Ideals in Europe." *Population Research and Policy Review* 22(5–6): 479–496.

Guinnane, Timothy W., Barbara S. Okun, and James Trussell. 1994. "What Do We Know About the Timing of Fertility Transitions in Europe?" *Demography* 31(1).

Gutmann, Myron P., Glenn D. Deane, Emily R. Merchant, and Kenneth M. Sylvester, eds. 2011. *Navigating Time and Space in Population Studies*. Dordrecht: Springer.

Hagewen, Kellie J., and S. Philip Morgan. 2005. "Intended and Ideal Family Size in the United States, 1970–2002." *Population and Development Review* 31(3): 507–527.

Hajnal, John. 1965. "European Marriage Patterns in Perspective." In D. V. Glass and D. E. C. Eversley, eds., *Population in History*. London: Arnold.

Harcourt, W. 1999. "Reproductive Health and Rights and the Quest for Social Justice" [editorial]. *Development* 42(1).

Hardee, K., K. Agarwal, N. Luke, E. Wilson, M. Pendzich, M. Farrel, and H. Cross. 1999. "Reproductive Health Policies and Programs in Eight Countries: Progress Since Cairo." *International Family Planning Perspectives* 25, Suppl. S.

Hartmann, Betsy. 1995. *Reproductive Rights and Wrongs: The Global Politics of Population Control*. Boston, MA: South End Press.

Haub, Carl. 2013. "Trends in Adolescent Fertility a Mixed Picture." Retrieved August 31, 2013. http://www.prb.org/Publications/Articles/2013/adolescent-fertility.aspx Washington, DC: Population Reference Bureau.

Haub, Carl, and James Gribble. 2011. "World at 7 Billion." *Population Bulletin* 66(2). Washington, DC: Population Reference Bureau.

Hauser, Philip M. 1967. "Family Planning and Population Programs: A Book Review Article." *Demography* 4(1).

Hawkes, Kristen. 2003. "Grandmothers and the Evolution of Human Longevity." *American Journal of Human Biology* 15(3): 380–400.

Heer, David M., and Jill S. Grigsby. 1992. *Society and Population*. 3rd ed. Englewood Cliffs, NJ: Prentice-Hall.

Henry, Louis. 1961. "Some Data on Natural Fertility." *Eugenics Quarterly* 8(1).

Hill, Kim, and A. Magadalena Hurtado. 1991. "The Evolution of Premature Reproductive Senescence and Menopause in Human Females: An Evaluation of the 'Grandmother' Hypothesis." *Human Nature* 2(4): 313–350.

Hirschman, Charles, and Marilyn Butler. 1981. "Trends and Differentials in Breastfeeding: An Update." *Demography* 18(1).

Hoyert, D. L. 1996. "Cigarettes and Fetal Mortality as Reported in 1990 Vital Statistics." *American Journal of Health Behavior* 20(3).

Jackson, Emily, and Anna Glasier. 2011. "Return of Ovulation and Menses in Postpartum Nonlactating Women: A Systematic Review." *Obstetrics & Gynecology* 117(3): 657–662.

Jacobsen, Linda A., Mark Mather, and Genevieve Dupuis. 2012. "Household Changes in the United States. *Population Bulletin* 67(1).

Jain, A. K., and John Bongaarts. 1980. "Socio-biological Factors in Exposure to Childbearing, Breastfeeding and Its Fertility Effects." Paper presented at the World Fertility Survey Conference, London, July 7–11.

Jeon, Yongil, and Michael P. Shields. 2005. "The Easterlin Hypothesis in the Recent Experience of Higher-Income OECD Countries: A Panel-Data Approach." *Journal of Population Economics* 18(1): 1–13.

Jolly, Carole L., and James N. Gribble. 1993. "The Proximate Determinants of Fertility." In Karen A. Foote, Kenneth H. Hill, and Linda G. Martin, eds., *Demographic Change in Sub-Saharan Africa.* Washington, DC: National Academy Press.

Kinsella, Kevin, and Wan He. 2009. "An Aging World: 2008." *U.S. Census Bureau, International Population Reports.* Washington, DC: U.S. GPO.

Klein, Herbert S. 2012. *A Population History of the United States.* 2nd ed. New York: Cambridge University Press.

Knodel, John, and Nibhon Debavalya. 1981. "Breastfeeding Trends in Thailand and Their Demographic Impact." *Intercom* 9(3).

Kohler, Hans-Peter, Francesco C. Billari, and Jose Antonio Ortega. 2002. "The Emergence of Lowest-Low Fertility in Europe During the 1990s." *Population and Development Review* 28(4): 641–680.

Kowal, Małgorzata, Łukasz Kryst, Agnieszka Woronkowicz, Jan Sobiecki, Janusz Brudecki, and Ryszard Żarów. 2013. "Long-Term Changes in BMI and Adiposity Rebound among Girls from Kraków (Poland) Over the Last 30 Years from 1983 to 2010." *American Journal of Human Biology* 25(3): 300–306.

Kristof, Nicholas D., and Sheryl WuDunn. 2010. *Half the Sky: Turning Oppression into Opportunity for Women Worldwide.* New York: Vintage Books.

Lanzieri, Giampaolo. 2013. "Towards a 'Baby Recession' in Europe? Differential Fertility Trends During the Economic Crisis." *Eurostat: Statistics in Focus* 13.

Leridon, Henri. 2004. "Can Assisted Reproduction Technology Compensate for the Natural Decline in Fertility with Age? A Model Assessment." *Human Reproduction* 19(7): 1548–1553.

Lesthaeghe, Ron J. 1983. "A Century of Demographic and Cultural Change in Western Europe: An Exploration of Underlying Dimensions." *Population and Development Review* 6(4).

———. 1995. "The Second Demographic Transition in Western Countries: An Interpretation." In K. O. Mason and A. M. Jensen, eds., *Gender and Family Change in Industrialized Countries.* Oxford: Clarendon Press.

Lewis, Carol. 2003. "HHS Blueprint to Boost Breast-Feeding." *FDA Consumer Magazine* 37(3). Washington, DC: U.S. Department of Health and Human Services.

Lindstrom, David P., and Silvia Giorguli Saucedo. 2007. "The Interrelationship of Fertility, Family Maintenance, and Mexico–US Migration." *Demographic Research* 17: 821–857.

Livingston, Gretchen. 2011. *In a Down Economy, Fewer Births.* Retrieved August 8, 2013. http://www.pewsocialtrends.org/files/2011/10/12/in-a-down-economy-fewer-births/ Washington, DC: Pew Social & Demographic Trends.

London, K. A., J. Cushing, S. O. Rutstein, J. Cleland, J. E. Anderson, L. Morris, and S. H. Moore. 1985. "Fertility and Family Planning Surveys: An Update." *Population Reports Series M, Special Topics.*

Lutz, Wolfgang, Vegard Skirbekk, and Maria Rita Testa. 2006. "The Low Fertility Trap Hypothesis: Forces That May Lead to Further Postponement and Fewer Births in Europe." *Vienna Yearbook of Population Research* 2006: 167–192.

Macaluso, Maurizio, Tracie J. Wright-Schnapp, Anjani Chandra, Robert Johnson, Catherine L. Satterwhite, Amy Pulver, and Stuart M. Berman et al. 2010. "A Public Health Focus on Infertility Prevention, Detection, and Management." *Fertility and Sterility* 93(1).

MacDorman, Marian F., and Sharon Kirmeyer. 2009. "The Challenge of Fetal Mortality." *NCHS Data Brief* (16).

Magadi, M. A., and A. O. Agwanda. 2010. "Investigating the Association between HIV/AIDS and Recent Fertility Patterns in Kenya." *Social Science & Medicine* 71(2): 335–344.

Maheshwari, Abha, Mark Hamilton, and Siladitya Bhattacharya. 2008. "Effect of Female Age on the Diagnostic Categories of Infertility." *Human Reproduction* 23(3): 538–542.

Mascarenhas, Maya N., Seth R. Flaxman, Ties Boerma, Sheryl Vanderpoel, and Gretchen A. Stevens. 2012. "National, Regional, and Global Trends in Infertility Prevalence Since 1990: A

Systematic Analysis of 277 Health Surveys." *PLoS Med* 9(12): e1001356. doi:10.1371/journal.pmed.1001356.

Mason, Karen Oppenheim. 1997. "Explaining Fertility Transitions." Presidential Address to the Population Association of America. *Demography* 34(4).

Matorras, Roberto, Francisco Matorras, Antonia Expósito, Lorea Martinez, and Lorena Crisol. 2011. "Decline in Human Fertility Rates with Male Age: A Consequence of a Decrease in Male Fecundity with Aging?" *Gynecologic and Obstetric Investigation* 71(4): 229–235.

Max Planck Institute for Demographic Research. 2013. *New Forecast: Lifetime Fertility on the Rise* (Press release). Retrieved August 10, 2013. www.popcouncil.org/pdfs/MediaCenter/2013NewsRelease_MaxPlanckInstPDR.pdf

Menken, Jane, James Trussell, and Ulla Larsen. 1986. "Age and Infertility." *Science* 233(4771): 1389–1394.

Menken, Jane, James Trussell, and Susan Watkins. 1981. "The Nutrition and Fertility Link: An Evaluation of the Evidence." *Journal of Interdisciplinary History* 11(3).

Meston, Cindy M., and Tierney Ahrold. 2010. "Ethnic, Gender, and Acculturation Influences on Sexual Behaviors." *Archives of Sexual Behavior* 31(1): 179–189.

Moore, Maurice, and Martin O'Connell. 1978. *Perspectives on American Fertility*. U.S. Census Bureau, Current Population Reports, Special Studies, Series P-23, no. 70. Washington, DC: GPO.

Morgan, S. Philip. 2003. "Is Low Fertility a 21st-Century Demographic Crisis?" *Demography* 40(4).

Murthy, Padmini, and Clyde Lanford Smith, eds. 2010. *Women's Global Health and Human Rights*. Sudbury MA: Jones and Bartlett Publishers.

Nag, Moni. 1980. "How Modernization Can Also Increase Fertility." *Current Anthropology* 21(5).

Nallella, Kiran P., Rakesh K. Sharma, Nabil Aziz, and Ashok Agarwal. 2006. "Significance of Sperm Characteristics in the Evaluation of Male Infertility." *Fertility and Sterility* 85(3): 629–634.

National Institute on Aging. 2013. "AgePage: Menopause." *Health & Aging*. Last Updated July 25, 2013. Retrieved August 12, 2013. www.nia.nih.gov/health/publication/menopause

NCHS (National Center for Health Statistics). 1998. "Report of Final Natality Statistics." *Monthly Vital Statistics Report* 46(1).

———. 2002. "Vital Statistics of the United States, 2000." *National Vital Statistics Reports* 50(5).

———. 2003. "Teen Birth Rate Continues to Decline; African-American Teens Show Sharpest Drop." December 17. http://www.cdc.gov/nchs/pressroom/03facts/teenbirth.htm

———. 2005a. "Births: Final Data for 2003." *National Vital Statistics Reports* 54(2). http://www.cdc.gov/nchs/products/pubs/pubd/nvsr/nvsr.htm

———. 2005b. "Preliminary Births for 2004." http://www.cdc.gov/nchs/products/pubs/pubd/hestats/prelim_births/prelim_births04.htm

———. 2013. "Births: Final Data for 2011." *National Vital Statistics Reports* 62(1). http://www.cdc.gov/nchs/data/nvsr/nvsr62/nvsr62_01.pdf

Nicolosi, Alfredo, Edward O. Laumann, Dale B. Glasser, Edson D. Moreira Jr., Anthony Paik, and Clive Gingell. 2004. "Sexual Behavior and Sexual Dysfunctions after Age 40: The Global Study of Sexual Attitudes and Behaviors." *Urology* 64(5): 991–997.

Notestein, Frank. 1953. "Economic Problems of Population Change." *Proceedings of the Eighth International Conference of Agricultural Economics*. London: Oxford University Press.

OECD (Organisation for Economic Co-Operation and Development). 2012. "CO1.5: Breastfeeding Rates." *OECD Family Database*. Retrieved August 22, 2013. http://www.oecd.org/social/family/database Paris: OECD.

Office of the Surgeon General. 2011. *The Surgeon General's Call to Action to Support Breastfeeding*. Washington, DC: U.S. Department of Health and Human Services.

Ombelet, Willem, Ian Cooke, Silke Dyer, Gamal Serour, and Paul Devroey. 2008. "Infertility and the Provision of Infertility Medical Services in Developing Countries." *Human Reproduction Update* 14(6): 605–621.

Parent, Anne-Simone, Grete Teilmann, Anders Juul, Niels E. Skakkebaek, Jorma Toppari, and Jean-Pierre Bourguignon. 2003. "The Timing of Normal Puberty and the Age Limits of Sexual Precocity: Variations around the World, Secular Trends, and Changes after Migration." *Endocrine Reviews* 24(5): 668–693.

PRB (Population Reference Bureau). 2012. *U.S. Teen Birth Rate Hits New Low, Still Higher than Europe's*. Retrieved August 12, 2013. http://www.prb.org/Publications/Articles/2012/us-teen-birth-rate.aspx

———. 2014. *2014 World Population Data Sheet*. Washington, DC: Population Reference Bureau.

Preston, Samuel H., Patrick Heuveline, and Michel Guillot. 2001. *Demography: Measuring and Modeling Population Processes*. Oxford: Blackwell Publishing.

Quesnel-Vallée, Amélie, and S. Philip Morgan. 2003. "Missing the Target? Correspondence of Fertility Intentions and Behavior in the U.S." *Population Research and Policy Review* 22(5–6).

Rah, Jee H., Abu Ahmed Shamim, Ummeh T. Arju, Alain B. Labrique, Mahbubur Rashid, and Parul Christian. 2009. "Age of Onset, Nutritional Determinants, and Seasonal Variations in Menarche in Rural Bangladesh." *Journal of Health, Population and Nutrition* 27(6): 802–807.

Rashad, Hoda, Magued Osman, and Farzaneh Roudi-Fahimi. 2005. *Marriage in the Arab World*. Washington, DC: Population Reference Bureau.

Rasmussen, Kathleen M., and Sheela R. Geraghty. 2011. "The Quiet Revolution: Breastfeeding Transformed with the Use of Breast Pumps." *American Journal of Public Health* 101(8): 1356–1359.

Reher, David, and Roger Schofield. 1993. *Old and New Methods in Historical Demography*. Oxford: Clarendon Press.

Robinson, W. C. 1997. "The Economic Theory of Fertility Over Three Decades." *Population Studies* 51(1).

Ruggles, Steven. 2012. "The Future of Historical Family Demography." *Annual Review of Sociology* 38(1): 423–441.

Ryder, Norman B. 1959. "Fertility." In Philip M. Hauser and Otis Dudley Duncan, eds., *The Study of Population: An Inventory and Appraisal*. Chicago: University of Chicago Press.

———. 1979. "The Future of American Fertility." *Social Problems* 26(3).

Sadik, Nafis, ed. 1991. *Population Policies and Programmes: Lessons Learned from Two Decades of Experience*. United Nations Population Fund. New York University Press.

Schwartz, David A. 2013. "Challenges in Improvement of Perinatal Health in Developing Nations: Role of Perinatal Pathology." *Archives of Pathology & Laboratory Medicine* 137(6): 742–746.

Sedgh, Gilda, Susheela Singh, Iqbal H. Shah, Elisabeth Åhman, Stanley K. Henshaw, and Akinrinola Bankole. 2012. "Induced Abortion: Incidence and Trends Worldwide from 1995 to 2008." *The Lancet* 379(9816): 625–632.

Shane, Barbara. 1997. *Planning Saves Lives*. 3rd ed. Washington, DC: Population Reference Bureau.

Sharma, R. K., S. O. Rutstein, M. H. Labbok, and G. Ramos. 1991. *Trends and Differentials in Breastfeeding: Findings from the World Fertility Survey and the Demographic and Health Surveys*. Unpublished manuscript.

Shorter, Edward, John Knodel, and Etienne van de Walle. 1971. "The Decline of Non-marital Fertility in Europe, 1880–1940." *Population Studies* 25(3).

Shryock, Henry S., and Jacob S. Siegel. 1976. *The Methods and Materials of Demography*. Condensed edition by Edward G. Stockwell. New York: Academic Press.

Sievert, Lynnette Leidy. 2006. *Menopause: A Biocultural Perspective*. New Brunswick, NJ: Rutgers University Press.

Simmons, George B. 1986. "Family Planning Programs." In Jane Menken, ed., *World Population and U.S. Policy: The Choices Ahead*. New York: W. W. Norton.

Singh, Susheela, and Jacqueline E. Darroch. 2012. *Adding It Up: Costs and Benefits of Contraceptive Services—Estimates for 2012.* Guttmacher Institute and United Nations Population Fund (UNFPA). Retrieved August 12, 2013. www.guttmacher.org/pubs/AIU-2012-estimates.pdf

Singh, Susheela, Jacqueline E. Darroch, Michael Vlassoff, and Jennifer Nadeau. 2003. *Adding It Up: The Benefits of Investing in Sexual and Reproductive Health Care.* New York: UNFPA.

Sipsma, Heather L., Elizabeth H. Bradley, and Peggy G. Chen. 2013. "Lactational Amenorrhea Method as a Contraceptive Strategy in Niger." *Maternal and Child Health Journal* 17(4): 654–660.

Slack, Tim, and Leif Jensen. 2008. "Birth and Fortune Revisited: A Cohort Analysis of Underemployment, 1974–2004." *Population Research and Policy Review* 27(6): 729–749.

Sobotka, T., M. A. Hansen, T. K. Jensen, A. T. Pedersen, W. Lutz, and N. E. Skakkebæk. 2008. "The Contribution of Assisted Reproduction to Completed Fertility: An Analysis of Danish Data." *Population and Development Review* 34(1): 79–101.

Sussner K. M., A. C. Lindsay, and K. E. Peterson. 2008. "The Influence of Acculturation on Breast-Feeding Initiation and Duration in Low-Income Women in the U.S." *Journal of Biosocial Science* 40: 673–696.

Tafari, N., and G. Zerihun. 1993. "The Effect of Age, Parity, and Socioeconomic Factors on Perinatal Mortality and Long-Term Morbidity." In J. David Baum, ed., *Birth Risks.* New York: Raven Press.

Thompson, W. S. 1930. *Population Problems.* New York: McGraw-Hill.

Thornton, Arland, and Thomas E. Fricke. 1987. "Social Change and the Family: Comparative Perspectives from the West, China, and South Asia." In J. M. Stycos, ed., *Demography as an Interdiscipline.* Oxford: Transaction Publishers.

Trussell, James, and Charles F. Westoff. 1980. "Contraceptive Practice Trends in Coital Frequency." *Family Planning Perspectives* 12(5).

Tsuya, Noriko O., Feng Wang, George Alter, and James Z. Lee, et al. 2010. *Prudence and Pressure: Reproduction and Human Agency in Europe and Asia, 1700–1900.* Cambridge, MA: MIT Press.

United Nations. 2010. *The World's Women 2010: Trends and Statistics.* Department of Economic and Social Affairs. ST/ESA/STAT/SER.K/19. New York: United Nations.

———. 2011a. "United Nations' Message to Mothers: Breastfeeding Can Save Your Baby's Life." *UN News Centre.* August 1, 2011. Retrieved August 12, 2013. http://www.un.org/apps/news/story.asp?NewsID=39203&Cr=child&Cr1=health#.UgmMCBbB7G5

———. 2011b. *World Contraceptive Use 2011.* Population Division of the Department of Economic and Social Affairs. Retrieved August 8, 2013. http://www.un.org/esa/population/publications/contraceptive2011/wallchart_front.pdf

———. 2011c. *World Fertility Policies 2011.* Population Division of the Department of Economic and Social Affairs. ST/ESA/SER.A/303. Retrieved August 13, 2013. http://www.un.org/en/development/desa/population/publications/pdf/fertility/worldFertilityPolicies2011.pdf

———. 2011d. *World Fertility Report 2009.* Population Division of the Department of Economic and Social Affairs. ST/ESA/SER.A/304. New York: United Nations.

———. 2012. *World Contraceptive Use 2012.* Population Division of the Department of Economic and Social Affairs. POP/DB/CP/Rev2012. Retrieved August 13, 2013. http://www.un.org/esa/population/publications/WCU2012/MainFrame.html

———. 2013a. *World Abortion Policies 2013.* Department of Economic and Social Affairs. Retrieved August 12, 2013. http://www.un.org/en/development/desa/population/publications/pdf/policy/WorldAbortionPolicies2013/WorldAbortionPolicies2013_WallChart.pdf

———. 2013b. *World Population Prospects: The 2012 Revision.* Population Division of the Department of Economic and Social Affairs. http://esa.un.org/wpp/

UNFPA (United Nations Population Fund). 2005. *State of World Population 2005.* http://www.unfpa.org/swp/2005/english/ch1/index.htm

————. 2012. *State of World Population 2012. By Choice, Not By Chance: Family Planning, Human Rights and Development.* New York: United Nations Population Fund.

USAID. 2009. "USAID's Family Planning Guiding Principles and U.S. Legislative and Policy Requirements." *Restrictions on Support for Abortion.* Last Updated June 2, 2009. Retrieved August 12, 2013. http://transition.usaid.gov/our_work/global_health/pop/restrictions.html

————. 2013. "Global Health: Family Planning." *What We Do.* Last Updated July 31, 2013. Retrieved August 12, 2013. http://www.usaid.gov/what-we-do/global-health/family-planning

U.S. Census Bureau. 2009. *An Aging World: 2008.* International Population Reports P95/09-1. Washington, DC: U.S. GPO.

U.S. Department of Health and Human Services. 2013. "Maternal, Infant, and Child Health." *HealthyPeople.gov: 2020 Topics & Objectives.* Last Updated April 10, 2013. Retrieved August 12, 2013. http://www.healthypeople.gov/2020/topicsobjectives2020/overview.aspx?topicid=26

van Bavel, Jan. 2004. "Detecting Stopping and Spacing Behaviour in Historical Demography. *Population* 59(1):117–128.

van de Walle, Etienne, and John Knodel. 1980. "Europe's Fertility Transition: New Evidence and Lessons for Today's Developing World." *Population Bulletin* 34(6). Washington, DC: Population Reference Bureau.

van Poppel, Frans, Niels Schenk, and Ruben van Gaalen. 2013. "Demographic Transitions and Changes in the Living Arrangements of Children: The Netherlands 1850–2010." *Population Research and Policy Review* 32(2): 243–260.

Vavasseur, C., A. Foran, and J. F. Murphy. 2007. "Consensus Statements on the Borderlands of Neonatal Viability: From Uncertainty to Grey Areas." *Irish Medical Journal* 100 (8): 561–564.

Watson, Walter B. 1982. "Family Planning Programs: Developing Countries." In John A. Ross, ed., *International Encyclopedia of Population.* New York: Free Press.

Wetstein, Matthew E. 1996. *Abortion Rates in the United States: The Influence of Opinion and Policy.* Albany, NY: SUNY Press.

White, Kari, and Joseph E. Potter. 2013. "The Impact of Out Migration of Men on Fertility and Marriage in the Migrant-Sending States of Mexico, 1995–2000." *Population Studies* 67(1): 83–95.

WHO (World Health Organization). 2007. *Planning Guide for National Implementation of the Global Strategy for Infant and Young Child Feeding.* Geneva: World Health Organization.

————. 2012. *Trends in Maternal Mortality: 1990 to 2010 - WHO, UNICEF, UNFPA and The World Bank Estimates.* Geneva: World Health Organization.

Wilcox, Allen J., Clarice R. Weinberg, and Donna D. Baird. 1995. "Timing of Sexual Intercourse in Relation to Ovulation—Effects on the Probability of Conception, Survival of the Pregnancy, and Sex of the Baby." *New England Journal of Medicine* 333: 1517–1521.

Willigan, J. Dennis, and Katherine A. Lynch. 1982. *Sources and Methods of Historical Demography.* New York: Academic Press.

Zohoori, Namvar, and Barry M. Popkin. 1996. "Longitudinal Analysis of the Effects of Infant-Feeding Practices on Postpartum Amenorrhea." *Demography* 33(2).

8

Unions and Householding

Rapidly changing fertility patterns detailed in the previous chapter have been accompanied by equally dramatic changes in family formation and householding. The longer life expectancies and smaller completed family sizes brought about by the demographic transition have transformed the social and economic roles of men and women. This has been most apparent in MDRs, but these changes have also begun in many LDRs. People are spending less of their lives as parents of young children and the meaning of marriage has changed considerably. Under conditions of high fertility and high mortality, women spent most of their adult lives reproducing and raising children. In conditions of low fertility and low mortality, childbearing has become an often passing or optional phase of marriage. Women's lifestyle choices have increased and women's working roles frequently extend beyond the domestic realm. Increased women's economic independence and a reduced reproductive orientation have led to a transformation of marriage from necessity to a lifestyle choice. In turn, traditional family forms are giving way to many different types of lives. Many people delay marriage to older ages and some people never marry at all. People divorce and remarry, sometimes multiple times. Single-parent households are becoming more common, as are households formed by unmarried partners.

Why are these seemingly personal lifestyle preferences of interest to the demographer? **Households**, and the families who reside together in them, are social units. They act together to raise children, to move, and to help each other survive. That is, they act collectively to influence the processes of fertility, migration, and mortality. They also act collectively in other social and economic behaviors. While they may not be units of economic production as much as they once were, they still are units of consumption. In addition, recent lifestyle changes have a direct impact on fertility levels. Nontraditional households often produce fewer or no children, and the delay and interruption of traditional marital unions also can result in smaller families. In fact, many demogra-

279

phers are now referring to these changes as part of a **second demographic transition** (van de Kaa, 1987; Lesthaeghe and van de Kaa, 1986; Lesthaeghe, 2010). Some argue that the second demographic transition is less of a theory than a description of the continuing family changes started in motion by the first demographic transition. However, it does appear to notably differ from the first transition in specific ways. The second transition is differentiated by (1) a shift from near universal and traditional marriage to the acceptance of a wide variety of nonmarital family structures, and (2) unpredictable but low fertility levels that often fall *below* replacement levels. These trends are unfolding in securalizing and affluent countries.

There are so many aspects of families and households that we could describe in this chapter that we must put some aside for lack of space. We have chosen a set of topics centering around what demographers call **nuptiality**. This means that we will focus on the formation and breakup of marriages. However, in addressing nuptial patterns, we also devote attention to related second demographic transition trends that stem from recent changes in marital behavior, such as **cohabitation** and the decoupling of childbearing from marriage. After a section dealing with methodological concerns, we will deal with international and historical variations in the process of marriages and unions. Then we will focus on two features of the second demographic transition process, using the United States as an example: (1) changing patterns of widowhood, divorce, cohabitation, and nonmarital fertility; and (2) the changing family life course.

Definition and Measurement

Definitions

The best way to introduce you to the terms used in the study of nuptiality is to take you through the imaginary marital history of a birth cohort (Cherlin, 2010b, 1981). Figure 8-1 graphs this history schematically.

Everyone starts her or his life as **never-married**, or **single.** Since this is a marital history, we will ignore for the moment alternatives to marriage, such as cohabiting. However we want to mention that cohabitation is becoming increasingly common across many industrialized nations, especially for couples aged twenty to thirty-four, who are in prime fertility years. In some countries, such as in Denmark and Finland, cohabiting partners can enter into a legalized civil union, and records show that roughly three out of ten prime-age couples live in such civil unions (OECD, 2012). In the case of the United States, formal marriage continues to be quite prevalent, with 90% of the population eventually marrying (Cherlin, 2010b). As Figure 8-1 shows, many of these never-married cohort members experience, sooner or later, an event called **first marriage**, thereby entering the status of currently married, or **married**, for short. Demographers generally include the legally separated (but not yet divorced) in the category of currently married.

Moving up the chart, we see that some married cohort members have their marriages dissolve: some cohort members die, leaving their spouses as **widowed**. Other married cohort members decide to end their marriages, putting both in the status of being **divorced**.

Figure 8-1

Schematic Marital History of a Birth Cohort

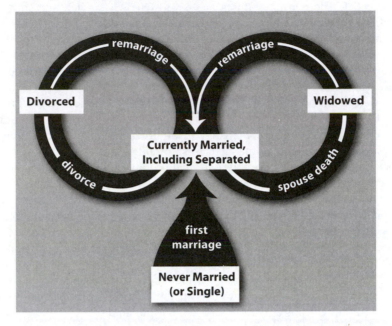

Widowed or divorced cohort members can rejoin the currently married by the process of remarriage. Once they are back in the currently married status, they may reenter a new cycle of nonmarriage by the death of their new spouse or by divorce.

Some of these statuses combine into larger categories. For instance, demographers use the term **unmarried** or nonmarried to combine never-married, divorced, and widowed. **Ever-married** includes the currently married, divorced, and widowed. *Formerly married* means those currently divorced or widowed.

Similarly, the processes of first marriage and remarriage combine to make up the process of **marriage**. The processes of spouse mortality and divorce combine to make up the process of **marital dissolution**.

This scheme emphasizes the legal and public statuses of individuals and changes from one status to the other; it does not pretend to capture the complexity of sexual unions and cohabitation. It does not record entering into nonsanctioned sexual unions in many countries, such as consensual unions, same-sex unions, common-law marriages, or "living together." Being consistently legalistic, the scheme views a marriage that is annulled as a marriage that never existed; and it does not capture the leaving of a consensual union or the separation, without divorce, from a legal marriage.

One part of the history of the birth cohort is not represented in Figure 8-1: the mortality of the cohort member him- or herself. The number of original members currently in any one of these marital statuses is determined not only by the processes of transition (first marriage, spouse mortality, divorce, remarriage, and so on) but also by attrition due to their own deaths. Members of any status can and do die.

Data on Marriage and Divorce

Let us distinguish between individuals' **marital statuses** and their marital *events* in Figure 8-1. The marital statuses are never-married (single), currently married (married), divorced, and widowed. The marital events mark the transitions from one status to the other: first marriage, divorce, spouse death, and remarriage. On an aggregate level, these two aspects are seen respectively as marital status *compositions* and marriage *processes*. Data about these two aspects of marriage conventionally come from different sources.

Censuses and intercensal surveys, such as the American Community Survey and the Current Population Survey provide most marital *status* information. As you may remember from chapter 2, the United Nations (2008) recommends that marital status questions be asked in national censuses. Although most countries follow this advice, it does not necessarily assure internationally comparable information. "Marriage" refers to a legal recognition of a sexual union, and which unions enjoy legal standing varies somewhat from country to country. For example, some recognize same-sex marriage (mostly European, but also South Africa, Argentina, Brazil, Uruguay, New Zealand, the U.S., and Canada), but most do not. Questions regarding marriage can change from census to census as the cultural significance of marriage changes in a country.

Ideally, direct information about marital *events*, on the other hand, comes from the civil registration system. Just as births and deaths are certified by legal authorities, so are marriages and divorces. And in all these cases the additional step involved, for demographic purposes, is to report these events to a central office where they can be accumulated, tabulated, and reported. However, in most Western countries the registration of marriages and divorces is notoriously less complete than the registration of either births or deaths. Indeed, the United States stopped collecting standardized marriage and divorce registration information in 1996. The lack of direct registration data often forces demographers to rely upon census and survey data for estimating the marital events and processes, as well as statuses.

Censuses and surveys can give two kinds of data on marital processes. First, current marital status data taken over time (e.g., successive surveys or censuses) can be combined with age reports and used for inferring the timing of marital events in the histories of cohorts. Second, retrospective questions on age at marriage can provide estimates of marriage behavior among (surviving) individuals.

Most Western censuses have included such retrospective questions for decades. That information is used to describe the age-timing of the marriage processes, as well as to pinpoint marital occurrences within the context of other important events, such as childbearing, school enrollment, employment, etc. By asking additional questions regarding household composition and relationships, censuses also provide the basis for indirect estimates of *living arrangements* that can be an alternative or precursor to marriage, such as cohabitation and same-sex unions.

In the less-developed countries, the main vehicles for survey questions on marriage are fertility and family-planning surveys. Interview schedules about fertility include questions about marital history. The advantage of such surveys is that they link marital information about individuals with other information about their childbearing, economic status, and the like. A disadvantage is that complete marriage histories usually are still not asked for men, except as they enter into the lives of the women respondents.

In the United States, data on families and living arrangements are collected periodically through four different nationwide surveys; the American Community Survey (ACS), the Current Population Survey (CPS), the Survey of Income and Program Participation (SIPP), and the decennial censuses. Collected data on marriage, marital status, and living arrangements are disseminated through the Census Bureau's *Family and Living Arrangements* website and via reports produced by the Census Bureau or Bureau of Labor Statistics (U.S. Census Bureau, 2012a) and is further analyzed in Population Division working papers (e.g., Kreider, 2006; Bachu, 1999a). Most media articles monitoring changes in the U.S. marital situation are based on these reports.

Marital Status Composition

The main technique for describing marital status composition—or composition in general—is by means of percentage distributions. To find the percentage of the population in any given status category, we take the number of persons in that category, divide it by the number in the total population, and multiply by 100 to obtain a percentage. The upper panel of Table 8-1 gives percentage distributions by the four major marital statuses, according to the 1950–2000 U.S. censuses and the 2010 Current Population Survey.

Since the 1950s, men and women in the United States have experienced a steady increase in the proportion never-married and a corresponding decline in the proportion married. The proportion widowed has generally declined since 1950, while divorce among men and women has increased steadily over the past six decades. The crude divorce rate reached its peak in about 1980 and has flattened since (Cherlin, 2010a; Goldstein, 1999). Younger Americans, born since 1980, have the lowest divorce rates due to the increasing selectivity of marriage (Kennedy and Ruggles, 2014). Even so, divorce rates in the United States (and in Eastern European countries) remain the highest in the world (United Nations, 2012; U.S. Census Bureau, 2011).

Table 8-1   Marital Status of the U.S. Adult Population, by Sex, 1950 through 2010

	Male (%)					Female (%)				
	1950	**1970**	**1990**	**2000**	**2010**	**1950**	**1970**	**1990**	**2000**	**2010**
Marital Status	**(1)**	**(2)**	**(3)**	**(4)**	**(5)**	**(6)**	**(7)**	**(8)**	**(9)**	**(10)**
Unstandardized										
Never Married	26.2	28.1	30.9	31.3	34.2	19.6	22.1	23.5	25.1	27.4
Married	68.0	66.7	59.7	57.9	52.8	66.1	61.9	55.1	54.7	49.9
Widowed	4.2	2.9	2.6	2.5	2.5	12.2	12.5	12.0	10.0	9.1
Divorced	1.7	2.2	6.9	8.3	10.5	2.2	3.5	9.5	10.2	13.7
Age Standardized[a]										
Never Married	26.2	23.9	29.5	32.1	36.2	20.0	19.3	24.1	26.8	30.2
Married	67.4	70.8	60.8	57.4	51.5	63.9	64.9	55.7	54.6	49.6
Widowed	4.7	3.0	2.6	2.2	2.0	14.0	12.0	10.3	8.4	6.9
Divorced	1.7	2.4	7.1	8.3	10.2	2.1	3.8	9.8	10.2	13.4

[a]Standardized to 1960 age-sex distribution.

Sources: U.S. Census Bureau, 1976. *Social Indicators,* table 2-3; U.S. Census Bureau, 1998. *Marital Status and Living Arrangements;* Fields and Casper, 2001. "America's Families and Living Arrangements: 2000"; U.S. Census Bureau, 2010. *America's Families and Living Arrangements: 2010.*

One cause of a changing marital status composition could be a changing age structure during the period covered. The age structure of the U.S. population changed considerably between 1950 and 2010. Demographers have developed techniques for discounting the influence of such age-structure differences in making marital-status composition comparisons. These also are illustrated in Table 8-1.

A first step is to confine the analysis to the segment of the age distribution at risk. For instance, in Table 8-1 (and in most tabulations of marital status), adolescents are excluded, on the assumption that they are rarely at risk of being anything besides single (never-married).

A more complete method of controlling for the effects of age composition is age **standardization**. It attempts to answer the following hypothetical question: If the age structures of all populations being compared were the same (some specified percentage distribution by age), then what percentage would fall into each of the marital status categories?

The bottom panel of Table 8-1 presents such standardized percentages. The age structure used as a standard was that for 1960; therefore, the bottom panel of the table shows the percentages that would fall into each of the marital status categories if the populations of 1950, 1970, 1990, 2000, and 2010 all had the age structure (for each sex) of the population of 1960.

The standardized percentages in Table 8-1 show that changes in the age composition, largely caused by the baby boom, affected marital status composition in the 1970s. Although the unstandardized percentage of those married decreased in 1970 for men and women, the standardized percentages married actually increased. The opposite is true for the proportion single; the unstandardized proportion single increased while the standardized proportion actually decreased. This difference is due to the largely young and still single baby-boom cohort in the 1970s. The increase in single status and decrease in married status in 1970 thus were due to changing age structures.

The choice of the standard population is somewhat arbitrary. When comparing more than one population, one choice is to select a standard population close to the average of the populations being compared. However, the use of multiple standards confuses statistical comparisons, so there is an advantage in choosing some convention. Government agencies, for example, frequently choose a single standard which is then used to allow comparisons across different publications or studies. The year 2000 population has now been widely adopted as the standard.

Standardization is a very flexible and useful technique in demography, not confined to the study of marital status or to standardization of age. We most frequently see standardization of age because age influences so many other demographic characteristics and processes. The same basic process also can be used in standardizing for race, education, and so on. Exercise 1 at the end of the chapter demonstrates one technique of age standardization.

Annual Rates

One can measure the processes of marriage and marital dissolution with rates (just as one does the vital processes of mortality and fertility), using crude rates, refined rates, specific rates, or total rates. Refined rates are favored, however. In refined rates, the numerator contains *all* of the specified marital events that occurred in the year, while the denominator includes not the total population but rather a segment of it considered to be at risk of experiencing that event.

Clearly, not everybody in the population is equally at risk of being first married, divorced, widowed, or remarried. Some age categories can be eliminated as being "not at risk." For example, in most societies those under fifteen can be considered not at risk for all marital events. Moreover, what can happen to an individual, marriage-wise, depends on that person's present status. Looking back at Figure 8-1, we see confirmation of some obvious points: A first marriage can happen only to those who never have married; only those currently married can get divorced or widowed; only those divorced or widowed can be remarried. Therefore, refined rates for these processes confine their denominators to the population in the proper marital status category, as well as the respective age categories.

The set of refined rates for nuptiality has not been conventionalized. Instead demographers tend to be pragmatic and flexible, using the limited data at hand in a given situation. This makes for a certain lack of exact comparability between reported rates. The "divorce rate" does not mean the same thing in all reports. It is necessary for the reader to always check for definitions of the rates being employed.

World Variations in First Marriage

Since we all are born single, the first nuptial event we can encounter is first marriage. How many of us take that step, and when, varies considerably from culture to culture and cohort to cohort. We start this section describing something that is shared: the first-marriage curve. Then we demonstrate the current wide international variation in other aspects of the first-marriage process. Turning to history, we then trace the changes that have accompanied the modernization of the West, ending with specific attention to the United States.

The First-Marriage Curve

Let us once again use the example of a hypothetical birth cohort and follow it through a marital process, this time the process of first marriage alone. For simplicity, let us suppose that we are dealing with a cohort of women only. Somewhere around age fifteen, cohort women start to marry, gradually at first, changing their status from never-married to ever-married. During the next few years, first marriage spreads through the "surviving" singles in the cohort, changing the status of most to ever-married before their thirtieth birthday. The first-marriage trend spends itself as it runs out of singles and finds the few remaining singles harder to marry (or uninterested in doing so). Demographers have found that individuals who are never-married at the age of fifty are very unlikely to marry at all.

Figure 8-2 on the following page graphs this process for five different countries at five historical time points. Coale (1971) chose these countries and these times to present a wide variety of marital patterns for which data were available.

What is striking is the similarity in the *form* of the curve, given the variety of cultures involved. In all countries graphed, the proportions ever-married increase in an S-shaped curve, but not a symmetrical one. The left side is compressed; the right side is spread out.

Figure 8-2

Proportions of Women Ever-Married, by Age, Selected Populations

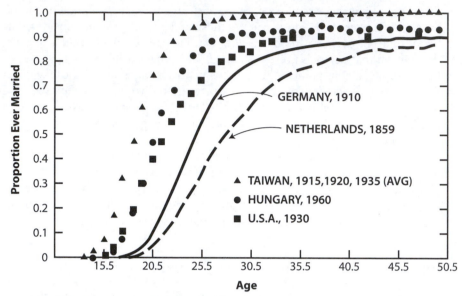

Source: Coale, 1971. "Age Patterns of Marriage," figure 3.

Coale and his team started investigating the prevalence of this form after noticing it in all of the European demographic transitions they happened to be studying. Intrigued by the regularity, Coale attempted, unsuccessfully, to find exceptions to the pattern outside of the region and time he had been studying. He observed:

> The most puzzling feature of the common pattern . . . is its very prevalence. We have seen evidence of the same basic curve . . . in cohorts that marry early and cohorts that marry late, in cohorts in which marriage is virtually universal and in cohorts in which one-quarter remain single. Moreover, the uniform age structure of nuptiality occurs in societies in which most marriages are arranged by families with little regard for the preference of bride and groom and in societies in which marriages result from self-selection of mutually preferred partners. (Coale, 1971, p. 203)

Figure 8-2 dramatizes the formal similarity among countries in historical first-marriage processes, but it also alerts us to the ways in which countries have varied in this process. First, the countries varied in the proportions of women who ever married, represented by the heights of the curves at their termination at the right of the figure. The proportion ever-married at about age fifty ranged from virtually 100% in Taiwan to between 80–90% in the Netherlands. Second, the countries varied in the age at which nuptiality began and peaked. The steepest part of the curve was earliest for Taiwan and latest for the Netherlands. Finally, countries differed in the speed with which marriage spread though the nubile population. That is, the steepness of the curve varied, again from a very rapid pace in Taiwan and Hungary to a slower pace in the Netherlands.

Current Variations among Less-Developed Countries

Table 8-2 on the following page presents data about the timing of marriage in selected less-developed countries. Not all countries of the world have enough information even for estimates. From among those countries that do, only a few have been chosen to represent each of the world's subregions. Generally, we have included the country with the second youngest marriage pattern and the country with the second oldest for women in the subregion; therefore, the countries in the table demonstrate not only the variety *among* less-developed regions when it comes to age at marriage, but also the variety *within* subregions.

The table uses two measures. Column 3 shows the proportion of women aged fifteen through nineteen in a marital union. This measure reflects the prevalence of very early marriage among women.

The other measure is the **singulate mean age at marriage**, computed separately for men and women. The first step in computing one of these means is to array the five-year age categories from fifteen through forty-nine sequentially, and to tabulate the percentage single for each category. The data usually come from a census, sometimes from a survey. We interpret the array of percentages as though it were the history of a hypothetical cohort. Then we estimate what the mean age at marriage must be for a cohort that left such a trail. The computation methodology is beyond the scope of an introductory text, but readers may remember this general line of thinking from both our treatment of life expectancy in chapter 5 and the total fertility rate in chapter 6.

The age of marriage has increased globally over time, from a singulate mean age of twenty-two to twenty-nine in developed countries, from age twenty-two to twenty-four in developing countries, and from age eighteen to twenty-one in the least developed countries since 1970 (United Nations, 2011). Age at marriage is an important indicator generally of female autonomy and often indicative of the age at childbearing in any given society. One can make several preliminary generalizations from Table 8-2. In all the countries, men normally marry later than women. In most countries this age difference is roughly between two and five years of age, with some exceptions such as in Guyana and Niger where gender differences are even greater. There usually is less variation among the countries with respect to male average age at marriage than with respect to women's average age at marriage. For example, women's age at marriage varies from seventeen all the way to thirty-three. Therefore, the age gap between the husband and the wife at marriage tends to be greatest where female marriage is earliest, such as the case in Niger. But no single table can fully capture the LDR variety in marital patterns. What follows, therefore, is a region-by-region summary of the timing of marriage and trends in that timing.

Africa.   In Africa, proportions of people of reproductive ages who are married vary considerably, ranging from only 30% in South Africa where cohabitation is common to 67% in Nigeria, where cohabitation is relatively uncommon (The World Family Map, 2013; Rashad et al., 2005; Westoff, 2003). Alternative unions are more common in some African countries. In Botswana and Namibia, for example, many women are in *stable childbearing relationships* that do not involve either marriage or regular cohabitation. These alternatives to marriage confound the measurement of marriage patterns by simple indicators such as the percentage ever marrying or singulate mean

Table 8-2   Estimated Age at Marriage, Selected Countries from LDRs

| Region and Country | Singulate Mean Age at Marriage | | % Females Married Ages 15–19 |
	Male (1)	Female (2)	(3)
Africa			
North			
Morocco	31.2	26.4	11.1
Algeria	33.0	29.5	1.8
South			
Lesotho	27.3	22.5	17.9
Namibia	30.2	28.3	5.4
East			
Malawi	23.6	19.0	36.2
Djibouti	30.8	27.7	5.3
Niger	25.1	17.6	60.7
Ghana	26.6	22.4	13.7
Middle			
Chad	24.5	18.3	45.3
Gabon	26.2	22.1	22.4
Asia			
East			
Mainland China	25.1	23.3	1.2
Hong Kong	32.8	30.3	0.4
West			
Yemen	25.4	22.2	17.2
Lebanon	31.4	27.4	5.3
Southeast			
Laos	24.7	21.7	19.8
Singapore	30.1	26.9	0.6
South Central			
Nepal	22.4	19.4	32.3
Sri Lanka	27.6	23.8	10.8
Latin America			
Caribbean			
Cuba	25.3	21.1	23.1
Jamaica	34.8	33.2	0.5
South			
Guyana	26.5	19.6	21.6
Chile	27.7	24.6	8.7
Central			
Nicaragua	24.4	20.6	28.4
Costa Rica	27.6	24.1	10.8

Source: United Nations, 2011. *World Fertility Report: 2009*. Used with permission.

ages of marriage. They also have led to very different estimates of the proportion of women in a union, depending on whether survey questions ask whether women are "married," "living with a man," or have a "partner." Although the second demographic transition trends occurring in many MDRs are sometimes described as a unique facet of modernization, it is notable that some specific SDT trends, such as alternative unions to marriage, have long been common in various LDR countries.

Even for women who are married, there are considerable variations in the types of marriage across Africa. In specific regions marriage is sometimes polygamous. **Polygamy** means a marriage that includes more than two partners. Where the multiple partners are women, it is called **polygyny** and where the partners are male it is called **polyandry**. While both are rare today, the former is more common than the latter. Generally, polygyny occurs among older generations and is less prevalent among the urban and more highly educated (Westoff, 2003). As an example, almost half of married women age fifty or greater in Burkina Faso and Cameroon are in polygynous unions.

The timing of first marriage is generally early in Africa but varies widely. In sub-Saharan Africa marriage occurs at younger ages than in Northern Africa, although Table 8-2 demonstrates the great range in the sub-Saharan region, with women in Chad marrying at age 18 compared to Namibian women who marry on average at age 28. Sub-Saharan countries where polygyny is more prevalent also tend to have higher percentages of women married before age twenty. For example, 61% of women aged fifteen to nineteen in sub-Saharan Niger are married, as are 45% of such women in Chad. In contrast, few young women in Northern Africa and the Near East marry now as teenagers. Today only 2% of women under twenty in Algeria marry.

Differences in the timing of marriage across regions of Africa have grown larger over the past four decades as later marriage ages in Arab countries have increased differences between Northern and sub-Saharan Africa. Age at first marriage has risen in every Arab country since the 1970s.

Asia. Regions of Asia also vary dramatically in the timing of first marriage for women. At one extreme, women in most countries of South Central Asia (e.g., the Indian subcontinent) marry very early. At the other extreme, marriage patterns in most countries of East Asia (e.g., Japan, South Korea, Taiwan, Singapore, and Hong Kong) are more similar to those of Europe in terms of late average age at marriage, with only a small proportion of women marrying early. Between these extremes are the countries of Southeast Asia and West Asia.

The rising age of marriage in Arab countries also has increased differences among countries within West Asia. The percentage of women aged fifteen to nineteen who are married has declined in some West Asian Arab countries as it has in many Arab countries of Northern Africa. Only 5% of women ages fifteen to nineteen are married in Lebanon, for example, while 17% of this age group is married in nearby Yemen.

Although Asian women vary regionally in terms of the timing of their first marriages, as can be seen in Table 8-2, most of them eventually do marry. Among the Central, South, and Southeast Asian countries covered by the Demographic and Health Surveys (DHS), the proportions still single at age forty-five through forty-nine are universally low. The highest reported was 6.1% for Cambodia in 2010; the lowest, 0.2% for Bangladesh in 2011 (ICF International, 2012). Cohabitation is uncommon in most of

Asia (The World Family Map, 2013) except for in Japan. There, premarital cohabitation among younger generations is now almost as widespread as in the United States and Europe (Lesthaeghe, 2010).

Consanguineous marriage, or marriage between blood relatives, is respected and sometimes preferred in many communities across North Africa, the Middle East, and West Asia. Intrafamilial unions account for 20–50% or more of marriages in these regions with the most common being marriage among first cousins. In countries like Sudan and Syria, an estimated 50% of marriages occur between first cousins and other relatives (Hamamy et al., 2011). Consanguineous marriage further illustrates the variability of cultural marriage patterns throughout the world and is of interest to demographers because of possible biological impacts on mortality and fertility.

Latin America. There are two conventional types of sexual unions coexisting side by side in many Latin American countries: marriage, which has legal or religious sanction, and consensual unions, which differ in their cultural meaning from region to region. Unlike the stable unions without cohabitation in Botswana and Namibia (discussed earlier), consensual unions in Latin America most often involve cohabitation. Cohabitation is most common in Latin American countries (The World Family Map, 2013).

Table 8-2 indicates that age at marriage in Latin America varies widely, as in Asia. Obviously, this is only part of the picture. In many Latin American countries the proportion of women cohabiting is greater than those marrying, especially at younger ages. And fertility rates for women aged fifteen through nineteen are high enough to suggest marriage data alone undercount stable sexual unions. In the Dominican Republic, for example, only 0.8% of women aged fifteen to nineteen are married, but quite a bit more in that age range are cohabiting (ICF International, 2012). Cohabitation ranges from about 12% of all women of reproductive ages in Chile to 39% in Colombia.

International contrasts illustrated. The previous summaries make the point that marital patterns vary immensely, not only among less-developed regions but also within regions. To dramatize these cultural contrasts, Figure 8-3 gives extreme examples of three different marriage patterns, selected from the countries of Africa and Latin America.

The first graph illustrates the pattern of polygyny in one African country, Burkina Faso. Each bar of the graph shows the percentages of married women at a given age by the type of marital union, monogamous and polygynous (cohabitation remains rare). Polygyny involves approximately two out of every ten married women over age thirty. Polygynous marriages are more common among older generations, indicating the declining practice of polygyny in more recent marriages.

The second graph shows another African country, Cameroon. Unlike Burkina Faso, however, cohabitation in Cameroon has become fairly common. The graph shows that marital polygynous and monogamous unions have declined in younger age groups, with cohabiting unions emerging in their place. The number of cohabiting adolescent women was double that of cohabiting women aged thirty to thirty-four. As ages at marriage begin to rise in the less-developed world, informal unions are beginning to emerge, most often as a precursor to marriage, just as they have in MDRs. Cameroon is

Figure 8-3

Type of Marital Union in Three Countries

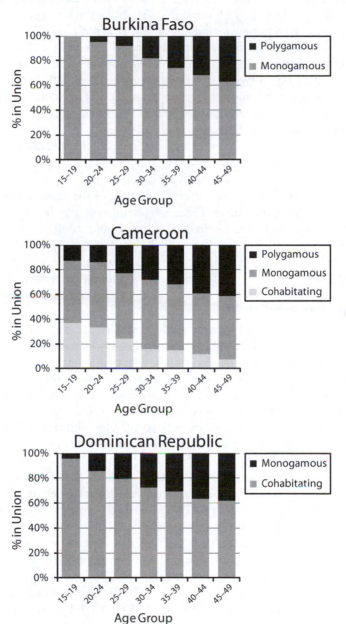

Source: Data from ICF International, 2012. *Demographic and Health Surveys.* Graphs created by Eiko Strader.

an unusual example of more modern forms of unions (cohabitation) coexisting along-side very traditional unions (polygynous marriage).

In a few LDRs, cohabitation is more prevalent than in MDRs. Informal unions both as an alternative and a forerunner to traditional marital unions characterize some Latin American countries, including Bolivia, Brazil, Colombia, Paraguay, and Peru, as well as those in the Caribbean. Unions among women of the Dominican Republic, for example, are shown in the third graph of Figure 8-3. At every age, cohabitation is the predominating union type. As in most countries, it is still most common among the youngest generations, involving more than 90% of all adolescent women living in unions. In this case, it makes more sense to consider married and cohabiting women together in studying the formation of sexual unions.

These three unusual cases serve to remind us of the variation in marriage practices and patterns throughout the world. The nature of sexual unions and the age pattern of different types of unions vary widely across countries.

At the same time, we should not lose sight of the common features of marriage across countries and cultures. Three are worth remembering: (1) Most people in general are in heterosexual stable marital/sexual unions; (2) there are worldwide similarities in the general form of the cumulative marriage distribution; and (3) where marriage behaviors have begun to undergo change, recent trends are in the direction of cohabitation, rising age of marriage, and declining universality of marriage.

Europe, Past and Present

As we have done with fertility and mortality, we might reasonably ask how the marriage patterns and trends of currently less-developed countries compare with the historical marriage patterns of Europe. Were rising marriage ages and declining universality of marriage features of historical modernization and demographic transitions in the presently more-developed countries? If so, are there changes in marriage we might expect to accompany demographic transitions that are now underway throughout much of the less-developed world? What did mid-transition European censuses of, say, 1870 through 1900 find with respect to the timing and universality of first marriage?

In Europe, too, there were regional variations. Scholars consistently observed a geo-historical split between Northwestern and Eastern Europe, the dividing line running roughly from Leningrad to Trieste (Hajnal, 1965, p. 101). Historically, scholars characterized Northwestern Europe as less family centric, where more women remained unmarried throughout their lives, and those who did marry did so later (Thornton and Philipov, 2009; Sovič, 2008; Thornton, 2005; Anderson, 1995). In this region, the average age of women at first marriage must have been about twenty-four years or older. In most of these countries, 10 to 20% of women aged forty-five through forty-nine were never-married (Hajnal, 1965, p. 102). By contrast, in Eastern Europe more women married and more married earlier. Central Europe was characterized by intermediary family and marriage patterns somewhere between the Northwestern and Eastern European patterns (Thornton and Philipov, 2009). Although statements about times prior to the mid-1800s have to rely on considerably more scanty and heterogeneous information plumbed by the various techniques of historical demography, the birth and spread of this unique marriage pattern can be traced back as far as the 17th century in the general European population.

Regional divergence in Europe peaked around the end of the 19th century and then began to converge. This was due largely to the retreat by Northwestern European countries from their unique pattern of late marriage, especially during the "marriage boom" that followed World War II (Hajnal, 1953; Watkins, 1981). Between 1950 and 1970 the average age at first marriage for both women and men continued downward in almost all the countries of Europe.

But starting in the last part of the 20th century, the Northwestern European marriage boom became a bust. Since the 1970s and along with the decline of Communism in the East, the second demographic transition spread rapidly throughout Europe. Women's age at marriage and never-marrying rates increased, but unlike in centuries past, cohabitation is now prevalent. However, remnants of the regional variation of the past, namely in differences between Eastern and Northwestern Europe, persist.

Table 8-3 presents some typical cases from the current European scene. Comparing regions of Europe, the singulate mean age at marriage for women is still somewhat younger in the East than in other parts of Europe, though it ranges greatly across countries (from 21.9 for women in the Republic of Moldova to 29.7 for Hungarian women, for example). In addition, the percentage married at young ages is considerably higher in some countries of the East, such as in Bulgaria where more than 10% of women ages fifteen to nineteen are currently married or have ever been married. The percentage of older women never married in the East is still much lower than in other regions. Trends toward later and less universal marriage do not suggest, of course, that the young in Europe have been avoiding sexual unions. The average age at sexual initiation in Europe is seventeen and cohabitation has increased within many of these

Table 8-3   Marital Trends, Selected European Countries

Region, Country, and Survey Year	Singulate Mean Age at Marriage		Percent Ever Married Ages 15–19		Percent Never Married Age 45 and Over	
	Male	Female	Male	Female	Male	Female
Europe						
North						
Norway 2007	34.0	31.9	0.0	0.2	24.9	17.6
Sweden 2006	34.3	32.2	0.1	0.4	33.6	25.3
West						
Luxembourg 2001	30.6	27.8	0.3	1.4	11.1	8.2
France 2006	33.4	31.6	0.0	0.2	22.1	16.7
East						
Bulgaria 2001	27.5	24.2	2.0	10.0	8.2	3.4
Hungary 2007	32.0	29.7	0.1	0.7	15.1	6.4
South						
Italy 2006	33.3	30.0	0.0	0.6	15.4	11.6
Spain 2001	31.6	29.3	0.4	1.2	13.0	10.2

Source: United Nations, 2011. *World Fertility Report: 2009.* Used with permission.

countries as marriage has been pushed back to later ages or foregone altogether (The World Family Map, 2013; Santelli and Schalet, 2009; Kiernan, 2001; Festy, 1980). Most Europeans who cohabit eventually marry, although not always before childbearing (Sobotka, 2008).

Not surprisingly, as young European adults spend more of their lifetimes unmarried, or in some cases all of their lives, childbearing has become less tied to marriage than it once was. Until recently, **nonmarital births** were commonly referred to as "illegitimate" births. This change in terminology reflects both the increasing occurrence of nonmarital births in many MDRs as well as their growing social acceptance. Births occurring outside of marriage in various European countries between 1960 and 2011 are shown in Figure 8-4. While there is wide variation in current levels of nonmarital fertility, the overall proportion of nonmarital births has risen consistently across all of the countries over the last fifty years. In 1960, nonmarital childbearing comprised 10% or less of births in most of these countries. By 2010, nonmarital childbearing had risen substantially, becoming the most common birth context for a third of the countries shown. Generally, European countries with higher nonmarital fertility rates also have higher overall TFRs (Eurostat, 2013).

Even though nonmarital births are commonly assumed to take place in a single-parent setting, this is not the case in many European countries. In countries where nonmarital childbearing has become common, most occur within cohabiting partner-

Figure 8-4

Births Outside Marriage in Selected European Countries, 1960–2011

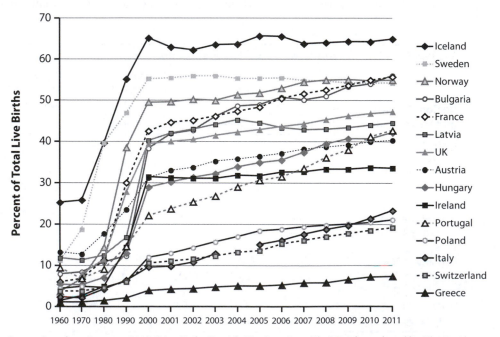

Source: Data from Eurostat, 2013. "Live Births Outside Marriage Data File." Graph produced by Eiko Strader.

ships. The vast majority of babies born outside of marriage in Sweden, for example, are to parents who live together (Sobotka, 2002, 2008).

When it comes to nonmarital childbearing, rates are increasing in all European countries. Generalized regional patterns can be discerned in Figure 8-4, although with plenty of exceptions. Northern European countries tend to have the highest proportion of births outside of marriage. Indeed Norway, Sweden, and Iceland fall beyond the 50% mark in the figure, although Bulgaria and France joined the ranks in the past five years or so. Western and Eastern European countries are clustered below those of their northern neighbors in nonmarital childbearing, but at still more than one-third of all births. Southern European countries generally have the lowest incidence of nonmarital childbearing in Europe, with Greece at only 7% for example. Switzerland and Poland also fall on the lower side, along with Italy, with about 20% nonmarital fertility. Although it is debated whether all European nonmarital fertility trends will eventually converge to the higher rates seen in the figure (Lesthaeghe and Surkyn, 2006), regional variation has generally been explained by differences in cultures and public policies. The role of organized religion is stronger in Southern Europe than in many other European countries and gender roles continue to be more conservative there. Young southern Europeans commonly live at home with their parents well into adulthood instead of moving out on their own before marriage. Many Northern and Western European governments provide universal family benefits such as child care, per-child allowances, and part-time work policies that enable parents of all marital statuses to balance employment and parenting; in Southern Europe, government-provided family benefits and family-friendly policies are more limited. The irony, as some have pointed out (Dalla Zuanna, 2001), is that traditional family cultures in Southern Europe are leading to among the lowest overall fertility levels in Europe.

The United States, Past and Present

Regarding timing of first marriage in the United States, we have census figures starting in 1890 but have to make an educated guess about prior times. As of then, the median age at first marriage was 26.1 years for men and 22.0 years for women. That would imply that U.S. women were marrying about two years earlier than their Western European contemporaries. Since U.S. age at marriage declined for decades after 1890, it is tempting to suppose that it also declined before 1890, but fragmentary data do not confirm such a prior trend (Davis, 1972). The safest guess is that there had not been much variation from the 1890 level in prior decades (Monahan, 1951).

Figure 8-5 shows men's and women's median ages at first marriage, estimated from historical censuses and the Current Population Survey through 2010. Before we discuss the rising and falling age of marriage over the past century, note one consistent trend: The age difference between husbands and wives has shrunk steadily over the century. In 1890 husbands were on average more than four years older than their wives; by 2010 they were only 2.1 years older. Other trends in age at first marriage have been anything but consistent over the century. In general, we can see that the long time span of Figure 8-5 is best broken in the middle, after World War II, and that trends vary considerably before and after that war.

From 1890 to the 1950s, the overall trend in the United States was toward earlier marriage. That trend was strongest up to 1920. In the 1920s and 1930s, through the

Depression years, marital age leveled off for men and even rose slightly for women. By 1940, the stage was set for even more dramatic changes.

Just as Europe experienced a marriage boom early in the optimistic postwar years, so too did the United States. The female median age at first marriage dropped from 21.5 in 1940 to an estimate of 20.3 in 1950; the male drop was even more extreme, from 24.3 in 1940 to 22.8 years in 1950. Not only did the average age at first marriage plummet, but also most marriages tended to cluster around those averages; variation diminished. Early marriage appeared to be in fashion.

Then, just as dramatic as the prewar decline in age at marriage, came its reversal after 1960. Figure 8-5 shows resurgent median age at first marriage for men and women since the 1960s. Since 1960, the median age at first marriage has gone up by more than five years for men and women to the highest level ever recorded for the U.S. population.

At this point perhaps we should take a lesson from the variety of sexual unions we have documented worldwide. The recent trend toward later marriage should be interpreted in the context of increasing cohabitation and stable sexual unions in the absence of marriage; otherwise, one gets an exaggerated picture of the degree to which young adults are delaying setting up sexual unions. Women who cohabit are also more likely to marry and to begin childbearing than those who do not (Musick, 2007; Brien et al., 1999).

Tracking such nontraditional unions can pose methodological problems. Even though cohabitation became both more common and more acceptable in the 1970s, the U.S. Census Bureau and American Community Survey did not collect data on it until the 1990s. The census now includes a category for unmarried partners, as differentiated from housemates or roommates.

Figure 8-5

Estimated Median Age at First Marriage for U.S. Men and Women, 1890–2010

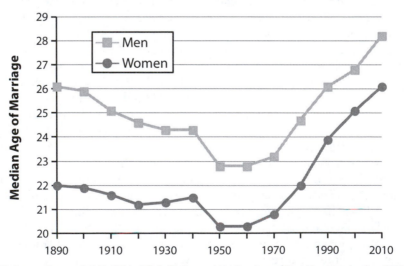

Source: U.S. Census Bureau, 2012b. Table MS-2, "Estimated Median Age of First Marriage, by Sex: 1890 to the Present." Graph created by Eiko Strader.

The changing nature of couple householding can be seen in Figure 8-6. In this graph the percentage of households that included a married couple declined from over 75% of all households in 1940 to just below half of all households in 2010. Figure 8-6 graphs the rise in households with other forms of families and nonfamilies during this same period. The percentage living as single parents has more than doubled since 1940. Single-parent households are most often headed by mothers (Lofquist et al., 2012). These households are emerging both from divorce and nonmarital childbearing in the United States.

Cohabiting couple households have also increased significantly, although household distinctions used in the census measurements shown in Figure 8-6 are not straightforward. Cohabiting couples with a child are counted in the "other family" category. In the past, this category also comprised more extended family arrangements than cohabiting arrangements. Unmarried couples without children are counted in the "other nonfamily" category, and this type of household has tripled over the period shown. Given that we know that cohabitation has become common, you might be surprised by how small the "other family" and "other nonfamily" percentages are in this figure. This is mainly about measurement. Compared to marriage, cohabitation trends in the United States are more transitory, often ending quickly in either union dissolution or marriage. As a result, even though most young adults in the United States have cohabited in their lives (and 40% of children have lived in a cohabiting union), actual

Figure 8-6

Household Types, United States, 1940–2010

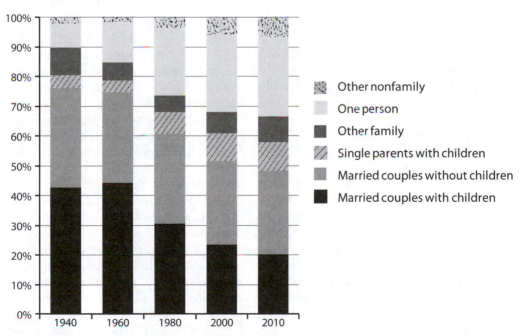

Source: U.S. Census Bureau, 2012a. "Data on Families and Living Arrangements." Graph created by Eiko Strader.

numbers of individuals cohabiting at any given year are small (Lofquist et al., 2012; Kennedy and Bumpass, 2008).

Another notable change in household structure is the emergence of people living alone, which has quadrupled since 1940. This trend is due not only to people living single for longer periods in young adult life, but also due to the significant increase in the number of people ages sixty-five and older living on their own. Studies have shown that improved health and financial conditions of elders may have contributed to this increase, with single or widowed elderly now less dependent on other family members (Jacobsen et al., 2012).

Figure 8-6 does not distinguish how cohabitation breaks down into same-sex couple householding. Current measures show that 1% of all households are comprised of same-sex couples (Lofquist, 2011; Simmons and O'Connell, 2003), although there are well-known underreporting and mismeasurement problems with this category (Lofquist et al., 2012).

Not all segments of the population are equally likely to live together unmarried. People without a college degree are now twice as likely as the college educated to co-reside in an unmarried household, a pattern in keeping with decreasing marriage rates among this group (Fry and Cohn, 2011). Cohabitation is not only less common among more educated Americans, but it is coming to serve different purposes for different social classes. Most college-educated Americans cohabit as a precursor to marriage; but they still tend to marry before having children. Non-college educated Americans are much more likely to have children in cohabiting unions. Given that such cohabiting unions tend to be less financially secure and, perhaps as a result, are more likely to dissolve than marriages, there is growing American inequality among children born in each type of household (Cherlin, 2010a).

As married-couple households have declined in the United States, a tremendous variety of householding arrangements are replacing these traditional households and the child-rearing role they have fulfilled in the past. Cohabitation is but one adaptation. Although Figure 8-6 showed the remarkable increase over time in people living alone, as young adults wait longer to marry, they are now living with their parents longer and returning more frequently to their parents' home after attending college. This is particularly true following the Great Recession of 2007–2009 (Mykyta and Macartney, 2012). Of American families that live in *multifamily households*, the majority are comprised of adult children living with the householder. A much smaller proportion consists of parents or grandchildren of the householder.

Increasing proportions of nonmarital births are shown by the darker shading in Figure 8-7. In 1943, such births comprised only a small percentage of all births (about 3%) but by the end of the century nonmarital births had become a sizeable minority, rising to 36% of all births (Shattuck and Kreider, 2013). Although nonmarital fertility in the United States is still not as high as that in a number of European countries (see Figure 8-4), what sets it apart is how many more U.S. nonmarital births take place in single-parent households rather than in cohabiting unions. About half of nonmarital births in the United States are to single parents (Mather and Lavery, 2010; Chandra et al., 2005).

The increase of U.S. nonmarital fertility shown in Figure 8-7 is attributable to changing marital norms. As increasing numbers of individuals delay marriage to older ages and, to a lesser extent, do not marry at all, the likelihood that births will take place

Figure 8-7

Numbers of Total Births and Nonmarital Births to American Women, 1943–2010

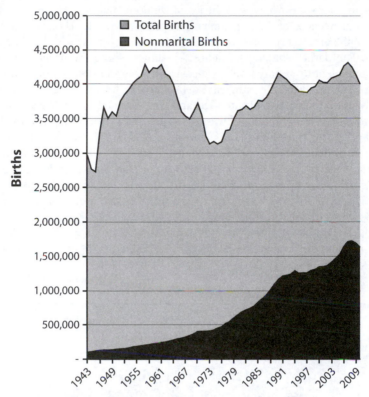

Sources: NCHS, 2000. "Vital Statistics of the United States, 2000: Volume I, Natality," data from table 1-17. For years 2001 to 2010, CDC, 2010. "Birth Tables by Characteristics of Mothers." Graph produced by Eiko Strader.

outside of marriage rises. This is due in part to accidental pregnancies that are no longer being "legitimated" by normative expectations of marriage. In the past, the majority of premarital pregnancies resulted in "shotgun marriages," but today such hastily arranged unions are much less common than they once were (Cherlin, 2010a; Musick, 2007; Bachu, 1999b; Akerlof et al., 1996).

In addition, some women are simply less willing to put off childbearing as long as they might have to wait to find a marriageable partner. A recent survey shows that younger generations may value parenthood more highly than marriage (Wang and Taylor, 2011). This is helped by the fact that women no longer must rely on a husband for financial resources in order to raise a family. Nevertheless, mothers still experience a motherhood penalty in pay, whereas fathers benefit from a wage premium in many countries depending on the cultural and policy contexts (Killewald and Gough, 2013; Budig et al., 2010; Hodges and Budig, 2010). This effect of marriage and childbearing on wages varies across education levels. For example, women's increased economic autonomy in the face of men's declining earnings in the non-college labor market makes marriage simply less advantageous for less educated people (Cherlin, 2010b). Thus, as we noted earlier, there is growing social class inequality in this respect.

These trends are all part of the second demographic transition (SDT). Just as the SDT is moving across European countries at different paces, there is also variation *within* countries. Because of the size and cultural diversity of the U.S., we might expect to find some of the greatest regional variation there and, in fact, we do (Lesthaeghe and Neidert, 2006). The darker shading in Figure 8-8 shows where the American SDT has become most prevalent by county level, as measured in standard deviations from the U.S. mean. These SDT trends, such as marital delay, fertility postponement, and cohabitation, are clearly most common in urban areas and concentrated in the Northeast, the West Coast, and in some areas of the Southwest. As evidenced by the areas with the lightest shading, they are least common in the South and Midwest. Utah stands out as the state with the lowest prevalence of SDT indicators, most likely due to its large Mormon population.

Incidentally, these spatial SDT indicators also map onto ideational and economic trends that vary by region in the United States. Demographers have noticed that the areas with the strongest SDT trends are those where individuals are more highly educated, with greater disposable incomes, and where labor is more unionized (Michigan Population Studies Center, 2013). They have also noted a U.S. political correlation to SDT measures in recent decades, with lower SDT localities more likely to vote Repub-

Figure 8-8

Map of the Overall "Second Demographic Transition" Factor (SDT) in the U.S. by County

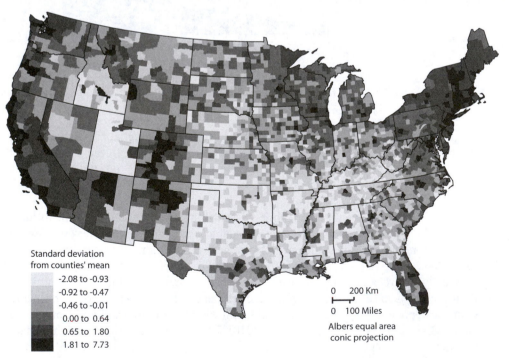

Standard deviation
from counties' mean

-2.08 to -0.93
-0.92 to -0.47
-0.46 to -0.01
0.00 to 0.64
0.65 to 1.80
1.81 to 7.73

0   200 Km

0   100 Miles

Albers equal area
conic projection

Source: Adapted from Neidert and Lesthaeghe, 2014.

lican and higher SDT localities more likely to vote Democrat. The rise in single-parent households, together with increases in unmarried partner unions and people living alone, is challenging the idea of one "normal" type of household in the United States. This has been cited with alarm by the popular media as evidence for the demise of marriage, making the institution obsolete (Popenoe and Whitehead, 1999; Elliott et al., 2012). This is only a somewhat accurate characterization and only then if our baseline for comparison is the 1950s and 1960s. This era is a common comparison reference point but the trends during this era are statistically anomalous when considered within the larger context of American demographic history (Elliott et al., 2012; Coontz, 2000). Marriage is still quite common in the United States, and has always been historically higher than in most of Europe. Recent changes in marriage primarily reflect "decline" only in that marriage is occurring later in the life course, but *eventual* marriage remains an almost universal stable form of sexual union within the United States.

How do demographers measure the eventuality of marriage? Conventionally, they do so by the percentage of men or women age forty-five and older who have ever married. From the late 1800s through most of 20th century it has hovered around 90%. Today's forty-five and older adults are just as likely to be married as your great, great grandparents were at the same age.

What will happen in the future to universality of marriage is anybody's guess. One thing we do know is that current marriage rates are at an all-time low, with only about half of American adults currently married. Is this evidence for marriage delayed or marriage foregone? That is, will those young men and women now putting off marriage end up opting out of it entirely? The popular media has pointed a finger at the recession of 2007–2009; however, demographers note that annualized marriage rates began declining long before the recession due to rising ages at marriage (Grusky et al., 2011; Cohn, 2010). We will have to wait for today's twenty and thirty-year-olds to age beyond forty-five in order to tell. Has the "need" to marry fallen as fertility has declined and the economic independence of women has risen? Will those delaying marriage eventually revert to the traditional U.S. pattern of almost universal marriage? Or will the dividing line between married and cohabiting unions become so unimportant, as it has in some European countries, that we will begin to think of households simply in terms of unions and non-unions?

Marital Dissolution Trends in the United States

Let us look back at Figure 8-1 to remind ourselves of the processes involved in marital dissolution. The population at risk of marital dissolution is the currently married population only. Current marriages can dissolve through either of two events, death of a spouse (thrusting the surviving spouse into widowed status) or divorce (thrusting both spouses into the divorced status). In either case, individuals can reenter the marriage market and change those statuses by remarriage, thus reentering the currently married population and again being at risk of marital dissolution.

By implication, there are demographic limits on the number of marital dissolutions. How many divorces or widowings occur depends on how many people get married in the first place. The number of divorced or widowed people depends not only on the rates

Box
8-1

The Marriage Market in the United States

Demographers sometimes refer to the composition of the marriageable population as a **marriage market**. Try to imagine such a market. For heterosexual marriages, it contains all the women and men who, at a given time and place, are eligible as mates for each other. This is similar to a dating market except perhaps more selective since the stakes are higher. Each sex in the market has its own population composition with respect to traits that make them more or less eligible and desirable as marriage partners for others. For one thing, both female and male components have age structures. Moreover, each society has its own rules of **endogamy** with respect to characteristics beyond age, which often include such traits as kinship, religion, race and ethnic identity, and socioeconomic status.

We can say that a marriage market is *efficient* to the degree that individual women and men have an easy time finding mates with acceptable combinations of marriage-significant traits. Efficient markets, on the aggregate level, tend to be ones where there is minimal delay in finding mates and thus—everything else being equal—potentially earlier marriage.

Efficiency can be enhanced in several ways. The market can increase in size through a breakdown of localism, greater mobility of population, and easier communication or transportation. All of these broaden one's options, effectively increasing the size of one's pool of eligible mates. The size of the pool of potential mates also can be increased by high divorce rates, thus inserting divorced persons back into the market. Beyond that, the pool can be increased by relaxing **exogamy** limitations: for instance, increasing intermarriage across racial, ethnic, religious, or socioeconomic lines. Something also can happen to equalize in a category the number of men and women who are eligible to each other.

Until the mid-20th century, most married couples met through family; today the most common way of meeting is through friends, followed by bars and online contexts (Rosenfeld and Thomas, 2012). Potential partners no longer are confined to their family and neighborhood social network, but have become increasingly free to roam the country—or surf online dating sites—to find partners. Increasing proportions of young people are clustering in those local dating markets we call colleges and universities, which account for the fifth most common way that American married couples meet (just after the workplace setting). Divorces and the number of individuals not currently married have risen, also increasing the marriage market. Religious, racial, and ethnic exclusiveness have also declined, allowing greater intermarriage across those lines.

The efficiency of marriage markets can be limited in various ways, something that demographers refer to as a **marriage squeeze**. Most societies have cultural norms regarding the relative ages of husbands and wives, with husbands being generally a few years older than wives. Since another feature of societies experiencing transition or change is a population pyramid with age-specific bulges and busts (see chapter 4), the combined result of these two features can be a chronic age-related marriage squeeze in the heterosexual market. For every bulge moving up the population pyramid, the female component will hit its prime marriage ages before the males do; when that male bulge hits its prime ages, women a few years younger may be in a bust. Heterosexual marriage squeezes are also caused by trends that disproportionately affect the population size of one sex over another even within the same age range. A historical example: World War II resulted in significant losses to the young male population in many countries, which impacted subsequent marriage and fertility patterns (Bethmann and Kvasnicka, 2013). A future example: ongoing sex selective practices that favor male babies are projected to lead to a 50% surplus of Chinese and Indian bachelors by mid-century (Guilmoto, 2012).

of spouse death and of divorce, but also on the mortality rates for widowed and divorced former spouses. More forcefully, the number of former spouses divorced and left widowed at a given moment depends on the rates of marriage, including remarriage.

Although there are some obvious similarities between widowhood and divorce, there also are some important differences. Both create unmarried spouses, but divorce creates two, whereas spouse mortality creates one. Widowhood happens later in life on the average than does divorce. Among first marriages, the median age at divorce is thirty-three to thirty-five whereas the median age at widowhood is over sixty (James and Shafer, 2012). Divorced individuals remarry more quickly than widowers. The cause of widowhood is involuntary, whereas the cause of divorce is voluntary, although that distinction may not be as clear-cut as it sounds. Partially because of the differing age patterns of incidence, the number and ages of the children left in the household with only one parent at a time varies from widowhood to divorce.

Modernization has considerably changed the relative roles of widowhood and divorce in the marital dissolution process. We have chosen the United States as a dramatic example. There are several reasons for this choice. One is that the United States presents an extreme case of high divorce along with relatively low spouse mortality. Looking at one country alone also avoids the difficulties of noncomparable definitions of divorce, separation, annulment, and so on, which bedevil international comparisons. Furthermore, partially because of U.S. concern over its rising divorce rate, this country has kept relatively good statistics over a long period of time.

Widowhood in the United States

Let us start with a description of the present situation in the United States. Table 8-4 shows the percentage of persons widowed in 2012, by sex, for all adult age classes. It presents the same information for the divorced, both for contrast and for future reference.

The difference between the patterns for widowhood and divorce is dramatic. Widowhood is overwhelmingly a female phenomenon. In the fifteen-and-over population, there are almost four times as many widows as widowers, and sizable differentials in that direction hold true in every age category. For fifteen-and-over women the prevalence of widowhood is only slightly less than that of divorce, while widowhood is far less common than divorce for men.

If widowhood and divorce are both so common for adult women, why do we carry around the idea that divorce is the major cause of marital dissolution? One explanation probably has to do with the age patterns of widowhood and divorce. After retirement ages, widowhood—and especially female widowhood—rises to considerable proportions; being divorced, on the other hand, is more evenly spread over the age distribution, peaking somewhat in the middle ages. Why would this age differential affect our consciousness of divorce relative to widowhood? A likely reason is that marriages ended by divorce are much more likely to involve parents of still-dependent children than are marriages broken by widowhood, at least in modern times. Societal concern over the well-being of these children tend to focus the spotlight on divorce.

Which historical demographic changes have produced this age and sex pattern of widowhood? As the life expectancy of everyone in the United States went up, so did the average age of the dying spouse and that of the surviving mate at the time of that death. This in itself was the major factor in pushing widowhood back to the senior years.

Table 8-4   Percentage Widowed and Divorced by Sex and Age, United States, 2012

	Widowed		Divorced	
Age	Male	Female	Male	Female
15–17 years	0.0	0.0	0.1	0.1
18–19 years	0.1	0.3	0.3	0.3
20–24 years	0.1	0.2	0.6	1.1
25–29 years	0.1	0.3	2.9	4.4
30–34 years	0.1	0.3	6.0	8.1
35–39 years	0.4	0.8	9.0	11.5
40–44 years	0.3	1.4	11.8	13.9
45–49 years	0.8	2.2	13.8	16.2
50–54 years	1.2	4.1	15.0	17.7
55–64 years	2.5	8.2	15.6	18.1
65–74 years	6.3	21.9	11.6	15.6
75–84 years	13.9	46.1	6.9	9.3
85 and Over	36.3	73.0	3.4	4.8
15 and Over	2.4	8.8	8.9	11.1

Source: U.S. Census Bureau, 2012a. "Data on Families and Living Arrangements 2012," Table A1.

Another aspect of the mortality decline would be, of course, the remaining life expectancy due the surviving spouse. The direction of change in this factor, however, is not quite so clear. Although remaining life expectancy at every age was going up, the death of the spouse also was occurring later in the surviving spouse's life.

Another historical demographic trend to take into account is the sex difference in mortality declines. For most of the mortality transition, male longevity did not improve as rapidly as did female, and thus female widowhood did not decrease as rapidly as did male. The present extreme imbalance between male and female widowhood is a generally modern phenomenon. These differences have, however, declined in recent decades as the gap between male and female longevity has narrowed (see chapter 5).

The net results of demographic changes in developed countries like the United States have been an overall decline in the prevalence of widowhood and telescoping of widowhood to the elderly population, especially the female elderly. For elderly women, the decline in the proportion widowed has been minor at best, and we should be reminded that the segment of our total population that is growing most rapidly is the elderly. Issues raised by widowhood, therefore, are not about to go away.

Divorce in the United States

Figure 8-9 traces the U.S. annual crude divorce rates from 1920 to 2011. This rate measures the annual number of divorces in the numerator divided by the total U.S. population in the denominator. It is a crude rate because the denominator ignores who is married and thus at risk of divorce. Crude divorce rates experienced a relatively steady, but slow, increase for more than a half century leading up to 1920 (Cherlin, 1981). The overall trend since 1920 also is clearly upward, dramatically so. But within that upward trend there have been sharp fluctuations, lasting from a year or so to

Figure 8-9

Annual Crude Divorce Rates, United States, 1920–2011

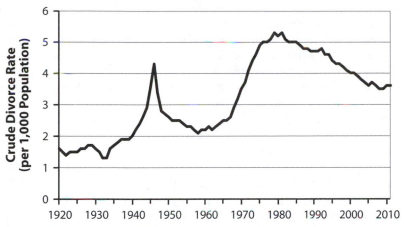

Source: CDC, 2013. "National Marriage and Divorce Rate Trends, 2000–2011."

decades. Remember, these are annual rates, which are extremely sensitive to external events that might encourage couples to break up (or postpone a breakup) in particular years. After major wars, for instance, there normally have been some temporary rises in the divorce rate, the peak after World War II being the most dramatic example in Figure 8-9. On the other hand, there was a temporary retreat from divorce during the depths of the Depression. After the post–World War II temporary peak, there was a rather unprecedented holiday from upward divorce trends between 1950 and 1962. Since that time, however, and especially through the 1970s, the upward trend in divorce rates resumed with a vengeance. Although the divorce rate remains higher than at any time prior to 1975, it has declined slightly since its peak in 1979.

Though not so dramatic as during the Depression, divorce rates decreased during the recent recession. Like marriage and fertility, divorce is also dampened by hard times. Although this may seem counterintuitive since we know that economic distress is a common cause of divorce, in the midst of economic downturns couples tend to postpone divorce because dividing assets and setting up separate households can be a costly business (Chowdhury, 2013).

It should be noted that the divorce process ideally should be measured by a *refined* rate, called the **general divorce rate**, rather than a crude rate like that depicted in Figure 8-9. Unfortunately, the U.S. Center for Health Statistics suspended collection of detailed marriage and divorce data in 1996, making refined divorce rates more difficult to come by. In the refined general divorce rate, the total events (divorces) compose the numerator, but only those at risk of participating in the event are in the denominator. Actually, the "population" at risk is marriages, not people. Since there is one married woman in each such couple, the number of married women of adult age is used as a denominator. The crude divorce rate underestimates the true rate of divorce because the denominator includes both members of married couples, as well as the entire unmarried portion of the population not at risk of divorce. Nevertheless, the shape of the general divorce rate and the crude divorce rate over time are generally very similar, even if the former is more than twice as high as the latter. The second exercise at the end of the chapter allows you to calculate for yourself how the general divorce rate differs from the crude divorce rate.

Demographers sometimes use a **cohort perspective** rather than a *period* perspective in studying or measuring divorce. The purpose is to estimate the lifetime chances of divorce implicit in period rates. Since current cohorts in a population have not completed their marital history, an estimate of their lifetime chances of divorce requires projecting the future marriage behavior of the cohort. This is done in the same way that life tables are used to project the future mortality of a cohort (see chapter 5). A group of married women are aged forward in time assuming they experience the same age-specific divorce rates that the current population does. Using such a method allows demographers to spell out the implications of sequences of rates for the marital life chances of individuals belonging to particular cohorts (see Bogue et al., 1993, vol. 4).

Again using the United States as an example, Figure 8-10 presents cohort measures of divorce for women who were ever married by 2003 from the cohorts of couples married between 1950 and 2003. For each cohort across the graph, the lines show the percent of those marriages that may end in divorce in years since the wedding took place. The graph suggests that the percentage of first marriages ending in divorce will peak with the marriage cohort of 1970–1979, and fall for younger cohorts. Of course, these projections may change as years go by and newer data become available. Cohort

Figure 8-10

First Marriages Ending in Divorce by Year of Marriage

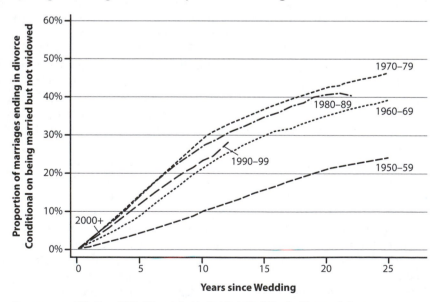

Source: Stevenson and Wolfers, 2011. "Trends in Marital Stability." Used with permission.

projections of divorce are not generally reliable. Projecting the chances of divorce into the future for a cohort makes the unlikely assumption of stable divorce rates over time. The dramatic variability in divorce rates in Figure 8-9, in contrast, suggests divorce is highly responsive to contemporary, or period, events. As predictions, these projections are very tentative.

For a more accurate measure of lifetime chances of divorce, taking a completed history approach to an actual cohort is obviously best; however, it is unclear *when* a marriage cohort is considered to be no longer at risk of divorce. A longitudinal analysis of marriage cohort data in the National Survey of Family Growth examined the *survival probabilities* of marriages from a cohort that had married twenty years prior. It found that 45% of such marriages had dissolved within two decades (Copen et al., 2012). Although most divorces take place within the first twenty years, some additional divorces will probably still occur among this cohort in the remaining decades. Thus, the popularly quoted "half of all marriages end in divorce" statistic is probably close to the truth. The cohort study showed that marriage survival varies considerably by the demographic characteristics of the couple. For example, marriages among college graduates are almost twice as likely to survive as those among non-college graduates. It also depends on the generation of the cohort. A recent study shows that marriages among the youngest generations are significantly more stable than those among the baby boomers (Kennedy and Ruggles, 2014).

With levels of divorce near historically high levels, how does the United States compare with other countries? International comparisons relying on legal divorce statistics are difficult to make. In those countries where many unions are consensual rather than official, unions can be dissolved voluntarily without ever being recorded. Indeed, census reports from Latin American countries imply that many people who have gone through this process (without remarriage) describe themselves as "single" rather than "divorced." Beyond that there is the process in some predominantly Catholic countries of erasing the record of a legal marriage by annulment. There is also the vague category of "separation," which may involve large proportions of the population but is poorly and inconsistently reported.

All this is to say that it is more precise to say that the United States has peaked at one of the highest divorce rates in the world, rather than to say that it has one of the highest rates of marital breakup. As Andrew Cherlin (2010b) points out, it is ironic that the United States has one of the highest divorce rates in the Western world at the same time that marriage is so idealized there. Marital rights are at the epicenter of an American battleground over lesbian and gay civil liberties, and it is the only country whose government actively promotes marriage using federal funds.

The total rate of marital dissolution, from divorce and widowhood combined, remained remarkably stable over most of the 20th century until rising during the divorce boom of the 1970s (Cherlin, 1981, 2010b). In terms of rates, widowhood declined and divorce rose over this same period. It is tempting—probably too tempting—to interpret these rates as suggesting that divorce has simply replaced widowhood as a form of marital dissolution as spouses live longer. It was, perhaps, easier to keep the vow of marital commitment "til death do us part" when that terminal date was due in a couple of decades, rather than in half a century. Thus, there may now be reluctance to confine oneself to only one long-term partnership over the extended life course.

Careers in Demography

Ron Lesthaeghe

Emeritus Professor of Demography & Social Science Research Methods
  Free University of Brussels (VUB)

Fellow, Class of Social Sciences, Royal Flemish Academy of Belgium of Arts
  & Sciences.

Life Time Award Recipient, International Union of the Scientific Study of
  Population (IUSSP), 2008

How did you decide that being a demographer was the career path for you?

After a bit of an overdose of law and history during the first two years at the university, I discovered Roland Pressat's textbook *L'analyse Démographique*, which was a striking example of methodological clarity, all based on the unifying analytic use of the Lexis diagram. At that time demography proved to me the ideal window to the world of social change as experienced by successive generations. My own world was already so different from that of my parents and even more so from the traumatic life experience of my grandparents. Furthermore, not any hyperbolic description with anecdotal evidence, but a clear text based on an analysis of representative data was what attracted me.

What kind of education and training did you pursue to get to where you are in your career?

During the 1960s Belgian universities had not yet "balkanized" the social sciences, but offered general undergraduate programs combining law, history, sociology, macroeconomics, statistics, and social science research methods. That proved to be a major asset as it prevented me from ever thinking "within any box."

With an interest in both demography and wider horizons, I applied for a Fulbright travel stipend and admission to an American university, and after graduating from the University of Ghent in 1967, I continued at Brown University, where Robert Potter and Sid Goldstein were my MA supervisors. With a Belgian National Science Foundation Fellowship and far better insights in formal demography, I returned to start my PhD thesis studying the age-structure changes and waves caused by a fertility transition. That dissertation led me to the Office of Population Research (OPR) at Princeton, where Ansley Coale and Etienne van de Walle had started the European Fertility Project.

Two years later, the Belgian monograph on the fertility and nuptiality transition was finished, and I was married as well. Although it was Christmas Day 1971, Ansley and Sue Coale provided their home and the Princeton township judge, whereas OPR organized a surprise wedding party shortly thereafter. The superb atmosphere at OPR and the friendships that budded there have been a major stimulus all the way. Demography had become "family."

Describe your work/research as a demographer. What do you consider your most important accomplishments?

While working for the Population Council stationed in Lagos, Nigeria, my wife Hilary Page and I embarked on fieldwork in all corners of that city, gathering data on the birth-spacing aspects of fertility. This culminated in a book with several colleagues and an article on the analysis of breast-feeding, amenorrhea, and postpartum abstinence durations. In tandem with the later World Fertility Survey data, this line of work was prolonged with a small team of junior researchers and graduate students at the VUB in Brussels, and this led to a second book on the impact of different types of social organization, religious traditions, and patterns of structural modernization on sub-Saharan fertility and marriage. For me, that also connected demography to ethnography.

In the meantime, it became more and more evident that cultural elements (religion and secularization, political aspect, ideational and ethical "revolutions") are an indispensable part of any story of demographic change. This was also brought home in a forceful way by studying the fertility, marriage, and acculturation patterns of Turkish and Moroccan immigrants and their second generation in Belgium. Hence, back I went to the Boolean model underlying Ansley Coale's succinct three-conditions paradigm, also known as the "Ready, Willing and Able" model of social innovation. And this would then lead to a short Dutch language article co-authored by Dirk van de Kaa with the title "Is There a Second Demographic Transition?" (note the question mark), proposing that the "cultural revolutions" of the 1960s would permit the development of new lifestyles.

In modern democracies, the strength of the principle of individual freedom of choice and the concomitant tolerance for diversity would foster demographic changes characterized by cohabitation, postponement of parenthood, and sustained structural "below replacement fertility," even in periods of strong economic growth. At that time, i.e. 1986, we did not predict the dip to "lowest-low fertility" with TFRs below 1.3, but merely the continuation of fertility below two children for more decades into the 21st century.

And that sparked a major debate with initial reactions often being of the type "not us, we're different." In other words, the "second demographic transition" (SDT) would only remain an idiosyncratic Western European feature. However, evidence from Japan and Taiwan, and especially from Latin America, by now indicates that the SDT is no longer a "provincial European phenomenon" but a much wider one, be it that different sub-patterns are equally unfolding. Current research with colleagues in Barcelona using the Latin American census data now begin to reveal how pervasive the SDT changes can be, even in areas where cohabitation was not grafted on older historical patterns. All of this makes me jealous of my younger colleagues who can now delve into this gold mine for research currently offered by the diverse unfolding patterns of the SDT!

What do you see as the field's most important contribution as well as its greatest challenge?

On the technical side, I would single out two major innovations in demography since the 1960s. Firstly, the use of life-table techniques and hazard analyses to all demographic phenomena, and not solely to mortality. Secondly, the broadening of stable population theory into "multi-state" demography has opened up so many possibilities, not only because of the incorporation of migration, but also because of its massive potential to all studies involving transitions of both a cultural and a structural nature. But there are dangers as well: quickly constructed, but widely used synthetic "period" measures can produce distortions, especially in periods of rapid change. By contrast, more sensitivity to measures that respect the longitudinal sequences of events during the life course of successive generations is essential.

The challenges for the future are precisely the attractions for the incoming cohorts of demographers: the high resolution capturing of the course followed by humankind anywhere in the world, by stimulating high quality data gathering and engaging in fine-tuned comparative analyses. It's a thoroughly scientific vocation, which may not offer the prospect of great financial gain, but instead assures a front row seat in the "theatre of history." Furthermore, the quintessential multidisciplinary nature of demography, involving scientists and colleagues with the widest range of backgrounds, is a joy forever.

Welcome to the multi-faceted world of demography!

Family Life Course Trends in the United States

One notion that demographers and sociologists employ in the cohort study of the family is that of a life course perspective, sometimes referred to as the **family life cycle**. A family life cycle or course specifies a sequence of events that might occur in the life of a nuclear family, such as first union, bearing children, and death of both spouses. In a given society and time period, a whole array of sequences will have been experienced by families, with varying frequencies. It is the relative frequency of these sequences that is of primary interest. A second important aspect of a life course is the *timing* of those events that make up the sequence.

As we saw with estimating the lifetime probability of divorce, a chronic problem with employing such cohort perspectives is that recent cohort histories are yet incomplete. That means family life-course descriptions of *real* cohorts will be limited to those cohorts who might have experienced all the specified family events. To describe the life-course implications of current marital event rates we have to employ the strategy of hypothetical cohorts, just as we did in constructing life tables (chapter 5).

We provide examples of each of these strategies below, necessarily describing somewhat different time periods. Uhlenberg's pioneering work (1978) dealt with a sequence of *real* cohorts and compares their family life-course arrays. The latest cohort represented, however, was born in 1930, roughly the generation of the grandparents of most of our college-age readers. The work by Schoen and Weinick (1993) provides more contemporary information, but necessarily about *hypothetical* cohorts. From their work, we have chosen three recent years whose rates they interpret, 1970 (before the peak in the divorce rate), 1980 (the approximate peak in that rate), and 1988 (after the divorce peak). The emphasis in Uhlenberg's study is on the *array* of event sequences involved; the emphasis in the study by Schoen and Weinick is on the *timing* of events.

Changes in Completed Family Life Courses

Using a combination of census and vital statistics data, Uhlenberg (1978) described the changing array of marital life courses in the United States for historical birth cohorts that had reached, or neared, average life expectancy by the end of the 20th century. Table 8-5 presents the data for women (he also calculated rates for men, which were similar in trend). Each row is a birth cohort selected at twenty-year intervals from 1870 to 1930. One can read down a given column in order to see the direction of any trend in marital experiences across the cohorts. The numbers in the column for each life-course type tell how many (per 1,000 women in the birth cohort who reached age twenty) experienced a specified life-course sequence.

A major conclusion is that the proportion who experienced the "normatively expected course" (column 5) consistently *increased* over that half century. This life course involves marrying, bearing children, and surviving to age fifty with marriage still intact. The major reason for the ascendance of the normatively expected pattern was the decline of early death (column 1). As a result, more, not fewer, women lived out the cultural ideal.

The three remaining life-course types offer a variety of trends. "Never Married" (column 2), surviving never-married to age fifty, declined dramatically in prevalence.

Table 8-5   Distribution of 1,000 White Women in the United States, by Type of Life Course Experiences, Birth Cohorts from 1870–1930

Birth Cohort	Early Death (1)	Never Married (2)	Childless (3)	Unstable Marriage with Children (4)	Normatively Expected (5)
1870	235	80	70	175	440
1890	170	85	115	170	460
1910	90	60	145	185	520
1930	50	45	40	265	600

Note: Confined to those who survived to age 20.

Source: Uhlenberg, 1978. "Changing Configurations in the Life Course," table 2.5.

"Unstable marriage with children" (column 4), defined as having a marriage with children end by divorce or death of the husband before the woman reaches age fifty, increased dramatically. "Childless" (column 3), marrying and surviving without having any children, first went up during these decades and then decreased dramatically.

Several well-known demographic trends during this period are behind the changing patterns of life course experience. Foremost was the decline in mortality associated with the demographic transition. Fewer women died between ages fifteen and fifty, shrinking the "early death" column. Aside from mortality, marriage became more universal in the later cohorts, reducing the number of never-married women. Rising marriage also raised the percentage of the population at risk for each of the last three columns of the table. The increase in the "unstable marriage with children" column reflects increased divorces, separations, and widowings among rising numbers of marriages. In the table, childless women are considered only if married, so the rise and fall of percentages in the "childless" column also reflect an initial rise in marriages (column 5) and a later rise in marriage dissolution (column 4).

Generations who lived out their family life cycle in the 20th century therefore *increased* the likelihood of living out the culturally normative life course across these cohorts. Much of the 20th-century change in the life-course experience was due to declining mortality coupled with a rise in the universality of marriage.

Recent Changes in Timing of Marital Events

To examine marital timing during recent times, we will use marital-life tables computed from period rates of marriage, divorce, and widowhood. We have seen (in Figure 8-9) the dramatic rise in crude divorce rates that occurred between 1970 and 1980 and the subsequent drop in those rates thereafter. To examine the effects of these changes on marital timing, Table 8-6 on the following page presents selected marital life-table estimates from before the divorce peak, during the peak, and post peak computed by Schoen and Weinick (1993) and Schoen and Standish (2001). (We trust the reader will remember that these life-table estimates are only what would *hypothetically* occur if a cohort were to experience the period rates of 1970, 1980, or 1995, respectively, over the

Table 8-6   Marital Life Table Estimates 1970 to 1995, United States

	Males			Females		
	1970	1980	1995	1970	1980	1995
Marriage						
Percent ever marrying	92.9	87.4	82.1	94.1	89.3	87.8
Average age at first marriage	23.4	26.3	28.6	21.8	24.1	26.6
Average duration of marriage	26.5	23.8	25.7	26.8	24.4	25.7
Divorce						
Percent ending in divorce	37.3	44.4	43.7	35.7	42.9	42.5
Average age at divorce	36.4	37.1	39.7	33.9	33.1	37.3
Average duration of divorced status	4.3	6.0	8.4	9.4	10.8	14.5
Widowhood						
Percent ending in widowhood	18.7	17.1	14.1	45.3	40.0	43.4
Average age at widowhood	67.8	71.1	77.8	65.2	67.9	72.0
Average duration of widowhood	7.4	7.7	6.9	14.8	15.0	13.2
Remarriage						
Percent of divorced remarrying	86.0	82.7	78.1	80.2	78.3	68.7
Average age of remarriage for divorced	37.3	38.5	42.5	35.5	34.7	39.7
Percent of widowed remarrying	27.0	20.8	12.3	10.3	7.6	4.8
Average age of remarriage for widowed	58.8	61.9	65.6	53.9	56.0	56.9

Source: Schoen and Standish, 2001. "The Retrenchment of Marriage," table 1. Used with permission.

cohort's life course.) The first three columns of the table give estimates for males in each of the three periods while the next three columns provide similar figures for females.

The first three rows of the table give marriage and marriage timing estimates. For both sexes, the percentage ever marrying (first row) declined and the average age at first marriage (second row) rose substantially throughout. Comparing gender differences, American men marry at slightly lower levels than women and at older ages. Although cohabitation is not included in these estimates, its rise as a precursor to marriage is the subtext behind why age at marriage (and remarriage) has increased. The average duration of marriages (third row) declined as divorce rose, but then rose slightly as divorce rates fell after 1980. Marriages became less universal, occurred at an older age, and lasted a shorter number of years across the three life marriage cohorts.

The next three rows provide divorce estimates. Not surprisingly, the percentage of marriages ending in divorce rose as divorce rates rose and declined slightly after 1980 as divorce rates fell. The average age at divorce rose over the three periods. These trends echo the balance between changes in the age and duration of marriages. Most importantly, the average duration of divorced status rose considerably across all three periods and for both sexes, indicating that immediate remarriage has become less common (in part because cohabitation has become more common). The time spent living as divorced steadily increased regardless of whether divorce rates increased or fell.

As divorce rose, the percentage of marriages ending in widowhood declined. Yet the age at widowhood increased steadily, which is largely explained by rising life expectancy. The average duration of widowhood has decreased accordingly, in part because as widowhood gets pushed back later in life, the surviving spouse lives a shorter period in this status. The percentage remarrying after either divorce or widowhood declined for both sexes just as first marriages declined. The age at remarriage after divorce fell for women who both divorced and remarried at younger ages during the divorce peak, and then rose. The age at which divorced men remarry rose steadily, as did the average age at remarriage for widows of both sexes.

Table 8-6 demonstrates that the timing of the marital life course was clearly affected by the rising divorce rates from 1970 to 1980. However, these estimates also reveal that during these dramatic changes in divorce, the marital life course was also profoundly shaped by two more consistent trends, a decline in marriage (both universal and early marriage), and an increasing life expectancy. It is important, however, to remember these images are drawn from period rates and that younger women during these years have not yet completed their marital life course. Some of the trends seen, especially the declining universality of marriage, may well change in the future if individuals who remained single turn out to be only delaying, rather than foregoing, marriage.

Which Household Union Trends Are Problems?

Apparently, it is universal to feel nostalgic when judging any current marriage trends. This is not new. For example, in 1889, a British politician and a devout advocate of the Church of England, William Ewart Gladstone, wrote a controversial article titled "The Question of Divorce" in the *North American Review*, in response to increasing prevalence of divorce in the United States at the time:

> For I incline to think that the future of America is of greater importance to Christendom at large than that of any other country; that the future, in its highest features, vitally depends upon the incidents of marriage; and that no country has ever been so directly challenged as America now is. (Quoted in Phelps, 1890, p. 36)

The family always has seemed to be on the decline and in disarray at any given moment, as compared with the past. Because family institutions and the roles associated with them are central to all cultures, any change can seem threatening because it requires compensating changes in many interconnected cultural norms, including some of our most deeply held values.

On the other hand, in periods of social change, some members of society might find family changes to be in keeping with the other changes in their lives. To them, the old family pattern often may seem an anachronism and a bad fit. Thus, in a changing culture there is not likely to be much agreement on the definition of "problems" associated with changes in marriage and marital dissolution, not nearly as much as there is concerning trends in mortality, for example. We do not even find well-articulated problem definitions held by sizable segments of the public. Instead, we seem to have widespread ambivalence or a mix of opposing views about almost any given trend.

Nevertheless, the four trends in American families that have received the most scrutiny are as follows: (1) increased proportions of children living in single-parent families due to union dissolution and childbearing outside of unions, (2) increased proportions of nontraditional living arrangements, (3) increased women's labor force participation across the life course, and (4) an increasing number of people living alone, especially at the older ages. We will briefly discuss the impacts of these trends and why some are labeled "problems."

1. *More children are living in single-parent families.* Children in single-parent families have fewer economic resources and represent one of the most rapidly growing groups living in poverty. This is in large part because of the absence of a second household income, but also because of the gender gap in pay that still penalizes women (and the vast majority of single-parent households are still headed by women). Two parents can also provide other types of resources and support to mitigate the burdens of child rearing and balancing employment at the same time. In answer to these problems, one of America's policy responses has been to encourage more marriage with the Healthy Marriage Act. But given that families most vulnerable to dissolution are poor and working class whose members have little access to decent-paying jobs, improving educational and job opportunities may be a more effective policy response than to encourage marriage in the absence of such supports. These problems also arise from the abdication of responsibility to children by society at large, such as lack of affordable child care, preschool, paid maternity leave, and so on. Indeed, the United States has among the highest child poverty rates in the MDRs (Gornick and Jäntti, 2010). As Sam Preston (1984) first pointed out and has been verified repeatedly since, many more U.S. public funds are now funneled toward elderly dependents than toward child dependents (Isaacs et al., 2011).

2. *More couples are living together in nontraditional ways.* Some segments of the population believe that traditional marital commitments, referred to as "family values" by proponents, are being undermined by the increasing acceptance of cohabitation, divorce, and nontraditional family arrangements. On the other hand, nonmarital cohabitation among the young may reinforce the stability of marriage when it does occur, by providing a trial marriage and delaying marriage until people generally less committed to marriage are somewhat more mature. Many nontraditional living arrangements may also provide social and economic stability for individuals who are legally barred from forming a traditional union, for example gay and lesbian families in some U.S. states. Others point out that eroding governmental and extended family support, longer periods of educational investment leading to later ages at marriage, greater geographic dispersion of families, rising social and economic independence of women, greater acceptability of same-sex couples, and similar social trends all require more flexible household arrangements. Often the stated concern about nontraditional households is their impact on children who are being raised in them. It is true that cohabiting unions are shorter in duration than marital unions and thus can be less stable settings for children.

3. *More women are working (for wages) before marriage, after marriage, and as mothers of young children.* Some segments of the population view women working outside the home as the root of marriage decline. There is evidence to support that view, and it is more positive than negative. Women's economic independence allows marriage to become more of a lifestyle choice than an economic necessity for women. Working before marriage often increases the likelihood marriage will be delayed, and working

during marriage provides economic resources allowing women to exit marital unions if they choose to do so. Female employment also reduces married women's traditional domestic roles and fertility levels. In the United States only 23% of married-couple households with children under fifteen are comprised of the traditional male earner and female homemaker, while 0.8% are the reverse—female earner/male homemaker (U.S. Census Bureau, 2013). Implicit in this critique of women entering the wage labor force is the assumption that marital decline and changing gender roles are in themselves problems. Others genuinely lament the loss of respect for the domestic labor women traditionally have provided and the economic and social benefits it afforded the family. Married-couple breadwinner/homemaker families are an economic option for a decreasingly small segment of the U.S. population. At the same time, others point to the economic benefits (and often necessity) of a dual-income family, the overall satisfaction a career may bring to a woman, the role model working mothers provide to their children, and so forth. But some women (and perhaps also some men) might prefer the satisfactions and time spent parenting in a more traditional domestic lifestyle to the stress or dissatisfaction of a wage-labor job.

4. *More people are now living alone.* When the census first released reports that more Americans were living alone than ever before in recorded history, popular media tended to paint a depressing picture of lonely Americans living out solitary lives. In fact, this trend mostly represents a positive development—greater autonomy and less dependence of young adults and the elderly. Adult children are more financially able to move out of their parents' homes soon after they turn eighteen than they were historically. Elderly, often widowed, adults now have the health and financial security to live independently rather than with their adult children or in a nursing home. The rise of the single householder in America is the product of delayed marriage and longer life spans. The other, less sanguine, cause of this rise in individualism is divorce. While divorce may be liberating for some, the consequences of divorce for others can be quite negative. Aside from the possible negative impact of union instability on child well-being, adult divorcees often lose social networks and related supports that are important not just for their mental well-being, but also for their physical well-being. Divorced individuals, particularly men, have a 30% greater risk of early mortality than the married (Shor et al., 2012).

SUMMARY

Marriage remains the most common form of stable sexual union in nearly all countries, but it is experiencing great transformation in many. The general pattern of eventual spread of first marriage through a birth cohort still appears nearly universal. Yet societies differ in terms of when the process starts, the proliferation of differing unions forms, how fast it spreads once started, and how many never marry. Rising ages at marriage, increasing proportions of people never married, and living in nontraditional households, including cohabiting partners and single parents, are all becoming part of the modern landscape in many MDRs. The relationship between these trends away from marriage and toward very low fertility levels is referred to as the second demographic transition. Although there is considerable variety among the less-developed regions, some LDRs are also beginning to experience signs of this second transition.

As a birth cohort matures, its members experience demographic events (marriage, divorce, death of spouse) that place them for periods of time in different marital statuses or sexual unions (single, married, divorced, separated, widowed, remarried, cohabiting, noncohabiting stable sexual unions, multiple unions, etc.). Societies track changes in population composition with respect to stable sexual unions by means of censuses and interim sample surveys. They sometimes track the transitional events by civil registration and by retrospective survey or census questions. As registration systems have been curtailed in the United States, sample surveys have added greatly to the fund of information for the demographic study of nuptiality and sexual unions.

Over the past several centuries, Europe developed a distinctive pattern of late marriage of women combined with high proportions never marrying. More recently, both Europe and the United States have experienced a pattern of marriage booms and busts, perhaps facilitated by the increasingly voluntary nature of marriage and responding to demographic compositional swings.

In the United States, marriage has increasingly been delayed and the universality of marriage has declined as cohabitation and nonmarital fertility have risen. Widowhood now occurs later in the life course mainly for women, due to the gendered increase in longevity during the mortality transition. Divorce has taken over as the cause of marital dissolution during the young and middle ages, and the trend rose sharply in the 1970s before leveling and now declining among younger age groups. Nevertheless, U.S. divorce rates remain at a high plateau, among the highest in the world.

These changes have had their impact on the family life courses followed by successive cohorts in the United States. Perhaps surprisingly, the proportion of women and men who lived out the culturally-normative sequence of events—getting married, having at least one child, and having the marriage survive until their fiftieth birthday—has actually increased over past cohorts. It's the timing of these events that has changed over more recent decades, and marriage in cohorts still living out their marital histories has become later, less universal, and shorter in duration. The time spent living as divorced has continued to increase.

Some nostalgia for the supposedly better family life of the past seems universal. Yet the pros and cons of any given marriage trend in a changing society is debatable, and debated. For example, we summarized the debate surrounding four salient trends in the United States. Individuals who value traditional arrangements view some of these trends as problematic, while those who value flexible alternatives welcome them.

EXERCISES

1. Age Standardization

   Suppose you are making a historical contrast between the 1890 and the 2015 U.S. male marital status compositions. You are aware that one reason for a change in marital status composition might be an aging population during the past century (see chapter 4). You might want to know how much of the marital status change is attributable to changes to age structure. Thus, you might ask what the 1890 marital status composition would have been if it had that older 2015 age structure. To do this you could *standardize* 1890 to the 2015 age distribution using the *direct method,* as follows.

First, record different information about the two dates in a standardization table, such as Table E8-1. The number of men in each age category (excluding those under age fourteen) for the standard population of 2015 would be recorded in column 1 of the top panel in Table E8-1. For the 1890 population, record the proportion in each age category falling into each marital status (see columns 2, 3, 4, and 5 of the top panel of Table E8-1).

Using these source data, make the following computations, filling in the blanks in the exercise table.

a. Multiply each of the proportions for 1890 in columns 2 through 5 against the 2015 population for the appropriate age category found in column 1. Record the resulting expected numbers upon 1890 standardization in the middle panel of Table E8-1.

Table E8-1   Calculation of Percent Distribution by Marital Status for U.S. Males in 1890, Standardized by Age to the 2015 U.S. Male Population Distribution

| Age | Male Population Midyear 2015 (1) | Proportional Distribution by Marital Status, 1890 | | | |
		Single (2)	Married (3)	Widowed (4)	Divorced (5)
15–19	10,690,310	0.9957	0.0042	0.0001	0.0001
20–24	11,227,724	0.8081	0.1889	0.0025	0.0005
25–29	11,209,657	0.4607	0.5278	0.0099	0.0016
30–34	11,037,036	0.2655	0.7140	0.0181	0.0024
35–44	20,513,724	0.1537	0.8102	0.0327	0.0035
45–54	21,316,584	0.0915	0.8400	0.0602	0.0043
55–64	19,491,715	0.0683	0.8245	0.1024	0.0048
65 and over	20,495,685	0.0561	0.7063	0.2335	0.0040
		Expected Number upon Standardization to 1890			
15–19	10,690,310	10,644,342	44,899	1,069	1,069
20–24	11,227,724	9,073,124	2,120,917	28,069	5,614
25–29	11,209,657		5,916,457	110,976	17,935
30–34	11,037,036			199,770	26,489
35–44	20,513,724	3,152,959			71,798
45–54	21,316,584	1,950,467	17,905,931		
55–64	19,491,715	1,331,284	16,070,919	1,995,952	
65 and over	20,495,685	1,149,808	14,476,102	4,785,742	81,983
Total	**125,982,435**				
		Percent in Status			
2015 Standardized 1890 Unstandardized		44	52	4	0.2

Sources: Shryock and Siegel, 1976. *The Methods and Materials of Demography,* table 10-2; U.S. Census Bureau, 2013. *International Data Base.*

b. For each marital status, accumulate the expected numbers, at all ages, at the foot of columns 2 through 5. Together, these totals form the expected frequency distribution by marital status.

c. Convert this frequency distribution into a percentage distribution. Divide the expected number in each status category by the expected number in all categories combined (125,982,435).

The bottom row of Table E8-1 presents, for comparison, the actual (nonstandardized) percentage distribution by marital status of the 1890 male population aged fourteen and over. What are the differences from the standardized 2015 population and why?

2. Calculating Annual Rates

Table E8-2 contains data to compute the Japanese crude marriage and divorce rates

Table E8-2   Calculation of Marriage and Divorce Rates, Japan, 2010 and 2005

	Year	
	2010	2005
Total Population (1,000s)	128,057	127,768
Married Females 15 Years Old and Over (1,000s)	31,927	32,323
Marriages	706,000	714,265
Divorces	251,000	
Crude Marriage Rate		5.59
Crude Divorce Rate		2.05
General Divorce Rate		8.10

Source: Statistics Japan, 2013. *Decennial Census Data.*

(per 1,000 population) and the more refined general divorce rate (per 1,000 married adult women) for the years 2010 and 2005. Complete the table by filling in the blank cells for each rate in 2010 and the number of divorces in 2005.

3. Age at Marriage

Go to Exercise 3 under the exercise section of the Chapter 8 tab on the textbook website at www.demographytextbook.com. This interactive graph shows age at first marriage among women over time across three countries, Algeria, Canada, and the Philippines.

a. Which country has the latest age at marriage in 1966, 1986, and 2005?

b. How would you explain these trends?

c. Now focus just on Canada and pull back the time bar to 1915. How do Canadian age-at-marriage trends play out over the time period?

PROPOSITIONS FOR DEBATE

1. Rising proportions of people living as officially "single" in the United States demonstrate a fundamental decline in the desire to live as a couple.

2. We should expect marriage to decline and divorce to rise as fertility decreases.

3. We should expect both the age at first marriage and the divorce rate to rise as life expectancy increases.

4. The divorce rate will fall again as the population grows older.

5. We should expect the divorce rate to rise as more women enter into the labor force and are gaining greater economic independence.

6. Cohabitation, same-sex couples, and nonmarital childbearing will continue to rise in the MDRs.

7. The Second Demographic Transition will sweep across all countries in the future.

REFERENCES AND SUGGESTED READINGS

Akerlof, G. A., J. L. Yellen, and M. L. Katz. 1996. "An Analysis of Out-of-Wedlock Childbearing in the United States." *Quarterly Journal of Economics* 111(2).

Anderson, Michael. 1995. *Approaches to the History of the Western Family 1500–1914*. Cambridge: Cambridge University Press.

Bachu, Amaru. 1999a. "Is Childlessness Among American Women on the Rise?" Population Division Working Paper No. 37. Washington, DC: U.S. Census Bureau.

———. 1999b. "Trends in Premarital Childbearing, 1930 to 1994." *Current Population Reports*, Series P23, no. 197. Washington, DC: GPO.

Bethmann, Dirk, and Michael Kvasnicka. 2013. "World War II, Missing Men, and Out of Wedlock Childbearing." *The Economic Journal* 123(567): 162–194.

Bogue, Donald J., Eduardo Arriaga, and Douglas L. Anderton, eds. 1993. *Readings in Population Research Methodology*. Chicago: UNFPA/Social Development Center.

Brien, Michael J., Lee A. Lillard, and Linda J. Waite. 1999. "Interrelated Family-Building Behaviors: Cohabitation, Marriage and Nonmarital Conception." *Demography* 36(4).

Budig, Michelle J., Joya Misra, and Irene Boeckmann. 2010. "The Wage Penalty for Motherhood in a Cross-National Perspective: Relationships with Work-Family Policies and Cultural Attitudes." Paper presented at the Population Association of America, Dallas, TX.

CDC (Centers for Disease Control). 2010. "Birth Tables by Characteristics of Mother." *VitalStats*. Retrieved September 2013. Last Updated January 2010. http://www.cdc.gov/nchs/VitalStats.htm

———. 2013. "National Marriage and Divorce Rate Trends, 2000–2011." *National Vital Statistics System*. Retrieved September 10, 2013. Last Updated February 19, 2013. http://www.cdc.gov/nchs/nvss/marriage_divorce_tables.htm

Chandra, A., G. M. Martinez, W. D. Mosher, J. C. Abma, and J. Jones. 2005. "Fertility, Family Planning, and Reproductive Health of U.S. Women: Data from the 2002 National Survey of Family Growth." *Vital Health Statistics* 23(25). Washington, DC: GPO.

Cherlin, Andrew J. 1981. *Marriage, Divorce, and Remarriage*. Cambridge, MA: Harvard University Press.

———. 2010a. "Demographic Trends in The United States: A Review of Research in the 2000s." *Journal of Marriage and Family* 72(3): 403–419.

———. 2010b. *The Marriage-Go-Round: The State of Marriage and the Family in America Today*. New York: Vintage.

Chowdhury, Abdur. 2013. "'Til Recession Do Us Part: Booms, Busts and Divorce in the United States." *Applied Economics Letters* 20(3): 255–261.

Coale, Ansley J. 1971. "Age Patterns of Marriage." *Population Studies* 25(2).

Cohn, D'Vera. 2010. *Is the Recession Linked to Fewer Marriages?* Pew Research Center. Retrieved September 9, 2013. http://www.pewresearch.org/2010/10/22/is-the-recession-linked-to-fewer-marriages/

Coontz, Stephanie. 2000. *The Way We Never Were: American Families and the Nostalgia Trap*. New York: Basic Books.

Copen, Casey E., Kimberly Daniels, Jonathan Vespa, and William D. Mosher. 2012. "First Marriages in the United States: Data from the 2006–2010 National Survey of Family Growth." *National Health Statistics Report* 49 (March 22).

Dalla Zuanna, Gianpiero. 2001. "The Banquet of Aeolus: A Familistic Interpretation of Italy's Lowest Low Fertility. *Demographic Research* 4(5): 133–161.

———. 2004. "Few Children in Strong Families: Values and Low Fertility in Italy." *Genus* 60(1): 39–70.

Davis, Kingsley. 1972. "The American Family in Relation to Demographic Change." In Charles F. Westoff and Robert Parke, Jr., eds., *Demographic and Social Aspects of Population Growth*. Vol. 1. Washington, DC: GPO.

Elliott, Diana B., Kristy Krivickas, Matthew W. Brault, and Rose M. Kreider. 2012. "Historical Marriage Trends from 1890–2010: A Focus on Race Differences." *SEHSD Working Paper 2012–12*. Washington, DC: U.S. Census Bureau.

Eurostat. 2013. "Live Births outside Marriage (tps00018) Data File." Last updated August 13, 2013. Retrieved August 31, 2013. http://epp.eurostat.ec.europa.eu/portal/page/portal/statistics/search_database

Festy, Patrick. 1980. "On the New Context of Marriage in Western Europe." *Population and Development Review* 6(2).

Fields, Jason, and Lynne M. Casper. 2001. "America's Families and Living Arrangements: 2000." *Current Population Reports*, P20-537. Washington, DC: U.S. Census Bureau.

Fry, Richard, and D'Vera Cohn. 2011. "Living Together: The Economics of Cohabitation." *Social & Demographic Trends*. Washington, DC: Pew Research Center.

Goldstein, Joshua R. 1999. "The Leveling of Divorce in the United States." *Demography* 36(3).

Gornick, Janet C., and Markus Jäntti. 2010. "Child Poverty in Upper-Income Countries: Lessons from the Luxembourg Income Study." *From Child Welfare to Child Well-Being* 1: 339–368.

Grusky, David B., Bruce Western, and Christopher Wimer, eds. 2011. *The Great Recession*. New York: Russell Sage Foundation.

Guilmoto, Christophe Z. 2012. "Skewed Sex Ratios At Birth and Future Marriage Squeeze in China and India, 2005–2100." *Demography* 49(1): 77–100.

Hajnal, John. 1953. "The Marriage Boom." *Population Index* 19(2).

———. 1965. "European Marriage Patterns in Perspective." In D. V. Glass and D. E. C. Eversley, eds., *Population in History*. London: Arnold.

Hamamy, Hanan, et al. 2011. "Consanguineous Marriages, Pearls and Perils: Geneva International Consanguinity Workshop Report." *Genetics in Medicine* 13: 841–847.

Hodges, M. J., and M. J. Budig. 2010. "Who Gets the Daddy Bonus? Organizational Hegemonic Masculinity and the Impact of Fatherhood on Earnings." *Gender & Society* 24(6): 717–745.

ICF International. 2012. *Demographic and Health Surveys (Various Years) [Datasets]*. http://www.measuredhs.com/Data/. Calverton, Maryland: ICF International.

Isaacs, Julia, Heather Hahn, Stephanie Rennane, C. Eugene Steuerle, and Tracy Vericker. 2011. *Kids' Share 2011: Report on Federal Expenditures on Children through 2010*. Washington, DC: Urban Institute and Brookings.

Jacobsen, Linda A., Mark Mather, and Genevieve Dupuis. 2012. "Household Change in the United States." *Population Bulletin* 67(1). Washington, DC: Population Reference Bureau.

James, Spencer L., and Kevin Shafer. 2012. "Temporal Differences in Remarriage Timing: Comparing Divorce and Widowhood." *Journal of Divorce & Remarriage* 53(7): 543–558.

Kennedy, Sheela, and Larry Bumpass. 2008. "Cohabitation and Children's Living Arrangements: New Estimates from the United States." *Demographic Research* 19: 1663–1692.

Kennedy, Sheela, and S. Ruggles. 2014. "Breaking Up Is Hard to Count: The Rise of Divorce in the United States, 1980–2010." *Demography* 51(2): 587–598.

Kiernan, K. 2001. "The Rise of Cohabitation and Childbearing outside Marriage in Western Europe." *International Journal of Law Policy and the Family* 15(1).

Killewald, Alexandra, and Margaret Gough. 2013. "Does Specialization Explain Marriage Penalties and Premiums?" *American Sociological Review* 78(3): 477–502.

Kreider, Rose M. 2006. "Marital Status in the 2004 American Community Survey." *Population Division Working Paper No. 83*. Washington, DC: U.S. Census Bureau.

Lesthaeghe, Ron. 2010. "The Unfolding Story of the Second Demographic Transition." *Population and Development Review* 36(2): 211–251.

Lesthaeghe, Ron J., and Lisa Neidert. 2006. "The Second Demographic Transition in the United States: Exception or Textbook Example?" *Population and Development Review* 32(4): 669–698.

Lesthaeghe, Ron, and Johan Surkyn. 2006. "When History Moves On: The Foundations and Diffusion of a Second Demographic Transition." In Rukmalie Jayakody, Arland Thornton, and William G. Axinn, eds., *International Family Change: Ideational Perspectives*. Mahwah, NJ: Lawrence Erlbaum Associates.

Lesthaeghe, Ron., and D. J. van de Kaa. 1986. "Twee Demografische Transities?" (Three Demographic Transitions?) In R. Lesthaeghe and D. J. van de Kaa, eds., *Bevolking: Groei en Krimp* (Population: Growth and Decline). Mens en Maatschappij book supplement. Deventer: Van Loghum-Slaterus.

Lofquist, Daphne. 2011. "Same-Sex Couple Households." *American Community Survey Brief*. ACSBR/10-03. Washington, DC: GPO.

Lofquist, Daphne, Terry Lugaila, Martin O'Connell, and Sarah Feliz. 2012. "Households and Families: 2010." *2010 Census Briefs*. C2010BR-14. Washington, DC: GPO.

Mather, Mark, and Diana Lavery. 2010. "In U.S., Proportion Married at Lowest Recorded Levels." Retrieved September 6, 2013. http://www.prb.org/Publications/Articles/2010/usmarriagedecline.aspx

Michigan Population Studies Center. 2013. *SDT: Second Demographic Transition (Website)*. Retrieved September 6, 2013. http://sdt.psc.isr.umich.edu

Monahan, Thomas P. 1951. *The Age at Marriage in the United States*. Philadelphia: Stephenson.

Musick, Kelly. 2007. "Cohabitation, Nonmarital Childbearing, and the Marriage Process." *Demographic Research* 16(9): 249–286.

Mykyta, Laryssa, and Suzanne Macartney. 2012. "Sharing a Household: Household Composition and Economic Well-Being: 2007–2010." *Current Population Report* P60-242. Washington, DC: GPO.

NCHS (National Center for Health Statistics). 2000. "Vital Statistics of the United States, 2000: Volume I, Natality." http://www.cdc.gov/nchs/datawh/statab/unpubd/natality/natab2000.htm

Neidert, Lisa, and Ron Lesthaeghe. 2014. Population Studies Center, University of Michigan. Retrieved from http://sdt.psc.isr.umich.edu/pubs/maps/map_tfr_sdt.pdf

OECD (Organisation for Economic Cooperation and Development). 2012. "SF3.3: Cohabitation Rate and Prevalence of Other Forms of Partnership" *OECD Family Database*. Retrieved August 25, 2013. http://www.oecd.org/social/family/database Paris: OECD.

Phelps, E.G. 1890. "Ought Divorced People to Re-Marry?" In William Thomas Stead, ed., *The Review of Reviews* 1(1): 36-37. London: The Review of Reviews.

Popenoe, David, and Barbara Dafoe Whitehead. 1999. *The State of Our Unions: The Social Health of Marriage in America*. National Marriage Project Report. New Brunswick, NJ: Rutgers University.

Preston, Samuel H. 1984. "Children and the Elderly: Divergent Paths for America's Dependents." *Demography* 21(4): 435–457.

Rashad, Hoda, Magued Osman, and Farzaneh Roudi-Fahimi. 2005. *Marriage in the Arab World.* Washington, DC: Population Reference Bureau.

Rosenfeld, Michael J., and Reuben J. Thomas. 2012. "Searching for a Mate: The Rise of the Internet as a Social Intermediary." *American Sociological Review* 77(4): 523–547.

Santelli, John S., and Amy T. Schalet. 2009. "A New Vision for Adolescent Sexual and Reproductive Health." *ACT for Youth Center of Excellence: Research fACTs and Findings.*

Schoen, Robert, and Nicola Standish. 2001. "The Retrenchment of Marriage: Results from Marital Status Life Tables for the United States." *Population and Development Review* 27(3).

Schoen, Robert, and Robin M. Weinick. 1993. "The Slowing Metabolism of Marriage: Figures from 1988 U.S. Marital Status Life Tables." *Demography* 30(4).

Shattuck, Rachel M., and Rose M. Kreider. 2013. "Social and Economic Characteristics of Currently Unmarried Women with a Recent Birth: 2011." *American Community Survey Reports.* ACS-21. Washington, DC: GPO.

Shor, Eran, David J. Roelfs, Paul Bugyi, and Joseph E. Schwartz. 2012. "Meta-Analysis of Marital Dissolution and Mortality: Reevaluating the Intersection of Gender and Age." *Social Science & Medicine* 75(1): 46–59.

Shryock, Henry S., and Jacob S. Siegel. 1976. *The Methods and Materials of Demography.* Condensed ed. by Edward G. Stockwell. New York: Academic Press.

Simmons, Tavia, and Martin O'Connell. 2003. *Married-Couple and Unmarried-Partner Households: 2000.* Census 2000 Special Reports. CENSR-5. Washington, DC: U.S. Census Bureau.

Sobotka, Tomáš. 2002. "Demotrends: Non-Marital Births in Europe and in the United States." *Issues* 7 (July).

———. 2008. "Overview Chapter 6: The Diverse Faces of the Second Demographic Transition in Europe." *Demographic Research* 19(8): 171–224.

Sovič, Silvia. 2008. "European Family History Moving Beyond Stereotypes of 'East' and 'West.'" *Cultural & Social History* 5(2): 141–163.

Statistics Japan. 2013. *e-Stat: Portal Site of Official Statistics of Japan.* Retrieved September 12, 2013. http://www.e-stat.go.jp

Stevenson, Betsey, and Justin Wolfers. 2011. "Trends in Marital Stability." In Lloyd R. Cohen and Joshua D. Wright, eds., *Research Handbook on the Economics of Family Law.* Cheltenham, UK: Edward Elgar.

Thornton, Arland. 2005. *Reading History Sideways: The Fallacy and Enduring Impact of the Developmental Paradigm on Family Life.* Chicago: University of Chicago Press.

Thornton, Arland, and Dimiter Philipov. 2009. "Sweeping Changes in Marriage, Cohabitation and Childbearing in Central and Eastern Europe: New Insights from the Developmental Idealism Framework." *European Journal of Population* 25(2): 123–156.

Uhlenberg, Peter. 1978. "Changing Configurations in the Life Course." In Tamara K. Hareven, ed., *Transitions: The Family and Life Course in Historical Perspective.* New York: Academic Press.

United Nations. 2008. *Principles and Recommendations for Population and Housing Censuses, Revision 2.* Series M, No.67/Rev.2. New York: United Nations.

———. 2011. *World Fertility Report 2009.* Population Division of the Department of Economic and Social Affairs. New York: United Nations.

———. 2012. *Demographic Yearbook/Annuaire Démographique 2011.* B.13.XIII.1 H New York: United Nations.

U.S. Census Bureau. 1976. *Social Indicators, 1976.* Washington, DC: GPO.

———. 1998. "Marital Status and Living Arrangements: March 1998 (Update)." *Current Population Reports*, Series P-20, no. 514. Washington, DC: GPO.

———. 2010. *America's Families and Living Arrangements: 2010.* Retrieved September 17, 2013. http://www.census.gov/population/www/socdemo/hh-fam/cps2010.html

———. 2011. *2012 Statistical Abstract of the United States.* 131st Edition. Washington, DC: GPO.

———. 2012a. "Data on Families and Living Arrangements." *Families and Living Arrangements Main*. Last Revised November 13, 2012. Retrieved August 25, 2013. http://www.census.gov/hhes/families/data/

———. 2012b. "Table MS-2. Estimated Median Age at First Marriage, by Sex: 1890 to the Present." *Families and Living Arrangements: Marital Status*. Last Revised November 13, 2012. Retrieved August 25, 2013. http://www.census.gov/hhes/families/data/marital.html

———. 2013. *Families and Living Arrangements Main*. Last Revised August 23, 2013. Retrieved September 20, 2013. http://www.census.gov/hhes/families/

van de Kaa, D. J. 1987. "Europe's Second Demographic Transition." *Population Bulletin* no. 42. Washington, DC: Population Reference Bureau.

Wang, Wendy, and Paul Taylor. 2011. "For Millennials, Parenthood Trumps Marriage." *Social & Demographic Trends*. Washington DC: Pew Research Center.

Watkins, Susan C. 1981. "Regional Patterns of Nuptiality in Europe, 1870–1960." *Population Studies* 35(2).

Westoff, Charles. 2003. *Trends in Marriage and Early Childbearing in Developing Countries*. DHS Comparative Report no. 5. Calverton, MD: ORC Macro.

The World Family Map. 2013. *World Family Map 2013: Mapping Family Change and Child Well-Being Outcomes*. Washington, DC: Child Trends.

9

Migration

In this chapter we introduce the remaining component of population growth, migration. Thereafter, in chapters 10 and 11, we discuss two major consequences of migration: urbanization and population diversity. This chapter starts with the knotty problem of defining migration. It then proceeds to describe the major patterns of international and internal migration and theories about the causes or determinants of migration. Finally, we address the consequences and policy concerns of international migration, especially the flow of population from the less-developed regions to the more-developed regions of the world.

What Is Migration?

Migration is more difficult to define than is mortality or fertility. Whereas all births contribute to fertility and all deaths contribute to mortality, not all moves contribute to migration. A vacation trip, a move to a neighboring apartment, an errand to the store, a daily commute to work: these moves are *not* migrations.

Which Moves Are Migrations?

So, which moves do demographers consider migrations? One answer to this question can be seen in the population growth equation of chapter 1. **Migrations** are those population movements that add or subtract from the *members* of a population or society. For demographers, membership in a population is closely linked to the idea of *residence*. Residence, in this context, means more than just being physically present at a geographic location at a moment in time; it implies being socially *affiliated* with a population.

By this limitation, we focus on those moves which are demographically and socially important. The society in the **area of origin** (the *sending* society) wants to know how many people, of what kind, it is losing. The society in the **area of destination** (the *receiving* society) wants to know how many people, of what kind, it is gaining. And, from the perspective of individuals, changes in residence that involve the tearing up of old roots and the setting down of new ones are psychologically, socially, and economically more important than casual moves.

Migration, or change in population membership, is then demographically identified as a change in **residence**. Being more precise, demographers require a move to satisfy three conditions to qualify as a migration: (1) It must involve a permanent or semi-permanent change in one's residence; (2) it must cross some administrative boundary; and (3) it must occur during a given time or period (Pressat, 1985). This is the simplest definition of migration, a change in residence across some geopolitical boundary in a given period of time.

Note that this definition of migration uses neither distance nor duration as criteria, at least not directly. A change in residence by moving across the street might be a migration if it crosses administrative boundaries, while a vacation trip around the world might not. A citizen of one country might live for years in another without changing his citizenship, while a refugee might immediately adopt her new home as a country of residence. Demographers may use distance of move and duration of stay—or even intended duration—as a proxy or indicator for the change of residence, but reaffiliation remains the underlying criterion.

Which kinds of moves are left out of this demographic definition of migration? One exclusion would be moves of people who have no geographically durable residence, either before or after the moves, such as nomadic or homeless populations. Another exclusion would be short-term movements of a periodic sort, for instance, commuting to and from work or annual vacation trips. Another categorical exclusion would be a change of residence within a geopolitical unit, such as moving from one's present house to another in the same administrative area.

This last exclusion raises a complication in our definition. Determining which moves are going to be called migrations depends on the scale of geopolitical units one is considering, the **migration-defining area** (Pressat, 1985). If we are dealing with international migration, we do not count the moves that might take place between provinces or states within nations. When dealing with interprovince or interstate migration, moves between communities within states or provinces are not counted.

Because of this ambiguity, demographers are careful to specify which scale of migration they are talking about. For instance, they universally distinguish between international and internal migration, and within internal migration, they are careful to specify further. Within the United States, for example, they distinguish between interregional, interstate, and intercounty migration.

Which Dimensions of Migration Are Important?

The vocabulary of migration is more easily introduced when looking at the simplified migration schematic diagram shown in Figure 9-1. We have two areas, A and B, each with a specified residential population at the beginning of a year. During that year, one set of people crosses from area A to area B and another set crosses from area B to area A. Let us assume that these border crossings mean changes of residence—that they are migrations.

Figure 9-1

Schematic Diagram of Migration between Two Areas

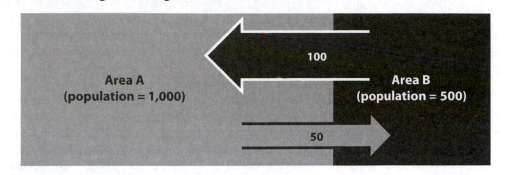

This migration situation can be viewed either from a wide perspective or from a narrow one. Broadly, we can think of areas A and B as parts of some larger whole, such as when studying migration among regions of a country. More narrowly, we can identify with only one of the areas and view the migration only in terms of its impact on that one area, such as how most nations view their international migration.

Let us start with the wider perspective and introduce its terms. The focus of interest is likely to be on migration streams. A **migration stream** consists of the people who migrate from one specified area to another in a given period of time. The arrows in Figure 9-1 show two streams. The numbers within the arrows tell how many people are in the stream and the size of the arrow represents the size of the stream. Each stream has an area of origin and an area of destination. Demographers sometimes are concerned about the collective force of the two streams, and sometimes about the balance between the two streams; that is, they might focus upon **gross migration** (or the *volume* of migration), the sum of the two streams (150 in our figure), or the **net migration**, the differences between the two streams (50 in our figure).

From a narrow, local perspective, priorities are different. Let us take, for a moment, the position of area A, and let us say that areas A and B are nations (albeit tiny ones). From that position, the 100 who move from area B to area A represent **immigration**; the 50 who move from area A to area B represent **emigration.** If the areas were not nations but subunits (that is, if the migration were internal), then the processes might be labeled **out-migration** rather than emigration, and **in-migration** rather than immigration. The net migration for area A would be the in-migration (100) minus the out-migration (50), for a gain of 50 people. Net migration for area B would be *minus* 50. Exercise 1 at the end of this chapter provides practice in applying these concepts.

Migration *rates* can be computed for each of these aspects of migration, but their meaning tends to be less clear than either death rates or birth rates. Emigration (or out-migration) rates make some sense. The total resident population in an area bears some resemblance to the number of people who could move out. So crude, or even age-specific, rates can be used to measure emigration (or out-migration) relevant to a resident population at risk of leaving. But the rate of immigration (or in-migration) among current residents makes less sense. The resident population is not at risk of immigration, and its absolute size has little to do with the number of people who could move into the area. When immigration (in-migration) rates are constructed, it is usually to indicate the rate at which immigration *impacts* the resident population in the area of destination. Similarly, the rate of net migration frequently is used to indicate the net impact of immigration and emigration on the population in the area of destination. Generally, however, you will see demographers using migration rates sparingly and reporting instead the absolute size of migration movements (Shryock and Siegel, 1976).

One more important dimension of this process is **selective migration**. Demographers, you will remember, are interested not only in changes of population size but also in population *composition*. To the degree that the composition of the net migration stream differs from the composition of the resident population of the destination area, migration will have an impact on the composition of the resident population; the same will be true at the origin area. Exercise 2 at the end of this chapter gives readers a closer look at this process of selective migration.

Data Sources

Of the three population processes in the growth equation (i.e., fertility, mortality, and migration), our data on migration are the least complete. Among migration data, those on international migration, and especially undocumented international migration, are the worst.

One reason for this negative distinction is that we do not have a world government. Such an authority could insist on all nations cooperating in tracking moves from one country to another, just as some nations track moves among their regions, provinces, and states. Instead, what we have is a mishmash of differing national definitions, priorities, and procedures, mostly based on national rather than international concerns; leaving us unable to answer some crucial questions, such as the effect of migrant labors on source and host countries and the consequence of different immigration policies.

It is helpful to remind ourselves what would constitute ideal data, as applied to international migration. Ideally, we would have the same kind of information on migrations that we are supposed to have about births and deaths. All moves that might later be classed as migrations should be recorded, as well as the time of each move. Enough information about the ultimate reaffiliation (change of residence, membership) of the mover should be gathered so that later decisions can be made as to which moves were migrations. Enough information also should be gathered about the characteristics of the migrants so that, minimally, the composition of migrant populations could be compared with the composition of resident populations. Simply to describe the ideal is to warn the reader that we fall woefully short, especially on the international plane. The description also reminds us how unlikely it is to achieve such an ideal anytime soon, so let us return to the real world.

Estimates of both international and internal migration typically come from four main sources, and the weight placed on these data sources differs between the study of international and internal migration: (1) administrative records, (2) inferences made from past and present residences as reported in censuses or surveys, (3) surveys that specifically target immigrants, and (4) estimations of migration made from knowledge of growth and the other components of growth (Henning and Hovy, 2011; Zlotnik et al., 2010; Santo Tomas et al., 2009; United Nations, 1998a). Below, we discuss the latest developments and limitations in immigration data collection.

Administrative Records

Administrative sources of migration data include population registers, registers of foreigners, applications (for visas, residence, and work permits), exit clearances, border control statistics and registrations, and any other source of information generated by the bureaucratic processing of movers. Administrative data generally are available for international migrations, though the number of countries that publish relevant administrative data is still limited. In addition, they are not designed primarily to collect migration information and are of limited use for that purpose. Moreover, because different bureaucratic agencies are involved in the data-collection process, comparability of administrative data is rather questionable (Zlotnik et al., 2010; United Nations, 1998a).

For example, the Office of Immigration Statistics of the Department of Homeland Security collects immigration data in the United States based on administrative records. These records provide some information on entry patterns and characteristics of those who possibly stay beyond the specified length of stay, because almost all administrative records provide information on the (documented) arrival of long-term immigrants and foreigners who are admitted for temporary stays. However, these records do not capture the movement of undocumented migrants, unless they are apprehended within the United States, and they do not collect data at the moment of arrival for those who change their immigration status halfway through (Massey, 2010; Massey and Capoferro, 2004).

In the absence of data on departures, we cannot estimate the size of immigration accurately within a country, but as more countries disseminate administrative records to international data agencies, comparison of origin-country and destination-country records may become possible (Santo Tomas et al., 2009). For example, the International Labour Office (ILO) collects data on the admission of migrant workers, and the Organization for Economic Cooperation and Development (OECD) has been compiling data on residence permits issued within the member states. The Office of the High Commissioner for Refugees (UNHCR) also collects information on refugees based on the administrative records of the countries of asylum (Zlotnik et al., 2010).

Registering Border Crossings

An especially useful type of administrative records is the registration of border crossings. One way to track a demographic process—be it mortality, fertility, or migration—is to register the events making up the process as they occur. Data collected at border crossings occur at the time of movements and have the advantage of being frequently collected for both foreigners and citizens. Unfortunately, most border statistics provide unreliable data on international migration.

One problem springs from the fact that officials at the border do not know, at the time of crossing, what the mover ultimately will do. The United Nations (1998a, table 1) recommends asking how long the migrants lived at their prior residences and how long they *intend* to live at their new residences, to distinguish immigrants and emigrants (with long previous and expected durations of residence) from other types of travelers. Even following such guidelines, border officials would know only the mover's stated intentions, and intentions change.

A related problem is that the two nations involved—that of origin and that of destination—might differ in their priorities and in their records. Nations tend to be more concerned with detailed information about people who are joining them (immigrants) than about people who are leaving them (emigrants). Moreover, decisions about how to determine residence (or affiliation) and which characteristics of movers are important to record vary from nation to nation. The upshot is that the two countries involved in any given migration stream are likely to record it differently. This makes combining their data to estimate net migration difficult.

Another category of problems is logistical. Simply recording all the border crossings that later might prove to be migrations can be a difficult job. It is easier for nations whose ports of entry and exit are limited, such as islands. At the other extreme, some countries have long land borders that normally are not fully patrolled, such as the northern and southern borders of the United States. And, finally, the borders of political units within the nation are usually relatively unimportant, so nations seldom monitor the crossings of internal borders as they do external ones.

However, there are some developments around the use of border crossing records. The Mexican Migration Project (MMP) and the Latin American Migration Project (LAMP) help to overcome challenges associated with recording border crossings by incorporating ethnographic fieldwork in the source country and the destination country (more discussion in the Survey section below).

Retrospective Census Questions

Most governments rely on household inquiries, in the form of censuses and surveys, to estimate migration. Between 2005 and 2010, seventy-eight countries conducted a population census, and fifty-nine of those collected information on country of birth, country of citizenship, year of arrival, or a combination of these questions (Zlotnik et al., 2010). Some, like recent U.S. censuses, ask about residence at some specified prior time, say five years ago or one year ago. Where the current residence differs from the place of birth or prior residence, some move must have occurred, probably a migration. This indirect measurement of migration from census data thus far has been the most comparable data on international migration (Zlotnik et al., 2010). Because these methods identify migrants but not the exact timing of migration, they are more useful in measuring the size of a population's stock of international migrants than they are for measuring the migration flow.

But this method is not airtight. People can and do conceal their foreign origins. More importantly, some kinds of moves are not recorded, such as moves by those who emigrate and are abroad at the time of the census, by those who emigrate but return to the same location before the census, and by those who immigrate but leave or die before the census. The method is particularly limited in measuring emigration, requiring a complex procedure of comparing censuses over time to identify those who have left and those with death records to identify people lost to emigration rather than death.

If national censuses ask similar questions about place of birth or prior residence for more detailed geographic areas within the nation, then internal migration can be estimated. United States censuses since 1850 have asked state or country of birth. Since 1940 the U.S. census and the Current Population Survey have asked detailed place-of-residence questions either one or five years prior to the census. Asking such questions in censuses is highly recommended by the United Nations and is becoming more widespread.

There are advantages to asking place-of-prior-residence (over place-of-birth) questions: The shorter period between the prior-residence data and the census date means fewer intervening moves will go unrecorded. Moreover, the timing of those that are recorded is bracketed more narrowly and recent migrations are often of greatest interest. The disadvantage is that the data refer to a very limited calendar period.

Another major concern is the ability of a country to carry out a full census. Both in developed and less-developed countries, the recent global economic crisis has affected the census budget to nontrivial degrees. In some cases, countries also may be paralyzed from natural disasters and humanitarian crises, and others may simply avoid counting or providing information on migrants for discriminatory reasons (Zlotnik et al., 2010). Indeed, even the most trusted source of immigration data also suffers from many challenges.

Surveys

Because sample surveys are less costly than censuses, they can be used to probe more deeply into the migrations of their fewer respondents. On the other hand, surveys have the weakness of not supplying information about every local area, only those that are included in the sample. The ideal balance seems to be to include as many questions as can be afforded in decennial censuses or large national samples, and then to supplement those with periodic and more intensive surveys. This is the practice in the United States, where the Current Population Survey has contained detailed questions about prior residence and decennial censuses have asked general questions about prior residence in earlier periods.

Intensive *retrospective* migration surveys attempt to record the entire sequence of lifetime moves for respondents, the areas of origin and destination, the timing of migration, and related life-course events that may reveal the determinants or consequences of migrations. Alternately, repeated surveys, which follow a cohort through time (e.g., the National Longitudinal Surveys), can trace the history of individuals' migration as it unfolds.

Globally, the World Bank's Africa Migration Project has been collecting data on international migration and remittances, and the ILO has been assisting governments to collect data on migrant labors. The European Union has routine surveys that collect labor-force behavior of international migrants and has been publishing data publicly through the Eurostat system. Other unique surveys, such as the MMP and the LAMP, produce rich information on migrants by taking specialized household surveys and in-depth interviews in both the source and the destination countries.

While these specialized surveys provide valuable in-depth data on immigration, they also face many challenges exactly because they are specialized. Often, specific researchers or institutions carry out these surveys based on different priorities and motives, so they may adopt different definitions of migration and ask specific questions that are not comparable to others. They also are conducted on an ad-hoc basis due to limited budgets. In addition, because they are specialized, not all data is available for public use (Zlotnik et al., 2010).

Estimating from Intercensal Growth

If a country has repetitive censuses and either ongoing counts or estimates of mortality and fertility, it can use these to deduce *net* migration. Because this strategy does not involve the actual counting of moves as they happen, or even inferring particular moves from changes in reported residence, these techniques have been called *indirect* or *residual* (Bogue, 1993).

One technique is the **vital statistics method**. Remember the growth equation from chapter 1? It was stated as

$$P_2 - P_1 = (B - D) + M$$

For estimating net migration, the equation can be converted to

$$M = (P_2 - P_1) - (B - D)$$

That is to say: The net migration between censuses (M) is equal to the total growth between the censuses ($P_2 - P_1$) minus the natural increase between the censuses ($B - D$). Since most countries are relatively confident of their census totals and have developed methods for making at least rough estimates of their total deaths and births, this method is usually considered the most reliable for gauging *net* migration (Bogue, 1993). Exercise 3 at the end of the chapter illustrates the use of this vital statistics method.

Aside from being limited to net migration, the vital statistics method also can be inaccurate. Censuses do err, and the estimates of fertility and mortality can be approximate. Moreover, since the migration component in the equation is usually small compared with those of growth and natural increase, even a small absolute error in those other components can result in a large proportional misestimation of net migration (Bogue, 1993).

A refinement of the same strategy makes estimates for one age-sex class at a time. If we know the size of a given living cohort at the end of the interval and at the beginning of the interval, and if we can estimate the deaths that occurred to that age class in between, then we can infer the net migration of that cohort. The logic is precisely the same as for the vital statistics method, but applied to one category at a time.

These methods are also applicable for geographic units smaller than nations, where separate data are available for such units. Additional options for estimation are afforded when there is demographic information on a whole set of contiguous geographic areas, such as regions within a nation. For instance, we can use multiregional life tables for inferring not only net migration but also migration flows among regions. A method requiring less data is the **national growth rate method**, which compares the growth in any subnational area with that in the nation as a whole and attributes deviations to net migration (Shryock and Siegel, 1976).

Accuracy aside, indirect methods are limited in the completeness of information they provide. They estimate net migration but do not describe migration streams unless supplemented with other data. They do not automatically identify the composition of the residual net migrant population unless they are applied to birth, death, and population data available separately for each such group. Yet, in the imperfect world of migration statistics, they play a major role.

Table 9-1 illustrates the application of the vital statistics method to estimate net migration for world regions during the year preceding 2015. Column 1 of the table shows the population at the end of the period. Columns 2 and 3 record estimates of the births and deaths in the preceding year (using the annual averages from the five years 2010–2015). Column 4 is the natural increase resulting from the excess of births over deaths, obtained by subtracting column 3 from column 2. The population growth in column 5 is the difference between the 2015 population and the preceding year's population (estimated by subtracting the average annual growth over the preceding five years). Subtracting natural increase, column 4, from the total growth, column 5, then leaves a residual change that must be due to net migration—column 6.

Table 9-1   Net Migration into World Regions, 2014–2015, Estimated by the Vital Statistics Method Using the 2010–2015 Annual Averages

(In Thousands) Region	P_2 2015 Population (1)	B Births (2)	D Deaths (3)	B–D Natural Increase (4)	P_2–P_1 Total Growth (5)	M Net Migration (6)
World	7,324,782	695,605	287,010	408,595	408,599	
More-Developed Regions	1,259,588	70,215	64,735	5,480	18,653	13,173
Less-Developed Regions	6,065,194	625,390	222,275	403,115	389,945	–13,170
Africa	1,166,239	195,020	57,385	137,635	135,155	–2,480
Asia	4,384,844	379,200	152,635	226,565	219,404	–7,161
Europe	743,123	40,030	43,110	–3,080	2,815	5,895
Latin America and the Caribbean	630,089	55100	18,100	37,000	33,898	–3,102
Northern America	361,128	23,015	14,485	8,530	14,627	6,097
Oceania	39,359	3245	1290	1,955	2,700	745

Note: Because these estimates are rounded to thousands, they may not add up to 100%.

Source: United Nations, 2013d. *World Population Prospects: The 2012 Revision.* Used with permission.

We will elaborate on the substantive global net migration pattern revealed in Table 9-1, but we can use the table as a global preview now. We can see that less-developed regions lost migrants (i.e., had a negative net migration) to the more-developed regions. Asia had the largest negative net migration, in absolute numbers; Africa had the smallest. Europe and Northern America were the regions with the greatest net gain of migrants, with fewer going to Oceania.

Estimating Undocumented Immigration

The data sources discussed so far are not completely satisfactory in measuring even documented migration, so one can imagine how difficult it is to estimate *undocumented* migration, where the migrant usually has the intention of remaining uncounted. The United Nations (1998a) cites efforts in the United States as illustrating the best attempt to document illegal immigration. The U.S. Citizenship & Immigration

Services (USCIS) has greatly improved its estimates since the early 1990s. And since the 2001 terrorist attacks, the USCIS has devoted increasing attention to authenticating potentially fraudulent immigration documentation and tracking immigrants once in the United States.

The most common estimation method for counting undocumented immigration is the *residual method*. The procedure counts all of the documented foreign-born population (naturalized citizens, legal permanent residents, refugees, and temporary legal residents) and subtracts this total from the total foreign-born population counted in the census. The leftover residual population is the undocumented immigrant population (Passel and Cohn, 2011). The USCIS further hones this estimate down using administrative records on immigrants who entered legally but overstayed their permitted visit, mortality among undocumented immigrants, and so on. Border-crossing data are used to identify visits not completed by subsequent departures. Censuses and Current Population Surveys are used to adjust foreign-born populations for undercounting. More complex procedures are used to estimate the departures, or emigration, of arriving undocumented populations. Although the integration of these data sources and estimation methods allows for considerable error, the latest U.S. estimates ranged from 10.7 to 13.9 million depending on the assumptions made (Hoefer et al., 2012).

Few countries have invested as much effort in estimating undocumented migration streams as has the United States. However, all countries use the same basic types of data to estimate migration trends and make some efforts to monitor otherwise undocumented migrations.

International Migration

Much of the history of human migration, of course, occurred before demographers ever began collecting data on migration. To place our discussion in a historical context, it is useful to briefly review these prehistoric and historic migration patterns. In this section we trace the different forms, or types, of human migration from prehistoric to modern times. We end our discussion with a more detailed treatment of modern migration streams and their impacts on receiving nations.

Prehistoric and Historic Variety

The earliest human populations migrated. We believe that the first humans were game hunters and wanderers, gatherers of plants, nuts, and berries. Many of these movements were long enough to cross continental and regional boundaries; some would have been international if there had been nations then. Yet the nature and meaning of human migration has changed over time—with respect to the migratory forces that cause people to move, the typical size of the social unit doing the moving (e.g., groups, families, individuals, or masses), and the degree of choice enjoyed by the movers.

Primitive migration refers to moves forced by an ecological push, such as a deterioration in the resources necessary to support a people. Many prehistoric migrations were likely of this sort. A more technically advanced people might have responded with innovations that would have enabled them to adapt to the changing environment; peoples with primitive technologies historically have responded by collectively moving.

Early primitive migrations probably could be called *wandering*, moving away from one place but without a definite destination. For instance, those people who most likely moved from Siberia to Alaska over the land bridge between 26,000 and 8000 BCE probably were not aiming to settle in North America; they likely knew nothing of it. More contemporary forms of primitive migration would be groups of people (clans, tribes) *ranging* over perhaps fixed traditional routes, gathering food in season or, more prevalently now, raising cattle as *nomads*. Another contemporary form of primitive migration would be illustrated by rural peoples, where the agricultural land has been overused or overpopulated, who flee to the cities.

Forced or impelled migration in various forms results, indirectly or directly, from state expansions and conflicts. Expanding nations often set up trading outposts, such as did the Phoenicians and the Greeks around the Mediterranean. A step up in scale would be the establishment of colonies, such as during Europe's mercantile period. American readers, of course, are familiar with this kind of immigration, which occurred during their colonial history. On a larger and more dramatic scale would be invasions, such as the Roman conquest of Gaul and Britain. There are many modern examples as well. In these, the invading state's intention is not necessarily to move large numbers of its people into the new territory, but rather to subdue, control, and extract resources. Increasingly important refugee movements of modern times bear witness to the persistence of forced migrations.

Slavery and *indentured servitude* are further examples of forced migrations. Slavery in the Western Hemisphere was dominated in premodern times by the trade of Africans to the New World, extending from the late 15th century to the abolition of slavery at various dates in the 19th century (Eltis, 2007). It is estimated that about 12 million slaves were imported into the Americas between 1550 and 1850, the vast majority to the Caribbean (4 million) and Brazil (5.5 million) (Trans-Atlantic Slave Trade Database, 2013). The relatively smaller number of African slaves imported to the United States, however, has had a disproportionately greater impact on its current population diversity (see chapter 11). As for indentured servitude, there are a very limited number of artifacts that chronicles the experiences of indentured servants from their perspectives. Below is a rare firsthand narrative account, taken from a letter Richard Frethorne, an indentured servant, wrote in 1623 to his parents:

> And I have nothing to comfort me, nor is there nothing to be gotten here
> but sickness and death, except [in the event] that one had money to lay out
> in some things for profit. But I have nothing at all no, not a shirt to my back
> but two rags, nor clothes but one poor suit, nor but one pair of shoes, but
> one pair of stockings, but one cap, [and] but two bands [collars]. My cloak
> is stolen by one of my fellows, and to his dying hour [he] would not tell me
> what he did with it; but some of my fellows saw him have butter and beef
> out of a ship, which my cloak, I doubt [not], paid for. So that I have not a
> penny, nor a penny worth, to help me too either spice or sugar or strong
> waters, without which one cannot live here. For as strong beer in England
> doth fatten and strengthen them, so water here doth wash and weaken
> these here [and] only keeps [their] life and soul together. But I am not half
> [of] a quarter so strong as I was in England, and all is for want of victuals;
> for I do protest unto you that I have eaten more in [one] day at home than I

have allowed me here for a week. You have given more than my day's allowance to a beggar at the door; and if Mr. Jackson had not relieved me, I should be in a poor case. But he like a father and she like a loving mother doth still help me. (Frethorne, 1623 taken from Murrell, 2000)

Free migration is the kind of migration with which American readers are most familiar. The outstanding example was the migration of some 60 million Europeans between the 16th and 20th centuries. Principal destinations were the United States, Argentina, Canada, Brazil, Australia, New Zealand, South Africa, and the British West Indies. The surge in European emigration corresponded with two important changes. One was the demographic transition in Europe, the reduction in the death rate prior to a lowered birth rate, resulting in national population explosions first in Northern and Western Europe and then in the rest of Europe. The other was the improvement in transportation, such as the invention of the steamship. The important thing for readers to keep in mind is that this immense wave of free migration was something of an isolated phenomenon in the long prehistory and history of human migration.

Premodern Migration Streams, 1500–1965

Figure 9-2 maps the major intercontinental net migration streams from 1500 until the beginning of the modern migration period in 1965 (adapted from Woytinsky and Woytinsky, 1953). The seven major, largely intercontinental, migration streams of the premodern period are numbered on the map.

The first three streams identified were primarily made up of free migrations: (1) the mass migration from all parts of Europe to North America, (2) the north-to-south migration from Latin countries of Europe to Central and South America, and (3) the migrations of colonial expansion from Great Britain to Africa and Australia. However, colonial expansions did include indentured servants, forced migration of slaves and convicts, and so on. While much of the migrations in these three streams were freely motivated, it often led to the forced relocation or genocide of indigenous people living in those locations.

Two of the migration streams identified were exclusively or largely forced migrations: (4) the importation of slaves from the western parts of Africa to the Caribbean, South America, and North America, and (5) the (partly intercontinental, partly intracontinental) migrations from China and India abroad. While migrations from China and India included free migrations, we identify them with forced migration because of the substantial role of indentured labor in these migration streams.

Also shown on the map are two important streams of interregional but internal migration: (6) the westward and then southward movement of the population within the United States, and (7) the eastward and northward movements in Russia to settle northern environs (later to be government sponsored). Especially in North America, these internal migrations were frequently simple extensions of the great transatlantic voyages. It is not so much that the eastern U.S. population moved westward as that the destinations for transatlantic immigrants moved westward.

The list of migration streams in Figure 9-2 is not exhaustive; population movements are widespread, continual, and fluctuating over this premodern period. Even the listed streams were far from constant over time. The mass migration from Europe to North America (numbered 1 in Figure 9-2) is an example.

Figure 9-2

Major World Migration Streams, 1500–1965

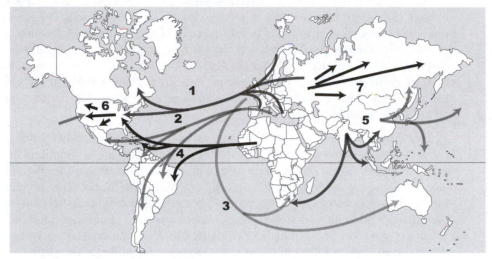

1. From all Europe to North America
2. Latin European countries to Central and South America
3. Great Britain to Africa and Australia
4. African slavery to Caribbean, Latin America, and North America
5. China and India abroad (inter- and intracontinental)
6. American westward and southward expansion
7. Russian eastward and northern expansion

Sources: Adapted from Woytinsky and Woytinsky, 1953. *World Population and Production*; McEvedy and Jones, 1978. *Atlas of World Population History.*

   This immigration stream, familiar to U.S. readers, actually consisted of a series of migration *waves* (Martin and Midgley, 1994). The first wave occurred from 1790 to 1820 and consisted primarily of English, as well as Scotch, Scotch-Irish, German, Dutch, French, and Spanish immigrants seeking religious and political freedoms or economic betterment. The second wave, from 1820 to 1860, consisted of German, British, and Irish immigrants, many displaced by the industrial revolution in Europe and local hardships such as the Irish famines. The third wave, from 1880 to 1914, came largely from countries of Southern and Eastern Europe and flowed into the eastern and midwestern United States (at more or less the same time as the migration from Asian countries, numbered 5 in Figure 9-2, flowed into the western United States). More than with earlier waves, the promise of a better life in the rapidly industrializing United States constituted a pull, rather than a push, underlying this third migration wave. After these three great waves, nativist legislation was passed curbing Southern and Eastern European immigration, and barring completely almost all from Asia. There was a rise of World War II-related migration, but when immigration restrictions were finally eased in the mid-1960s, a fourth wave of modern immigration began which has lasted until the present.

Modern Migration Streams

With continuous and changing streams, choosing a starting point to introduce *modern* migration is difficult. We have chosen 1965 to separate Figures 9-2 and 9-3, although the shift from premodern to modern migration patterns actually spanned the period from the end of World War II until then. During this couple of decades, migration patterns underwent a fundamental change from migrations largely influenced by European population expansion and political history, to migrations increasingly influenced by globalization, the demographics of post-Soviet transition countries, and refugee movements from conflicts and civil war. Figure 9-3 maps the major migration streams of the modern period.

Free migration. In the United States, as we have observed, when immigration restrictions were eased in the mid-1960s, the 20th-century lull in immigration gave way to a fourth wave. The countries from which the fourth wave of immigrants has come, however, are vastly different than before or during the World Wars. Immigration to the United States from Europe continued, but at diminished levels (labeled number 1 in Figure 9-3). In the Americas, the dominant stream of migration changed from Europeans going to South and North America to Latin Americans going to North America, with slowing immigration around the recent Great Recession period.

In Europe, the postwar political realignments, rebuilding, and prosperity of Western Europe drew immigrants from Eastern Europe, lasting until the dissolution of the Soviet Union. Prosperity in Europe and the aging of the European workforce have attracted immigrants from northern Africa and the Mideast (labeled number 3), although these flows stalled temporarily during the 2007–2009 recession and its aftermath. These changes have resulted in a shift, as in the Americas, from north-south to south-north migration streams.

Although the causes are quite different, a similar reversal of migration patterns occurred in the Russian Federation and Commonwealth of Independent States. Following the breakup of the Soviet Union, the former migration streams to settle the less-developed regions to the north and south have been reversed by migrations back to central Russia and by ethnic minorities returning to ancestral homelands (labeled number 4 in Figure 9-3). In 1991 some 25 million Russians were living in non-Russia successor states. Return migration to Russia from the Transcaucasian Republics (Armenia, Azerbaijan, and Georgia) alone peaked at nearly 600,000 in 1993. Despite differences, this change has some similarities to the European and American cases.

In all three areas described above, pre-WWII migration streams that had flowed from the more-developed regions into the less-developed ones shifted their direction. In modern times migration streams to MDRs now mostly flow from LDRs. This change in direction is one hallmark of modern migration patterns. However, we should note that there are very early signs of initial immigrant streams of LDR immigrants into nontraditional destinations, such as the emerging economies of China, South Africa, and Brazil, in recent years (Migration Policy Institute, 2012). Internal migration streams between European countries have also grown steadily with the rise of the European Union (EU) and its opening of within-EU borders.

Modern migrations differ from the pre-WWII migration streams in other ways. Not all these migrations are permanent relocations in the sense that an arduous transatlan-

Figure 9-3

Major World Migration Streams, 1965–2005

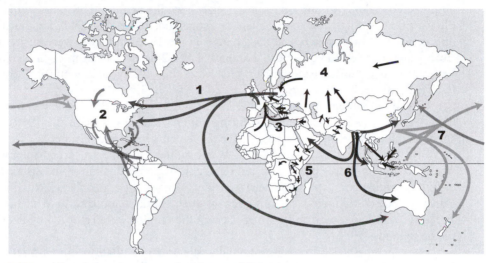

1. Slowed European migration to American and Oceania
2. Latin America and Canada to the United States and Japan*
3. North Africa, developing countries and Eastern Europe to Western Europe*
4. Returns to Central Russia after breakup of the USSR
5. Refugees (e.g., African, Afghan, Balkan, Pakistani, Iranian, Palestinian, and Southeast Asia)
6. Bangladesh, Pakistan, and Sri Lanka abroad*
7. Philippine and Asian abroad*

*Including temporary labor migrations
Note: Political boundaries circa 1965.

Sources: Zlotnick, *International Migration 1965–96*, 1998; National Geographic, "Migration," 1998; United Nations, *World Population Monitoring 1997*, 1998a (and updated with Stephen Castles and Mark Miller, *The Age of Migration*, 2003 and Martin and Widgren, "International Migration: Facing the Challenge," 2002).

tic crossing once implied. Temporary migrations and refugee moves outnumber permanent migrations by more than ten to one in modern times. It is also important to note that most LDR to MDR migration streams are highly selective, given the distances and resources required to relocate, as well as substantial barriers to migration that many MDRs now impose. In fact, only 20% of LDR migration is to MDRs. Most migrants from LDRs migrate to neighboring countries, usually other LDRs (UNCTAD, 2012).

Forced migration. A second major change in the modern migration period is a shift in the levels and patterns of forced migration. Since the end of World War II the size of forced migration has increased. The global refugee population, for example, increased from under 2 million in 1965 to more than 15 million persons by 2013 (United Nations, 2013b; UNHCR, 2005). These are individuals who must leave their homes for their own safety or survival, often due to war or natural disaster. When including the number of people who have also been internally-displaced, the number of refugees climbs to an estimated 43 million worldwide (United Nations, 2013b). The sources of refugee movements have also changed: in the 1940s and 1950s forced migrations were mostly consequences of the European wars and declining European empires. Forced migrations today have largely been the result of U.S. wars in the Middle East and conflicts among some less-developed countries. The changing global origins of refugees over time reflect this change: in the 1950s, refugees were largely from European countries; in 2012 more than half of all refugees were from Afghanistan and Iraq or from countries experiencing civil war, such as Syria, Sudan, and Somalia (UNHCR, 2013a, 2005).

Forced migrations during and after World War II (e.g., millions of Jews streaming from Germany as political refugees during Hitler's rise to power in the 1930s) foreshadowed the rising importance of refugee movements in the modern period. The close of World War II and the ensuing Cold War resulted in immense forced migrations. About 20 million people in Eastern and Central Europe were involved in various kinds of flights, exchanges, expulsions, and transfers. Most of these people relocated within Europe; some ended up in North America or other frontier countries. In Asia, 3 million Japanese who had moved to far-flung parts of the empire were returned by decree to the homeland.

Postwar emergence from the colonial system also resulted in forced migrations. The partition of India and Pakistan in 1947, for example, resulted in about 7 million Hindus fleeing to India and an equal number of Muslims fleeing to Pakistan. In 1948, following the establishment of the state of Israel, about 700,000 Palestinian Arabs fled. The Communist victory in China in 1949 caused the migration of uncounted millions to elsewhere in Asia, such as Taiwan. The Cuban revolution sent a wave of migrants across the South Atlantic to the shores of Florida and beyond. The Indo-Pakistani war in 1971 gave birth to the state of Bangladesh and triggered the exchange of millions more among that country, India, and Pakistan.

The establishment of postcolonial African states, with boundaries arbitrarily designated by former colonial powers, resulted in massive migrations and set the stage for future conflicts in the region. Such streams are labeled number 5 in Figure 9-3. Conflicts among, and civil wars within, African states have resulted in significant refugee migrations in Somalia, Sudan, the Democratic Republic of the Congo, and Mali, among others. The U.S. invasion of Afghanistan and Iraq, the Arab-Israeli conflict, and conflict in Syria have sparked other refugee movements. As a result, most refugee populations tend to cluster in neighboring LDR countries, with MDRs taking in only a small proportion (19%) of refugees (UNHCR, 2013a). Figure 9-4 shows the percentages of refugees per world region to illustrate this tendency. Asian countries host almost half of the world's refugees, many of whom are Afghans displaced by the U.S.-Afghanistan war. African countries also host a substantial proportion, over 30%, of refugees.

In addition to refugee migration, another type of forced migration is modern-day **human trafficking**. Trafficking in humans is defined as recruitment by force or deception for purposes of sexual exploitation or forced labor. Figure 9-5 on p. 342 shows the regional origins of transnationally trafficked victims. Arrows point to countries where demand is most prevalent. Wealthier regions, such as North America, Western Europe, and the Middle East fuel much of the demand for trafficked migration, while most of the victims come from poorer regions, such as East and South Asia, Eastern Europe, and sub-Saharan Africa. In Europe, Africans are the most commonly trafficked victims, whereas in the Americas it is East Asians. Trafficking victims in the Middle East are from a wide variety of regional origins. It is estimated that 20.9 million people are human trafficking victims globally, 27% of whom are children (UNODC, 2012). Because it is a clandestine activity and not defined as a crime in all countries, the prevalence and severity of human trafficking is underestimated. But the phenomenon is gaining increasing international attention, with 134 countries officially criminalizing the practice. The United Nations Office on Drugs and Crime is aggressively pushing awareness of trafficking activity and now collects systematic data to assist countries in, first, recognizing the phenomenon and, second, prosecuting traffickers and repatriating victims.

Temporary voluntary labor migration. The third major change creating modern migration patterns has been the rise of large-scale temporary labor force

Figure 9-4

World Refugee Population by UN Region at the End of 2012

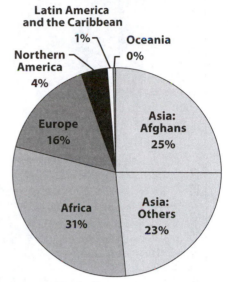

Source: Data taken from UNHCR, 2013b. Figure created by Eiko Strader.

relocations from the less-developed to the more-developed economies. This is often referred to as "circular" migration undertaken by "guest workers." International streams of this sort have become sizable in the modern day context of globalization and high-speed transportation systems.

The same conditions that have attracted free immigration into Europe and North America (i.e., an aging labor force and relative prosperity), when coupled with immigration restrictions, encourage the importation of foreign migrants with a nonpermanent, guest worker, or **undocumented** status to fulfill labor-force needs. Migration streams into these countries from less-developed regions (labeled 2 and 3 in Figure 9-3) include substantial temporary labor migrations. In the oil-rich Gulf countries, very large percentages of the population are comprised of guest-worker immigrants. In some of these countries, such as Kuwait, Qatar, and the United Arab Emirates, immigrants comprise a *majority*. The first waves of immigrants were mainly recruited from poorer Middle Eastern countries, such as Palestine, Yemen, and Jordan, but the majority of temporary workers in the Gulf states today are now recruited from Asia (Kapiszewski, 2006).

Two migration streams from Asia consist substantially of temporary labor migrations. The first of these streams has been from South Central Asia (e.g., Bangladesh, India, Pakistan, and Sri Lanka) to other Asian countries and abroad to the Middle East and Oceania (labeled number 6 in Figure 9-3). Another major migration stream is that from Southeast Asia (e.g., Indonesia, the Philippines, and Thailand) and eastern Asia (e.g., China and Korea) to western Asia and abroad (labeled number 7).

Figure 9-5

Regional Origins of Victims Detected in Major Destination Regions, 2007–2010

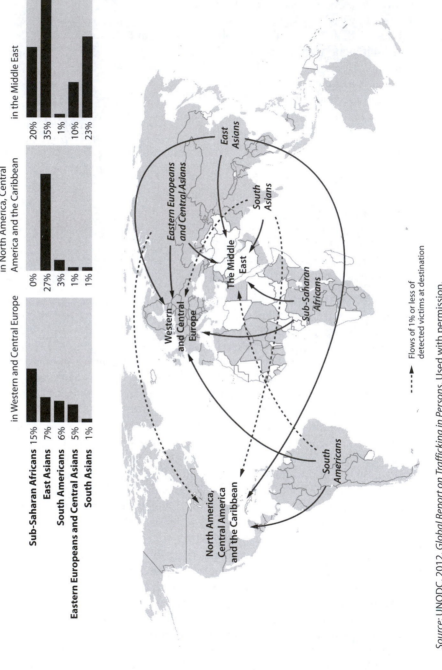

Source: UNODC, 2012. *Global Report on Trafficking in Persons.* Used with permission.

Not all labor-force migration streams are temporary migrations, of course, and even those that begin as temporary in intent may not remain so. These migration streams are, however, a salient part of modern migration patterns. As we shall see in the next section, they can pose problems for both host countries and the immigrant due to the ambiguity of their temporary status.

Impact on Resident Populations

Let us turn from the study of international migration as a population process to the study of the impact of that process on population size and composition. It is these net results, rather than the movements themselves, that cause the most concern, especially in countries of destination.

Table 9-1 introduced a method of estimating net migration. Let us use it now to summarize net migration for world regions currently. We can see that the less-developed regions lost migrants and that the more-developed regions gained the same migrants. Asia had the largest negative net migration, with most other net migration loss coming from Africa, Latin America, and the Caribbean. Europe and Northern America (U.S. and Canada) were the regions with the greatest net gain of migrants. Oceania was less heavily involved numerically in either plus or minus net migration.

Table 9-2 allows us to assess roughly the impact of net migration on destination region populations during the modern period. Specifically, it tells the percentages of regional populations that were foreign born in 1965 and in 2010, and the increase (or decrease) between those two years.

The more-developed regions have a greater proportion of foreign born than do the less-developed, and the gap has widened over the modern period. Note that the impact of net migration on a country or region is influenced not only by the number of net migrants it receives, but also by the size of the resident receiving population. Oceania (dominated by Australia-New Zealand) dramatizes this point. Although it was singled

Table 9-2   Migrants as a Percent of World Regional Populations, 1965–2010

Region	Foreign-Born Population as Percent of Region's Population		
	1965	2010	Increase
World	2.3	3.1	0.8
Africa	2.5	1.9	−0.6
Asia	1.7	1.5	−0.2
Latin America and Caribbean	2.4	1.3	−1.1
Northern America	6.0	14.5	8.5
Europe	3.6	9.5	5.9
Oceania	14.4	16.4	2.0

Sources: United Nations, 1998a. *World Population Monitoring,* table 6; UNHCR, 2013a. "Displacement: The New 21st Century Challenge."

out in Table 9-1 as a low importer of net migrants numerically, it stands out in Table 9-2 in terms of the impact of those immigrants on its small resident population.

The high proportion of MDR populations that are foreign born, then, is a result of both a numerically large net migration and a numerically small resident population. For many European countries, net in-migration exceeds their natural growth, keeping them from shrinking in population size (Robustillo et al., 2013). High national net migration rates in the MDRs are altering the ethnic compositions and diversity of more-developed countries, as we will detail in chapter 11.

Internal Migration: The U.S. Case

Which internal moves (that is, intranational moves) are migrations? **Internal migration** can be interregional, interstate, interprovince, intercounty, intercommunity, and even interneighborhood. Again, whom you call a migrant depends on which kind of boundaries you are using and how fine a net you are casting over the movers.

Of all the patterns of internal migration that nations could study, three are of particular interest. One is interregional migration, as typified by the shifting regional population of the United States, which we address here. Another is rural-to-urban (and sometimes urban-to-rural) migration. We are saving separate treatment of that for chapter 10. The third is the migration and spatial distribution of ethnic populations within countries, a subject we will address in more detail in chapter 11.

We focus here on the example of regional migration salient to most readers—that within the borders of the United States. By choosing interregional migration, we are viewing the "big picture" of internal migration. Remember, however, that a demographer advising local community planning officials, for example, might zoom in on a different level of internal migration, such as state, community, or even neighborhood.

A Brief History of U.S. Interregional Migration

Initial settlement of the thirteen colonies concentrated on what is now the East Coast of the United States. At the time Thomas Jefferson supervised the first census in 1790, the population was equally divided among the northern and southern states. Although northeastern states attracted immigrants from abroad, they lost population, partially through out-migration, to other regions. The percentage of the national population in the Northeast steadily declined over the past two centuries and is now less than one-fourth of the population.

The opening of rich croplands in the Ohio River valley initially drew migrants from New England. Later, migration to the Midwest boomed as industry in the region expanded after the Civil War. At its peak in 1890, the Midwest held more than one-third of the country's population, and in the 1940s midwestern cities drew substantial numbers of black Americans migrating northward from the southern states, as they now attract immigrants from Latin America and the Caribbean. Yet throughout the 20th century the Midwest grew more slowly than did the rest of the country.

For the past two centuries, the population of the South grew much more slowly than the other American regions. But in recent decades, internal and international migration has brought about a resurgence of southern and southwestern growth.

Meanwhile, increasing immigration from Latin America and the Caribbean to both urban and rural areas has also contributed to rapid growth in the South. The South has, at this time, gained the greatest share of the nation's population, at 37% compared to 23% in the West, 22% in the Midwest, and 18% in the Northeast (Mackun and Wilson, 2011).

Western states were admitted to the union between 1848 (California) and 1959 (Hawaii). The West attracted in-migration continuously since 1848 with the California gold rush, Depression-era dustbowl migrations westward, and the postwar economic boom. It owes recent growth to a share in more recent internal Sunbelt migrations and to immigration from Latin America and Asia. At the time of the Civil War, only one in fifty residents lived west of the Rocky Mountains; in 2010 one in four residents lived in the West. Today the West has a larger population than both the Northeast and Midwest.

Although international migration and natural increase (births minus deaths) can affect the distribution of the nation's population across regions, internal migration accounts for many of these U.S. regional changes. The western flow of the population out of the Northeast, and later out of the Midwest, has been sustained. The other major net migration stream flowed from the South to the North until after World War II. During its prime it had a heavy component of African Americans and poor whites seeking opportunity in the industrializing Northeast and Midwest. By the 1960s when the U.S. began deindustrializing, the net flow reversed and migration from the northeastern and midwestern Rustbelt states to the southern Sunbelt states became well-established. By the beginning of the 21st century, even the southern exodus of the African American population to the North reversed itself, so that for every African American who left the South, two others moved in (Rastogi et al., 2011; Schachter, 2003; Frey, 1998; see also chapter 11). More African Americans than whites relocate to the American South today, and these migration streams tend to be more highly educated and disproportionately comprised of women (Hunt et al., 2013).

Current Interregional Net Migration

Table 9-3 on the following page lists Census Bureau estimates of interregional migration in the United States for 2011 to 2012. Looking at the number of domestic migrants in the left half of the table, we see that the Northeast and Midwest continued to have net out-migration while the South and West continued to gain from internal migration. The biggest losses were in the Northeast and the biggest gains in the West.

However, interregional migration is only one factor influencing the regional distribution of population. Especially in a country with heavy international migration, such as the United States, migration also can be a major determinant. Immigration from abroad (column 2) has profoundly altered the impacts of U.S. internal migration over the past decade. Domestic loss in the Midwest was canceled out, while losses in the Northeast would have been much greater were it not for immigration gains. Meanwhile, the internal migration gains in the South and the West were more than quadrupled due to immigration from abroad.

Several demographers suggest that, recently, there is a close connection between international migration and subsequent internal migration (White and Liang, 1998; Frey and Liaw, 1998; Frey, 1996). According to this argument, as immigrants enter population centers they increase the supply of labor in an area, especially lower-skilled

Table 9-3   Interregional Migration, United States, 2011 to 2012

Region	Net Domestic (1)	From Abroad (2)	Total (3)
Northeast	−324,000	273,000	−51,000
Midwest	−99,000	563,000	464,000
South	164,000	1,064,000	1,228,000
West	260,000	839,000	1,099,000
	Rate (per 1,000 Residents)		
Northeast	−5.96	5.02	−0.94
Midwest	−1.52	8.62	7.10
South	1.44	9.37	10.81
West	3.63	11.71	15.33

Note: Ages 1 year and older.

Source: U.S. Census Bureau, 2012. "Geographical Mobility: 2011 to 2012 Data."

labor. An oversupply of labor may then encourage domestic internal migration out of the region by those in the same labor market. Evidence for this migration pattern is, however, mixed. Recent out-migration from urbanized areas of California and Northeastern states, for example, is largely middle class, and unlikely threatened by competition with low-skill immigrant labor. More likely, they are escaping high living costs and rapid urban development. Frey has compared this movement to the post–World War II flight of middle-class Americans (primarily white at the time) from cities to suburbs (Frey, 2003). Many are settling in more suburbanized metropolitan areas that stretch in a geographical swath from southeastern states like North Carolina and Georgia to western states like Nevada and Utah. Frey has coined this region the "New Sunbelt," and it is growing faster than any other part of the country (Frey, 2002, 2003). Between 1990 and 2000, for example, Atlanta increased its black share of the population by 60% and its white share of the population by 175%. High growth rates in nontraditional sunbelt geographical regions continued into the 21st century, but the 2007–2009 recession led to a five-year hiatus in migration to these areas (Frey, 2009). Early signs show that migration to these destinations is recovering. Table 9-4 shows the top ten population growth rates for U.S. metropolitan areas in 2010–2011 and 2011–2012. All of these fast-growing areas are located in the American South and West. Between the two periods, growth rates are generally increasing as the economy and housing market recovers from the recession.

Effect of Population Age Composition

The changing age composition of the United States (see chapter 4) also affects internal migration. The chances that a person will migrate are highest for those entering the labor market, normally young adults. Since these young adults often have families, the next most likely group to migrate is children. In the United States, there also is a tendency for individuals to migrate at retirement ages.

As an example of internal migration age selectivity, Figure 9-6 analyzes migration in two periods, prior to the recession and during the recession.

As expected, the individuals with the highest migration rates (measured as moves per 100 residents) were those of entry labor-force ages, from twenty to thirty. The second highest rates of migration are among those under five years old, and there is a small retirement bump around age sixty to sixty-five. Comparing trends during the

Table 9-4   Highest U.S. Growth Rates, 2011–2012

Growth Rank	Metro Area	Percent Population Change 2011–2012	Percent Population Change 2010–2011
1	Austin-Round Rock, TX	3.01	3.07
2	Charleston-North Charleston, SC	2.31	2.11
3	Orlando-Kissimmee-Sanford, FL	2.24	1.66
4	Raleigh, NC	2.23	2.23
5	Cape Coral-Fort Myers, FL	2.17	1.77
6	Houston-The Woodlands-Sugar Land, TX	2.07	1.74
7	Dallas-Fort Worth-Arlington, TX	2.01	1.80
8	San Antonio-New Braunfels, TX	1.93	1.79
9	Provo-Orem, UT	1.93	1.95
10	Phoenix-Mesa-Scottsdale, AZ	1.82	1.01

Note: For metropolitan areas where end of period group population exceeds 50,000.

Source: Frey, 2013. "Economic Improvement Nudges U.S. Migration to Normal." Brookings Institute.

Figure 9-6

Interstate Migration Rate by Age, United States, 2000–2001 and 2008–2009

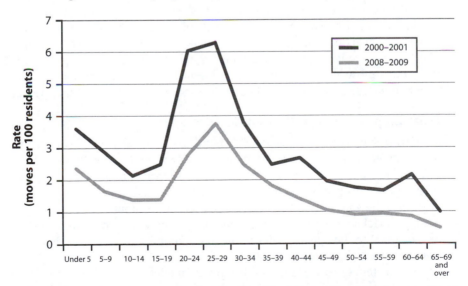

Source: Frey, 2009. "The Great American Migration Slowdown," fig. 3. Metropolitan Policy Program, Brookings Institute.

recession, it is notable that internal migration trends on the whole are notably lower, particularly among young adults entering the labor market who faced less cross-regional employment opportunities. The retirement bump is all but absent during the recession period, reflecting fewer retirements as well as lessened real estate elasticity.

What is the relevance of such age selectivity to internal migration in the United States? Over the past several decades the impact of the baby-boom generation on the age structure and thus on internal migration has been significant. During the 1970s the baby boom reached employment ages and the migration streams out of the Northeast and Midwest to the South and West generated levels of net migration nearly three times those of the previous two decades (Plane, 1992). Yet many of the baby boomers delayed moving (as they delayed marriage and fertility) and then moved during the 1980s, keeping internal migration high during that decade (Plane and Rogerson, 1991). In the 1990s, internal migration declined in all regions as the baby boomers settled in (the exception being a recent increase in out-migration from the Midwest (U.S. Census Bureau, 1998). In the 21st century, many baby boomers have reached retirement ages just as the recession made retirement-related migration less likely than originally projected. If the economy fully recovers, we can expect a rise in internal migration among baby boomers who are moving to their final retirement destinations.

Migration is selective not only with age, but potentially with gender, education, and other migrant characteristics. For example, the Americans most likely to make interstate migrations are often college-educated professionals because their labor markets are often more national than local. Empirical generalizations about selectivity in migration are presented in the next section.

Determinants of Migration

Why do people migrate? The *theoretical* study of migration began with observations that (1) not everybody is equally likely to move—indeed the vast majority of people in the world do not migrate internationally, and (2) knowing which people are most likely to move might help us understand the forces underlying migration. Identifying the groups most likely to migrate provides empirical generalizations about migration which might then contribute to theoretical explanations of migration (Pressat, 1985).

From Empirical Generalizations to Theories

The first empirical generalizations of this sort were those of E. G. Ravenstein, who wrote his editions of "Laws of Migration" in 1885 and 1889 (Pressat, 1985). Ravenstein's observations attempted to describe the general characteristics of migration and migrants. He also provided the basis for the *size-distance* rule, a concept later developed into the *gravity model* of George Zipf and S. A. Stouffer (see Pressat, 1985). The gravity model simply states that the number of migrants over a given distance will be proportional to the opportunities at the destination but inversely related to opportunities at a nearer distance.

Ravenstein's observations and the gravity model's notion of intervening influences were expanded upon by other demographers including E. S. Lee (1966, pp. 52–56), whose reformulation is quoted here. On the volume of migration, Lee states:

1. The volume of migration within a given territory varies with the degree of diversity of areas included in that territory.
2. The volume of migration varies with the diversity of people.
3. The volume of migration is related to the difficulty of surmounting the intervening obstacles.
4. The volume of migration varies with fluctuations in the economy.
5. Unless severe checks are imposed, both volume and rate of migration tend to increase with time.
6. The volume and rate of migration vary with the state of progress in a country or area.

On migration streams and *counterstreams*, he asserts:

1. Migration tends to take place largely within well-defined streams.
2. For every major migration stream, a counterstream develops.
3. The efficiency of the stream (the ratio of the stream to the counterstream) is high if the major factors in the development of a migration stream were minus factors at origin.
4. The efficiency of stream and counterstream tends to be low if origin and destination are similar.
5. The efficiency of streams will be high if the intervening obstacles are great.
6. The efficiency of a migration stream varies with economic conditions, being high in prosperous times and low in times of depression.

Lee went on to observe that migration is not only selective, but the degree of selectivity varies (1966, pp. 56–57). Where migration is influenced mostly by the attractions to the area of destination, then migrants are likely to be **positively selected**. That is, those who are most likely to win in the competition for those attractive qualities (e.g., jobs) are most likely to migrate. On the other hand, where migration is impelled mostly by negative forces at the area of origin (such as political upheaval or natural calamity), then the emigration is likely to be less selective. Obstacles between the area of origin and destination—distance, legal barriers, threats to survival—tend to make the migration more selective. And, over time, there is a tendency for selectivity in a migration stream to erode, as in pioneer migrations, in which adventurous young adults start the stream and later on send for their families and friends.

Lee also observed that migration is especially likely at transitions between life's stages: getting married, entering the workforce, when the children leave home, getting divorced, retiring, becoming widowed, and so on. As we have seen, one expression of this is the nearly universal age selectivity of migration as young adults enter the labor force. Migration also selects by sex, but the nature of that selection varies, depending on such things as the definition of gender roles. Traditionally, migration has selected for young men seeking work or fortunes abroad. But sex selectivity is becoming more varied as barriers to women's participation in the labor market are reduced, and particularly due to the globalization of demand for care workers (UNCTAD, 2012; Chant and Radcliffe, 1992). International migrants from MDRs are now majority female, and half of all global immigration is comprised of women (United Nations, 2005; UNFPA, 2006).

Despite this, policy debates on immigration still treat it as though it is a primarily male-driven phenomenon (Batalova, 2009). Culturally and politically defined identities (e.g., race and ethnicity, religion) may affect mobility directly, or indirectly through differences in occupation or educational opportunity, societal incorporation or cultural preferences, and the momentum created by existing migration streams (see chapters 10 and 11).

Lee incorporates these observations into a broad conceptual model of migration selectivity in *individual, voluntary* migration. The model is presented as Figure 9-7. Lee explains his *push-pull* migration model as follows:

> In every area there are countless factors which act to hold people within that area or attract people to it, and there are others which tend to repel them. These are shown in the diagram as + and – signs. There are others, shown as 0s, to which people are essentially indifferent. Some of these factors affect most people in much the same way, while others affect different people in different ways. (1966, p. 50)

Figure 9-7

E. S. Lee's Model of Voluntary Migration

Origin and Destination Factors and Intervening Obstacles in Migration

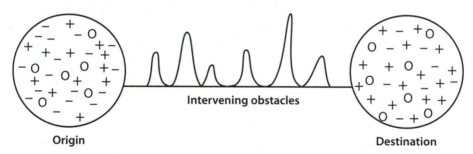

Source: Based on Lee, "A Theory of Migration," chart 1.

Between the two locations is a set of "intervening obstacles," which can be viewed as "costs" involved in moving from the origin to the destination. An abundance of pluses at the destination would attract migrants (a **migration pull**), while an abundance of minuses at the origin would repel migrants (a **migration push**). Intervening obstacles decrease the potency of these effects.

Migration Theories

Migration theory has been one of the most fruitful and rapidly developing areas of demography in recent decades. Several authors have recently reviewed and assessed the prevailing theories of migration (e.g., Brettell and Hollifield, 2007; Castles, 2007; United Nations, 1998a, 1998b; Stahl, 1995; Massey et al., 2005, 1994). A review of the major current migration theories is presented below.

Neoclassical economics (macro theory).   One of the earliest migration theories, the neoclassical economic theory attempts to explain the relationship between labor migration and economic development by theorizing that mass migration will tend to flow from countries with an oversupply of labor to those with unmet demands for labor. In theory, capital, including highly skilled human capital, also will tend to migrate from areas of abundance to those of scarcity where it can earn higher returns (i.e., usually moving in the opposite direction of mass labor migrations). Left unrestricted, migration of labor and capital will continue until an international equilibrium of labor supply and demand is reached. This is a macro theory in the sense that it does not pay much attention to the characteristics or motivations of migrants except for their skill, or human capital, and the wages available to them in different areas.

Neoclassical economics (micro theory).   Related to the macro theory, this view is formulated at the level of the individual migrant. According to this theory, individuals make rational choices on whether to migrate based on cost-benefit calculations. These calculations are not limited to immediate gains and losses but also include future expectations (see chapter 10 for a discussion of how this impacts rural-urban migration). In theory, and barring migration restrictions, a migrant will move to where the expected value of future returns is greatest. As demographers have noted, this micro-level theory leads to somewhat different conclusions than does macro-level neoclassical theory (Massey et al., 2005). Two important differences are that the micro-level model affords some explanation of differential migration within countries (not simply between countries) and that individuals may migrate based on future expectations (not just current wage differences).

New economics of migration theory.   This viewpoint challenges the conclusions of neoclassical economic theory and assumes that not only individuals but also social units such as families and households make migration decisions. Such units are able to make more complex migration plans because of the potential for diversification of family labor. Some family members can remain working at home, for example, while others migrate to distant labor opportunities and may send earnings, or remittances, back to their families. Especially in developing countries, these strategies can be used to minimize risks faced by a family. Sending a family member abroad can provide a source of income to insure against local hard times from unemployment, crop failures, falling crop prices, lack of capital, and so on. This suggests that the source, not just the amount, of income matters. Household members may migrate for the insurance that remittances provide, even when wage differences are small, and would not result in migration according to neoclassical theories. Similarly, a family's sense of relative deprivation influences migration decisions in ways not explained by wages alone. If, for example, economic development raises lifestyle expectations in a community, individuals may have greater motivation to seek gains from migration even if their wage has also improved during the development.

Dual labor market theory.   This theory explains migration as a result of labor force needs and migration policies of modern industrial societies. Developed, post-industrial countries often evolve dual labor markets, with a high-skill, high-wage, and capital-intensive sector affording attractive job opportunities and a low-skill, low-wage, and labor-intensive sector affording the least attractive employment. More-developed countries find it increasingly difficult to fill low-status jobs from their high-aspiration native labor pool. Demographic trends in developed countries compound the shortage of less skilled labor. Fertility declines have lowered the proportion of young unskilled laborers willing to temporarily take low-status jobs. Later marriage, rising divorce rates, and access to higher education have encouraged women to enter the primary high-skill labor force, also making them less willing to take low-status jobs. Acceptable raises in wages will not sufficiently improve the relative status of low-skill jobs and may simply push the entire wage scale and aspirations even higher. So, to fulfill needs for low-skill labor, developed economies recruit migrant labor from abroad, which does not require raising wages. In fact, wages are most often held in check through institutional mechanisms and migration policies. To the extent that migrant populations are unofficial, as in the case of U.S. migration where one-third of migrants lack documentation, employers often profit by being able to pay laborers lower wages than the legal minimum wage and consumers often profit by paying less for goods and services. As a result, wages are not likely to rise with greater demand but may fall with increased supply, increasing the gap between sectors.

World systems theory.   This applies a broad-sweeping view of global development to explain migration movements. A theory of migration based in world-systems analysis theorizes that migration simply follows from the political and economic organization of an ever-expanding capitalist world market or world division of labor. Capitalist penetration into the developing economies creates disruptive development and an uprooted mobile population at the periphery of the world economy. The use of force by capitalist countries seeking to protect investments abroad and to expand the world economy can also create dislocated refugee populations. At the same time, strong material and cultural ties are formed with the core countries during capitalist penetration (and earlier colonial rule). International migration of disrupted populations then flows in the opposite direction of capital penetration, toward the newly familiar culture, aspirations, and opportunities in the core economies. Economic considerations may influence migrants' decisions, but they are not the primary cause of migration. The impetus for migration in developing countries is the dislocation of population arising from capitalist penetration.

Migration systems theory.   This theory is somewhat different from the other theories in that it focuses on the self-perpetuation of migration streams. Once a migration stream has begun, systematic effects can arise that support continuing migration. Whatever the original cause of migration, it may become less important as these migration systems become stronger. Network theory, for example, emphasizes that social networks are a form of social capital. When enough migrants with a common social identity arrive in an area they may constitute a network that can then offer aid to new arrivals—from material comfort to simply lowering the psychic costs of migrating to a strange place. Members of the network also retain ties to their community of origin and can reach out to offer information or assistance to prospective migrants. In both ways networks contribute to a self-sustaining immigration stream. Institutional theory emphasizes the similar role of social organizations ranging from voluntary humanitarian organizations to private black-market immigration services. Like networks, these institutions can perpetuate, and sometimes profit from, migration regardless of the initial reasons for the migration stream. Both of these theories reflect cumulative causation where each migration decision changes the context in which subsequent decisions are made, usually perpetuating migration (Massey et al., 2005; Massey, 1990). Our discussion of relative deprivation illustrates cumulative causation: As some families in an area of origin receive remittances from a family member working abroad, others will see a fall in their income relative to these neighbors and will, in turn, be more likely to then send a family member abroad, and so on (Stark and Taylor, 1991). Migration systems and cumulative causation can explain significant migration effects that are not explained well by the other major theories. Some of these explanations are now well-developed theories such as network theory. Others, however, are more nearly empirical generalizations. This remains a developing area of demographic theory.

With several major migration theories to choose from we might naturally ask, which theory is correct? However, migration theories are not so much contradictory as they are potentially complementary. As Massey and his colleagues conclude:

> Our review produced little substantial evidence that would lead to the rejection of any of the theoretical models we have surveyed. On the contrary, each model received at least some empirical support, suggesting that each theory captures an element of the truth. . . . What is unclear is how well the various models perform against each other, and how much of an independent contribution to explanatory power each model might retain in a simultaneous examination. (1994, p. 739)

Each of the major migration theories can be used to explain internal as well as international migration. As internal and international migration become more inseparable due to increasing globalization, there is utility in theorizing the two types of movements as part of the same phenomenon (King and Skeldon, 2010). The study of internal migration does, however, have unique concerns that have given rise to a number of specific *middle-range* theories (e.g., United Nations, 1994; Frey, 1998; Fokkema et al., 1993; Todaro, 1997). Some of these internal migration theories are taken up in later chapters on urbanization (chapter 10) and population diversity (chapter 11).

Migration Problems and Policies

Consequences of migration are felt both by individual migrants and by the social collectivities (e.g., nation states) they leave and join. On the individual level, most migration theories suggest we would ultimately expect a positive effect for immigrants and employers who hire them. That, supposedly, was the expectation of the individual migrants, at least in free migration. However, population problems and policies usually are defined on a collective level.

What are the collective effects of migration on origin and destination populations? Obviously, moving numbers of people about can directly affect the size and growth rates of both origin and destination populations. Migration also can change the size and composition of the labor force in both countries. An exchange of residents between populations also alters the social and cultural composition of each.

Are these collective consequences population problems? Using the questions we identified in chapter 1 as our guides, we will ask *who* views these consequences as a source of problems, what the perceived problems are, and *why* they are considered to be problems.

Careers in Demography

Douglas S. Massey

Henry G. Bryant Professor of Sociology and Public Affairs, Princeton University

Director, Office of Population Research, Woodrow Wilson School, Princeton

President, American Academy of Political and Social Science, 2006–2015

President, American Association of Sociology, 2000–2001

President, Population Association of America, 1996

How did you decide that being a demographer was the career path for you?

I was always interested in people, their behavior, and their social organizations and so was drawn to the social sciences when I entered college. It was 1970 and the zeitgeist of the 1960s was still very much in the air. Economics was uncool and psychology was in, so I started off taking psych courses.

I did quite well and ultimately finished a major in psychology, but experiments conducted in laboratories gradually came to seem too far removed from the real world for me, even if they were conducted on people rather than rats. Psychology prized the ability to make causal statements even if their generalization to the real world was dubious. So I swung 180° around and began to study anthropology, which investigated people in their real-world settings. I liked physical anthropology quite a lot, but in those days cultural anthropology was in the grip of cultural relativism, at least in my department, and since everything was relative one could not draw final conclusions about anything, which in the end seemed to lead nowhere.

In my senior year, however, I discovered demography, which was precise and made strong statements about causal processes but at the same time was intimately grounded in the real world, grappling with fundamental issues such as birth, death, marriage, childbearing, migration, and belonging. I first studied demography as a reading course and then took a formal class—my first course in sociology (I've never taken intro sociology)! That was when demography became my calling.

What kind of education and training did you pursue to get to where you are in your career?

After discovering demography I decided I needed to improve my quantitative training, so I delayed graduation until the next year and used the extra time to learn computer programming, take calculus and linear algebra, and completed the graduate statistics sequence in psychology as well as the graduate course in factor analysis and undergraduate methods course in sociology.

I also started doing my own research and submitted my first paper for publication while I was still an undergraduate (it appeared in *Population Studies*). I then applied to demographic training programs around the country and ended up going to Princeton, where I entered in the fall of 1975.

In my first year I took the two-semester demography sequence with Ansley Coale and completed my general examination in demography during the spring of 1976. In my second year I finished all remaining required courses and general exams, and in the third year I completed my dissertation, which was the first nationwide analysis of Hispanic residential segregation. I then spent an additional year as a postdoctoral fellow at Princeton, where I developed my interest in international migration, and then moved to a second postdoc at UC Berkeley in 1979–1980. I began my academic career as Assistant Professor of Sociology at the University of Pennsylvania in the fall of 1980, where I was part of its Population Studies Center and Graduate Group in Demography.

Describe your work/research as a demographer. What do you consider your most important accomplishments?

I have always had diverse interests in social science and one of the reasons I chose demography is because it is inherently interdisciplinary and provides a framework for learning and investigation across a variety of fields. From the very beginning I pursued two parallel lines of research in residential segregation and international migration, and over time these dovetailed into broader interests in Mexican society, stratification, education, and methodology.

I currently run two large data-collection and dissemination projects on Latin American migration in collaboration with my longtime colleague Jorge Durand at the University of Guadalajara, the Mexican Migration Project, and the Latin American Migration Project, which provide basic data on documented and undocumented migrants to the U.S. to thousands of users and also supports our own research. I also co-direct the New Immigrant survey, which is a longitudinal survey of the cohort of legal immigrants who entered the United States in 2003, with a follow-up survey in 2008. It has also become a key data resource in migration studies. Finally, with Camille Charles at the University of Pennsylvania I established the National Longitudinal Survey of Freshmen to study processes of minority under-achievement at selective colleges and universities. Like all my projects, the NLSF is publicly available from the web and has sponsored numerous studies by a diverse collection of data users.

I have certainly had no scarcity of recognition as a social scientist—prizes, presidencies, awards, grants, and prestige positions—but while recognition is nice, the accomplishments that are really important are the products I have produced and the effects that they have had inside and outside the academy. I have already spoken of the data products, which help literally thousands of people conduct reliable research on important topics.

I have also produced a body of work on racial segregation culminating in the book *American Apartheid*, which has become a basic source in thinking about stratification and poverty in the United States and led to testimony before Congress in hearings that ultimately led to legislation strengthening the Fair Housing Act. I have also produced a body of work on Mexican immigration, including the book *Beyond Smoke and Mirrors*, which has led to multiple testimonies before both the House and Senate on behalf of immigration legislation.

What do you see as the field's most important contribution as well as its greatest challenge?

Ultimately demographic trends underlie every facet of human society. Sociology, economics, and political science all rest on demographic foundations and demographers have something of interest to contribute to virtually all social science disciplines. The great challenge now is to bring demographic insights to bear in the study of biosocial interactions—the interplay between biological and social processes in determining human outcomes and behavior.

In the future it will be very important for demographers and other social scientists to be a part of ongoing research in neuroscience, epigenetics, and epidemiology, studying how the social environment shapes brain development, gene expression, and biological functioning within human beings; and of course the traditional subjects of fertility, mortality, nuptiality, migration, and ecology will grow no less important in the world to come. All in all, it is an exciting time to be a demographer.

Spread of National Policies

Let us start with the first of these questions: Who views the consequences of migration as problematic? This question is the easiest one to answer. Although international immigration is generally viewed as a positive for both sending and receiving nations, an increasing number of countries view at least some consequences of immigration and emigration as significant problems (United Nations, 2013a). This is seen in a growing tendency of countries to intervene politically in immigration and emigration streams; that is, a declining willingness to leave migration unchecked.

Figure 9-8 shows the percentage of countries intervening to either raise or lower their immigration levels in 1976 and in 2011 (not shown are the percentages without policies on immigration or that have policies to maintain current levels). On the left side of the figure are the percentages of countries that had policies in place to raise immigration and on the right side are percentages with policies to lower the levels of immigration into their country. In 1976, when the United Nations began monitoring governments' policies on the level of immigration, developed countries were more apt to have policies in place to discourage immigration, while developing countries had policies in place to encourage immigration. By 2011, this pattern had flipped. Today, a larger proportion of MDRs than LDRs have immigration policies intended to *raise* immigration, not lower it. On the other hand, more LDRs have policies to *lower* immigration. The reversal in this trend over the time period reflects differences in growth rates in MDRs and LDRs. MDRs are increasingly recognizing immigration as a way to offset slowing growth rates, while LDRs may see less value in immigration as long as their own growth rates remain high.

The situation is somewhat different for *emigration*, shown in Figure 9-9 on the following page. The percentage of more developed countries with interventionist emigration policies changed little and even decreased somewhat over the period. But in the

Figure 9-8

Percentage of Countries with Intervention Policies to Either Raise or Lower Immigration, 1976 and 2011

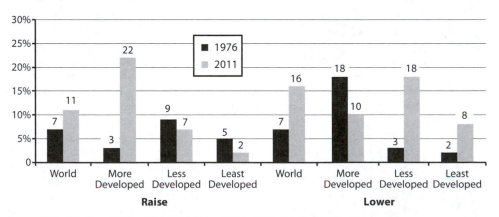

Source: United Nations, 2013c. *World Population Policies 2011.* Used with permission.

Figure 9-9

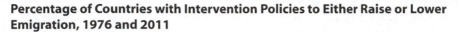

Percentage of Countries with Intervention Policies to Either Raise or Lower Emigration, 1976 and 2011

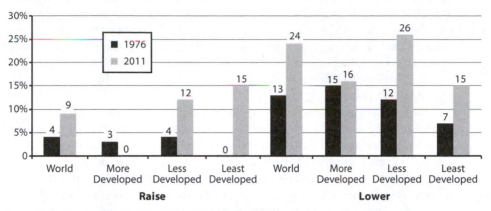

Source: United Nations, 2013c. *World Population Policies 2011.* Used with permission.

less-developed and least-developed regions, the percentage with emigration intervention policies has more than doubled, whether targeted at increasing or decreasing emigration. Some LDCs may benefit from high emigration rates, particularly if their population growth outpaces their infrastructure or if they have a well-developed remittance-capturing system in place. But in other countries disproportionately large numbers of highly skilled professionals emigrate each year, a phenomenon sometimes referred to as "brain drain." In this instance, governments are more likely to view emigration as a problem that needs to be reduced. One would think that MDRs would also be concerned about emigration, particularly because population loss might aggravate problems arising from their already aging populations and slow growth rates. But MDRs tend to be less concerned than LDRs about emigration, in part because their emigration streams are smaller and more negligible in impact.

What specific migration consequences are viewed as problems, and why are they considered differently between more- and less-developed regions? To answer these questions we will need to discuss the general consequences of migration in a bit more detail.

Impact on Size and Growth Rates

International migration increases the size and growth rate of the population in the country of destination and decreases them in the country of origin. It is obvious that net migration from one population to another would decrease the origin population by the same absolute number that it would increase the destination population. Less obviously, the degree of impact on the *growth rate* of the two populations would *not* be the same. That impact depends on the size of the net migrant population *relative to* the size of the resident population. Net migration from a small to a large population, for example, would cause a greater decrease in the growth rate of the small origin population than increase in the growth rate of the larger destination population. Conversely, net migration from a large to a small population would have a greater impact on the growth rate of the destination country.

The point is not trivial. It implies that the degree to which social units experience growth or shrinkage depends somewhat on how narrowly focused the migrant streams are, either at their origin or destination. A small village, for example, might have its population devastated by sending most of its former inhabitants to a large, more-developed city, whereas that city's inhabitants might hardly feel the addition. Conversely, a particular destination city might feel overwhelmed by its growth if it became the exclusive destination of a migrant stream (which, as we will see in chapters 10 and 11, is frequently the case).

Indirect effects of migration also can alter growth rates. Separations, costs of migration, and especially age selectivity can change fertility, nuptiality, and mortality rates in both origin and destination populations. Higher levels of migrant fertility (see chapter 11) also operate indirectly to increase growth rates in destination countries. As we have shown in previous chapters, immigration is what is keeping some MDR populations from declining in size. In international migration streams most effects operate in the same direction—to *increase* the population size and growth rates of the receiving more-developed countries while decreasing those in the less-developed countries.

Impact on the Labor Force

Of more immediate concern has been the impact on the composition of the populations, especially in the receiving countries. One focus of this concern has been the effect of composition changes on the labor force. It turns out that the labor force effects of international migration are anything but simple. Let us start with the least complicated effect, that of *age selectivity*, then proceed to the complications.

Theoretically, immigration to more-developed countries from less-developed ones explicitly selects young adults. Since MDRs have older resident populations, they gain the benefit of a needed increase in their young labor force. In contrast, LDRs have very young populations and removal of working-age adults would make already high age-dependency ratios even worse. In general, destination MDRs benefit from the age selectivity of migration while LDRs suffer.

International immigration also generally favors *employable* adults who are needed in the destination countries. Depending on the migration stream, it might favor highly educated and high-skill labor (as in the case of migration from other developed countries to the United States, Canada, and Australia) or less educated low-skill labor (as with migrant farm workers in the United States and Asian laborers in the Persian Gulf States). Theoretically then, international migration of workers benefits economies of destination countries, but there is great debate over how and to what extent destination economies benefit from such immigration. In the U.S. case, immigration has been shown to boost GDP (Martin and Midgley, 2010). While undocumented immigrants may use local social services that they do not pay into, like schools for their children and emergency room healthcare, they pay sales tax and often contribute to social security and Medicare that they are never able to collect (Donato and Armenta, 2011). The impact of U.S. immigration on wages, however, is more hotly debated, with some studies showing a depressant effect, and other studies showing no relationship.

The impact of skill selectivity on the labor force of origin countries is equally complex. Theoretically, origin economies would gain from emigration; it could, for example, boost the demand for workers remaining in LDR labor forces, and thus their employment rates and wage levels. However, those most likely to emigrate are the most skilled.

The loss of the most highly educated individuals to migration (brain drain) is of concern to many countries. The impact of such a drain would be greatest in those regions already facing shortages of highly skilled workers and stagnating economies. Recent studies, however, have shown that the benefits of skilled labor emigration may carry more benefits than negatives for sending societies (Clemens, 2009). The key is to develop programs and infrastructure that facilitate return migration or sustained investment by emigrant diasporic communities so that they can use their labor skills and experiences as a "brain gain" for their sending countries (UNCTAD, 2012).

Although emigration is likely to select the most employable from a country of origin, these "positively selected" migrants may still suffer by comparison with the resident workforce in the destination country. In fact, the theory of dual economies suggests that immigrants will tend to be among the least skilled, least educated, and lowest-paid laborers in the destination country. Wages of migrant workers, for example, are only about three-fourths those of the native population in Germany and the United States, and less than half those of the native population working in many of the same industries in South Korea (Duleep and Dowhan, 2008; United Nations, 1998a). The low-skilled native laborers in destination countries may also suffer from decreased competitiveness and inability to bargain for higher wages, ultimately increasing the wage-status gap in the dual economy.

Migration contributes to global development. Because of household migration strategies, many workers abroad send **remittances** (earnings) to their families, which reduces poverty, has multiplying effects on the national economy, and provides an important source of foreign exchange. The flow of capital involved should not be underestimated. In 2012 remittances to LDCs amounted to $406 billion, far exceeding what many such countries receive in development assistance or foreign investment (UNFPA, 2013; Martin and Widgren, 2002). These amounts are underestimated since they rely on official reports from banks and other financial institutions but not informal transfers made by migrants directly. Although women immigrants tend to earn less than men, they send home a higher proportion of their wages to family members (UNFPA, 2013). For some countries immigrant remittances comprise an important portion of the gross domestic product. For example, remittances sent back to Haiti, Samoa, Liberia, Moldova, Tajikistan, Rwanda, and Nepal were all over 20% of each country's GDP in 2012 (UNCTAD, 2012).

Remittance flows are not a simple case of economic exchange from MDRs to LDRs. Since most international immigrants move to neighboring countries in their regions, not MDRs, the majority of remittances are from slightly wealthier LDCs to other LDCs. Countries which depend heavily on such remittances leave themselves vulnerable to changes in employment conditions and/or immigration policies at the country of destination. In addition, relative deprivation and social inequality in the home community can be widened by unequal access to remittances. In short, the labor force effects of migration are mixed. In general, the economies of destination MDRs benefit from net immigration even though some segments of their populations, especially new immigrants, may suffer; and in general the economies of origin LDRs gain through remittances from abroad but may suffer from the immediate loss of skilled workers, particularly in health fields. Such a complex picture does not easily lead to migration policy formulation.

Impact on Social Composition

It is hard to review past and present MDR popular debates over immigration policies without suspecting that they are motivated strongly by **xenophobia**. This fear of ethnically distinct foreigners has resulted in many groups of migrants being viewed as "problems" by the populations in countries of destination, and rationalized with negative ethnic stereotyping in the policy debates. Indeed, nearly all immigrant groups with any identifiable difference from the host population have been discriminated against in migration policies, differing mainly in degree (see, e.g., Menjívar and Abrego, 2012; Bloemraad et al., 2008; Massey, 2009; Korteweg and Yurdakul, 2009; Cummings and Lambert, 1998; Layton-Henry, 1994; S. Cohen, 1995). Immigration policies and national debates regarding them have, in turn, perpetuated and solidified discriminatory attitudes toward immigrants (Hopkins, 2010; Fassin et al., 1997).

Such discrimination is easier to justify publicly if it is supported by rationalizations. Migrants have been characterized at various times, for example, as a danger to public health, a threat to job security, a drain on social welfare systems, as criminals and terrorists, and a threat to the dominant groups or cultures of the host country. Such sentiments toward migrants are more likely to affect migration policy if they are plausible, whether or not they are true.

At various times in history some discriminatory concerns with the composition of migrant streams were clearly plausible. A historical example is the quarantine of migrants. Quarantines from specific countries with widespread endemic diseases, for example, have been justifiable, even if discriminatory, in some past cases. If the recent Ebola outbreak had been accompanied by migrant streams from the countries impacted, receiving societies would have set up quarantines or even temporary migration bans. Yet, in other cases, the same reason has been used to detain migrants without plausible evidence of a public health threat.

It is also important to recognize that at any given time the view of migrants as a "social problem" may be genuine for some and an excuse for discrimination by others. For example, fears that importation of foreign labor might result in falling wages for low-skill occupations in the host country is a currently held *belief* among many—a genuine concern for some and an excuse to discriminate for others. It would be naive of us to limit our discussion of migration by ignoring the evidence that migration policies throughout history—and in the present—have been profoundly shaped by these sentiments among host populations. The United States is no exception.

Immigration Policy: The U.S. Case

We will use the case of migration policies in the United States to illustrate immigration concerns and policies in the more-developed regions. Although the United States case does not represent all more-developed countries, it is a reasonable representative of the frontier receiving nations, such as Australia and Canada. Focusing on one case will allow us to provide specific examples of past migration issues and policies.

A Brief History

Immigration policies in the United States have gone through several distinct stages (Olzak, 2003; Martin and Midgley, 1994; Ong Hing, 1993; Keely, 1982), moving back and forth between more welcoming and more restrictive eras. We describe them serially as follows.

Laissez faire: 1790 to 1875. A welcoming viewpoint held sway for the first century of the nation's life. Until 1875, there were no federal laws abridging or forbidding immigration. Exceptions were very specific and minor. In 1808, the importation of slaves was prohibited, although slavery was not outlawed until 1865. In 1798, the Alien and Sedition Act empowered the president to deport any alien he deemed dangerous, but this power was not renewed two years later. The influx of Roman Catholics in the 1840s set off the first organized anti-foreign movement in the country against Irish immigrants, the "Know Nothing" movement, but it did not result in congressional action on immigration.

Qualitative restrictions: 1875 to 1920. The Supreme Court in 1876 held that Congress was empowered by the interstate commerce clause to regulate immigration. During the next forty-five years, Congress passed three kinds of laws restricting certain types, or quality, of immigrants. The first excluded people with various physical and mental diseases or who had criminal, moral, or political orientations that made them unfit. Second were the contract-labor laws, prohibiting persons contracted abroad to work in the United States, the intent being to reduce competition with American labor.

Third, foreshadowing the future, was the categorical exclusion of groups because of race or nationality, specifically Asiatic race and nationality. In 1882 Congress passed the Chinese Exclusion Act. In 1907 came the "Gentleman's Agreement," which required Japan to refuse passports to the United States for Japanese laborers. In 1917, Congress set up an Asiatic Barred Zone that declared any native of India, Burma, Siam, the Malay States, the East Indies, or the Polynesian Islands to be inadmissible to the United States. As the decades passed, exclusionist sentiment held sway but the target changed. Immigration policy also became more politically savvy, employing quantitative restrictions rather than qualitative restrictions, which indirectly targeted groups according to their national origin.

Quantitative restrictions: 1921 to 1965. Immigration quota acts passed in 1921 and 1924 were responding to popular fears regarding the "racial impurity" of immigrants from Southern and Eastern Europe (primarily Italians and Jewish Poles and Russians). These acts changed the basis for limiting immigration from the countries outside the Western Hemisphere and reserved fixed proportions of the total visa allotment for natives of specific countries. Asian immigrants continued to be barred. The first quota act, passed in 1921, limited migrants from Europe to a small annual percentage of their non-U.S.-born compatriots enumerated in the U.S. census as of 1910. The Immigration Act of 1924 went even further, lowering the percentage and basing it

Figure 9-10

Give Me Some of Your Tired, Your Poor . . .

Source: © 1981 John Trever, *Albuquerque Journal.* Used with permission of John Trever.

not on the most current census but that of 1890, when the population composition of the country had been less influenced by recent immigration from Southern and Eastern Europe. The 1952 McCarran-Walter Act continued the restrictionist emphasis; however, the fact that it had to be passed over President Truman's veto implies that anti-restrictionist sentiment was rising. Immigration restrictions have continued in some quantitative form to the present; the basis of these restrictions, however, has changed.

Family reunion and labor needs: 1965 to 1980. In 1965 national-origin quotas were relaxed and replaced with those giving preference to close relatives of U.S. citizens and those with special skills. Public Law 89-236 went into full effect in 1968. There remained in place a form of earlier quantitative restrictions. No more than 20,000 immigrants were to come from any single country. Initially the Eastern Hemisphere as a whole could send no more than 170,000 immigrants (with no limit on those from the Western Hemisphere). In 1978 these hemispheric limits were abolished and a worldwide ceiling was established. A complicated and fluid system of preferences was used to determine qualification and priority for migration.

The Refugee Act (1980) gave special status to refugees, a tacit acknowledgment that many people become refugees as a result of U.S. economic and political policies around the world. It empowered the attorney general to admit for up to two years any persons whose entry was deemed in the national interest. Further, it enlarged the definition of **refugee** to conform to the United Nations definition—basically, any person who faces persecution or who has a well-founded fear of persecution on account of race, religion, nationality, political beliefs, or membership in a social group.

Recent Immigration Reforms

The recent era of immigration reform in the United States has shifted to a focus on undocumented immigration and attempting to control it. Between 1986 and 2003, Congress enacted a number of major reforms: the Immigration Reform and Control Act of 1986 (IRCA), the Personal Responsibility and Work Opportunity Reconciliation Acts and the Illegal Immigration Reform and Immigrant Responsibility Acts of 1996 (PRWORA and IIRIRA), and the post–9/11 transfer of immigration border control and security to the jurisdiction of the Department of Homeland Security. Not surprisingly, most of these reforms have served to address rising modern migration streams and issues related to undocumented immigration and terrorism.

The Immigration Reform and Control Act (1986) was intended to reduce the number of undocumented migrants resident in the country. The act legalized most undocumented workers then employed in the country and followed this with harsh sanctions on employers for hiring new unauthorized workers. The dramatic impact of IRCA on U.S. immigration can be seen in Figure 9-11 on the next page, labeled IRCA legalization. The tremendous peak in admissions, exceeding any other time in the 20th century, reflects amnesty granted to undocumented workers through IRCA.

IRCA, however, had modest success in its objectives. Fraud was considerable. More than two-thirds of those admitted as agricultural workers did not satisfy the program's requirements (Martin and Midgley, 2003). Employers rarely were sanctioned for continuing to recruit and hire undocumented migrants. The legalization of 2.7 million undocumented laborers through IRCA also reinforced immigrant networks, resulting in a backlog of green card applications from family members, and encouraged additional undocumented immigrations with the anticipation that more amnesties might be applied in the future. One of the major deficits of IRCA was that it did not put policies in place to meet the continuously growing demand by U.S. employers for unskilled laborers, such as a visa system for temporary guest workers. As a result, undocumented migrant labor simply continued to respond to the unofficial demand for labor.

In 1996, Congress passed a series of immigration reforms that reflected continued frustration with undocumented immigration, as well as growing public distrust of immigrants' alleged abuse of the social welfare system. The Personal Responsibility and Work Opportunity Reconciliation Act and the Illegal Immigration Reform and Immigrant Responsibility Act made most immigrants ineligible for welfare benefits, regardless of their legal or illegal resident status. The combined acts also raised the annual income threshold required of U.S. resident sponsors of immigrants while significantly increasing border control funding and doubling the number of border patrol agents at the 2,000-mile long U.S.-Mexico border. Despite increased border security, undocumented immigration continued to grow. Studies have shown that the primary impact of border militarization was to reduce Mexican return flows and keep undocumented immigrants in the United States; but increased security had little impact on the initial probability of migrating from Mexico to the U.S. (Donato and Armenta, 2011).

Table 9-5 on the following page presents the Homeland Security Office of Immigration Statistics estimates of undocumented immigration populations in the United States

Figure 9-11

Immigration to the United States, 1820 to Present

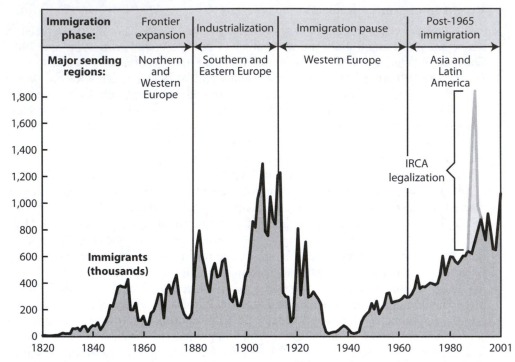

Note: IRCA refers to the amnesty provisions of the Immigration Reform and Control Act of 1986, under which 2.7 million unauthorized foreign residents obtained legal immigrant status.

Source: Martin and Midgley, 2003. "Immigration: Shaping and Reshaping America," figure 2.

Table 9-5   Estimated Undocumented Immigrant Population for the Top 10 Countries of Origin and States of Residence, United States, 2011

Country of Origin (1)	Population (2)	State of Residence (3)	Population (4)
All Countries	11,510,000	All States	11,510,000
Mexico	6,800,000	California	2,830,000
El Salvador	660,000	Texas	1,790,000
Guatemala	520,000	Florida	740,000
Honduras	380,000	New York	630,000
China	280,000	Illinois	550,000
Philippines	270,000	Georgia	440,000
India	240,000	New Jersey	420,000
Korea	230,000	North Carolina	400,000
Ecuador	210,000	Arizona	360,000
Vietnam	170,000	Washington	260,000

Source: Hoefer et al., 2012. "Estimates of the Unauthorized Immigrant Population Residing in the United States: January 2011."

as of 2011. The panel on the left presents the top ten countries from which undocumented immigrants originated, and the number from each country. The panel on the right presents the top ten states in which undocumented immigrants resided as of 2011. According to this table, the origins of undocumented immigration to the United States were largely in the Western Hemisphere and geographically close. However, a significant portion also came from Asia. Almost two-thirds of all undocumented immigrants to the United States came from Mexico. Not surprisingly, about two-fifths reside in California and Texas, both border states with Mexico. Other states in which undocumented immigrants reside have large metropolitan areas with substantial foreign-born populations.

Not shown in Table 9-5 is a fact that some readers may find surprising. Only half of undocumented immigrants enter the United States via a surreptitious border crossing. The majority of undocumented immigrants residing in the United States are those who entered legally (or, less frequently, with fraudulent documentation) but overstayed their permitted visas (Martin and Midgley, 2010). It is partly for this reason that, even in the face of substantially increased resources directed at tightening our borders, undocumented immigration has continued to rise. Just since 2000 the number of undocumented immigrants is estimated to have risen from 8.6 million to 11.5 million (Hoefer et al., 2012). The September 11, 2001 terrorist attacks drove this point home when it was revealed that all nineteen hijackers entered the United States on legal tourist, business, and student visas. As a result, post–2001 immigration reform, while still diverting subsequent funds toward border control, has also turned its focus toward background checks of legal immigrants and the tracking of foreigners once inside the country.

The dissolution of the Immigration and Naturalization Service and transfer of its border security functions to the domain of Homeland Security's Immigration and Customs Enforcement symbolized a cultural and political shift toward the association of labor immigration with criminality. A combination of legislation was passed from 2001 through 2003, the most famous being the Uniting and Strengthening America by Providing Appropriate Tools Required to Intercept and Obstruct Terrorism Act (USA PATRIOT). These served not only to increase border security and personnel but also to significantly expand the government's ability to track and detain foreigners within the United States. Undocumented immigrants can now be detained without charge, universities must keep tabs on their foreign students, and visa applications are cross-checked through the CIA and the FBI. Hundreds of thousands of undocumented immigrants have been detained and many are sent to prison-like detention centers where they lack access to legal counsel and are subject to excessive force by law enforcement authorities (MIS, 2012; Donato and Armenta, 2011).

For the past decade, Congress has been locked in stalemate over further immigration reform. At the center of the debate is what to do about the estimated 11.5 million undocumented immigrants currently living in the United States. Because of federal gridlock, some states and cities have begun passing their own legislation, much of which further criminalizes the presence of undocumented immigrants and attempts to enforce laxly applied laws from IRCA and USA PATRIOT (as in Arizona). Of particular concern was the spike of undocumented children migrants who overwhelmed U.S. border officials in May and June of 2014 (Chishti and Hipsman, 2014). These minors were fleeing poverty and violence in Central American countries and are currently awaiting deportation trials as this textbook goes to press. Of equal concern are the 1.7

million undocumented immigrant children who were brought to the United States by their parents and who are now unable to legally access routes to higher education and jobs. Federal bipartisan legislation to address this issue, the DREAM Act, has been debated in Congress with no resolution since 2001.

The most recent iteration of the act would provide a path to legal status for undocumented young adults who arrived in the U.S. as children and who obtain two years of college or serve in the military, among other requirements. Further illustrating the increasing federal-state divide over U.S. immigration policy action, California and Illinois have passed their own versions of the DREAM Act, allowing undocumented immigrants access to some college scholarships.

Whether immigration reforms of the past decades will have any substantial impact remains to be seen. The most telling non-policy impact on immigration was the 2007–2009 recession, which resulted in an unprecedented standstill of migration to the U.S.—both documented and undocumented. Clearly, migration ceases when economic demand for immigrant labor in the United States ceases—or when economic conditions in sending countries stabilize and the supply is no longer interested in meeting the demand. In the meantime, the lesson of recent immigration reforms appears to be that migration streams such as the current south-to-north flow from Latin America are much easier to start than they are to stop.

Summary

Migration is harder to define than the other demographic growth processes, mortality and fertility. Not all moves across geographic boundaries are migrations, since not all of them involve changing residence (that is, reaffiliation with a new population). Nor are there consistent attempts to register all moves across geographic borders as they occur. Thus, demographers rely on indirect information to infer migration. One such method is to note changes in residences reported at succeeding times. Another is to measure the degree of population growth, deduct the amount of natural increase, and infer the net migration that must have occurred.

International migration has taken widely various forms throughout history. The voluntary migration, both individual and mass, that has been so prominent in modern Western history is unusual in the overall picture. Patterns of migration have shifted rapidly in the modern period and probably will continue to do so. Temporary labor migrations have grown to significantly outnumber permanent migrations. Former migration streams from more-developed countries to less-developed countries have reversed. Conflicts, increasingly within less-developed regions, have increased the numbers of people forced to migrate as refugees.

People migrate for a variety of reasons, of course, but there are regularities. Differential rates relate to stage in the life cycle (age), employment status, ethnic identity, gender, and so on. Young adults entering the labor force and their offspring are the most likely to move. The most general model for interpreting migratory motivation is one that features a place of origin and a place of destination, each with attractive *pull* and unattractive *push* qualities, separated by a series of intervening *obstacles*. These empirical generalizations about migration have given rise to several modern migration theories which increasingly reflect the complexity of migration.

Migration theoretically favors population growth at the place of destination at the expense of growth at the place of origin, both directly through the simple exchange of population and indirectly through age selectivity and differential fertility. In the long term, migration generally benefits the workforce at the place of destination. Selectivity will bring younger laborers and skills in demand to the destination's workforce while removing these from the population of origin, which can sometimes result in "brain drain." However, remittances to less-developed countries are substantial and may provide families with some insurance against economic risks while providing much needed capital to less-developed economies.

Large-scale migration into more-developed countries can involve difficult adjustments, at least in the short term, for both migrants and destination communities. Resistance to immigration in MDRs can reflect concerns over alleged burdens of new immigrants on social services, loss of jobs and lowered competitiveness among less skilled workers, and so forth. Recent events and legislation have also led to an increasing conflation of migration with terrorism and crime in the public eye. But much of the resistance to immigration seems the result of xenophobia and fears over the loss of dominance by majority cultural and political groups in the population of destination. These concerns have found expression in the immigration policies of many countries.

The United States is an example of a developed destination country with a history of immigration policies that have shifted back and forth between encouraging and then discouraging immigration. Despite recent reforms, the greatest challenge to contemporary U.S. immigration policies is that of controlling migration streams that it originally welcomed, but that turned into substantial undocumented migration streams once such migration was no longer welcomed.

EXERCISES

1. Table E9-1 is a matrix showing U.S. regions of residence for those who migrated between 2011 and 2012, according to the Census Bureau's Current Population Survey. Define as an *interregional migrant* anyone who had a different U.S. region of residence in 2012 than she or he reported for 2011. Answer the following questions:

   a. The migration *stream* from the Northeast to the South had 362,000 people. How many were in the migration stream from South to Northeast?

Table E9-1   Region of Residence for Those Who Migrated between Regions, 2011 to 2012, United States

	Residence March 2012			
	Northeast	Midwest	South	West
Residence March 2011				
Northeast	—	52	362	184
Midwest	53	—	373	237
South	178	304	—	419
West	43	207	329	—

Note: In thousands, ages 1 year and older.

Source: U.S. Census Bureau, 2012. "Geographical Mobility: 2011 to 2012 Data."

b. The *volume* of (gross) migration between the South and the Northeast was 540,000 people. What was the volume of migration between the Midwest and the South?

c. The *net* migration from the Northeast to the South was plus 184,000. What was the net migration from the South to the Northeast?

d. What was the *net* migration from the Midwest to the South?

2. Suppose you had the hypothetical interregional migration situation in Table E9-2.

a. What would be the resulting net migration stream (in raw numbers) to Area B from Area A? (Specify plus or minus.)

of men _____

of women _____

b. What would be the influence of this sex-selective net migration on the sex ratio of the new resident population of Area A? (Check one.)

_____ raise it

_____ lower it

_____ no influence

c. The influence would be in the opposite direction in Area B, but would the *degree* of effect be more, or less, in Area B, given Area B's larger initial resident population? (Check one.)

_____ more

_____ less

_____ the same

Table E9-2   Resident and Interregional Migration Populations between Areas A and B, by Sex, 2010 to 2015

Sex	Resident, Area A, Jan. 2010 (1)	Resident, Area B, Jan. 2010 (2)	Migrant, 2010–2015, Area A to B (3)	Migrant, 2010–2015, Area B to A (4)
Male	1000	2000	300	100
Female	1000	2000	100	300
Ratio	100	100	300	33

Note: In thousands, hypothetical illustration.

3. Lacking direct counts of migration, nations often infer net migration between censuses by the vital statistics method. The appropriate formula is

$$M = (P_2 - P_1) - (B - D)$$

You may recognize this as a transformation of the growth equation presented in chapter 1.

Table E9-3 shows the required calculations of net migration for the United States from 2012 to 2013. Following that model, estimate the net migration for Mexico from 2012 to 2013. Enter your answers in the blank spaces in the table.

Table E9-3   Estimating Net Migration by the Vital Statistics Method

Components of Population Change, 2012–2013

	Population 2012 (1)	Population 2013 (2)	Net Change (3) = (2) – (1)	Births (4)	Deaths (5)	Natural Increase (6) = (4) – (5)	Estimated Net Migration (7) = (3) – (6)
United States	313,847,465	316,668,567	2,821,102	4,293,433	2,633,180	1,660,253	1,160,849
Mexico	114,975,406	116,220,947	1,245,541	2,169,586	563,379		

Source: U.S. Census Bureau, International Data Base, 2013.

If these estimates are to be believed, which country had the higher crude *rate* of net migration, on the average, for the years 2012 to 2013? (Check one.)

_____ Mexico

_____ U.S.

PROPOSITIONS FOR DEBATE

1. "Seasonal migration" of agricultural workers from Mexico to the United States should not be defined as true migration.

2. The country of destination loses and the country of origin wins through international migration.

3. More-developed countries have no right to restrict immigration from less-developed countries.

4. Economic pull and push factors completely explain undocumented immigration.

5. As the U.S. baby boomers enter their senior years, age selectivity of interregional migration will decrease.

6. International migration promotes [or reduces] economic inequalities among countries.

7. International migration streams probably will continue to increase even if population growth in the less-developed countries continues to decline.

8. In the next few decades, population "problems" will be defined increasingly around migration and decreasingly around fertility.

REFERENCES AND SUGGESTED READINGS

Batalova, Jeanne. 2009. "Immigrant Women in the United States." *US in Focus.* Retrieved September 24, 2013. http://www.migrationinformation.org/usfocus/display.cfm?ID=763. Washington, DC: Migration Policy Institute.

Bloemraad, Irene, Anna Korteweg, and Gökçe Yurdakul. 2008. "Citizenship and Immigration: Multiculturalism, Assimilation, and Challenges to the Nation-State." *Annual Review of Sociology* 34: 153–179.

Bogue, Donald J., ed. 1993. "Spatial Mobility and Migration Research." In D. J. Bogue, E. Arriaga, and D. L. Anderton, eds., *Readings in Population Research Methodology*. United Nations Fund for Population Activities, Chicago: Social Development Center.

Brettell, Caroline, and James Hollifield, eds. 2007. *Migration Theory: Talking Across Disciplines*. New York: Routledge.

Castles, Stephen. 2007. "21st Century Migration as a Challenge to Sociology." *Journal of Ethnic and Migration Studies* 33(3): 351–370.

Chant, S., and S. A. Radcliffe. 1992. "Migration and Development: The Importance of Gender." In Sylvia Chant, ed., *Gender and Migration in Developing Countries*. London: Belhaven Press.

Chishti, Muzaffar, and Faye Hipsman. 2014. *Unaccompanied Minors Crisis Has Receded from Headlines But Major Issues Remain*. Migration Policy Institute. September 25, 2014. http://www.migrationpolicy.org/article/unaccompanied-minors-crisis-has-receded-headlines-major-issues-remain

Clemens, Michael. 2009. "Skill Flow: A Fundamental Reconsideration of Skilled-Worker Mobility and Development." *Working Paper* 180. Retrieved September 24, 2013. http://www.cgdev.org/content/publications/detail/1422684. Washington, DC: Center for Global Development.

Cohen, S. 1995. "The Mighty State of Immigration Controls." *Social Policy Review* 7.

Cummings, S., and T. Lambert. 1998. "Immigration Restrictions and the American Worker: An Examination of Competing Interpretations." *Population Research and Policy Review* 17(6).

Donato, Katharine M., and Amada Armenta. 2011. "What We Know About Unauthorized Migration." *Annual Review of Sociology* 37: 529–543.

Duleep, Harriet Orcutt, and Daniel J. Dowhan. 2008. "Research on Immigrant Earnings." *Social Security Bulletin* 68(1). Washington, DC: Social Security Administration.

Eltis, David. 2007. "A Brief Overview of the Trans-Atlantic Slave Trade." *Voyages: The Trans-Atlantic Slave Trade Database via Emory University*. Retrieved September 24, 2013. http://www.slavevoyages.org/tast/assessment/essays-intro-01.faces

Fassin, D., A. Morice, and C. Quiminal. 1997. *The Laws of Inhospitality: Immigration Policies and the Test Posed by Undocumented Immigrants*. Paris, France: Editions La Decouverte.

Fokkema, T., G. J. De Jong, and P. Nijkamp. 1993. *Internal Elderly Migration: An Exploration of the Literature*. NIDI Report no. 32. The Hague, Netherlands: Netherlands Interdisciplinary Demographic Institute.

Frey, William H. 1996. "Immigrant and Native Migrant Magnets." *American Demographics* 18(11).

———. 1998. "Black Migration to the South Reaches Record Highs in 1990s." *Population Today* 26(2).

———. 2002. "Metro Magnets for Minorities and Whites: Melting Pots, the New Sunbelt, and the Heartland." PSC Research Report no. 02-496, February. Population Studies Center, University of Michigan.

———. 2003. "The New Migration Equation." http://www.brookings.edu/metro/20031109_frey.htm. Originally published in the *Orlando Sentinel*, November 9.

———. 2005. Communication with author on forthcoming research. http://www.brookings.edu/metro. Washington, DC: Brookings Institute.

———. 2009. *The Great American Migration Slowdown: Regional and Metropolitan Dimensions*. Retrieved September 24, 2013. http://www.brookings.edu/~/media/research/files/reports/2009/12/09%20migration%20frey/1209_migration_frey.pdf. Washington, DC: Brookings Institute.

———. 2013. "Economic Improvement Nudges U.S. Migration to Normal." *Opinion*. Retrieved September 24, 2013. http://www.brookings.edu/research/opinions/2013/03/15-us-migration-economics-frey. Washington, DC: Brookings Institute.

Frey, W. H., and K. L. Liaw. 1998. "The Impact of Recent Immigration on Population Redistribution within the United States." In J. P. Smith and B. Edmonston, eds., *The Immigration Debate: Studies on the Economic, Demographic, and Fiscal Effects of Immigration.* Washington, DC: National Academy Press.

Henning, Sabine, and Bela Hovy. 2011. "Data Sets on International Migration." *International Migration Review* 45(4): 980–985.

Hoefer, Michael, Nancy Rytina, and Bryan Baker. 2012. "Estimates of the Unauthorized Immigrant Population Residing in the United States: January 2011." *Population Estimates* (March). Washington, DC: Homeland Security.

Hopkins, Daniel J. 2010. "Politicized Places: Explaining Where and When Immigrants Provoke Local Opposition." *American Political Science Review* 104(1): 40–60.

Hunt, Matthew O., Larry L. Hunt, and William W. Falk. 2013. "Twenty-First-Century Trends in Black Migration to the US South: Demographic and Subjective Predictors." *Social Science Quarterly.*

Kapiszewski, Andrzej. 2006. "Arab Versus Asian Migrant Workers in The GCC Countries." *United Nations Expert Group Meeting On International Migration And Development In The Arab Region, Beirut, 15–17 May.* UN/POP/EGM/2006/02. Department of Economic and Social Affairs, Population Division. Geneva: United Nations.

Keely, Charles B. 1982. "Illegal Migration." *Scientific American* 246(3).

King, Russell, and Ronald Skeldon. 2010. "'Mind the Gap!' Integrating Approaches to Internal and International Migration." *Journal of Ethnic and Migration Studies* 36(10): 1619–1646.

Korteweg, A., and G. Yurdakul. 2009. "Islam, Gender, and Immigrant Integration: Boundary Drawing in Discourses on Honour Killing in the Netherlands and Germany." *Ethnic and Racial Studies* 32(2): 218–238.

Layton-Henry, Z. 1994. "Britain: The Would-Be Zero-Immigration Country." In Wayne A. Cornelius, Philip L. Martin, and James F. Hollifield, eds., *Controlling Immigration: A Global Perspective.* Stanford: Stanford University Press.

Lee, Everett S. 1966. "A Theory of Migration." *Demography* 3(1).

Mackun, Paul, and Steven Wilson. 2011. "Population Distribution and Change: 2000 to 2010." *2010 Census Briefs.* C2010BR-01. Washington, DC: GPO.

Martin, Philip, and Elizabeth Midgley. 1994. "Immigration to the United States: Journey to an Uncertain Destination." *Population Bulletin* 49(4). Washington, DC: Population Reference Bureau.

———. 2003. "Immigration: Shaping and Reshaping America." *Population Bulletin* 58(2). Washington, DC: Population Reference Bureau.

———. 2010. "Immigration in America 2010." *Population Bulletin Update.* Washington, DC: Population Reference Bureau.

Martin, Philip, and Jonas Widgren. 2002. "International Migration: Facing the Challenge." *Population Bulletin* 57(1). Washington, DC: Population Reference Bureau.

Massey, Douglas S. 1990. "Social Structure, Household Strategies, and the Cumulative Causation of Migration." *Population Index* 56(1).

———. 2009. "Racial Formation in Theory and Practice: The Case of Mexicans in the United States." *Race and Social Problems* 1(1): 12–26.

———. 2010. "Immigration Statistics for the Twenty-First Century." *The ANNALS of the American Academy of Political and Social Science* 631: 124–140.

Massey, Douglas S., Joaquin Arango, Graeme Hugo, Ali Kouaouci, Adela Pellegrino, and J. Edward Taylor. 1994. "An Evaluation of International Migration Theory: The North American Case." *Population and Development Review* 20(4).

———. 2005. *Worlds in Motion: Understanding International Migration at the End of the Millennium.* New York: Oxford University Press.

Massey, Douglas S., and Chiara Capoferro. 2004. "Measuring Undocumented Migration." *International Migration Review* 38(3): 1075–1102.

Menjívar, Cecilia and Leisy J. Abrego. 2012. "Legal Violence: Immigration Law and the Lives of Central American Immigrants." *American Journal of Sociology* 117(5): 1380–1421.

Migration Policy Institute. 2012. "The Top 10 Migration Issues of 2012, Issue #1: Migration Flows Rise, Diversify as Global Economy Stumbles Toward Recovery." *Feature Story.* http://www.migrationinformation.org/top10_2012.cfm. Washington, DC: Migration Policy Institute.

MIS (Migration Information Source). December 2012. "Major Immigration Countries Take a Crack at Addressing Thorny Issue of Immigrant Detention." Retrieved October 23, 2012 from: http://www.migrationinformation.org/Feature/display.cfm?ID=923

Murrell, Amy. 2000. Machine-Readable Version of Richard Frethorne's Letter to His Father and Mother, March 20, April 2 and 3, 1623. Retrieved September 24, 2013. http://etext.lib.virginia.edu/etcbin/jamestown-browse?id=J1012. Charlottesville, VA: Virginia Center for Digital History.

Olzak, Susan, 2003. "Racial Policy and Racial Conflict in the Urban United States, 1869–1924." *Social Forces* 82(2): 481–517.

Ong Hing, Bill. 1993. *Making and Remaking Asian America Through Immigration Policy, 1850–1990.* Stanford, CA: Stanford University Press.

Passel, Jeffrey S., and D'Vera Cohn. 2011. "Unauthorized Immigrant Population: National and State Trends, 2010." http://www.pewhispanic.org/files/reports/133.pdf. Washington, DC: Pew Hispanic Center.

Plane, D. A. 1992. "Age-Composition Change and the Geographical Dynamics of Interregional Migration in the U.S." *Annals of the Association of American Geographers* 82(1).

Plane, D. A., and P. A. Rogerson. 1991. "Tracking the Baby Boom, the Baby Bust, and Echo Generations: How Age Composition Regulates U.S. Migration." *Professional Geographer* 43(4).

Pressat, Roland. 1985. *The Dictionary of Demography*, edited by Christopher Wilson. New York: Basil Blackwell Ltd.

Rastogi, Sonya, Tallese D. Johnson, Elizabeth M. Hoeffel, and Malcom P. Drewery, Jr. 2011. "The Black Population: 2010." *2010 Census Briefs.* C2010BR-06. Washington, DC: GPO.

Ravenstein, E. 1889. "The Laws of Migration." *Journal of the Royal Statistical Society* 52.

Robustillo, Silvia Andueza, Veronica Corsini, Monica Marcu, Katya Vasileva, and Ettore Marchetti. 2013. "EU Employment and Social Situation, Quarterly Review." *Special Supplement on Demographic Trends.* Luxembourg: European Union.

Santo Tomas, Patricia A., Lawrence H. Summers, and Michael Clemens. 2009. *Migrants Count: Five Steps Toward Better Migration Data.* Washington, DC: Center for Global Development.

Schachter, Jason P. 2003. *Migration by Race and Hispanic Origin: 1995 to 2000.* Census 2000 Special Reports, CENSR-13, U.S. Census Bureau.

Shryock, Henry S., and Jacob S. Siegel. 1976. *The Methods and Materials of Demography.* Condensed edition by Edward G. Stockwell. New York: Academic Press.

Stahl, C. W. 1995. "Theories of International Labor Migration: An Overview." *Asian and Pacific Migration Journal* 4(2–3).

Stark, O., and J. E. Taylor. 1991. *Relative Deprivation and Migration: Theory, Evidence, and Policy Implications.* World Bank Policy, Research and External Affairs Working Paper no. WPS 656. Washington, DC: World Bank.

Todaro, Michael P. 1997. *Urbanization, Unemployment, and Migration in Africa: Theory and Policy.* Policy Research Division Working Paper no. 104. New York: Population Council.

Trans-Atlantic Slave Trade Database. 2013. "Estimates Database." *Voyages: The Trans-Atlantic Slave Trade Database via Emory University.* Retrieved September 24, 2013. http://www.slavevoyages.org/tast/assessment/estimates.faces

UNCTAD (United Nations Conference on Trade and Development). 2012. *The Least Developed Countries Report 2012: Harnessing Remittances and Diaspora Knowledge to Build Productive Capacities.* Geneva, Switzerland: United Nations.

UNFPA (United Nations Population Fund). 2006. *State of World Population 2006: A Passage to Hope, Women and International Migration.* New York: UNFPA.

———. 2013. "Migration: A World on the Move." *Linking Population, Poverty And Development.* Retrieved October 1, 2013. http://www.unfpa.org/pds/migration.html

UNHCR (United Nations High Commissioner for Refugees). 2005. *2004 Global Refugee Trends: Overview of Refugee Populations, New Arrivals, Durable Solutions, Asylum-Seekers, Stateless and Other Persons of Concern to UNHCR.* June 17. Population and Geographical Data Section, Division of Operational Support. Geneva: UNHCR. http://www.unhcr.ch/cgi-bin/texis/vtx/statistics/opendoc.pdf?tbl=statistics&id=42b283744

———. 2013a. "Displacement: The New 21st Century Challenge." *UNHCR Global Trends 2012.* Retrieved September 24, 2013. http://www.unhcr.org/51bacb0f9.html

———. 2013b. *UNHCR Population Statistics Database.* Accessed September 24, 2013. http://popstats.unhcr.org

United Nations. 1994. *The Migration of Women: Methodological Issues in the Measurement and Analysis of Internal and International Migration.* Santo Domingo: International Research and Training Institute for the Advancement of Women.

———. 1998a. *World Population Monitoring 1997: International Migration and Development.* Population Studies, no. 169, ST/ESA/SER.A/169. New York: United Nations.

———. 1998b. *Population Distribution and Migration,* ST/ESA/SER.R/133. New York: United Nations.

———. 2005. *2004 World Survey on the Role of Women in Development: Women and International Migration.* Department of Economic and Social Affairs, Division for the Advancement of Women. A/59/287Add.1, ST/ESA/294. New York: United Nations.

———. 2013a. *International Migration Policies 2013.* Retrieved September 24, 2013. http://www.un.org/en/development/desa/population/publications/policy/international-migration-policies-2013.shtml. New York: United Nations.

———. 2013b. "Refugees: The Number." *Resources for Speakers on Global Issues.* Retrieved September 24, 2013. http://www.un.org/en/globalissues/briefingpapers/refugees/index.shtml

———. 2013c. *World Population Policies 2011.* ST/ESA/SER.A/327. Department of Economic and Social Affairs, Population Division. New York: United Nations.

———. 2013d. *World Population Prospects: The 2012 Revision.* Department of Economic and Social Affairs, Population Division. http://esa.un.org/unpd/wpp/index.htm

UNODC (United Nations Office on Drugs and Crime). 2012. *Global Report on Trafficking in Persons.* Vienna, Austria: UNODC.

U.S. Census Bureau. 1998. *State Population Estimates and Demographic Components of Population Change: Annual Time Series, July 1, 1990 to July 1, 1998.* Press Release CB98-242 and Data File ST-98-7.

———. 2012. "Geographical Mobility: 2011 to 2012 Data." *Geographical Mobility/Migration.* Retrieved September 24, 2013. Data Last Revised October 11, 2012. http://www.census.gov/hhes/migration/data/cps/cps2012.html

———. 2013. *International Data Base.* http://www.census.gov/population/international/data/idb/informationGateway.php

White, M. J., and Liang Z. 1998. "The Effect of Immigration on the Internal Migration of the Native-Born Population, 1981–1990." *Population Research and Policy Review* 17(2).

Woytinsky, Wladimir S., and E. S. Woytinsky. 1953. *World Population and Production.* New York: The Twentieth Century Fund.

Zlotnik, Hania, Philip Guest, Bela Hovy, and Sabine Henning. 2010. "Data and Analysis: Partnering to Better Understand and Address the Human Development Implications of Migration." *Background Paper for the Global Migration Group Practitioners Symposium.* Retrieved September 22, 2013. http://www.un.org/esa/population/migration/data-analysis-undesa-bpaper.pdf

10

Urbanization

The history of civilization has also been a history of urbanization, the concentration of populations in cities and suburban communities. In modern times, the industrial revolution has triggered a veritable urban explosion, first in the world's more-developed regions and then in the less-developed ones. The UN now projects that by the year 2025, 78% of the population in the more-developed regions and 47% of the population in the less-developed regions will reside in urban areas (United Nations, 2011).

This ongoing evolution in human settlement patterns is so important that we devote a separate chapter to it. We start the chapter with a descriptive history of world urban growth and urbanization. We soon discover that the process of urbanization is different in the less-developed regions of the world than in the more-developed ones, and so we provide separate sections on urbanization trends in each of the two regional categories.

World Urbanization: Past, Present, and Future

Definition and Measurement

Before one can measure urbanization or urban growth, one has to define "urban." What characteristics of a population settlement allow us to call it a "city" or a "town"? In demographic terms, the fundamental criteria are the size and concentration of the population settlement: An **urban place** is one that has a relatively large population density settled in an area surrounded by a less dense settlement. Other good answers could easily refer to (1) politically designated areas such as towns or cities, (2) the location of central features in an urban lifestyle, (3) a concentration of economic activities or occupations, or (4) the presence of specific local institutions (Pressat, 1985). These are certainly all correlates of the demographic criteria.

Population size and density are matters of degree, and so is being urban. How do we determine the cut-off point between the smallest urban community and the largest rural community? There is some minimum community size below which the style of life, the occupational structure, and the political institutions clearly are rural, but that cut-off point varies somewhat from culture to culture. Therefore, we rely on the national census bureaus to establish their cut-off points. Most countries use some combination of the criteria mentioned above. This reliance on national censuses introduces a bothersome lack of standardization into international comparisons (OECD, 2010). For this reason, we tend to have more confidence in comparative statements about cities of larger population sizes, such as 100,000 and above, or one million and above because everyone could agree that these should be considered as cities.

If we have decided what "urban" means, then what is **urbanization**? Actually, it has two meanings. One is a present condition, or the *degree* of urbanization. This conventionally is measured as the percentage of the total population residing in places that are categorized as urban. The other meaning is urbanization as a process, or the *pace* of urbanization. This pace often is measured by the rate of change over time in the percentage of the population residing in urban places (Arriaga, 1982).

Urbanization should be distinguished from **urban growth**. Just as the total population of a country has its growth rate, so do the rural population and the urban population. It is the *relative* speed of urban versus rural population growth that determines the pace of urbanization. But a country can have rapid urban growth without necessarily having rapid urbanization; the rural population may be growing at about the same speed as the urban. Moreover, rapid urban growth, the multiplication of cities and the increase in their size, can have its own consequences, above and beyond the consequences of urbanization. So it is important that we keep these concepts separate.

A final aspect of the process worth noting is which *size of city* seems to be growing most rapidly. Being urban, remember, is a matter of degree. A particularly important aspect of the modern urban explosion has been the disproportionate growth of metropolitan mega-cities, first in the more-developed and now in the less-developed regions.

History of Urbanization

Towns, and even some great cities, have been with us since antiquity. In the first century CE, for example, Rome had a population estimated at over one million, nearly as large as London in 1800 or Philadelphia in 1900 (Hopkins, 1978). Pre-industrial population centers were, of course, very different from what we think of as a modern city. Ancient cities generally were concentrations of political power that lived off the surplus of agricultural activities in rural areas and colonies. In contrast, industry brought the center of economic activity into the heart of the city, and as nonagricultural enterprises gained in importance, so did the cities.

As economic activity moved into towns and cities, people followed, with hopes of securing livelihood there. The *pull* of cities was often compounded by a *push* from agricultural areas, as prime farming lands and agricultural work for growing rural populations were in increasingly short supply. Industrialization, providing livelihoods not tied to the ownership of land, opened the new urban frontier for settlement.

However, the first industrial cities were not necessarily technologically modern. The early industrial revolution even hindered modernization through difficult labor conditions and harsh social inequalities within emergent cities (Wrigley, 1981). Rapid urban growth, especially in the new industrial cities, brought with it problems of disease and severe population crowding (Melosi, 2000). After the industrial revolution, most of the world's population still lived in rural areas and worked in agricultural occupations, even in countries that were becoming more-developed.

The tremendous growth of urban areas was shaped by the MDR population boom and the "second industrial revolution" that would expand the horizons of urban growth and tilt the balance to bring a majority of the world's population into the cities. This happened first in the regions of the world that industrialized first—the present-day MDRs. In the United States this urban explosion began after the Civil War. In 1860 less than 20% of U.S. residents were urban dwellers; by 1930 a majority of the U.S. population lived in metropolitan areas (Hobbs and Stoops, 2002).

Technology was once again key to rapid urban growth. In the thirty years after the Civil War, more than twelve times as many inventions were patented as in the entire history of the country to that time (Flanders, 1998). Two crucial developments were the shift from steam to electrical power and the concurrent rise of the steel industry. Electricity and steel, in turn, shaped the skyline of the emerging modern city. The first steel-framed skyscraper, a "towering" twenty-two stories, was completed in New York City in 1904 as elevators opened a new vertical habitat. Less than ten years later, the fifty-five-story Woolworth building dominated the skyline.

Urban growth was as explosive as the urban skyline. By the turn of the 20th century, three U.S. cities had more than a million residents each: New York with 3.4 million; Chicago with 1.7 million; and Philadelphia with 1.3 million. By 1950 New York had more than doubled in size and these three cities had gained as many residents as they have today (U.S. Census Bureau, 2012a; Flanders, 1998). The influence of these industrial and technological revolutions worldwide is graphed in Figure 10-1 on the following page.

Figure 10-1 charts the estimated, observed, and projected increase in urbanization from 1650 to 2025. The top line refers to the percentage of the world's population living in all urban areas. The line below that refers to the percentage of the population living in cities of one million or more, and the lowest line gives the percentage living in cities of more than 10 million. Historical time goes from left to right in the graph in equal fifty-year intervals, the time spans before 1800 being largely estimates based on historical observation, those from 1950 to 2010 being direct observations for most countries, and those from 2015 to 2025 being projections. The height of each line tells us the *degree* of urbanization in different-sized cities.

The slope of each line shows the *pace* of urbanization. We see that the overall pace of urbanization increased slowly but steadily up to 1800. Then, with the coming of the first industrial revolution, the pace of urbanization increased dramatically and remained nearly constant into recent decades, where it has slowed slightly.

The population living in urban areas did not increase substantially until 1850, with the second industrial revolution, when the pace of growth in cities increased rapidly. Cities with one million people or more took off in the period between 1900 and 1950. More recent growth in mega-cities exploded in the latter half of the 20th century. The continuing growth of mega-cities has surpassed even recent expectations. In just the next decade, between 2015–2025, the number of mega-cities of over 10 million is pro-

Figure 10-1

World Urbanization by City Size, 1650–2025

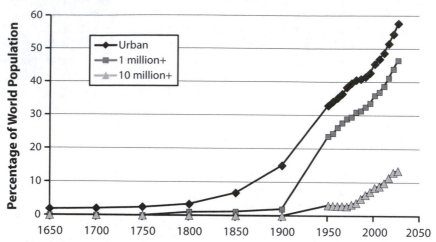

Sources: United Nations, 2012c. *World Urbanization Prospects: The 2011 Revision*, table 17c; Golden, 1981. *Urbanization and Cities*. Figure produced by Eiko Strader.

jected to increase from twenty-one to thirty-seven (or by 22%) and the population living in mega-cities by 28% (United Nations, 2011).

In 2007, something unprecedented happened. A majority of the world's people became urban dwellers, a first in the history of the human population. Figure 10-2 illustrates the growth in the percentage of urban population for the world, for more-developed regions, and for less-developed regions. Rapid urbanization and the modern city skyline emerged first in the more-developed countries. By the 1950s a majority of the population in MDRs lived in urban areas. Only later did the urban explosions start in the less-developed regions. The current percentage of LDR urban populations is still considerably less than what it was for the MDRs in 1950. At the current rate of growth in urban areas, more than two-thirds of the world population will be urban by 2050.

Although urbanization in the less-developed regions has historically lagged behind that in the more-developed regions, the recent *pace* of LDR urbanization has been higher than that of the MDRs and is projected to continue. In Figure 10-2 there is only a slightly higher absolute yearly increase in the urban percentage of the less-developed regions compared with the more-developed regions—but that increase represents a greater proportional change: For the LDRs, the 2050 figure is about 40% greater than the 2010 figure; for the MDRs, that increase is only about 10%. Still, MDRs will continue to have a more urban population. By 2050, 86% of the population in MDRs will live in urban areas compared to 66% of LDRs. As we will see later in this chapter, the definition of an urban population in MDRs is more expansive, with many living not just in large cities but also in smaller cities and suburban regions.

Figure 10-2

Percentage of Urban Population in MDRs and LDRs, 1950–2050

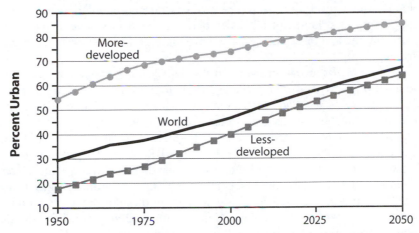

Source: United Nations, 2012c. *World Urbanization Prospects: The 2011 Revision*, table 2. Figure produced by Eiko Strader.

The Components of Urban Growth

What has produced the rapid growth in the percentage of populations living in urban areas throughout the world? To answer this question we must first ask how urban populations grow.

Urban growth must come from either natural increase of the urban population or the net movement of people who were not previously urban residents into urban areas. The movement of population into urban areas occurs in two ways. First, individuals can become urban residents by migrating to existing urban areas (from rural areas or from abroad). Second, they may live in rural areas which grow to the point where an entire area and its population are reclassified from rural to urban. Thus, (1) urban natural increase, (2) net migration, and (3) reclassification are the three components of urban population growth. Being more specific, we might ask whether the rapid growth of urban populations is a result of natural increase in existing urban centers or of net migration and reclassification into urban areas.

To begin to answer this question it is important to consider stages in the history of urban areas. In the early history of urban settlements the population is relatively small, and migration may have a dramatic impact on growth. New York City at the turn of the 18th century provides an example. The small city population, only 33,131 in 1790, nearly doubled over the next ten years, almost entirely from migration. During this early stage of city growth, it does not take a large number of migrants to contribute substantially to the growth of the urban population. However, as an urban population grows this situation changes. It takes a much larger migration stream to have such large effects on the size of the urban population. Some 220 years later, in 2010, the population of New York City was over 8.3 million. This larger city population would not have doubled even if all the immigrants to the United States over the next decade came only to New York City. As cities grow large, migration tends to make proportionately less of a contribution to urban growth; and, if demographic behavior does not change, the natural increase of the very large urban population becomes proportionately more important. But other demographic behaviors have changed as cities have grown larger, and these changes also have had significant effects on the components of urban growth.

In the MDRs, urban growth and the demographic transition have worked in tandem. During early stages of urban growth both the small size of urban populations and their high mortality made migration a very significant component of urban growth. Then, as many MDR cities grew to have large populations, mortality also declined, the combination of which made urban natural increase more significant in urban growth. Currently, as urban areas grow over time in MDRs, a greater proportion of that growth is likely to come from natural increase rather than migration. This is especially true when legal barriers or economic conditions impede migration. Indeed, research indicates a slightly greater role of natural increase in recent urban growth than anticipated, with 60% due to natural increase (United Nations, 2007). In LDRs, the main component of growth into the future will also be natural increase, although rural to urban internal migration rates continue to be significant contributors to LDR urbanization.

Regional Urbanization Trends

Degree of urbanization. Table 10-1 presents the percentage of the total population of various world regions that was urban in 1950, 1975, and 2000, and is projected to be urban in 2025 and 2050. For the world as a whole, half of the population already lives in urban places. The more-developed regions are the more urban, with nearly three of every four persons in the MDRs living in urban areas, compared with less than half of those in LDRs. The degree of urbanization is increasing in both more- and less-

Table 10-1   Percentage Urban Population, World Regions, 1950 to 2050

| | Percentage Urban | | | | |
Region[a]	1950 (1)	1975 (2)	2000 (3)	2025[b] (4)	2050[b] (5)
World	29.4	37.7	46.7	58.0	67.2
More-Developed Regions	54.5	68.7	74.1	81.1	85.9
Less-Developed Regions	17.6	27.0	40.1	53.6	64.1
North America	63.9	73.8	79.1	85.0	88.6
Latin America and Caribbean	41.4	60.7	75.5	82.5	86.6
Europe	51.3	65.2	70.8	76.1	82.2
Oceania	62.4	71.9	70.4	71.1	73.0
Asia	17.5	25.0	37.4	53.1	64.4
Africa	14.4	25.6	35.6	45.3	57.7

[a]Sorted in order of percentage urban in 2000.
[b]Projections.

Source: United Nations, 2012c. *World Urbanization Prospects: The 2011 Revision*, table 2. Used with permission.

developed regions and is projected to continue to do so. Some of these results already have been presented graphically in Figure 10-2.

What is different in Table 10-1 is the comparison among specific world regions. We have ranked the regions from most urban to least urban as of 2000. The three more-developed regions (North America, Latin America and the Caribbean, and Europe) are the most urbanized. Oceania was one of the most urbanized regions in 1950 but has not experienced the same increase in urbanization over the last half of the 20th century as other MDRs or Latin America and the Caribbean. The world as a whole became a majority urban population in 2007. The percentage urban has more than doubled for Asia and Africa in the past half century. The majority of Asia's population is projected to be urban by 2020, while the majority of Africa's population is projected to be so by 2035. By 2050 more than two-thirds of the world population will be urbanized. By that time Japan will consist of almost 100% urban dwellers!

Urban growth and the pace of urbanization. Urban growth has its own consequences, and the balance between urban and rural growth determines the pace of urbanization. Table 10-2 presents the average annual rate of change for urban and rural populations for world regions during the periods 1950 to 1975, 1975 to 2009, and projected forward to 2025. Until 2009 the world's population as a whole continued to grow, but more so in the urban areas, increasing world urbanization. By 2025, the pace of urban growth will have slowed considerably, and growth rates for rural areas of the world will be nearing zero or negative. In fact, by 2050 there is likely to be negative rural growth rates in some regions (United Nations, 2010).

The pace of world urbanization varies across Table 10-2's time span. From 1950 to 1975 the average annual rate of change for urban populations was twice that of the rural population. Then, from 1975 to 2009, as lower levels of fertility spread throughout much of the world (see chapter 5), growth slowed in both urban and rural areas.

Table 10-2   Average Annual Rate of Change, Urban and Rural Populations, World Regions, 1950–1975, 1975–2009, and 2009–2025

| | Average Annual Rate of Change (Percent) | | | | | |
| | 1950–1975 | | 1975–2009 | | 2009–2025 | |
Region	Urban (1)	Rural (2)	Urban (3)	Rural (4)	Urban (5)	Rural (6)
World	2.91	1.39	2.40	0.85	1.76	0.12
More-Developed Regions	1.97	−0.39	0.82	−0.35	0.58	−1.01
Less-Developed Regions	3.96	1.77	3.30	1.01	2.15	0.22
Africa	4.77	1.88	3.85	1.98	3.14	1.20
Asia	3.66	1.73	3.24	0.84	2.04	−0.03
Latin America and the Caribbean	4.17	1.03	2.51	−0.15	1.22	−0.66
Oceania	2.60	0.88	1.44	1.63	1.20	1.02
Northern America	1.96	0.09	1.37	−0.01	1.11	−0.64
Europe	1.81	−0.51	0.55	−0.46	0.34	−1.10

Note: Sorted in order of annual urban change 1975–2009.

Source: United Nations, 2010. *World Urbanization Prospects: The 2009 Revision*, tables 1, 7. Used with permission.

However, the decline in rural growth was more severe than the decline in urban growth, resulting in an increase in the pace of urbanization even as urban growth slowed. The ratio of urban to rural growth from 1975 to 2009 increased to about 2.8 and is projected to increase exponentially by 2025.

Table 10-2 reveals complex regional differences in the postwar pace of urbanization. For the more-developed regions as a class, the pace of urbanization was fastest in the earlier period, owing mainly to growth in urban centers. Despite the slowing of the pace of urban growth in MDRs over time, rural populations are projected to shrink at faster rates. This has kept the pace of urbanization higher than it otherwise would be.

For the less-developed regions, both urban and rural growth rates were considerably higher than in the MDRs over the last half century, and the very high urban growth rates resulted in relatively rapid urbanization. Between 1975 and 2009, growth in rural areas fell considerably more than in urban areas, increasing the pace of LDR urbanization during this period. But by 2050, the pace of urban growth in LDRs is projected to drop below the current levels of urban growth in MDRs as more and more of the entire world's population is already urban in nature (United Nations, 2010).

Table 10-2 also reveals some considerable difference among LDRs. Asia has experienced the greatest increase in the pace of urbanization as rural growth has turned negative since 2000. As a result, the latest estimate suggests that the rural growth rate for LDRs as a whole will turn negative by 2030, but urban growth will remain high for quite awhile (United Nations, 2014). Growth in rural and urban Africa has not changed considerably from 1975 to 2009, but rural growth is projected to slow down in the near future. In Latin America and the Caribbean urban growth has actually slowed more than the decline in rural growth, slowing urbanization.

City Size, Mega-Cities, and Urban Corridors

So far in this section, we have dealt with the simple dichotomy between urban and rural. But cities come in many sizes, from small towns to mega-cities. Has urban growth been spread evenly over the range of city sizes, or has it favored mega-cities?

The postwar picture is complex. The biggest change has occurred at the high ranges of the city-size distribution, with a rapid increase of urban dwellers living in **mega-cities** of over 10 million. Since 1950, the proportion of people living in mega-cities has more than tripled (United Nations, 2011, table 17c). Despite the fast growth of mega-cities over the latter half of the 20th century and the great amount of popular attention given to them, just over a tenth of the world's urban population are mega-city dwellers; roughly half of the global urban population lives in cities with fewer than 500,000 residents (United Nations, 2011, table 17c). By 2025 about one of every eight urban dwellers is expected to live in a mega-city (United Nations, 2011).

The disproportionate growth of mega-cities is not equally strong worldwide. Table 10-3 shows the number of mega-cities for regions of the world in 1975, 2010, and projected to 2025. Most of the growth in mega-cities occurred between the first two time periods in less-developed regions like Asia, and growth in mega-cities for the immediate future will be almost exclusively in the less-developed regions of the world (United Nations, 2011, table 17a). As the number of mega-cities in Asia and elsewhere grows, they are more likely to merge and integrate into even larger global **urban corridors** (United Nations, 2012c; Lo and Yeung, 1998). Regional urbanization is so common in

Table 10-3   Number of Mega-Cities in World Regions, 1975, 2010, and 2025

| | Number of Mega-Cities | | |
| | 1975 | 2010 | 2025 |
Region	(1)	(2)	(3)
World	3	23	37
More-Developed Regions	2	6	8
Less-Developed Regions	1	17	29
Asia	1	13	22
Latin America and the Caribbean	1	4	6
Northern America	1	2	3
Europe	0	2	3
Africa	0	2	3

Note: Regions sorted in order of the number of mega-cities in 2010.

Source: United Nations, 2012c. *World Urbanization Prospects: The 2011 Revision.* Used with permission.

Asian countries, for example, that some demographers have argued that the European notion of separate cities is not appropriate in less-developed countries (Lin, 1994). Instead, they argue, we should consider broad regional urbanization trends in the LDRs. The Pear River Delta-Yangtze River Delta-Beijing-Shenyang-Seoul-Tokyo-Taipei urban corridor and the Singapore-Kuala Lumpur corridor are two examples of linked mega-cities of regional urbanization in Asia. The Tokaido corridor stretching between Tokyo and Osaka, and the high-speed Shinkansen (bullet train) system that connects the two metropolises, epitomize the high level of urbanization in Japan. The Boston-New York-Washington, DC axis, the Chicago-Pittsburgh corridor, the Rhine Valley, and the London network are all examples of urban corridors in more-developed countries.

One result of this clustering in less-developed regions will be a change in the hierarchy of the world's largest cities. This is dramatized in Table 10-4 on the next page, showing the largest fifteen cities in 1950 and as projected in the year 2025. In 1950 the top five cities, and most of the rest of the list, were in the more-developed countries. By 2025, only three MDR cities will be left on the list of most populous cities. The rest have been replaced by LDR cities that were not even on the list in 1950.

In 2025, all of the top cities will be mega-cities. These new mega-cities will be headed by Tokyo, which is projected to have 38.7 million people. To give you a sense of scale, if Tokyo were a country, not a city, it would rank as the 35th most populous country in the world. Los Angeles (including Long Beach and Santa Ana), near the bottom of the list, is projected to have a mere 15.7 million!

Urbanization "Problems" and Policies in the Less-Developed Regions

Governmental Concerns

Until recently, governments of less-developed countries did not generally consider urban growth to be a problem. International agreements about urban growth, such as

Table 10-4   World's Largest Urban Agglomerations, Ranked by Size, 1950 and 2025

City (1)	1950 Population in Millions (2)	City (3)	2025 Population in Millions (4)
New York	12.34	Tokyo	38.66
Tokyo	11.27	Delhi	32.94
London	8.36	Shanghai	28.40
Paris	6.28	Mumbai (Bombay)	26.56
Moscow	5.36	Mexico City	24.58
Buenos Aires	5.10	New York	23.57
Chicago	5.00	São Paulo	23.17
Calcutta	4.51	Dhaka	22.91
Shanghai	4.30	Beijing	22.63
Osaka-Kobe	4.15	Karachi	20.19
Los Angeles	4.05	Lagos	18.86
Berlin	3.34	Calcutta	18.71
Philadelphia	3.13	Manila	16.28
Rio de Janeiro	2.95	Los Angeles	15.69
Saint Petersburg	2.90	Shenzhen	15.54

Sources: 1950 column from United Nations, 1998a. *World Urbanization Prospects: The 1996 Revision*, table 3; 2025 column from United Nations, 2012c. *World Urbanization Prospects: The 2011 Revision*, table 3. Used with permission.

the United Nations' *Agenda 21* (United Nations, 1996), led to the United Nations Conference on Sustainable Development (or RIO+20) resolution *The Future We Want* (United Nations, 2012a), which encourages urban growth but in the form of more sustainable cities. Urban settlements are credited for 80% of the world's Gross Domestic Product (GDP) (United Nations, 2012a). However, while the positive urban-GDP relationship may apply to overall trends, a recent report from the World Bank showed no clear relationship between urbanization and GDP growth in sub-Saharan African countries (World Bank, 2012). By the 21st century, urban growth of the degree that many countries have experienced has been increasingly recognized as unsustainable. Grave concerns have emerged over many city problems, such as urban poverty, homelessness, unemployment, crime, inadequate sanitation, and so on, which have resulted from rapid urban growth. As a result, much of the international policy regarding urbanization for the last several decades has focused on sustainable management of urban growth, ways to address urban poverty, and bridging the divide between urban and rural areas (United Nations, 2012a).

Because urbanization is occurring so rapidly in the developing world, LDR governments have been more alarmed than MDRs about the problems of urbanization. Indeed, 83% of LDR countries report concern over their urbanization patterns compared to 58% of MDRs (United Nations, 2012a). These concerns have produced (1) policies to control out-migration from rural areas through transforming the rural economy, (2) policies to limit the growth of large cities through migration control, and (3) policies that try to slow the growth of large cities by redirecting migration flows to mid-sized cities and smaller urban centers (United Nations, 2012c, 1998b). Unfortunately, these policies have had limited success. Over the past decades, internal migration to the major cities has grown steadily and trends toward rapidly developing urban centers and population concentration therein have continued unabated. What specific demographic concerns have led governments to pursue these policies, and why have they largely failed?

Out-Migration from Rural Areas

In discussing the pros and cons of international migration in chapter 9, we noted that the country of origin can suffer from the selective loss of its young adults, especially because emigrants often are the best educated and perhaps the most ambitious. This also is the case in most rural-to-urban migrations. Because of the agrarian nature of most rural areas, the loss of productive agricultural workers is of special concern to the communities of origin and to the rest of the nation.

On the positive side, migrants to urban areas often remain in contact and send remittances back to their families or villages, and migrants from many rural areas often move to urban areas only on a temporary basis, returning for seasonal agricultural labor. However, when agricultural productivity suffers from out-migration, the negative impact on those remaining in rural areas is only partly compensated by remittances sent back by migrants (United Nations, 1998b). Moreover, many who do migrate and who maintain contact with home tend to become a successful elite from the village perspective. Providing financial support to their kin can exacerbate income disparities and relative deprivation at the village level, spurring others from the village to migrate in turn.

In-Migration to the Cities

Rural-to-urban migrants in LDRs are usually motivated either by a desire to have a better job or to get a better education. Obviously many succeed in these goals; otherwise the migration streams would eventually dry up. Positive selection of the most educated and ambitious from the villages contributes to a more productive urban workforce. Thus, in the long term, receiving cities should benefit. If that is so, then why are rural-to-urban migration and rapid city growth considered problematic?

Part of the problem is simply coping with the speed of population growth and the resulting infrastructure needs in the short term. Rapidly growing cities in the LDRs seem never to catch up with the need for rapidly developing social services, health needs, housing, infrastructure, and especially employment opportunities; and they characteristically develop budget deficits in their attempts. City economies may grow more slowly than urban populations and are thus incapable of providing immediate employment opportunities for all migrants. Although many migrants may benefit from moving to urban areas, others enter the informal sector and do not earn a sufficient wage to avoid poverty, or they remain unemployed.

The problem of supplying urban jobs relates to a concern over "premature" urbanization. Urbanization on a massive scale occurred fairly late in the industrialization and technological development of the present MDRs. In LDR cities, however, the massive influx from villages came before cities had industrial economy jobs for migrants to fill. A symptom of this is the large proportion of the workforce in LDR cities in service jobs, as opposed to manufacturing jobs. Optimistically, these cities—with their surpluses of labor—will be motivated to evolve a style of development that is labor-intensive rather than capital-intensive.

Maldistribution of Cities

Another concern relates to LDR city size and location. There is a tendency for a country's largest city and/or its capital to grow disproportionately large. This polarizing of the urban population in a few huge agglomerations means that whatever benefits come from urbanization are not spread throughout the country.

Urban problems also are generally easier to manage in mid-sized cities. The dominant cities in many LDRs were located primarily for the convenience of colonial powers. What may be needed are decentralized cities located more favorably to the development of the domestic economy and tied more closely to the largely rural domestic resources that support any large urban agglomeration.

Another concern over particularly large concentrations of urban populations is their vulnerability to natural disasters. Of urban centers with one million people or more, 60% are exposed to one or more natural hazards, namely flooding and drought, but a substantial number are also located in cyclone or earthquake zones (United Nations, 2012c). Such was the case for the 2011 Tohoku earthquake and tsunami in Japan.

Reasons for Limited Migration Policy Success

Why have policies to limit LDR rural-to-urban migration and urban growth had limited effect? Three major reasons probably explain much of the difficulty: (1) the strength of the attraction that urban areas have for migrants, (2) the weak and conflicting commitments governments have made to controlling population redistributions, and (3) high rates of natural increase in less-developed countries.

Expected eventual benefits of urban migration.   In chapter 9 we discussed migration theories that emphasized the role of expected eventual benefits in migration decisions. Such calculations appear to play a large part in migration from rural to urban areas in the LDRs. Migrants often enter the unfamiliar landscape of the large city only to find themselves at a social and economic disadvantage, and many end up joining the ranks of the urban poor. Why would they migrate to such dismal prospects?

The answer involves both the push from rural areas and the pull of urban areas. It is not only the *current* push-and-pull factors but also the prospects for the future that matter. Many rural areas appear to provide very limited possibilities for the future while growing urban centers seem to offer boundless opportunity. Migrants continue to face the costs of migration and move to the urban areas because the *expected* benefits from such a move seem high.

Figure 10-3 schematically illustrates such migration decisions. The figure shows two patterns of expected income in the years after deciding whether to migrate. If potential migrants choose simply to remain in the rural area, they might expect little change in income over the coming years unless the rural economy changes drastically. If they choose to migrate they may expect to encounter costs of moving, interruption of employment, retraining, and so on; so for the first few years they may expect to actually experience a loss of income. However, if they have high expectations for the future,

Figure 10-3

Expected Value of Rural-to-Urban Migration Decisions

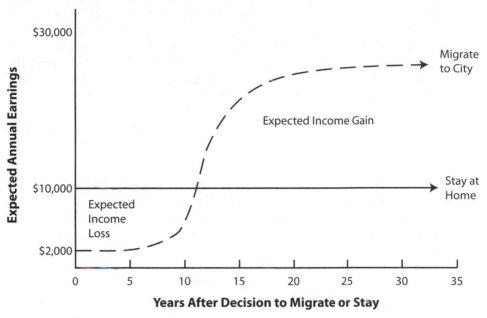

Source: Adapted from Martin and Midgley, 1994. "Immigration to the United States," figure 4.

their expected income may eventually rise to much higher levels than if they had not moved to the city. If these expectations are sufficiently high, then they will likely decide to make the move and suffer the temporary costs of migration. Because the decision to migrate is a personal judgment, migration to urban areas may continue even when the immediate prospects for migrants are dismal and their future uncertain. So long as rural dwellers believe the promise of urban futures are brighter than the more well-known and predictable drudgeries of remaining at home, they will continue to move to the growing urban centers. Such migration decisions can also be household-level strategies to broaden labor opportunities and lessen risks. That is, if one member of the family continues to work in the rural labor economy while another family member goes to the city to find additional work, the family will be less reliant on the vicissitudes of a single local labor market.

Direct limits on migration to urban areas have had only limited success where migrants continue to perceive future benefits of migration, and it is difficult for a government to change the conditions of rural and urban life to the extent required for people to have a different vision of their possible future in these areas. It is equally difficult to resist a spreading dominance of capitalism's *urban culture*, which increases the value placed on the fast-paced, gleaming, technological urban lifestyle and neglects or denigrates the slow, pastoral, agricultural rural life.

If the poor are more likely to migrate and their prospects in the city are uncertain, is the migration of the rural poor into the cities the cause of urban poverty? It may be tempting to think so, but there is little evidence to support this conclusion. Urban poverty does not increase in proportion to urbanization in the less-developed countries, and in fact the development of cities has been identified as a major influence in the fight against global poverty (United Nations, 2012a; Hjerppe and Berghäll, 1996). The proportion of poor actually tends to decline as city size increases; and a much larger proportion of the world's rural population than of the city population is poor. New immigrants to the city also are no more likely to be excluded from the formal economy than are others. In the absence of urbanization, poverty might, in fact, be much worse. Urban poverty is the result of disadvantages in education, health, nutrition, family planning, and so on and, although some migrants may bring such disadvantages with them, decisions to move to urban areas generally benefit migrants socioeconomically. So long as that remains the case, it is difficult for government policies to reverse the rural-to-urban migration stream.

Conflicting aims and weak commitments.   What might a comprehensive LDR policy require to discourage and/or accommodate rural-to-urban migration? To reduce the push from rural areas, investments in rural economies would be needed. More importantly, support for the informal economies of cities is required to expand the employment opportunities of newly arriving migrants. Decentralization would require the creation of new mid-sized urban centers—but such investments have difficulty competing with the other national development priorities, and resulting weak commitments and limited funding for such programs have led to the dismal record of rural-urban migration policies in LDRs.

Policies to decentralize urbanization from very large cities to medium-sized ones offer an example (United Nations, 2012c). Relocation of industrial activities to outlying areas has, instead of decreasing urbanization, tended simply to increase the boundaries of urban areas. Simply relocating administrative or industrial activities to entirely new or small cities has failed to attract populations away from the large urban areas where migrants perceive greater opportunities and social services. The success of such programs generally would require much more ambitious, and costly, economic development programs.

A growing amount of attention over the past decade has been devoted toward policies to increase the sustainability of urban centers and to design cities that accommodate all segments of the population, rather than discouraging urban growth (United Nations, 2011). Indeed, policies to reduce rural-urban migration have not only been of limited success, they may even contradict aspects of accepted economic development policy. As less-developed countries struggle to expand their international economies they are led further in the direction of developing export-oriented industries within major urban centers (United Nations, 1996, 1998b, 2012c). At the same time, attempts to modernize agriculture have promoted a green revolution that has decreased, rather than increased, the demand for rural labor. These efforts to enhance national development have amplified rather than limited urbanization, rural-to-urban migration, and the growth of large cities.

In the face of competing demands and priorities, migration policies have been weakly funded and conflicted. Governments have not made (and perhaps cannot make) the large investments that would be required to reverse the push-pull forces underlying rural-urban migration streams. There is considerable controversy about whether policies to decentralize urban centers or those to concentrate and accommodate large cities are most compatible with sustainable land development efforts and investment in quality of urban life (United Nations, 2011). Even given the means to address urban growth, many governments may not wish to limit patterns of urbanization that contribute to national development and rising standards of living overall.

> In 1976, 44 per cent of developing countries reported having implemented such policies and by 2011, that proportion had increased to 72 per cent. At the same time, among developed countries, the proportion having policies to reduce migrant flows to large cities declined from 55 per cent in 1976 to 26 per cent in 1996 but increased later to 34 per cent in 2009. (United Nations, 2012c, p. 15)

These regional differences and volatile trends in policy reflect the international ambiguity concerning the costs and benefits of continuing urban growth.

Continued population growth.   A major reason for the failure of many migration policies in the less-developed countries has been their high rate of natural increase. Urbanization is a direct outcome of the demographic transition, and just as the mortality transition and population growth has occurred more rapidly in the LDRs than the MDRs, urbanization is also occurring at much faster rates (Dyson, 2011). As populations increase, the expanding opportunities of urban areas provide an outlet for such growth while rural areas and agricultural enterprises have limited abilities to absorb growing populations. In many countries that have attempted to improve rural retention through land reform, for example, these programs have simply been overwhelmed by continuing population growth, and land reforms have not improved the problem of land scarcity. As increasing proportions of the population live in urban areas, their own natural increase also contributes to the growth and reclassification of urban communities. Consequently, attempts to decentralize have resulted in cities which have been absorbed into new, even larger, urban corridors and metropolises (United Nations, 2011).

There is also a potentially negative ecological impact of rapid urbanization in concentrated settings. But if we are able develop sustainable urban infrastructure in tandem with growth, city living actually has the potential to reduce our global ecological footprint (see chapter 3). In fact, studies show that per capita greenhouse gas emissions are lower in cities than elsewhere (Dodman, 2009). Cities offer the potential for high-density residential and employment structures with mass transit systems and collectivized waste management, recycling, and other services, which lessens the overall per-person demand on land and resources. Urbanization is also associated with rapid fertility decline, which, as we have seen in previous chapters, reduces population growth.

Urbanization "Problems" in the More-Developed Regions

It is ironic that the most salient and troublesome urbanization trends for the more-developed regions are almost the opposite of those typical for less-developed regions.

Careers in Demography

Myron P. Gutmann
Professor of History and Director, Institute of Behavioral Science, University of Colorado, Boulder
Assistant Director, SBE of the National Science Foundation, 2009–2013
Director, Inter-University Consortium for Political and Social Research, 2001–2009

How did you decide that being a demographer was the career path for you?

I suspect that I began to really think of myself as a demographer when I got settled as a young faculty member at the University of Texas at Austin (UT-Austin) in the late 1970s. Prior to that I was comfortable as a historian who dabbled in a lot of approaches, one of which was demography. Being thrown into an environment at the Texas Population Research Center, where everyone else thought of themselves as demographers, made a big difference, giving me confidence that my knowledge and skills were up to the task.

What kind of education and training did you pursue to get to where you are in your career?

I discovered demography as an undergraduate at Columbia University, but I came to it as a historian. In the late 1960s historians were beginning to make use of quantitative approaches to the study of society, and as a young social historian I was drawn to those approaches. At the same time, I was engaged by an emerging community of French historians who made use of innovative research sources and methods. My most important mentor at that time, the Dutch historian J. W. Smit, introduced me to this literature and encouraged me to think about it.

My real demographic training came at Princeton, with Ansley Coale and Etienne van de Walle. That solid training in core concepts of demography has stood me in good stead ever since. I used some of it in my dissertation (on 17th and 18th century Belgian and Dutch history of the social, demographic, and economic consequences of war), and expanded that knowledge later. As I was finishing my dissertation, I worked on Etienne's La Hulpe population register project, and together with him, Susan Watkins, and George Alter we developed and refined methods for working with longitudinal data in historical settings that are used widely today. These approaches are at the core of the summer workshop on longitudinal approaches to historical demographic data that George and I led from 2006 to 2013.

Describe your work/research as a demographer. What do you consider your most important accomplishments?

Chance plays a big role in the development of everyone's career, and mine is no exception. In the mid-1980s one of my colleagues at the University of Texas asked me to think about new approaches to teaching, and I decided that teaching the micro-historical approaches that I had developed for the study of European communities would be useful, but that teaching about the U.S. would be easier and more interesting for my students. This shifted my interests to the western U.S., and taught me lessons about the ways that population processes were different in Europe and the Americas. I became especially interested in the role of migration, ethnicity, and environment on demographic processes, which are less complex in the American context. The ideas I developed teaching about the social and demographic history of Texas led me to spend time on a micro-historical study of six Texas counties in that time period, work that I did with the late Kenneth Fliess. Later, the interest I developed in ethnicity and migration led to a series of incredibly interesting projects with Brian Gratton of Arizona State University on immigrants to the U.S. and their demographic and family behavior.

Working with students always gives me new ideas and spurs new insights. When I became interested in the relationship between population and environment my then-student (now faculty at the University of Saskatchewan) Geoff Cunfer pushed me to have extremely ambitious ideas, through which we would study the whole Great Plains region instead of just a few communities. That spur has led to nearly two decades of research with a large number of collaborators across many disciplines. It also finally pulled me away from my emphasis on single communities and micro-level studies to the largest kind of regional, macro-study, with the county as the unit of analysis. That work has produced no shortage of great ideas, valuable research, and real pleasure in collaborations, especially with Cunfer, Bill Parton, Glenn Deane, Susan Hautaniemi Leonard, Ken Sylvester, Emily Merchant, Dan Brown, and many, many others.

All these collaborations are my greatest accomplishment.

From 2001 to 2009 I was director of ICPSR. Leadership jobs often limit scientific energy, but that job did exactly the opposite for me. Not only did the work on the Great Plains project continue and flourish, but I developed a real interest in how to think about protecting the confidentiality of survey and census respondents, and what to do in order to ensure that protection, especially where geospatial information was involved. All that arose out of the requirement as a manager to think hard about data, and from the relationships I developed at the University of Michigan with researchers who were deeply involved in large-scale survey projects.

After ICPSR I spent four years as Assistant Director of the National Science Foundation, responsible for NSF's portfolio—and Directorate—for the Social, Behavioral and Economic Sciences. Work at NSF gave me a unique insight into the breadth of scientific research done in the United States, and of the important place that demographic research has as part of that breadth. It also helped me understand the strong connections between the basic scientific research that demographers (especially historical demographers) do, and both more applied scientific research and development, and the formulation of public policy. It showed just how great are our abilities to contribute to better lives in the U.S. and around the world.

What do you see as the field's most important contribution as well as its greatest challenge?

Demography is deeply embedded in everything that we need to know about society, and vice versa. Explicating those relationships makes demography exciting. Its breadth and integration with the rest of science and our understanding of the world allow for great accomplishments, but also provide substantial challenges. How do we engage society in a world where questions of human behavior are contentious, and where many of the things that we study (marriage, reproduction, the provision of health services) are the cause of strident debate and misunderstanding? Overcoming those challenges will keep us busy long into the future.

In my role at NSF I found myself neatly positioned between ideas of social science as a "basic" science, generating and testing general hypotheses about human behavior, and a more applied science that solves immediate societal or economic problems. What I say to students about demography is that it is uniquely qualified as an area of study to allow them to stay in that attractive middle ground, where what they do allows them to understand the fundamentals of human behavior while contributing ideas that will lead to the betterment of society. That's a great place to be.

The LDRs generally are plagued by rapid urbanization, especially metropolitanization at the cost of infrastructure development. While MDRs also experienced urbanization, it took place over a longer period of time, beginning after the industrial revolution and peaking by the mid-20th century. In the latter 20th century, many MDR countries were surprised by a phenomenon called **urban deconcentration**, with population flowing out of their largest cities and into the suburbs or smaller agglomerations. This exodus resulted in inner-city blight and decay in many core centers, creating an urban underclass mired in poverty.

Upon the turn of the 21st century there appeared to be signs of a slowing to this deconcentration trend, and in some cases even a reversal. The nascent movement of people back to large cities has been referred to as **reurbanization**. Unfortunately, the global recession appears to have cut short this trend in many countries, with an overall slowdown in internal migration. It is unclear whether the trend toward reurbanization will pick up again in the future.

Urbanization and Deconcentration in More-Developed Regions

In the 1970s and again in the 1990s there was a net out-migration from the largest cities (Illeris, 1990; Frey, 2012). This broad deconcentration was, in part, due to rapid changes in industrial activities and changing job opportunities across geographic regions of the MDRs (Illeris, 1990; Frey, 1995, 2012; Kasarda, 1995; United Nations, 1998b, 2012c). Now, however, internal migration in many MDRs is experiencing some stagnation, or decline, in population movement to, or between, urban areas and regions. While the global recession is likely to be blamed for this, a number of other reasons could also be contributing factors. For example, the relatively radical restructuring of industrial economies during the end of the last century may have already had its major impacts on population redistribution. The rising costs of urban housing in prime destinations, transportation limits within urban sprawl, a growth in telecommuting, a decrease in regional job specialization, and a greater distribution of urban amenities to suburban and rural areas have all been raised as hypotheses for the slowing internal migration in more developed countries (Molloy et al., 2011).

There is, of course, variation by region. In Europe, both economic development and population redistribution have been influenced by industrial restructuring and development of the European Union. Around 2010, many EU countries reported that between a third and two-thirds of foreign immigrants came from other EU countries (Eurostat, 2013). In the United States, industrial restructuring has continued but at a much slower pace and in some cities has contributed to continuing declines or stagnation in the growth of urban populations. Although urban deconcentration slowed somewhat due to high growth rates in the Sunbelt and northwestern United States, many old midwestern industrial cities experienced negative growth and cities in the Northeast experienced very little growth. It remains to be seen whether the same forces that have curtailed urban growth in the developed regions will come into play in the mega-cities of less-developed regions. Indeed, such mega-cities as Cairo, Lagos, Abidjan, and Johannesburg began to experience deconcentration trends around the turn of the 21st century (El-Shakhs, 1997).

Detailed comparative study of urbanization, urban deconcentration, and internal migration is a methodologically daunting task. Not only do countries lack a standard definition of "urban," but they also lack standard classifications of various sizes of cities. Even within given countries, definitions change over time. And, the distinction of urban migration from urban annexation, the legal process permitting cities to expand their official borders, is often difficult to track. To further explore the major trends of urban deconcentration in the more-developed countries requires careful consideration of the way in which urban centers are defined and deconcentration measured. For example, in Japan "urban" is defined as 50,000 people or more whereas in Norway urban is defined as 200 or more! (see Haub's 2013 blog piece for more on this). To simplify the matter, we will narrow our focus for the moment to the United States and its most recent trends.

Metropolitan Growth: The U.S. Case

Definition and measurement.   A **metropolitan area** consists of a large population nucleus and adjacent counties that are socially or economically integrated with the population center. Despite changing terminology over the years, that core meaning has remained in U.S. census designations since 1910. Census data in 2010 distinguished three types of metropolis: counties defined as *core-based statistical areas* (CBSAs), independent *metropolitan statistical areas* (MSAs), and *primary metropolitan statistical areas* (PMSAs) making up the huge urban belts of the United States.

Within metropolitan areas, data are available for a variety of geographic subdivisions including the central cities of the MSA, other urban fringe areas, and adjacent rural areas in the counties. Cities and places within the metropolitan areas also are distinguished by size. These complex geographic designations provide considerable detail on the movement of population between not only rural and urban areas, but between different types of more- and less-urbanized areas.

One can see from the way in which metropolitan areas are defined that it is important to distinguish the *concentration* of population, or clustering in areas of high density surrounded by areas of lesser density, from *centralization*, or the functional connection of many areas with a central economy. We will use *deconcentration* to refer to the decline of a population's urban concentration. It could be evident in a smaller proportion of the population living in metropolises, or movement from center cities to the rings around them or to less densely settled metropolitan areas.

Regional contrasts.   The major story of the American city has been an urban peak at mid-century followed by a trend toward major urban deconcentration in the late 20th century. More recently there was a slight uptick in reurbanization, but it is unclear if this will become a major trend. As is so often the case, there is important variation at the regional level. A major contrast is between the so-called *Frostbelt* cities of the Northeast and north central regions and the *Sunbelt* cities of the South and western regions. Table 10-5 on the following page shows the population growth in selected metropolitan statistical areas of both categories from 1950 to 2010.

Since the postwar period, metropolitan growth and new metropolitan areas have been concentrated in the Sunbelt states. Most Sunbelt MSAs continued to grow rapidly throughout the 1970s. In contrast, metropolitan areas in the Frostbelt experienced a net population loss during the urban deconcentration of the 1970s. The Frostbelt MSAs slowly recovered to have small population gains in the 1990s, the greatest decade of growth for many Frostbelt cities since the 1940s (Simmons and Lang, 2003). Notably,

Table 10-5 Population Growth in Selected U.S. Sunbelt and Frostbelt Metropolitan Areas, 1950–2010

Area	Percent Growth in Decade										
	1900–1910	1910–1920	1920–1930	1930–1940	1940–1950	1950–1960	1960–1970	1970–1980	1980–1990	1990–2000	2000–2010
United States	21.0	14.9	6.1	7.2	14.5	19.0	13.3	11.4	9.5	8.7	9.7
Sunbelt MSAs											
Atlanta	—	—	—	17.5	29.7	39.9	36.7	27.4	32.5	38.6	24.0
Dallas/Ft. Worth	—	—	—	19.3	56.4	69.7	39.9	28.3	32.5	29.3	23.4
Denver	—	—	—	—	38.3	51.8	32.1	30.7	13.6	30.0	16.7
Houston	—	—	—	47.2	52.5	54.1	40.0	45.3	20.7	25.8	26.1
Los Angeles	183.5	85.3	133.2	25.3	49.8	54.4	16.4	6.2	18.5	12.7	3.7
Miami	—	—	—	—	—	88.9	35.6	28.3	19.2	16.3	11.1
Phoenix	—	—	—	—	—	100.0	45.8	55.3	39.9	45.3	28.9
San Diego	—	—	—	—	92.4	85.5	31.4	37.1	34.2	12.6	10.0
Frostbelt MSAs											
Chicago	31.5	27.9	32.8	3.2	13.9	20.1	12.2	1.8	2.3	11.6	4.0
Cleveland	43.3	47.2	27.9	1.9	15.6	22.6	8.1	-8.0	-3.3	2.2	-3.3
Detroit	43.8	112.7	66.7	9.2	26.9	24.7	11.6	-1.9	-4.4	4.1	-3.5
New York	39.6	20.5	27.9	7.4	10.7	11.9	8.2	-8.6	3.3	9.0	3.1
Philadelphia	19.9	19.7	15.6	2.0	14.7	18.3	10.9	-2.2	2.9	3.6	4.9
St. Louis	25.3	13.5	19.3	5.3	17.4	19.8	12.3	-2.3	3.2	4.5	4.2

Note: Data begin with the decade when the metropolitan area first attained a population of 500,000. Prior to 1950 data represent metropolitan area boundaries recognized in 1950. After 1950 data refer to boundaries in effect at the end of each decade.

Source: Long, 1983. "Population Redistribution in the U.S.," table 1; U.S. Census Bureau, 1998. "Statistical Abstract of the United States," table 43; U.S. Census Bureau, 2005. *Census 2000 Redistricting Data Summary File,* 2005 and 1990 Census; U.S. Census Bureau, 2011. *2010 Census Population and Housing Tables CPH-T-2.*

without international immigration many of these Frostbelt cities would have had lower, or even negative, rates of growth. Frostbelt cities again had low growth rates compared to the Sunbelt in the 2000s, with several major cities—e.g. Detroit, Cleveland, and Pittsburgh—experiencing negative growth (Frey, 2012).

Of course, the Frostbelt cities not only are colder, but also tend to be older, with economies that at one time were based on heavy industry. Many of these cities are in the "Rustbelt" of declining heavy-industry economies. The difference between slow or stagnating growth of the Rustbelt cities and sustained growth in the Sunbelt cities during the 20th century is largely explained by a shift in employment opportunities out of the primary industries of the Rustbelt and into non-unionized and low-paid manufacturing and service sectors in the Sunbelt. The stagnation in internal migration has recently curtailed the role of migration from the north to south in the growth of the Sunbelt cities. Sunbelt cities have also been significantly impacted by the housing foreclosure crisis, which is likely to seriously impede their future growth.

Suburbanization. A major characteristic of deconcentration has been the relatively slow growth of central cities compared to surrounding areas. Since the 1940s, the rings immediately around the center cities of metropolises have been growing relatively rapidly; this is known as **suburbanization**. The emergence of terms like "edge city," "exurbia," and "sprawl" describe ever-expanding zones of settlement occurring in the peripheral cities. Such new settlement patterns are increasingly blurring the distinction between traditional urban and rural classifications used by demographers (United Nations, 2013; Champion and Hugo, 2004).

In the United States, suburbs grew more rapidly than central cities throughout most of the 20th century. Figure 10-4 shows the percentage of people living in U.S. sub-

Figure 10-4

Percent of U.S. Population Living in Central Cities and Suburbs: 1910 to 2010

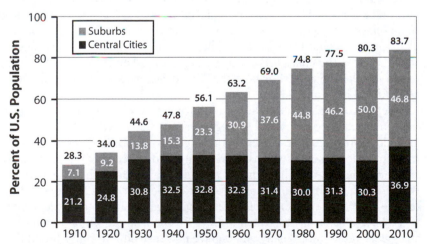

Sources: Short, John Rennie. 2012. "Metropolitan USA: Evidence from the 2010 Census," *International Journal of Population Research;* Hobbs and Stoops, 2002. *Demographic Trends in the 20th Century.* Figure produced by Eiko Strader.

urbs compared to central cities over the 20th century. By 1930, growth in central cities had plateaued to levels that lasted until the turn of the 21st century, with around 30% of the total U.S. population consisting of central-city dwellers. Suburbanization, on the other hand, grew significantly. By 1970, more Americans were living in the suburbs than in the cities. This suburbanization trend continued through the turn of the century, leveling off slightly in the most recent decade as central cities experienced significant growth for the first time since the early 20th century. Notably, the percentage of Americans living in suburbs declined in size for the first time ever in 2010. This reflects a 21st-century reurbanization trend that has also begun in other western countries. Although more Americans still live in suburbs than in center cities, this latest trend suggests that the American love affair with suburban life may be coming to an end.

Metropolitan "Problems": The U.S. Case

When Americans think of urban problems, what come first to mind probably are the everyday struggles of urban life—such as crowds, traffic, smog, crime, and noise. But do these collectively constitute the major urban problem? Rusk, for example, thinks not:

> Jobs, housing, streets and highways, water and sewer systems, pollution, and revenues are common issues for urban areas everywhere, but collectively they do not seem to add up to America's urban problem. In fact, compared with most urban populations throughout the world, America does not really have an urban problem as such. Most urban Americans are better employed, better housed, better served by transportation systems and public facilities, and live in better environmental conditions than the rest of the world. America's *real* urban problem [italics ours] is the racial and economic segregation that has created an underclass in many of America's major urban areas. (Rusk, 1993, p. 1)

Although there has been a lessening of racial segregation in recent decades, black-white segregation remains the most common form of segregation and the dissimilarity index (see chapter 11) is still very high (Parisi et al., 2011). Residential segregation by social class has proven to be among the most intractable of all segregation for non-black groups in the United States. There is a high degree of consensus among social scientists that the *concentration of poverty* within central cities is the single greatest urban problem for individuals in the United States (Kneebone et al., 2011; Massey et al., 2009; Massey and Denton, 1993).

Selective migration into and out of urban areas has played a central role in shaping the nature of poverty and segregation in the city today. The composition and geographic distribution of socioeconomic groups in U.S. cities reflect the effects of migrations long past as well as current migration streams. U.S. cities have historically had larger numbers of immigrants and minorities than other parts of the country. At the end of the 20th century many of America's largest cities became majority nonwhite for the first time (Berube, 2003). Immigrants, minorities, and the socially disadvantaged have historically migrated to the metropolis in search of a better life. Most have struggled, yet found it; many others have not. Instead, they have found themselves in a city segregated across social groups and with barriers blocking the social mobility of the disadvantaged, the different, and the disabled (see chapter 11).

Although poverty is still more than twice as high in cities as in suburbs, it is notable that poverty, segregation, and crime are rising in the suburbs—even prior to the Great Recession (Kneebone and Berube, 2013). Because more people live in the suburbs than in cities, the *absolute* number of poor suburban people is higher than in cities, but the *relative* percentage is still lower. More immigrants also now live in American suburban areas (51%) than live in cities (33%). This reflects economic restructuring where the regional demand for workers in construction and low-skilled industries has shifted away from typical immigrant gateway cities (Frey, 2012). These suburban trends mirror the uptick in reurbanization that occurred around the same time. As more people moved back into cities, housing became more expensive there. The subprime mortgage market also gave more people of wider income levels access to home ownership for the first time.

Many in-migrants to the cities already face social disadvantages such as language barriers, lower skill or education levels, less access to financial capital, and so forth. Facing such disadvantages, living in ethnic enclaves has historically been a choice of immigrant groups who have benefited from the support that a cultural and residential community of like individuals can offer. But more often segregation is not voluntary at all. Historically, discriminatory housing practices kept minority groups in the least desirable areas of cities and apart from white residents. Although such practices are illegal today, evidence shows that racial segregation continues due to informal discrimination by landlords and real estate agents, as well as inequalities in mortgage lending practices (Roscigno et al., 2009).

Patterns of urban out-migration and urban deconcentration have compounded the problem. One of these is the phenomenon of "white flight" where white residents move out of neighborhoods that are becoming racially diverse due to prejudice and/or fear of falling housing values. In the post-World War II decades, many middle-class and affluent whites moved out of the city to mass housing tracts in the suburbs when southern black Americans migrated to northern cities (Boustan, 2010; Massey and Denton, 1993). This exodus was enabled by a combination of factors: affordable home loans for primarily white World War II veterans; government subsidization of the mass highway system; and the availability of the automobile to the average middle-class family. White flight still occurs and recent research has shown that white flight is often followed by working-class minority flight, leaving such neighborhoods with highly concentrated poverty (Reibel, 2011).

Involuntary segregation has had lasting and negative effects. Many of the disadvantaged in the city, recent arrivals or long-term residents, face few employment opportunities, poor school systems, underfunded social services, and declining infrastructure. This state of affairs has resulted in an urban underclass isolated from opportunity in high-poverty neighborhoods (Jargowsky, 1997; Wilson, 2012, 2007; Massey, 1996).

Economic opportunities can sometimes lead to a deconcentration of urban minority populations. For instance, almost half of the nation's largest minority group, Hispanics, resided in just eight large metropolitan areas in 2000. Yet, by 2010, 107 other smaller metropolitan areas had nearly doubled their Hispanic population, largely due to demand for workers in construction and low-skilled industries in other rapidly growing parts of the country (Frey, 2012). These trends fell victim, however, to the failing economy at the end of the decade.

The same inner-city decay problems that have affected urban dwellers had a fiscal impact on city governments and their ability to provide for the social needs of their citizens. As deconcentration has led to a movement of many but the poorest out of numerous cities, the tax base and fiscal health of many metropolitan areas has been negatively impacted. Older, densely populated cities like those in the Northeast—surrounded by competing cities—are *inelastic* and cannot readily expand to include new rapidly growing suburbs. In contrast, many cities, especially those in the South and West, are more elastic and are able to expand through the annexation and incorporation of the growing suburbs. As economic growth expands in the suburbs and dwindles or stagnates in central cities, inelastic cities cannot expand to encompass this activity and garner the tax revenues required to address the needs of the central city. Rusk (2006, 1993) argues that metropolitan growth is inhibited in inelastic cities and that when their growth through expansion stops, deconcentration begins and the concentration of poverty worsens. This is evident in the recent example of Detroit, a declining Rustbelt city that filed for bankruptcy in 2013.

The dominant trend in the United States over the last half of the 20th century has clearly been the rise of suburbia (Landis, 2009). But a strong urban revalorization movement arose in resistance to this trend. This "new urbanist" perspective was powerfully influenced by Jane Jacobs, author of the well-known *The Death and Life of Great American Cities* (1961). With the recent stabilization in population loss from many urban areas starting in the 2000s, as well as nascent signs of population resurgence in a few cities, e.g. Boston, Chicago, D.C., Philadelphia, and Minneapolis, optimistic dialogue has re-emerged on how best to revive cities (Short and Mussman, 2013). The dramatic drop in crime in many cities since the 1980s has helped to invigorate this conversation. A prominent theory suggests that cities should strive to attract a "creative class" (Florida, 2002, 2012). This class consists of professionals working in high-tech or knowledge-based occupations, as well as artists, who will breathe new life into cities due to economic stimulation, their innovative ideas, and their alleged appreciation for cultural diversity. Although many policy makers and city planners quickly embraced creative class revitalization polices, it is not yet clear that the theory works in practice (Hoyman and Faricy, 2009). Furthermore, the creative class thesis has received criticism for encouraging the negative elements of **gentrification** (Shaw and Sullivan, 2011; Hoyman and Faricy, 2009), such as the displacement of poor and working-class urban dwellers due to rising housing costs brought on by the settlement of wealthier residents.

SUMMARY

Although the world had been moving toward urbanization throughout history, industrialization triggered an urban explosion. The present more-developed regions industrialized and started their urban explosions first, and at the moment they are the most urbanized. The less-developed regions, however, now have the more rapid growth of their urban populations; they also have the more rapid pace of urbanization, as urban population growth far outstrips that of rural population. This rapid pace of urbanization is projected to continue in the LDRs. Moreover, we can expect the largest mega-cities and urban corridors of the near future to be found in the LDRs. Net migration always has been the major demographic cause of urbanization and it continues to be so, although now urban natural increase also contributes to urban growth, just as it does to rural growth, in the LDRs.

There is widespread concern in less-developed countries about the consequences of massive rural-to-urban migration. Migrations may improve the circumstances of the individual, and in the long run the receiving community may gain desirable kinds of migrants. Yet, the constant immediate strain of rapid urban growth can mask any such benefits. Migration policies to control this rural-to-urban migration stream have, however, had little effect. One reason for the inefficacy of migration policies is the strong expectation many migrants have that the city offers a more promising eventual future, regardless of the immediate costs of migration. Another reason migration policies have had little impact is that they often conflict with economic development policies that encourage continuing economic growth in urban areas, which in turn lowers the demand for agricultural labor in rural areas. Policies that emphasize sustainable growth in cities are now shaping LDR strategic urban planning.

Ironically, while the less-developed regions are concerned with too-rapid metropolitan growth, the more-developed regions have experienced extensive urban deconcentration. Some of the largest U.S. cities have begun to shrink. Trends toward suburbanization and regional shifts in industrial activities and employment opportunities from the Frostbelt states to those in the Sunbelt were causes. Over past decades, urban growth continued to favor the Sunbelt while several Frostbelt cities, including Detroit, have continued to lose population.

Suburbanization involved the flight of more affluent residents out of the central cities and into metropolitan-edge cities and suburbs, where economic opportunities are increasingly concentrated, remote from the problems of urban life. Meanwhile, segregation, discrimination, and persistent social disadvantage have all contributed to a concentration of high-poverty neighborhoods and urban decay in the inner cities. Cities that cannot expand to incorporate the economic growth at their fringes see their social needs grow as their tax revenues dwindle.

In the early 21st century there have been signs of a slight reurbanization movement back to city life. However, the global recession of 2007–2009 has led to stagnation in growth and regional population movements. Impacted by hard economic times, it is perhaps not surprising to see some of the oldest, most venerable, U.S. cities facing the greatest fiscal crises of their history. One thing, however, is certain. The global trend toward urbanization—both in central cities and suburbs—throughout the 20th century is likely to continue unabated on a world scale, and an increasing percentage of the world's population will live the urban experience.

EXERCISES

1. Watch Hans Rosling's four-minute video on urbanization under the exercises section of the Chapter 10 tab on this text's website at www.demographytextbook.com and answer the following questions:

   a. In two sentences summarize the trends he shows.

   b. What is the urban challenge he refers to?

   c. What does he think the advantages of urbanization are?

2. Compute measures of the degree of urbanization in China, using the data and examples in Table E10-1.

   a. Compute the percentage of the total population living in urban places for 1990 and 2020, rounding to one decimal place, and record them in the blank spaces of the table.

   b. Compute the ratio of the urban population to the rural population for 2000 and 2030, rounding to one decimal place, and record them in the blank spaces in the table.

Table E10-1   Degree of Estimated and Projected Urbanization in China, 1980–2030

Population (in 1,000s)	1980	1990	2000	2010	2020	2030
Urban	190,320	302,817	455,325	660,286	846,363	957,649
Rural	792,851	842,379	813,792	681,049	541,428	435,427
Total	983,171	1,145,195	1,269,117	1,341,335	1,387,792	1,393,076
Percent Urban	19.4		35.9	49.2		68.7
Ratio Urban/Rural × 100	24.0	35.9		97.0	156.3	

Sources: United Nations, 2012c. *World Urbanization Prospects: The 2011 Revision;* 2004, *World Urbanization Prospects: The 2003 Revision.*

3. Compute measures of the pace of Chinese urban growth and of urbanization, using the data in Table E10-1 and examples in Table E10-2.

Table E10-2   Pace of Urban and Rural Growth and of Urbanization in China, 1980–2030

	1980–1990 (1)	1990–2000 (2)	2000–2010 (3)	2010–2020 (4)	2020–2030 (5)
		Decade Growth Ratio (× 100)			
Urban	159.11		145.01		113.15
Rural	106.25		83.69		80.42
		Ratio of Urban Growth Ratio to Rural Growth Ratio (× 100)			
		155.65		161.24	140.69

Source: Derived from Table E10-1.

   a. Compute ratios of urban growth for 1990–2000 and 2010–2020. Do this by dividing the later urban population by the earlier urban population and multiplying the quotient by 100. Round to one decimal place and record in the blank spaces in Table E10-2.

   b. Compute the ratios of rural growth for 1990–2000 and 2010–2020, using the same procedure. Round to one decimal place and record in the blank spaces in Table E10-2.

c. Compute the ratio of the urban-growth ratio to the rural-growth ratio for 1980–1990 and for 2000–2010. Multiply by 100, round to the nearest whole number, and record in the blank spaces of Table E10-2. This is one measure of the pace of urbanization.

d. If the figure in the bottom row for a given decade were less than 100, that would mean that (check one):

_____ the urban growth ratio was less than the rural growth ratio.

_____ the urban population did not grow.

_____ less than half the population lived in urban places during the decade.

_____ all of the above.

4. Compute net total migration for the United States between 2011 and 2012 using the data in Table E10-3.

Table E10-3   Migration for Metropolitan and Nonmetropolitan Areas, United States, 2011–2012

	Net Internal Migration (1)	Migrants from Abroad (2)	Net Total Migration (3)
Metropolitan Areas	8,714,000	1,078,000	9,792,000
Principal Cities	5,420,000	580,000	
Suburbs	3,294,000	498,000	
Nonmetropolitan Areas	1,260,000	76,000	

Source: U.S. Census Bureau, 2012b. "Geographical Mobility: 2011 to 2012."

a. Compute the net total migration for principal cities, suburbs, and nonmetropolitan areas in column 3. Enter your answers in the blank spaces of the table.

PROPOSITIONS FOR DEBATE

1. In countries where population growth is rapid, urbanization also tends to be rapid, everything else being equal.

2. On balance, less-developed countries actually are better off if their urbanization is rapid.

3. One of the reasons for the urban deconcentration of the U.S. population in recent decades may have been the change in marriage and family norms.

4. Any problems resulting from urban deconcentration in the U.S. have been minimized by the steady arrival of international migrants into metropolitan areas.

5. Deconcentration is a stage of a city's life cycle; all old cities eventually will stop growing and will experience deconcentration.

6. Since problems of racial and ethnic relations seem most severe in metropolitan central cities, the United States should welcome any deconcentration of its metropolitan populations.

7. Mega-cities are a potential remedy to environmental problems of population growth and resource waste.

REFERENCES AND SELECTED READINGS

Arriaga, Eduardo. 1982. "Urbanization: Measurement." In J. A. Ross, ed., *International Encyclopedia of Population*. Vol. 2. New York: Free Press.

Berube, Alan. 2003. "Racial and Ethnic Change in the Nation's Largest Cities." In B. J. Katz and R. E. Lang, eds., *Redefining Urban and Suburban America: Evidence from the 2000 Census*. Vol. 1. Washington, DC: Brookings Institution Press.

Boustan, Leah Platt. 2010. "Was Postwar Suburbanization 'White Flight'? Evidence from the Black Migration." *The Quarterly Journal of Economics* 125(1): 417–443.

Champion, T., and G. Hugo, eds. 2004. *New Forms of Urbanization: Beyond the Urban-Rural Dichotomy*. Aldershot: Ashgate.

Dodman, D. 2009. "Blaming Cities for Climate Change? An Analysis of Urban Greenhouse Gas Emissions Inventories." *Environment and Urbanization* 21: 185–201.

Dyson, T. 2011. "The Role of the Demographic Transition in the Process of Urbanization." *Population and Development Review* 37: 34–54.

El-Shakhs, S. 1997. "Towards Appropriate Urban Development Policy in Emerging Mega-Cities in Africa." In Carole Rakodi, ed., *The Urban Challenge in Africa: Growth and Management of Its Large Cities*. Tokyo: United Nations University Press.

Eurostat. 2013 (March). *Migration and Migrant Population Statistics*. Retrieved from http://epp.eurostat.ec.europa.eu/statistics_explained/index.php/Migration_and_migrant_population_statistics

Flanders, Carol M. 1998. *Atlas of American Migration*. New York: Facts on File Inc.

Florida, Richard. 2002. *The Rise of the Creative Class: And How It's Transforming Work, Leisure, Community and Everyday Life*. New York: Perseus Book Group.

———. 2012. *The Rise of the Creative Class: Revisited*. New York: Basic Books.

Frey, William H. 1995. "The New Geography of Population Shifts: Trends Toward Balkanization." In Reynolds Farley, ed., *State of the Union: America in the 1990s*. Vol. II, Social Trends. New York: Russell Sage Press.

———. 2012. "Population Growth in Metro America since 1980: Putting the Volatile 2000s in Perspective." *Metropolitan Policy Program* (March). Washington, DC: Brookings Institution.

Golden, Hilda H. 1981. *Urbanization and Cities*. Lexington, MA: D.C. Heath.

Haub, Carl. 2013. "What Does Urbanization Really Mean?" on Demographics Revealed! http://demographicsrevealed.org/2013/06/13/what-does-urbanization-really-mean/#more-148

Hjerppe, R., and P. E. Berghäll. 1996. "The Urban Challenge." Research Paper 96–3. Helsinki: World Institute for Development Economics Research.

Hobbs, Frank, and Nicole Stoops. 2002. *Demographic Trends in the 20th Century*. Census 2000 Special Reports. CENSR-4. Washington, DC: U.S. Census Bureau.

Hopkins, Keith. 1978. "Economic Growth and Towns in Classical Antiquity." In Philip Abrams and E. A. Wrigley, eds., *Towns in Societies*. Cambridge: Cambridge University Press.

Hoyman, M., and C. Faricy. 2009. "It Takes a Village: A Test of the Creative Class, Social Capital, and Human Capital Theories." *Urban Affairs Review* 44(3): 311–333.

Illeris, S. 1990. "Counter-Urbanization Revisited: The New Map of Population Distribution in Central and North-Western Europe." *Norwegian Journal of Geography* 44(1).

Jacobs, Jane. 1961. *The Death and Life of Great American Cities*. Random House Digital, Inc.

Jargowsky, Paul A. 1997. *Poverty and Place: Ghettos, Barrios, and the American City*. New York: Russell Sage Foundation.

Kasarda, John D. 1995. "Industrial Restructuring and the Changing Location of Jobs." In Reynolds Farley, ed., *State of the Union: America in the 1990s*. Vol. I, Economic Trends. New York: Russell Sage Press.

Kneebone, Elizabeth, and Alan Berube. 2013. *Confronting Suburban Poverty in America*. Washington, DC: Brookings Institution Press.

Kneebone, E., C. Nadeau, and A. Berube. 2011. "The Re-Emergence of Concentrated Poverty." *Brookings Institution Metropolitan Opportunity* Series.

Landis, J. 2009. "The Changing Shape of Metropolitan America." *The Annals of the American Academy of Political and Social Science* 626(1): 154–191.

Lin, G. C. 1994. "Changing Theoretical Perspectives on Urbanisation in Asian Developing Countries." *Third World Planning Review* 16(1).

Lo, Fu-chen, and Yue-man Yeung, eds. 1998. *Globalization and the World of Large Cities*. Tokyo: United Nations University Press.

Long, Larry H. 1983. "Population Redistribution in the U.S.: Issues for the 1980s." *Population Trends and Public Policy*, no. 3. Washington, DC: Population Reference Bureau.

Martin, Philip, and Elizabeth Midgley. 1994. "Immigration to the United States." *Population Bulletin* 49(4).

Massey, Douglas S. 1996. "The Age of Extremes: Concentrated Affluence and Poverty in the Twenty-First Century." *Demography* 33(4).

Massey, Douglas, and Nancy Denton. 1993. *American Apartheid: Segregation and the Making of the Underclass*. Cambridge, MA: Harvard University Press.

Massey, D. S., J. Rothwell, and T. Domina. 2009. "The Changing Bases of Segregation in the United States." *The Annals of the American Academy of Political and Social Science* 626(1): 74–90.

Melosi, Martin V. 2000. *The Sanitary City*. Baltimore: The John Hopkins University Press.

Molloy, Raven, Christopher L. Smith, and Abigail Wozniak. 2011. "Internal Migration in the United States." *Journal of Economic Perspectives* 25(3): 173–196.

OECD (Organization for Economic Cooperation and Development). 2010. *Trends in Urbanisation and Urban Policies in OECD Countries: What Lessons for China?* China Development Research Foundation. OECD Publishing.

Parisi, Domenico, Daniel T. Lichter, and Michael C. Taquino. 2011. "Multi-scale Residential Segregation: Black Exceptionalism and America's Changing Color Line." *Social Forces* 89(3): 829–852.

Pressat, Roland. 1985. *The Dictionary of Demography*, Christopher Wilson, ed. New York: Basil Blackwell Ltd.

Reibel, Michael. 2011. "White Flight/Black Flight: The Dynamics of Racial Change in an American Neighborhood." Ithaca, NY: Cornell University Press.

Roscigno, Vincent J., Diana L. Karafin, and Griff Tester. 2009. "The Complexities and Processes of Racial Housing Discrimination." *Social Problems* 56(1): 49–69.

Rusk, David. 1993. *Cities Without Suburbs*. Washington, DC: Woodrow Wilson Center Press.

———. 2006. *Annexation and the Fiscal Fate of Cities*. Washington, DC: The Brookings Institution. http://www.brookings.edu/metro/pubs/20060810 fateofcities.pdf

Shaw, S., and D. M. Sullivan. 2011. "White Night": Gentrification, Racial Exclusion, and Perceptions and Participation in the Arts. *City & Community* 10(3): 241–264.

Short, John Rennie. 2012. "Metropolitan USA: Evidence from the 2010 Census." *International Journal of Population Research*. doi:10.1155/2012/207532

Short, J. R., and M. Mussman. 2013. "Population Change in U.S. Cities: Estimating and Explaining the Extent of Decline and Level of Resurgence." *The Professional Geographer*, forthcoming.

Simmons, Patrick A., and Robert E. Lang. 2003. "The Urban Turnaround." In B. J. Katz and R. E. Lang, eds., *Redefining Urban and Suburban America: Evidence from the 2000 Census*. Washington, DC: Brookings Institution Press.

United Nations. 1996. *United Nations Conference on Human Settlements (Habitat II)*. A/CONF. 165/14 (part). New York: United Nations.

———. 1998a. *World Urbanization Prospects: The 1996 Revision*. Population Division of the Department of Economics and Social Affairs, ST/ESA/SER.A/170. New York: United Nations.

———. 1998b. *Population Distribution and Migration*. ST/ESA/SER.R/133. New York: United Nations.

———. 2004. *World Urbanization Prospects: The 2003 Revision*. New York: United Nations.

———. 2005. *World Population Prospects: The 2004 Revision*. Population Division of the Department of Economic and Social Affairs. http://esa.un.org/unpp

———. 2007. *State of World Population 2007: Unleashing the Potential of Urban Growth*. United Nations Population Fund (UNFPA). New York: United Nations.

———. 2008. *World Urbanization Prospects: The 2007 Revision*. New York: United Nations.

———. 2010. *World Urbanization Prospects: The 2009 Revision*. New York: United Nations.

———. 2011. *Population Distribution, Urbanization and Internal Migration: An International Perspective*. Department of Economic and Social Affairs. http://www.un.org/esa/population/publications/PopDistribUrbanization/PopulationDistributionUrbanization.pdf

———. 2012a. *The Future We Want*. U.N. Resolution A/RES/66/288 (http://sustainabledevelopment.un.org/futurewewant.html)

———. 2012b. *UN System Task Team on the Post-2015 UN Development Agenda: Sustainable Urbanization, Thematic Think Piece*. UN-Habitat. New York: United Nations.

———. 2012c. *World Urbanization Prospects: The 2011 Revision*. Department of Economic and Social Affairs, Population Division. ESA/P/WP/224. New York: United Nations.

———. 2013. *United Nations Statistics Division* website. http://unstats.un.org/unsd/demographic/sconcerns/densurb/densurbmethods.htm

———. 2014. *World Urbanization Prospects: The 2014 Revision*, CD Rom edition. New York: United Nations.

U.S. Census Bureau. 1998. *Statistical Abstract of the United States, 1998*. Washington, DC: GPO.

———. 2005. *Census 2000 Redistricting Data* (Public Law 94-171) Summary File 2000. PL/00-6 (RV). Washington, DC: U.S. Census Bureau.

———. 2011. *2010 Census Population and Housing Tables*. CPH-T-2. Washington, DC: U.S. Census Bureau.

———. 2012a. *2012 Population Estimates*. Washington, DC: U.S. Census Bureau.

———. 2012b. *Geographical Mobility: 2011 to 2012*. Retrieved October 21, 2013. www.census.gov/hhes/migration/data/cps/cps2012.html. Washington, DC: U.S. Census Bureau.

Wilson, William J. 2007. *When Work Disappears: The World of the New Urban Poor*. New York: Vintage Press.

Wilson, William Julius. 2012. *The Truly Disadvantaged: The Inner City, the Underclass, and Public Policy*. Chicago: University of Chicago Press.

World Bank. 2012. *World Development Report 2013: Jobs*. Washington, DC: World Bank.

Wrigley, E. A. 1981. "The Process of Modernization and the Industrial Revolution in England." In Theodore K. Rabb and Robert I. Rotberg, eds., *Industrialization and Urbanization*. Princeton: Princeton University Press.

11

Population Diversity

Throughout history one effect of migration has been to bring people from diverse origins and cultures into contact with one another. Globalization has led to increased levels of migration worldwide. This, combined with subsequent growth of immigrant groups, means that most countries of the world now have a population with considerable diversity. Cultural diversity, therefore, is a fundamental dimension of population composition of interest to demographers.

Demographic Terminology

The identification and labeling of culturally diverse groups can be, with good reason, a sensitive undertaking. In the past, such categorizing of cultural groups has too often been used to stereotype minority populations and to facilitate discrimination against those marked as different. Thus, even the most innocent attempts at classification are understandably met with suspicion. In such an atmosphere, it is important to recognize what is, and what is not, implied by demographers in the labels they use to identify culturally diverse groups.

Race, Ethnicity, and Ancestry

The concept of **race** offers perhaps the clearest illustration of an abused demographic concept. During the early 20th century race was regarded as an objective trait reflecting biological heredity and inherent social differences between identified racial groups (Soloway, 1990). The use of race often reflected an underlying ideology of *racism* (i.e., that humans are divided into genetic physical types with traits intrinsically related to their cultures and to their physical or cultural superiority). As the world recoiled from the horrors of World War II and Hitler's quest for a master race, growing scientific evidence of genetic commonality across—and of cultural variability within—identified race groups cast increasing doubt on the biological validity of race categories. Identified races differ from culture to culture and across history, lending recognition of race as an essentially cultural, rather than biological, definition of social groups. Race as a concept is clearly more useful for understanding how social groups construct difference. Yet, even as a reference to social groups, race is not without problems. The use of the term "race" is so arbitrary and so emotionally charged that it is difficult to employ in any useful analytical fashion. Adding to the confusion, race categories, such as black or white, are sweeping combinations of very different cultural populations.

> As a result of its confusing usage and questionable scientific validity, many sociologists and anthropologists have dispensed entirely with the term race and instead use *ethnic group* to describe those groups commonly defined as racial . . . [or,] for those groups that are particularly divergent from the dominant group . . . the term *racial-ethnic group*. (Marger, 2000, pp. 25–26)

Although the terms **ethnic group** and **ethnicity** are now familiar, these terms did not appear in standard English dictionaries until the 1960s. What constitutes an ethnic group is still not entirely clear. Martin Marger (2000), for example, identifies ethnic groups as subcultures that have unique cultural traits (e.g., language, religion), a sense of community, varying degrees of ethnocentrism, most often ascribed membership, and frequently some distinct territoriality or regional concentration.

Ethnic group identity is sometimes, but not always, related to **ancestry**, in the simplest case defined as the birthplace of one's parents. In a broader sense, however, ancestry can refer to more remote heritages than one's own parents. People often claim ancestry, such as Irish-American, Italian-American, or African-American, many generations removed from any contact with ancestral homelands and after such heritage is blurred by repeated intermarriage with those of different ancestries. Self-identified ancestries are often so strong that the individuals involved have a strong sense of community and constitute an ethnic group. In contrast, many first-generation foreign-born residents with a clearly identified ancestry may become thoroughly involved and assimilated in the dominant culture with little cultural identity as an ethnic group.

Population diversity among race, ethnic, or ancestry groups clearly depends on exactly how these subgroups are defined and measured. It also is likely that the importance of population diversity in one culture will not be the same as that in another. Discussions around race and ethnicity in India, for example, are considerably different from those in the United States.

For that reason we will focus more narrowly on the United States in this chapter than we have in earlier chapters. We will begin with issues of defining and measuring population diversity in the U.S. We then provide a brief demographic comparison of major racial and ethnic groups in the United States with respect to the topics of earlier chapters: growth, age and sex structure, mortality, morbidity, health, fertility, marriage, migration, and urbanization. The chapter ends with the problems and policies that sometimes spring from those demographic comparisons.

Definition and Measurement in the United States

By the end of the 19th century, the growing cultural diversity of the population had led to concerns about whether the census's race, ethnicity, and ancestry questions were sufficient to reflect the population's heterogeneity. Since ethnic and racial groups are culturally defined and self-identities change over time, there are continuing questions about the best terminology to identify any one group. For example, should the census refer to African American or black? Use the term Hispanic or Latino? Ask about Guamanians or Chamorro? Distinguish Hawaiian or Native Hawaiian? These are not equivalent identities, and changes in question wording can result in incomparability across successive censuses. Yet, because such labels are socially constructed and do change over time, in the long run the census has little choice in the matter. As a result, the measurement of race, ethnicity, and ancestry has changed repeatedly over the centuries. Questions asked about these social distinctions in the 1870, 1970, and 2010 censuses are shown in Table 11-1 on the following page. In the earliest of these three censuses, race was defined as "color," and only four racial categories were used. By 1970, nine categories of race, six Hispanic-origin groups, and three ancestry questions were included. This was the first time that a Hispanic-origin question appeared on the U.S. census. By 2000, for the first time respondents could select more than one racial category, an acknowledgement that race is not a monolithic concept. Asian race categories were also expanded, and Hispanic origin (as a designation of ethnicity separate from race) was collected from all respondents. The 2010 census continued these multiracial response possibilities, with some fifteen racial categories, and changed some race category terms yet again. These most recent changes reflect continuing attention to the growing percentage of nonwhite residents in the United States, increasing population diversity, and evolving self-identity among social groups.

Sensitivity to racial categories and changes in categories is inevitable. For example, the reaction to the 2010 race and ethnicity categories was not all positive. Some critics considered re-introduction of the term "Negro" offensive, and others questioned why "Latino or Spanish" is not considered as a racial category. Indeed, one may ask "what is the race for those who identify as Latino?" In the race question their race continues to be primarily defined by the skin color options in the census question (black or white). If Latino is not included as a race, why then is there no category of brown, yellow, or other potentially more appropriate shades of "color." And, more to the point, if race is defined irrespective of skin color for some groups such as Korean, Japanese, Samoan, etc., then why is Latino or Spanish not included as a racial response? Given the contentious social ground of race and ethnicity in an increasingly multiracial and multiethnic society, these disputes are not likely to have a simple resolution and will continue to evolve from one census to the next. In the meantime, any discussion of race using census categories is hampered by constantly changing definitions, significant measurement error, and cultural ambiguity.

The ability to check more than one race meant that by the turn of the century Americans could select a racial identity from one to six races in combination and, if appropriate, with additional specification of a Hispanic/Latino/Spanish ethnic identification. Interestingly, even with this expanded questionnaire, only 2.9% of the population reported more than one racial identity in response to the race question. And, of those reporting multiple racial identities, 91.7% reported only two racial identities. This means for many population-level analyses in the United States at the moment, it is generally sufficient to either look at one and two-race groups, or to look at major one-race groups and identify the percentage with any additional racial identity reported.

Table 11-1   Race, Ethnicity, and Ancestry Questions on the U.S. Census Questionnaire, 1870, 1970, and 2010

1870 (1)	1970 (2)	2010 (3)
Color: White Black, mulatto Indian Chinese	**Race—Mark ONE:** White Negro or Black Indian (Amer.): print tribe Japanese Chinese Filipino Hawaiian Korean Other: print race	**Is This Person of Hispanic, Latino, or Spanish Origin?** No, not of Hispanic, Latino, or Spanish origin Yes, Mexican, Mexican-Am., Chicano Yes, Puerto Rican Yes, Cuban Yes, another Hispanic, Latino, or Spanish origin: print origin, for example, Argentinean, Columbian, Dominican, Nicaraguan, Salvadoran, Spaniard, and so on. **Race—Mark One *or More*:** White Black, African American, or Negro American Indian or Alaska Native: print name of enrolled or principal tribe. Asian Indian Chinese Filipino Japanese Korean Vietnamese Other Asian: print race. Native Hawaiian Guamanian or Chamorro Samoan Other Pacific Islander: print race Some other race: print race
Sample (Long Form) Items		
[None]	Where was this person born? What country was his father born in? What country was his mother born in? Is this person's origin or descent Mexican; Puerto Rican; Cuban, Central or South American, Other, Spanish; None of these? Is this person naturalized?	In what U.S. state or foreign country was this person born? Is this person a citizen of the United States? What is this person's ancestry or ethnic origin? Does this person speak a language other than English at home? How well does this person speak English? When did this person come to live in the U.S.?

For example, the Census Bureau produces a number of statistics like those in Figure 11-1. This figure shows less than three-fourths of the population, 72.4% of individuals, identified as white alone, which decreased from 75.1% in the 2000 census. The largest nonwhite racial category was black or African American, representing 12.6% of the population. The fastest growing racial identification in the United States was Asian, which rose from 3.6% to 4.8% of the population between the 2000 and 2010 censuses. Only 2.9% of census respondents indicated more than one racial identity. In contrast, while the figure shows only 0.2% of the population identified as Native Hawaiian or

Figure 11-1

Racial and Hispanic Groupings in the United States, 2010

Panel A: Racial Groups

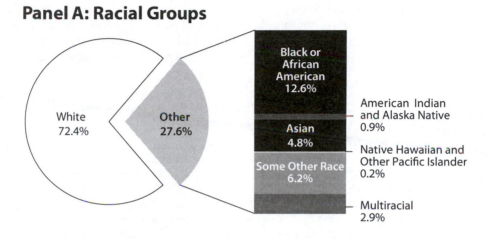

Panel B: Hispanics by Race

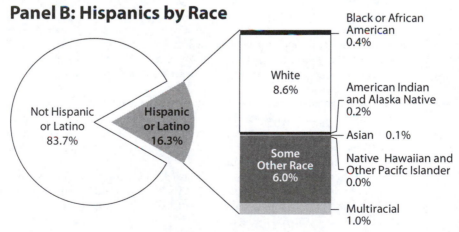

Source: Data from Humes et al., 2011. "Overview of Race and Hispanic Origin: 2010." *2010 Census Briefs.* Figure produced by Eiko Strader.

other Pacific Islander, more than half of these individuals, 55.9%, indicated multiple racial identities. Detailed census data is, of course, available for any combination of racial and ethnic identities even though census reports are often limited to the largest, or most common, combinations of racial and ethnic identities.

More than 50 million people, 16.3% of the U.S. population, identified themselves as Hispanic or Latino origin in the 2010 census. This was an increase of 43% since just the 2000 census. Most Hispanics identify themselves as either white (53%, or 8.6% of the total population) or, partly because of confusion over racial categories and ethnicity, as some other race (36.7%, or 6% of the total population). We discuss this further in Figure 11-3. Similarly, although not shown here, 7.4% of those who identified themselves as black or African American report themselves to be biracial or multiracial, and 43.8% of American Indian and Alaska Native people also identify themselves to be biracial or multiracial. Indeed, the census results point to complex racial and ethnic dynamics in the United State.

Throughout the rest of this chapter we will focus on the major racial groups as defined by the U.S. census, identified in Box 11-1. Where useful we will also focus on the Hispanic or Latino population alone, but remember that these individuals are

---

Box 11-1

2010 U.S. Census Racial Group Definitions

White refers to people having origins in any of the original peoples of Europe, the Middle East, or North Africa. It includes people who indicated their race or races as "white" or wrote in entries such as Irish, German, Italian, Lebanese, Arab, Moroccan, or Caucasian.

Black or African American refers to people having origins in any of the black racial groups of Africa. It includes people who indicated their race or races as "black, African Am., or Negro," or wrote in entries such as African American, Kenyan, Nigerian, or Haitian.

American Indian and Alaska Native refers to people having origins in any of the original peoples of North and South America (including Central America), and who maintain tribal affiliation or community attachment. It includes people who indicated their race or races as "American Indian or Alaska Native" or reported their principal or enrolled tribe, such as Navajo, Blackfeet, Inupiat, Yuk'ik, or Central American or South American indigenous groups.

Asian refers to people having origins in any of the original peoples of the Far East, Southeast Asia, or the Indian subcontinent. It includes, for example, people who indicated their race or races as "Asian Indian," "Chinese," "Filipino," "Korean," "Japanese," "Vietnamese," and "Other Asian," or wrote in other entries, for example Burmese, Hmong, Pakistani, Thai, etc.

Native Hawaiian and Other Pacific Islander refer to people having origins in any of the original peoples of Hawaii, Guam, Samoa, or other Pacific Islands. It includes people who indicated their race or races as "Pacific Islander," "Native Hawaiian," "Guamanian or Chamorro," "Samoan," or "Other Pacific Islander," or wrote in other entries such as Tahitian, Mariana Islander, or Chuukese.

Some other race includes all other responses not included in the above categories. This includes respondents who reported themselves as **multiracial**, mixed race, interracial, or as a Hispanic or Latino group (for example, Mexican, Puerto Rican, Cuban, or Spanish) in response to the race question.

Source: Humes et al., 2011. "Overview of Race and Hispanic Origin: 2010." *2010 Census Briefs.*

included among the various racial groupings. We will also refer to race and ethnicity interchangeably. Since racial and ethnic groups identified by the Census Bureau have changed over time, and vary in different reports, there is some variability in the data available. Most notably, some tabulations will further identify non-Hispanic whites from Hispanics as a whole. It is important to remember throughout this discussion that there are a considerable variety of racial and ethnic identities within any one of these major groups.

The Demography of U.S. Ethnic Groups

Relative Growth

A population's **diversity** rises as the variety of ethnic and racial subgroups increases or as people are spread more evenly across ethnic groups. Many of the more-developed regions have experienced substantial increases in diversity through immigration, lower birth rates of native populations, and a relatively young age structure among ethnic minorities conducive to higher rates of growth. The United States is a case in point.

There have always been diverse groups in the U.S. population. However, the variety of ethnic and racial groups and the percentage of the population expressing ethnic identities that differ from that of the majority are both increasing. Over the last half century the proportion of the U.S. population accounted for by "majority" non-Hispanic whites has declined as other groups have more than tripled in size. By the 1990s the "minority" nonwhite and Hispanic population of the United States was larger than the population of Great Britain, France, Italy, or Spain (Pollard and O'Hare, 1999). Until recently, four of every five people in the United States were non-Hispanic white and the largest minority ethnic group for much of U.S. history was the black population. As noted earlier, however, Hispanic and Asian populations have begun to increase at a much faster rate. Projections into the mid-21st century show rising percentages of these ethnic populations relative to the black and non-Hispanic population. Figure 11-2 on the next page shows the percentage composition of the United States population among five major ethnic groups identified by the census, combining the two questions by breaking down the black and white population to distinguish Hispanics from non-Hispanics. In 2000, traditional "majority" white, non-Hispanics were just under 70% of the population. By 2050, they are projected to be less than 50% of the U.S. population. The percentage of black non-Hispanics will not significantly decrease or increase. By contrast, the percentages of Hispanic and Asian populations will double, as Hispanics replace blacks as the largest ethnic minority, and as Asians become a substantial percentage of the population. These differences in growth are clearly seen in the 2010 census data.

There is complex diversity within these two major groups, which is largely attributable to recent migrations of Asians and Hispanics from a wide variety of countries. Figure 11-3 on p. 413 shows the national origins of Asians and Hispanics in the United States. Asians in particular represent a very diverse population, with great variation in languages and cultures. Although the Chinese population is the largest of the Asian groups at 23%, it is by no means the most dominant Asian group in the United States.

Figure 11-2

Projected Ethnic Composition of the United States Population, 2000-2050

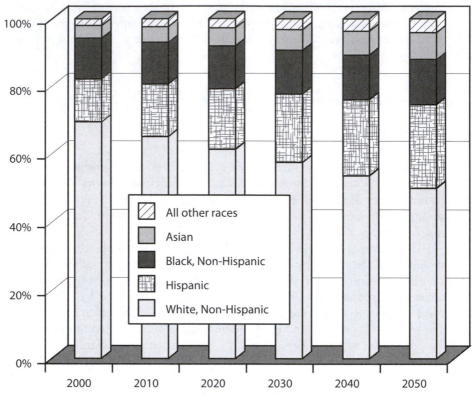

Source: U.S. Census Bureau, 2004. "U.S. Interim Projections by Age, Sex, Race, and Hispanic Origin."

Asian Indians, Filipinos, Vietnamese, Koreans, and Japanese also have a strong numerical presence in the Asian population. Hispanics, by comparison, are largely dominated by those originating from Mexico, 63%, with another 15.5% from the Caribbean.

Age and Sex Structures

In chapter 4 we saw that the age-sex structure of a population reflects its past mortality, fertility, and selective net migration. This is true of ethnic group populations as well as national populations. Moreover, ethnic groups within a nation can vary considerably in their structures. In turn, the varying age and sex structures of ethnic groups will influence their demographic futures.

Figure 11-4 on pp. 414–415 presents population pyramids (discussed in chapter 4) for several large U.S. ethnic groups. Each population pyramid is shaded in gray against that of the total population. The general shape of the total population (outlined in bold in each pyramid) shows a higher percentage of its population in the oldest age categories and a lower percentage in the youngest age categories compared to specific ethnic groups. The composition of the overall American population largely reflects patterns among non-Hispanic whites, since they comprise the majority of the populace as of 2010, and shows their recent declines in fertility and mortality.

Compared to the overall population, Asians have a population bulge at the working ages with fewer people at older and younger ages. This is in part due to age selectivity among immigrants and also due to recent fertility declines. The Hispanic population, in contrast, has the greatest percentages of population in the very young

Figure 11-3

National Origins Percentage Composition of U.S. Asians and Hispanics

Panel A: Asian Population

Source: Data from Hoeffel et al., 2012. "The Asian Population: 2010." *2010 Census Briefs*. Graph produced by Eiko Strader.

Panel B: Hispanic Population

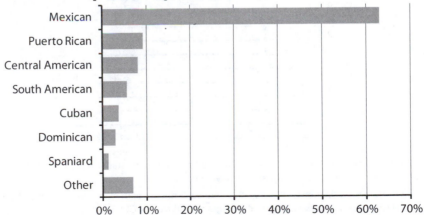

Source: Data from Ennis et al., 2011. "The Hispanic Population: 2010." *2010 Census Briefs*. Graph produced by Eiko Strader.

Figure 11-4

Estimated Population Pyramids of Selected U.S. Ethnic Groups, 2010

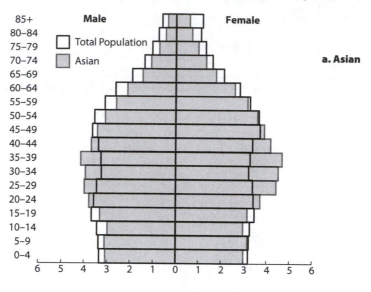

a. Asian

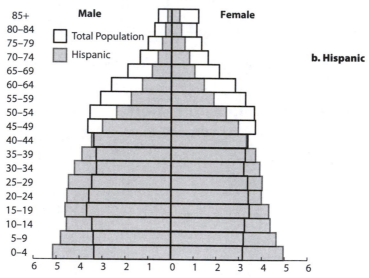

b. Hispanic

Note: Percent distribution. Data based on sample. For population estimates methodology statements, see http://www.census.gov/popest/methodology/index.html

Source: Data from U.S. Census Bureau, 2013. "Annual Estimates of the Resident Population by Sex, Age, Race, and Hispanic Origin for the United States." Figures produced by Eiko Strader.

Figure 11-4 *(cont'd).*

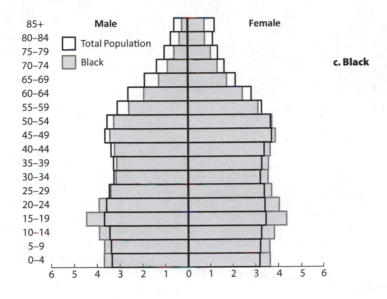

c. Black

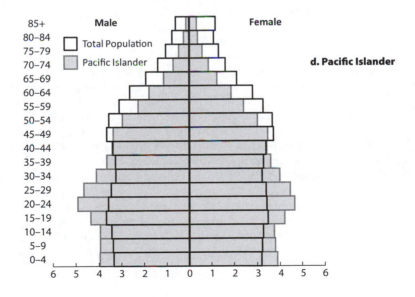

d. Pacific Islander

Careers in Demography

Ana L. Gonzalez-Barrera
Research Associate, Pew Research Center in Washington, DC
Past Director for Population Distribution and Sustainable Regional Development, Mexican Population Council (CONAPO)

How did you decide that being a demographer was the career path for you?

It all started when I came to the U.S. from Mexico for graduate school, during a summer internship researching Latino health demographics for the YMCA of the USA. I was given complete freedom to design my own research project, so I immersed myself in all relevant academic literature and available statistics regarding the health of Latinos.

I quickly found that there was a paradox: Hispanics as a group had lower educational attainment and income than other groups in the U.S., yet they also had some of the lowest rates of morbidity. My gut feeling, however, was that this paradox was hiding a selectivity bias. Unfortunately, there wasn't enough data to test this paradox, nor had there been enough experiments or studies testing it. Furthermore, finding statistically reliable information about the well-being of undocumented immigrants was simply impossible. I knew most undocumented immigrants were included in government surveys, but there was no way to distinguish them from other Hispanic immigrants. At the end of the internship, I had few recommendations and guidelines to give to my employers. I realized at that point that I wanted to help fill this void by studying the well-being of Latinos in the U.S. to better understand this seeming paradox.

What kind of education and training did you pursue to get to where you are in your career?

I received my BA in international relations from Universidad Iberoamericana in Mexico City in 2003. I had a very short stint in finance working as a junior broker until I realized I didn't want to be in a highly stressful job. I took up an offer from a former employer at Mexico City's Center for Research and Teaching in the Social Sciences (CIDE), where I had interned as a research assistant during my junior year of college. There I had the opportunity to help develop a groundbreaking national survey on public opinion and foreign policy, the first of its kind in Mexico, which compared the views of the Mexican public with the views of the U.S. public. The way I see it now, I was just lucky enough to be there at the right moment when this big project was born. Not only did I enjoy learning about questionnaire development, but I was also thrilled at helping to analyze the survey results. Drawing conclusions and providing policy recommendations based on the actual views of the people was very fulfilling.

Under the guidance of my supervisor and mentor, Susan Minushkin, I learned about scholarship opportunities and graduate programs in the United States. I decided to attend the University of Chicago as a Fulbright Scholar where I received my master's degree in public policy in 2008.

Describe your work/research as a demographer. What do you consider your most important accomplishments?

After completing my master's and spending a year as research analyst at Pew Research Center, I was hired back by CIDE as an affiliated professor and researcher. Besides coordinating the team working on the 2010 installment of the Mexico, the Americas, and the World Foreign Policy survey being fielded in several countries in Latin America, I continued doing quantitative research on Mexico-U.S. immigration patterns and coauthored a piece on the educational selectivity of Mexican immigrants to the U.S. with professors Carla Pederzini and Alfredo Cuecuecha. I was then hired as a Director at the National Population Council (CONAPO), which is the main entity in the Mexican government that performs demographic research for public policy and is tasked with developing all the demographic guidelines for the National Development Plan. I oversaw the publication of the 2010 Marginalization Index and the 2010 Delimitation of Metropolitan Statistical Areas of Mexico. Both products are fundamental instruments to the policy-making process in Mexico. The Mexican congress in particular uses these instruments as guidelines to assign money for all social development and metropolitan urbanization programs.

Since late 2011, I have worked at the Pew Research Center in Washington, DC as a Research Associate for the Hispanic Trends Project and I have been lucky enough to participate in some of the most important and groundbreaking studies we have produced. This includes a report I coauthored with our senior demographer Jeffrey Passel and senior writer D'Vera Cohn, which used all U.S. and Mexican governmental data available at the time to estimate immigration and outmigration flows of Mexican citizens from 1990 to 2010, concluding that Mexican immigration to the U.S. was at a net zero flow in 2010 and might have even reversed by 2011. Even though a number of researchers studying U.S.-Mexican immigration had hinted at this based on ethnographic research and some partial evidence of the flows on one side or the other of the border, we were able to ascertain this with concrete numbers from both sides of the border and produce an estimate of the flows of Mexican immigrants into the U.S. and back to Mexico. This report received a great deal of popular attention from the U.S. and Mexican media, as well as from Mexican President Calderon, who kept quoting our results as evidence of the success of his social development policies. Even Jay Leno mentioned our results in a monologue at the beginning of his show. I felt like a total rock star, in a very nerdy fashion, of course!

What do you see as the field's most important contribution as well as its greatest challenge?

The most important contribution of demography is producing population estimates and making projections that become guidelines for policy making that improves the well-being of the entire population and helps countries plan ahead. Even though demographic projections are fallible, as they rely on a number of assumptions and may be affected by the shortcomings of the available data, they are the best instrument we have to design and plan public policy in the long term. I think one of the field's biggest challenges is figuring out how to transfer statistics and projections into regular people's jargon, and how to actually be heard and understood by the individuals for whom these data are most useful—average people whose everyday decisions might be crucial to furthering the overall well-being of the population.

ages, reflecting the higher fertility of this population. The Hispanic pyramid also shows that Hispanic working-age males outnumber Hispanic females, the opposite of the overall population and Asians. This is an artifact of historical Hispanic male-dominated migration streams.

The population pyramid for blacks almost resembles that of the overall population with a slight population bulge at the lower half of the working-ages, which reflects a younger age structure than the larger American population. Another characteristic of the black pyramid is the dearth of black males relative to black females in the middle-adult age range. We discuss this in more detail when we review Table 11-2. The population pyramid for Pacific Islanders is similar in shape to the Asian population pyramid, though this is not due to migration. The bulge in the lower half of the working-age population reflects higher fertility than the overall population up until the recent past. However, even with the recent fertility decline among Native Hawaiians and other Pacific Islanders, percentages of population in the very young ages are much larger than those of the total population.

Measures introduced in chapter 4, the age-dependency ratio and the sex ratio, can be used to summarize ethnic group contrasts in age-sex structure. Table 11-2 presents these ratios. The bulge of working-age population among the Asian group is reflected in their remarkably low age-dependency ratio, just as the higher fertility of Hispanics is reflected in higher age-dependency ratios. Due to recent declines in fertility, a larger proportion of blacks and Native Hawaiians/Other Pacific Islanders are now in the working-age population, while more whites have moved into the older age-dependency categories.

While most groups have low sex ratios in Table 11-2 due to the higher old age survivorship of females, Asians and blacks have among the lowest sex ratios. This relative shortage of the black and Asian male population has differing explanations for each group. For Asians, it is primarily driven by sex-selective migration of more women than men. For blacks, it is due in part to higher risks of mortality among black males, and this was also evident in Figure 11-4. The notably higher sex ratio among Hispanics,

Table 11-2   Age-Dependency and Sex Ratios of Selected U.S. Race and Ethnic Groups

Ethnic Group	Age-Dependency Ratio (1)	Sex Ratio (2)
Total Resident Population	48.97	96.70
Race (Non-Hispanic)		
White	48.99	96.73
Black	45.59	91.01
Asian	38.54	90.61
Native Hawaiian and Other Pacific Islander	41.62	101.70
American Indian or Alaskan Native	46.24	97.23
Hispanic Origin		
Hispanic Total	51.74	103.06
Hispanic White	50.95	103.39

Source: U.S. Census Bureau, 2013. "Annual Estimates of the Resident Population by Sex, Age, Race, and Hispanic Origin for the United States."

however, has two sources: a higher percentage at young ages where biological sex ratios at birth favor a temporary surplus of males, and sex selectivity among migrants reinforcing this difference into older ages.

Mortality, Morbidity, and Health

There also are substantial differences in the mortality and morbidity experiences of American ethnic groups. As Table 11-3 shows, for example, life expectancy in 2011 was 79.0 years for whites and 75.3 for blacks, revealing a declining, but still substantial, difference in life expectancy. Table 11-3 also presents preliminary life expectancy and age-standardized mortality rates separately for males and females of selected ethnic groups in 2011. The reader may recall that age standardization is a method for controlling the effects of age composition when making comparisons across populations (see chapter 8). Overall, age-standardized mortality is higher for males, but this is dramatically more so for black males. For both sexes, black mortality is higher.

Figure 11-5 on the following page charts the trends in life expectancy for major race and ethnicity groups from 2006 to 2011. These data show that males have had a larger increase in life expectancy over recent years than females, in part because of the already long female life expectancy. There is also ethnic variation within the male life expectancy. Non-Hispanic black males continue to have a dramatically lower life expectancy despite an increase in longevity over recent years.

Hispanics (and, in data not shown, Asians) have dramatically lower mortality rates resulting in the longer life expectancy shown in Figure 11-5. There is a great deal of debate over why this may be, since Hispanics tend to have lower socioeconomic status than non-Hispanic whites. This is known as the Hispanic "health paradox." Some researchers have attributed low mortality rates for Hispanics (and Asians) to the effect of immigrant selectivity, where healthier people are more likely to immigrate than

Table 11-3   U.S. Age-Standardized Mortality Rates by Race and Sex, 2011

	All Races (1)	White (2)	Black (3)
All Deaths	2,513,171	2,153,864	290,135
Male	1,253,716	1,070,817	146,843
Female	1,259,456	1,083,046	143,292
Age-Adjusted Death Rate	740.6	738.1	877.4
Male	874.5	869.3	1,067.3
Female	631.9	629.7	740.1
Life Expectancy at Birth	78.7	79.0	75.3
Male	76.3	76.6	72.1
Female	81.1	81.3	78.2
All Infant Deaths	23,910	15,438	7,234
Infant Mortality Rate	6.05	5.11	11.42

Note: Death rates are per 100,000 U.S. population and infant mortality rates are deaths under age 1 year per 1,000 live births.

Source: Hoyert and Xu, 2012. "Deaths: Preliminary Data for 2011." *National Vital Statistics Reports.*

Figure 11-5

U.S. Life Expectancy at Birth by Hispanic Origin, Race for Non-Hispanics, and Sex

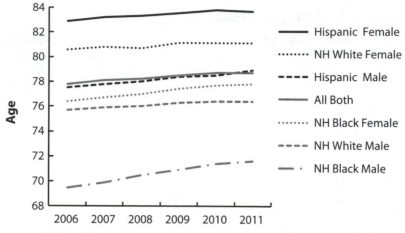

Source: Hoyert and Xu, 2012. "Deaths: Preliminary Data for 2011." *National Vital Statistics Reports.*

unhealthy people, and also to the "salmon effect," where migrants who become sick return to their home country, leaving behind a healthier migrant pool (Palloni and Arias, 2004; Palloni and Morenoff, 2001; Abraido-Lanza et al., 1999). However, much of this may be attributable simply to poor data quality, which tends to underestimate the mortality rates of immigrants (Smith and Bradshaw, 2006; Rosenberg et al., 1999). The sizeable population of undocumented immigrants in the United States who are reluctant to report health problems and thus avoid use of healthcare systems means that we do not have accurate data on their true mortality and morbidity patterns. American Indian mortality estimates, in particular, are known to suffer from misclassification and underestimation. But in more precise measurements that focus on those American Indians living on reservations, the death and morbidity rates are much higher than that for the overall U.S. population due to poverty and limited access to quality healthcare (Office of Minority Health, 2012).

What is responsible for the higher mortality of some racial and ethnic groups? In chapter 5 we suggested that one way to identify vulnerable groups was to look at cause-specific mortality rates to see if certain segments of the population suffer disproportionately from mortality that is premature and largely preventable. The National Center for Health Statistics (Murphy et al., 2013) identified the two causes of death in 2010 that were most significantly higher among the black population as HIV/AIDS and homicide. Figure 11-6 shows the crude death rates for these two causes among the ethnic populations of the United States in 2010. The bar charts in this figure show that the crude death rate for both causes was more than five times higher for blacks than for whites (eight times and five times higher using age-standardized rates). The crude cause-specific death rates for homicide among Hispanics and American Indians (and HIV/AIDS also for Hispanics) were also considerably higher than for whites but still

Figure 11-6

Age-Adjusted Death Rates for Four Major Causes in U.S. Ethnic Groups, 2010

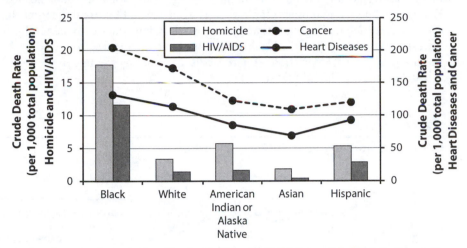

Source: Data from Murphy et al., 2013. "Deaths: Final Data for 2010." *National Vital Statistics Reports.* Figure produced by Eiko Strader.

significantly lower than for blacks. These two cause-specific mortality differences are important because they are the two largest ethnic differences in leading causes of death, and because they both identify preventable causes of mortality among vulnerable groups. An analysis of homicide and HIV/AIDS by socioeconomic status and race (Singh et al., 2013) confirms the continuing existence of these disparities among nonwhite groups for U.S. youth aged fifteen to twenty-four.

Although HIV/AIDS and homicide are relatively rare mortality risks in the United States, it is important to remember that even among the fifteen leading causes of death, mortality rates are often higher in the black population than among whites (Murphy et al., 2013). The trend lines in Figure 11-6 show that black Americans are disadvantaged in the two leading causes of death, ischemic heart diseases and cancer. As can be seen by comparing the left y-axis to the right y-axis in the figure, overall rates of heart disease and cancer are much higher than rates of HIV/AIDS and homicide. These racial disparities indicate that ischemic heart diseases and cancer are major contributors to the difference in life expectancy between black and white populations (Kochanek et al., 2013). Figure 11-6 also shows that other ethnic groups have notably lower mortality rates than either blacks or whites from cancer and heart disease.

A general indicator of differences in health conditions among population groups (introduced in chapter 5) is the infant mortality rate. The reader may recall that deaths in the first year are particularly preventable through medical care, and that infant mortality is often used as an index of general medical and public health conditions. Infant mortality rates in the United States are higher among socioeconomically disadvantaged populations and among some ethnic groups. As Table 11-3 shows, the infant mortality rate for black Americans is more than double the rate for whites. Infant mortality rates for all groups are declining, and declining most rapidly for the black non-His-panic population (CDC, 2013). Nevertheless, large differences remain between groups. Figure 11-7 charts the decline in infant mortality rates for non-Hispanic black, non-Hispanic white, and all other ethnic groups from 1995-2009. By the end of the period racial disparities had only somewhat narrowed. Asian Americans generally have the lowest infant mortality, while black Americans have the highest, followed by American Indian groups. This persistent difference is a troubling reminder of major health inequalities in the United States.

Figure 11-7

U.S. Infant Mortality Rates by Race of Mother

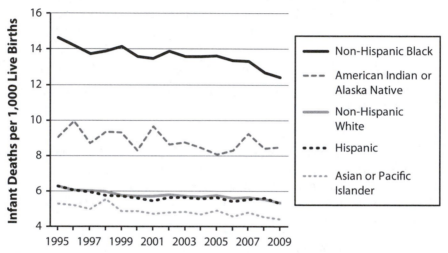

Source: Data from Mathews et al., 2006 for 1995–2003 period and from Mathews et al., 2013 for 2004–2009. Figure produced by Eiko Strader.

General patterns of ethnic morbidity are similar to those of mortality. In Figure 11-8, self-assessed health status in the United States is given for selected ethnic groups of all ages. These data are drawn from the National Health Interview Survey (see chapter 6). The age-sex-adjusted percentages of those who consider themselves to be in excellent or very good health are bar graphed for race-ethnicity groups. White Americans are most health advantaged. More than 70% of whites report excellent or very good health compared to only 60.7% of blacks and 57.6% of Hispanics.

One major morbidity measure introduced in chapter 6 is the *years of potential life lost*, or YPLL. Figure 11-9 shows these estimates for the years of life lost before age sixty-five for various ethnic groups in the United States. These YPLL rates are also age adjusted to remove the effects of age composition on morbidity comparisons. Consistent with trends we noted earlier in the textbook (chapter 3), males have much higher YPLLs than females across all ethnicities. Non-Hispanic black males have, by far, the greatest estimated YPLL, followed by Native American and Alaska Native groups. Non-

Hispanic black women lose nearly the same years of life before age sixty-five as white men. Asian Americans, both men and women, have the lowest estimated years of potential life lost.

What is the cause of race and ethnic health disparities? Some researchers examine genetic predispositions toward medical conditions as an explanation for ongoing racial disparities in health (e.g., Sheppard and Risch, 2003; Van den Oord and Rowe, 2000). However, these race-based approaches are problematic for reconstructing taxonomical classifications despite evidence that genetic variation is insignificantly patterned along racial

Figure 11-8

Age-Sex-Adjusted Percentage of Americans Who Report Excellent or Very Good Health, by Race and Ethnicity

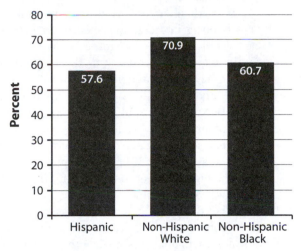

Source: CDC, 2013. *Early Release of Selected Estimates Based on Data from the January–March 2013 National Health Interview Survey,* fig. 11.4.

Figure 11-9

Years of Potential Life Lost before Age 65 for Selected Ethnic Groups by Sex, United States

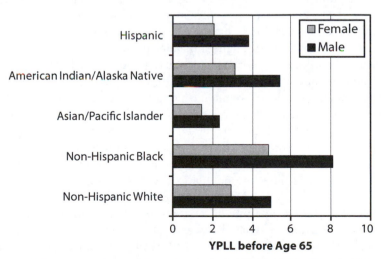

Source: Data from National Center for Injury Prevention and Control, 2013. *WISQARS Years of Potential Life Lost Reports.* Graph produced by Eiko Strader.

lines (David and Collins, 2007; Frank, 2001). Overwhelmingly, mortality differences in the United States are social in origin. Studies showing that foreign-born blacks, for instance, do not suffer from the same high mortality rates as native-born blacks suggest that health disparities stem from societal inequality and are therefore preventable (Read and Emerson, 2005).

These differences in health and morbidity among ethnic groups are clearly related to differences in access to socioeconomic resources (Hummer and Chinn, 2011). The legacies of slavery and ongoing inequality and racial discrimination have resulted in continuing black inequality in the U.S. (Hummer and Chinn, 2011). For example, black American households have substantially lower average median incomes than whites, and black adults are half as likely to have graduated from college (Crissey, 2009; DeNavas-Walt et al., 2010). Compared to whites, black Americans face twice as high unemployment, are less likely to own a home, and their median wealth, perhaps the greatest indicator of intergenerational disadvantage, is twenty times less than whites' (Taylor et al., 2011; U.S. Dept. of Labor, 2012). Asian Americans, who generally have the highest socioeconomic status due to immigration selectivity, also tend to have the best health outcomes.

What does socioeconomic status have to do with health? One obvious link is that socioeconomically disadvantaged groups have less purchasing power and thus have less access to high-quality healthcare and health insurance. As the United States moves toward more accessible healthcare it is hoped that there will be reductions in racial health disparities. But low socioeconomic status disadvantages groups in other ways as well. For example, they are less able to buy housing in safe and healthy environments. In fact, a major issue contributing to racial health disparities is continuing high rates of residential racial segregation, which limits access to community-level resources and worsens socioeconomic inequality (Williams and Sternthal, 2010). A study on some of the few racially integrated communities in the U.S. shows promising signs of significantly reduced racial disparities in health outcomes, such as in diabetes (LaVeist et al., 2009). Other socioeconomic pathways leading to poorer health are more indirect, such as the influence of education on healthier, preventative lifestyles and lesser mental stress throughout the life course.

Some health-behavior risk factors also are associated with ethnic identity. Cigarette smoking and alcohol consumption, for example, are most common according to white ethnicity and least common among many ethnic minorities (Trinidad et al., 2011). As we learned in chapter 6, tobacco and alcohol-related diseases are among the biggest killers of Americans. Figure 11-10 shows the percentage of people who have never smoked and who never consume alcohol for selected ethnic groups. The figure shows that the age-adjusted proportion of lifetime abstainers is highest among Asians and lowest among the white population. As for lifetime smoking status, whites and American Indian or Alaska Native adults are most likely to have smoked at some point in their lives. Yet even despite lower use rates, African Americans suffer from smoking-related and alcohol-related diseases at higher rates than whites (Webb, 2010; National Institute on Alcohol Abuse and Alcoholism, 2013). This stems from higher abuse rates among those who do not abstain as well as racial disparities in healthcare and treatment.

Figure 11-10

Age-Adjusted Percent Distribution of Lifetime Alcohol Consumption and Cigarette Smoking Status for Adults Aged 18+, United States

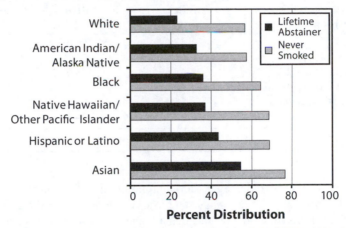

Source: Data from Schoenborn et al., 2013. "Health Behaviors of Adults: United States, 2008–2010." *Vital and Health Statistics.* Graph produced by Eiko Strader.

Fertility

Table 11-4 on the following page summarizes differences in fertility for selected ethnic groups, using three different fertility measures introduced in chapter 7: the crude birth rate (CBR), the general fertility rate (GFR), and the total fertility rate (TFR) for 2012. The Hispanic rates are highest, although as we will see below, they are still only just barely above replacement-level fertility. Focusing on the general fertility rate, a GFR of over 74.4 births to every 1,000 women of childbearing age suggests that approximately one of every 13 Hispanic women in these ages gives birth each year. Non-Hispanic blacks have the second highest GFR, 65.0, and American Indian/Alaska Natives have the lowest, 47.0, or about one of every 21 women per year giving birth.

The TFR in the third column of Table 11-4 gives the average number of children that would be born alive to a woman during her lifetime if she were to pass through all her childbearing years conforming to the current age-specific fertility rates of her ethnic group (see Table 7-1 for an example of the TFR computation). According to the TFR, Hispanic women might be expected to have close to an average of 2.2 children over their life course (just over replacement fertility of roughly 2.1 children per woman), while most other ethnic groups could be expected to have well below replacement-level fertility.

A glance back at the population pyramids in Figure 11-4 provides indirect evidence of historic fertility changes in the ethnic groups. All ethnic groups other than Hispanics have population booms, or bulges, at post-childhood ages. These births occurred before recent declines in fertility to replacement levels or below. The age of individuals in these bulges indicates how recently fertility has declined for these groups. Whites and Asians have had lower fertility for a longer period of time and thus have population

Table 11-4   Crude Birth, General Fertility, and Total Fertility Rates for Selected Ethnic Groups, United States, 2012

Ethnic Group	Crude Birth Rate (1)	General Fertility Rate (2)	Total Fertility Rate (3)
Total	12.6	63.0	1.88
Non-Hispanic White	10.7	58.7	1.76
Non-Hispanic Black	14.6	65.0	1.90
American Indian/Alaska Native	10.5	47.0	1.35
Asian/Pacific Islander	15.1	62.2	1.77
Hispanic	17.1	74.4	2.19

Source: Hamilton et al., 2013. "Births: Preliminary Data for 2012," table 1, *National Vital Statistics Reports.*

bulges at somewhat older ages. Younger population bulges in black and Hawaiian/Pacific Islander populations suggest a more recent decline to lower fertility levels. And, Hispanics will likely soon develop such a bulge from their most recent fertility declines.

Over recent history demographers have been concerned with high fertility among women of very young ages. Each year roughly a half million pregnancies occur to American teenagers between fifteen and nineteen years of age. These pregnancies are often unintended and sometimes have negative consequences for both mother and child. For example, adolescent childbearing is associated with a higher incidence of birth complications as well as reduced maternal educational attainment (Hoffman and Maynard, 2008; Mathews et al., 2003). The number of teenage pregnancies has declined significantly in recent years, but the prevention of teenage pregnancies nevertheless remains a major concern and national health initiative.

Ethnic group teenage birth rates from 2000 and 2012 are given in Figure 11-11. Over this period, teenage birthrates for all groups declined substantially. Because of the more significant decline among groups with the highest teenage birth rates, ethnic differences have narrowed over this period. For example, the gap in teen Hispanic and black birth rates has almost completely closed. Variations among other ethnic groups, however, remain wide. The fertility rate for Hispanic and black teens is still more than twice that of non-Hispanic whites. And, teenage birth rates of Asians are less than half that for non-Hispanic whites.

Differences in fertility rates reflect only the difference in pregnancies that result in a live birth. Like adolescent fertility, the U.S. abortion rate has declined steeply over recent decades for all groups (see chapter 7), but there remain significant ethnic differences. Pregnancies among Hispanic and black women respectively are two and five times as likely to end in abortion as are pregnancies among non-Hispanic white women, which reflects ethnic disparities in unintended pregnancy (Cohen, 2008; U.S. Census Bureau, 2012).

As we learned in chapter 7, fertility research suggests that differences in ethnic fertility levels will probably continue to decrease over time as all groups of women move to lower fertility levels. Past and present fertility differences are the source of some of the demographic contrasts among ethnic groups noted previously. They help explain

Figure 11-11

Fertility Rates over Time among Mothers Aged 15–19 for Selected Ethnic Groups, U.S.

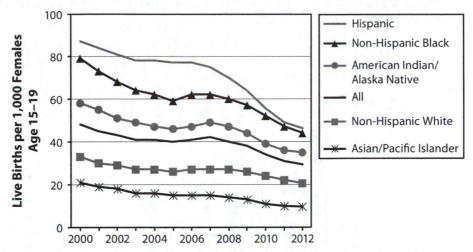

Source: Data from Hamilton et al., 2013 for years 2011 and 2012 and from Hamilton et al., 2011 for years 2000 to 2010. Graph produced by Eiko Strader.

differences in growth rates among these groups, and thus the ethnic composition of the population. They also help explain the differences in age composition of ethnic groups, differences that have their own social and cultural consequences as well as demographic ones.

Marriage

Marital status. There are, as we have seen in chapter 8, tremendous cultural differences in the prevalence and acceptability of different types of stable sexual unions among different countries. Not surprisingly, there are also significant differences in the marital and cohabitation patterns of ethnic groups within most countries, including the United States. The percentages of U.S. adults in each major marital status are given in Figure 11-12 (on the next page) for white, black, Asian, and Hispanic populations. Since 1990 the percentage of all groups married has decreased, but differences remain. Among adults, Asians and whites are most likely to be living in marital unions. Black adults are the least likely of these four groups to be living as married couples and indeed are more likely to be living as never married than married. White and black adults are also more likely to be currently divorced than are either Asians or Hispanics. As we saw in chapter 8, cohabitation is also now quite prevalent and we can assume that some of those listed as never married are instead in cohabiting unions. Although they are not shown in Figure 11-12, cohabitation rates are now similar across all racial groups (Manning, 2013).

Differences in the marital status of adults influence the living arrangements of children. Figure 11-13 on the following page shows the percentage of families with children under age eighteen in various living arrangements among white, black, Asian,

Figure 11-12

Marital Statuses of the Population Age 18 and Older by Race and Hispanic Origin, United States, 2010

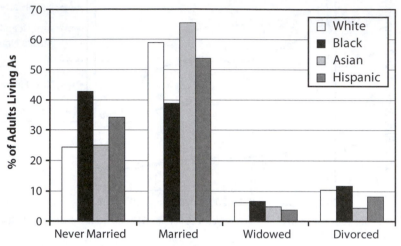

Source: U.S. Census Bureau. 2012. *Statistical Abstract of the United States, 2012.*

Figure 11-13

Living Arrangements of U.S. Children under Age 18 by Race and Hispanic Origin

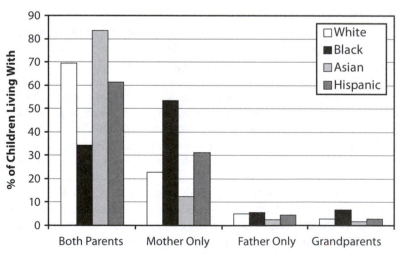

Source: Data from U.S. Census Bureau, 2012. *Statistical Abstract of the United States, 2012.* Graph produced by Eiko Strader.

and Hispanic populations of the United States. Given ethnic differences in the marital status of adults, it is not surprising that white and Asian children are more likely to live with both parents than are Hispanic and black children.

Ethnic intermarriage.   Intermarriage is a significant demographic mechanism through which ethnic identities are combined and changed over time. In 1970, less than 1% of all marriages were interethnic; by 2010 such marriages had increased to more than 10% (Kreider, 2012). Despite the increase, interethnic marriage would be much more common if people were paired randomly. It is often debated whether low rates of interracial marriage reflect same-race preferences in partners (homophily) or whether the low rates simply reflect lessened exposure to potential partners in a society that remains highly racially segregated at the neighborhood, school, and occupational levels. Recent research gets around this preference-versus-exposure question by looking at interracial behaviors among online daters and finds that same-race preference appears to be the driving factor behind low rates of interracial coupling (Lin and Lundquist, 2013).

Nearly half of all U.S. ethnic intermarriages (45%) involved a marriage between a non-Hispanic and a Hispanic person. The next most common type of ethnic intermarriage (16%) was between a single-race person and a multiracial spouse. This suggests that some of the reported increase in ethnic intermarriage is due to changing classifications; that is, the ability of partners in such a marriage to report their multiracial identity with evolving census categories. Intermarriages between Asians and whites were the third most common category (14%), followed by black-white pairings (8%). Although whites have been least likely to intermarry with blacks compared to with other groups, black-white unions are now increasing at a quicker pace than other groups (Qian and Lichter, 2011).

Figure 11-14 on the next page shows the percentage of men and women in each ethnic group that are intermarried. Not surprisingly, the intermarriage rate is highest for the numerically smallest ethnic group represented—American Indian and Alaska Native—and lowest for the largest ethnic group, non-Hispanic whites. While men and women are equally likely to marry outside of their ethnicity among many groups, there appear to be gender discrepancies among Asians and blacks. As Figure 11-14 shows, Asian women are more than twice as likely as Asian men to marry non-Asians, while the reverse is true of blacks, with twice as many black men as black women marrying outside their ethnicity.

Ethnic intermarriage is not equally common in all parts of the country. Hawaii had the highest proportion of married-couple households with a householder and spouse of different races (about 37%), followed by Oklahoma and Alaska (both about 17%). These higher intermarriage rates are believed to be due to the larger presence of Native Hawaiian, Pacific Islander, American Indian, and Alaska Natives in these states (Lofquist et al., 2012). Not surprisingly, interethnic unions are more common among younger generations. We also know that interethnic couples are more likely to be in cohabiting unions than marriages (Qian and Lichter, 2011). Recent data has also indicated that same-sex householders are more often in interethnic unions than are different-sex householders (Rosenfeld and Kim, 2005; Schwartz and Graf, 2009).

These interethnic unions are producing increasing numbers of children with multiethnic cultural identities. Across several generations the multiplicity of ethnic influences may become very complex or even fade in importance. Ethnic divisions, for

Figure 11-14

Percent Intermarried by Race and Sex, United States, 2010

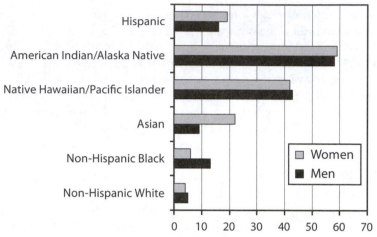

Source: Krieder, 2012. "A Look at Interracial and Interethnic Married Couple Households in the U.S. in 2010."

example, among European immigrants (e.g., Irish, Polish, Russian, German, English, Italian) to the United States were once far more stark than they now appear. It is not uncommon to find traditional ethnic identities are of greater importance to older generations than to younger ones. Ultimately, significant intermarriage blurs the boundaries of ethnic diversity and complicates any simple view of the origins and intergenerational transmission of ethnicity.

Migration

Ethnicity affects both international and internal migration streams. Just as there is age and sex selectivity to migration (noted in chapter 9), not all ethnic groups are equally likely to emigrate from, or immigrate to, an area. In this section, we will focus on the impact of this ethnically selective immigration on the diversity of the U.S. population.

Ethnic selectivity in international migration, of course, potentially affects the population composition of both the country of origin and of destination. Historically, however, the ethnic impacts of international migration have been greater for receiving countries. The purely demographic effects of forced migration and slavery on population composition have been, for example, far greater on the North American and Brazilian population than they were on European nations. Contemporary impacts of immigration on MDR population compositions are pronounced. This is because, as in the United States, the ethnic composition of the recent immigrant populations to the MDRs is often very different from that of the resident population.

Let us first address the ethnic composition of the documented immigrant population. Country of birth is often used as a proxy for ethnic origins of immigrants, although it is a crude measure since many different ethnic groups may have been born in any given country of origin. Table 11-5 classifies documented immigrants admitted to the United States in 2012 by place of birth. The largest groups of immigrants are

Table 11-5   Immigrants Admitted to the United States by Region and Selected Countries of Birth

Region/Country	% Total Immigration	% Regional Immigration
Africa	10.05	
Asia	40.37	
China		18.77
India		15.20
Philippines		13.31
Vietnam		6.62
Korea		4.99
Europe	8.43	
United Kingdom		16.03
Russia		11.63
Germany		7.74
Poland		6.93
Yugoslavia		5.16
The Americas	39.71	
Mexico		35.47
Dominican Republic		10.14
Cuba		7.95
Colombia		4.95
Canada		4.92
Oceania	0.54	
Unspecified	0.90	

Source: U.S. Department of Homeland Security, 2013. *Yearbook of Immigration Statistics: 2012.*

those from Asia and the Americas, followed by Europe. Of those immigrants born in the Americas, most were born in Mexico. Indeed, Mexican-born immigrants account for 14.1% of documented immigrants admitted to the United States. This migration has, however, decreased significantly since the recession of 2007–2009. Overall, about two of every five immigrants come from an Asian country. These selective immigration patterns obviously contribute to the high rate of increase in the Hispanic and Asian populations described earlier.

As we suggested in chapter 9, the impact of immigration on population diversity is also determined by where immigrants locate once they come to the United States. As Figure 11-15 on the next page shows, one of every five immigrants intended to reside in the state of California. About half of the immigrants admitted in 2012 planned to settle in just four states: California, New York, Florida, or Texas. This concentration of ethnic immigrants in specific states is largely a result of migration into enclaves, areas that already have a large population of immigrants with a similar background. This tendency has created greater regional differences in ethnic diversity, with large concentrations of various ethnic groups in some places and few in others.

The recent regional distribution of ethnic groups in the United States is largely the product of contemporary and historical ethnically-selective migrations. Table 11-6 on the following page describes that distribution. Non-Hispanic whites are the most widely diffused population. In contrast, over half of the black population resides in the southern United States. Almost half of the Asian population and the vast majority of the Pacific Islander population live in the western states, which are traditional destinations of Pacific transoceanic migration. Nearly half of the American Indian/Alaskan Native population lives in the western states, both as a result of native populations in that region and the forced progressive displacement of eastern Native Americans to western reservations. The higher percentage of Hispanics in the South and West is similarly a result of their migration history and proximity to the southern borders of entry to the United States.

Although the regional distribution of ethnic populations is revealing, it also can be somewhat misleading. Over one-fourth of the foreign-born population resides in Cali-

Figure 11-15

Immigrants Admitted to the United States by Intended State of Residence, Top Ten States of Destination, 2012

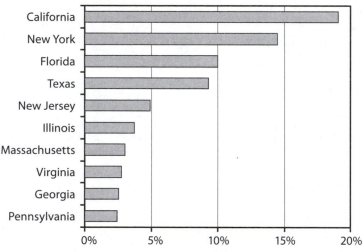

Source: Data from U.S. Department of Homeland Security, 2013. *Yearbook of Immigration Statistics: 2012.* Graph produced by Eiko Strader.

Table 11-6   Estimated Regional Distribution of United States Ethnic Groups

Region % Distribution:	White (1)	Black (2)	Hispanic (3)	American Indian/ Alaska Native (4)	Asian (5)	Pacific Islander (6)
Northeast	19.31	16.05	13.85	5.24	20.97	2.81
Midwest	26.47	18.16	9.24	17.27	11.85	5.18
South	34.91	57.26	36.11	32.86	21.92	13.97
West	19.31	8.53	40.80	44.63	45.26	78.05
Total	100.00	100.00	100.00	100.00	100.00	100.00

Source: U.S. Census Bureau, 2010 Census.

fornia alone, with more than one-tenth in New York and Texas (Grieco et al., 2012). Even within these states most immigrants initially locate in metropolitan areas, and, although the concentration of immigrants in the major metropolitan areas has declined in recent years, Los Angeles, New York City, Miami, Chicago, and San Francisco still contain 38% of all immigrants in the United States while 85% reside in the largest 100 metropolitan regions (Singer, 2011). One exception is the recent trend among Hispanic immigrants who have increasingly been migrating to smaller metropolitan areas and even rural destinations in the South over the past decade. Although the vast majority of Hispanics still settle in traditional urban gateway cities like Los Angeles and Dallas, the fastest rates of Hispanic growth have been taking place in towns and small cities in the American Sunbelt (see chapter 9).

Problems and Policies

Our procedure in earlier chapters has been to discuss the demographic problems arising from trends discussed, and to approach these problems by first questioning who considers them to be problematic. Relatively few people consider population diversity itself to be a demographic problem. At the same time, there are a variety of specific demographic issues and policy concerns that have been associated with different ethnic subpopulations. We will limit ourselves here to discussing a few general demographic concerns that apply broadly across many ethnic minorities and that have received considerable demographic attention over recent decades. These central concerns are about the grievous persistence of segregation, the poorer health among ethnic groups, and accommodating changing patterns of ethnic immigration.

Urban Segregation

Since international migrants tend to locate in major urban areas, we might expect that over time ethnic minorities would also be more likely to concentrate in urban areas. Unfortunately, given the continuing discrimination against minority populations in many societies across the globe, we might also expect that these populations are likely to live in segregated urban enclaves. Many different national studies confirm these expectations. Minority populations in European countries and Canada are more likely to be urban residents and to live in segregated urban areas (Musterd and Ostendorf, 2013; Myles and Hou, 2004). Minorities are also more likely to live in urban areas of the former Soviet republics (Harris, 1993) and areas of Southeast Asia (Banister, 1992). However, in some cases, most notably China, minorities are more likely to live in rural, outlying, or even border areas (Cao, 2010).

In the United States, all large minority groups, except American Indians and Alaska natives, are more likely than whites to live in metropolitan areas. In many of the largest U.S. cities, ethnic "majority" whites are actually numerical minorities.

Table 11-7 on the following page shows the ten metropolitan statistical areas with the largest numbers of black and Hispanic residents in the United States as of 2010. In column 1 of this table we can see that New York, Atlanta, Chicago, Washington, DC, and Philadelphia were the five metropolitan areas with the largest black populations. Column 3 gives the percentage within each MSA (metropolitan statistical area) that is

Table 11-7 Metropolitan Statistical Areas with the Largest Numbers of Black and Hispanic Residents

MSAs with Largest Black Populations (1)	Percent of Total Black Population (2)	Percent of MSA that is Black (3)	MSAs with Largest Hispanic Populations (4)	Percent of Total Hispanic Population (5)	Percent of MSA that is Hispanic (6)
Total U.S. (38,929,319)	12.6	—	Total U.S. (50,477,594)	16.3	
New York, NY	8.6	17.8	Los Angeles, CA	11.3	44.4
Atlanta, GA	4.4	32.4	New York, NY	8.6	22.9
Chicago, IL	4.2	17.4	Miami, FL	4.6	41.6
Washington, DC	3.7	25.8	Houston, TX	4.2	35.3
Philadelphia, PA	3.2	20.8	Riverside, CA	4.0	47.3
Miami, FL	3.0	21.0	Chicago, IL	3.9	20.7
Houston, TX	2.6	17.2	Dallas, TX	3.5	27.5
Detroit, MI	2.5	22.8	Phoenix, AZ	2.4	29.5
Dallas, TX	2.5	15.1	San Antonio, TX	2.3	54.1
Los Angeles, CA	2.3	7.1	San Diego, CA	2.0	32.0

Source: U.S. Census Bureau, 2012, table 23.

black. Even though New York contains the largest proportion of the black population, they are still a minority at 17.8%. Given the relatively small proportion of blacks in the United States, the degree of racial concentration in some of these cities is apparent. In half of all the MSAs shown in Table 11-7, blacks comprise 20% or more of the population. This is most apparent in Atlanta, where the MSA is nearly one-third black. The largest populations of Hispanics are in Los Angeles, New York, and Miami, and they are near majorities in several cities and a majority in San Antonio, Texas. In all of these cities they are overrepresented relative to their proportion of the overall population.

Within the cities in which they live, ethnic groups often are segregated from other populations. In general, black Americans experience the highest levels of residential segregation, followed by Hispanics, Asians, Pacific Islanders, and American Indians in that order. Much of black American segregation is the result of the historical legacy of slavery and continued discrimination in housing and employment opportunities, which persists despite African American gains into the middle class (Massey et al., 2009, 1993).

Migration also plays a role. Post-World War II migrations by black Americans to northern cities often reinforced and sometimes worsened historical patterns of segregation. The influx of immigrants into cities that are major ports of entry in particular can significantly increase residential segregation in these cities (Charles, 2003; Pollard and O'Hare, 1999). Segregation can also reflect migrants' choices of destination (Massey, 2001; South and Crowder, 1998). Hispanic segregation is more heavily influenced by recent immigration. There is great variation among Hispanic groups in levels of segregation, with Puerto Ricans experiencing the highest levels.

Demographers have several different indices to measure how segregated populations are. Measuring segregation involves a comparison of how a specified minority is distributed across the neighborhoods (usually census tracts or block areas) of a city compared to the majority population. A commonly used measure of segregation is the **dissimilarity index**. As an equation, the index is simply

$$D = \frac{1}{2} \sum_{i=1}^{n} |m_i - o_i|$$

where m_i is the percentage of the city's total minority population that lives in neighborhood i and o_i is the percentage of the total of all other city residents who live in the neighborhood. If every neighborhood has the same proportion of the city's minority residents as it has of the city's other residents, then the two populations are equally distributed and the dissimilarity index will be zero. At the other extreme, if minority and majority populations live in entirely different neighborhoods, the index will be 100. Although few would propose forced migrations to resolve segregation, the value of the dissimilarity index is easily interpreted as the percentage of minority residents who would have to move to other neighborhoods for them to have the same distribution as the rest of the population. (See Exercise 11-2 for an example of computing the dissimilarity index.)

Table 11-8 on the next page lists dissimilarity indices for both non-Hispanic blacks and Hispanics in the largest metropolitan statistical areas of the United States. In column 1 the MSAs are ordered from those in which non-Hispanic blacks are most segregated, such as New York, Chicago, and Detroit, to those in which they are least segregated, such as Portland, San Bernadino, and Phoenix. Segregation in most major metropolitan areas has decreased over the past two decades as minority populations have grown. It is apparent that the most segregated cities for blacks are generally those in the old industrial North while the least segregated are those in the West and South. Blacks migrating to the North in search of employment, and to escape from southern segregation, instead found discriminatory housing and employment practices (Sugrue, 1996). The resulting segregation persists to the present. Looking at column 2, for example, the dissimilarity index for New York suggests that nearly eight of ten non-Hispanic blacks in the city would have to change residence to achieve an equal integration of neighborhoods in the city. Even in the least segregated of these MSAs, Phoenix, more than four of ten non-Hispanic blacks would have to relocate to achieve an equal integration.

Columns 3 and 4 give similar data for Hispanics. The regional nature of segregation is less consistent for Hispanics; the most segregated of these MSAs are either major Hispanic cities in the South or cities of the old industrial North. Also apparent from column 4 is the fact that Hispanics are in general less segregated than non-Hispanic blacks. Not shown in Table 11-8 are dissimilarity indices for Asians. Segregation levels are generally lower for Asians (in the mid-forties); however, their dissimilarity indices rose between 2000 and 2010, due mostly to increases in immigration.

Why is segregation a problem, and who considers it a problem? The answer may seem self-evident to many of our readers. There is a long history of demographic research showing that segregation limits opportunities and results in a spatial concentration of poverty and economic inequality (as we reviewed in chapter 10). The concentration of poverty in segregated ethnic neighborhoods is both a cause and a consequence of limited social and economic opportunities for individuals in these areas worldwide.

The limits segregation places upon population groups are universally acknowledged as social problems. At the same time, as we've seen in Figure 11-15, many ethnic immigrants choose to live in the same areas as other members of the same ethnic group. First generation immigrants may wish to live in the specific neighborhoods, or enclaves—such as "Little Havana" in Miami, Florida—where others share the same culture and social networks. These voluntary assortative residential decisions must be distinguished from segregation, which is the imposed or forced separation of popula-

Table 11-8   Segregation of Non-Hispanic Blacks and Hispanics in the Largest Metropolitan Statistical Areas,[a] United States

Non-Hispanic Blacks		Hispanics	
Metropolitan Statistical Area (1)	Dissimilarity Index (2)	Metropolitan Statistical Area (3)	Dissimilarity Index (4)
New York	78.0	Los Angeles	62.2
Chicago	76.4	New York	62.0
Detroit	75.3	Boston	59.6
Cleveland	74.1	Miami	57.4
St. Louis	72.3	Chicago	56.3
Cincinnati	69.4	Philadelphia	55.1
Philadelphia	68.4	Houston	52.5
Los Angeles	67.8	Cleveland	52.3
Pittsburgh	65.8	Dallas	50.3
Baltimore	65.4	San Diego	49.6
Miami	64.8	San Francisco	49.6
Boston	64.0	Atlanta	49.5
Denver	62.6	Phoenix	49.3
Washington	62.3	Denver	48.8
San Francisco	62.0	Washington	48.3
Houston	61.4	San Antonio	46.1
Kansas City	61.2	Kansas City	44.4
Atlanta	59.0	Detroit	43.3
Sacramento	56.9	Minneapolis	42.5
Dallas	56.6	Riverside/San Bernardino	42.4
Tampa	56.2	Tampa	40.7
Minneapolis	52.9	Orlando	40.2
San Diego	51.2	Baltimore	39.8
Orlando	50.7	Sacramento	38.9
Seattle	49.1	Cincinnati	36.9
San Antonio	49.0	Portland	34.3
Portland	46.0	Seattle	32.8
Riverside/San Bernardino	45.7	St. Louis	30.7
Phoenix	43.6	Pittsburgh	28.6

[a]Excluding Washington, DC, and metropolitan statistical areas with population size below 2 million.

Source: Frey, 2013. "New Racial Segregation Measures for Large Metropolitan Areas: Analysis of the 1990–2010 Decennial Censuses." *Brookings Institution and University of Michigan Social Science Data Analysis Network.*

tion groups. However, decisions to live in an ethnic enclave may limit some long-term opportunities and reinforce segregation even as it fulfills short-term desires.

There is considerable interest among demographers in the trends of ethnic segregation and their possible causes. There have been some recent declines in U.S. segregation for blacks, yet Table 11-8 shows that segregation is still highly prevalent (Frey, 2013).

Inequities in Health

Although the health of the U.S. population has improved dramatically in the past fifty years, as we have seen in chapters 5 and 6, some ethnic minority groups still have poorer health and higher mortality. Ethnic health inequities are a social problem for all who see these differences in health as a reflection of more basic social injustices. Indeed, much of the difference in ethnic group health arises from the lower socioeconomic status, racially segregated living conditions, and more limited access to healthcare among ethnic minorities. Fewer American blacks and Hispanics than whites have health insurance (AHRQ, 2012). These inequities are also of special epidemiological concern to public health officials who see the greatest potential for overall improvement in public health in lowering the high morbidity and mortality of these more vulnerable groups. Quality of care received among minorities is a similar concern. According to one recent report (AHRQ, 2012), black Americans received worse care than whites for 41% of healthcare quality measures and Hispanics received worse care than non-Hispanic whites for 39% of measures. Although not quite as disparate, Asians and American Indians received worse care than whites for nearly 30% of quality measures. With a persistently higher infant mortality rate than that of whites, reducing infant mortality among black Americans, for example, is critical to continued overall declines in health inequities.

Social inequities are reflected in many specific health problems that disproportionately burden ethnic minorities, as we saw earlier in this chapter. These health problems reflect the less adequate residential environs and socioeconomic resources than the more privileged non-Hispanic white population enjoys. These inequities in health will not be eliminated as long as basic social inequality persists.

Accommodating Ethnic Immigrants

Immigration is a major component of growth in the ethnic populations of the United States. This means that many people in these ethnic groups came to this country recently. In fact, two-thirds of Asian Americans were not born in the United States (Immigration Policy Center, 2012).

Who considers this immigration a problem? Of course, there are some people and politicians who simply have a xenophobic fear of immigrants and view all immigration as a problem. However, many others have more specific concerns over the changing nature of ethnic immigration.

One concern is the young age structure of some ethnic groups, resulting from age-selectivity in migration and higher fertility after arrival. On the one hand, this young ethnic population is already serving as an antidote for the aging, non-Hispanic workforce. However, Pollard and O'Hare note there are special concerns with preparing this new generation to fulfill their role as the future workforce of the United States:

Careers in Demography

Zhenchao Qian
Chair, Department of Sociology
Ohio State University

How did you decide that being a demographer was the career path for you?

After studying English in college in Shanghai, I was assigned a job in the Shanghai Statistics Bureau. Little did I know that it marked the beginning of my career as a demographer. After a few months in the National Bureau of Statistics honing my professional English skills, I spent six months in Japan in 1984 at the Statistical Institute for Asia and the Pacific, learning survey methods and statistics.

I met Dr. Sam Preston when he attended the China Census Workshop in 1985. He later became my advisor in graduate school, although I never knew then that our paths would cross again. I participated in China's In-Depth Fertility Survey, the last project of the World Fertility Survey (WFS). I learned survey operations, questionnaire designs, and sampling in the WFS headquarters in London, and data analysis at the International Statistical Institute in the Hague. I had the pleasure of learning from, and providing language interpretation for demographers John Casterline, John Cleland, Gabriele Dankert, Noreen Goldman, Barbara Vaughan, Vijay Verma, and Zeng Yi. I was so fascinated with population issues that I often went beyond my role as a translator.

What kind of education and training did you pursue to get to where you are in your career?

I went to the University of Pennsylvania in 1989 and received a joint PhD degree in demography and sociology in 1994. I was fortunate to work with several great demography scholars at Penn. Working with Phil Morgan, I completed my master's thesis on marriage transitions in China using data from the China In-Depth Fertility Survey, the data I had helped collect. I was Herb Smith's research assistant and conducted field research for his project, Introducing New Contraceptives in Rural China. Under the advising of Sam Preston, I wrote my second year paper and the dissertation on changes in American marriage and assortative mating patterns. I have worked on these research areas ever since.

Describe your work/research as a demographer. What do you consider your most important accomplishments?

I study "who marries whom" and "who cohabits with whom," their patterns, trends, and consequences. I explore who is available in marriage markets and how men and women pair up to form marital and cohabiting unions in terms of age, educational attainment, race and ethnicity, and nativity. This research agenda fits squarely in the area of demography and social stratification.

I'm interested in marriage patterns and the extent to which they reflect social structure, social stratification, and the extent of openness in societies. Indeed, mate selection reflects the dynamics of social structure in many areas. This line of work contributes to the sociological knowledge of inequality in family resources and intergenerational transmission of social statuses.

My work on mate-selection patterns examines how education and race affect mate selection. I published my first article in this area with Sam Preston. We have examined temporal changes in marriage and cohabitation by men's and women's age and educational attainment. This work disaggregates recent changes in marriage into changes in population structure and changes in the "force of attraction."

I have continued to conduct research in this area, revealing how cultural shifts in addition to economic factors have played a prominent role in changing marriage rates. This work contributes to the demographic understanding of rapid changes in marriage and cohabitation in the past decades and how these changes are related to improvement in women's educational attainment and increases in female labor force participation.

My long-time collaborator, Daniel T. Lichter, and I have published several articles on changes in interracial marriage. Interracial marriage not only indicates that marital partners of different racial and ethnic backgrounds treat each other as social equals, but also reflects race relations, racial residential patterns, and racial inequality in American society more broadly. We have shown that intermarriage with whites is more likely for Hispanics and Asian Americans than for African Americans. Our results reveal the effects of rapid immigration, rising cohabitation, and educational upgrading on intermarriage patterns. This line of research contributes to the understanding of salience of race in American society and diversity of race and ethnicity in social distance.

I'm also interested in exploring who marries, who cohabits, and who makes transitions from cohabitation to marriage in order to better understand the role cohabitation plays in increasing selectivity of marriage. Some of my current work investigates how assortative mating patterns, changes in marital status, and marital transitions influence individuals' well-being.

What do you see as the field's most important contribution as well as its greatest challenge?

One of demography's important contributions is to help understand the role social context, structure, and composition play in socioeconomic outcomes. It provides a larger picture of how changes in social structure matter when we examine a particular social phenomenon. A case in point is my 2007 article with Dan Lichter published in *American Sociological Review*, entitled "Social Boundaries and Marital Assimilation: Interpreting Trends in Racial and Ethnic Intermarriage." In this article, our focus is to examine changes in interracial marriage over the past decades. A simple examination of such changes may miss the large picture of social change in America. In this article, we identify changes in racial classification (i.e., in the 2000 census, for the first time, Americans were allowed to indicate one or more racial categories) that are likely to confound changes in interracial marriage.

In addition, we take into account the massive influx of new immigrants especially from Latin America and Asia (which replenishes the marriage pool for their U.S.-born counterparts), the rise in cohabitation (which may depress rates of interracial marriage), and changes in the educational composition of some racial/ethnic groups (which may change the dynamics of marriage markets). Controlling for structural and compositional changes, we were able to reveal changes in interracial marriages, a strong barometer of social distance among various racial/ethnic groups.

The field's great challenge and opportunity, in my view, is statistical software. Statistical software has made demographers' research much easier as it faithfully runs every single model. While formal demography emphasizes controls through standardizations, demographers work through these techniques with a good sense of how structures and compositions influence socioeconomic outcomes. Statistical software is like a black box that churns out statistical results. I always encourage students to run statistical models with care and think beyond what statistical controls mean in a larger picture of demographic standardizations.

> Minorities' growing share of U.S. children—the future workforce—has implications for American businesses and public policy. Minorities have lower educational attainment and higher poverty rates than whites, on average. Because such a large percentage is immigrants or the children of immigrants, many Asian and Hispanic children have limited English skills and require special language classes. Policy makers will need to ensure that minority children from disadvantaged homes receive adequate education, nutrition, and health care in order to provide the nation with a trained and competitive workforce in the years ahead. (1999, p. 7)

Many have voiced concern over the ethnic minority status of immigrants and their prospects for successful assimilation in a society that still discriminates on the basis of skin color (Portes and Rumbaut, 2001; Gans, 1992). Despite such concerns over downward acculturation, socioeconomic studies of the second immigrant generation as they move into adulthood show that most groups are doing as well if not better than their parents (Alba and Nee, 2003; Kasinitz et al., 2009). The group that continues to face the greatest challenges to equal treatment and resources, however, is native-born black Americans. Racial disparities in health and socioeconomic mobility will continue until social equality in America is fully achieved.

SUMMARY

Diversity refers to the variety of cultural groups in a population and the even distribution of the population across these groups. Ethnicity, race, and ancestry are common demographic terms that refer to diverse cultural groups. Some countries, such as Ethiopia (with over thirty official ethnic groups), have been diverse since their national inception, but most nations have experienced rapidly increasing population diversity over the past century. Growth in international migration has been the greatest source of this increasing population diversity.

Because ethnicity, race, and ancestry are culturally defined, groups identified vary from one national population to another. Definitions also change dramatically over time within nations. These unstandardized and often arbitrary definitions complicate the measurement of diversity over time and across populations.

Nonetheless, it is clear that in the United States diversity is increasing. Since the mid-20th century, the "minority" ethnic population (i.e., nonwhites and Hispanic groups) has more than tripled in size. By 2050 it is projected that half of the country's population will be non-Hispanic white. Hispanics and, now especially, Asian Americans are the fastest growing ethnic groups in the country—and Hispanics have already overtaken non-Hispanic blacks as the largest ethnic minority in the country.

Most racial and ethnic minorities in the United States have had a younger age composition and high growth rates. More recently, fertility has declined among all ethnic groups and age-composition effects are shifting into the working ages. Because of recently young ethnic populations, diversity in the working-age population is even greater than in the total population and will increase rapidly in the near future. Diversity of young adults is also producing an increase in ethnic intermarriage, further expanding ethnic identities in the 21st century.

There appears to be a general Hispanic paradox with regard to health, where otherwise disadvantaged Hispanic groups are healthier than expected. Asian health outcomes are also very good; however, this is more clearly a selection function of Asian immigrants' higher socioeconomic status upon immigrating. Some minority groups, such as black Americans, Puerto Ricans, and Native Americans, experience poorer health and higher mortality on average. This is particularly true of native-born African American populations, whose migration history and subsequent societal incorporation was uniquely disadvantageous. While black-white racial disparities have improved over time, the continued poorer health of the black populations is largely due to continued societal inequality and residential segregation, which results in lower average socioeconomic status and inadequate access to healthcare.

Most ethnic immigrants migrate to relatively few states, and largely to major metropolitan areas within them, reinforcing differences between regions of the United States and concentrating ethnic populations within major urban areas. Concentration in urban areas and in ethnic enclaves in the cities has contributed to the persistence of urban segregation in recent decades. Residential segregation, in turn, has historically resulted in concentrated pockets of poverty and social disadvantage that are difficult to escape.

Rising diversity is a major demographic trend, not only in the United States but also in more-developed regions generally, as resident populations age and younger ethnic immigrants arrive. Because these arriving cultural groups often have different demographic behaviors, diversity will impact the demography of many countries throughout the 21st century. Changes in population diversity will present both new challenges and new opportunities to these nations. Given changing demographics in the U.S., America's future rests on ethnic youth as the nation's future leadership and workforce. Racial and ethnic inequality must be remedied before this social contract can be fairly carried out.

EXERCISES

1. The projected age composition of several ethnic groups in 2025 is summarized in Table E11-1. Using this information, and formulas from chapter 4, compute and fill in the missing age-dependency ratios for Hispanics and blacks.

   a. Which ethnic group will probably have the highest dependency ratio in 2025?

   _____

   b. Which ethnic group will probably have the lowest dependency ratio in 2025?

   _____

Table E11-1   Projected U.S. Ethnic Populations (in 1,000s) by Age Group

Age Group	Hispanic Origin		White (3)	Black (4)	Asian (5)
	Hispanic (1)	Non-Hispanic White (2)			
0–14	18,441	30,687	46,362	10,044	1,087
15–64	46,238	120,450	161,273	30,352	2,988
65+	6,295	48,421	54,126	6,668	537
Age-Dependency Ratio		65.68	62.31		54.35

Source: U.S. Census Bureau, 2012. "Table 1. Projected Population by Single Year of Age, Sex, Race, and Hispanic Origin for the United States: 2012 to 2060." *2012 National Population Projections: Downloadable Files.* http://www.census.gov/population/projections/data/national/2012/downloadablefiles.html.

2. The calculation of dissimilarity indices from the turn of the century are illustrated for two small university towns in Table E11-2 (neither town is highly segregated). Computations for the town of Amherst, Massachusetts are complete. Fill in the blanks to complete the computations of the dissimilarity index in Morgantown, West

Table E11-2   Segregation in Two Small University Towns, United States Census Data

	Black			Hispanic		
Census Tract Number	Percent of Black Population Residing in Tract (1)	Percent of Non-Black Population Residing in Tract (2)	Absolute Value of Difference |(1) − (2)| (3)	Percent of Hispanic Population Residing in Tract (4)	Percent of Non-Hispanic Population Residing in Tract (5)	Absolute Value of Difference |(4) − (5)| (6)
Amherst, MA						
8201.01	0.72	10.51	9.80	2.43	10.54	8.11
8201.02	1.99	6.43	4.44	5.36	6.32	0.96
8202.02	1.02	2.43	1.41	1.00	2.44	1.44
8202.03	3.78	13.36	9.58	5.02	13.41	8.39
8202.04	1.58	9.21	7.62	2.86	9.24	6.38
8203	14.15	11.54	2.61	18.53	11.31	7.22
8204	30.08	16.39	13.69	19.10	16.74	2.36
8205	10.98	9.82	1.16	10.54	9.83	0.71
8206	4.19	2.49	1.70	3.01	2.53	0.48
8207	12.10	6.95	5.15	12.27	6.89	5.39
8208.01	19.36	10.88	8.48	19.88	10.76	9.12
8208.02	0.05	0.00	0.05	0.00	0.00	0.00
		Total of Differences =	65.69		Total of Differences =	50.56
			÷ 2			÷ 2
		Dissimilarity Index =	32.8		Dissimilarity Index =	25.3
Morgantown, WV						
101	21.20	14.26	6.93	17.31	14.46	2.85
102	8.28	7.74	0.54	12.34	7.70	4.64
103	5.17	3.50	1.66	7.05	3.52	3.54
104	4.64	6.88	2.24	2.88	6.86	3.97
105	3.23	4.59	1.36	5.77	4.53	1.24
106	12.39	10.94	1.45	13.62	10.95	2.67
107	10.75	6.39	4.36	8.33	6.51	1.82
108	2.11	4.54	2.42	3.37	4.47	1.11
109.01	11.04	6.42	4.62	8.33	6.55	1.78
109.02	3.41	4.02	0.62	4.33	4.00	0.33
110	11.27	5.63	5.64	3.85	5.84	2.00
118.01		14.04		6.25	13.79	7.54
118.02	0.03			6.57	10.83	4.25
		Total of Differences =	42.20		Total of Differences =	37.74
			÷ 2			÷ 2
		Dissimilarity Index =			Dissimilarity Index =	18.9

Source: U.S. Census Bureau, 2001. *Census 2000 Redistricting Data (Public Law 94-171) Summary File 2000.*

Virginia. (Use the fact that the first two columns of this table should total to 100% to derive the missing entries in those columns.) Then, answer the following questions about the results:

a. In which town were the tracts in which blacks reside more dissimilar from those in which whites reside? _____

b. Were blacks or Hispanics more segregated in Morgantown, West Virginia? _____

PROPOSITIONS FOR DEBATE

1. The 2010 census shows that the "more than one race" classifications were utilized only by a relatively small percentage of the population. Therefore, the Census Bureau should give up this multiracial identity undertaking as futile and meaningless.

2. Since most ethnic groups in the United States have similar demographic characteristics, it is safe to treat them as a homogeneous class of "minority" populations.

3. Ethnic differences in mortality and health in the United States are largely genetic in origin.

4. Current U.S. racial and ethnic categories will no longer be in use by 2050.

5. Immigration and the increasing diversity of the U.S. population will continue to decrease ethnic segregation in urban areas.

6. The United States is becoming a more divided nation because of the large concentration of immigration in a few states.

7. Segregation is no longer caused by overt discrimination and limited opportunities but simply because minority groups most often prefer to live with others of similar cultural background.

8. The Hispanic or Latino identification should be classified as a race by the U.S. Census Bureau instead of a separate category as an ethnic group to allow more accurate multiracial identifications.

REFERENCES AND SELECTED READINGS

Abraido-Lanza, A. F., B. P. Dohrenwend, D. S. Ng-Mak, and J. B. Turner. 1999. "The Latino Mortality Paradox: A Test of the 'Salmon Bias' and Healthy Migrant Hypotheses." *American Journal of Public Health* 89.

AHRQ (Agency for Healthcare Research and Quality). 2012. *Innovations and Emerging Issues Portfolio.* Last updated September 2012. Retrieved November 3, 2013. http://www.ahrq.gov/cpi/portfolios/innovations/index.html

Alba, Richard D., and Victor Nee. 2003. *Remaking the American Mainstream: Assimilation and the New Immigration.* Cambridge, MA: Harvard University Press.

Banister, Judith. 1992. "Vietnam: Population Dynamics and Prospects." U.S. Census Bureau, Center for International Research, Staff Paper no. 65.

Cao, H. 2010. "Urban–Rural Income Disparity and Urbanization: What is the Role of Spatial Distribution of Ethnic Groups? A Case Study of Xinjiang Uyghur Autonomous Region in Western China." *Regional Studies* 44(8): 965–982.

CDC (Centers for Disease Control). 2013. *Early Release of Selected Estimates Based on Data From the January-March 2013 National Health Interview Survey.* Released September 24, 2013. http://www.cdc.gov/nchs/nhis/released201309.htm

Charles, Camille Zubrinsky. 2003 "The Dynamics of Racial Residential Segregation." *Annual Review of Sociology* 29.

Cohen, Susan A. 2008. "Abortion and Women of Color: The Bigger Picture." *Guttmacher Policy Review* 11(3). http://www.guttmacher.org/pubs/gpr/11/3/gpr110302.html

Crissey, S. R. 2009. *Educational Attainment in the United States: 2007.* U.S. Census Bureau. Retrieved from http://www.census.gov

David, R., and J. Collins Jr. 2007. "Disparities in Infant Mortality: What's Genetics Got to Do with It?" *Journal Information* 97(7).

DeNavas-Walt, C., B. D. Proctor, and J. C. Smith. 2010. *Income, Poverty, and Health Insurance Coverage in the United States: 2009.* Washington, DC: U.S. GPO.

Ennis, Sharon R., Merarys Rios-Vargas, and Nora G. Albert. 2011. "The Hispanic Population: 2010." *2010 Census Briefs.* C2010BR-04. Washington, DC: U.S. Census Bureau.

Frank, R. 2001. "The Misuse of Biology in Demographic Research on Race/Ethnic Differentials: A Reply to Van den Oord and Rowe." *Demography* 38: 563–567.

Frey, William H. 2013. "New Racial Segregation Measures for Large Metropolitan Areas: Analysis of the 1990–2010 Decennial Censuses." *Brookings Institution and University of Michigan Social Science Data Analysis Network's Analysis of 1990, 2000, and 2010 Census Decennial Census Tract Data.* Retrieved November 3, 2013. http://www.psc.isr.umich.edu/dis/census/segregation2010.html

Gans, Herbert J. 1992. "Second-Generation Decline: Scenarios for the Economic and Ethnic Futures of the Post-1965 American Immigrants." *Ethnic and Racial Studies* 15(2): 173–192.

Grieco, Elizabeth M., Yesenia D. Acosta, G. Patricia de la Cruz, Christine Gambino, Thomas Gryn, and Luke J. Larsen et al. 2012. "The Foreign-Born Population in the United States: 2010." *American Community Survey Reports.* ACS-19. Washington, DC: U.S. Census Bureau.

Hamilton, Brady E., Joyce A. Martin, and Stephanie J. Ventura. 2011. "Births: Preliminary Data for 2010." *National Vital Statistics Reports* 60(2).

———. 2013. "Births: Preliminary Data for 2012." *National Vital Statistics Reports* 62(3).

Harris, C. D. 1993. "A Geographic Analysis of non-Russian Minorities in Russia and its Ethnic Homelands." *Post-Soviet Geography* 34(19).

Hoeffel, Elizabeth M., Sonya Rastogi, Myoung Ouk Kim, and Hasan Shahid. 2012. "The Asian Population: 2010." *2010 Census Briefs.* C2010BR-11. Washington, DC: U.S. Census Bureau.

Hoffman, Saul D., and Rebecca A. Maynard (Eds.) 2008. *Kids Having Kids: Economic Costs and Social Consequences of Teen Pregnancy.* Washington, DC: The Urban Institute Press.

Hoyert, Donna L., and Jiaquan Xu. 2012. "Deaths: Preliminary Data for 2011." *National Vital Statistics Reports* 61: 6.

Humes, Karen R., Nicholas A. Jones, and Roberto R. Ramirez. 2011. "Overview of Race and Hispanic Origin: 2010." *2010 Census Briefs.* C2010BR-02. Washington, DC: U.S. Census Bureau.

Hummer, Robert A., and Juanita J. Chinn. 2011. "Race/Ethnicity and U.S. Adult Mortality: Progress, Prospects, and New Analysis." *Du Bois Review* 8(1): 5–24.

Immigration Policy Center. 2012. *Asians in America: A Demographic Overview.* Released April 26, 2012. Retrieved November 3, 2013. http://www.immigrationpolicy.org/just-facts/asians-america-demographic-overview

Kasinitz, P., J. H. Mollenkopf, M. C. Waters, and J. Holdaway. 2009. *Inheriting the City: The Children of Immigrants Come of Age.* New York: Russell Sage Foundation.

Kochanek, Kenneth D., Elizabeth Arias, and Robert N. Anderson. 2013. "How Did Cause of Death Contribute to Racial Differences in Life Expectancy in the United States in 2010?" *NCHS Data Brief* 125.

Kreider, Rose, M. 2012. *A Look at Interracial and Interethnic Married Couple Households in the U.S. in 2010.* Posted on April 26, 2012. Retrieved November 3, 2013. http://blogs.census.gov/2012/04/26/a-look-at-interracial-and-interethnic-married-couple-households-in-the-u-s-in-2010/

LaVeist, T., R. J. Thorpe, J. E. Galarraga, K. M. Bower, and T. L. Gary-Webb. 2009. "Environmental and Socioeconomic Factors as Contributors to Racial Disparities in Diabetes Prevalence." *Journal of General Internal Medicine* 24:1144–1148.

Lin, Ken-Hou, and Jennifer Lundquist. 2013. "Mate Selection in Cyberspace: The Intersection of Race, Gender, and Education." *American Journal of Sociology* 118 (6).

Lofquist, Daphne, Terry Lugaila, Martin O'Connell, and Sarah Feliz. 2012. "Households and Families: 2010." *2010 Census Briefs.* C2010BR-14. Washington, DC: GPO.

Manning, Wendy D. 2013. "Trends in Cohabitation: Over Twenty Years of Change, 1987–2010." *National Center for Family & Marriage Research, Family Profiles Series.* FP-13-12. Retrieved November 3, 2013. http://ncfmr.bgsu.edu/pdf/family_profiles/file130944.pdf

Marger, Martin N. 2000. *Race and Ethnic Relations: American and Global Perspectives.* 5th ed. Belmont, CA: Wadsworth/Thomson Learning.

Massey, Douglas S. 2001. "Residential Segregation and Neighborhood Conditions in U.S. Metropolitan Areas." In Neil Smelser, William Julius Wilson, and Faith Mitchell, eds., *America Becoming: Racial Trends and Their Consequences.* Washington, DC: National Academy Press.

Massey, D. S., J. Rothwell, and T. Domina. 2009. "The Changing Bases of Segregation in the United States." *The Annals of the American Academy of Political and Social Science* 626(1): 74–90.

Mathews, T. J., F. Menacker, and M. F. MacDorman. 2003. "Infant Mortality Statistics from the 2001 Period Linked Birth/Infant Death Data Set." *National Vital Statistics Reports* 52(2).

———. 2006. "Infant Mortality Statistics from the 2003 Period Linked Birth/Infant Death Data Set." *National Vital Statistics Reports* 54(16).

———. 2013. "Infant Mortality Statistics from the 2009 Period Linked Birth/Infant Death Data Set." *National Vital Statistics Reports* 61(8).

Murphy, Sherry L., Jiaquan Xu, and Kenneth D. Kochanek. 2013. "Deaths" Final Data for 2010." *National Vital Statistics Reports* 61(4).

Musterd, S., and W. Ostendorf. (Eds.). 2013. *Urban Segregation and the Welfare State: Inequality and Exclusion in Western Cities.* New York and London: Routledge.

Myles, John, and Feng Hou. 2004. "Changing Colours: Spatial Assimilation and New Racial Minority Immigrants." *The Canadian Journal of Sociology* 29(1).

National Center for Injury Prevention and Control. 2013. *WISQARS Years of Potential Life Lost Reports.* http://webappa.cdc.gov/sasweb/ncipc/ypll10.html

National Institute on Alcohol Abuse and Alcoholism. 2013. *Minority Health and Health Disparities.* Retrieved November 3, 2013. http://www.niaaa.nih.gov/alcohol-health/special-populations-co-occurring-disorders/minority-health-and-health-disparities

Office of Minority Health. 2012. "American Indian/Alaska Native Profile." *Data/Statistics.* Retrieved November 15, 2013. Last Updated September 17, 2012. http://minorityhealth.hhs.gov/templates/browse.aspx?lvl=2&lvlID=52

Palloni, Alberto, and Elizabeth Arias. 2004. "Paradox Lost: Explaining the Hispanic Adult Mortality Advantage." *Demography* 41(3).

Palloni, A., and J. Morenoff. 2001. "Interpreting the Paradoxical in the 'Hispanic Paradox': Demographic and Epidemiological Approaches." In M. Weinstein, A. Hermalin, and M. Stoto, eds., *Population Health and Aging.* New York: New York Academy of Sciences.

Pollard, Kelvin M., and William P. O'Hare. 1999. "America's Racial and Ethnic Minorities." *Population Bulletin* 54(3).

Portes, A., and R. G. Rumbaut. 2001. *Legacies: The Story of the Immigrant Second Generation*. Berkeley and Los Angeles: University of California Press.

Qian, Zhenchao, and Daniel T. Lichter. 2011. "Changing Patterns of Interracial Marriage in a Multiracial Society." *Journal of Marriage and Family* 73(5):1065–1084.

Read, Jennan Ghazal, and Michael O. Emerson. 2005. "Racial Context, Black Immigration and the U.S. Black/White Health Disparity." *Social Forces* 84(1).

Rosenberg, H. M., J. D. Maurer, P. D. Sorlie, N. J. Johnson, M. F. MacDorman, and D. L. Hoyert et al. 1999. "Quality of Death Rates by Race and Hispanic Origin: A Summary of Current Research, 1999." *Vital and Health Statistics*, Series 2(128). Hyattsville, MD: National Center for Health Statistics.

Rosenfeld, M., and B. S. Kim. 2005. "The Independence of Young Adults and the Rise of Interracial and Same-Sex Unions." *American Sociological Review* 70 (4): 541–562.

Schoenborn, Charlotte, Patricia F. Adams, and Jennifer A. Peregoy. 2013. "Health Behaviors of Adults: United States, 2008–2010." *Vital and Health Statistics* 10(257).

Schwartz, C. R., and N. L. Graf. 2009. "Assortative Matching among Same Sex and Different Sex Couples in the United States, 1990-2000." *Demographic Research* 21: 843–878.

Sheppard, D., and N. Risch. 2003. "The Importance of Race and Ethnic Background in Biomedical Research and Clinical Practice." *New England Journal of Medicine* 348(12).

Singer, Audrey. 2011. "Immigrants in 2010 Metropolitan America: A Decade of Change." Speech, October 24, 2011. Retrieved November 3, 2013. The Brookings Institution. http://www.brookings.edu/research/speeches/2011/10/24-immigration-singer

Singh, Gopal K., Romuladus E. Azuine, and Mohammad Siahpush. 2013. "Widening Socioeconomic, Racial, and Geographic Disparities in HIV/AIDS Mortality in the United States, 1987–2011." *Advances in Preventive Medicine* 657961.

Smith, David P., and Benjamin S. Bradshaw. 2006. "Rethinking the Hispanic Paradox: Death Rates and Life Expectancy for US Non-Hispanic White and Hispanic Populations." *American Journal of Public Health* 96(9): 1686–1692.

Soloway, Richard A. 1990. *Demography and Degeneration: Eugenics and the Declining Birthrate in Twentieth-Century Britain*. Chapel Hill: University of North Carolina Press.

South, Scott J., and Kyle D. Crowder. 1998. "Leaving the 'Hood: Residential Mobility between Black, White, and Integrated Neighborhoods." *American Sociological Review* 59(1).

Sugrue, Thomas J. 1996. *The Origins of the Urban Crisis: Race and Inequality in Postwar Detroit*. Princeton, NJ: Princeton University Press.

Taylor, P., R. Fry, and R. Kochhar. 2011. *Wealth Gaps Rise to Record Highs between Whites, Blacks, Hispanics*. Retrieved from http://www.pewsocialtrends.org/2011/07/26/wealth-gaps-rise-to-record-highs-between-whites-blacks-hispanics

Trinidad, Dennis R., Eliseo J. Pérez-Stable, Martha M. White, Sherry L. Emery, and Karen Messer. 2011. "A Nationwide Analysis of US Racial/Ethnic Disparities in Smoking Behaviors, Smoking Cessation, and Cessation-Related Factors." *American Journal of Public Health* 101(4): 699–706.

U.S. Census Bureau. 2001. *Census 2000 Redistricting Data (Public Law 94-171) Summary File 2000*. PL/00-1 (RV). Washington, DC: U.S. Census Bureau.

———. 2004. "U.S. Interim Projections by Age, Sex, Race, and Hispanic Origin." http://www.census.gov/ipc/www/usinterimproj

———. 2012. *Statistical Abstract of the United States, 2012*. Washington, DC: GPO. http://www.census.gov/compendia/statab/

———. 2013. *Annual Estimates of the Resident Population by Sex, Age, Race, and Hispanic Origin for the United States*, April 1, 2010 to July 1, 2012. Washington, DC: U.S. Census Bureau.

U.S. Department of Homeland Security. 2013. *Yearbook of Immigration Statistics: 2012*. Washington, DC: U.S. Department of Homeland Security, Office of Immigration Statistics. Retrieved November 20, 2013. https://www.dhs.gov/yearbook-immigration-statistics

U.S. Department of Labor. 2012. *The African-American Labor Force in the Recovery*. Washington, DC: U.S. Department of Labor. Retrieved August 21, 2014. http://www.dol.gov/_sec/media/reports/BlackLaborForce/BlackLaborForce.pdf

Van den Oord, E., and D. C. Rowe. 2000. "Racial Differences in Birth Health Risk: A Quantitative Genetic Approach." *Demography* 37:285–98.

Webb, Monica S. 2010. "Addressing Tobacco-Associated Health Disparities through Behavioral Science." *American Psychological Association: Psychological Science Agenda, May 2010*. Retrieved November 3, 2013. http://www.apa.org/science/about/psa/2010/05/sci-brief.aspx

Williams, David R., and Michelle Sternthal. 2010. "Understanding Racial/Ethnic Disparities in Health: Sociological Contribution." *Journal of Health and Social Behavior* 51(1): S15–27.

Glossary

abortion termination of a pregnancy after the implantation of the blastocyst (fertilized egg) in the endometrium (uterine wall) but before the fetus is viable. Includes both spontaneous and induced abortions. (chapter 7)

abortion rate a rate whose numerator is the estimated number of induced abortions in a given year and whose denominator is some estimate of the at-risk population of women. Thus potentially there can be crude, general, and age-specific abortion rates analogous to birth and fertility rates. However, abortion rate, unmodified, usually means the number of induced abortions per 1,000 women aged 15–44, analogous to the general fertility rate. (chapter 7)

abortion ratio a ratio whose numerator is the estimated number of induced abortions in a given year and whose denominator is some measure of the pregnancies at risk of being aborted. The at-risk population can be either the number of live births in the given year or the number of live births plus the legal abortions in that year. Abortion ratios can be either crude—for the total population—or specific—for an age (or other) category. (chapter 7)

African American see **black**. (chapter 11)

age-dependency ratio the number of people in the economically dependent ages (conventionally, younger than fifteen and sixty-five or older) per one hundred people in the economically productive ages (conventionally, fifteen through sixty-four). Synonym: dependency ratio. (chapter 4)

age heaping the tendency of respondents to report age, or date of birth, as years ending in zero, five, or even numbers, sometimes especially avoiding numbers that are culturally taboo. (chapters 2, 4)

age-sex pyramid see **population pyramid**. (chapter 4)

age-sex-specific rate a rate referring to the performance of a subset of the population defined by age and sex. Examples: *age-sex-specific death rates*, *age-specific fertility rates* for females. (chapters 4, 7)

age-sex structure the composition of a population with respect to age and sex; the distribution of a population among categories defined by a combination of age and sex. (chapter 4)

age structure the composition of a population with respect to age; the distribution of a population among age categories. (chapter 4)

aging of a population increase in the median age of a population. (chapter 4)

Alaska Native   a person whose race has its origin in any of the original peoples of North and South America (including Central America), and who maintains tribal affiliation or community attachment. (chapter 11)

American Community Survey   a survey that is distributed to 250,000 households each month, rather than just once every ten years, and which will provide detailed information on American cities and towns annually that used to be available only on a decadal basis in the Census long form. (chapter 2)

American Indian   a person whose race has its origin in any of the original peoples of North and South America (including Central America), and who maintains tribal affiliation or community attachment, such as those designating themselves Rosebud Sioux, Chippewa, or Navajo. (chapter 11)

ancestry   narrowly defined, the birthplace of one's parents; broadly defined, the ethnic group from which one claims biological descent. (chapter 11)

area of destination   in the context of migration, the area where the migration ended; the location of the host or receiving society. Synonym: place of destination. (chapter 9)

area of origin   in the context of migration, the area from which the migration started; the location of the sending or donor society. Synonym: place of origin. (chapter 9)

Asian   a person whose race has its origin in any of the original peoples of the Far East, Southeast Asia, or the Indian subcontinent, including a designation of Asian Indian, Chinese, Filipino, Korean, Japanese, or Vietnamese, or Burmese, Hmong, Pakistani, or Thai. (chapter 11)

assisted reproductive technologies   the use of medical techniques, such as drug therapy, in vitro fertilization, and/or cryopreservation of ova or sperm, to circumvent infertility. (chapter 7)

at-risk population   that set of people who could have produced a specified kind of population event, for example, a death, a birth, or a migration. (chapter 6)

average   in statistical usage, the arithmetic mean, the total of all scores divided by number of cases. More casually, the one value that best represents all cases in a set. Another measure is a median, the score above which and below which one-half the cases fall.

baby boom   in the United States, the increase in fertility that extended from the late 1940s through the early 1960s, peaking in 1957. (chapter 7)

birth cohort   a set of people having similar birth dates and current ages, also known as a generation. (chapter 4)

biodemography   a branch of demography that examines the complementary biological and demographic determinants and interactions between the birth and death processes that shape individuals, cohorts, and populations. (chapter 1)

birth control   measures taken to delay or avoid a birth, including contraception and induced abortion. (chapter 7)

black   a person whose race has its origin in any of the black racial groups of Africa, including a designation of Negro, African American, Nigerian, or Haitian. (chapter 11)

carrying capacity   the maximum population size within a given area that can sustain itself indefinitely without environmental degradation, given its technology and consumption patterns. (chapter 3)

cause of death   the principal cause of death as recorded by the responsible authority in the registration process. Ideally, the immediate cause (such as homicide, cancer, heart attack) as contrasted with secondary or contributing causes (murder motive, smoking, high cholesterol buildup). (chapter 5)

cause-specific death rate/mortality rate   a mortality rate indicating the number of deaths attributable to a specific cause per 100,000 population in a given year. (chapters 6, 11)

census a complete count of every inhabitant of a given geographic entity at a given time. (chapter 2)

cohabitation the living together of two persons of opposite sex in a conjugal, usually non-marital, union. Sometimes includes same-sex couples presumed equivalent in social function to cohabiting heterosexual couples. (chapter 8)

cohort generally, a set of people defined on the basis of experiencing some specified population event during the same short period of time. Thus, a *birth cohort* is a set of people having similar birth dates and current ages, also known as a generation. When demographers use the term cohort unmodified, they usually mean birth cohort. (chapter 4)

cohort-completed fertility the average number of children born per woman in a birth cohort surviving the childbearing period. Can be measured by a *cohort-completed fertility rate*. Synonym: completed family size. (chapter 7)

cohort-completed fertility rate the average number of children born per woman in a cohort by the end of their childbearing years. A measure of cohort-completed family size. Analogous to a total fertility rate, but constructed for a real cohort rather than a hypothetical one. (chapter 7)

cohort-component projection a population projection in which each birth cohort is projected separately, resulting in a projection of age-sex structure as well as size. (chapter 4)

cohort perspective the viewing of a population process longitudinally, as the cumulative life experience of a cohort. Used in cohort analysis or generational analysis. Contrast with period perspective. (chapter 8)

components of population growth the only events by which a population's size can be influenced directly: births, deaths, and migrations. See **growth equation.** (chapter 1)

conception the fertilization of an ovum by a sperm, marking the beginning of pregnancy or gestation. (chapter 7)

consanguinity marriage between blood relatives. (chapter 8)

consensual union a non-marital sexual union that is relatively socially recognized and stable. (chapter 8)

contraception measures taken to prevent coitus from resulting in conception. (chapter 7)

crude birth rate the number of live births per 1,000 total population in a given year. Sometimes called simply the birth rate. (chapters 1, 7)

crude death rate the number of deaths per 1,000 total population in a given year. Sometimes called simply the death rate. (chapters 1, 6)

crude rate a period rate whose denominator is the total population. (chapter 1)

de facto residence a person's residence at a given moment, such as a census moment. Contrast with de jure residence. (chapter 2)

de jure residence the residence where a person usually or habitually lives. Contrast with de facto residence. (chapter 2)

demographic description characterizing past or present populations in terms of their demographic variables, taken either singly or in combination. (chapters 1, 8)

demographic dividend the potentially accelerated economic growth that begins with changes in the age structure of a country's population as it transitions from high to low birth and death rates. Also known as a demographic bonus. (chapter 3)

demographic transition transition from a situation where fertility and mortality are high and uncontrolled to a situation where fertility and mortality are low and controlled. (chapters 3, 7)

demographic variables dimensions of variation among populations with respect to their size, growth and components of growth, and composition. (chapter 1)

demography the scientific study of human population, its size and composition, dynamic life-course processes that change this composition (birth, death, marriage, migration, etc.), and relationships of population composition and change with social and physical environments. (chapter 1)

density see **population density**.

dependency ratio see **age-dependency ratio**.

determinants causes.

differential in the context of studying the population processes, differences among the members of a set of compositional categories with respect to the incidence of the specified process. For instance, differential mortality, differential fertility, or differential migration.

disability adjusted life-years lost the sum of years of life lost and years lived with disability, giving a total picture of morbidity and mortality impacts due to a specific cause. (chapter 6)

dissimilarity index a measure of residential segregation based on comparing the distribution of members of a group among a set of residential areas in comparison with the distribution of non-members of that group. (chapter 11)

distribution in a statistical context, the numbers of cases falling within a series of categories. In a **frequency distribution**, each category is represented by the absolute number of cases; in a **percentage distribution**, each category is represented by a proportion of the total cases. See also population distribution. (chapters 1, 4)

diversity see **population diversity**.

divorced a marital status category, usually meaning currently not married by reason of civil dissolution of marriage from last spouse. (chapter 8)

doubling time the time it would take for a population to double at a given annual growth rate. (chapter 3)

early fetal death pregnancy loss during the first 28 weeks; corresponds to the popular notion of miscarriage. (chapter 7)

echo effect the tendency toward repetition, one generation hence, of any span of abnormally high (or low) fertility, caused by the effect of the initial fertility level upon the age structure. (chapter 7)

ecological footprint the per capita amount of resource consumption relative to the environment's ability to regenerate needed resources. (chapter 3)

emigration migration out of a nation. See **out-migration**. (chapter 9)

endogamy marrying within the same race, ethnicity, or socioeconomic class. (chapters 4, 8)

epidemic a mass outbreak of a disease that spreads and then disappears within a fairly short time. Where it appears in a large number of countries it is called a *pandemic*. Both contrast with endemic disease, which is a condition that more or less permanently affects substantial segments of a population. (chapter 5)

epidemiological transition a part of the demographic transition in which mortality declines from a high, variable, and uncontrolled level to a low, constant, and controlled level. (chapter 6)

epidemiology the study of the distribution of diseases or conditions in human populations. (chapter 6)

ethnic group a group sharing a common subculture with unique cultural traits (e.g. language, religion) and, to some degree, a sense of community, ethnocentrism, ascribed membership, and distinct territoriality. (chapter 11)

ethnicity reflecting a common subculture with unique cultural traits (e.g., language, religion) and, to some degree, a sense of community, ethnocentrism, ascribed membership, and distinct territoriality. (chapter 11)

European marriage pattern   the pattern that distinguished Western Europe during the 18th and 19th centuries, namely late marriage and large proportions never marrying. (chapter 7)

ever-married   a marital status combining (currently) married, divorced, and widowed. (chapter 8)

exogamy   intermarriage across racial, ethnic, or socioeconomic lines. (chapter 8)

family life cycle/life course   the normal sequence of marital status and family formation changes occurring in a society, along with their timing. (chapter 8)

family planning   attempts by couples to regulate the number and spacing of their births. (chapter 7)

family-planning program   a government-sponsored effort to provide the information, supplies, and services for modern fertility control to those interested. (chapter 7)

family reconstitution   the linking of birth, marriage, and death dates of each married couple and their children, taken from administrative records (e.g. vital records or parish registers) into a chronology of vital events for family members. (chapter 7)

fecundity   the biological capacity of a man, a woman, or a couple to produce a live birth. (chapter 7)

fertility   the childbearing performance of individuals, couples, or groups as indicated by the frequency with which birth occurs in a population. (chapter 7)

fertility rate   see **general fertility rate**.

fertility transition   a part of the demographic transition in which fertility declines from a high, constant, and uncontrolled level to a low, variable, and controlled level. (chapters 3, 7)

fetal death/fetal mortality   death of a fetus, usually after at least four weeks of pregnancy and including both spontaneous abortions or miscarriages—deaths before 28 weeks of pregnancy—and stillbirths—deaths after that period. (chapter 7)

forced or impelled migration   migration in which individuals are compelled by authorities or events to move. Includes flight or displacement and the creation of refugees. Historically also would include migration for slavery and involuntary indentured servitude. (chapter 9)

formal demography   the study of demographic variables separate from related nondemographic variables. To be distinguished from population studies. (chapter 1)

free migration   migration resulting from the initiative and free choice of the migrants, either individually or as a mass. Synonym: spontaneous, voluntary migration. (chapter 9)

frontier regions/nations   in the context of world regions, those MDRs that have received large-scale immigration from Europe in recent centuries: North America, Australia, and New Zealand. (chapter 3)

gender   the socially constructed role assigned by society to women and men, as opposed to sex, which is defined as biological and physiological characteristics of females and males. (chapter 4)

general divorce rate   number of divorces in a given year divided by the number of married women of adult age. (chapter 8)

general fertility rate   the number of live births per 1,000 women aged fifteen to forty-four (or fifteen to forty-nine) in a given year. Sometimes called simply the fertility rate. (chapter 7)

gentrification   the transition from a working-class, poor, or vacant area of the central city to a middle class residential and/or commercial use area. (chapter 10)

geographical information systems (GIS)   a system for capturing, storing, checking, and displaying data related to geographical locations. (chapter 2)

gestation period duration of pregnancy. (chapter 7)

grandevity extremely old ages. (chapter 4)

gross migration the sum of migration into and out of a given area. In the context of migration streams, the sum of the migration streams in both directions between two areas. Synonym: volume of migration. Contrast with net migration. (chapter 9)

gross reproduction rate the average number of daughters that would be born to a set of women during their lifetimes if they passed through their childbearing years conforming to the age-specific fertility rates of a given year. Like the total fertility rate but not counting sons. (chapter 7)

growth equation the formula that specifies the components of growth during a specified time:

$$P_2 - P_1 = B_{(1, 2)} - D_{(1, 2)} + M_{(1, 2)}$$

Sometimes called (redundantly) the *balancing equation*. (chapter 1)

growth rate the ratio of the total change in a population during a period to the average population (usually the midpoint population) during that period. (chapter 3)

health-adjusted life expectancy (HALE) a measure of life expectancy at birth minus the number of years of life spent in poor health or injured. (chapter 6)

Hispanic a person of Cuban, Mexican, Puerto Rican, South or Central American, or other Spanish culture or origin regardless of race. (chapter 11)

historical demography the application of demographic methods to datasets from the past. (chapter 7)

HIV/AIDs human immunodeficiency virus/acquired immune deficiency syndrome, a disease of the immune system transmitted through body fluids, most often via sexual contact or contaminated needles. (chapter 6)

household a set of individuals who reside together, whether related or not. Commonly defined in censuses as those who make common provision for food and living essentials. (chapter 8)

Human Development Index (HDI) an international development index that provides a composite score of life expectancy, education, and country income used to rank countries into various tiers of human development. (chapter 3)

human trafficking the illegal forced (or by deception) migration for purposes of sexual exploitation or forced labor. (chapter 9)

hypothetical cohort an imaginary set of people traced through a series of specified risks in order to detail the cumulative impact of those risks. This strategy is used in the construction of life tables and the computation of life expectancy, as well as the construction of total fertility rates. Synonym: synthetic cohort. (chapters 5, 6)

immigration migration into a nation. See **in-migration**. (chapter 9)

incidence rate the number of persons contracting a disease as a proportion of the population at risk, per specified unit of time. (chapter 6)

induced abortion an abortion that is assumed to result from action intended to cause it. (chapter 7)

inequality an uneven distribution of population groups across categories such as income, opportunity, treatment, or status, generating or reflecting social or economic disparities. (chapter 11)

infant mortality the mortality among live-born children who have not yet reached their first birthday. (chapter 5)

infant mortality rate the number of deaths among infants under one year of age, per 1,000 live births in the same year. (chapter 5)

in-migration migration into an area usually smaller than a nation. See **immigration**. (chapter 9)

intermediate variable   if a change in one variable results in a change in a second variable, which in turn results in a change in a third variable, then the second variable is called the intermediate variable. In the context of fertility explanation, intermediate variables are those proximate determinants of fertility that are intermediate between sociocultural and economic determinants on the one hand, and fertility itself on the other. (chapter 7)

internal migration   migration between parts of a nation or smaller geographic units. (chapter 9)

late fetal death   pregnancy loss after the twenty-eighth week; corresponds to the popular notion of stillbirth. (chapter 7)

less-developed countries (LDCs)   those countries with technologically less developed or pre-industrial economies. Synonyms: developing countries, Third-World countries. (chapter 3)

less-developed regions (LDRs)   world regions consisting largely of less-developed countries (LDCs). The UN version of this classification includes Africa, Asia (less Japan), Oceania (less Australia and New Zealand), Latin America, and the Caribbean. (chapter 3)

life course/life cycle   the sequence of sociodemographic stages through which individuals pass from birth to death, usually with an emphasis on householding, marriage, schooling, and employment. Synonyms: life cycle, life history. (chapter 8)

life expectancy   the average (mean) number of years yet to be lived by people attaining a given age, according to a given life table. If the age is unspecified, it is assumed to be zero, in which case life expectancy means life expectancy at birth. (chapter 5)

life table   a table used for tracing the cumulative effect of a specified series of age-sex-specific death rates over a life cycle for a hypothetical cohort; the table used to compute life expectancy. (chapter 5)

longevity   the length of an individual life. Collectively, average length of life of a cohort. (chapter 5)

Malthusianism/Malthusian transition   based upon the writings of Thomas Malthus; specifically, believing that population tends to outstrip the means for its subsistence. (chapters 3, 7)

marital dissolution   the combined processes of spouse mortality and divorce. (chapter 8)

marital fertility   the fertility of married persons. Synonym: legitimate fertility. (chapter 7)

marital status   one's status with respect to marriage. See **single**, **never-married**, **married**, **widowed**, **divorced**. (chapters 8, 11)

marriage   legal recognition of a sexual union. The combined processes of first marriage and remarriage. (chapter 8)

marriage cohort   a set of people identified on the basis of being married at about the same time. (chapter 8)

marriage market   all the men and women who, at a given time and place, are potential marital partners for each other. (chapter 8)

marriage squeeze   a restriction in the marriage market caused by imbalance between the sizes of succeeding birth cohorts, combined with persistent norms regarding relative ages of brides and grooms. (chapter 8)

marriage, timing of   conventionally measured by the average age at first marriage or the proportion ever-married by age. (chapter 8)

married   marital status currently married, usually even if separated. (chapter 8)

Marxist   based upon the writings of Karl Marx.

maternal mortality   female mortality (female death) associated with pregnancy, labor, or the puerperium (the period immediately following childbirth). (chapter 5)

maternal mortality rate the number of maternal deaths per 100,000 live births in a specified year. Synonym: maternal death rate. (chapter 5)

mega-city city with a population of over 10 million people. (chapter 10)

megalopolis a term denoting an interconnected group of cities in connecting urbanized bands. (chapter 10)

menarche the beginning of the female reproductive, or childbearing, period, signaled by the first menstrual flow. (chapter 6)

menopause the end of the female reproductive or childbearing period, signaled by the cessation of menstruation. (chapter 6)

metropolis a very large and/or important city. (chapter 10)

metropolitan area a large concentration of population usually consisting of a central city and surrounding settlements. (chapter 10)

metropolitanization the relative growth of metropolitan-area population, compared with other population. (chapter 10)

migrant an individual who migrates. (chapter 9)

migration a change in residence (involving social reaffiliation) across some specified geopolitical boundary. (chapters 2, 9)

migration pull attraction by a place of destination, for a migrant. (chapter 9)

migration push repulsion by a place of origin, for a migrant. (chapter 9)

migration stream the people who migrate from a given area of origin to a given area of destination in a given period of time. (chapter 9)

misreporting in a census, misallocation of an enumerated person among compositional categories. A form of content error. (chapters 2, 4)

mobility in a geographic or spatial context, the quantity of movement among geographic units, including not only migration but also temporary moves such as commuting, transit across units, tourism, and seasonal movements. (chapter 9)

morbidity the state of illness and disability in a population. Specifically, the incidence and/or prevalence of a disease or disability in a population. (chapter 6).

more-developed countries (MDCs) countries with technologically developed, industrial economies. Synonym: developed countries. (chapter 3)

more-developed regions (MDRs) world regions consisting almost entirely of more-developed countries (MDCs). The UN version of this classification includes North America, Europe, Japan, Australia, and New Zealand. (chapter 3)

mortality the frequency with which death occurs in a population. (chapter 5)

mortality transition a part of the demographic transition in which mortality declines from a high, variable, and uncontrolled level to a low, constant, and controlled level. (chapters 3, 5)

multiracial relating to or made up of many human races. (chapter 11)

Native Hawaiian and Other Pacific Islander a person whose race has its origin in any of the original peoples of Hawaii, Guam, Samoa, or other Pacific Islands, including a designation of Native Hawaiian, Guamanian or Chamorro, Samoan, or Other Pacific Islander, or Tahitian, Mariana Islander, or Chuukese. (chapter 11)

natural increase births minus deaths. (chapter 1)

neo-Malthusianism believing (as Thomas Malthus did) in the tendency for population to outstrip the means for its subsistence and advocating (as Malthus did not) the promotion of birth control as a solution to this dilemma. (chapters 3, 7)

net migration migration into an area minus migration out of that area. (chapters 1, 9)

never-married single in marital status and not having been married previously. (chapter 8)

nonmarital fertility/nonmarital birth fertility of persons not currently married and births resulting therefrom. Synonym: illegitimate fertility/illegitimate birth. (chapter 8)

nuptiality   the formation and dissolution of marriages and other stable sexual unions. (chapters 1, 8)

Oceania   Australia, New Zealand, the Malay Archipelago, and the islands of the southern, western, and central Pacific Ocean, including Melanesia, Micronesia, and Polynesia. (chapter 3)

old-age dependency   the proportion of the population judged too old to be fully economically productive; usually measured as the percent aged sixty-five or over in the dependency ratio. Similarly, the *oldest old dependency ratio* measures the percent aged eighty and over and the *prospective old-age dependency ratio adjusts* for generational differences in life expectancies across generations. (chapter 4)

out-migration   migration out of an area smaller than a nation. See **emigration**. (chapter 9)

pandemic   an outbreak of disease that involves large proportions of the population, devastating it briefly. (chapter 5)

parity   the number of children previously born alive to a woman. (chapter 7)

period perspective   the viewing of a population process cross-sectionally, as the combined experience of cohorts in a specified short period of time, normally one year. Employed in period analysis or cross-sectional analysis, usually involving period rates. See **cohort perspective.** (chapter 8)

period rate   a rate measuring the incidence of a population event during a specified short period of time, such as one year for an annual rate. (chapter 1)

polyandry   the condition or practice of having more than one husband at a time. (chapter 8)

polygamy   marriage that includes more than two partners. (chapter 8)

polygyny   the condition or practice of having more than one wife at one time. (chapter 8)

population   a set of people residing in a given area at a given time.

population composition/structure   the distribution of a population among a set of distinct status categories, such as sex (gender), age, and marital status. (chapters 1, 4)

population density   the relationship between the size of a population and the size of the area in which it lives. (chapters 1, 3)

population distribution   comparison of the sizes of populations resident in a set of geographic areas or other relevant categories. See **distribution**. (chapters 1, 3)

population diversity   the variety of cultural groups represented, in significant proportions, within a population and the evenness of the population distribution across these groups. (chapter 11)

population events   individual events that alter the size or composition of a population. (chapter 1)

population explosion   a dramatic increase in population size; often, those increases associated with demographic transitions. (chapter 3)

population growth   change in population size, in either a positive or negative direction. Sometimes called population change. (chapters 1, 3)

population momentum   generally, the resistance to change in crude birth rates caused by an age structure resulting from the prior fertility regime. Currently, in LDRs, it is the lag between a decline of total fertility rates and decline in growth rates caused by large proportions of women still being in their childbearing years due to past high total fertility rates. (chapter 4)

population problem   a believed consequence of a population trend or characteristic that is negatively valued. A social problem of which a population trend or characteristic is the perceived cause. (chapter 1)

population pyramid   a conventional form of bar graph representing the age-sex structure of a population, so named because of its normal pyramidal shape in LDRs. Synonym: age-sex pyramid. (chapter 4)

population register   the continuous recording of population events for individual members of a population in such a way that a current reading of all members' demographic characteristics is always available. (chapter 2)

population studies   the study of demographic variables, including their relationships with nondemographic variables. To be distinguished from formal demography. (chapter 1)

positive checks   in Malthusian theory, those checks on population growth operating through increase in the death rate. (chapter 3)

positive selectivity   migration in which those people with traits especially valued in the area of destination are overrepresented in the migrant stream. (chapter 9)

postpartum   immediately after the end of a pregnancy. (chapter 7)

postpartum amenorrhea   the temporary disappearance of menstruation in the period immediately following childbirth, usually prolonged by breast-feeding. (chapter 7)

prevalence rate   the number of persons having a particular disease at a given point in time per 1,000 population at risk. (chapter 6)

preventive checks   in Malthusian theory, those checks on population growth operating through decrease in the birth rate. (chapter 3)

primitive migration   the kind of migration caused by an ecological push, including wandering, ranging, and nomadic movements. (chapter 9)

projection   a population projection specifies the future size of a population by employing assumptions about future fertility, mortality, and migration. (chapters 3, 4)

pronatalist   advocating increased fertility. (chapter 7)

proximate cause or proximate determinant   the most immediate cause of some population process. See, for example, **cause of death** and **intermediate variable**. (chapters 5, 6)

race   an ambiguous term referring to a culturally defined social or ethnic group classified together on the basis of common history, nationality, or geographic distribution but with a supposedly shared unique genetic heritage. (chapter 11)

ratio   comparison of the sizes of two categories in a series by dividing one by the other. Examples: sex ratio, age-dependency ratio. (chapter 4)

reclassification   the process of changing population composition by moving members from one category to another, such as by aging or marriage. (chapter 1)

refined rate   a rate whose numerator contains all of the specified population events in a given year but whose denominator contains not the total population but some subset more narrowly defining the at-risk population. Example: general fertility rate. (chapter 6)

refugee   one who has migrated in response to strong pressure because his continued stay in his country of origin may have exposed him to danger of persecution. (chapter 9)

registration   the recording of population events on a continuous basis for all members of a population. Took the form of parish registers in Western history; takes the form of civil registration in current national data systems. (chapters 2, 7)

remittance   earnings sent back to the families of those family members who have migrated to distant labor opportunities. (chapter 9)

replacement-level fertility   the level of fertility at which a cohort of women, on the average, have just enough daughters to replace themselves in the population at current mortality levels. (chapter 7)

residence   the location with which an individual is affiliated, where they usually or habitually live. (chapters 2, 9)

retrospective questions   questions asking about events that have happened in the past, perhaps the remote past. Sometimes employed in censuses or sample surveys, but not in registration of population events. (chapter 2)

reurbanization   recent (21st-century) movement of people back to large cities. (chapter 10)

rural   not urban. (chapter 10)

second demographic transition   a shift from near universal and traditional marriage to a wide variety of marital and nonmarital family structures, and unpredictable fertility levels that often fall below replacement levels. (chapters 3, 8)

segregation   the policy, practice, or results of imposing a separation of social groups such as racial or ethnic groups, especially as a result of discrimination. (chapter 11)

selective migration   migration in which the composition of the migrant population differs from the composition of the specified resident population. (chapters 9, 11)

sex ratio   the number of males per one hundred females in a population or a part thereof. Synonym: masculinity ratio. (chapter 4)

sex structure   the composition of a population with regard to sex (gender); the distribution of a population between the two sexes. (chapter 4)

single   not in a marital union, usually never-married in marital status. (chapter 8)

singulate mean age at first marriage   the mean age at first marriage which would produce a specified distribution of percentages single by age. A method of estimating mean age at first marriage from period marital-status data. (chapter 8)

size of population   the number of people residing in a geographical location. Synonym: absolute size of population. (chapter 1)

social demography   that part of population studies that specifies the relationships among demographic and sociological variables. (chapter 1)

specific rate   generally, any rate for some subset of the population rather than the total population (as in a crude rate). See **age-sex-specific rate**. (chapter 4)

standardization   a set of statistical procedures that control the effect of compositional factors that may contaminate the comparison of populations. (chapter 8)

stunting   where a child's height relative to their age is more than two standard deviations lower than the reference population of children, indicating severe malnutrition (chapter 6).

suburbanization   increase in the proportion of the urban population living in rings immediately around central cities. (chapter 10)

surveillance systems   organized efforts to detect, characterize, and inform policy responses to reportable diseases. (chapter 6)

survival   in the context of mortality, not dying. (chapter 5)

synthetic cohort   see hypothetical **cohort**.

theory   a clear statement of the hypothesized relationships among certain variables.

total fertility rate   the average number of children that would be born alive to a group of women during their lifetime if they were to pass through all their childbearing years conforming to the age-specific (female) fertility rates of a given year. (chapter 7)

tragedy of the commons   depletion of a shared resource by individuals that goes against the long-term best interest of the group of individuals as a whole (chapter 3).

underenumeration   undercounting population in a census. A form of coverage error. (chapter 4)

underpopulation   description of a geographic entity that would benefit from having a larger population size. (chapter 3)

undocumented migration   migration that lacks authorized documentation and conflicts with the laws of a country, governing entry or departure of migrants. (chapter 9)

universality of marriage   the proportion of a population which can marry that does.
Distinguished from timing of marriage. (chapter 8)

unmarried   marital status combining single (never-married), divorced, and widowed.
Synonym: non-married. (chapter 8)

urban corridors   regional urbanization creating a swath of development between
once separated cities. (chapter 10)

urban deconcentration   the process of population flow out of large cities to suburban
areas. (chapter 10)

urban growth   the growth of the urban population. (chapter 10)

urban place/urban area   a place having a relatively large resident population densely
settled and surrounded by a less densely settled area. (chapters 2, 10)

urban population   the part of the population residing in urban places. (chapter 10)

urbanism   having a lifestyle characteristic of urban places. (chapter 10)

urbanization   as a condition, the proportion of the total population that lives in urban
places. Synonym: degree of urbanization. As a process, the increase in this proportion. Synonym: pace of urbanization. (chapter 10)

variable   a characteristic that varies from one unit to another.

vital statistics   processed results of registrations of vital events. Strictly speaking, vital
events are deaths and births only, but the term often is broadened to include other
population events captured by a registration system, such as marriages and
divorces. (chapter 2)

vital statistics method   estimating net migration between censuses as the total growth
between the censuses minus the natural increase between the censuses expected
from vital statistics records. (chapter 9)

widowed   a marital status of currently unmarried by reason of last spouse's death.
(chapter 8)

xenophobia   fear of ethnically distinct foreigners. (chapter 9)

years lived with disability   years of life lived with, and lost to, health disabilities of
known severity and duration. (chapter 6)

years of life lost   how many more years persons might have lived if they had not died
from a particular illness or cause. (chapter 6)

years of potential life lost (YPLL)   a gauge of premature mortality occurring before
the age of 75. (chapter 6)

youth (or **young-age**) **dependency**   the proportion of the population judged too young
to be fully economically productive, usually measured as the percent under age fifteen. (chapters 3, 4)

Index